MAKING TREATIES WORK

There is an increasing focus on the need for national implementation of treaties. International law has traditionally left enforcement to the individual parties, but more and more treaties contain arrangements to induce States to comply with their commitments. This book examines three forms of such mechanisms: dispute settlement procedures in the form of international courts, non-compliance procedures of an administrative character, and enforcement of obligation by coercive means. Three fields are examined, namely, human rights, international environmental law, and arms control and disarmament. These areas are in the forefront of the development of current international law and deal with multilateral, rather than purely bilateral issues. The three sections of the book on human rights, international environmental law and arms control contain a general introduction and three or four case studies of the most relevant treaties in the field. The book finishes with three concluding articles.

GEIR ULFSTEIN is Professor of Law and Director of the Norwegian Centre for Human Rights, University of Oslo.

THILO MARAUHN is Professor of Public Law, International Law and European Law at the Justus-Liebig-Universität Gießen, and a Research Fellow at the University of Luzern.

ANDREAS ZIMMERMANN is Professor of Law and Director of the Walter-Schücking-Institute for International Law, University of Kiel.

MAKING TREATIES WORK

Human Rights, Environment and Arms Control

Edited by
GEIR ULFSTEIN

in collaboration with
THILO MARAUHN and
ANDREAS ZIMMERMANN

CAMBRIDGE UNIVERSITY PRESS
Cambridge, New York, Melbourne, Madrid, Cape Town, Singapore,
São Paulo, Delhi, Dubai, Tokyo, Mexico City

Cambridge University Press
The Edinburgh Building, Cambridge CB2 8RU, UK

Published in the United States of America by Cambridge University Press, New York

www.cambridge.org
Information on this title: www.cambridge.org/9780521153928

© Cambridge University Press 2007

This publication is in copyright. Subject to statutory exception
and to the provisions of relevant collective licensing agreements,
no reproduction of any part may take place without the written
permission of Cambridge University Press.

First published 2007
First paperback printing 2010

A catalogue record for this publication is available from the British Library

ISBN 978-0-521-87317-8 Hardback
ISBN 978-0-521-15392-8 Paperback

Cambridge University Press has no responsibility for the persistence or
accuracy of URLs for external or third-party Internet Web sites referred to in
this publication, and does not guarantee that any content on such Web sites is,
or will remain, accurate or appropriate.

CONTENTS

Preface and acknowledgments	*page* xi
Notes on the contributors	xiii
Table of cases	xvi
Table of treaties and other international instruments	xix

INTRODUCTION

Introduction	3
GEIR ULFSTEIN, THILO MARAUHN AND	
ANDREAS ZIMMERMANN	
The significance of treaties	3
Compliance with treaty obligations	4
General international law	5
Treaty mechanisms	6
Dispute settlement procedures	7
Non-compliance procedures	9
Enforcement	11
The structure of the book	12

PART I   INTERNATIONAL HUMAN RIGHTS

1 Dispute resolution, compliance control and enforcement in human rights law	15
ANDREAS ZIMMERMANN	
1.1 General questions and introduction	15
1.2 Dispute resolution	16
1.3 Compliance control	22
1.4 Enforcement	38
1.5 Overall evaluation	47

2 The International Covenant on Civil and Political Rights 48

MARTIN SCHEININ

2.1	General issues	48
2.2	Dispute resolution	53
2.3	Compliance control	57
2.4	Enforcement	64
2.5	Overall evaluation	66

3 The European Convention on Human Rights 70

MARK E. VILLIGER

3.1	Introduction	70
3.2	The Court and its procedures	74
3.3	The Court's judgments	80
3.4	Overall evaluation	87

4 The European Convention on the Prevention of Torture compared with the United Nations Convention Against Torture and its Optional Protocol 91

RENATE KICKER

4.1	General issues	91
4.2	Defining the task	101
4.3	Dispute resolution	103
4.4	Compliance control	104
4.5	Enforcement	107
4.6	Overall evaluation	109

PART II INTERNATIONAL ENVIRONMENTAL LAW

5 Dispute resolution, compliance control and enforcement in international environmental law 115

GEIR ULFSTEIN

5.1	Introduction	115
5.2	Dispute settlement procedures	118
5.3	Compliance control	124
5.4	Enforcement	128
5.5	Overall evaluation	131

CONTENTS

6 The Convention on International Trade in Endangered Species of Wild Fauna and Flora (CITES)   **134**

ROSALIND REEVE

6.1	Introduction	134
6.2	Compliance control	136
6.3	Enforcement	148
6.4	Effectiveness of the compliance and enforcement mechanisms	152
6.5	Dispute resolution	157
6.6	Lessons learned	158

7 The Convention on Long-Range Transboundary Air Pollution   **161**

TUOMAS KUOKKANEN

7.1	General	161
7.2	Dispute resolution	165
7.3	Compliance control	166
7.4	Enforcement	172
7.5	Overall evaluation	173
	Annex: Structure and Functions of the Implementation Committee and Procedures for Review of Compliance	175

8 The Convention on Access to Information, Public Participation in Decision-Making and Access to Justice in Environmental Matters (Aarhus Convention)   **179**

VEIT KOESTER

8.1	Introduction	179
8.2	Summary contents of the Aarhus Convention and the nature of the Convention	182
8.3	Dispute resolution	183
8.4	Rules of the Convention and MoP decisions on reporting and compliance control	189
8.5	Bodies responsible for monitoring compliance	192
8.6	Procedures of the Compliance Committee	197
8.7	Determination of non-compliance and decision on non-compliance response measures	203
8.8	The relationship between settlement of disputes and review of compliance	213

viii CONTENTS

8.9 Do the compliance and the dispute settlement
mechanisms constitute a self-contained regime? 214
8.10 Overall evaluation 215

**9 The Convention on Environmental Impact Assessment
in a Transboundary Context (Espoo Convention)** 218
TIMO KOIVUROVA
9.1 Dispute resolution 220
9.2 Compliance control 226
9.3 Overall evaluation 235

PART III INTERNATIONAL ARMS CONTROL

**10 Dispute resolution, compliance control and
enforcement of international arms control law** 243
THILO MARAUHN
10.1 Introduction 243
10.2 Consolidation rather than crisis? 247
10.3 Negative and positive incentives to comply with
arms control agreements 250
10.4 Dispute settlement in arms control agreements 255
10.5 Compliance control in arms control agreements:
verification and inspections 257
10.6 Enforcement 266
10.7 Perspectives 271

**11 The Convention on the Prohibition of the Development,
Production, Stockpiling and Use of Chemical Weapons and
on their Destruction (Chemical Weapons Convention)** 273
LISA TABASSI
11.1 Introduction 273
11.2 Dispute resolution 274
11.3 Compliance control 279
11.4 Enforcement 290
11.5 Overall evaluation 298
11.6 Conclusion 300

12 The Treaty on the Non-Proliferation of Nuclear Weapons (NPT) and the IAEA Safeguards Agreements   301

LAURA ROCKWOOD

12.1	The IAEA's safeguards system	302
12.2	The Treaty on the Non-Proliferation of Nuclear Weapons	304
12.3	Comprehensive NPT Safeguards Agreements	306
12.4	Verification	308
12.5	Dispute resolution	312
12.6	Compliance	314
12.7	Enforcement	319
12.8	Overall evaluation	321

13 The Convention on the Prohibition of the Use, Stockpiling, Production and Transfer of Anti-Personnel Mines and on their Destruction (Ottawa Convention)   324

KATHLEEN LAWAND

13.1	Negotiating history of the Ottawa Convention	325
13.2	Key obligations, achievements and challenges	327
13.3	Compliance control, dispute resolution and enforcement mechanisms managed by the States parties	329
13.4	The involvement of non-State actors in compliance control	341
13.5	Conclusions: assessing the strengths and weaknesses of the Ottawa Convention's compliance control regime	343

GENERAL COMMENTS

14 Dispute resolution   351

ANDREAS L. PAULUS

14.1	Dispute settlement in a fragmented legal order	351
14.2	International human rights	356
14.3	Environment	362
14.4	Arms control	365
14.5	Conclusion	368

15 Compliance control		373
JUTTA BRUNNÉE		
15.1	Reporting	374
15.2	Monitoring and assessment of compliance	376
15.3	Compliance bodies	380
15.4	Outcomes	388
15.5	Conclusion	390
16 Enforcement		391
CHRISTIAN J. TAMS		
16.1	Terminology and basic distinctions	319
16.2	Enforcement in the different treaty systems	396
16.3	The role of State responsibility	407
Index		411

PREFACE AND ACKNOWLEDGMENTS

This book is the outcome of a joint research project undertaken by the editors. The underlying theme was to analyze how various regulatory regimes can facilitate the implementation of relevant treaty obligations undertaken by States parties. The editors had decided to invite specialists working in three fields of international law, namely, human rights, international environmental law and arms control, in order to provide analyses of arrangements for dispute settlement, compliance control and enforcement. These contributions were supplemented by introductions from the editors and concluding chapters by well-known academics.

Thilo Marauhn and Geir Ulfstein applied for financing from the Deutsche Forschungsgemeinschaft (German Research Foundation) and the Norwegian Research Council, respectively, and the editors are grateful to both these institutions for the support they provided which made this endeavour a reality. Drafts of the respective reports were presented and discussed at a workshop held at the Walther-Schücking-Institute for International Law, University of Kiel, from 20 to 23 January 2005, which Andreas Zimmermann had undertaken to organize. Geir Ulfstein secured the contact with the authors and the publisher with a view to finalizing the book.

The editors would like to thank particularly all the contributors for their dedication, for allocating their precious time to this project, and for the open discussions during the workshop. We would like to give our special appreciation to Sarah Isabelle Reich, Justus Liebig University, Gießen, for her support in preparing the application to the Deutsche Forschungsgemeinschaft, to the staff of the Walther-Schücking-Institute, in particular Carmen Thies, for having organized the workshop in such a professional manner, and, finally, the scientific assistants, Janne Kaasin, Karin Kaasen and Andreas M. Kravik, for their great efforts and skills in making the manuscript ready for publication.

Finally, thanks go to Cambridge University Press and its staff, first and foremost Finola O'Sullivan who ever since we first approached her has been an effective decision-maker.

NOTES ON THE CONTRIBUTORS

Jutta Brunnée is Professor of Law and Metcalf Chair in Environmental Law, University of Toronto.

Renate Kicker is Associate Professor at the Institute of International Law and International Relations, University of Graz, Austria; a Member of the European Committee for the Prevention of Torture and Inhuman or Degrading Treatment or Punishment (CPT) since September 1997; and Director of the European Training and Research Centre for Human Rights and Democracy (ETC).

Veit Koester was a civil servant with the Danish Ministry of Environment until 2002. He is External Professor at Roskilde University Centre, Denmark, and Visiting Professor at United Nations University's Institute of Advanced Studies, Yokohama, Japan and a guest lecturer at Copenhagen University, Faculty of Law. He is chairman of the Compliance Committee of the Aarhus Convention and chairman of the Compliance Committee of the Cartagena Protocol on Biosafety. He is a member of the Steering Committee for the IUCN (the World Conservation Union) Commission on Environmental Law and a member of the Conseil Europeen du Droit de l'Environnement (CEDE).

Timo Koivurova is Research Professor of Arctic Environment and Minority Law, and Director of the Northern Institute for Environmental and Minority Law (NIEM/Arctic Centre).

Tuomas Kuokkanen is Counsellor, Ministry of Environment of Finland; was a member of the Implementation Committee under the Convention on Long-Range Transboundary Air Pollution from 1999 to 2005; and is a part-time Professor of International Environmental Law at the University of Joensuu.

Kathleen Lawand is Legal Adviser, Mines-Arms Unit, International Committee of the Red Cross (ICRC).

Thilo Marauhn is Professor of Public Law, International Law and European Law at the Justus-Liebig-Universität Gießen, and Research Fellow at the University of Luzern.

Andreas Paulus is Lecturer, Institute for International Law, Ludwig-Maximilians-University München, Germany.

Rosalind Reeve is Associate Fellow of the Sustainable Development Programme, Chatham House, UK, and adviser to the David Shepherd Wildlife Foundation and the International Fund for Animal Welfare.

Laura Rockwood is Principal Legal Officer, Section Head for Non-Proliferation and Policy Making, Office of Legal Affairs, International Atomic Energy Agency.

Martin Scheinin is Professor of Constitutional and International Law and Director of the Institute for Human Rights at Åbo Akademi University, Turku, Finland. He was a member of the Human Rights Committee from 1997 to 2004.

Lisa Tabassi is Legal Officer, Technical Secretariat of the Organisation for the Prohibition of Chemical Weapons (OPCW).

Christian J. Tams is Lecturer, Walther-Schücking-Institute for International Law, University of Kiel, Germany.

Geir Ulfstein is Professor of Law and Director of the Norwegian Centre for Human Rights, University of Oslo. He is Deputy Director of the Board, Norwegian Branch of the International Law Association. He is also a member of the International Law Association's Committee on Human Rights Law and Practice, and a member of the IUCN (the World Conservation Union) Commission on Environmental Law.

Mark Villiger is a Judge of the European Court of Human Rights, and is Titularprofessor of International and European Law at the University of Zurich.

Andreas Zimmermann is Professor of Law and Director of the Walter-Schücking-Institute for International Law, University of Kiel. From 1999 to 2001 he was a member of the expert commission for the drafting of a Code of Offences Against International Law at the German Ministry of Justice. In 1997/8 he was a member of and legal adviser to the German delegation at the Preparatory Committee for, and at the United Nations Diplomatic Conference of Plenipotentiaries on, the Establishment of an International Criminal Court.

TABLE OF CASES

Permanent Court of International Justice

Mavrommatis Palestine Concessions Case (Greece v. United Kingdom), 1924   255, 352

International Court of Justice

Application of the Convention on the Prevention and Punishment of the Crime of Genocide (Bosnia and Herzegovina v. Yugoslavia), 1996   18

Application of the Convention on the Prevention and Punishment of the Crime of Genocide (Croatia v. Yugoslavia), 2002   18

Armed Activities on the Territory of the Congo (Democratic Republic of the Congo v. Rwanda), 2002   18

Avena and Other Mexican Nationals (Mexico v. United States), 2004   354, 357, 359

Barcelona Traction, Light and Power Company Ltd (Belgium v. Spain), 1970   39, 354, 364

Case Concerning Armed Activities on the Territory of the Congo (Democratic Republic of the Congo v. Uganda), 2005   43

Certain Property (Liechtenstein v. Germany), 2005   352, 353, 355

East Timor (Portugal v. Australia), 1995, 90   352, 354, 364

Fisheries Jurisdiction Case (Spain v. Canada) 1998   371

Gabcikovo–Nagymaros Dam case (Hungary v. Slovakia), 1997   119, 362, 363

LaGrand (Germany v. US), 2001   354, 357

Land and Maritime Boundary between Cameroon and Nigeria (Cameroon v. Nigeria), 1998   352

Legal Consequences of the Construction of a Wall in the Occupied Palestinian Territory, Advisory Opinion, 2004   42, 54, 353, 354, 360

Legality of the Threat or Use of Nuclear Weapons, Advisory Opinion, 1996   54, 252, 355, 360, 363, 367, 368

Questions of Interpretation and Application of the 1971 Montreal Convention arising from the Aerial Incident at Lockerbie (Libya v. UK), 1998   352, 372

South West Africa Cases, 1962   255

Vienna Convention on Consular Relations (Paraguay v. US), 1998   371

TABLE OF CASES

Arbitration

Behring Sea Fur Seals Arbitration, Moore's *International Arbitration Awards* 755, 1898
119

Lake Lanoux case, 24 ILM 101, 1957   119

MOX Case: Dispute Concerning Access to Information under Article 9 of the Ospar
Convention (Ireland v. United Kingdom), Permanent Court of Arbitration,
2003   120, 384

Southern Bluefin Tuna Arbitration, 39 ILM 1359, 2000   119

Trail Smelter (US v. Canada), 3 UNRIAA 1905 (1941); (1939) 33 AJIL 182   119, 362

WTO Dispute Settlement Body

EC – Asbestos: European Communities – Measures Affecting Asbestos-Containing
Products, 2001, WT/DS135/AB/R   361, 370

EC – Bananas: Report of the Appellate Body on the European Community Regime for
the Importation, Sale and Distribution of Bananas, 1997, WT/DS27/AB/R   354

US – Shrimps: United States – Importation of Certain Shrimp and Shrimp Products,
1998, WT/DS58/AB/R   361

US – Steel: United States – Imposition of Countervailing Duties on Certain Hot-
Rolled Lead and Bismuth Carbon Steel Products Originating in the United
Kingdom, 2000, WT/DS/138/AB/R   361

International Labour Organization Administrative Tribunal

Judgment 2032 (2001)   278
Judgment 2232 (2003)   279
Judgment 2256 (2003)   278
Judgment 2327 (2004)   279
Judgment 2328 (2004)   279

UN Human Rights CommitteeReports

A v. Australia, 1993   64
Apirana Mahuika et al. v. New Zealand, 1984   61
Bernard Ominayak, Chief of the Lubicon Lake Band v. Canada, 1984   49, 60, 61
Dante Piandiong et al. v. Philippines, 1999   63
A Publication and a Printing Company v. Trinidad and Tobago, 1989   60

European Commission on Human Rights

Austria v. Italy, 1961   18
Denmark, Norway, Sweden and the Netherlands v. Greece, 1968   22

xviii

TABLE OF CASES

European Court of Human Rights

Akkoc v. Turkey, 1993   106
Amuur v. France, 1996   104
Austria v. Italy, Application, 1960   79
Belilos v. Switzerland, 1988   80
Broniowski v. Poland, Application, 1996   83
Brumarescu v. Romania, Application, 1995   83
Corigliano v. Italy, 1982   81
Cyprus v. Turkey, 2001   22, 79
Denmark, Norway, Sweden and the Netherlands v. Greece, 1967   79
France, Norway, Denmark and Sweden v. Turkey, 1982   79
Gençel v. Turkey, Application, 1999   83
Ilascu v. Moldova and Russia, Application, 1999   82
Ireland v. United Kingdom, 1978   22, 79
Kalashnikov v. Russia, 2002   106
Le Compte, Van Leuven and de Meyere v. Belgium, 1982   82
Lorsé v. Netherlands, 2001   106
Mamatkulov v. Abdurasulovic v. Turkey, Applications, 1999   72
Moreira de Azevedo v. Portugal, 1991   81
Tyrer v. United Kingdom, 1978   88
Van der Ven v. Netherlands, 2003   106
X etc. v. Netherlands, 1984   73

Inter-American Court of Human Rights

Advisory Opinion, 1999   359
Barrios Altos Case, 2003   27

Netherlands

LJN: AU8685, Rechtbank 's-Gravenhage, 09/751003-04   298

United Kingdom Privy Council

Tangiora v. Wellington District Legal Services Committee (2000) 4 LRC 44   45

TABLE OF TREATIES AND OTHER INTERNATIONAL INSTRUMENTS

General Instruments

1945 UN Charter
    art. 2(3)   353
    art. 2(4)   267
    art. 33   7, 255, 353
    art. 39   269, 270, 304, 406
    art. 41   270
    art. 42   270
    art. 48   304
    art. 53   392
    art. 96   354
    Chapter VII   251, 266, 295–6, 297, 304

1945 ICJ Statute
    art. 36(1)   17
    art. 36(2)   17
    art. 63(2)   123

1963 Vienna Convention on Consular Relations, 596 UNTS 291   4, 371
    art. 36   357

1969 Vienna Convention on the Law of Treaties, 1155 UNTS 331   46
    art. 3   207
    art. 28   76
    art. 31   44
    art. 31(3)(a)   233
    art. 60   5, 129, 212, 214, 393
    art. 60(1)(a)(i)   85
    art. 60(2)(c)   122, 269, 409
    art. 60(5)   212, 214

xix

XX   TABLE OF TREATIES AND INTERNATIONAL INSTRUMENTS

1998 Statute of the International Criminal Court (Rome Statute), 2187 UNTS 3   298,
    358
    art. 12   359
    art. 13   359

2001 Articles on State Responsibility   5
    art. 33(2)   39
    art. 41   42
    art. 42   6, 42, 122, 409
    art. 42(11)   364
    art. 42(b)(ii)   409
    art. 48   6, 42, 409
    art. 48(1)   408
    art. 48(7)   364, 365, 409
    art. 49   6, 42, 43
    art. 54   6, 42, 43, 408

General regional instruments

1948 Charter of the Organization of American States, 119 UNTS 3
    art. 9   46

1948 Statute of the Council of Europe
    art. 3   23, 24, 85
    art. 4   23
    art. 7   31, 85
    art. 8   31, 46, 85, 109
    art. 23(a)   31

1972 European Convention on State Immunity, ETS No. 074A
    Additional Protocol 1972   89
        art. 1   89
        art. 2   89
        art. 4   89

2000 Constitutive Act of the African Union, OAU Doc. CAB/LEG/23.15
    art. 30   46

2000 Cotonou Agreement [2000] OJ L317/3   403
    art. 9   402
    art. 96(2)   402

TABLE OF TREATIES AND INTERNATIONAL INSTRUMENTS xxi

Human rights

1948 Convention on the Prevention and Punishment of the Crime of Genocide, 78 UNTS 177
   art. IX   17

1948 Universal Declaration of Human Rights, UN Doc. A/810 (1948) 71   15, 48, 88
   art. 3   97

1950 European Convention for the Protection of Human Rights and Fundamental Freedoms, ETS No. 5   15, 70–90, 384
  art. 3   77, 93, 105, 110, 396
  art. 6(1)   83
  art. 8   77
  art. 10   77
  art. 11   77
  art. 15   45
  art. 19   74
  art. 21   74
  art. 22   74
  art. 23   75
  art. 24   37
  art. 25   75
  art. 26   76
  art. 28   75, 76
  art. 29   75
  art. 30   72, 75
  art. 33   79, 407
  art. 34   76, 78, 79
  art. 35   77
  art. 35(2)(b)   17, 76
  art. 35(3)   76, 77
  art. 36(3)   87
  art. 37(1)(a)   75
  art. 38(1)(b)   78
  art. 39   78
  art. 40   78
  art. 41   81, 82, 83
  art. 45   78
  art. 46   80
  art. 46(1)   33, 71, 80
  art. 46(2)   33, 71, 84, 85, 400
  art. 46(3)   86

xxii   TABLE OF TREATIES AND INTERNATIONAL INSTRUMENTS

art. 46(4)   87
art. 52   26
art. 54   33
art. 55   41
art. 59(2)   74
Protocol 1, art. 1   83
Protocol 11   17, 70, 80
Protocol 12   70–1
Protocol 14   34, 72, 74, 76, 77, 80, 86–7
  art. 8(2)   34

1960 Unesco Convention Against Discrimination, 429 UNTS 93
art. 17   25

1966 Convention on the Elimination of All Forms of Racial Discrimination (CERD),
  660 UNTS 195
art. 9   25
art. 11   20
Optional Protocol   68

1966 International Covenant on Civil and Political Rights (ICCPR), 999 UNTS 171
  15, 48–69, 89, 375, 376, 377, 380, 381, 382, 384
art. 1   48, 49
art. 2   50, 65
art. 2(3)   51
art. 3   50
art. 4   45
art. 6   48, 49
art. 7   49, 97, 396
art. 8   49
art. 9   49, 64
art. 10   48–9
art. 11   49
art. 12   49
art. 13   49
art. 14   49
art. 15   49
art. 16   49
art. 17   49
art. 18   49
art. 19   49
art. 20   49

TABLE OF TREATIES AND INTERNATIONAL INSTRUMENTS xxiii

art. 21 49
art. 22 48
art. 23 49
art. 24 49
art. 25 48
art. 26 48
art. 27 48, 50
art. 28 19, 50, 52, 64, 126
art. 29 126
art. 30(4) 52
art. 31 19
art. 39(2) 53, 64
art. 40 25, 50, 52, 53, 64, 65
art. 40(1) 51, 57
art. 40(2) 51, 57
art. 40(4) 53
art. 41 17, 20, 50, 51, 54, 55, 56, 407
art. 41(1) 19, 20
art. 42 50, 51, 54, 55, 56
art. 42(6)(c) 52
art. 44 18, 54
Protocol 1 on Individual Complaints 49, 50, 52, 63–4, 68
   art. 4 19
   art. 4(2) 62
   art. 5(1) 56, 62
   art. 5(3) 62
   art. 5(4) 20, 52, 63
   art. 5(a) 199

1966 International Covenant on Economic, Social and Cultural Rights (ICESCR), 993
   UNTS 3 15, 47, 48
art. 16 25

1969 American Convention on Human Rights, 1144 UNTS 123 89
art. 26 28
art. 27 45
arts. 34–40 19
art. 34 19
art. 35 19
art. 41(f) 36
art. 42 28
art. 43 28

art. 45   17, 37
art. 48   19
art. 49   20
art. 50   20, 36
art. 51   20
art. 52   19
art. 62   17
art. 63   20

1973 International Convention on the Suppression and Punishment of the Crime of
    Apartheid
    art. VI   25

1979 Convention on the Elimination of All Forms of Discrimination Against Women
    (CEDAW), 1249 UNTS 13   15, 357, 375, 377, 380, 382, 384, 387
    art. 18   25
    art. 29   357
    Optional Protocol   47, 68, 357
        art. 8   29

1979 Statute of the Inter-American Commission on Human Rights
    art. 20(b)   36
    art. 44(1)   36

1981 African Charter on Human and Peoples' Rights, 1520 UNTS 217   89
    art. 30   19
    art. 31   19
    art. 45   17
    art. 47   19, 37
    art. 49   37
    art. 51(2)   19
    art. 52   20
    art. 53   20, 35
    art. 58   35
    Protocol
        art. 3   17
        art. 11   19
        art. 26(2)   19
        art. 27   20
        art. 29(2)   35
        art. 31   35

TABLE OF TREATIES AND INTERNATIONAL INSTRUMENTS

1984 Convention Against Torture and Other Cruel, Inhuman or Degrading Treatment or Punishment (UN CAT), 1465 UNTS 85   15, 384, 387, 396
- art. 1   97
- art. 3   100
- art. 17   19
- art. 19   25, 98
- art. 20   29, 99
- art. 21   20, 98
- art. 21(1)(a)   19
- art. 21(1)(h)   20
- art. 22   17, 98
- art. 22(4)   98
- art. 24   100
- art. 28   29
- Optional Protocol 2002   99, 110–11, 379

1987 European Convention for the Prevention of Torture and Inhuman or Degrading Treatment or Punishment (ECPT), ETS No. 126   27, 91–111, 374, 379, 396
- Preamble   104–5
- Preamble   89
- art. 3   94, 101
- art. 8(5)   93, 107
- art. 9   105
- art. 10   93
- art. 10(2)   94, 107
- art. 11(2)   28, 94
- art. 14(3)   103
- Protocol 1   91

1987 European Convention on Human Rights and Biomedicine, ETS No. 164
- art. 29   89

1989 Convention on the Rights of the Child, 577 UNTS 3   15
- art. 44   25

1990 United Nations Convention on the Protection of the Rights of All Migrant Workers and Members of their Families, 2220 UNTS 3
- art. 23   38

1992 European Charter for Regional or Minority Languages, ETS No. 148
- art. 17   24–5, 27

xxvi TABLE OF TREATIES AND INTERNATIONAL INSTRUMENTS

1995 Framework Convention for the Protection of National Minorities, ETS No. 157
44
art. 26   27

1996 European Social Charter (Revised), ETS No. 163   25
art. 25   31
art. 29   27
Protocol on Collective Complaints 1995, ETS No.   34
art. 1(b)   21

Environmental protection

1971 Convention on Wetlands of International Importance Especially as Waterfowl
Habitat, Ramsar, 2 February 1971, 996 UNTS 243   158

1973 Convention on International Trade in Endangered Species (CITES), 993 UNTS
243   117, 134–60, 363, 374, 376, 378, 382, 383, 384, 385, 387, 389, 392, 398
art. II   135
art. III   135
art. VIII   136
art. VIII(1)   144
art. VIII(6)   137
art. VIII(7)   137, 145
art. IX(1)   144
art. XI   136
art. XII   136, 138, 139–40
art. XIII   136, 143
art. XV   142
art. XVI   142
art. XVIII   119, 157, 158
art. XXIII   142
Appendix I   135
Appendix II   135, 145, 149
Appendix III   135

1974 Nordic Environment Protection, 13 ILM 352 (1974)
art. 12   223, 236

1979 Convention on the Conservation of European Wildlife and Natural Habitats, ETS
No. 104   195, 397

1979 ECE Convention on Long-Range Transboundary Air Pollution (LRTAP), 18 ILM
1442 (1979)   117, 161–78, 186, 213, 374, 376, 378, 381, 383, 385, 388

art. 10(1)   162
art. 13   119, 165, 235–6
Annex V
  § 6   127
Protocol on Co-operation (EMEP) 1984   163
  art. 7   165
Protocol on Sulphur 1985   163, 172
  art. 8   165
Protocol on Nitrogen Oxide Emissions 1988   163, 166, 167, 169, 172
  art. 12   165
Protocol on Volatile Organic Compounds 1991   163, 168. 169, 170, 172
  art. 3(3)   164
Protocol on Sulphur 1994   125, 163, 168, 172
  art. 7   164
  art. 9   165
  art. 9(5)   165
Protocol on Persistent Organic Pollutants 1998   163
  art. 11   164
  art. 12   165
Protocol on Heavy Metals 1998 (Aarhus Protocol)   163
  art. 8   164
  art. 11   165
  art. 12   362
Protocol to Abate Acidification etc. 1999 (Gothenburg Protocol)   163
  art. 9   164
  art. 11   119
  art. 11(5)   119, 165

1980 Convention on the Conservation of Migratory Species of Wild Animals (Bonn
    Convention), 19 ILM 15 (1980)   118

1985 Vienna Convention for the Protection of the Ozone Layer, 1513 UNTS 293   184,
    186, 235
  art. 11   364

1987 Montreal Protocol on Substances that Deplete the Ozone Layer, 26 ILM 1550
    (1987)   117–18, 184, 211, 213, 364, 383, 385
  art. 8   125

1989 Basel Convention on the Control of Transboundary Movement of
    Hazardous Wastes and their Disposal 1989, 28 ILM 657 (1989)   121, 159, 184,
    186, 213

xxviii TABLE OF TREATIES AND INTERNATIONAL INSTRUMENTS

1991 Convention on Environmental Impact Assessment in a Transboundary Context
(Espoo Convention), 90 ILM 802 (1991)   117, 186, 213, 218–39, 378, 384, 385,
387
art. 2   219
art. 3   219
art. 3(1)   223
art. 3(7)   120, 199, 223
art. 4   219
art. 6   219
art. 6(1)   222
art. 7   219
art. 11(2)   227
art. 14(6)   230
art. 14(7)   227
art. 14*bis*   228
art. 15   221, 362
art. 15(2)   119, 222
Annex IV   120
Annex VII § 15   123
Appendix I   223, 224
Appendix IV   199, 223, 224
    § 1   225
    § 2   224
    § 3   224, 225, 226
    § 4   225
    § 6   224
    § 7   224
    § 9   225
    § 12   225
    § 13   225, 226
    § 14   225
Appendix V   219
Appendix VII   221, 222
SEA Protocol. *See* 2003 Protocol (below)

1991 Convention on the Protection of the Alps, 31 ILM 767 (1992)   195, 202

1992 Convention for the Protection of the Marine Environment of the North-East
Atlantic (OSPAR Convention)
art. 9   120, 384
art. 32(1)   120

TABLE OF TREATIES AND INTERNATIONAL INSTRUMENTS xxix

1992 Convention on Biological Diversity, 31 ILM 818 (1992)   118, 186, 220
   art. 27   235

1992 Convention on the Protection and Use of Transboundary Watercourses and
     International Lakes
   Protocol on Water and Health 1999   216, 239
     art. 20   236

1992 Helsinki Convention on the Transboundary Effects of Industrial Accidents, 31
     ILM 1330 (1992)
   art. 4(2)   237
   art. 21   236
   art. 22   236
   Annex II   237

1992 Rio Declaration
   art. 7   115
   art. 10   217

1992 United Nations Framework Convention on Climate Change, 1771 UNTS 107
     129, 184, 377–8, 389
   art. 14   235, 362

1997 Convention on the Law of Non-Navigational Uses of International Watercourses,
     Doc. A/5/869
   art. 33   237

1997 Kyoto Protocol to the United Nations Convention on Climate Change, 37 ILM 22
     (1998)   118, 184, 186, 210, 376, 383, 389
   art. 7   378
   art. 17   212, 399
   art. 18   130, 191

1998 Convention on Access to Information, Public Participation in Decision-Making
     and Access to Justice in Environmental Matters (Aarhus Convention), 2161
     UNTS 447   117, 179–217, 362, 383, 387
   Preamble   182, 188, 189
   art. 1   182
   art. 2   182
   art. 3   182
   art. 3(9)   182, 215
   art. 4   182, 183, 215

art. 5   182
art. 6   182, 183, 195
art. 6(11)   181
art. 6*bis*   181
art. 7   182
art. 8   182
art. 9   182
art. 9(1)   183
art. 10   182
art. 10(1)   192
art. 10(2)   181, 189, 192
art. 10(2)(d)   194
art. 10(3)   210
art. 10(5)   363
art. 11   212
art. 12   182, 192
art. 15   125, 181, 191, 194, 207, 216
art. 16   184, 213, 236
art. 16(1)   212
art. 16(2)   119, 186
Annex 1   182
Annex 1*bis*   181
Annex 2   184, 185
   § 1   186
   § 15   186
PRTR Protocol 2003   181, 186
   art. 22   191

1998 Rotterdam Convention on the Prior Informed Consent Procedure in Certain
   Hazardous Chemicals and Pesticides in International Trade, 38 ILM 1 (1999)
   159, 184

2000 Cartagena Protocol on Biosafety to the Convention on Biological Diversity, 1760
   UNTS 79   159, 186, 199, 203, 213
   art. 34   191

2001 Stockholm Convention on Persistent Organic Pollutants, 40 ILM 532 (2001)
   159, 184
   art. 17   191

2003 Protocol on Civil Liability and Compensation for Damage Caused by the
   Transboundary Effects of Industrial Accidents on Transboundary Waters
   art. 26   236

TABLE OF TREATIES AND INTERNATIONAL INSTRUMENTS   xxxi

2003 Protocol on Strategic Environmental Assessment to the Convention on Environmental Impact Assessment in a Transboundary Context, Doc. ECE/MP.EIA/2003/2   218, 220
  art. 5   219, 220
  art. 6   220
  art. 7   220
  art. 8   220
  art. 9   220
  art. 10   219, 220, 223
  art. 13   220
  art. 14   235
  art. 20   221

Arms control

1925 Protocol for the Prohibition of the Use of Asphyxiating, Poisonous or Other Cases, and of Bacteriological Methods of Warfare, 94 LNTS (1929) No. 2138   273, 298

1956 IAEA Statute, 276 UNTS 3 (No. 3988)   301
  art. III(A)(5)   302
  art. III(B)(4)   302, 318, 320
  art. XII   405, 406
  art. XII(A)   303
  art. XII(C)   303, 315, 317, 318, 403

1959 Antarctic Treaty, 402 UNTS 71
  art. VII(5)   260

1963 Treaty Banning Nuclear Weapon Tests in the Atmosphere, in Outer Space and Under Water (Limited Test Ban Treaty), 480 UNTS 43   4
  art. IV   268

1967 Tlatelolco Treaty for the Prohibition of Nuclear Weapons in Latin America, 634 UNTS 326
  art. 7   260
  art. 14   260
  art. 15   260
  art. 25   256
  art. 31(1)   268
  Protocol II
    art. 1   253
    art. 3   253

xxxii TABLE OF TREATIES AND INTERNATIONAL INSTRUMENTS

1968 Treaty on the Non-Proliferation of Nuclear Weapons (NPT), 729 UNTS 161
    245, 248, 298–9, 301–23, 354, 366, 379, 381, 386, 388, 403, 405
  art. I   305, 306
  art. II   305, 306
  art. III   306
  art. III(1)   305
  art. III(2)   305, 309
  art. IV   306
  art. VI   249, 252, 253, 305
  art. VII   252, 253, 268
  art. X   306

1971 Treaty on the Prohibition of the Emplacement of Nuclear Weapons and Other
    Weapons of Mass Destruction on the Sea-Bed and the Ocean Floor and in the
    Subsoil Thereof, 955 UNTS 115
  art. VIII   268

1972 Convention on the Prohibition of the Development, Production, and Stockpiling
    of Bacteriological (Biological) and Toxin Weapons and on their Destruction
    (BTWC), 1015 UNTS 163   245, 248, 300
  art. VI   269, 365–6
  art. VII   253
  art. XIII   268

1972 Treaty between the United States and the Union of Soviet Socialist Republics on
    the Limitation of Anti-Ballistic Missile Systems (ABM Treaty), 944 UNTS 13
  art. XII   259
  art. XIII   255–6
  art. XV(2)   268

1974 Treaty between the United States and the Union of Soviet Socialist Republics on
    the Limitation of Underground Nuclear Weapons Tests, 13 ILM 906 (1974)
  art. II   259

1976 Treaty between the United States and the Union of Soviet Socialist Republics on
    Underground Nuclear Explosions for Peaceful Purposes, 15 ILM 891 (1976)
  art. IV   259

1980 UN Convention on Conventional Weapons which may be deemed to be
    Excessively Injurious or to have Indiscriminate Effects (CCW Treaty), 1324
    UNTS 137   247, 318, 325–6, 367
  Protocol II   326

TABLE OF TREATIES AND INTERNATIONAL INSTRUMENTS xxxiii

Protocol V (2003)
  art. 11 366

1985 South Pacific Nuclear Free Zone Treaty, Rarotonga, 1445 UNTS 177
  art. 9 260
  art. 13 268

1987 Treaty between the United States and the Union of Soviet Socialist Republics on the Elimination of their Intermediate Range and Shorter-Range Missiles (INF Treaty), 27 ILM 183 (1988)
  art. XI 263
  art. XII 259
  art. XIII 256, 260

1990 Conventional Armed Forces Treaty (CFE Treaty), 30 ILM 1 (1991) 245, 265, 379, 380, 384–5, 386
  art. XIII 261
  art. XV 259

1991 Treaty between the United States of America and the Union of Soviet Socialist Republics on the Reduction and Limitation of Strategic Offensive Arms (START 1), 729 UNTS 161
  art. IX 259
  art. XV 256
  Lisbon Protocol 245

1992 Treaty on Open Skies 259

1993 Convention on the Prohibition of the Development, Production, Stockpiling and Use of Chemical Weapons and on their Destruction (CWC Treaty), UN Doc. A/RES/47/39 245, 248, 273–300, 374, 375, 379, 380, 381, 382, 384, 385, 392, 403, 404
  art. I 308
  art. III 261
  art. III(1) 308
  art. IV(6) 290
  art. IV(11) 254
  art. IV(12) 254
  art. VI 261
  art. VI(2) 291
  art. VII 293, 294, 296
  art. VII(1) 291

art. VII(2)   254, 291
art. VII(5)   293
art. VIII   282
art. VIII(1)   274
art. VIII(36)   284, 294–5, 296, 378, 386
art. VIII(37)   263
art. IX   277, 285
art. IX(1)   285
art. IX(2)   285
art. IX(4)(b)   280
art. IX(5)   280
art. IX(8)   243, 265, 286
art. IX(17)   266
art. IX(22)   286
art. IX(23)   286
art. X   254
art. XII   270, 271, 277, 295, 296, 403, 406
art. XII(1)   271
art. XII(4)   269, 405, 406
art. XIV   275, 276, 278, 366
art. XV(5)   289
art. XVI(2)   404
Schedule 1   280, 289
Schedule 2   280
Schedule 3   280
Confidentiality Annex   277, 283
Verification Annex   291–2
   Part II § 65   284
   Part IV   261
   Part IV § 26   290
   Part IV(A) §§ 20–3   254
   Part IV(A) §§ 24–8   254
   Part VI   261
   Part VI § 30   265

1996 Comprehensive Nuclear Test Ban Treaty (CTBT), 35 ILM 1439 (1996)   245,
   252
art. IV   257, 259
art. V   257
art. V(4)   269
art. VI(6)   257

TABLE OF TREATIES AND INTERNATIONAL INSTRUMENTS   XXXV

1997 Convention on the Prohibition of the Use, Stockpiling, Production and Transfer of Anti-Personnel Mines and on their Destruction (Ottawa Convention), 36 ILM 1507 (1997)   245, 324–47, 379, 380, 386

Preamble   327, 341

art. 1   327, 345

art. 2   346

art. 3   345

art. 3(1)   327

art. 4   327, 329

art. 5   327, 330

art. 5(1)   327

art. 5(2)   328

art. 6   328, 333

art. 7   329, 330, 335–7

art. 8   330, 337–9, 366

art. 8(19)   340

art. 9   340

art. 10   339–40, 366

art. 11   330

art. 11(1)   330

1999 Inter-American Convention on Transparency in Conventional Weapons   247

Introduction

Introduction

GEIR ULFSTEIN, THILO MARAUHN AND
ANDREAS ZIMMERMANN

While States traditionally could resolve their problems by adopting legislation and other domestic measures, they are increasingly facing the fact that finding solutions to a given problem is beyond their national control. Current examples of such a development include international trade, security issues, the protection of the environment, cultural exchange and the protection of human rights.

This development has also changed the character of international law. In the 1960s, Wolfgang Friedmann had argued that international law had moved away from a 'law of coexistence' towards a 'law of co-operation'.[1] This means that States no longer are concerned only with the preservation of their sovereignty from international interference, but more and more engage in positive co-operation through treaties and international organizations. As of today, it might even be possible to refer to an emerging international 'constitutionalism'. This concept refers to the increased significance of international institutions, which apply checks and balances comparable to those known from domestic law.[2]

The significance of treaties

Notwithstanding this development, treaties remain the most important instrument for regulating international affairs and the intercourse between States. Bruno Simma has accordingly called treaties the 'workhorse' of

---

[1] Wolfgang Friedmann, *The Changing Structure of International Law* (London: Stevens & Sons, 1964), pp. 60–2.

[2] Anne Peters, 'Compensatory Constitutionalism: The Function and Potential of Fundamental International Norms and Structures' (2006) 12 *Leiden Journal of International Law*, forthcoming, with further references.

international law.[3] They may be used for regulating any bilateral or multilateral relationship between States, be it the demarcation of a boundary, the establishment of a customs regime, the protection against climate change or the setting up of an international organization. But, as Simma notes, multilateral treaties are increasingly used to deal with common problems of the whole international community. At the same time, the content of treaties changes from consisting essentially of bilateral obligations (e.g. the two Vienna conventions on diplomatic and consular relations) to containing obligations so interwoven that each obligation has to be performed in relation to all treaty parties (the Nuclear Test Ban Treaty of 1963 being a case at hand). Indeed, treaties may also contain obligations that are not primarily intended to regulate inter-State relations, but aim at a uniform domestic practice that may involve conferring rights on third parties, for example the rights contained in human rights treaties.[4]

Compliance with treaty obligations

The current system of international law experiences an ever-increasing focus on compliance with treaty obligations. The first reason for this concern is obviously that the objectives of a given treaty may already be in jeopardy if any of the States parties does not fulfil its commitments. But breach of the treaty may create a snowball effect in the sense that States may not accept other States as free-riders. They may consequently also suspend or terminate their own treaty obligations, and thereby further reduce the likelihood of achieving the treaty objectives. This development may be of even more importance as treaty obligations become more demanding, in both economic and political terms. The possibility that States may take advantage of the possibility of non-fulfilment of their obligations may even prevent the successful outcome of the negotiations of future treaties. These are some of the essential backdrops for including legal mechanisms to ensure compliance with treaty obligations – which is the focus of this book.

It may of course be asked to what extent there is a need to design treaty mechanisms to promote compliance with the commitments States have previously undertaken voluntarily. Louis Henkin's formulation, that 'almost all nations observe almost all principles of international law and

---

[3] B. Simma, 'From Bilateralism to Community Interest in International Law' (1994-VI) 250 *Recueil des Cours* 221–384, at 322–3. [4] *Ibid.*, pp. 336–7.

INTRODUCTION

almost all of their obligations almost all of the time, has often been cited.[5] While this may generally be true, it does not provide an answer as to how compliance may be improved in cases where this is crucial to achieve the treaties' very objectives. Thomas M. Franck has argued that the legitimacy of international obligations may exert a significant pull towards compliance.[6] While this is also true, the question arises to what extent such pull may be assisted by specially designed procedural treaty mechanisms.

General international law

International law has traditionally left the enforcement of treaty obligations to individual States parties. As is well known, article 60 of the Vienna Convention on the Law of Treaties allows States to suspend or terminate a treaty if it is violated. This possibility is, however, only open in cases of certain qualified violations constituting a material breach thereof. Individual parties may suspend the treaty in whole or in part if they are 'specially affected' or if the breach by one party 'radically changes the position of every party with respect to the further performance of its obligations under the treaty'. But, if the parties want to act collectively, suspension or termination normally requires unanimous agreement by all other non-defaulting parties. Furthermore, there is little point in suspending or terminating treaties aimed at the protection of collective interests such as the protection of the environment or the reduction of armaments. And, finally, these remedies are not available at all in relation to provisions 'relating to the protection of the human person contained in treaties of a humanitarian character'.

States may also invoke the law of State responsibility and thereby claim reparation for injury and apply counter-measures against a State violating its international obligations. Under the articles on State responsibility adopted by the International Law Commission (ILC) in 2001, the right to request reparations and to use counter-measures is, at the outset, limited to the 'injured' State(s). But the ILC at least seems somewhat to open the possibility for their use also by other concerned States to protect collective

---

[5] Louis Henkin, *How Nations Behave* (New York: Columbia University Press, 1979), p. 47.
[6] Thomas M. Franck, *The Power of Legitimacy Among Nations* (Oxford: Oxford University Press, 1990), p. 25. See also Thomas M. Franck, *Fairness in International Law and Institutions* (Oxford: Oxford University Press, 1995).

6 INTRODUCTION

interests.[7] The law of State responsibility, however, provides no generalized normative system by which States parties to a multilateral treaty may act as a collective entity. It is against this background that the book undertakes to analyze selected treaty systems in order to determine whether indeed specific conventions in the field of disarmament, environmental protection and human rights contain an answer to this question.

Treaty mechanisms

While the foremost function of treaties has been to establish the substantive obligations of the parties, they are increasingly used also to design mechanisms to induce compliance with such obligations. This book examines three forms of such mechanisms. First, dispute settlement procedures aimed at solving legal disputes through negotiation, mediation, conciliation, or binding settlement through arbitration or international courts will be examined. Secondly, the book examines non-compliance procedures that have been established to apply a facilitative approach in persuading States to comply with their obligations through 'soft' enforcement, such as 'naming and shaming' or by offering financial and technological assistance. Finally, treaties may open the way for different forms of 'hard' enforcement, *inter alia* in the form of suspension of rights and privileges, or by different forms of sanctions. The book does not purport to provide definitive conclusions on the effectiveness of the relevant treaties, be it in terms of the implementation of relevant obligations or achieving the overall objectives of the treaties. The treaty mechanisms can, however, be seen as reflections of what States parties have considered desirable and realistic in inducing and pressuring States to comply with treaty obligations, and thereby enhancing effectiveness. At least, the mechanisms show what it is politically possible to achieve with co-operation between States parties.

Three fields of international law are examined, namely, human rights, international environmental law, and arms control and disarmament. The reason for choosing these areas is, first, that they are in the forefront of the development of current international law, and constitute those parts of

---

[7] Draft arts. 42, 48, 49 and 54. See James Crawford, *The International Law Commission's Articles on State Responsibility: Introduction, Text and Commentaries* (Cambridge: Cambridge University Press, 2002). On the approach taken by the United Nations General Assembly, see James Crawford and Simon Olleson, 'The Continuing Debate on a UN Convention on State Responsibility' (2005) 54 *International and Comparative Law Quarterly* 959–73.

modern international law where recent trends in law-making and law-enforcement are most obvious. Secondly, the importance – both legally and politically – of these respective fields cannot be understated, given that the protection of the environment, the protection and furtherance of human rights, as well as the issue of arms control, are of vital importance for the very survival of mankind and for securing core rights for individual human beings. Finally, all three fields have common features, since none of them deals with purely bilateral relationships, but rather focus on common interests in the respective field by all States parties to a given treaty.

A comparative approach is also important since individual international legal scholars more and more tend to focus their attention on their respective fields, but have difficulties in considering how these very same issues are being addressed in other areas of international law. This study therefore describes and compares compliance mechanisms within each of the three legal fields, but also between these areas of law by trying to answer the following questions:

- To what extent may common patterns be discerned?
- Are the respective treaty arrangements inspired by other treaties, and are there possible lessons to be learned?
- What is the relationship between treaty law and general international law on treaties and on State responsibility, including the notion of 'self-contained regimes'?[8]
- And, finally, do these treaties reveal more general tendencies in the development of international law?

Dispute settlement procedures

Under article 33 of the United Nations Charter, States shall settle their international disputes by peaceful means, including negotiation, inquiry, mediation, conciliation, arbitration or international courts. While the disputing States retain control over the outcome in negotiations, inquiry, mediation and conciliation, these approaches to dispute settlement involve a gradually increasing role for a third party, be it other States, international

---

[8] On self-contained regimes, see the Report on the Study Group of the International Law Commission, 'Fragmentation of International Law: Difficulties Arising from the Diversification and Expansion of International Law', Report of the International Law Commission, 56th Session, 2004, GAOR Supp. No. 10 (A/59/10), pp. 281–305, at pp. 288–93.

organizations or a conciliation committee. Furthermore, the role of law rather than political considerations becomes more important, the apex being international arbitration or courts, which will resolve the dispute on the basis of international law, unless a different mandate is explicitly given by the parties.

The prime advantages of using international courts and tribunals for dispute settlement are that they represent impartial organs with legal expertise, and have a procedure well suited to resolving legal disputes. They provide binding and final decisions in the form of *res judicata*, and may impose obligations of restitution and payment of reparations for damage suffered. While there has been a steady increase in the number of cases brought before the International Court of Justice, the number of States accepting its compulsory jurisdiction remains at some sixty States out of the current 191 Member States of the United Nations. New international courts have, however, been established in the recent decades, such as the International Tribunal for the Law of the Sea and the Dispute Settlement Body of the World Trade Organization. Such courts may be specially designed for the issue at hand and States may more readily accept their compulsory jurisdiction in a limited field.

In all of the three areas covered by this study, specific arrangements for the settlement of disputes have been developed. First, we find examples of obligations to undertake negotiations or conciliation. While the only examples of special courts established in these fields are regional human rights courts, there are several examples of treaties referring to the use of arbitration or pre-existing international courts. The respective studies examine to what extent the use of dispute settlement mechanisms is compulsory or whether instead it requires the *ad hoc* consent of both disputing parties in each case. It is of particular interest to reveal examples of compulsory binding settlement in the form of arbitration or court procedures.

Furthermore, multilateral treaties raise the question of 'standing' in the sense that it may be a question whether all States may bring a claim before the respective dispute settlement mechanisms, or whether some form of qualified injury is required. For instance, such injury may be more difficult to demonstrate if a State violates its human rights obligations towards its own citizens than if environmental damage is suffered as a result of a breach of an environmental agreement. While individuals have standing before regional human rights courts, the role of individuals in other forms of dispute settlement requires scrutiny (e.g. do individuals have standing or may they appear as *amicus curiae*, etc.). Similarly, the legal status of non-governmental organizations (NGOs), both in human rights procedures and in international environmental law and arms control, will be analyzed.

If special dispute mechanisms are established, their structure, composition and procedures must also be addressed. These are relevant issues both in relation to conciliation procedures and arbitration, and in relation to existing regional human rights courts.

Finally, the question to what extent such mechanisms are used in cases of disputes is examined. By whom are the mechanisms used (e.g. only by particular groups of States or also by other actors), and what have been the outcomes? If they are not used, what are the reasons: is it the multilateral rather than the bilateral character of the co-operation, the lack of standing, or the character of what is to be protected (human rights, the environment, the prevention of increased armaments)? Should individuals be given a more prominent role also in matters other than human rights? Should this also be the case for NGOs? If the procedures are not extensively used, may dispute settlement procedures serve as *ultima ratio* if other mechanisms have failed?

Non-compliance procedures

A characteristic feature of human rights treaties is supervisory organs consisting of independent experts. Several multilateral environmental agreements have set up non-compliance committees, although usually consisting of representatives of the States parties. Arms control treaties may provide the secretariat and the plenary body with the responsibility to check compliance by the parties.

These developments may be seen as a reflection of the need to supplement or replace dispute settlement procedures with organs possessing a more facilitative quality, consonant with the view of those claiming that a 'managerial approach' rather than an 'enforcement approach' is needed in order to address non-compliance questions.[9] It has furthermore been

---

[9] On the managerial and enforcement approaches, see Abram Chayes and Antonia Handler Chayes, *The New Sovereignty: Compliance with International Regulatory Agreements* (Cambridge, MA: Harvard University Press, 1995). The authors claim that '[a] century of experience with international adjudication leads to considerable skepticism about its suitability as an international dispute settlement method and, in particular, as a way of securing compliance with treaties' (p. 205). See further, on the two approaches, Kyle Danish, 'Book Review: The New Sovereignty' (1997) 37 *Virginia Journal of International Law* 789; Harold Hongju Koh, 'Review Essay: Why Do Nations Obey International Law?' (1996–7) 106 *Yale Law Journal* 2599; Kal

argued that the bilateral character of dispute settlement procedures is inherently ill-suited to dealing with multiparty problems, such as the ones dealt with in this book. Treaty organs may also be better designed towards prevention rather than reparation of possible damage caused by non-compliance. Finally, it may be added that there may be a danger that confrontational approaches might undermine the co-operative spirit in ongoing international co-operation under the same treaties.

These may be some of the reasons why non-compliance procedures are established in treaties. An alternative explanation, however, is that States prefer non-compliance procedures because – instead of leaving decisions to a third party in the form of a court or an arbitral tribunal – they allow States more control over the process and its outcome. Furthermore, a decision resulting from a non-compliance procedure is not final in the form of *res judicata*, and may therefore be seen as less intrusive on State sovereignty.

A fundamental requirement for assessing compliance with international obligations is information about relevant facts, be it the emission of relevant polluting substances, the treatment of human beings, or the manufacturing and storage of weapons. States have traditionally been responsible for providing such data through reporting obligations. It is therefore examined to what extent the parties to treaties in the three fields under scrutiny have an obligation to report their implementation of substantive obligations. There may exist, however, a need to supplement State reporting with information provided by other sources, such as monitoring from other States or from international bodies. Such arrangements may be found in treaties on the prevention of torture, certain environmental treaties and arms control.

The establishment of international organs to deal with possible non-compliance issues may serve to disclose or possibly prevent non-compliance, and to develop common approaches to non-compliance issues among States parties. Relevant questions addressed are:

- What are the mandates for compliance bodies, i.e. to what extent may such mechanisms assess both factual and legal questions?

Raustiala and Anne-Marie Slaughter, 'International Law, International Relations and Compliance', in Walter Carlsnaes, Thomas Risse and Beth A. Simmons (eds.), *Handbook of International Relations* (London: Sage Publications, 2002), pp. 538–59; and Jutta Brunnée and Stephen J. Toope, 'Persuasion and Enforcement: Explaining Compliance with International Law' (2002) 13 *Finnish Yearbook of International Law* 1–14.

INTRODUCTION

- What are the structures, compositions and procedures of such mechanisms as compared to regular dispute settlement mechanisms?
- What are the trigger procedures, i.e. may cases of non-compliance be brought by treaty organs, States, or individuals and non-governmental organizations?
- What are the roles of non-governmental organizations in dealing with non-compliance issues in such treaty bodies?
- What is the legal status of the findings of non-compliance organs, i.e. are they legally binding under international law?
- What is the relationship between non-compliance procedures and dispute settlement? May such procedures be regarded as 'self-contained regimes' in the sense that their existence prevents the applicability of other forms of action against a non-complying State?
- What are the experiences concerning the effectiveness of non-compliance procedures?

It will be of interest to consider whether the differences between the three fields and within each field may be explained by the character of the substantive problem addressed by the respective treaty regime, such as the differences between arms control and human rights, or between torture and other forms of human rights violations. It is, moreover, worthwhile to see whether there are more general developments in the non-compliance procedures, for example to what extent there is a development towards more due process requirements in treaties providing for sanctions against non-complying States. It may also be questioned whether the non-compliance procedures establish a distinct new feature in international law and embody an aspect of its further constitutionalization as well as its legalization.[10]

Enforcement

To the extent that pressure on States is desirable to ensure compliance, one may ask which measures can be effective in an essentially horizontal international legal system. First, it may be asked to what extent compliance

---

[10] On legalization in international law, see K. W. Abbott *et al.*, 'The Concept of Legalization' (2000) 54 *International Organization* 401–19; M. Kahler, 'The Causes and Consequences of Legalization' (2000) 54 *International Organization* 661–85; R O. Keohane *et al.*, 'Legalized Dispute Resolution: Interstate and Transnational' (2000) 54 *International Organization* 457–89; and M. Finnemore and S. J. Toope, 'Alternatives to "Legalization": Richer Views of Law and Politics' (2001) 55 *International Organization* 743–58.

organs may provide assistance to non-complying parties. Furthermore, the finding of non-compliance may serve as 'naming and shaming' ('soft' enforcement). But the crucial question is whether treaty organs may also, should the case arise, decide to use negative consequences in the form of sanctions in cases of non-compliance ('hard' enforcement). If so, what are the sanctions available, for example to what extent may the suspension of rights or the imposition of obligations – such as payment of compensation, or even financial penalties – be used? And, how effective is soft as compared to hard enforcement under the respective treaty regimes?

Finally, what is the proper role of unilateral approaches to enforcement, as opposed to multilateral approaches? Can traditional bilateral enforcement mechanisms such as breach of treaty or counter-measures not only apply, but also play a significant role? Or are the regimes self-contained in the sense that only measures devised by the regimes are available? If State responsibility applies, which States are then in a position to enforce obligations arising under the respective regimes, e.g. are we dealing with obligations *erga omnes inter partes*?

The structure of the book

The three sections of the book, on human rights, international environmental law and arms control, contain a general introduction and three or four case studies of the most relevant treaties in the field. The case studies cover both global and regional treaties and – while by no means exhaustive – are considered to provide a representative expression of the mechanisms applied in the relevant field. The editors have each written one of the three introductions, but the case studies are written by specialists, either working in the secretariat of the relevant treaty or having intimate knowledge of the practical operation of the treaty. The case studies are based on a common template, but the authors have been given considerable freedom regarding both content and format. The book finishes with three articles discussing conclusions that may be drawn on dispute resolution, compliance control and enforcement, respectively. Most of the contributions were discussed at a workshop held at the Walther-Schücking-Institute in Kiel on 21 and 22 January 2005, and comments have been exchanged subsequently. But, of course, each of the authors bears responsibility for his or her contribution.

PART I

International human rights

1

Dispute resolution, compliance control and enforcement in human rights law

ANDREAS ZIMMERMANN[*]

1.1 General questions and introduction

International law has seen a vast and far-reaching development of human rights law, starting with the adoption of the Universal Declaration of Human Rights,[1] to the entry into force of regional human rights conventions such as the European Convention on Human Rights,[2] to the two Covenants on Civil and Political and on Social and Economic Rights[3] and later specific subject-matter-oriented treaties such as the United Nations Convention Against Torture,[4] the Convention on the Rights of the Child[5] and finally the Convention on the Elimination of All Forms of Discrimination Against Women.[6]

Yet, if one considers the daily reality of international life, one might wonder whether this development of substantive rules and the attempt to codify existing rules has led to an increased level of *de facto* protection of human rights.[7] Thus the issue arises how the various treaties guaranteeing

---

[*] Thanks go to Björn Elberling for his very valuable help in finalizing the manuscript.

[1] Universal Declaration of Human Rights, New York, 10 December 1948, GA Res. 217 A (III), UN Doc. A/810 (1948), p. 71.

[2] European Convention for the Protection of Human Rights and Fundamental Freedoms, Rome, 4 November 1950, ETS No. 5 (hereinafter, ECHR).

[3] International Covenant on Civil and Political Rights, New York, 16 December 1966, 999 UNTS 171 (hereinafter, ICCPR); International Covenant on Economic, Social and Cultural Rights, New York, 16 December 1966, 993 UNTS 3 (hereinafter, ICESCR).

[4] Convention Against Torture and Other Cruel, Inhuman or Degrading Treatment or Punishment, New York, 10 December 1984, 1465 UNTS 85 (hereinafter, UN CAT).

[5] Convention on the Rights of the Child, New York, 20 November 1989, 1577 UNTS 3 (hereinafter, CRC).

[6] Convention on the Elimination of All Forms of Discrimination Against Women, New York, 18 December 1979, 1249 UNTS 13 (hereinafter, CEDAW).

[7] For a critical view on the effectiveness of human rights protection in general, see Oona A. Hathaway, 'Do Human Rights Treaties Make a Difference?' (2002) 111 *Yale Law Journal*

human rights by the same token also provide for mechanisms of dispute settlement, enforcement and compliance control.

This presentation will focus mainly on dispute resolution, enforcement and compliance control as contemplated by the various treaty regimes, in particular those treaty regimes which are not the subject of more specific case reports.[8] In addition, some general remarks are also warranted relating not to treaty regimes, but to issues of general international law in the context of human rights protection, such as diplomatic protection and State responsibility.

In the field of human rights protection, the three notions of dispute resolution, compliance control and enforcement overlap to a certain degree. This is because each and every decision or recommendation by a dispute settlement body created under a given treaty necessarily entails a determination of whether the State concerned has fulfilled its obligations under that treaty. Thus any dispute settlement mechanism also carries with it – at least to some extent and on an individualized basis – the potential to serve as a compliance control mechanism. Already the determination by an international court or tribunal or a similar institution that there has been a treaty violation not only carries with it the obligation to carry out the relevant decision, but also highlights the fact that the State concerned has not abided by its obligations under the treaty. This fact alone normally induces most States to change their behaviour. Thus any such decisions also serve as a method to bring about increased compliance. Still, for the sake of clarity, an attempt will be made to distinguish the three notions of dispute resolution, compliance control and enforcement as much as possible.

1.2 Dispute resolution

1.2.1 Arrangements for compulsory dispute settlement

While quite a number of human rights treaties provide for some form of dispute settlement by a treaty body, either in the form of legally binding

---

1935–2042. See also the reply by Ryan Goodman and Derek Jinks, 'Measuring the Effects of Human Rights Treaties' (2003) 14 *European Journal of International Law* 171–83; as well as the further reply by Oona A. Hathaway, 'Testing Conventional Wisdom' (2003) 14 *European Journal of International Law* 185–200.

[8] See also the overview by C. Heyns, D. Padilla and L. Zwaak, 'A Schematic Comparison of Regional Human Rights Systems: An Update' (2005) 5 *African Human Rights Law Journal* 308.

judgments or in the form of non-binding 'views', in most cases this settlement is *optional* only. This is especially true with regard to treaties adopted under the auspices of the United Nations, but also in the Inter-American and African systems as far as the jurisdiction of the respective Court, as opposed to Commission, is concerned.[9]

The only notable exception in the field of human rights *stricto sensu* seems to be the European Convention on Human Rights (ECHR) as amended by Protocol No. 11. Regarding human rights treaties in a broader sense, one should refer to the Genocide Convention,[10] which in its article IX provides for the jurisdiction of the International Court of Justice (ICJ).

1.2.2 Use of ordinary courts and tribunals instead of special institutions and procedures for the settlement of disputes

As human rights treaties usually set up a specific dispute settlement body, the use of regular courts, and in particular the ICJ, to settle disputes arising under the respective treaty is not, as such, foreseen – the Genocide Convention being the rare exception. One general question that might arise is whether, by establishing a given dispute settlement mechanism for a treaty, the parties to that treaty have also excluded the possibility of referring a case to the ICJ, even where the ICJ would otherwise have jurisdiction under general rules.[11]

As far as can be seen, the ECHR is the only human rights treaty which even addresses this issue. According to its article 35(2)(b), the ECHR shall not deal with an application which is 'substantially the same as a matter that . . . has already been submitted to another procedure of international investigation or settlement and contains no relevant new information'. With regard to other conventions, in the absence of any prohibitive norm,

---

[9] ICCPR, art. 41; UN CAT, art. 22; American Convention on Human Rights, 1144 UNTS 123 (hereinafter, ACHR), art. 45 (on the Commission) and art. 62 (on the Court); African Charter on Human and Peoples' Rights, 1520 UNTS 217 (hereinafter, African Charter), art. 45 (on the Commission); Protocol to the African Charter on Human and Peoples' Rights on the Establishment of a Court on Human and Peoples' Rights, Ouagadougou, Burkina Faso, 10 June 1998, OAU Doc. OAU/LEG/EXP/AFCHPR/PROT (III) (hereinafter, Protocol to the African Charter), art. 3 (on the Court).

[10] Convention on the Prevention and Punishment of the Crime of Genocide, New York, 9 December 1948, 78 UNTS 277.

[11] I.e. either by virtue of two matching declarations under art. 36(2) of the Court's Statute or under a compromissory clause, as mentioned in art. 36(1) of the Statute, contained in a general bilateral or multilateral treaty.

18   INTERNATIONAL HUMAN RIGHTS

parties are free to submit disputes arising under such treaties to other general dispute settlement procedures, in particular to the ICJ. In fact, article 44 of the International Covenant on Civil and Political Rights (ICCPR) specifically provides that the provisions of the Covenant 'shall not prevent the States parties . . . from having recourse to other procedures for settling a dispute in accordance with general or special . . . agreements in force between them'.

Still, in practice, apart from the Genocide Convention,[12] States have so far almost never seized the ICJ or any other arbitral tribunal with disputes arising under one of the major human rights treaties.[13]

1.2.3 Mandate, composition and procedures of dispute settlement institutions

1.2.3.1 Mandate

When seized of an individual case and thus serving in its dispute settlement function in the strictest sense, the respective treaty body is mandated to undertake a case-specific determination of whether in the given case the State has abided by its obligations under the respective human rights treaty. The situation is somewhat different when – as provided for in certain treaty regimes – such body is seized with an inter-State complaint, as for example in the Greek case before the Strasbourg institutions. In such cases, the respective institution usually has to give an overall evaluation of the situation in a given country and thus must take into account a significantly broader picture.[14]

---

[12] See e.g. *Application of the Convention on the Prevention and Punishment of the Crime of Genocide* (*Bosnia and Herzegovina* v. *Yugoslavia*), Preliminary Objections, Judgment of 11 July 1996, ICJ Reports 1996, pp. 595 *et seq.*; *Application of the Convention on the Prevention and Punishment of the Crime of Genocide* (*Croatia* v. *Yugoslavia*), www.icj-cij.org/icjwww/idocket/icry/icryframe.htm.

[13] But see *Armed Activities on the Territory of the Congo (New Application: 2002)* (*Democratic Republic of the Congo* v. *Rwanda*), Judgment of 3 February 2006, www.icj-cij.org/icjwww/idocket/icrw/icrwframe.htm, where the applicant State *inter alia* relied on alleged violations of the UN CAT, the Genocide Convention, the International Convention on the Elimination of All Forms of Racial Discrimination (New York, 7 March 1966, 660 UNTS 195) (hereinafter, CERD) and CEDAW.

[14] See e.g. Jochen A. Frowein and Wolfgang Peukert, *Europäische MenschenRechtsKonvention – EGMR-Kommentar* (Kehl: N. P. Engel, 2nd edn, 1996), art. 24, marginal notes 12 and 13. The only exception to this rule was a case brought by Austria against Italy concerning a single criminal trial in Italy (European Commission on Human Rights, *Austria* v. *Italy*, Decision of 11 January 1961, http://hudoc/.echr.coe.int/hudoc/).

1.2.3.2 Composition

It is quite striking that almost all human rights treaty bodies and courts are composed in a rather similar manner. First, they normally consist of individuals being elected in their individual capacity, and not as State representatives, for a given period.[15] Secondly, the number of members is either equivalent to the number of States parties – for those treaties with a limited number of contracting parties – or otherwise limited to a certain number.[16] In the latter case, the composition takes into account an equitable geographic distribution among the various geographic groups represented in the United Nations.[17]

1.2.3.3 Procedures

An in-depth analysis of the procedures provided for in the various human rights treaties would go beyond the scope of this contribution. Some common features might be discerned, however. The focus will be laid only on those procedures where the respective body deals with an individual application either by an individual or a State, given that, where the respective treaty body is considering a State report, one cannot speak of dispute settlement *stricto sensu.*

After the application has been lodged, the State concerned is usually granted the right to take a position.[18] Usually, an oral hearing takes place, allowing the State concerned to present its own position.[19] Furthermore, the applicant or in some cases a third party representing the applicant's interests – such as the European Commission on Human Rights under the old ECHR regime – also has the right to present its views.[20] Finally, the respective dispute settlement body will render a decision, either in the form

---

[15] ICCPR, arts. 28 *et seq.*; UN CAT, art. 17; ACHR, arts. 34–40 (on the Commission) and art. 52 (on the Court); African Charter, arts. 30 and 31 (on the Commission); Protocol to the African Charter, art. 11 (on the Court).

[16] ICCPR, art. 28; UN CAT, art. 17; ACHR, arts. 34 and 35 (on the Commission) and art. 52 (on the Court); African Charter, art. 31 (on the Commission); Protocol to the African Charter, art. 11 (on the Court).   [17] ICCPR, art. 31; UN CAT, art. 17.

[18] ICCPR, art. 41(1)(a); First Additional Protocol to the ICCPR, 999 UNTS 302, art. 4; UN CAT, art. 21(1)(a); ACHR, art. 48(1)(a) (on the Commission); African Charter, art. 47 (on the Commission); Protocol to the African Charter, art. 26(2) (on the Court).

[19] ICCPR, art. 41(1)(g); UN CAT, art. 21(1)(g); ACHR, art. 48(1)e (on the Commission); African Charter, art. 51(2) (on the Commission).

[20] ICCPR, art. 41(1)(g); UN CAT, art. 21(1)(a); African Charter, art. 51(2) (on the Commission); Protocol to the African Charter, art. 26(2) (on the Court).

20   INTERNATIONAL HUMAN RIGHTS

of a formal, legally binding judgment or in the form of a non-legally binding 'view'.[21]

1.2.4 Standing of States to bring cases before the respective mechanism

No uniform picture can be discerned with regard to the standing of States to bring complaints. There are a significant number of human rights treaties which grant States the right, in line with the *erga omnes* character of the underlying rights,[22] to bring cases against other contracting parties for alleged violations of the respective treaty provisions.[23] On the other hand, there are also other major human rights treaties which do not contain such clauses, e.g. the Convention on the Rights of the Child (CRC) or the Convention on the Elimination of All Forms of Discrimination Against Women (CEDAW), including its optional protocol.

1.2.5 Standing and role of individuals and NGOs (as complainants or amici curiae)

Individuals are granted standing before dispute settlement bodies more often than States, at least *vis-à-vis* those States that have accepted the jurisdiction of the respective body in cases of optional dispute-settlement systems.

In order to lodge a complaint, the complainant must usually be considered a 'victim' of a violation of the respective treaty. Accordingly, NGOs may not, as a matter of principle, bring claims on behalf of third parties. In other words, an *actio popularis* is not available before most treaty bodies. There are, however, two major exceptions. Article 44 of the American Convention on Human Rights (ACHR) grants NGOs the right to lodge complaints with the Inter-American Commission on Human Rights.[24] Similarly, under the

---

[21] ICCPR, art. 41(1)(h); First Additional Protocol to the ICCPR, art. 5(4); UN CAT, art. 21(1)(h); ACHR, arts. 49–51 (on the Commission) and art. 63 (on the Court); African Charter, arts. 52–53 (on the Commission); Protocol to the African Charter, art. 27 (on the Court).

[22] On the *erga omnes* concept, and its relevance for human rights proceedings, see generally Christian J. Tams, *Enforcing Obligations Erga Omnes in International Law* (Cambridge: Cambridge University Press, 2005), especially at pp. 69 *et seq.* and pp. 158 *et seq.*

[23] Such rules are, *inter alia*, contained in ICCPR, art. 41; UN CAT, art. 21 (provided that the respondent State has recognized the jurisdiction of the committee in that regard); and CERD, arts. 11 *et seq.*

[24] See Ruth Wedgwood, 'Legal Personalities and the Role of Non-Governmental Organizations and Transnational Enterprises in International Law and the Changing Role of the State', in

Additional Protocol to the European Social Charter, certain NGOs – namely, those which have been granted consultative status with the Council of Europe and accredited by the assembly of contracting parties – may lodge complaints against States claiming violations of the European Social Charter.[25]

In some of the treaty regimes which do not allow NGOs to institute claims, such organizations still have the possibility of otherwise influencing the decision-making process. In particular, they have been granted the right to participate as *amici curiae* in proceedings before both the European and the Inter-American Courts of Human Rights.[26] With regard to human rights instruments adopted under the umbrella of the United Nations, the respective rules of procedure usually enable the treaty body to request information from NGOs, such information being particularly important when a State report is being considered.

1.2.6 Extent of usage of arrangements for dispute settlement

On the question of usage, a distinction must be made between individual complaints and inter-State proceedings. In those treaty regimes which grant individuals the right to bring claims, this option has been used to quite some extent;[27] the most prominent example being the overwhelming, maybe too overwhelming,[28] success of the European Court of Human Rights.

Rainer Hofman (ed.), *Non-State Actors as New Subjects of International Law – From the Traditional State Order Towards the Law of the Global Community* (Berlin: Duncker & Humblot, 1999), pp. 21–36, at pp. 24–5; Martin Ölz, *Die NGOs in Recht des internationalen Menschenrechtsschutzes* (Vienna: Verlag Österreich, 2002), pp. 332–3.

[25] Additional Protocol to the European Social Charter Providing for a System of Collective Complaints, Strasbourg, 9 November 1995, ETS No. 58, art. 1(b).

[26] Hervé Ascensio, 'L'amicus curiae devant les juridictions internationales' (2001) 105 *Revue Générale de Droit International Public* 897–930, at 902.

[27] In the UN system, the Human Rights Committee has so far dealt with 1,279 cases, with 287 still pending (OHCHR, Statistical Survey of Individual Complaints, www.unhchr.ch/html/menu2/8/stat2.htm), the Committee Against Torture has dealt with 283 cases, 47 cases are pending (OHCHR Statistics, www.ohchr.org/english/bodies/cat/stat3.htm) and the Committee under CERD has dealt with thirty-five cases, three cases are pending (OHCHR Statistics, www.ohchr.org/english/bodies/cerd/stat4.htm). The Committee under CEDAW has so far dealt with two individual communications (www.un.org/womenwatch/daw/cedaw/protocol/dec-views.htm). The Inter-American Commission on Human Rights has received 1,080 complaints in 2003 and 1,329 complaints in 2004 (Annual Report of the Inter-American Commission on Human Rights 2004, OAS Doc. OAE/Ser.L/V/II.122 Doc. 5 rev. 1 (23 February 2005)).

[28] Over 38,000 applications were lodged with the Court in 2003; this figure rose to over 44,000 applications in 2004 (Survey of Activities 2005, www.echr.coe.int/ECHR/EN/Header/Reports+and+Statistics/Reports/Annual+surveys+of+activity/). In fact, fears of the Court being

In sharp contrast, States have been very reluctant to bring inter-State complaints. Even within the framework of the ECHR, probably for a long time the most highly integrated and least heterogeneous system for the protection of human rights, such examples were rare[29] and only occurred either where the political situation between the complainant and the respondent States were already rather difficult[30] or where, as in the Greek case,[31] the respective treaty violations were both blatant and widespread. It seems to be quite obvious that the reason for this reluctance to bring inter-State complaints is that other national interests by and large overshadow the political interest in bringing about treaty compliance. Besides, in many cases, States seem to have the feeling that there are other, more promising ways to settle disputes concerning compliance by other States.[32]

1.3 Compliance control

Compliance control usually presupposes that States have already undertaken obligations with which they have to comply, and this is indeed the usual form of compliance control concerning human rights treaties. The Council of Europe, however, also utilizes a particular system of compliance control by which possible new Member States of the Council are 'screened' before being admitted as new members, and their admission is made subject to certain commitments undertaken in the field of human rights protection.

1.3.1 Ex ante *compliance control in the Council of Europe system*

The idea behind these procedures is that the Council of Europe (CoE) should admit as new members only those States which are perceived as

> overwhelmed by applications led to the adoption of Protocol No. 14, striving for more streamlined procedures and some limitations on the right of application. On this protocol, see Tilmann Laubner, 'Relieving the Court of Its Success? Protocol No. 14 to the European Convention on Human Rights' (2004) 47 *German Yearbook of International Law* 691–721.

[29] See Frowein and Peukert, *Europäische MenschenRechtsKonvention*, art. 24, marginal note 2, for a list of the ten cases brought up to the end of 1999.

[30] E.g. European Court of Human Rights, *Ireland* v. *United Kingdom*, Judgment of 18 January 1978, Ser. A No. 25; *Cyprus* v. *Turkey*, Judgment of 10 May 2001, ECHR 2001-IV, pp. 1–235.

[31] European Commission on Human Rights, *Denmark, Norway, Sweden and the Netherlands* v. *Greece*, Decision of 24 January 1968, http://hudoc/.echr.coe.int/hudoc/.

[32] Scott Leckie, 'The Inter-State Complaint Procedure in International Human Rights Law: Hopeful Prospects or Wishful Thinking?' (1988) 10 *Human Rights Quarterly* 249, at 252.

being able and willing to fulfil certain obligations, namely, those contained in article 3 of the CoE Statute, as well as obligations they will incur when becoming parties to the ECHR. The basis for this approach can be found in article 4 of the CoE Statute, which provides that the ability and willingness to fulfil the provisions of article 3 are pre-conditions to membership in the Council. It is against this background that the Council of Ministers has undertaken a screening of States applying for membership in order to evaluate whether they indeed fulfil the criteria contained in article 3.

1.3.1.1 Screening

This screening of applicant States before they are admitted as members of the Council of Europe is a relatively new phenomenon. Until 1989, the Council of Europe had not put into place any such procedure – not even with regard to States such as Spain and Portugal which had only installed or reinstalled democratic systems of governments very shortly before applying for membership in the Council.[33] It was only after the dramatic changes occurring in and after 1989 that such a procedure was put into place; and in at least one case, that of the Federal Republic of Yugoslavia, an application for membership was rejected due to an internal situation considered not in conformity with the standard foreseen in article 3 of the CoE Statute.[34]

Technically speaking, it is for the Committee of Ministers to decide upon any application for membership in the Council, as contemplated in article 4 of the CoE Statute. Yet, since the very beginning of the existence of the Council, the Parliamentary Assembly has always played a decisive role. The Committee of Ministers has regularly invited the Assembly to give its opinion, and it is hardly conceivable that the Committee of Ministers would disregard a negative opinion of the Assembly. The Parliamentary Assembly in turn usually invites rapporteurs – usually former or current members of the European Commission or the European Court of Human Rights – whose task is to examine the compatibility of the respective domestic legal system with applicable Council of Europe standards.[35] This process is often in itself

---

[33] Portugal and Spain were both admitted on 24 November 1976, less than two years after the first free general election in Portugal on 25 April 1975 and even before the first such election in Spain on 15 June 1977.

[34] Decisions of the Committee of Ministers (Deputies), 639th meeting (7–9 September 1998), Item 2.4; Vladimir Djeric, 'Admission to Membership of the Council of Europe and Legal Significance of Commitments Entered into by New Member States' (2000) 60 *Zeitschrift für ausländisches öffentliches Recht und Völkerrecht* 605–29, at 608.

[35] Djeric, 'Admission to Membership of the Council of Europe', 609.

24 INTERNATIONAL HUMAN RIGHTS

a sufficient catalyst for improving the situation in the applicant State, since the prospect of becoming a member of the Council of Europe is a great incentive, and considered a major step towards European integration.

Still, one must acknowledge that the Council organs have a certain margin of appreciation as to the question whether a given State fulfils the criteria contained in article 3 of the CoE Statute, since the text refers to the fact that such State must be *deemed*[36] to be able and willing to fulfil the provisions of article 3. One pertinent example is the admission of the Russian Federation, where the report of the rapporteur was rather critical regarding the human rights situation, but where political considerations nevertheless tipped the balance in favour of admission.[37]

1.3.1.2 Pre-accession undertakings

The screening procedure is further supplemented by requesting the candidate State to enter into certain commitments when adhering to the Council of Europe. Ever since the admission of Malta in 1965,[38] the political organs of the Council of Europe have made reference to the ECHR in the relevant accession documents. Later, adhering States expressed their intention to sign and ratify the Convention upon accession. It was, however, only when the Central and Eastern European States knocked on the Council's door that this practice became more formalized.

Since then, States are not only required to undertake formal commitments to ratify the ECHR and its protocols – including the 12th and 13th Protocols, some of which have not even been ratified by all current Member States – they also have to make other commitments. To give one example, the latest newly admitted member, Serbia and Montenegro,[39] was required to ratify the European Convention for the Prevention of Torture and Inhuman or Degrading Treatment or Punishment, the European Charter

---

[36] '[C]onsidéré capable' in the French version.

[37] See Council of Europe, Parliamentary Assembly, Opinion No. 193 (1996) on Russia's request for membership of the Council of Europe adopted by the Assembly on 25 January 1996 (7th Sitting), http://assembly.coe.int/Mainf.asp?link=/Documents/AdoptedText/ta96/EOPI193. tm.

[38] See Council of Europe, Parliamentary Assembly, Opinion No. 44 (1965)[1] on the accession of Malta to the CoE adopted by the Assembly on 25 January 1965 (17th Sitting), http://assembly.coe.int/Mainf.asp?link=/Documents/AdoptedText/ta65/EOPI44.htm.

[39] Federal Republic of Yugoslavia, Application for Membership in the Council of Europe, Doc. 9533, 5 September 2002, See CoE, Parliamentary Assembly, Opinion No. 239 (2002). The Federal Republic of Yugoslavia's application for membership of the CoE was adopted by the Assembly on 24 September 2002 (26th Sitting), http://assembly.coe.int/Mainf.asp?link=/Documents/AdoptedText/ta02/EOPI239.htm.

for Regional or Minority Languages, the European Charter of Local Self-Government, and the European Social Charter, and furthermore to bring its domestic law and policies into line with Council of Europe standards.

The legal character of such commitments is not easy to determine. The practice of both the Parliamentary Assembly and the Committee of Ministers seems to distinguish between 'obligations' arising under the Statute of the Council of Europe and 'commitments' entered into in the context of admission. Therefore, one must probably qualify these 'commitments' as being of a solely political nature, unless the relevant documents emanating from the relevant organs could exceptionally be understood as a binding unilateral declaration.[40] Given the non-legal nature of such 'commitments', it is even more important to stress the relevance of post-accession compliance control by both the Parliamentary Assembly and the Committee of Ministers.

1.3.2 *Reporting obligations with regard to the implementation of substantive obligations*

1.3.2.1 Universal level

The International Labour Organization was the first to establish a reporting system in respect of rights coming within its mandate and based on international instruments adopted under its auspices. Similarly, practically all human rights treaties within the UN system by now contain reporting obligations.[41] It should be noted, however, that a significant number of States are in significant arrears with regard to their reports – by the late 1990s, some parties to the ICCPR had been in arrears for thirteen years and had disregarded twenty-five reminders by the Human Rights Committee.[42]

While providing for regular reporting obligations, as developed in the practice of the Human Rights Committee,[43] has the advantage of being

---

[40] Djeric, 'Admission to Membership of the CoE', 625–8.

[41] Art. 40 of the ICCPR; art. 16 of the ICESCR; art. 9 of CERD; art. 18 of CEDAW; art. 19 of the UN CAT; art. VI of the International Convention on the Suppression and Punishment of the Crime of Apartheid, GA Res. 3068 (XXVIII) of 30 November 1973; art. 44 of the CRC; and art. 17 of the UNESCO Convention Against Discrimination in Education, Paris, 14 December 1960, 429 UNTS 93.

[42] Human Rights Committee, Provisional Agenda and Annotations, UN Doc. CCPR/C/126 of 28 August 1997, pp. 4–7.

[43] See Human Rights Committee, Decision on Periodicity, UN Doc. CCPR/C/19 of 22 July 1981; Vojin Dimitrijevic, 'State Reports', in Gudmundur Alfredsson *et al.* (eds.), *International Human Rights Monitoring Mechanisms – Essays in Honour of Jakob Th. Möller* (The Hague: Martinus Nijhoff, 2001), pp. 185–200, at p. 193.

perceived as impartial and thus inducing States to participate in the process,[44] it can also create the idea that all States which do report also abide by applicable human rights standards to the same extent. To dispel such misconceptions, almost all treaty bodies have amended their rules of procedure so as to empower the respective chairperson to request a report in case of an exceptional situation, even where the body as such is not currently in session.[45]

It should be noted in conclusion that the complete or partial failure of a State to fulfil its reporting obligations *ipso facto* gives rise to a violation of an obligation arising under the respective treaty – a violation which may be treated as such by the respective supervisory mechanism and/or other States parties.

The respective supervisory bodies regularly request that State reports should indicate factors and difficulties affecting the degree of fulfilment of the obligations which the State party has undertaken. They also request information on what measures have been adopted to implement the provisions of the Convention. The respective treaty body normally also adopts concluding comments with regard to a State party after having exchanged views with the State representatives. In those comments, it indicates its views on the degree of compliance by the State concerned. Thus, such a reporting system and its follow-up procedure indeed serves as a compliance control system, albeit with no real enforcement mechanism of its own.

1.3.2.2 Regional systems

With regard to regional human rights systems, the situation as to reporting mechanisms is somewhat more nuanced.

Europe   The ECHR does not, as such, contain a general reporting obligation. Yet, under its article 52, the Secretary-General of the Council of Europe may request one, several or all of the contracting parties to furnish

---

[44] *Ibid.*, pp. 193–4.

[45] The Human Rights Committee amended its Rules of Procedure to empower its chairperson, acting in consultation with other members, to request a report in the case of an exceptional situation and when the Committee is not session (new Rule 66.2). For a similar decision of the Committee on the Rights of the Child, see CRC/C/10, paras. 54–8. For proposals in the same vein by the Committee on Economic, Social and Cultural Rights, see E/C.12/1992/CRP.1/Add.11, paras. 18–20. For the Committee under CERD, see CERD/C/1993/Misc.1/Rev.2, para. 10(h).

information on the implementation of the Convention.[46] In practice, until the late 1980s, the Secretary-General had only addressed five general enquiries to all contracting parties.[47] After the accession of new members, however, the Secretary-General has also used the article 52 powers to address specific requests to certain countries. *Inter alia*, in 2002, the Secretary-General requested an explanation from Moldova reacting in particular to the suspension of a political party,[48] and most recently he requested all Member States of the Council of Europe to furnish explanations in relation to alleged secret detention centres on their territories and related irregular inter-State transport of prisoners.[49]

Unlike the ECHR, other human rights treaties adopted within the framework of the Council of Europe, such as the European Social Charter[50] or the two minority protection treaties, all contain 'classical' reporting systems similar to that contained in the ICCPR, with, however, an enhanced role for the Committee of Ministers. According to article 29 of the European Social Charter, if the Committee of Experts concludes that a State does not comply with the Charter, and the State takes no action on these conclusions, the Committee may address a recommendation to the respective State, asking it to alter the situation. Similarly, in the case of the two minority protection treaties, the respective reports are first considered by a committee of experts acting as an advisory committee, which then reports to the Committee of Ministers of the Council of Europe.[51]

In this regard, the structure and task of the European Committee for the Protection of Torture (CPT) set up by the European Convention on the Prevention of Torture (ECPT)[52] is unique. As outlined in more detail by Renate Kicker in chapter 4 below,[53] the work of the European

---

[46] On this procedure, see Frowein and Peukert, *Europäische MenschenRechtsKonvention*, art. 57; Paul Mahoney, 'Separation of powers in the Council of Europe: The Status of the European Court of Human Rights vis-à-vis the Authorities of the Council of Europe' (2003) 24 *Human Rights Law Journal* 152–61, at 153.

[47] Frowein and Peukert, *Europäische MenschenRechtsKonvention*, art. 57, marginal note 2.

[48] See CoE, 'Recent Developments Between the Council of Europe and Moldova', CoE Doc. SG/Inf(2002)11 revised 28 March 2002.

[49] For further details, see www.coe.int/T/E/Com/Files/Events/2006-cia/.

[50] European Social Charter (Revised), Strasbourg, 3 May 1996, ETS No. 163.

[51] European Charter for Regional or Minority Languages, Strasbourg, 5 November 1992, ETS No. 148, art. 17; Framework Convention for the Protection of National Minorities, Strasbourg, 1 February 1995, ETS No. 157, art. 26.

[52] European Convention for the Prevention of Torture and Inhuman or Degrading Treatment or Punishment, Strasbourg, 26 June 1987, in force 1 February 1989, ETS No. 126.

[53] See pp. 91–6 below.

Committee for the Protection of Torture is not based on periodic State reports. Instead, the Committee – after having visited a given contracting party either as part of its programme of periodic visits or when it appears to be required by specific circumstances – shall draw up a report on the situation in the relevant State, to which the State concerned may then make comments. While the ECPT itself does not refer to a hard-law obligation to comment, subsequent practice seems to indicate that States always use the opportunity to make such comments. In this regard, it is also important to note that, while article 11(2) provides for the publication of both the CPT report and the governmental comments only upon request by the government, they have, ever since the creation of the CPT, been regularly published. The CPT procedure must therefore be considered as a hybrid between a reporting and a compliance control mechanism.

Americas The American Convention on Human Rights (ACHR) contains only a *nucleus* of reporting obligations, namely, articles 42 and 43. Under article 42, States parties shall submit copies of reports that they prepare for other organs of the Organization of American States (OAS), namely, the Inter-American Economic and Social Council and the Inter-American Council of Education, Science and Culture. Such reports, however, only focus specifically on the rights enshrined in the Convention to the extent that article 26 of the Convention refers to the OAS Charter. Article 42 has therefore been of little relevance in practice, even though article 62 of the Commission's Rules of Procedure empowers the Commission to submit formal requests to governments if they do not abide by their reporting obligation.

In addition, under article 43 of the Convention, the Commission may request that a State supplies information on the implementation of the ACHR in that State. However, just like article 42, this provision – which is *mutatis mutandis* identical to article 52 of the ECHR – has been of little practical importance. One has to note, however, that the Inter-American Commission has developed the practice of on-site investigations as part of its monitoring powers.

Africa Unlike the European and the Inter-American systems, the African Charter on Human and Peoples' Rights does not contain any reporting mechanism.

1.3.3 Arrangements for the monitoring of compliance and mandate, composition and procedures of non-compliance organs

The issue of compliance monitoring can be sub-divided into two categories, namely, on the one hand, securing compliance with general standards as contained in the respective underlying treaty and/or customary law, and, on the other hand, securing compliance with case-specific, individualized decisions of the respective treaty organ.

1.3.3.1 General compliance monitoring systems

Universal level Apart from the reporting system previously outlined, most universal human rights treaty systems do not contain generalized mechanisms for monitoring compliance. It is noteworthy, however, that the Optional Protocol to CEDAW empowers the Committee established under CEDAW to start an investigation if it receives reliable information about gross or systematic violations of the Convention by a State party.[54] This is a procedure modelled along the so-called '1503-procedure' dealt with below. Another notable exception is provided for by article 20 of the United Nations Convention Against Torture (UN CAT). Under this provision, whenever the Committee set up by the Convention receives reliable information indicating that torture is being systematically practised in a given State, it shall invite the State to co-operate in the examination of the information and to submit observations. The Committee may then undertake a confidential inquiry, which may include a visit to the State concerned, provided that the State agrees. Finally, the Committee may make comments and suggestions to the respective contracting party. All steps of this procedure are of a confidential nature, but the Committee may decide to include a summary account of its respective proceedings in its annual report. Unlike the system provided for in the European Convention for the Prevention of Torture, the system of visits as provided for in the UN CAT possesses more of a compliance control character, given that it presupposes concrete and specific allegations of torture being systematically committed in a given State, in order for the Committee to undertake an investigation and eventually an on-site visit.[55]

---

[54] Optional Protocol to CEDAW, New York, GA Res. 54/4 of 6 October 1999, art. 8.

[55] It should be noted, however, that quite a number of States made use of the option, under art. 28 of UN CAT, of entering a reservation concerning art. 20, which establishes the Committee's powers. See www.ohchr.org/english/countries/ratification/9.htm#reservations.

30 INTERNATIONAL HUMAN RIGHTS

Besides these treaty-specific monitoring mechanisms, the so-called '1503-procedure', as developed and revised by the former Commission on Human Rights and the Economic and Social Council,[56] also served in the past[57] as a generalized monitoring tool, highlighting those States where there is 'a consistent pattern of gross and reliably attested violations of human rights'. This process also served as a more general compliance control mechanism, since the reference by the Working Group on Communications of the Sub-Commission on the Promotion and Protection of Human Rights established by virtue of Resolution 1503 (as amended) to the Working Group on Situations already presupposes a finding in that regard. The same is true for the further reference by the Working Group on Situations to the Commission on Human Rights, which in turn could then take a decision concerning each situation, including eventually appointing an independent expert in order to enter into contact with the respective State or to appoint a Special Rapporteur. While the whole procedure, as a matter of principle, remained confidential, the Chairperson of the Commission on Human Rights publicly announced the names of those States that were under examination. The Commission could furthermore decide to take the matter up in public. It remains to be seen how the newly created Human Rights Council will further develop this supervisory mechanism.

Regional level: the example of the Council of Europe Within the system of the Council of Europe, the Parliamentary Assembly has set up a Monitoring Committee in order to verify whether in particular new Member States honour both the obligations incurred by membership in the Council and the pre-accession commitments mentioned above.[58] A similar mechanism has also been set up by the Committee of Ministers in pursuance of a Committee of Ministers' Declaration of 10 November 1994.[59]

---

[56] Resolution 1503 (XLVIII) of 27 May 1970, revised by Resolution 2000/3 of 16 June 2000; on this procedure, see generally María Francisca Ize-Charrin, '1503: A Serious Procedure', in Alfredsson *et al.*, *International Human Rights Monitoring Mechanisms*, pp. 293–310.

[57] The Human Rights Council replaced the Commission on Human Rights, which was formally abolished on 16 June 2006 while the first meeting of the Human Rights Council took place on 19 June 2006, see GA Res. A/Res/60/251 of 15 March 2006.

[58] CoE, Parliamentary Assembly, Resolution 1115 (1997) on the setting up of an Assembly committee on the honouring of obligations and commitments by Member States of the Council of Europe (Monitoring Committee).

[59] See generally Andrew Drzemczewski, 'Monitoring by the Council of Europe', in Alfredsson *et al.*, *International Human Rights Monitoring Mechanisms*, pp. 525–32.

The statutory basis for the monitoring work of the Committee of Ministers may be found in articles 7 and 8 of the CoE Statute, under which the Committee may decide upon the suspension and eventual expulsion of a Member State in case of a serious violation of the rule of law and human rights standards contained in article 3 of the Statute. This presupposes that the Committee of Ministers also has an inherent power to monitor these obligations. Similarly, the Parliamentary Assembly has been granted the power, under article 23(a) of the CoE Statute, to discuss and make recommendations upon any matter referred to it by the Committee of Ministers. Given that the Committee of Ministers has decided that it shall seek the advice of the Parliamentary Assembly[60] before inviting a member of the Council to withdraw from membership, it follows that the Assembly also has monitoring powers.

The compliance monitoring system as developed by the Committee of Ministers also foresees that, every other year, the Secretary-General shall provide the Committee with a factual overview of compliance with the commitments undertaken by Member States. This overview will then be discussed by the Committee of Ministers on the basis of confidentiality.[61]

Finally, with regard to the monitoring of the European Social Charter, the reports of the Committee of Experts created by the Charter are communicated to a subcommittee of the Council of Europe, reviewed by the Parliamentary Assembly and communicated to the Committee of Ministers, which may then finally make recommendations to the State concerned.[62]

1.3.3.2 Case-specific compliance monitoring systems

The other dimension of compliance monitoring is the monitoring in specific cases, i.e. after an individual case has been dealt with by a treaty body. This issue obviously arises only with regard to those treaties which grant such bodies the right to decide individual cases.

Universal level   With regard to those universal human rights treaties that grant individuals the possibility to bring a claim, the resulting treaty body's 'views' on individual cases, even if they are not as such legally binding, will also recommend which measures ought to be taken by the respective

---

[60] CoE, Committee of Ministers, Statutory Resolution (51) 30 of 3 May 1951.   [61] *Ibid.*
[62] European Social Charter, art. 25.

contracting party to remedy a breach.[63] The various rules of procedure of such treaty bodies all contain specific provisions on the follow-up and implementation of their decisions.[64]

The first question that arises is whether – given the lack of specific authorization for such follow-up in the respective treaty – the respective treaty body is indeed empowered to provide for such follow-up when adopting or amending their rules of procedure. It is probably correct to assume that, even without a legally binding force of their own, contracting parties are under an obligation to take the respective decisions of the treaty bodies into account as part of their overall obligation to abide by and implement their general treaty obligations *in casu*. And, if that is true, the respective treaty body must also possess the implied power to verify how and to what extent such decisions are respected, since every procedure of international dispute settlement in the larger sense must be able to verify whether a settlement has been reached.[65]

It is against this background that the various rules of procedure either provide that the State party concerned shall simply be invited to inform the Committee of the action it takes in conformity with the Committee's recommendations,[66] or go further by providing for the designation of a rapporteur or a working group to ascertain the measures taken by States parties to give effect to the Committee's views and recommendations, which may then take appropriate action to be reported back to the treaty body at large.[67]

The only sanction in case a State party does not implement the 'views' of the respective treaty body, however, lies in the ability of the treaty body to

---

[63] Markus G. Schmidt, 'Follow-up Procedures to Individual Complaints and Periodic State Reporting Mechanisms', in Alfredsson *et al.*, *International Human Rights Monitoring Mechanisms*, pp. 201–15.

[64] Rules of Procedure of the Human Rights Committee, 22 September 2005, UN Doc. CCPR/C/3/Rev.8, Rule 101; Rules of Procedure of the Committee Against Torture, 9 August 2002, UN Doc. CAT/C/3/Rev.4, Rule 114; Rules of Procedure of the Inter-American Commission on Human Rights, as amended in October 2003, www.cidh.org/Basicos/basic16.htm, arts. 43–46.

[65] Schmidt, 'Follow-up Procedures to Individual Complaints', p. 202; Markus G. Schmidt, 'Portée et suivi des constatations du Comité des droits de l'homme des Nations Unies', in Frédéric Sudre (ed.), *La Protection des droits de l'homme par le Comité des droits de l'homme – les communications individuelles* (Montpellier: IDEDH, 1995), pp. 157–69, at pp. 159–60.

[66] Rules of Procedure of the Committee under CERD of 1 January 1989, UN Doc. CERD/C/35/Rev.3, Rule 95(5).

[67] Rules of Procedure of the Human Rights Committee, Rule 95, paras. 1 and 3; Rules of Procedure of the Committee under CEDAW, UN Doc. A/56/38, Annex 1, Rule 73, paras. 4–6; Rules of Procedure of the Committee Against Torture, Rule 114.

include information on its follow-up activities and the respective reactions thereto in its annual report.

Europe In Europe, the only conventions adopted under the umbrella of the Council of Europe which provide for individual complaints, are the ECHR and the European Social Charter as amended. The ECHR possesses the most sophisticated compliance control mechanism.

Under article 46(1) of the ECHR, States parties are under an obligation to abide by a judgment of the European Court of Human Rights. While there might be doubts about the exact limits of the legal effects of such a judgment *vis-à-vis* other States parties or in parallel cases involving the same State,[68] there can be no doubt that, at the very least with regard to the case at hand, the respective contracting party is obliged to follow up on those measures indicated by the European Court of Human Rights in its holding.

Article 46(2) provides that the judgment shall be transmitted to the Committee of Ministers, which supervises its execution.[69] Under the rules adopted by the Committee of Ministers for that purpose,[70] where the Court has found a violation in a given case, it is inscribed on the agenda of the Committee of Ministers without delay, and the defendant State is under an

---

[68] See Frowein and Peukert, *Europäische MenschenRechtsKonvention*, art. 53, marginal notes 7 *et seq.*; and Mark E. Villiger, *Handbuch der Europäischen Menschenrechtskonvention (EMRK)* (Zurich: Schulthess, 1993), p. 150, for a view in favour of a binding effect beyond the actual case in question; for the contrary view, see Eckart Klein, 'Should the Binding Effect of the Judgments of the European Court of Human Rights be Extended?', in Paul Mahoney (ed.), *Protection des droits de l'homme: la perspective européenne: mélanges à la mémoire de Rolv Ryssdal* (Cologne: Heymann, 2000), pp. 705–13.

[69] See, on this issue, Fredrik G. E. Sundberg, 'Control of Execution of Decisions under the ECHR – Some Remarks on the Committee of Ministers' Control of the Proper Implementation of Decisions Finding Violations of the Convention', in Alfredsson *et al.*, *International Human Rights Monitoring Mechanisms*, pp. 561–85; Rolv Ryssdal, 'The Enforcement System Set up under the European Convention on Human Rights', in Mielle Bulterman *et al.* (eds.), *Compliance with Judgments of International Courts* (The Hague: Martinus Nijhoff, 1996), pp. 49–66; Georg Ress, 'Article 54', in Louis-Edmond Pettiti *et al.* (eds.), *La convention européenne des droits de l'homme: commentaire article par article* (Paris: Economica, 1995), pp. 857–69; Hans-Jürgen Bartsch, 'The Supervisory Functions of the Committee of Ministers under Article 54 – A Postscript to Luedicke-Belkacem-Koç', in Franz Matscher and Herbert Petzold (eds.), *Protecting Human Rights: The European Dimension* (Cologne: Carl Heymann, 1988), pp. 47–55. See also Resolution DH (83) 4 of 23 March 1983 of the Committee of Ministers of the Council of Europe.

[70] Rules adopted by the Committee of Ministers for the application of art. 46(2) of the European Convention on Human Rights, adopted on 10 January 2001, http://cm.coe.int/imntro/e-rules46.htm.

obligation to inform the Committee about its implementing measures. Until the State concerned has provided sufficient information on the execution of the judgment and this fact has been noted by the Committee of Ministers,[71] the case is, as a matter of principle, placed on the agenda of each human rights meeting of the Committee. A point of particular importance is that the Committee of Ministers is entitled to receive information from the injured party as to execution of a judgment in a given case,[72] and that information provided by the State to the Committee shall generally be made available to the public. It is also worth noting that, under the recently adopted Protocol No. 14 to the ECHR, the Court will possess the power to determine that a State has not abided by its obligations to implement a previous judgment of the Court.[73]

The situation is similar with regard to the European Social Charter in the context of findings by the Committee of Independent Experts concerning individual complaints. Thus, under article 8(2) of the Protocol,[74] the Committee of Independent Experts shall draw up a report including a finding whether or not the party has ensured the satisfactory application of the provision of the Charter referred to in the complaint. This report is then transmitted to the Committee of Ministers, the organization that lodged the complaint and the contracting party concerned.

If the Committee of Independent Experts has found that the Charter has not been applied in a satisfactory manner, the Committee of Ministers shall then adopt a recommendation addressed to the contracting party concerned. One major difference from the ECHR is owed to the collective character of the underlying rights and the fact that any violation will almost always necessitate significant legislative and/or administrative changes. The contracting party is therefore granted more time for implementation – in the next report which it submits to the Secretary-General under the European Social Charter the party is solely under an obligation to provide information on measures taken to give effect to the recommendation.

Africa   In Africa, the monitoring of compliance with judgments of the African Court on Human and Peoples' Rights, for those States that have

---

[71] *Ibid.*, Rule 8.   [72] *Ibid.*, Rule 6(a).

[73] See Tilmann Laubner, 'Relieving the Court of Its Success? Protocol No. 14 to the European Convention on Human Rights' (2004) 47 *German Yearbook of International Law* 691–721, at 711.

[74] Protocol Amending the European Social Charter Providing for a System of Collective Complaints, Strasbourg, 9 November 1995, ETS No. 158.

ratified the founding treaty of the Court, is modelled after the European Court of Human Rights. Under article 29(2) of the Protocol creating the Court, the Council of Ministers of the African Union shall monitor the execution of the Court's judgments on behalf of the Assembly. Article 31 furthermore provides that the annual report of the Court submitted to the Assembly shall in particular specify the cases in which a State has not complied with a judgment of the Court.

For the remaining members of the African Union, i.e. those which have not ratified the Protocol creating the Court, the African Charter in its original version remains in force. Were the African Commission to find a violation of the Charter in an inter-State complaint, it could make recommendations it deems useful to the Assembly of Heads of States and Governments.[75] The Charter is, however, silent as to the role of the Assembly in that regard, and given that so far there has been no inter-State complaint there is no relevant practice either.

With regard to communications emanating from individuals, the Commission may consider that those indicate the existence of multiple, serious or massive breaches of rights guaranteed by the Convention. In such cases, the Commission may draw the Assembly's attention to these situations, and the Assembly may permit the Commission to undertake an in-depth study, which would include making recommendations.[76] However, the Charter is again completely silent on the possible monitoring by the Assembly of the implementation of any such recommendations.

Americas   In the Americas, the Inter-American system for the protection of human rights is rather complex since one has to distinguish between those OAS Member States which have ratified the ACHR and those which have not. In addition, one also has to distinguish between the ACHR members which have recognized the jurisdiction of the Inter-American Court of Human Rights in contentious cases, and those which have not done so and are therefore subject only to the jurisdiction of the Inter-American Commission on Human Rights.

The first issue is the monitoring of compliance with decisions of the Inter-American Commission on Human Rights. With regard to all OAS Member States, the Commission may examine communications submitted

---

[75] African Charter on Human and Peoples' Rights, Nairobi, June 1981, 1520 UNTS 217, art. 53.
[76] *Ibid.*, art. 58.

36 INTERNATIONAL HUMAN RIGHTS

to it, address the respective government and make recommendations.[77] With regard to contracting parties of the ACHR, a similar basis can be found in article 41(f) of the ACHR, under which it may take action on petitions. In both scenarios, the Commission handles them in much the same fashion.[78]

When such communication is brought with regard to States not party to the ACHR, the Commission may prepare a 'final decision'.[79] This 'decision' may include recommendations and a deadline for its implementation. Neither the OAS Charter nor any other relevant instrument provides for the monitoring of compliance. In cases where a State does not 'comply' with the recommendations, the Commission may publish its decision and mention it in its annual report.[80] This empowerment of the Commission implies an inherent power to supervise compliance.

With regard to contracting parties of the ACHR, the Commission may similarly, in its report, issue recommendations to the respective State on the basis of article 50 of the ACHR. If the case is not then brought before the Court, the Commission may adopt the report and set a deadline for its implementation. Once this period has expired, the report may once again be published in the annual report of the Commission. Once a report becomes part of the overall annual report of the Commission, the General Assembly of the OAS may discuss the matter and eventually adopt a resolution in that regard.

Finally, the Commission may also, when dealing with a communication concerning a State that has accepted the jurisdiction of the Inter-American Court of Human Rights, refer the case to the Court, which then renders a binding judgment.[81] Summaries of such judgments are then included in the Court's annual report, which is submitted to the General Assembly of the OAS. The summaries shall in particular specify the cases in which a State has not complied with the Court's ruling.[82] In addition, the Court itself considers that it is one of the inherent attributes of its jurisdictional functions to monitor compliance with its decisions. It has therefore

---

[77] Statute of the Inter-American Commission on Human Rights, October 1979, OAS Res. 447 (IX-0/79), art. 20(b).

[78] Thomas Buergenthal, 'Implementation in the Inter-American Human Rights System', in Rudolf Bernhardt et al. (eds.), *International Enforcement of Human Rights* (Heidelberg: Springer, 1985), pp. 57–75, at p. 67.   [79] Rules of Procedure, art. 53.

[80] Rules of Procedure, arts. 45 and 46.

[81] Statute of the Inter-American Commission on Human Rights, art. 44(1).

[82] Buergenthal, 'Implementation in the Inter-American Human Rights System', p. 71.

frequently issued post-judgment orders with regard to the details of implementation of it judgments.[83]

1.3.4 Standing to raise non-compliance issues

As a matter of principle, States have two ways of raising the issue of non-compliance with treaty-based human rights standards: either by invoking the State responsibility of the State which allegedly violated its obligations, or, where such possibility exists, to bring an inter-State complaint before the respective dispute settlement body. Thus, the first question that arises is whether the existence of an inter-State complaint procedure *ipso facto* excludes any reference to the general law of State responsibility, in other words whether such human rights treaties constitute a self-contained regime with regard to non-compliance issues. In this regard, it is particularly worth quoting the Human Rights Committee's General Comment,[84] which rightly states that:

> the mere fact that a formal interstate mechanism . . . exists . . . does not mean that this procedure is the only method by which States Parties can assert their interest in the performance of other States Parties. On the contrary, [this] should be seen as supplementary to, not diminishing of, States Parties' interest in each other's discharge of their obligations . . . To draw attention to possible breaches of Covenant obligations by other States Parties and to call on them to comply with their Covenant obligations should . . . be considered as a reflection of legitimate community interest.

Apart from this general option of bringing a claim of non-compliance by virtue of general principles of the law of State responsibility, most human rights treaties provide for either mandatory or optional inter-State complaint mechanisms.[85] This is even true of those treaties which only possess a relatively weak compliance monitoring or enforcement system, like the African Charter on Human and Peoples' Rights.

---

[83] See e.g. Inter-American Court of Human Rights, *Barrios Altos* Case, Compliance with Judgment, Order of 28 November 2003, www.corteidh.or.cr/cumplipdf_ing/barrios_28_11_03_ing.pdf.

[84] Human Rights Committee, General Comment No. 31 (2004) on Article 2 of the Covenant: The Nature of the General Legal Obligation on States Parties to the Covenant, UN Doc. CCPR/C/21/Rev.1/Add.13 (2004).

[85] Art. 24 of the ECHR; arts. 47 and 49 of the African Charter; art. 45 of the ACHR.

1.4 Enforcement

1.4.1 General issues

1.4.1.1 Relationship between diplomatic protection and treaty-based procedures in the field of human rights

One question in the context of enforcement concerns the relationship between individual complaints mechanisms and diplomatic protection: where an individual brings a complaint against a State *other than his or her home State*, is the home State excluded from exercising diplomatic protection on behalf of its citizen? Even if one does not take the position of the Special Rapporteur of the International Law Commission, John Dugard, that 'to suggest that the universal human rights conventions . . . provide individuals with effective remedies for the protection of their human rights is to engage in a fantasy',[86] one must still admit that – seen from a worldwide perspective – only a limited number of individuals may obtain satisfactory remedies under the respective human rights treaties, and only for those rights coming within the scope of application *ratione materiae* of such treaty. Therefore, diplomatic protection remains an essential tool for securing compliance with applicable human rights standards for aliens, be they of a customary law nature or treaty-based.

Indeed, it seems that the exercise of diplomatic protection is without prejudice to possible recourse an individual may have to a relevant treaty body – and *vice versa*. This principle is contained, *inter alia*, in the 1991 Migrant Workers Convention,[87] which in its article 23 provides for both a monitoring body similar to the Human Rights Committee and an optional right of individual petition, as well as for the right of the State of origin to exercise diplomatic protection.

Thus, it may be rightly assumed that the International Law Commission was simply codifying pre-existing customary law when it provided in article 17 of its current 2004 Draft Articles on Diplomatic Protection that '[t]he present draft articles are without prejudice to the rights of . . . natural persons . . . to resort to actions or procedures under international

---

[86] John R. Dugard, First Report on Diplomatic Protection, UN Doc. A/CN.4/506 (2000), p. 8.
[87] United Nations Convention on the Protection of the Rights of All Migrant Workers and Members of Their Families, New York, 18 December 1990, 2220 UNTS 3.

law other than diplomatic protection to secure redress for injury suffered as a result of an internationally wrongful act'.[88]

This result is also in line with article 33(2) of the ILC Draft Articles on State Responsibility, which, *mutatis mutandis,* reaches the same result by stating that issues of State responsibility are without prejudice to any right, arising from the international responsibility of a State, which may accrue directly to a person. It is important to note, however, that the respective State of nationality of the victim is not under an international law obligation to exercise diplomatic protection. In that regard, it is quite telling that the Special Rapporteur of the International Law Commission on Diplomatic Protection in its First Report had still included a provision which stated that, 'unless the injured persons is able to bring a claim . . . before a competent international court or tribunal, the State of his or her nationality has a legal duty to exercise diplomatic protection on behalf of the injured person upon request, if the injury results from a grave breach of a *jus cogens* norm attributable to another State'.[89] Yet, even the Special Rapporteur considered the proposed norm to involve an exercise in progressive development of international law.[90] This is also owed to a pronouncement by the ICJ in 1970 in the *Barcelona Traction Case* that, even where an individual believes that his or her rights are not adequately protected by their State of nationality, he or she does not have a remedy in international law, and that State of nationality is the sole judge of whether its protection will be granted at all, to what extent it is granted, and when it will cease.[91] It is therefore not surprising that the proposed provision did not find its way into the ILC Draft Articles on Diplomatic Protection as adopted on first reading in 2004.

1.4.2 Enforcement by other States of (treaty-based) human rights standards by means not specifically provided for in the respective treaty

It is important to note, however, that, in most cases, the human rights violations do not occur with regard to aliens, but to nationals of the acting State. Thus, normally, there is no State which could exercise diplomatic

---

[88] UN Doc. A/CN.4/L.647 of 24 May 2004, art. 17.
[89] Dugard, First Report on Diplomatic Protection, UN Doc. A/CN.4/506, p. 27, Draft Art. 4(1).
[90] *Ibid.,* p. 33.
[91] ICJ, *Barcelona Traction, Light and Power Company Ltd (Belgium v. Spain)* Second Phase, Judgment of 5 February 1970, ICJ Reports 1970, p. 3.

protection. Therefore, the question arises whether at all, and if so to what extent and under what circumstances, third States still have the possibility to try to enforce human rights obligations.

At this stage I will only briefly discuss the functioning of enforcement mechanisms not expressly provided by the respective treaty, and their interrelationship with specific forms and mechanisms of enforcement specifically provided for in the respective treaty – such as inter-State complaints under the ICCPR, or the supervision of the implementation of judgments of the European Court of Human Rights by the CoE Committee of Ministers under article 46(2) of the ECHR.

1.4.2.1 Role of meetings of contracting parties

Where the human rights treaty under consideration has set up a specific monitoring body, the regular meetings of contracting parties are usually not concerned with the record of compliance of one or more States, and in particular they do not deal with country-specific conclusions and views of the monitoring body on the compliance record of a given State. Yet, the contracting parties still have the possibility to meet and consider any specific issues of non-compliance by one or more of the other contracting parties if they so desire. This is a view shared by some members of the Human Rights Committee, who have at least hinted at a more country-specific substantive role for such meetings.[92]

Thus, to cite an example not relating to human rights in the strictest sense, in 2001 a meeting of contracting parties to the Fourth Geneva Convention was convened by the depositary, the Swiss Government, to consider violations of obligations arising under the Convention.[93] In the same vein, on 8 December 2003, the General Assembly's Special Emergency Session adopted Resolution ES-10/14, which led to the advisory opinion of the ICJ on the Israeli security wall in the occupied Palestinian territories. One might consider this adoption as one form of fulfilment by parties to the Geneva Conventions of their obligation under common article 1 to ensure respect for the substantive obligations arising under the four Geneva Conventions.

---

[92] Sir Nigel Rodley, 'United Nations Human Rights Treaty Bodies and Special Procedures of the Commission on Human Rights – Complementarity or Competition?' (2003) 25 *Human Rights Quarterly* 882–908, at 887.

[93] See Conference of High Contracting Parties to the Fourth Geneva Convention, Declaration of 5 December 2001, www.icrc.org/Web/Eng/siteeng0.nsf/iwpList393/D86C9E662022D64E41256 C6800366D55#1.

But, even where the specific treaty does not entail such an *obligation erga omnes* to enforce the underlying obligations, the other contracting parties would still have the *right* to collectively consider possible violations by one or more of the other contracting parties. In that regard, it might be argued that, even where the respective treaty provides either for the compulsory jurisdiction of the ICJ, as does the Genocide Convention, or for inter-State complaints before the respective treaty body, an interpretation of human rights treaties focusing on their effective implementation leads to the conclusion that these options for addressing and eventually determining treaty violations are not exclusive. As a matter of fact, even article 55 of the ECHR, which provides that parties shall not submit disputes arising under the Convention to other dispute settlement mechanisms, does not seem to exclude direct State-to-State enforcement.[94] Indeed, the Yugoslav crisis provides an example where contracting parties of several human rights treaties took steps to try to enforce the implementation of obligations by the Federal Republic of Yugoslavia (FRY, now Serbia and Montenegro): after acts perceived as massive violations of ICCPR rights by the authorities of the FRY both within and outside Serbia and Montenegro, the contracting parties of the Covenant decided to deny the Yugoslav authorities the right to participate in meetings of the contracting parties.[95] Similar developments took place with regard to other human rights treaties.[96] In that regard, it is important to note that the approach was – at least as far as the Member States of the European Community were concerned – not based on the argument that the FRY, as one of the successor States to the former Yugoslavia, was no longer a contracting party. Rather, it was perceived as a means to bring about compliance with regard to treaty obligations which the FRY was perceived to have incurred by virtue of State succession.

1.4.2.2 Enforcing human rights by relying on general norms of State responsibility

Not abiding by treaty-based or customary human rights standards obviously constitutes an internationally wrongful act in the sense of article 2 of

---

[94] For a contrary view, see Frowein and Peukert, *Europäische MenschenRechtsKonvention*, art. 62.

[95] UN Doc. CCPR/SP/SR.18 of 4 April 1994, pp. 3–7; UN Doc. CCPR/SP/SR.19 of 9 December 1994, pp. 6–9.

[96] See e.g. UN Doc. CAT/SP/SR.7 of 5 December 1995, pp. 2–6 UN Doc. CRC/SP/SR.7 of 17 October 1994, pp. 4 *et seq.*

42INTERNATIONAL HUMAN RIGHTS

the ILC Draft Articles on State Responsibility, entailing the international responsibility of the respective State.

It is first important to note that, according to article 41 of the ILC's Draft Articles on State Responsibility, all States are under a duty to positively act and co-operate with each other in order to end violations of *jus cogens* norms. According to the view of the ILC, which is in turn largely based on holdings of the ICJ,[97] this category includes not only the prohibition of slavery, genocide, racial discrimination and apartheid, but also the prohibition of torture and the right to self-determination.

Yet, under article 41 of the ILC's Draft Articles on State Responsibility, this obligation shall, even in the view of the ILC itself, only apply to gross or systematic violations of such norms. Moreover, article 41 was considered a progressive development of international law – it is thus questionable whether such an obligation now exists under international law. On the other hand, a similar positive obligation to enforce compliance with *jus cogens* norms was recently derived by the ICJ from the common article 1 of the four Geneva Conventions.[98] If or when there is no such duty to act against violations of human rights, the question arises which State has the right to invoke the responsibility of the said State – a question regulated by the interplay of articles 42, 48, 49 and 54 of the ILC's Draft Articles. By virtue of article 42, States are considered as injured by wrongful acts when they are specifically affected by it. With regard to human rights violations, it is hard to see how a certain State is particularly affected by a given violation, unless such violations lead to the influx of refugees into its territory or the violation of fundamental human rights of a group of persons with whom the State invoking the responsibility has specific ties, such as nationality.

Even those States which are not considered to fall into the category of 'injured States' may, under article 48 of the ILC's Draft Articles on State Responsibility, formally invoke the responsibility of the State violating applicable human rights standards in case of violations of *erga omnes*

---

[97] See ILC, Commentaries to the Draft Articles on Responsibility of States for Internationally Wrongful Acts, arts. 40 and 41, UN Doc. A/56/10 (2001), pp. 282–92, and the references to ICJ judgments contained therein.

[98] *Legal Consequences of the Construction of a Wall in the Occupied Palestinian Territory*, Advisory Opinion of 9 July 2004, ICJ Reports 2004, pp. 136–271; Andrea Bianchi, 'Dismantling the Wall: The ICJ's Advisory Opinion and Its Likely Impact on International Law' (2004) 47 *German Yearbook of International Law* 343–91.

obligations, and thus in particular request cessation and/or reparation.[99] The crucial point is, however, whether, in such a situation, such third States may also take counter-measures. This question was deliberately left open by articles 49 and 54 of the ILC's Draft Articles on State Responsibility. On the one hand, article 49 limits the right to resort to counter-measures to *injured States* within the meaning of article 42 and, therefore, in the case of human rights violations, to States specifically affected by such human rights violations. However, article 54, in turn, underlines at the same time that the right of *any* State to invoke the responsibility of another State for violations of obligations *erga omnes* and therefore to take *lawful* measures against the violating State is not touched upon. The crucial point is, however, whether such third States may then also resort to counter-measures, i.e. to acts otherwise illegal under international law, but which are permitted in order to induce the violating State to cease its violation and make appropriate reparation.[100]

1.4.2.3 Special non-treaty-based procedures established by the United Nations Commission on Human Rights

The UN Commission on Human Rights has developed special procedures to address country-specific instances of human rights violations. Such procedures may include the creation of working groups or special rapporteurs on torture, enforced disappearances and arbitrary detention, to name just a few.[101] There seems to be an extensive osmotic relationship between country-specific findings of special rapporteurs and the concluding observations of treaty bodies such as the Human Rights Committee or the Committee Against Torture – in particular in situations where the respective rapporteur has recently undertaken an on-site investigation or where, *vice versa*, the Committee Against Torture has undertaken a mission to a country later visited by the special rapporteur on torture. In some cases,

---

[99] *Case Concerning Armed Activities on the Territory of the Congo (Democratic Republic of the Congo v. Uganda)*, Judgment of 19 December 2005, Separate Opinion of Judge Simma, www.icj-cij.org/icjwww/idocket/ico/icoframe.htm; Institut de Droit International, Resolution of 27 August 2005, www.idi-iil.org/idiE/resolutionsE/2005_kra_01_en.pdf.

[100] For further debate on this issue, see Tams, *Enforcing Obligations Erga Omnes in International Law*, pp. 198–251.

[101] For further details, see Beate Rudolf, *Die thematischen Berichterstatter und Arbeitsgruppen der UN-Menschenrechtskommission: Ihr Beitrag zur Fortentwicklung des internationalen Menschenrechtsschutzes*, pp. 29 *et seq.* and *passim*.

44   INTERNATIONAL HUMAN RIGHTS

special rapporteurs have also urged the government concerned to 'comply' with findings of treaty bodies.[102]

Typically, the special procedures undertake several forms of activities to ensure compliance, namely, country visits, urgent appeals, and the possibility to investigate specific cases. While country visits have become standard practice for most special procedures, they continue to depend on the acceptance of the respective territorial State. Yet, the continuous practice of the contracting parties of the European Framework Convention for the Protection of Minorities to allow the Committee of Experts access, demonstrates that treaty systems may be further developed through relevant subsequent State practice within the meaning of article 31 of the Vienna Convention on the Law of Treaties, even where the treaty text itself is silent on the matter. As a matter of fact, more than fifty States have now or in the past given blanket prior agreement to visits by any special procedure established by the UN Human Rights Commission.[103]

Generally speaking, one might be tempted to say that these special procedures, as developed by the UN Commission for Human Rights, indeed show certain special features of implementation, which complement the otherwise existing procedures established under the various human rights treaties and which help to foster enforcement in particular where the States represented in the Human Rights Commission support their efforts politically.

1.4.3 Ability to make binding determinations of non-compliance

Here, one must once again distinguish between individual and general determinations on non-compliance. In individual cases, most human rights treaties provide for the possibility of determinations by the respective treaty body on whether or not the State concerned has complied with its obligations. However, the views of treaty bodies established under the UN system are usually not binding. With regard to the issue of *general*

---

[102] For a recent example, see the Report on the Right of Everyone to the Highest Attainable Standard of Physical and Mental Health, Mission to Peru, UN Doc. E/CN.4/2005/51/Add.3, para. 59: 'The Special Rapporteur also urges the Government to comply with the precautionary measures requested by the Inter-American Commission in the case of San Mateo.'

[103] It should be noted, however, that most of these States have not renewed their standing invitations after 2002. See OHCHR, List of Standing Invitations, www.ohchr.org/english/bodies/chr/special/invitations.htm.

non-compliance, views or comments by treaty bodies in the UN system are not as such binding. In the European system, the supervision of general compliance is of a less formalized legal nature.

Two remarks remain to be made. First, one might consider whether treaty organs are not, by their very nature and regardless of their character as court, tribunal or solely committee, empowered to provide for an authentic interpretation of the respective treaty. If this was the case, one could then argue that the contracting parties are – by virtue of being bound by the underlying treaty – also bound by the interpretation given to the norms of this treaty by such treaty organ.[104] Secondly, where the respective treaty provides for the possibility of sanctions, such as the exclusion of a State from the treaty or the suspension of certain treaty-based rights, this necessarily presupposes the power to determine beforehand whether an instance of non-compliance has arisen.

1.4.4 *Power of treaty organs to set aside obligations to comply*

As far as can be discerned, human rights treaties do not empower the respective supervisory body to set aside obligations to comply. On the one hand, this is because at least some of the core guarantees of most treaties are not subject to derogation even in instances of emergency.[105] On the other hand, it is for each contracting party itself to decide whether, and if so to what extent, it wants to invoke such emergency provision as is contained in the treaty, while treaty organs such as the respective depositary would only duly take note of such action.

---

[104] On the relevance of treaty body statements for the interpretation of human rights agreements, see generally Nihal Jayawickrama, *The Judicial Application of Human Rights Law* (Cambridge: Cambridge University Press, 2002), pp. 167–70. With respect to findings of the Human Rights Committee, the Privy Council noted in *Tangiora* v. *Wellington District Legal Services Committee* (on appeal from the Court of Appeal of New Zealand) (2000) 4 LRC 44: '[T]he findings of the Human Rights Committee are based on orderly proceedings during which the parties have a proper opportunity to present their cases, and its findings gain their authority from the standing of its judges and their judicial qualities of impartiality, objectivity and restraint. Its rulings are definitive, final and determinative of the issue before it.' For a more general assessment of treaty interpretation by treaty organs, see José E. Alvarez, *International Organizations as Law-Makers* (Oxford: Oxford University Press, 2005), pp. 465–85.

[105] Art. 15 of the ECHR; art. 4 of the ICCPR; art. 27 of the ACHR.

1.4.5 Possibility to provide assistance to non-complying parties ('soft' enforcement)

Human rights treaties usually do not contain generalized or specific provisions for furthering compliance by parties. Yet, where the respective treaty has been adopted within the framework of an international organization, this organization may, as part of its overall powers whether explicit or implied, provide assistance, financial or otherwise, to one of its members. It seems that, unlike in the case of environmental treaties, 'soft enforcement' has so far not played a significant role with regard to human rights treaties. With regard to treaties adopted within the framework of the United Nations, it should be noted that the work of the United Nations Programme of Technical Co-operation in the Field of Human Rights is focused on the strengthening of human rights protection in general and therefore not, as such, on treaty implementation.[106]

1.4.6 Possible sanctions to be applied by treaty organs in cases of non-compliance ('hard' enforcement)

Most universal human rights treaties do not provide for specific negative consequences to be applied by treaty organs in case of systemic instances of non-compliance. Accordingly, the regular rules of general international law as codified in the Vienna Convention on the Law of Treaties apply, the exclusion of the FRY from meetings of contracting parties being one example at hand. There are, however, examples where the respective treaty specifically provides for possible sanctions, such as the CoE Statute, which in article 8 provides for the suspension and eventual exclusion from the Council of Europe. Somewhat in contrast thereto, while the founding instruments of both the OAS and the African Union deal with the issue of non-democratic government and their status within the organization,[107] they do not tackle the issue of violations of human rights by any of its members and possible ensuing legal consequences resulting.

---

[106] See the description provided by the OHCHR, www.ohchr.org/english/countries/coop/. On technical co-operation in general, see Mona Rishmawi, 'Human Rights in Development: UN Technical Co-operation in the Field of Human Rights' (1997) 58–9 *The Review – International Commission of Jurists* 57–85.

[107] Charter of the Organization of American States, Bogota, 30 April 1948, 119 UNTS 3 (as amended by the 'Protocol of Managua' of 10 June 1993, reprinted in 33 ILM 1009), art. 9; Constitutive Act of the African Union, Togo, 11 July 2000, OAU Doc. CAB/LEG/23.15, art. 30.

1.5 Overall evaluation

It is not easy to give a general overview on the issue of possible interconnections and inspirations that the various treaty regimes draw from each other. It seems, however, that whether procedures for dispute settlement, compliance control and enforcement are taken over from one treaty to another is largely, if not exclusively, dependent on the political will of the States involved. Thus, it is probably, to refer to just one example, no surprise that the comparatively high standards of dispute settlement, compliance control and enforcement provided for in the ECHR have so far remained a rare example, and that, even the most recent supervisory mechanism provided for in a universal treaty, namely, the Optional Protocol to CEDAW, does not contain a very effective or satisfactory dispute settlement, compliance control and enforcement mechanism.

Furthermore, the variation in the various dispute settlement, compliance control and enforcement mechanisms is also, at least partially, due to the difference in the underlying rights being protected. For example, social and cultural rights as enshrined in the International Covenant on Economic, Social and Cultural Rights are, by their very nature, not (or not as) suitable for enforcement by way of a judicial or quasi-judicial procedure as are more classical freedom rights as, for instance, those contained in the International Covenant on Civil and Political Rights.

2

The International Covenant on Civil and Political Rights

MARTIN SCHEININ

2.1 General issues

2.1.1 Basic features

The International Covenant on Civil and Political Rights (ICCPR) was adopted by the United Nations General Assembly in 1966, and, after the required number of ratifications, it entered into force on 23 March 1976.[1] To a large extent the Covenant, together with the simultaneously adopted International Covenant on Economic, Social and Cultural Rights,[2] codifies in the form of a legally binding international treaty the human rights enshrined in the Universal Declaration of Human Rights of 1948.[3]

The rights protected under the Covenant range from the right to life (article 6) to the right of public participation (article 25), from the right of all peoples to self-determination (article 1) to rights of members of minorities (article 27). Despite its name, the Covenant is not restricted to 'civil and political rights' in the narrow sense. The above-mentioned provisions on self-determination and minority rights include important dimensions related to economic resources. The prohibition against discrimination (article 26) is overarching in nature, hence extending, for instance, to social, economic and cultural spheres. The provision on the right to freedom of association (article 22) explicitly covers also trade union rights. The right of all persons deprived of their liberty to humane treatment (article 10) addresses also the practical

---

[1] International Covenant on Civil and Political Rights, New York, 16 December 1966, in force 23 March 1976, 999 UNTS 171.

[2] International Covenant on Economic, Social and Cultural Rights, New York, 16 December 1966, in force 3 January 1976, 993 UNTS 3.   [3] GA Res. 217 A (III) of 10 December 1948.

conditions of detention and hence the obligation of the State to allocate economic resources to secure that its prison conditions meet international standards.

Most of the substantive provisions on human rights protected by the Covenant are to be found in Part III of the instrument (articles 6–27). In addition to the rights already mentioned above, they relate to the prohibition against torture and cruel, inhuman or degrading treatment or punishment (article 7), the prohibition against slavery, servitude and forced labour (article 8), the right to liberty and security of the person (article 9), the prohibition against imprisonment for inability to fulfil a contractual obligation (article 11), freedom of movement (article 12), procedural guarantees against expulsion (article 13), the right to a fair trial (article 14), the principle of legality in criminal law, including the prohibition against its retroactive application (article 15), the right to recognition as a person before the law (article 16), the protection of privacy, family, home and correspondence (article 17), the freedom of thought, conscience and religion (article 18), the freedom of opinion and expression (article 19),[4] the right of peaceful assembly (article 21), the protection of the family and the equality of spouses (article 23) and the rights of the child (article 24).

Although the provision on the right to life (article 6) includes several conditions and restrictions for the application of the death penalty, it does not on its own prohibit capital punishment. Such a prohibition is established by the Second Optional Protocol to the Covenant.[5]

Another substantive human rights provision outside Part III of the Covenant is the right of all peoples to self-determination (article 1). As a right of 'all peoples' it is a human right of truly collective nature and, according to the interpretation by the Human Rights Committee, not subject to the procedure for individual complaints under the Optional Protocol.[6] In contrast, the Covenant's unique provision on minority rights

---

[4] This provision is accompanied by art. 20, which establishes an obligation to prohibit propaganda for war as well as advocacy of national, racial or religious hatred.

[5] Concluded 15 December 1989, in force 11 July 1991, UN Doc. A/RES/44/128. As of 9 December 2002, there were forty-nine parties to the Second Optional Protocol.

[6] Optional Protocol to the International Covenant on Civil and Political Rights, New York, 16 December 1966, in force 23 March 1976, 999 UNTS 171; *Bernard Ominayak, Chief of the Lubicon Lake Band* v. *Canada* (Communication No. 167/1984), Views adopted 26 March 1990, Report of the Human Rights Committee, vol. II, GAOR, 45th Session, Supp. No. 40 (A/45/40), pp. 1–30.

50 INTERNATIONAL HUMAN RIGHTS

(article 27),[7] which is formulated as an individual right with collective dimensions, has given rise to a number of important cases under the Optional Protocol.

Article 2 is a provision on the general State obligations under the Covenant, including a general duty to 'respect and ensure' the rights enshrined in the Covenant without discrimination and an obligation to ensure an effective and enforceable remedy for any violation of the Covenant.[8] Article 3, in turn, supplements the Covenant's other provisions on equality and non-discrimination with an undertaking to ensure the equal enjoyment of all Covenant rights by men and women.[9]

The Covenant itself provides for two mechanisms of compliance control, namely, a periodic reporting procedure (article 40) and an inter-State complaint procedure (articles 41 and 42). Furthermore, the (first) Optional Protocol to the Covenant provides for a third mechanism, a procedure for individual complaints. There are 154 States parties to the Covenant and 106 of them are also parties to the Optional Protocol allowing for individual complaints.[10]

The Human Rights Committee is an independent expert body composed of eighteen persons elected by the States parties to the Covenant (see article 28). All mechanisms of compliance control are functions of the Committee.

The procedure for periodic reports is the only mandatory mechanism of compliance control under the Covenant. According to article 40, each State party is to submit an initial report within one year from the entry into force of the Covenant in respect of it, and thereafter a report whenever the Human Rights Committee so requests. The latter part of the provision is interpreted to give the Committee authority to request both regular periodic reports and, when the need arises, also so-called special reports that deviate from the normal cycle of periodicity. For a long time, the Committee requested all States parties to provide periodic reports every five years. Since 2001, this approach has been replaced by a system where

---

[7] 'In those States in which ethnic, religious or linguistic minorities exist, *persons belonging to such minorities* shall not be denied the right, *in community with the other members of their group*, to enjoy their own culture, to profess and practise their own religion, or to use their own language.' Emphasis added.

[8] General Comment No. 31 (80), adopted in 2004, UN Doc. HRI/GEN/1/Rev.7, pp. 192–7.

[9] General Comment No. 28 (68), adopted in 2000, UN Doc. HRI/GEN/1/Rev.7, pp. 178–84.

[10] See, Status of Ratifications of the Principal International Human Rights Treaties, 3 June 2005, available at www.ohchr.org.

the Committee decides for each State, at the end of its consideration of one periodic report, the due date of the following report.

According to article 40(1), States are to report on the measures they have adopted which give effect to the rights recognized in the Covenant and on the progress made in the enjoyment of those rights. According to paragraph 2 of the same article, reports shall indicate the factors and difficulties, if any, affecting the implementation of the Covenant.

The Covenant is silent on the modalities of the consideration of a report by the Human Rights Committee. In practice, a written report is translated into and issued in at least three United Nations languages and thereafter scheduled by the Committee for consideration during one of its three annual sessions. One session prior to this consideration, the Committee adopts a list of issues which is transmitted to the State party. That list of issues forms the basis for the oral consideration of the report in a public meeting of the Committee. As a rule, three meetings (nine hours) are allocated for an initial report and two meetings (six hours) for subsequent reports. Towards the end of the three-week session in which a report was considered, the Committee adopts, in closed meetings, its 'Concluding Observations' on the report. This document forms the basis of a follow-up dialogue between the Committee and the State party, and subsequently a starting-point for the preparation of the following periodic report.

The procedure for inter-State complaints is optional in nature. It is applicable only in respect of those States parties that have given a separate declaration to that effect under article 41. Furthermore, the procedure may be resorted to only by those States that have themselves given such a declaration. At the moment, forty-eight States have given the declaration under article 41, recognizing the competence of the Human Rights Committee to receive inter-State complaints that the declaring State is not fulfilling its obligations under the Covenant. So far, the procedure has never been resorted to. Hence, it is not possible to give a detailed account of how the provisions in articles 41 and 42 would be applied in practice. Textually, articles 41 and 42 point towards a procedure that is geared towards a friendly settlement,[11] includes oral hearings,[12] and restricts the role of the Committee to the establishment of the facts if no friendly settlement is reached,[13] unless the parties have consented to the establishment of an

---

[11] Art. 41(1)(b) and (e) and art. 42.   [12] Art. 41(1)(g).   [13] Art. 41(1)(h).

52 INTERNATIONAL HUMAN RIGHTS

ad hoc Conciliation Commission which thereby is authorized to formulate its views on the substance of a settlement even if the parties do not agree.[14]

The procedure for individual complaints is optional in nature, enabling the Human Rights Committee to receive and consider complaints by individuals subject to the jurisdiction of a State party to both the Covenant and its (first) Optional Protocol, claiming to be victims of a violation of any of their rights under the Covenant. The Optional Protocol spells out the conditions of admissibility of complaints as well as the basic rules related to the procedure. The proceedings are adversarial in nature and, at least so far, only in writing. The result of the procedure is either an inadmissibility decision by the Committee or a set of 'Views'[15] in which the Committee gives its reasoned assessment as to whether one or more provisions of the Covenant were violated. The Optional Protocol contains no provisions on the legal effect of the Views, the authority of which hence rests on the position of the Committee as the monitoring body established through article 28 of the Covenant. Nevertheless, it is to be noted that article 2(3) of the Covenant guarantees the right to an effective remedy whenever an individual has suffered a violation of his or her rights under the Covenant. With reference to this provision, the Committee systematically addresses the right to a remedy whenever it establishes a violation in its Views. The Committee has established a fairly informal follow-up procedure for its Views, based on the appointment of one member of the Committee as special rapporteur on follow-up under the Optional Protocol. This rapporteur engages in bilateral exchanges with States parties about the implementation of the Committee's Views and reports back to the Committee on these exchanges. In addition, the article 40 procedure for periodic reports serves as a follow-up mechanism in respect of Views adopted under the Optional Protocol.

2.1.2 Secondary norms and guidelines

Article 30(4) of the Covenant creates an institution of a meeting of States parties. However, that meeting has restricted itself to the task provided in articles 30–34, namely, the election of the members of the Human Rights Committee. Hence, only the Committee operates as an organ of compliance control, and only the Committee has issued secondary rules or

[14] Art. 42(6)(c).   [15] Optional Protocol, art. 5(4).

guidelines related to it. The Covenant provides a legal basis for two types of secondary rules: rules of procedure and general comments. In addition, the Committee has in practice adopted also other types of documents that serve as guidelines for its compliance control functions.

Article 39(2) of the Covenant authorizes the Committee to adopt its own Rules of Procedure.[16] These Rules of Procedure regulate the Committee's own work, and also regulate its mechanisms for compliance control. Part II of the Rules of Procedure includes the relevant rules on the functions of the Committee, so that Chapter XV (rules 66–73) deals with the procedure for State party reports, Chapter XVI with inter-State complaints (rules 74–83) and Chapter XVII with individual complaints (rules 84–104).

According to article 40(4) of the Covenant, the consideration of State party reports may lead to the adoption by the Committee of 'such general comments as it may consider appropriate'. To date, the Committee has adopted thirty-one General Comments, most of them on specific substantive provisions of the Covenant but some of them on cross-cutting issues such as reservations to the Covenant (General Comment No. 24). While the General Comments are legally binding neither for the Committee nor for the States parties, they nevertheless consolidate the lines of interpretation adopted by the Committee when dealing with State party reports or individual communications. General Comment No. 30 deals specifically with the modalities of the reporting procedure under article 40 of the Covenant.[17]

For the purposes of compliance control, the most important other guidelines adopted by the Committee are the Consolidated Guidelines for State party reports[18] and certain decisions on the Committee's own working methods. These documents are fairly technical in nature but nevertheless illustrate the practice of the Committee in the performance of its functions.

2.2 Dispute resolution

The Covenant does not provide for a compulsory mechanism of dispute settlement. Furthermore, the Covenant has no clause that would mention

---

[16] Currently, UN Doc. CCPR/C/3/Rev.7.

[17] UN Doc. CCPR/C/21/Rev.2/Add.12. For a compilation of general comments by the UN human rights treaty bodies, including the Human Rights Committee, see UN Doc. HRI/GEN/1/Rev.7.

[18] CCPR/C/66/GUI/Rev.2.

54 INTERNATIONAL HUMAN RIGHTS

the role of the International Court of Justice in the resolution of disputes that arise under it. Nevertheless, in two of its Advisory Opinions the ICJ has referred to the provisions of the Covenant, and to relevant General Comments and other pronouncements by the Committee.[19] According to article 44, the provisions for the implementation of the Covenant shall not prevent the States parties from having recourse to other procedures for settling a dispute in accordance with general or special international agreements in force between them.

Articles 41 and 42 of the Covenant provide for a mechanism for resolving disputes between States parties. Article 41 prescribes the modalities for a settlement procedure applied by the Human Rights Committee itself, while article 42 enables the establishment of a subsidiary body, an *ad hoc* Conciliation Commission. Although the fairly complex provisions of articles 41 and 42 are explained below in some detail, it must be pointed out that so far there has not been a single inter-State complaint submitted pursuant to them. Consequently, it is not possible to comment on issues of interpretation that may arise based on the treaty provisions.

Under article 41 of the Covenant, the handling of an inter-State complaint will proceed in the following manner:

1. As a first step, the complaining State shall bring the matter to the attention of the State subject to a complaint. The State subject to a complaint has three months in which to make a response (article 41(1)(a)).
2. After that three-month period and a subsequent period of another three months has elapsed, the complaining State may initiate the proceedings before the Human Rights Committee (article 41(1)(b)).
3. The Committee shall ascertain that all available domestic remedies have been exhausted, in accordance with the general principles of international law (article 41(1)(c)).
4. The Committee shall make available to the parties its good offices, in order to reach a friendly solution. The Committee has a duty to ensure that any friendly solution is based on respect for human rights and fundamental freedoms as recognized in the Covenant (article 41(1)(e)).
5. The Committee shall, within twelve months after the complaint was filed, issue a report on either the friendly solution reached or, if no

---

[19] International Court of Justice, Advisory Opinion of 8 July 1996 on the *Legality of the Threat or Use of Nuclear Weapons*; Advisory Opinion of 9 July 2004 on *Legal Consequences of the Construction of a Wall in the Occupied Palestinian Territory*.

such solution is reached, on the facts of the dispute. The text of the Covenant seems not to enable the Committee to take any substantive position to the dispute if no friendly solution is reached (article 41(1)(h)).

The *ad hoc* Conciliation Commission, established pursuant to article 42 of the Covenant, will consist of five persons who are not nationals of the States that are parties to the dispute but of other States that have accepted the competence of the Human Rights Committee under article 41. The members shall primarily be appointed with the approval of the parties to the dispute but if such approval is not reached within three months they shall be elected by the Committee from among its members. In any case, a Conciliation Commission may be resorted to only with the agreement of the parties to the dispute.[20]

The Conciliation Commission will proceed as follows:

1. It will make its good offices available to the parties with a view to reaching an amicable solution based on respect for the provisions of the Covenant (article 42(1)(a)).
2. The Commission will make use of the information already obtained by the Committee pursuant to article 41, but it may nevertheless obtain further submissions by the parties (article 42(6)).
3. Within twelve months, the Commission will submit through the chairperson of the Committee to the States parties a report the substance of which has three options:
   a. the Commission concludes that it is unable to complete its consideration of the matter within the prescribed period of twelve months, in which case its report is confined to a brief statement of the status of its consideration of the matter (article 42(7)(a));
   b. an amicable solution is reached and the report consists of a brief statement of the facts and of the solution reached (article 42(7)(b)); or
   c. in the absence of a solution the Commission moves to a report on its findings on all questions of fact relevant to the issues between the States parties concerned, and on its views on the possibilities of an amicable solution of the matter (article 42(7)(c)).

---

[20] Art. 42(1) and (2).

4. In the last-mentioned case, the States parties concerned shall, within three months of the receipt of the report, notify the chairman of the Committee whether or not they accept the contents of the report of the Commission (article 42(7)(d)).

According to article 41, a State party to the Covenant that has made the declaration under article 41 that it accepts the competence of the Human Rights Committee to receive inter-State complaints, is entitled to submit an inter-State complaint ('a communication') in respect of a similarly situated State party if it claims that that State is not fulfilling its obligations under the Covenant.

The Covenant provisions related to the inter-State complaint procedure (articles 41–42), as well as the Rules of Procedure, are silent as to *amici curiae*. However, the Committee has taken the position that autonomous third-party interventions are not accepted in the Optional Protocol procedure for individual complaints.[21] As article 5(1) of the Optional Protocol explicitly prescribes that the Committee shall base its decision on the written submissions by the parties, and as no corresponding provision exists in articles 41–42, the same approach does not necessarily apply in the inter-State complaint procedure.

Articles 41–42 of the Covenant have never been resorted to. Among the reasons why States have not made use of the inter-State complaint procedure are the following: (a) as the procedure is optional in nature and the number of States that have made the relevant declaration relatively small in comparison to the total number of States parties to the Covenant, the available permutations of a State party submitting a complaint and a State party subject to such a complaint may not be the most relevant ones; (b) as the procedure has never been resorted to and there therefore exists no precedent, States may feel reluctant to resort to this procedure before an independent expert body and choose instead to resort either to political procedures or to the International Court of Justice; and (c) as the Human Rights Committee is composed of eighteen members and there is no provision on *ad hoc* members appointed for the inter-State complaint procedure, States that resort to the procedure would not necessarily have a national on the Committee when it deals with the complaint.

---

[21] This was the practice of the Committee in 1997–2004 when the author was a member of the Committee.

2.3 Compliance control

2.3.1 The reporting procedure

Pursuant to article 40(1) of the Covenant, all States parties have a duty to report on their implementation of their substantive obligations under the treaty, initially within one year after the entry into force of the Covenant in respect of the State concerned and thereafter whenever the Human Rights Committee so requests.

The main function of the Human Rights Committee is to consider periodic reports by the States parties. The reporting obligation prescribed in article 40 of the Covenant is the main procedural obligation of States that have ratified the Covenant. Under the terms of article 40, an initial report is to be submitted within one year of the entry into force of the Covenant in respect of the State in question. Thereafter, periodic reports are due 'whenever the Committee so requires'. For a long time, the Committee applied a uniform periodicity of five years between the submission of two consecutive reports. In July 2001, however, the Committee adopted a new approach of specifying separately for each State the due date of its next periodic report. In addition, the Committee may request a so-called special report irrespective of the decided due date, for instance, if the human rights situation appears to deteriorate rapidly.[22]

In the terms of article 40, a periodic report shall consist of information on the measures adopted by a State party to give effect to the rights recognized in the Covenant and the progress made in the enjoyment of those rights (article 40(1)). Reports shall also indicate the factors and difficulties, if any, affecting the implementation of the Covenant (article 40(2)).

The modalities of the consideration of a report are not spelled out in the Covenant. In practice, the system of periodic reporting operates as a continuous cycle in which the consideration of a report in a public hearing before the Committee forms a high point, followed by the Committee's Concluding Observations. Usually, the Committee allocates two meetings (six hours) to each report, during which time a delegation sent by the reporting State answers written and oral questions posed by the Committee and its individual members. The Committee prepares for the oral hearing by hearing non-governmental and intergovernmental organizations, by studying written information from these and other sources and by drawing

---

[22] See also Rules of Procedure, rule 66.2.

up a written list of issues which is sent to the State party three to four months before the oral hearings. Since 2002, the Committee has appointed, from among its members, a so-called task force of four to six members to handle the consideration of a report.

The Concluding Observations adopted by the Committee after its consideration of a State party report[23] give recognition to positive aspects in the implementation of the Covenant but the main part of them is devoted to expressions of concern and recommendations. The State party is expected to publicize the Concluding Observations and to use them as a starting-point for the next reporting cycle. The reporting guidelines adopted by the Human Rights Committee recommend so-called focused reports, which are based on the Committee's Concluding Observations from the previous round and any new developments that emanate from the national human rights discussion. The due date of the next periodic report is set at the end of the Committee's Concluding Observations.

In 2002, two further reforms were introduced by the Human Rights Committee. First, the Committee has started to tackle the problem of long-overdue reports by scheduling a country to be considered by the Committee even in the absence of a report.[24] By mid-2005, this procedure had been applied in a handful of cases, either with the benefit of the presence of a delegation sent by the State party (Suriname) or with neither a report nor a delegation (Gambia). Contrary to its normal practice under article 40, the Committee does not issue public Concluding Observations in respect of non-reporting States but Provisional Observations that are transmitted to the State party concerned in order to assist it in performing its reporting obligation.[25] If the State party continues to fail in performing its reporting obligations, the Provisional Observations may be converted into public Concluding Observations.[26]

Secondly, the Committee instituted a follow-up procedure to its Concluding Observations.[27] At the end of the Concluding Observations, a follow-up submission is requested within twelve months on some of the concerns identified by the Committee. One member of the Committee serves as the Committee's Special Rapporteur on follow-up under article 40. Based on follow-up submissions received, the Special Rapporteur recommends to the Committee what further measures should be taken in

---

[23] *Ibid.*, rule 71.3. [24] *Ibid.*, rule 70. [25] *Ibid.*, rule 70. [26] *Ibid.*, rule 70.3.
[27] *Ibid.*, rule 72.

respect of a State party. These may include the adjustment of the due date of the next periodic report.

Although the mandatory reporting procedure under article 40 is initiated by the submission of a State party report, non-governmental organizations have several points of entry into the processing of a report. They may appear before the Committee in a separate NGO hearing held on the first day of a session; they may submit so-called shadow reports or commentaries to the State party report; they may arrange informal lunch-hour briefings for the Committee members; and they may attend the actual consideration of a State party report.

There is great variation in the degree of NGO involvement in the consideration of reports. In respect of some reports, there are no NGO submissions whatever, whereas on some occasions there might be a high degree of interest by both national and international human rights NGOs. From the perspective of the Committee, shadow reports or commentaries submitted several months before the consideration of a report are the most useful form of NGO involvement, as they can be taken into account in formulating the Committee's list of issues that is adopted one session ahead of the actual consideration and that largely shapes the agenda for the oral consideration. For media and domestic policy impact, however, the oral consideration of a report before the Human Rights Committee might be the most important moment for active NGO presence, although at that point it is usually too late to influence the actual questioning by Committee members.

The track record of the effectiveness of the reporting procedure is mixed. A majority of States parties to the Covenant are in delay in submitting their reports, such delays amounting to, in extreme cases, up to fifteen years. The Committee addresses the problem of failures or delays in reporting by issuing reminders and, in extreme cases, by scheduling a country for consideration even in the absence of a report. The current working methods of the Committee allow for the annual consideration of fifteen to eighteen reports, which is roughly half of the number of reports that should be submitted according to the decisions of the Committee. If all States were to submit their reports on time, the Committee would need to adjust its working methods, for instance by meeting in two parallel chambers simultaneously. This, in turn, would have financial implications.

In respect of reports that are submitted, the procedure functions fairly well and effectively. There is no backlog of submitted reports, although some delay is often caused by the process of translating the report into three

UN languages before it is scheduled for consideration and a task force is convened for drawing up the list of issues. In general, States parties and NGOs demonstrate considerable interest in the reporting procedure, thus contributing to the Committee's ability to examine the State's compliance with the Covenant and arrive at pertinent and focused Concluding Observations. Since the follow-up procedure of requesting the State party to address within twelve months selected concerns of the Committee was introduced, almost all concerned States have made use of this opportunity.

In sum, the reporting procedure functions well in respect of those States parties that wish to co-operate with the Committee in good faith. In general, they may not be the most problematic countries in respect of human rights violations. Nevertheless, in all countries, there is room for continuous improvement in the implementation of the Covenant, and the reporting procedure provides for an opportunity for regular review and feedback on the international level. This is highly conducive to a national discourse and the development of a culture of human rights in respective countries.

2.3.2 The procedure for individual complaints

Only individuals claiming to be victims personally of an alleged violation of the Covenant have the right to initiate the complaints procedure under the (first) Optional Protocol. Hence, corporations, associations or other juridical persons cannot initiate the proceedings on their own, neither in the form of *actio popularis* nor with the claim that the juridical person itself would have rights under the Covenant which would have been violated.[28] However, there is no obstacle to human rights NGOs or other juridical persons acting as the *representative* of the alleged individual victim. Such representation requires authorization, generally by the alleged victim but in some situations alternatively by a family member. Further, several individuals can jointly act as complainants and one person may due to his or her position in a community be entitled to initiate a complaint on behalf of all the members of the group.[29] Nevertheless, this possibility does not

---

[28] See e.g. *A Publication and a Printing Company* v. *Trinidad and Tobago* (Communication No. 361/1989), declared inadmissible on 14 July 1989, Report of the Human Rights Committee, GAOR, 44th Session, Supp. No. 40 (A/44/40), pp. 307–8.

[29] See e.g. the case of *Bernard Ominayak, Chief of the Lubicon Lake Band* v. *Canada* (Communication 167/1984), where the Committee treated Mr Ominayak as the author of the communication and the Lubicon Lake Band as the victim.

INTERNATIONAL COVENANT ON CIVIL AND POLITICAL RIGHTS 61

extend so far that it would enable complaints under the truly collective right of peoples to self-determination.[30]

The consideration of an individual complaint consists of the following phases:

1. Receipt and pre-registration considerations. The Human Rights Committee is assisted by a small Petitions Unit in the Office of the High Commissioner for Human Rights. This unit screens incoming correspondence for letters that explicitly or implicitly are individual communications under the Optional Protocol. If needed, the Petitions Unit corresponds with potential complainants in order to clarify whether a letter qualifies as such a communication.[31]

2. Registration. One member of the Committee acts as its Special Rapporteur on New Communications, and is authorized to decide on the registration of new cases. The Special Rapporteur may decline registration for manifest failure to meet the admissibility requirements, or seek more information from the author prior to registration.[32]

3. Possible transmission to the State party (main rule) or Special Rapporteur's draft on inadmissibility. Upon registration, a communication is usually transmitted to the State party in order to receive its submissions on the admissibility and merits of a communication.[33] However, sometimes, the Special Rapporteur instructs the Petitions Unit to proceed towards an inadmissibility decision by the Committee without hearing the State party.

4. Possible request for interim measures of protection. Requests for interim measures of protection due to the risk of irreparable damage to the alleged victim are usually dealt with at the stage of registration.[34] The Committee's Special Rapporteur on New Communications exercises this authority, most often in cases that involve the death penalty.

5. State party submission on admissibility and merits (main rule) or admissibility only and a request for a so-called 'split' (separation of admissibility and merits). After the registration of a communication

---

[30] *Bernard Ominayak, Chief of the Lubicon Lake Band* v. *Canada* (Communication 167/1984); *Apirana Mahuika et al.* v. *New Zealand* (Communication No. 547/1993), Views adopted 27 October 2000, Report of the Human Rights Committee, Vol. II, GAOR, 17th Session, A/56/40, pp. 11–29. However, in the latter case, it was recognized that the collective right of self-determination (ICCPR, art. 1) may affect the interpretation of other provisions of the ICCPR.

[31] See also Rules of Procedure, rules 84.2 and 86.   [32] *Ibid.*, rule 95.3.   [33] *Ibid.*, rule 97.

[34] *Ibid.*, rule 92.

and its transmission to the State party concerned, the State can either separately contest the admissibility of the communication within two months or present within six months its observations on both the admissibility and the merits of the case.[35] The main rule nowadays is that the plenary Committee deals only once with a communication, addressing at the same time its admissibility and, if appropriate, the merits of the case.

6. Possible Special Rapporteur's decision on a split. If a State party has separately addressed questions of admissibility, the Special Rapporteur on New Communications may decide on a 'split', whereafter the Committee will decide on admissibility prior to seeking the State party's observations on the merits. The admissibility requirements are prescribed in a fairly unsystematic way in articles 1, 2, 3 and 5 of the Optional Protocol and systematized in rule 96 of the Rules of Procedure. Some of the grounds for inadmissibility are recoverable in nature.[36]

7. Preparation of a draft decision on admissibility or of a joint decision on admissibility and merits, under the guidance of a Committee member acting as case rapporteur.

8. Consideration by a pre-sessional working group of the Committee.[37] The working group has the power to declare cases admissible, which means that a case need not be discussed in the plenary Committee before the merits stage.[38] Otherwise, the role of the working group is merely preparatory in respect of plenary consideration. In recent years, the pre-sessional working group has on occasion been replaced by an additional week of the plenary session, in order to deal with the backlog of cases ready for final decision.

9. Plenary consideration of a draft inadmissibility decision, or a joint decision on admissibility and merits, or a final decision on the merits where a separate admissibility decision has been taken earlier. When dealing with individual communications, the Committee has no oral hearings but restricts itself to 'written information made available to it by the individual and the State Party concerned'.[39] The Optional Protocol also specifies that the Committee 'shall hold closed meetings when examining communications'.[40] While these provisions do not

---

[35] Optional Protocol, art. 4(2); and Rules of Procedure, rule 97.
[36] See Rules of Procedure, rule 98.2.   [37] *Ibid.*, rule 95.   [38] *Ibid.*, rule 93.2.
[39] Optional Protocol, art. 5(1).   [40] *Ibid.*, art. 5(3).

legally exclude the possibility of having oral hearings as a preliminary phase before the submission of written final briefs by the parties and their examination in a closed meeting, the resource constraints on the work of the Committee and the backlog of communications have so far prevented the taking of this step. The final decision including the assessment of the merits of a case is called 'Views of the Human Rights Committee under article 5, paragraph 4, of the Optional Protocol to the International Covenant on Civil and Political Rights'. These Views include the Committee's reasoned determination whether there has been a violation of one or more provisions of the Covenant and, if so, what the State party should provide as the remedy.

10. The Views establishing a violation call for a follow-up response by the State party within a period of ninety days. The Committee also appoints one of its members as Special Rapporteur on Follow-up under the Optional Protocol.[41] Based on follow-up responses by States and actions taken by the special rapporteur, reports on follow-up are compiled for the plenary Committee which then decides to highlight positive experiences of best practices and problematic cases of non-compliance in its annual report to the General Assembly.

The assessment of the effectiveness of the procedure for individual complaints has many dimensions. Some States parties fail to provide their observations on the admissibility and merits of a communication, despite their voluntary ratification of the Optional Protocol. Such a failure to co-operate may often lead to considerable delays in the consideration of a case but does not prevent the Committee from assessing on the basis of materials submitted by the complainant whether there has been a violation of the Covenant.

In certain cases, States have failed to comply with the Committee's request for interim measures of protection. Some States have proceeded to the execution of a complainant subject to capital punishment, disregarding the Committee's request not to do so. In 2000, the Committee for the first time addressed the issue of the legal consequences of a State's non-compliance with a request for interim measures of protection. In the case of *Dante Piandiong et al.* v. *The Philippines*,[42] the Committee concluded that,

---

[41] Rules of Procedure, rule 101.

[42] *Dante Piandiong et al.* v. *Philippines* (Communication No. 869/1999), Views adopted on 19 October 2000, Report of the Human Rights Committee, Vol. II, GAOR, 17th Session (A/56/40), pp. 181–90.

by ratifying the Optional Protocol on the procedure for individual communications, a State undertakes to co-operate with the Committee in good faith so as to permit and enable it to consider the communication and that a State party commits a 'grave breach' of its obligations under the Optional Protocol if it acts to prevent or frustrate consideration by the Committee of a communication. Specifically, a State breaches its obligations under the Optional Protocol if, having been notified of the communication, it proceeds to execute the alleged victim. The Committee based itself directly on State obligations under the Optional Protocol and not on its own Rules of Procedure, which instrument, although based on a provision in the Covenant,[43] is not an international treaty binding on States.

Many States provide information on the individual and system-level measures taken subsequent to the adoption of Views establishing a violation of the Covenant. Some States have specific legislation (Colombia) or case law (Finland) providing the right to compensation in such cases. The annual reports by the Human Rights Committee include examples of best practice in the implementation of the Committee's Views. On the other hand, States may fail to report any measures taken, or they may challenge the interpretation or authority of the Human Rights Committee. The Committee addresses such challenges through its follow-up procedure under the Optional Protocol but also in the context of its consideration of a periodic report by the State party in question.[44]

2.4 Enforcement

There are no treaty provisions that would attach legally binding force to the findings made by the Committee. Article 28 of the Covenant on the establishment of the Committee and article 40 on the reporting procedure lack

---

[43] Art. 39(2).

[44] One example of such challenge is the case of *A* v. *Australia* (Communication No. 560/1993), Views adopted on 3 April 1997, Report of the Human Rights Committee, Vol. II, GAOR, 52nd Session, Supp. No. 40 (A/52/40), pp. 125–46. In this case, the government in question contested the Committee's interpretation of ICCPR, art. 9, after receiving the Views. The Human Rights Committee commented in its Concluding Observations on the report by Australia: 'The Committee is concerned over the approach of the State party to the Committee's Views in Communication No. 560/1993 (A v. Australia). Rejecting the Committee's interpretation of the Covenant when it does not correspond with the interpretation presented by the State party in its submissions to the Committee undermines the State party's recognition of the Committee's competence under the Optional Protocol to consider communications.' UN Doc. A/55/40, paras. 498–528, at para. 520.

any such element and appear deliberately vague in respect of the authority of the Committee. Under article 40, the Committee is empowered to 'consider' and 'study' State party reports, adopt 'general comments' and transmit these to the States parties and to ECOSOC. The post-1992 practice of adopting country-specific Concluding Observations, with findings of 'concern' or 'incompatibility' and with specific recommendations to the State party, is not even mentioned in the text of the treaty.

The Committee has no authority to set aside the treaty obligation to comply with the Covenant. Nevertheless, article 2 cf the Covenant uses the notion of 'jurisdiction' when prescribing the States parties' general obligation to respect and ensure the rights under the Covenant. Consequently, the Committee may take the position that a human rights violation has taken place in circumstances that are beyond the control of the State party and hence not within its effective jurisdiction. In the reporting procedure, such situations may be reflected in a section of the Concluding Observations entitled 'Factors and Difficulties' cr 'Introduction'.[45] The trend, however, has been towards commenting only on 'positive aspects' and on 'concerns and recommendations' in the implementation of the Covenant.

The follow-up procedures developed under both the reporting procedure and the procedure for individual complaints provide an opportunity for a direct exchange of information and views between the State party and the Committee member who exercises the respective follow-up mandate.

---

[45] See para. 3 of the Committee's Concluding Observations on Serbia and Montenegro (CCPR/CO/81/SEMO), 2004: 'The State party explained its inability to report on the discharge of its own responsibilities with regard to the human rights situation in Kosovo, and suggested that, owing to the fact that civil authority is exercised in Kosovo by the United Nations Interim Administration Mission in Kosovo (UNMIK), the Committee may invite UNMIK to submit to it a supplementary report on the human rights situation in Kosovo. The Committee notes that, in accordance with Security Council resolution 1244 (1999), Kosovo currently remains a part of Serbia and Montenegro as successor State to the Federal Republic of Yugoslavia, albeit under interim international administration, and the protection and promotion of human rights is one of the main responsibilities of the international civil presence (para. 11(j) of the resolution). It also notes the existence of provisional institutions of self-government in Kosovo that are bound by the Covenant by virtue of article 3.2(c) of UNMIK Regulation No. 2001/9 on a Constitutional Framework for Provisional Self-Government in Kosovo. The Committee considers that the Covenant continues to remain applicable in Kosovo. It welcomes the offer made by the State party to facilitate the consideration of the situation of human rights in Kosovo and encourages UNMIK, in co-operation with the Provisional Institutions of Self-Government (PISG), to provide, without prejudice to the legal status of Kosovo, a report on the situation of human rights in Kosovo since June 1999.'

Another form of 'soft enforcement' is the provision of training or other assistance by the Office of the High Commissioner for Human Rights. Members or former members of the Committee, as well as staff members familiar with the work of the Committee, may participate in such assistance, which is usually geared towards facilitating the respective government's ability to prepare its periodic report.

There are no real sanctions at the disposal of the Human Rights Committee. In principle, the findings made by the Committee could lead to action by the United Nations Security Council, including those available under Chapter VII.

2.5 Overall evaluation

The record of effectiveness of the monitoring mechanisms under the Covenant is mixed. There are huge problems in States' delays or outright failures to perform their reporting obligations. These failures can be remedied only in selected instances through requests for a special report or through proceeding to the examination of a country situation in the absence of a report. There are huge problems also in the implementation of the findings made by the Human Rights Committee in its Concluding Observations on countries. The same applies in respect of the implementation of Views adopted under the Optional Protocol procedure. Quite often, States simply choose to ignore the Views by not even reporting back to the Committee, let alone taking effective measures to remedy the human rights violation established by the Committee.

The other side of the coin, however, relates to a track record of success stories. In particular, in respect of States that choose to co-operate with the Committee in good faith, the periodic reporting procedure has developed into a regular stock-taking exercise that entails a critical assessment of treaty implementation and engages not only the Committee and the government of the country concerned but also a range of State and civil society entities in the respective country. At its best, exposure before an international expert body serves as a catalyst for domestic human rights discussion, review and reform. There are numerous instances where the findings by the Human Rights Committee have resulted in the amendment of domestic law.

Two more specific positive experiences of the effectiveness of the reporting procedure relate to the fairly recent modifications made to the procedure, namely, the possibility to schedule a country for consideration before the Committee even in the absence of a report, and the follow-up mechanism under the reporting procedure. In both cases, States parties have proven to be highly responsive. In almost all instances, States have made use of the possibility to submit a follow-up response within the twelve months after the Committee has adopted its Concluding Observations on a periodic report. Likewise, the scheduling of a country for consideration in the absence of a report has in a high proportion of the cases resulted either in the submission of a long-overdue report or in the appearance of a government delegation before the Committee even in the absence of a report.

The experiences under the procedure for individual complaints are similarly mixed. All Views by the Committee contribute to the accumulation of case law on the substantive interpretation of the material human rights provisions of the Covenant. Hence they may serve as a source of inspiration and even authority for the domestic courts all over the world by clarifying the evolving meaning of human rights provisions. Nevertheless, in a fairly large proportion of cases there is no track record whatever of amendments to the law or of an individual remedy to the victim after a finding of a violation. The follow-up procedure developed by the Committee under the Optional Protocol is fairly weak, as, in the absence of funds, it is primarily based on bilateral meetings between the respective members of the Committee and the Geneva- or New York-based diplomatic representatives of the State party. In relation to those States parties that participate in the reporting procedure in good faith, the consideration of a periodic report provides an additional opportunity for following up on individual cases and also on addressing the institutional framework the State party concerned has adopted in respect of implementing the Committee's Views. The flipside of these positive experiences is that many governments remain ignorant and do not even report on whether any measures were taken because of a finding of a violation.

One of the strongest arguments for the usefulness of the Optional Protocol procedure is its proven relevance for persons awaiting execution. Cases involving the death penalty represent one of the main categories of communications under the Optional Protocol. In a great majority of such cases, the Committee concluded that there was a violation of one or more substantive provisions of the Covenant and that the complainant's right to an effective remedy requires that he must not be executed. There is not a single case where a State party to the Optional Protocol has disregarded this

68   INTERNATIONAL HUMAN RIGHTS

aspect of the remedy by proceeding to the execution of an individual whose rights under the Covenant were found to be violated.

The reporting procedure under ILO Conventions was an important source of inspiration for drafting the treaty provisions on the reporting procedure under UN human rights treaties, and for their practical application. The drafting process of the Covenant was long, and during that time further treaties, for instance the European Convention on Human Rights[46] and the Convention for the Elimination of Racial Discrimination,[47] were drafted, including their provisions on monitoring mechanisms.

Within the UN human rights treaty framework, the practice of the Human Rights Committee has often served as a model for other treaty bodies. Hence, in spite of the fact that the legal basis in the treaties may be different, other treaty bodies have followed the Human Rights Committee in their decisions to start issuing country-specific Concluding Observations at the end of the consideration of a government report, as well as general comments or general recommendations.

The Optional Protocol to the Covenant has been an important source of inspiration in the drafting of the Optional Protocol to the Convention on the Elimination of Discrimination Against Women,[48] and the (future) Optional Protocol to the Covenant on Economic, Social and Cultural Rights. In both processes, lessons have been drawn not only from the text of the ICCPR's Optional Protocol but also from the evolving practice by the Human Rights Committee. Hence, deficiencies have also been identified and turned into stronger treaty provisions than those in the ICCPR's Optional Protocol. The provisions on admissibility requirements and interim measures of protection in the CEDAW Optional Protocol may be mentioned as examples of improvements made based on the experiences under the ICCPR's Optional Protocol.

The ICCPR Optional Protocol experience was also used in designing the World Bank Inspection Panel.

There are certainly several lessons to learn from the Covenant regime. One of them relates to the historical experience of living with fairly open-ended

---

[46] Convention for the Protection of Human Rights and Fundamental Freedoms, 4 November 1950, in force 3 September 1953, 213 UNTS 222.
[47] Convention on the Elimination of All Forms of Racial Discrimination, New York, 7 March 1966, in force 4 January 1969, 660 UNTS 195.
[48] Optional Protocol to the Convention on the Elimination of All Forms of Discrimination Against Women, New York, 6 October 1999, in force 22 December 2000, A/RES/54/4.

treaty provisions for more than twenty-five years. In this respect, the Covenant combines a set of legally binding and at best precise substantive human rights norms with weak treaty provisions on compliance control. The establishment and operation of an independent expert body has resulted in the accumulation of institutionalized practices of interpretation and a gradually expanding view of the competencies of the monitoring body. 'Implied powers' could be used as a doctrinal underpinning for the growing importance of the Human Rights Committee as an organ for compliance control.

A second lesson relates to the absence of treaty provisions and of institutionalized practice when it comes to the collective responsibility of the States parties, or of the political organs of the United Nations to come to the support of the implementation of the positions taken by the treaty-based expert body. In the absence of actual enforcement mechanisms in the treaty itself, it seems essential for the effective implementation of the findings made through an expert review that they should receive impartial and unconditional backing by the community of States parties or by an intergovernmental body with political authority. For this reason, it is not necessarily the lack of treaty provisions on the formally binding legal force of findings made by the Human Rights Committee that is the cause of the insufficiently efficient implementation. Equally efficient implementation could be achieved through providing systematic political backing for the findings made through the existing procedures of compliance control.

3

The European Convention on Human Rights

MARK E. VILLIGER[*]

3.1 Introduction

3.1.1 The European Convention on Human Rights

The European Court of Human Rights ('the Court') was set up by the 1950 European Convention on Human Rights ('the Convention').[1] Various protocols have been added to the Convention: these either contain substantive rights (Protocols Nos. 1, 4, 6, 7, 12 and 13) or relate to procedure (Protocols Nos. 2, 3, 5, 8–11 and 14). Originally, the Convention set up two bodies, the European Commission on Human Rights and the European Court of Human Rights, the latter acting as a quasi-body of appeal. Given the increased level of integration in Europe, the States of Europe decided to merge the two bodies, and in 1998 the reformed Court commenced its activities.[2]

The Convention contains a number of provisions enshrining fundamental human rights and freedoms, for example the right to life, the prohibition of inhuman treatment and torture, the right to liberty and security, the right to a fair trial, the right to respect for private and family life, freedom of thought, conscience and religion, freedoms of expression and of assembly and association, and the prohibition of discrimination. Protocol No. 12 (not yet in force) will include a general prohibition of

---

[*] The views expressed here are those of the author alone. This contribution is based on the author's *Handbuch der Europäischen Menschenrechtskonvention (EMRK)* (Zurich: Schulthess Polygraphischer Verlag, 2nd edn, 1999). The cases referred to can be found using the Court's search engine (HUDOC) at www.echr.coe.int.

[1] Convention for the Protection of Human Rights and Fundamental Freedoms, 4 November 1950, in force 3 September 1953, 213 UNTS 222; European Treaty Series (ETS) No. 5.

[2] Protocol No. 11 to the Convention for the Protection of Human Rights and Fundamental Freedoms, restructuring the control machinery established thereby, Strasbourg, 11 May 1994, in force 1 November 1998, ETS No. 155. The Protocol forms an integral part of the Convention.

discrimination.[3] In addition, and for the first time in the history of international human rights, the Convention sets up a system of protecting these rights. In particular, it sets up a complaints system whereby any individual or non-governmental organization (NGO) or group of individuals may submit an application to the Court against one of the forty-five Member States (right to individual application). A Member State may do the same in respect of other Member States (so-called inter-State applications). Thus, the Convention sets up the Court, defines its jurisdiction, lists the various conditions of admissibility for filing an application, and sets out the procedure to be followed.[4]

The Court will declare applications either admissible or inadmissible. If the application is admissible and a friendly settlement is not obtained, the Court will issue a reasoned judgment; if the application is inadmissible, the Court will issue a decision. Both the judgments and the decisions are binding. Thus, according to article 46(1) of the Convention, '[t]he High Contracting Parties undertake to abide by the final judgment of the Court in any case to which they are parties'. According to article 46(2), the Committee of Ministers of the Council of Europe (consisting of the foreign ministers of the Member States, or their delegates) shall supervise the execution of the judgments.

Indubitably, States have complied with the vast majority of judgments – which is not surprising, given the binding effect of judgments (article 46) and the fact that no State is obliged to join the Convention. Even occasional *causes célèbres*, where States at first did not appear to react, were sooner or later implemented.

3.1.2 Secondary texts

While the Convention contains the basic rules on the Court and its procedure, the most important secondary rules are the Rules of Court,[5] drafted by the Court itself, concerning various aspects of its organization, working

---

[3] Protocol No. 12 to the Convention for the Protection of Human Rights and Fundamental Freedoms, Rome, 4 November 2000, not yet in force, ETS No. 177.

[4] See on this subject generally L. Caflisch, 'Der Europäische Gerichtshof für Menschenrechte und dessen Überwachungsmechanismen: Vergangenheit, Gegenwart, Zukunft' (2003) 122 *Zeitschrift für Schweizerisches Recht* 125.

[5] The Rules of Court, including the amendments made by the plenary Court on 4 July 2005, in force 3 October 2005, are available on the Court's website at www.echr.coe.int/NR/rdonlyres/ D1EB31A8-4194-436E-987E-65AC8864BE4F/0/RulesOfCourt.pdf.

and procedure, as well as matters such as investigations and legal aid (it was last amended on 7 July 2003). The Rules of Court have been supplemented by so-called Practice Directions, which can be consulted on the Court's website.[6] These directions qualify as guidelines and have concerned, so far, requests for interim measures, the institution of proceedings, and written proceedings. The Court's competence to enact the Rules of Court is derived directly from the Court's competencies under the Convention.[7]

Protocol No. 14 to the Convention,[8] adopted on 13 May 2004, proposes various changes to the Convention's procedures. Its entry into force – in about three to four years' time – requires ratification by all forty-five Member States. As of November 2005, it has been signed by nineteen States and there are no ratifications. According to its preamble, the Protocol was adopted in view of the 'urgent need to amend certain provisions of the Convention in order to maintain and improve the efficiency of the control system for the long term, mainly in light of the continuing increase in the workload of the European Court of Human Rights'.[9]

The Court is not governed by precedent, there is no *stare decisis*. Previous judgments are not binding for the Court, and in theory it is free to depart from its previous case law. In practice, it will not do so lightly, and, indeed, article 30 requires the relinquishment of jurisdiction of a Chamber to the Grand Chamber if, *inter alia*, 'the resolution of a question before the Chamber might have a result inconsistent with a judgment previously delivered by the Court'. As a result, the vast body of judgments and decisions, including the case law of the previous European Commission on Human Rights, provides important signposts for the Court itself in its daily work.

As regards the effects of judgments *vis-à-vis* States, clearly, they are binding for the respondent government. As regards other States, the

---

[6] The Practise Directions are available on the Court's website at www.echr.coe.int/ECHR/EN/Header/Basic+Texts/Basic+Texts/Practice+directions/.

[7] This competence of the Court lies at the heart of the *Mamatkulov and Abdurasulovic* v. *Turkey* case (Application Nos. 46827/99 and 46951/99), currently pending before the Court's Grand Chamber. The case concerns, *inter alia*, the issue of whether or not Rule 39 of the Rules of Court provides for *binding* interim (provisional) measures and in particular whether this Rule finds a basis in the Convention. Previously, a judgment of Section IV in the same case had concluded that such measures were binding. See, on this topic, G. S. Letsas, 'International Human Rights and the Binding Force of Interim Measures' (2003) 5 *European Human Rights Law Review* 527–38.

[8] Protocol No. 14 to the Convention for the Protection of Human Rights and Fundamental Freedoms, amending the control system of the Convention, Strasbourg 13 May 2004, not yet in force.

[9] On this, see M.-B. Dembour, '"Finishing off" Cases: The Radical Solution to the Problem of the Expanding ECtHR Caseload' (2002) 5 *European Human Rights Law Review* 604–23.

judgments have important indirect effects. To begin with, if the Court has in a judgment resolved an issue concerning the legislation of one State, another State with the same legislation risks the Court reaching the same conclusion.[10] More importantly, given that the Court's case law is endowed with considerable authority, it provides the central, and essential, *acquis européen* of human rights. The case law thus has a constitutive-institutional function in that it influences legislation in Europe in all matters of modern society.[11]

The Committee of Ministers of the Council of Europe supervises the execution of judgments. For this purpose, it has prepared its own set of procedural rules. Furthermore, the Committee of Ministers and the Parliamentary Assembly of the Council of Europe have issued non-binding recommendations and declarations concerning the protection of human rights in Europe.[12]

The domestic practice of Member States, in particular of their highest courts (e.g. constitutional and supreme courts), is relevant for the Court in its interpretation and application of domestic law. It does so in view of the principle of subsidiarity, which prevails throughout the Convention.[13]

3.1.3 Dispute settlement under the Convention

The dispute settlement under the Convention becomes compulsory for Member States upon ratification of the Convention. Ratification includes in particular the State's acceptance of the right to individual application.[14]

---

[10] See, for instance, the judgments in *X etc.* v. *Netherlands*, 1984, Series A No. 77; and in the subsequent case of *Huber* v. *Switzerland*, 1990, Series A No. 188.

[11] On the subject of precedent and indirect effects, see L. Wildhaber, 'Precedent in the European Court of Human Rights', in Paul Mahoney, F. Matscher, H. Petzold and L. Wildhaber (eds.), *Protecting Human Rights: The European Perspective – Studies in Memory of Rolv Ryssdal* (Cologne: Heymann, 2000), pp. 1529 *et seq.*; F. Matscher, 'Bemerkungen zur extraterritorialen oder indirekten Wirkung der EMRK', in A. Donatsch, M. Forster and Ch. Schwarzenegger (eds.), *Festschrift St. Trechsel* (Zurich: Schulthess, 2002), pp. 25 *et seq.*

[12] For instance, in 2004, the Committee of Ministers issued recommendations, *inter alia*, on 'the European Convention on Human Rights in university education and professional training'; 'the verification of the compatibility of draft laws, existing laws and administrative practice with the standards laid down in the European Convention on Human Rights'; and 'the improvement of domestic remedies' (all recommendations adopted on 12 May 2004).

[13] See generally on subsidiarity P. G. Carozza, 'Subsidiarity as a Structural Principle of International Human Rights Law' (2003) 97 *American Journal of International Law* 38.

[14] The pre-1998 Convention required a further – facultative – declaration by means of which a State accepted the right to individual application for a certain period.

74 INTERNATIONAL HUMAN RIGHTS

In other words, at present, applications may be filed against each of the forty-five Member States. The obligation of a State to submit to an application filed against it by another Member State (so-called inter-State applications) has been compulsory since the Convention was adopted in 1950.

3.2 The Court and its procedures

3.2.1 The Court

The Court is called upon 'to ensure the observance of the engagements undertaken by the High Contracting Parties in the Convention and the Protocols thereto' (article 19). The seat of the Court is in Strasbourg, France, where it functions on a permanent basis. The Court consists of a number of judges equal to that of the Member States (the 'High Contracting Parties'), i.e. currently forty-five. According to Protocol No. 14 (not yet in force), the European Union may eventually accede to the Convention (revised Article 59(2)). The Convention sets out the profile of the judges, their elections and terms as follows:

1. The judges, who sit on the Court in their individual capacity, shall be of high moral character and must possess either the qualifications required for appointment to high judicial office or be jurisconsults of recognized competence. During their term of office, they shall not engage in any activity which is incompatible with their independence, impartiality or the demands of full-time office. All questions arising from the application of this provision shall be decided by the Court (article 21).

2. The judges are elected by the Parliamentary Assembly with respect to each High Contracting Party by a majority of votes cast from a list of three candidates (this is an aspect of democracy) nominated by the High Contracting Party (the aspect of State sovereignty). The same procedure shall be followed to complete the Court in the event of the accession of new High Contracting Parties and for filling casual vacancies (article 22).[15]

3. The judges shall be elected for a period of six years on a rotating basis, i.e. half the judges are rotated after three years. They may be re-

---

[15] On this subject, see A. Comber, 'Judicial Independence: Law and Practice of Appointments to the European Court of Human Rights' (2003) 5 *European Human Rights Law Review* 486–500.

elected. A judge elected to replace a judge whose term of office has not expired shall hold office for the remainder of his predecessor's term. The terms of office of judges shall expire when they reach the age of seventy. The judges shall hold office until replaced. They shall, however, continue to deal with such cases as they already have under consideration (article 23).

4. Judges have a registry at their disposal, the functions and organization of which are laid down in the Rules of the Court. Moreover, the Court is assisted by legal secretaries (article 25). The Court's staff currently comprises over 400 persons, among them managers, senior and junior case lawyers, assistants, secretaries, technical staff, messengers etc. The judges currently sit in formations of seventeen (Grand Chamber), seven (Chamber) and three judges (Committee). The Plenary Court has administrative functions.

5. The Grand Chamber decides cases relinquished to it by a Chamber raising 'a serious question affecting the interpretation of the Convention or the protocols thereto, or where the resolution of a question before the Chamber might have a result inconsistent with a judgment previously delivered by the Court' (article 30). The Grand Chamber may also function as a quasi-appeal body on judgments of a Chamber referred to it by a party to the case, provided a filtering panel of five judges has accepted the party's request. Finally, it may consider requests for advisory opinions.

6. Committees, according to article 28, are called upon solely to declare applications inadmissible by a unanimous vote, or to strike them out of the Court's list of cases (e.g. if the applicant has lost interest in the case, article 37(1)(a)).

7. Chambers, as provided by article 29, decide on the admissibility and merits of all other cases, both individual applications and inter-State cases.[16]

8. The Plenary Court has administrative functions. It elects its President and (currently) two Vice-Presidents for a term of three years. It also sets up Chambers, constituted for a period of three years. The Plenary elects the Presidents of the Chambers of the Court and the Registrar

---

[16] The formulation of art. 29(1), according to which the Chamber will decide 'if no decision is taken under article 28' (concerning Committee cases), may give rise to a misunderstanding: it is perfectly possible that an application goes directly before the Chamber without a Committee having taken a decision.

and (currently) one Deputy Registrar, and adopts the Rules of Court (article 26).

9. According to Protocol No. 14 (not yet in force), a single judge may in future exercise the functions of a Committee, in particular where such a decision can be taken without further examination. The Committees, on the other hand, will henceforth also be competent to declare a case admissible and even render a judgment on the merits if the underlying question in the case is 'already the subject of well-established case law of the Court' (revised article 28).

3.2.2 Conditions of admissibility

Various admissibility conditions must be complied with in order for the Court to be able to deal with an application. These are, in order of priority, *inter alia*:

1. The application shall not be substantially the same as a matter that has previously been examined by the Court (article 35(2)(b)). This requires in particular the same applicant and the same respondent State as well as the same facts and the same object of application.
2. The application shall not already have been submitted to another procedure of international investigation or settlement (article 35(2)(b)). By excluding an 'appeal' from one international body to another, the Convention presupposes the hierarchical equality of all international investigation and settlement procedures.
3. Compatibility *ratione personae* (article 34). Only individuals, NGOs or groups of individuals are entitled to raise an application against a Member State of the Convention. Moreover, the persons and organizations must claim to be a victim of a violation by one of the Member States (rather than, for instance, by another private person).
4. Compatibility *ratione temporis*. The Court is only competent to deal with a complaint concerning facts eventuating after a Member State's ratification of the Convention and its Protocols; according to the general principle of international law, the Convention has no retroactive effect.[17]
5. Compatibility *ratione materiae* (article 35(3)). The Court is only competent to entertain the alleged violation of rights and freedoms

---

[17] Art. 28 of the Vienna Convention on the Law of Treaties, Vienna, 23 May 1969, in force 27 January 1980, 1155 UNTS 331.

enshrined in the Convention. For instance, it is not competent to examine breaches of social and economic rights, the right to enter and reside in a State, tax proceedings, the right to institute criminal proceedings against third persons, issues arising out of military service, etc.

6. Exhaustion of domestic remedies (article 35). Before the Court can deal with a matter, the applicant must have raised her or his complaint before all competent domestic courts, from the first to the last instance (which is normally the constitutional or supreme court). This is the so-called vertical exhaustion of domestic remedies. Moreover, the applicant must approach the domestic courts correctly, i.e. comply with their respective procedural requirements. This is horizontal exhaustion. For instance, the applicant will not have complied with the requirement of domestic remedies if a domestic appeal is declared inadmissible on account of the expiry of a time-limit.

7. Six months' time-limit (article 35). The Court may only deal with an application within six months of the date of the decision of the last domestic court (which is normally the highest domestic court). In principle, the time-limit commences on the date when the applicant obtained the written reasons for the decision.

8. The application shall not be manifestly ill-founded (article 35(3)). The Court may employ this ground of inadmissibility where, for instance, it considers that the alleged inhuman treatment does not meet the thresholds of inhuman and degrading treatment within the meaning of article 3, or where it considers that a measure under articles 8–11 is not disproportionate within the meaning of paragraphs 2 of these provisions.

9. Protocol No. 14 (not yet in force) provides a further ground of inadmissibility, namely, that 'the applicant has not suffered a significant disadvantage, unless respect for human rights as defined in the Convention and the Protocols thereto requires an examination of the application on the merits and provided that no case may be rejected on this ground which has not been duly considered by a domestic tribunal' (revised article 35(3)(b)). It will be up to the Court to give meaning and scope to this new condition of admissibility, in particular whether the disadvantage shall be of a financial, moral, physical, psychological or other nature.

3.2.3 *Procedure in individual applications*

Court procedure consists of two parts. At the admissibility stage, the Court will examine whether the admissibility conditions have been complied with. The decision on inadmissibility is final, and an appeal is not possible. If a case is declared admissible, the Court will examine whether the application is well founded. If no friendly settlement is reached, the Court may, if necessary, undertake a further investigation (article 38(1)(b)); otherwise the case will proceed to judgment (article 45).

If a case is declared admissible, the parties have the possibility of reaching a friendly settlement of the case, as a result of which the Court will strike it out of its list of cases (article 39). A friendly settlement has no winners and no losers; in particular, there will be no determination of a violation of human rights. As a rule, the respondent government offers a sum of money, and the applicant withdraws her or his case.

The Rules of Court provide for a detailed set of rules for the Court's procedure. The following summary principles of procedure may be mentioned:

1. The Court's proceedings are in principle in writing, although, if need be, the Court may order a public and oral hearing (article 40).
2. There is strict equality between the parties.
3. The government must ensure the right to effective petition (article 34) and, where necessary, offer the necessary facilities if the Court undertakes an investigation (in particular fact-finding).
4. The applicant may at the outset file his or her application on his own; however, after a case has been communicated and in particular declared admissible, the applicant shall be represented by a lawyer.
5. The Court's official languages are English and French; the President of the Court or of a Chamber may, exceptionally, authorize the use of another language of a Member State.
6. The Court's proceedings are transparent. It is possible for everybody to consult at the Court's seat in Strasbourg the file of every case (excluding the minutes of the Court's deliberations and any correspondence or documents concerning attempts at a friendly settlement). Since this possibility benefits mainly individuals living in the vicinity of Strasbourg, in the future it is planned to scan these documents and to place them on the Court's website.

7. If the applicant is indigent and his or her application raises serious issues under the Convention, legal aid may be afforded by the Council of Europe.

3.2.4 Inter-State applications

States may at any time refer to the Court any alleged breach of the Convention and its Protocols against another Member State (so-called inter-State applications, article 33). In 1950, this possibility constituted the core of dispute settlement under the Convention. It offers States the possibility to ensure the European *ordre public* collectively. Inter-State applications have since been overtaken in importance – both in qualitative and quantitative terms – by individual applications. So far, twelve inter-State applications have been filed (there are different ways of counting the applications), including, *inter alia*, *Austria* v. *Italy* (filed in 1960); *Denmark, Norway, Sweden and the Netherlands* v. *Greece* (1967); *Ireland* v. *United Kingdom* (1971); *France, Norway, Denmark and Sweden* v. *Turkey* (1982); and *Cyprus* v. *Turkey* (1994).[18]

The low number of inter-State applications (compared with the high number of individual applications) may be explained, *inter alia*, by the fact that it is now largely considered an unfriendly act on account of the high level of European integration. Inter-State applications may also be considered cumbersome and indeed impractical in view of the well-established right to individual application. The procedure of inter-State applications resembles largely that of individual applications.

3.2.5 Position of individuals and NGOs

Individuals, NGOs or groups of individuals have the right to submit individual applications against one of the forty-five Member States of the Convention. However, they must claim to be a victim of a violation of the Convention (article 34). This excludes in particular a so-called *actio popularis*, e.g. complaints against legislation or generally about injustices in society that have not as such affected the individual complainant.

---

[18] *Austria* v. *Italy*, Application No. 788/60, Collection of Decisions 7, pp. 4–5; *Denmark, Norway, Sweden and the Netherlands* v. *Greece*, 1968, Collection of Decisions 25, pp. 92–116; *Ireland* v. *United Kingdom*, 1978, Series A No. 25; *France, Norway, Denmark and Sweden* v. *Turkey* (1982) Decisions and Reports (DR) 35, pp. 143 *et seq.* and DR 44, pp. 31 *et seq.*; *Cyprus* v. *Turkey*, 1996, DR 31 and Report of Judgments and Decisions 2001-IV.

80   INTERNATIONAL HUMAN RIGHTS

From 1953 until 31 December 2003, 133,158 individual applications had been registered by the Court's Registry (out of a total of 300,182 applications filed). These have resulted in 4,145 judgments of the Court (the remaining applications were declared inadmissible or were resolved by means of a friendly settlement). The number of applications has risen steadily – particularly since the 1980s – and the ratification of the Convention by States of Central and Eastern Europe has further boosted their numbers. Without doubt, the right to individual application has become highly popular in Europe – so much so that the Court can no longer deal with all the applications within a reasonable time. Protocol No. 11, which set up the present Court in 1998, aimed at speeding up proceedings. Recently, Protocol No. 14 (not yet in force) was adopted for the same purpose.

In all cases before a Chamber or the Grand Chamber, the President may invite any individual or NGO concerned to submit written comments or take part in hearings. In practice, NGOs occasionally submit third party briefs on pending cases.[19]

3.3 The Court's judgments

3.3.1 Binding nature of judgments

The Court's judgments, which are binding on the respondent State, state only whether there has been a violation of the Convention. The Court is not competent to quash domestic decisions, let alone to resolve a dispute. Given the binding nature of the Court's judgment (article 46(1)), a State is given a certain freedom in deciding how to bring its domestic legal order into conformity with the Convention as interpreted by the judgment in question. In the *Belilos* case, the Court held that 'the Court's judgment leaves to the State the choice of the means to be used in its domestic legal system to give effect to the obligation under Article 53 [now article 46]'.[20]

These considerations are a result of the principle of subsidiarity, which takes account of the many particularities of domestic law with regard to the implementation of the Court's judgments. In particular, if

---

[19] See C. E. Schwitter Marsiaj, *The Role of International NGOs in the Global Governance of Human Rights: Challenging the Democratic Deficit* (Zurich: Schulthess Polygraphischer Verlag, 2004), pp. 192 *et seq.* and *passim*.   [20] *Belilos* v. *Switzerland*, 1988, Series A No. 132, § 78.

the nature of the breach allows for *restitutio in integrum*, it is up to the respondent State to restore the original state of affairs as it was before the human rights violation took place. Overall, the obligation under article 46 concerns not only the executive, but all authorities of that State.[21]

3.3.2 Just satisfaction (pecuniary compensation)

Traditionally, the Court has not pronounced itself on *restitutio in integrum* but dealt solely with just satisfaction according to article 41. It may award pecuniary compensation (either in the same or in a subsequent so-called 'article 41 judgment'), if it has found that there has been a violation of the Convention. In this case, it can award material damage for any losses directly incurred because of the violation. Alternatively or cumulatively, it may award compensation for immaterial (non-pecuniary) damage for any suffering resulting from the violation.

The precise amount to be awarded is regularly established on an equitable basis, since non-pecuniary damage can only rarely be the object of concrete proof. On the other hand, it is reasonable to assume that applicants in respect of whom the Court has found a human rights violation have suffered some mental strain, distress and anxiety. In practice, the amount of just satisfaction (pecuniary and/or non-pecuniary damage) varies. The Court may even find that the judgment itself provides sufficient satisfaction at least for non-pecuniary damage.[22]

The Court has assumed the right to specify the currency in which the award is to be paid, in order to avoid the inconvenience of a currency that is rapidly depreciating. Currently, the awards are as a rule pronounced in euros. Since *Moreira de Azevedo* v. *Portugal*,[23] the Court has stated that the respondent

---

[21] See in particular E. Lambert-Abdelgawad, *The Execution of Judgments of the European Court of Human Rights*, Human Rights Files (2002) No. 19 (Strasbourg: Council of Europe Publication, 2002); see also L. Wildhaber, 'Article 41 of the European Convention on Human Rights: Just Satisfaction under the European Convention on Human Rights' (2003) 3 *Baltic Yearbook of International Law* 1; E. Klein, 'Should the Binding Effect of the Judgments of the European Court of Human Rights Be Extended?', in Mahoney *et al.* (eds.), *Studies in Memory of Rolv Ryssdal*, pp. 705 *et seq.*; J. Polakiewicz, *Die Verpflichtung der Staaten aus den Urteilen des Europäischen Menschenrechtsgerichtshofs* (Berlin: Springer, 1992); M. E. Villiger, 'Die Wirkungen der Entscheidungen der EMKR-Organe im innerstaatlichen Recht, namentlich in der Schweiz' (1985) 104 *Zeitschrift für Schweizerisches Recht* 469.
[22] See, for instance, the *Corigliano* v. *Italy* judgment, 1982, Series A No. 57, § 53.
[23] 1991, Series A No. 208-C.

State must pay the relevant amount within a certain period (normally three months). Owing to the delay with which certain States have paid the amounts due, the Court now also regularly makes orders for default interest.[24]

In addition, the Court is competent to award the applicant costs and expenses, which he or she incurred when bringing the case before the Court. To be entitled thereto, the injured party must have incurred the costs and expenses in order to seek, through the domestic legal order, prevention or rectification of a violation and to have the same established by the Court, or to obtain redress therefor. Furthermore, it has to be shown that the costs and expenses were actually incurred, that they were necessary and reasonable as to quantum. Often, this award occurs on an equitable basis.[25]

3.3.3 Restitutio in integrum

Where just satisfaction alone is insufficient, the respondent State may be called upon to remedy the situation. The first obligation of the State must be to put an end to a continuing violation (although admittedly this is of limited relevance, given the often lengthy procedures before the domestic authorities and the Strasbourg court). The second and more substantial obligation is to prevent a repetition of the violation, which may require the adoption of general measures in the domestic system. In particular, domestic courts may be called upon to amend their case law, or the authorities may be obliged to provide for legislative measures.

The step thereafter is to grant *restitutio in integrum*, i.e. that the State places the applicant in precisely that situation in which he or she was before the Court found a Convention violation. In theory, the Court has the possibility of ensuring such *restitutio*: the text of article 41 enables the Court to look through the so-called article 41 window into the domestic sphere and to decide on just satisfaction solely 'if the internal law of the High Contracting Party concerned allows only partial reparation to be made' (article 41). This would require the Court to separate its judgment on the merits from its article 41 judgment: after having rendered the former and before giving the

---

[24] As an example, in the recent case of *Ilascu* v. *Moldova and Russia*, Application No. 48787/99, the Court awarded each applicant a lump sum of Ä180,000 for pecuniary and non-pecuniary damage in respect of complaints about treatment and conditions occurring, *inter alia*, under arts. 3, 5 and 6, and an additional Ä10,000 to each applicant on account of a breach of the right to individual application according to art. 34.

[25] See, for instance, *Le Compte, Van Leuven and De Meyere* v. *Belgium*, 1982, Series A No. 54, § 17.

latter, it would have to satisfy itself that only partial reparation had been made. (Incidentally, this would be a strong tool of ensuring States' compliance with the judgment.) As pointed out above, so far the Court has been reluctant to do so. Exceptionally and more recently, the Court has commenced steering in this direction. Three examples may be mentioned:

1. In its 2001 *Brumarescu* v. *Romania* judgment,[26] concerning the deprivation of property according to article 1 of Protocol No. 1, the Court found 'that in the circumstances of the present case the return of the property in issue, as ordered in the final judgment of the Bucharest Court of First Instance of 9 December 1993, would put the applicant as far as possible in the situation equivalent to the one in which he would have been if there had not been a breach of Article 1 of Protocol No. 1'.[27]

2. In a number of cases since 2003 concerning proceedings before the Turkish State security courts, the Court has applied the so-called *Gençel* formula (going back to the 2003 *Gençel* v. *Turkey* judgment[28]), according to which '[w]here the Court finds that an applicant was convicted by a tribunal which was not independent and impartial within the meaning of Article 6 § 1, it considers that, in principle, the most appropriate form of relief would be to ensure that the applicant is granted in due course a retrial by an independent and impartial tribunal'.

3. The most recent example is the 2004 *Broniowski* v. *Poland* judgment,[29] concerning the deprivation of property of a potentially large number of applicants in Poland (and, therefore, of applicants in Strasbourg). The Court found that 'the respondent State should . . . through appropriate legal and administrative measures, secure the effective and expeditious realization of the entitlement in question in respect of the remaining . . . claimants, in accordance with the principles for the protection of property rights laid down in Article 1 of Protocol No. 1',[30] thereby hoping that the remaining claimants settle their cases in Poland rather than in Strasbourg!

3.3.4 *Examination by the Committee of Ministers*

Where the Court finds a violation of the Convention, the case is transmitted to the Committee of Ministers which will supervise its execution

---

[26] Art. 41; Application No. 28342/95.   [27] § 22.   [28] Application No. 53431/99.
[29] Application No. 31443/96.   [30] § 45.

(article 46(2)). In a Resolution of 10 January 2001, the Committee of Ministers adopted rules for the application of article 46(2), which may be summarized as follows:

1. The Committee of Ministers' supervision of the execution of judgments of the Court will in principle take place at special human rights meetings, the agenda of which is public (Rule 1 of the Committee of Minister's Resolution). The information provided to the Committee by the state concerned and the accompanying documents are made public. Only the deliberations of the Committee of Ministers remain secret.
2. When a judgment is transmitted to the Committee of Ministers in accordance with article 46(2) of the Convention, the case will be included on the agenda of the Committee of Ministers without delay (Rule 2).
3. When the Court has decided in the judgment that there has been a violation of the Convention and has awarded just satisfaction to the injured party, the Committee of Ministers will invite the State concerned to inform it of the measures which it has taken in consequence of the judgment (Rule 3).
4. When supervising the execution of a judgment by the respondent State, the Committee of Ministers will examine whether individual measures have been taken to ensure that the violation has ceased and that the injured party is put, as far as possible, in the same situation as that enjoyed prior to the violation of the Convention; and whether general measures have been adopted, preventing new violations similar to that or those found or putting an end to continuing violations (Rule 3).
5. Until the State concerned has provided information on the payment of the just satisfaction awarded by the Court or concerning possible individual measures, the case shall be placed on the agenda of each human rights meeting of the Committee of Ministers. If the State concerned informs the latter that it is not yet in a position to provide information that the general measures necessary to ensure compliance with the judgment have been taken, the case will be placed again on the agenda of a meeting of the Committee of Ministers taking place no more than six months later (Rule 5).
6. After having established that the State concerned has taken all the necessary measures to abide by the judgment (it may even check with the

defence that the sum of just satisfaction has been paid), the Committee of Ministers shall adopt a resolution concluding that its functions under article 46(2) of the Convention have been exercised (Rule 7).

7. Throughout, the Committee of Ministers receives considerable assistance from its own Secretariat and in particular from the Directorate-General II (the former Human Rights Directorate).

Interestingly, the Rules of the Committee of Ministers implicitly assume that States will implement the judgment. Indeed, in actual practice, States have complied without any difficulty with the overwhelming majority of the Court's judgments. Even occasional *causes célèbres* have eventually been resolved. Still, what could or should the Committee of Minister do if a State persistently refuses to execute a judgment? In such a situation, the Committee of Ministers could as a last resort expel the State from the Council of Europe according to articles 3 and 8 of the Statute of the Council of Europe.[31] In respect of the Convention, the other Member States could, in view of the State's persistent and material breach, unanimously agree to suspend the operation of the Convention or to terminate it in the relations between themselves and the defaulting State.[32]

3.3.5 Reopening of domestic proceedings

A particularly appropriate way for a State to comply with a judgment and grant *restitutio in integrum* is to reopen the domestic proceedings that led to the subsequent application in Strasbourg and the Court's ensuing finding of a violation of the Convention. Such reopening places the applicants again in the situation in which they found themselves before the violation occurred. Various difficulties arise here, not least that such reopening can cause harm to the rights of third parties. In particular, the

---

[31] Art. 3 of the Statute of the Council of Europe provides: 'Every member of the Council of Europe must accept the principles of the rule of law and of the enjoyment by all persons within its jurisdiction of human rights and fundamental freedoms, and collaborate sincerely and effectively in the realization of the aim of the Council as specified in Chapter I.' Art. 8 of the Statute provides: 'Any member of the Council of Europe which has seriously violated Article 3 may be suspended from its rights of representation and requested by the Committee of Ministers to withdraw under Article 7. If such member does not comply with this request, the Committee may decide that it has ceased to be a member of the Council as from such date as the Committee may determine.'

[32] Art. 60(1)(a)(i) of the 1969 Vienna Convention on the Law of Treaties; see M. E. Villiger, *Customary International Law and Treaties* (Dordrecht: Martinus Nijhoff Publishers, 1985), pp. 357 *et seq.*

original proceedings will long have obtained the status of *res judicata*. Member States are bound by their own decisions, and the traditional domestic grounds for reopening proceedings (errors, new facts, crimes etc.) do not encompass a judgment of the Strasbourg Court. Here, Member States are called upon to enact in their legislation that domestic proceedings may be reopened in view of a judgment of the Strasbourg Court. Reopening is not required in all cases of a violation of the Convention. Rather, it presupposes a substantive violation in particular of procedural guarantees which casts doubt on the outcome of the domestic proceedings complained of; the applicant must have suffered serious negative consequences on account of the domestic decision which has not been remedied sufficiently by the just satisfaction awarded.[33]

3.3.6 Protocol No. 14: a new role for the Court

Protocol No. 14 to the Convention (not yet in force) provides for far-reaching changes in the current system of supervision of the Court's judgments.[34] On the one hand, Protocol No. 14 authorizes the Committee of Ministers to refer a judgment back to the Court if its supervision of the execution of the judgment is hindered by a problem of interpretation of the judgment (revised article 46(3)). On the other hand, and more importantly, Protocol No. 14 aims at partly filling the gap of non-compliance currently to be found in the Committee of Ministers' supervision of the judgments by enabling the Court to determine at least whether a State has

---

[33] In its Recommendation of 19 January 2000, the Committee of Ministers exhorted Member States 'to examine their national legal systems with a view to ensuring that there exist adequate possibilities of re-examination of the case, including reopening of proceedings . . . especially where . . . the injured party continues to suffer very serious negative consequences because of the outcome of the domestic decision at issue, which are not adequately remedied by the just satisfaction and cannot be rectified except by re-examination or reopening, and . . . the judgment of the Court leads to the conclusion that . . . the impugned domestic decision is on the merits contrary to the Convention, or . . . the violation found is based on procedural errors or shortcomings of such gravity that a serious doubt is cast on the outcome of the domestic proceedings complained of'.

[34] See on the Protocol generally A. Scheidegger, 'Die Sicherstellung der Funktionsfähigkeit des Europäischen Gerichtshofs für Menschenrechte durch Protokoll Nr. 14 zur EMRK über die Änderung des Kontrollsystems der Konvention' (2005) 14 *Aktuelle Juristische Praxis* 172; F. Schürmann, 'Das Protokoll Nr. 14 zur EMRK: Jüngste Änderungen im Strassburger Kontrollmechanismus', in Astrid Epiney, Sarah Theuerkauf and Florence Rivière (eds.), *Schweizerisches Jahrbuch für Europarecht* (Zurich: Schulthess, and Bern: Staempfli, 2003), pp. 69 *et seq.*

complied with its obligations. Thus, if the Committee of Ministers considers that a Member State refuses to abide by a final judgment, it may refer to the Court the question whether that party has failed to fulfil its obligations (revised article 46(4)).

3.3.7 *European Human Rights Commissioner*

The European Human Rights Commissioner, elected by the Parliamentary Assembly, promotes education in and awareness of human rights in the Member States; identifies possible shortcomings in the law and practice of Member States with regard to compliance with human rights; and helps promote the effective observance and full enjoyment of human rights, as embodied in the various Council of Europe instruments. The Commissioner is a non-judicial institution that does not take up individual complaints, though he or she can draw conclusions and take initiatives of a general nature that are based on individual complaints. The Commissioner may encourage action by, and work actively with, national human rights structures and national ombudsmen or similar institutions. Protocol No. 14 postulates in the revised article 36(3) that, 'in all cases before a Chamber or the Grand Chamber, the Council of Europe Commissioner for Human Rights may submit written comments and take part in hearings'.

The purpose of the Commissioner's visits to various countries is to identify shortcomings in the legislation and practice of Member States, and to promote the effective observance of human rights (though not specifically directed towards compliance with the Convention). Visits are effected either on the invitation of the Member State in question or on the initiative of the Commissioner and usually involve meetings with senior government officials, representatives of civil society and the inspection of sites tending to the undermining of human rights. The Commissioner makes recommendations on how respect for human rights might be improved in certain areas.

3.4 Overall evaluation

3.4.1 *Reasons for the Court's success*

Different reasons may be suggested which explain the Convention's success over the past fifty years:

1. The Court's judgments are binding and have 'tangible results', including just satisfaction awards.
2. The high quality and authority of the Court's judgments.
3. The initial application may be filed informally by the applicant him- or herself.
4. The Convention rights are relevant. They concern all aspects of modern European society, and the Court has always interpreted the Convention as being a living instrument.[35]
5. The rights guaranteed in the Convention are capable of being judicially determined (they are justiciable), leaving no room for political decisions.
6. Most rights enshrined in the Convention are also protected in the domestic sphere. Since applicants must first raise their complaints before the domestic authorities (exhaustion of domestic remedies), it is comparatively simple for them, having been unsuccessful in the domestic courts, to continue and submit their complaint to the Strasbourg Court.
7. At times, governments will at the outset criticize the Court's judgments leading to a violation (though they will in the end comply with the judgments). In the eyes of many applicants, this confirms the independent and even powerful position of the Strasbourg Court.
8. Media publicity in the wake of judgments of the Court has boosted the Court's popularity.
9. Membership of the Convention has become an essential condition to obtain membership in the European Union.

3.4.2 The Convention and other international instruments

The fundamental guarantees enshrined in the Convention were inspired by the Universal Declaration of Human Rights proclaimed by the General Assembly of the United Nations on 10 December 1948.[36] On the other hand, the procedures in the Convention were largely innovatory in 1950. To a minor extent, they were influenced by the procedures for the protection of minorities within the League of Nations, in particular by the

---

[35] For instance, in the case of *Tyrer* v. *United Kingdom*, concerning the prohibition of corporal punishment of juveniles, the Court referred to 'developments and commonly accepted standards in the penal policy of the Member States of the Council of Europe' (1978, Series A No. 26, § 31).   [36] A/RES/217 A (III). See the second preambular paragraph to the Convention.

provisions on compatibility and admissibility, some of which the Convention has taken over verbatim.

Conversely, the Convention – and the successful operation of its Court – has indubitably influenced such international instruments as the 1966 International Covenant on Civil and Political Rights,[37] the 1969 American Convention on Human Rights,[38] the 1981 African Charter on Human and Peoples' Rights,[39] and the 1987 European Convention for the Prevention of Torture and Inhuman or Degrading Treatment or Punishment, which refers to the Convention in its second preambular paragraph.[40] The Council of Europe's 1997 Convention on Human Rights and Biomedicine envisages in its article 29 that the Court may give advisory opinions on legal questions concerning the interpretation of that Convention.[41] Mention may also be made of the 1972 Additional Protocol to the 1972 European Convention on State Immunity whose 'European Tribunal' consists of the judges of the Court.[42]

3.4.3 Future impact of the Convention

In the current state of international dispute settlement, setting up a new international court (or even instituting the right to individual petition)

[37] International Covenant on Civil and Political Rights, New York, 16 December 1966, in force 23 March 1976, 999 UNTS 171.

[38] American Convention on Human Rights, San José, Costa Rica, 22 November 1969, in force 18 July 1978, 1144 UNTS 123.

[39] African Charter on Human and Peoples' Rights, 27 June 1981, in force 21 October 1986, 21 ILM 58 (1982).

[40] European Convention for the Prevention of Torture and Inhuman or Degrading Treatment or Punishment, Strasbourg, 26 November 1987, in force 1 March 2002, ETS No. 126.

[41] Convention for the Protection of Human Rights and Dignity of the Human Being with Regard to the Application of Biology and Medicine: Convention on Human Rights and Biomedicine, Oviedo, 4 April 1997, in force 1 December 1999, ETS No. 164.

[42] Additional Protocol to the 1972 European Convention on State Immunity, Basle, 16 May 1972, in force 22 May 1985, ETS No. 074A. The Protocol establishes the European Tribunal in matters of State Immunity to determine cases brought before it, in particular where a domestic judgment has been given against a Convention party and that State does not give effect thereto (art. 1); or where a dispute arises between two or more Convention parties concerning the interpretation or application of the Convention (art. 2). According to art. 4, 'the European Tribunal shall consist of the members of the European Court of Human Rights and, in respect of each non-member State of the Council of Europe which has acceded to the present Protocol, a person possessing the qualifications required of members of that Court designated, with the agreement of the Committee of Ministers of the Council of Europe, by the government of that State for a period of nine years. The President of the European Tribunal shall be the President of the European Court of Human Rights.'

acceptable to States would be a formidable task. States hesitate to accept binding judgments in particular in view of their impact on States' sovereignty. It is true that the Convention was prepared comparatively speedily (the 1948 Hague Congress setting up the Council of Europe also instructed the preparation of the Convention which was adopted two years later in 1950). However, this effort must be appreciated against the backdrop of the atrocities of the Second World War. The Convention's subsequent success as from the 1970s as regards enlarged membership and the growing numbers of applications can be explained, *inter alia*, by its position within the process of European integration. Thus, membership of the Convention has become an essential condition for obtaining membership in the European Union. In addition, given the various existing international human rights instruments which were at least partly influenced by the Convention, there seems little room left in the international sphere for additional general human rights courts.

4

The European Convention on the Prevention of Torture compared with the United Nations Convention Against Torture and its Optional Protocol

RENATE KICKER

The focus of this essay lies on the European Convention on the Prevention of Torture[1] drawing on the author's practical experiences. The UN Convention Against Torture[2] and its procedures together with the newly adopted Optional Protocol[3] will only be looked at for the purpose of comparison as these procedures may be seen as complementary with a potential of overlapping.

4.1 General issues

4.1.1 The European Convention on the Prevention of Torture

4.1.1.1 Basic features

The European Convention for the Prevention of Torture and Inhuman or Degrading Treatment or Punishment (ECPT) was adopted by the Committee of Ministers of the Council of Europe on 26 June 1987 and opened for signature by Member States of the Council of Europe[4] on 26 November 1987; it entered into force on 1 February 1989.

---

[1] European Convention for the Prevention of Torture and Inhuman or Degrading Treatment or Punishment, Strasbourg, 26 June 1987, in force 1 February 1989, ETS No. 126. The text of the Convention and the Explanatory Report are published on the ECPT website, http://conventions.coe.int/Treaty/en/Treaties/Html/126.htm.

[2] Convention Against Torture and Other Cruel, Inhuman or Degrading Treatment or Punishment, New York, 10 December 1984, in force 26 June 1987. 1465 UNTS 85.

[3] Optional Protocol to the Convention Against Torture and Other Cruel, Inhuman or Degrading Treatment or Punishment, New York, 18 December 2002, in force 22 June 2006. GA Res. A/RES/57/199 of 9 January 2003.

[4] Protocol No. 1 to the European Convention for the Prevention of Torture and Inhuman or Degrading Treatment or Punishment, Strasbourg, 4 November 1993, in force 1 March 2002.

92 INTERNATIONAL HUMAN RIGHTS

The core provision of the Convention is the establishment of a European Committee for the Prevention of Torture and Inhuman or Degrading Treatment or Punishment (hereinafter, the 'Committee' or the 'European Committee' or 'CPT'). The Committee is composed of a number of members equal to that of the parties to the Convention.[5] The members are elected by the Committee of Ministers of the Council of Europe from a list of three candidates drawn up by the Bureau of the Parliamentary Assembly, which in turn is based on proposal made by the national delegations of the Members States. Members shall be independent and impartial,[6] and professional experts in the areas covered by the Convention. Reference is made in the annual general reports regarding professional expertise needed in its membership to inspire proposals for candidates.[7] When carrying out visits Committee members may be assisted by experts[8] and interpreters and are supported by members of the secretariat.[9]

The goal and mandate of the Committee are to strengthen the protection of persons deprived of their liberty against torture and inhuman or degrading treatment or punishment by non-judicial means of a preventative character. The Committee is authorized and even obliged[10] to visit detention

---

Since its entry into force, this Protocol forms an integral part of the Convention (ETS No. 126). Protocol No. 1 opened the Convention to non-Member States of the Council of Europe.

[5] As at 10 October 2006, the Committee was composed of forty-two members, while the seats in respect of five States parties remained vacant. At that date, forty-six Member States of the Council of Europe had ratified the Convention.

[6] Members serve in their individual capacity and not as representatives of their own country. The 'national member' does not take part in any visit to its home country, and as a matter of policy should not express any opinion concerning the dialogue between the Committee and the home country.

[7] See para. 35 of the 15th General Report on the Committee's activities, CPT/Inf (2005)17, the report can be accessed via the Convention website at www.cpt.coe.int/en/annual/rep-15.htm, where it is said that more members with first-hand knowledge of the work of law-enforcement agencies and of immigration issues, expertise in child psychiatry and more doctors with relevant forensic skills, in particular as regards the observation and recording of physical injuries are required.

[8] The assistance by experts became the rule. There is a small number of experts who are frequently asked to join a visiting delegation and who have carried out many more visits than any Committee member. Most of them are native speakers in one of the two official Council of Europe languages, English and French, and may offer support also in drafting final talks and draft reports.

[9] The secretariat forms an independent unit under the directorate of human rights in the Council of Europe and consists of a number of legally trained persons as well as administrative assistants originating from different European states: see Appendix 6 to the 16th General Report. CPT/Inf (2006) 35.

[10] Due to the political situation, the Committee has so far had no access to Northern Cyprus and Kosovo. When Serbia and Montenegro ratified the ECPT on 3 March 2004, Kosovo was not

centres in Member States and to examine the treatment of persons deprived of their liberty by a public authority. The Committee may carry out regular visits and such *ad hoc* visits as appear to it to be required in the circumstances. States parties on their side have to facilitate such visits to any place of detention within their jurisdiction.

Mention should be made that the Committee has accepted the request of the International Criminal Tribunal for the Former Yugoslavia (ICTY) to monitor the treatment of persons convicted by the Tribunal in a State that has agreed to accept the transfer of the prisoner concerned for the purpose of the enforcement of his or her sentence. Based on an Enforcement Agreement concluded between the United Kingdom and the ICTY, the first transfer of a prisoner occurred in December 2004 and the detention situation of the person concerned was monitored by the Committee during an *ad hoc* visit to the United Kingdom in July 2005.

At the end of a visit, the Committee may request the authorities to take action to remedy a situation that does not comply with the Committee's standards. These 'immediate observations'[11] made orally at the end of a visit by the visiting delegation are an important tool in situations which are close to being a violation of article 3 of the ECHR. Thus a State may be requested to provide within three months, or even within a shorter period of time, a report on the action taken in light of the 'immediate observations'.

The Convention stipulates that, after each visit, the Committee shall draw up a report on the facts found during the visit, taking account of any observations that may have been submitted by the party concerned. It shall transmit to the State party its report containing any recommendations it considers necessary.[12] Thus, the ECPT provides for a different reporting

---

excluded from the application of the Convention. As this area is under the United Nations Interim Administration Mission in Kosovo (UNMIK), a technical arrangement related to the Convention has been approved by the Committee of Ministers and signed by the representative of UNMIK and the Secretary-General of the Council of Europe in August 2004. Under this agreement, the Committee enjoys access to any place within Kosovo where persons are deprived of their liberty by an authority of UNMIK, under exactly the same conditions as those laid down in the Convention. However, before the Committee can commence its activities in Kosovo, similar arrangements of a binding nature must be concluded with the North Atlantic Treaty Organization (NATO) on the subject of places of detention in Kosovo administered by KFOR (the NATO military mission in Kosovo). Consultations are currently under way with NATO authorities on this subject. For the text of the agreement, see Appendix 8 to the 14th General Report on the Committee's activities, CPT/Inf(2004)28. The Appendix can be accessed at www.cpt.coe.int/en/annual/rep-14.htm#_Toc82840139. Concerning Northern Cyprus, the Committee has not been granted access to this part of the country which also falls under its mandate. [11] Art. 8(5). [12] Art. 10.

system than, for example, that laid down in the United Nations Convention Against Torture (UN CAT). The reports are issued by the expert body, requesting the State party concerned to respond to its comments and requests for information and, more importantly, to indicate the actions taken with respect to the recommendations made by the Committee for improvements regarding the protection of persons deprived of their liberty.

The Convention also refers to comments of the party concerned in relation to the Committee's reports.[13] Neither the Explanatory Report to the Convention nor the Rules of Procedure of the Committee elaborate on this provision. However, in practice, States have been required to respond to the Committee's recommendations, comments and requests for information in an interim report within six months and a final report within twelve months. The practice has changed in relations to States that have been visited several times, where only one final response is required within six months.

The main obligations arising from the ECPT for contracting parties are to co-operate with the independent expert body, the Committee, and to improve the situation in light of the Committee's recommendations.[14] The Committee, for its part, honours this co-operation by keeping its findings confidential unless the State concerned authorizes the publication of the Committee's report together with its own response. Authorization of publication has become the rule, with one notable exception.[15] Some States parties have even published the text of the final observations of a visiting Committee delegation, which are presented orally at the end of the visit and some time later delivered in writing.

If a State fails to co-operate or refuses to improve the situation in light of the recommendations made, the Committee may decide to set in motion a so-called article 10(2) procedure. This means that the Committee informs a State that it may be the subject of a public statement. Public statements have so far been issued only in relation to States where the Committee found allegations of torture and serious forms of ill-treatment backed up by medical evidence without sufficient action being taken by national

---

[13] Art. 11(2).   [14] Arts. 3 and 10(2).

[15] The Russian Federation has so far only authorized the publication of one of the ten reports drawn up by the Committee covering thirteen visits. See Appendix 4 to the 15th General Report producing a state-by-state table showing the number of visits by the Committee, visit reports sent to governments and reports published.

authorities to remedy such flagrant human rights violations.[16] In its most recent practice, the total lack of efforts to improve the situation or to provide specific answers detailing the action taken on all recommendations made or any other information required has led the Committee to 'threaten' a State with a public statement.[17]

4.1.1.2 Secondary rules and guidelines

The Explanatory Report to the Convention – the legal status of which formed part of a discussion between the Committee and the Committee of Ministers – clarifies and explains the provisions of the Convention in a rather detailed way. The Committee therefore formed the opinion that the Explanatory Report has the same legal force as the Convention itself, arguing that, according to the drafting history, it 'constitutes an instrument providing an authoritative interpretation of the text of the Convention'.[18] This stance helped the Committee in its practical work. By way of example, the Committee could refer to paragraph 32 of the Explanatory Report when visiting all parts of a psychiatric establishment and not only its closed section or private social care and elderly homes. The Explanatory Report clarifies that 'visits may be carried out in private as well as in public institutions', and, although 'the Committee may carry out visits only in relation to persons who are deprived of their liberty by a public authority, and not voluntary patients it should be possible for the Committee to satisfy itself that this was indeed the wish of the patient concerned'. In practice, States did not challenge this interpretation, which widened the scope of the Committee's activities.[19]

Another source of legal authority is the Rules of Procedure adopted by the Committee on 16 November 1989, with a few amendments.[20] These

---

[16] All in all, the Committee has issued four public statements, two in relation to Turkey in 1992 and 1996, and two in relation to the Russian Federation concerning the situation in Chechnya in 2001 and 2003.

[17] See e.g. the report to Latvia on the Committee's visit from 25 September to 4 October 2002, CPT/Inf(2005)8, para. 6.

[18] See the exchange of letters between the President of the Committee and the Chairman of the Ministers' Deputies published in Association for the Prevention of Torture, *The Prevention of Torture in Europe* (Association for the Prevention of Torture, Collected Texts, Brochure No. 1, Geneva, 1997), pp. 65–78.

[19] See the report to the German Government on the periodic visit in December 2000, CPT/Inf(2003)20, and the government's response, CPT/Inf(2003)21, where shortcomings in homes for elderly people are addressed. During the final talks, however, the German authorities had asked for a clarification of the CPT's mandate with respect to these institutions.

[20] Amendments were made in 1990, 1991 and 1997. See CPT/Inf/C(89)3 rev.1.

96INTERNATIONAL HUMAN RIGHTS

rules regulate the procedure concerning visits and the ongoing dialogue between the Committee and States parties in more detail.[21] They clarify the decision-making process and the procedure which leads to a public statement when a State refuses to co-operate with the Committee. Another provision[22] gives the Committee the possibility to lift confidentiality and to publish a report even if a party has not requested it to do so. This is the case 'if the Party itself makes the report public, but does not do so in its entirety' or 'if the Party concerned makes a public statement summarizing the report or commenting upon its contents'.[23]

The annual general report, which the Committee publishes each year in autumn, contains a record of its activities as well as developments in its working methods. The reports of the internal Working Group on Working Methods, which have already been declassified in line with the Council of Europe's new policy on access to documents,[24] are also important sources in relation to the visiting practice of the Committee.[25]

The 'substantive' sections of the Committee's general reports, drawn up in a single document, contain the Committee's views regarding the manner in which persons deprived of their liberty ought to be treated. It is a compilation of standards that form the basis of the assessment of the situation in a certain type of establishment (police custody, prisons, psychiatric establishments, detention centres for foreigners, and social care homes), and the recommendations the Committee addresses subsequently to the State concerned.

4.1.2 The UN Convention Against Torture

4.1.2.1 Basic features

The UN Convention Against Torture and Other Cruel, Inhuman or Degrading Treatment or Punishment (UN CAT) was adopted and opened for signature, ratification and accession by General Assembly Resolution 39/46 of 10 December 1984 and entered into force on 26 June 1987.[26] The

---

[21] Rules 29–45.   [22] Rule 42.   [23] See the only report published in relation to Russia.
[24] See the Committee of Minister's Resolution (2002) 6 of 12 June 2001.
[25] List of available documents, www.cpt.coe.int.
[26] For the drafting history, see J. H. Burgers and H. Danelius, *The United Nations Convention Against Torture: A Handbook on the Convention Against Torture and Other Cruel, Inhuman or Degrading Treatment or Punishment* (Dordrecht: Martinus Nijhoff Publishers, 1988), p. 152.

aim of this Convention is to strengthen the existing provisions[27] and procedures[28] as regards the prohibition against torture and other forms of ill-treatment. The main development in this field can be seen in defining the notion of 'torture' in article 1 of this Convention. A clear weakness of this definition is the 'legal sanction' clause, which excludes 'pain or suffering arising only from, inherent in or incidental to lawful sanctions'. States parties to the Convention are obliged to take effective legislative, administrative, judicial or other measures to prevent acts of torture in any territory under its legislation;[29] this applies in a rather restrictive manner also to other acts of cruel, inhuman or degrading treatment or punishment. Thus, the main provisions of the Convention are addressed to States parties to be implemented by national law.

A Committee Against Torture (hereinafter, the 'Committee' or the 'UN Committee') is established, consisting of ten members. These are independent experts of recognized competence in the field of human rights, who are nominated and elected for renewable terms of four years by States parties.[30] The recommendation made in the Convention itself – namely, to nominate candidates who are also members of the Human Rights Committee established under the International Covenant on Civil and Political Rights (ICCPR) in order to guarantee a consistent interpretation of the principle of the prohibition of torture – was followed in only a few cases. Two members of the UN Committee have at the same time been members of the European Committee.[31] The mandate of the UN Committee is to supervise the implementation of the Convention's obligations through receiving and reviewing State reports and by making general

---

[27] At the universal level, see art. 3 of the Universal Declaration of Human Rights of 10 December 1948, A/RES/217A (III); and art. 7 of the International Covenant on Civil and Political Rights (ICCPR), New York, 16 December 1966, in force 23 March 1976. 999 UNTS 171.

[28] The Human Rights Committee, established under the ICCPR, has the competence to supervise the implementation of the Convention's obligations through the review of State reports, and, based on the Optional Protocol, to receive complaints submitted by individuals. Under these procedures, the Human Rights Committee has developed an elaborate 'jurisprudence' in relation to the prohibition of torture; the same can be said for the visiting practice and reports of the Special Rapporteur on Torture.

[29] This raises the question whether this provision is literally restricted to the territory of a State party or whether it applies also to activities carried out in the territory of another State by nationals of a State party (participation in peacekeeping operations, international administrations etc.).

[30] For a detailed assessment, see Chris Ingelse, *The UN Committee Against Torture: An Assessment* (The Hague: Kluwer Law International, 2001), pp. 89 *et seq.*

[31] Bent Sorensen, and his successor in the UN Committee, Ole Vecel Rassmusen.

comments on them. The Committee may also carry out an inquiry if it receives reliable information which indicates that torture is being systematically practised in a Member State. It may also receive and consider communications by a State or an individual claiming that a Member State is not fulfilling its obligations under the Convention.

The complaint procedures initiated by a State or individuals are optional and can only be set in motion *vis-à-vis* a State that has made a formal declaration in this respect, which is clearly a strong concession to the States parties' sovereignty.[32] No State complaints have been addressed to the Committee so far and the figures on individual complaints are less than those received under the Optional Protocol to ICCPR relating to the article on the prohibition of torture.

The UN CAT provides further for a compulsory State reporting system. Article 19 stipulates that States parties shall submit to the Committee, within one year after accession, reports on the measures they have taken to give effect to their obligations under this Convention. Thereafter, supplementary reports are due every four years on new measures taken. The Committee may also request *ad hoc* reports. When considering reports by States parties on the implementation of the Convention's obligations, the Committee may make general comments on it.

In its only general comment in relation to article 3, the Committee states that it is not an appellate, a quasi-judicial or an administrative body, but rather a monitoring body created by the States parties themselves with declaratory powers only. It follows that, although considerable weight will be given, in exercising its jurisdiction pursuant to article 3 of the Convention, to findings of fact that are made by organs of the State party concerned, the Committee is not bound by such findings and instead has the power, provided by article 22(4) of the Convention, of free assessment of the facts based upon the full set of circumstances in every case.

The reporting as well as the complaints procedures are modelled after the procedures established under the ICCPR. In view of the fact that the Human Rights Committee has dealt with many more individual

---

[32] As at 21 May 2004, out of 146 States parties that have signed, ratified or acceded to the Convention, a total of fifty-one States parties have made the declarations provided for in arts. 21 and 22 (recognition of the competence of the CAT to receive and consider State as well as individual communications). Four States have made a declaration only in relation to art. 21 (State complaints), Japan, Uganda, the UK and the USA, and five States have accepted only the individual complaints procedure under art. 22, Burundi, Azerbaijan, Guatemala, Mexico and the Seychelles.

complaints in relation to the prohibition of torture and has issued more general comments, the question has been raised whether it was appropriate to establish another expert body – and furthermore one with less financial and institutional back-up.[33]

An innovative procedure is foreseen in article 20, which gives the Committee the mandate to carry out an inquiry if it receives reliable information that appears to it to contain well-founded indications that torture is being systematically practised in the territory of a State party. At all stages of the proceedings, the co-operation of the State party shall be sought and the inquiry may include a visit to its territory only with the agreement of the State concerned. While the whole procedure has to be carried out on a confidential basis, the Committee may decide after consultations with the State party to include a summary account of the results of this inquiry in its annual report. However, the Convention offers an opting-out clause (article 28) according to which a State may declare from the outset that it does not recognize the competence of the Committee provided for in article 20.[34]

Reference should also be made to the Optional Protocol to the United Nations Convention Against Torture, which entered into force in 2006. This will lead to the setting up of a Sub-Committee on the Prevention of Torture as well as national preventative mechanisms. Initially, the Sub-Committee will consist of ten expert members which will increase to twenty-five members upon the fiftieth ratification of the Protocol. The members will be elected by States parties from professionals with experience in various fields relevant to the treatment of persons deprived of their liberty for a renewable term of four years. The mandate of the Sub-Committee is, first, to carry out inspections and to make recommendations to States parties, secondly, to advise and assist them in regard to national visiting mechanisms, and, thirdly, to consult and co-operate with a view to avoiding duplication with international and regional bodies such as the European Committee. Given the small number of experts in relation to the Member States, it appears that the Sub-Committee will have to focus more

---

[33] See Ahcene Boulesbaa, *The UN Convention on Torture and the Prospects for Enforcement* (The Hague and Boston: Martinus Nijhoff Publishers, 1999); and Ingelse, *The UN Committee Against Torture.*

[34] As at 21 May 2004, a total of seven States parties have declared that they do not recognize the competence of the Committee provided for by art. 20 of the Convention; these are Afghanistan, China, Equatorial Guinea, Israel, Kuwait, Morocco and Saudi Arabia.

on defining criteria for the national mechanisms than on carrying out inspections of places of detention itself.

4.1.2.2 Secondary rules and guidelines

The Rules of Procedure[35] deal in its Part Two with the functions of the Committee, and elaborate in detail on the rules applicable concerning the reporting procedures, the inquiry function, and the handling of communications. The Committee has also adopted reporting guidelines to assist States parties in the preparation of initial and periodic reports.[36] The increasing number of ratifications and the practice developed in the performance of its functions has required the Committee to keep its Rules of Procedures under constant review, in order to enhance effectiveness and co-ordination. Thus, the Committee has in its most recent annual report published its working methods when considering reports under article 19 of the Convention.[37]

Another important source for the development of the working methods of the Committee in relation to its supervisory function is the annual reports on its activities according to article 24 of the Convention.

In relation to the complaints procedure, the Committee has adopted a general comment on the implementation of article 3,[38] in which it summarizes its case law concerning this provision. However, this has remained the only general comment so far and has been criticized in academic writing as a very meagre result in view of the desire for interpretation of the substantive provisions.[39]

Secondary rules in relation to its working methods can also be seen in what the Committee itself calls the follow-up procedures.[40] The Committee has recently appointed two rapporteurs, one to deal with the follow-up to conclusions and recommendations on State reporting, and one who takes care of the follow-up on individual cases where the Committee found

---

[35] The rules of procedure have been adopted by the Committee according to art. 18(2) of the Convention at its first and second session, and amended at its thirteenth, fifteenth and twenty-eighth sessions, see CAT/C3/Rev.4, 9 August 2002.

[36] General guidelines for initial reports, CAT/C/4/Rev.2.   [37] See A/59/44, Annex VI.

[38] A/53/44 (1998), Annex IX, General Comment No. 01: Implementation of Article 3 of the Convention in the Context of Article 22.

[39] See Chris Ingelse, 'The Committee Against Torture: One Step Forward, One Step Back' (2000) 18 *Netherlands Quarterly of Human Rights* 307–27.

[40] This information was provided by Carmen-Rosa Rueda-Castanon, member of the Secretariat of the Committee Against Torture, Support Services Branch, Office of the High Commissioner for Human Rights.

violations of the Convention. However, due to the Committee's workload, these activities have not been very prominent so far.[41]

4.2 Defining the task

The task of attributing the rules and procedures established under the two conventions under consideration here to the areas of dispute resolution, compliance control and enforcement of international obligations needs some reflection and preliminary decisions on how to define and distinguish these areas.

The regime as laid down in the European Convention on the Prevention of Torture (ECPT) is rather unique. It provides for a system of visits carried out by an independent expert body to a State party's territory with the intention of preventing the violation of an obligation that is stipulated in another treaty, namely, the European Convention on Human Rights in its article 3 on the prohibition of torture. In carrying out on-site inspections, the expert body by way of recommendations develops standards which eventually form the body of soft obligations for States parties, the observance of which is then monitored by the expert body in follow-up visits and an ongoing dialogue. As the experts are more or less creating the obligations, it is a standard-setting and at the same time a compliance control mechanism.

In contrast to the ECPT, the procedures regulated in the UN Convention Against Torture (UN CAT) share a common feature with other international human rights instruments, such as the International Covenant on Civil and Political Rights.[42] The UN CAT provides for communications by a State party to an independent expert body claiming that another State party is not fulfilling its obligation under the UN CAT, which could be seen as a means of peaceful settlement of a dispute concerning the interpretation or application of the UN CAT. Equally, communications from or on behalf of individuals who claim to be victims of a violation of the provisions of the UN CAT by a State party could be described as a form of international dispute resolution between individuals and States.[43] However,

---

[41] The terms of reference of the Rapporteurs for follow-up are reproduced in Annex IX to the 2001/2002 annual report (A/57/44). A description of the mandate of the Rapporteur on follow-up to individual complaints is also contained in the latest annual report (A/59/44), para. 264.

[42] See the contribution of Martin Scheinin, chapter 2 in this volume.

[43] See Henry J. Steiner, 'Individual Claims in a World of Massive Violations: What Role for the Human Rights Committee?', in Philip Alston and James Crawford (eds.), *The Future of UN Human Rights Treaty Monitoring* (Cambridge: Cambridge University Press, 2000), pp. 15–53.

both procedures are qualified as a means of compliance control in this book.[44] Clearly, the reporting system established under the CAT, where the reports are produced by the States, is a means of compliance control.

The question may be raised whether the inquiry system as foreseen in the UN CAT has any similarities with the visiting system established under the ECPT. Under the UN CAT, an independent expert body is mandated to react to reliable information of systematic violations of treaty obligations in the territory of a State party. Consequently, a general investigation into the situation is carried out which may include an on-site inspection. Compared with the European system, which is a preventative one, this is a reactive system and may be seen as a means of dispute settlement such as the State and individual communication procedures. However, the parties to the dispute are not clearly identifiable – they are potential victims and perpetrators. And, as the expert body looks into the general situation prevailing in the respective country, it appears to be justifiable to characterize this procedure as a compliance control mechanism. In practice, the difference from the European system is not so significant as the European Committee also bases its visiting programme partly on information provided by non-governmental organizations (NGOs) of cases of alleged ill-treatment.

Finally, the notion of enforcement also needs to be defined in order for it to be applied to this task. When speaking about 'soft' enforcement, it appears to be evident that any effective compliance control mechanism is at the same time a means of enforcement of treaty obligations. In relation to treaty-based human rights regimes, enforcement may also mean any act that can be undertaken by a treaty body without the consent of the State concerned, such as the unilateral/unauthorized publication of the findings of an expert body. Hard enforcement as a consequence of non-compliance with treaty obligations would mean restrictions on or loss of membership in an organization (exclusion as well as non-admission to the organization), in this case the Council of Europe and the United Nations. The experiences with Greece in the Council of Europe, however, have shown that such a measure entails totally losing control over a State and its torture practices.

To sum up, the ECPT as well as the UN CAT (together with its Optional Protocol) provide mainly for compliance control mechanisms and do not offer much in relation to dispute settlement and enforcement. The following, more detailed analysis will focus only on the ECPT.

---

[44] See Jutta Brunnée, chapter 15 in this volume.

4.3 Dispute resolution

There is no specific provision in the ECPT providing for a dispute settlement procedure. The question is whether the Convention gives rise to disputes at all, and, if so, between whom. In practice, questions about the interpretation of certain provisions of the Convention concerning Member States' obligations as well as the mandate of the Committee have arisen between the expert body and States parties.

A first issue concerned visa requirements for visiting delegations. Following a case where a State did not allow a visiting delegation entry into its territory without visas, the Committee formed the view that the article in the Convention that provides for 'exemption from any restrictions' on 'entry into . . . the country in which they exercise their functions' clearly rules out the application of visa requirement to any member of the Committee or expert assisting it, since the power of the Committee to carry out visits represents the very core of the Convention. Furthermore, the Committee considered it to be in accordance with the spirit of the Convention that members of the Secretariat and interpreters accompanying a visiting delegation should also be exempted from any visa requirements. The Committee asked the Secretary-General to raise this matter before the Committee of Ministers. A letter dated 7 September 1990 was sent by the President of the CPT to the Secretary-General of the Council of Europe raising the issue of visa requirements.

Even before the Ministers' Deputies responded to this letter, the Committee raised another issue in a letter of 9 November 1990. This letter was provoked by a State which objected to the participation in a visit of an expert assisting the Committee; this is possible under article 14(3), albeit only 'exceptionally'. When the Committee asked for the reasons for this refusal, the State took the view that there was no obligation on its side to provide such reasons. The Committee, however, referred to the Explanatory Report to the Convention, which makes it clear that an obligation to provide reasons is considered as flowing from the general principle of co-operation, which applies to all stages of the Committee's activities. The party in question denied the legally binding authority of the Explanatory Report and disagreed with the interpretation of its obligation under the Convention as defined by the Committee. Consequently, the Committee asked the Committee of Ministers to take a position in this 'dispute' and to interpret certain provisions of the Convention.

In response to both of the above letters, a report prepared by the Ministers' Deputies' Rapporteur Group on Legal Co-operation was forwarded to the Committee. First, the Rapporteur Group unanimously agreed that the Committee of Ministers is not empowered to give an authoritative interpretation of a treaty drawn up at the Council of Europe. It suggested that the Committee can always ask for a meeting to be convened of the contracting parties to the Convention which would be empowered to give an authoritative interpretation. Having said this, the Rapporteur Group gave its opinion on the questions raised by the Committee, in which it in the main agreed with the opinions expressed by the State party but at the same time showed a fair degree of sympathy for the Committee's views.[45] At the suggestion of the Committee, these documents were declassified by the Committee of Ministers and were published by the Association for the Prevention of Torture.[46]

Other questions of interpretation of the Committee's mandate arose in relation to the places the Committee may or may not visit (for example, transit zones in airports, open sections of psychiatric establishments, elderly and social care homes) as well as access to medical files and court records. These questions were partly resolved by the respective visiting delegation, by letters of the President, in high-level talks, and in the case of visiting transit zones in airports also by the European Court of Human Rights in its the judgment in *Amuur* v. *France*.[47]

4.4 Compliance control

The regime under the ECPT can be described as on-site inspections with the aim of improving detention conditions. It is explicitly of a preventive nature and not an inquiry system such as the one established under the UN CAT which aims primarily at establishing compliance or non-compliance with the commitments entered into by States when ratifying the Convention.

The question arises what are the material provisions that form the basis for the European Committee's monitoring function. The preamble to the

[45] Letter of 10 July 1991 from the President of the Committee to the Chairman of the Ministers' Deputies.
[46] See Association for the Prevention of Torture, *The Prevention of Torture in Europe* (Association for the Prevention of Torture, Collected Texts, Brochure No. 1, Geneva, 1997), pp. 65–78.
[47] *Amuur* v. *France* (Application No. 19776/92), judgment of 25 June 1996.

Convention recalls article 3 of the European Convention on Human Rights and notes that the machinery provided for in that Convention operates in relation to persons who allege that they are victims of violations of article 3. This part of the preamble, read alone, would suggest that the Committee is monitoring compliance with article 3 of the ECHR. However, the Explanatory Report makes clear that, although the case law of the European Court on article 3 provides a source of guidance, the Committee should not seek to interfere in the interpretation and application of article 3. It further states that the Committee's activities are aimed at future prevention rather than at the application of legal requirements to existing circumstances. In this way, the Committee has developed its own standards, compliance with which it is in fact monitoring during its visits. The Committee's standards are published in the 'substantive' sections of its general reports and are updated almost on an annual basis; the 14th annual report contains, for example, a chapter on 'combating impunity'. This indicates the dynamic development of the Committee's recommendations, which are *per se* not legally binding. The Committee consequently is monitoring compliance with its own 'soft' standards.

Although the inspection procedure is compulsory for the contracting parties, one exception in favour of the State is foreseen. Article 9 provides that: 'In exceptional circumstances, the competent authorities of the Party concerned may make representations to the Committee against a visit at the time or to the particular place proposed by the Committee.' It further stipulates that: 'Following such representations, the Committee and the Party shall immediately enter into consultations in order to clarify the situation and seek agreement on arrangements to enable the Committee to exercise its functions expeditiously.' This provision has been seen as a weakness in the Convention and a possible loophole for the effectiveness of the whole inspection system. In practice, however, States have so far never made use of this provision.

Concerning the effectiveness of its visiting practice, the Committee itself has not yet carried out a systematic assessment of the implementation of its recommendations. What can be said is that the Committee's recommendations have developed in a dynamic way – new types of establishments have been visited, such as social care homes, and new areas of concern, such as combating impunity, were focused upon. This reflects the Committee's intention to establish an 'ongoing dialogue' with Member States and to progressively improve the situation of detained persons. No single Member

State has implemented all the Committee's recommendations, or even been able to do so. However, the Committee is concerned if it has to 'recall' or 'reiterate' its recommendations made in previous reports, especially after a second or third regular or *ad hoc* visit. The reasons why States do not implement the Committee's recommendations differ and can be summarized under two main categories:

1. Repudiation of a particular Committee standard because of its perceived impracticality or lack of necessity in the overall context. Examples are introducing a code of conduct for police interrogation or establishing a body independent from the police to investigate complaints of police ill-treatment.
2. Acceptance of the Committee's standards in principle but difficulties in introducing the relevant legislation, such as access to a lawyer from the very outset of police custody, or implementing them, because of practical or financial reasons, such as absence of a functioning legal aid system.

The overall assessment in academic writing concerning acceptance of the Committee's standards is, however, positive. Two authors, who have followed the Committee's work from the very beginning, state that no government of a State party has yet suggested that the general approach to prevention reflected in the corpus of standards developed by the Committee is unacceptable. Moreover, they note that governments seem generally reluctant to challenge the recommendations made, even if they are slow to implement them.[48]

Finally, it should be mentioned that the European Court of Human Rights has frequently referred to the Committee's findings. On the one hand, the descriptions of detention situations and regimes in Committee reports have formed the factual basis of the Court's findings,[49] and, on the other hand, the standards for the treatment of detainees developed by the Committee have been integrated into the Court's case law.[50]

---

[48] See Rod Morgan and Malcolm Evans, *Combating Torture in Europe* (Strasbourg: Council of Europe Publishing, 2001).
[49] See the judgments of 4 February 2002 in the cases of *Van der Ven* v. *Netherlands* and *Lorsé* v. *Netherlands*, referring to the Committee's report on the visit to the Netherlands from 17–27 November 1997, CPT/Inf (98) 15.
[50] See e.g. the case of *Akkoc* v. *Turkey* (2000); or *Kalashnikov* v. *Russia* (2002).

4.5 Enforcement

Treaty rules on 'soft' enforcement, as defined in the preliminary remarks, may be seen in articles 8(5) and 10(2) of the ECPT. The first-mentioned article authorizes the Committee to make an 'immediate observation' at the end of a visit requesting the authorities to remedy an unacceptable situation and to report back within a short period of time. This appears to be the only means of enforcement, in the literal sense of the word; however, if a State does not act in accordance with an immediate observation, the Committee may threaten to issue a public statement.[51] A public statement means that the Committee may breach the principle of confidentiality as a consequence of non-compliance by a State party with the obligations arising from the Convention, namely, co-operation with the Committee and implementation of its recommendations.

The only sanction in cases of non-compliance with the Committee's recommendations is threatening and ultimately issuing a public statement.[52] By doing so, the Committee describes in detail the situation of detainees in the State concerned which usually makes clear that human rights principles and standards are being flagrantly violated. Thus, the Committee draws the attention of other organizations, States and non-governmental organizations to this problem, which might lead the latter to put pressure on the defaulting State, politically, morally, and economically, to improve the situation in line with the Committee's recommendations.

The two public statements in relation to Turkey were eventually effective in promoting positive changes, which were also motivated by the strong interest of Turkey in becoming a member of the European Union. The two public statements *vis-à-vis* Russia concerning the situation in Chechnya have so far not been effective. This is certainly related to the lack of political will by European States to put Russia under any pressure. The threat of terrorism and the general climate of anxiety are conducive to a higher degree of tolerance *vis-à-vis* anti-terror measures and have led certain States to introduce new legislation to combat terrorism.[53] Consequently, standards

---

[51] Art. 10(2).

[52] There have been two public statements *vis-à-vis* Turkey and two *vis-à-vis* the Russian Federation in relation to the situation in Chechnya.

[53] See the UK Crime, Security and Anti-Terrorism Act of 2000, which led the Committee to carry out two *ad hoc* missions to assess the situation of foreign nationals held under this law in indefinite detention without charge.

developed by the Committee were and are challenged in relation to terrorist suspects.[54]

The recommendations formulated by the Committee in its reports create an obligation on State parties to comply, under the principle of co-operation. However, not every single recommendation constitutes in itself an obligation; rather, the conclusions and recommendations at the end of any report as a whole form the basis of an assessment in follow-up missions and the respective report as to whether or not a State party has met its obligations.

On-site monitoring of the treatment of persons deprived of their liberty is not an end in itself; to be worthwhile, it must be accompanied by effective means of ensuring the implementation of the Committee's recommendations. It is first and foremost for the parties to the Convention to take decisive action to improve the situation in light of the Committee's recommendations.

As concerns the implementation of its recommendations, in particular those with financial implications, the Committee has already taken a more proactive approach and has engaged itself in facilitating a voluntary contribution from Luxembourg, which is being used to finance a project to improve living conditions for inmates in prison establishments in the Transnistrian region of the Republic of Moldova. Another project along similar lines is currently under consideration.[55]

Reference was made in the 14th General Report to the idea of organizing a pilot project in a limited number of countries among those experiencing difficulties with the implementation of the Committee's recommendations, especially those requiring significant financial investment.[56] A document fleshing out this proposal had been presented to the Committee of Ministers, and has been viewed favourably; it could do much to ensure that the Committee's recommendations lead to tangible results.

There are no means of 'hard' enforcement of Committee recommendations. The only 'hard' sanction in case a State party to the ECPT consistently does not comply with its obligations arising from this Convention

---

[54] See the preface to the 14th and 15th General Reports on the Committee's activities, in which the Committee raises its concern about the methods of detention and interrogation employed in the context of the fight against terrorism.

[55] This is a pilot project to assess the needs in three countries experiencing problems with the implementation of the Committee's recommendations, to identify concrete proposals for outside assistance and to present them to potential donors. See para. 13 of the 14th General Report on the Committee's activities. [56] Cf. CPT/Inf(2004), para. 13.

would be for the Committee of Ministers to invoke article 8 of the Statute of the Council of Europe. This article provides for a suspension of the rights of representation and a request by the Committee of Ministers to withdraw or if this request is not complied with to decide that a State has ceased to be a member of the Council. However, the 'voluntary' withdrawal of Greece following a discussion in the Council of invoking article 8 because of serious violations of human rights under the 'Obrist' regime has shown that by taking such a measure the Council loses all means of putting pressure on a State to comply with human rights principles. In the case of Russia, more political pressure from European institutions is needed to support the work of expert bodies in the field of human rights.

4.6 Overall evaluation

The principle of the prohibition of torture and other forms of ill-treatment was already laid down in the Universal Declaration of Human Rights of 1948 and became a legally binding obligation for States parties under the International Covenant on Civil and Political Rights as well as under the European Convention on Human Rights.[57] However, it was felt necessary to develop a specific Convention Against Torture and Other Cruel, Inhuman or Degrading Treatment or Punishment at the universal level. This Convention offers several procedures to monitor compliance with the obligations entered into by contracting parties, including a system of on-site inspections in relation to States where torture is allegedly systematically practised. However, to carry out such an inquiry, the consent of the State concerned is required.

These mainly reactive and repressive control measures appeared to be insufficient, as the anti-torture campaign launched by Amnesty International back in the early 1970s revealed. Reportedly, in two-thirds of the Member States of the United Nations, torture was systematically practised at that time. Based on this information, Jean-Jacques Gautier, a Swiss banker, developed the idea of establishing a universal system of regular inspections of places where people are deprived of their liberty with the aim of preventing torture and other forms of ill-treatment. A Swiss 'Committee Against Torture', a non-governmental organization, was

---

[57] See the procedures established under these Conventions to monitor the implementation of these principles in the essays of Mark E. Villiger (chapter 3) and Martin Scheinin (chapter 2) in this volume.

founded, and Gautier's idea was further developed. Inspired by the practice of the International Committee of the Red Cross in relation to prisoners of war, the project of a preventative system of visits to places of detention was eventually submitted by Costa Rica to the UN Commission on Human Rights and proposed as a draft optional protocol to the UN Convention Against Torture. In 1984, a pre-sessional working group was established at UN level to discuss this draft. As many objections were made by representatives of certain States against this draft at that time – because of the potentially far-reaching implications of such an inspection system on a State's sovereignty – the project was postponed for several years. In the meantime, the idea of a regional system of visits to prevent torture and ill-treatment and to improve the situation of detained persons was adopted in the Council of Europe. The European Convention on the Prevention of Torture was meant to complement the repressive judicial court procedure established under the European Convention on Human Rights in relation to the principle of the prohibition of torture as laid down in its article 3.

Eventually, the effective operation of the European system of preventing torture inspired the revision of the universal project, and, in December 2002, the General Assembly of the United Nations adopted the 1st Additional Protocol to the UN Convention Against Torture. This new system for the prevention of torture and ill-treatment established within the United Nations has now entered into force, and differs somewhat from the European one. However, the relationship between the ECPT and the Optional Protocol to the UN CAT is evident. Both documents regulate procedures to prevent the violation of the obligation to prohibit torture, which is stipulated in other conventions, namely, the European Convention on Human Rights as well as the UN Convention Against Torture. To avoid overlap between the future work of the Sub-Committee under the Optional Protocol and the Committee under the ECPT, the process of consultation and co-operation would be facilitated if a proposal made by the European Committee more than ten years ago, in its 3rd General Report, were to be accepted. The proposal was that parties to the ECPT which also ratify the Optional Protocol to the UN CAT agree that visit reports drawn up by the European Committee in respect of their countries, and their responses, be systematically forwarded to the Sub-Committee on a confidential basis. In this way, consultation between the Sub-Committee and the European Committee could be held in light of all the relevant facts. In the European

Committee's view, implementation of this measure should not require an amendment of its Convention.

Concerning the future relationship between the European Committee and the Sub-Committee, the European Committee stands ready to share its experience with those responsible for setting up the new mechanisms foreseen by the Optional Protocol. Representatives of the European Committee have already participated in meetings on this subject organized by the Association for the Prevention of Torture together with the Office of the UN High Commissioner for Human Rights. In these meetings, the President, Silvia Casale, stressed the importance of the principle of universality of standards and that the European Committee will hold to its standards and maintain the evolution of its jurisprudence, towards continuing rigorous standards for protection against ill-treatment of all persons deprived of their liberty, including in the context of the fight against terrorism. This clear message should indicate that a universal system must not undermine standards developed within the European system.

From the European Committee's point of view, the most interesting element in the Optional Protocol is the development of national monitoring mechanisms. The European Committee has long been recommending independent complaints mechanisms and independent inspection mechanisms. They are part of its standard jurisprudence for all custodial settings, including but not limited to police and prison settings. So far, these are, in most States, in the embryonic stage as far as full independence and the application to all custodial settings are concerned. However, there is a great potential for a major advance in human rights protection, if these mechanisms become fully operational.

International mechanisms such as the European Committee's programme of visits – in which periods of four to six years may elapse between visits – compare unfavourably with national monitoring mechanisms – in which inspections are carried out on a regular basis. At their best, national mechanisms provide a much fuller and more holistic picture of the scope and efficacy of human rights safeguards than is currently possible under international mechanisms. This would in turn greatly enhance the prospects for improving the protection of persons deprived of their liberty and reducing ill-treatment.

PART II

International environmental law

5

Dispute resolution, compliance control and enforcement in international environmental law

GEIR ULFSTEIN

5.1 Introduction

The world has experienced a growing awareness of environmental degradation since the 1960s. These concerns were reflected at the political level by the 1972 Stockholm Conference on the Human Environment, the 1992 Rio Conference on Environment and Development, and, finally, the 2002 Johannesburg World Summit on Sustainable Development. The legal response has been a steep proliferation in the number of multilateral environmental agreements (MEAs). While there is no environmental agreement setting out the general obligations of States to protect the environment, the MEAs represent a sectoral approach, covering diverse aspects of nature conservation and pollution prevention.

The agreements apply a 'sustainable development' approach to environmental protection, meaning that nature may be used in the interest of humankind, but such use should be sustainable in the long term. Furthermore, special consideration should be given to developing countries based on the principle of 'common but differentiated responsibilities', i.e. that the developed countries have accepted a special responsibility 'in view of the pressures their societies place on the global environment and of the technologies and financial resources they command'.[1] It should be noted that environmental protection is increasingly a matter of social and economic significance also in developed countries, such as restrictions on energy consumption in both industry and the private sector to protect against climate change.

MEAs are generally policy-oriented in establishing co-operative organs, in the form of a Conference of the Parties (COP), subsidiary bodies and a

---

[1] Art. 7 of the Rio Declaration, 13 June 1992, UN Doc. A/CONF.151/26Rev.1.

116 INTERNATIONAL ENVIRONMENTAL LAW

secretariat. The original MEA may have a framework character setting out the objectives and institutions of the co-operation. Subsequent protocols and decisions are developed through these institutions and adopted by the COP. While protocols will require ratification by States parties, binding or non-binding decisions may be adopted by COPs by consensus or majority vote. Binding decisions may be subject to subsequent reservations by the parties.

As a more comprehensive international legal framework has been developed, added emphasis has been directed towards effective implementation of the environmental obligations. The world's environmental ministers stated in 2000 that there is an 'alarming discrepancy between commitments and action'.[2] In 2001, The Governing Council of the United Nations Environment Programme (UNEP) called for 'speedy implementation of the legal commitments contained in the multilateral environmental agreements'.[3] As a result, a special session of UNEP's Governing Council adopted a set of guidelines on compliance with and enforcement of MEAs.[4] These guidelines recognize, however, that the parties to each treaty have the primary responsibility for designing effective mechanisms and procedures to ensure implementation.

Most MEAs contain dispute settlement procedures allowing parties to bring questions of violation of treaty obligations before an international court or arbitral tribunal. But use of such procedures will generally require consent from both parties, and this avenue is not commonly used. Instead, several MEAs have set up specialized bodies and procedures to deal with cases of non-compliance. A number of advantages of using such non-compliance mechanisms rather than more traditional dispute settlement procedures have been highlighted in the literature.[5] First, such mechanisms

---

[2] Malmö Ministerial Declaration, 2000, available at www.unep.org/malmo/malmo_ministerial.htm.

[3] UNEP Governing Council Decision 21/27, 'Compliance with and Enforcement of Multilateral Environmental Agreements', 2001.

[4] UNEP Governing Council Decision SS. VII/4. 'Compliance with and Enforcement of Multilateral Environmental Agreements', Report of the Governing Council on the Work of Its Seventh Special Session/Global Ministerial Forum, 13–15 February 2002. In the European context, the Fifth Ministerial Conference of Environment for Europe, 13–15 February 2002, endorsed the Guidelines for Strengthening Compliance with and Implementation of MEAs in the UNECE Region.

[5] See, from a large literature, J. Cameron, J. Werksman and P. Roderick (eds.), *Improving Compliance with International Environmental Law* (London: Earthscan, 1996); P. Széll, 'Compliance Regimes for Multilateral Environmental Agreements: A Progress Report' (1997) 27 *Environmental Policy* 304; E. B. Weiss and H. K. Jacobson (eds.), *Engaging Countries: Strengthening*

allow compliance issues to be addressed in a multilateral context, rather than through bilateral dispute settlement procedures. Secondly, non-compliance procedures may prevent potential violations rather than waiting for a breach to be established. Finally, non-compliance procedures may promote the resolution of compliance problems in a co-operative, rather than adversarial, manner through procedures designed to facilitate rather than enforce compliance. It has, however, been questioned to what extent there is a development from a 'managerial approach' to an 'enforcement approach' in MEAs, especially in treaties imposing environmental obligations with heavier economic and social costs.[6]

The following four MEAs have been selected as case studies: the 1973 Convention on International Trade in Endangered Species (CITES),[7] the 1979 ECE Convention on Long-Range Transboundary Air Pollution (LRTAP),[8] the 1991 Convention on Environmental Impact Assessment in a Transboundary Context (the Espoo Convention)[9] and the 1998 ECE Convention on Access to Information, Public Participation in Decision-Making and Access to Justice in Environmental Matters (the Aarhus Convention).[10] These MEAs cover nature conservation (CITES), pollution (LRTAP, Espoo, Aarhus), global (CITES) and regional (LRTAP, Espoo, Aarhus) issues, as well as having bilateral features (Espoo), trade related aspects (CITES) and agreements containing obligations towards civil society (Aarhus, Espoo).

We could have included the 1987 Montreal Protocol on Substances that Deplete the Ozone Layer,[11] which has served as a model for other MEAs

---

Compliance with International Environmental Accords (Cambridge, MA: MIT Press, 1998); D. G. Victor, K. Raustiala and E. B. Skolnikoff (eds.), *The Implementation and Effectiveness of International Environmental Commitments: Theory and Practice* (Cambridge, MA: MIT Press, 1998); R. Wolfrum, 'Means of Ensuring Compliance with and Enforcement of International Environmental Law' (1998) 272 *Recueil des Cours* 9–154; and M. A. Fitzmaurice and C. Redgwell, 'Environmental Non-Compliance Procedures and International Law' (2000) 31 *Netherlands Yearbook of International Law* 35–65.

[6] On the managerial and enforcement models, see A. Chayes and A. H. Chayes, *The New Sovereignty: Compliance with International Regulatory Agreements* (Cambridge, MA: Harvard University Press, 1995); K. Danish, 'Book Review: The New Sovereignty' (1997) 37 *Virginia Journal of International Law* 789; K. Raustiala and A.-M. Slaughter, 'International Law, International Relations and Compliance', in W. Carlsnaes, T. Risse and B. A. Simmons (eds.), *Handbook of International Relations* (London: Sage Publications, 2002), pp. 538–59; and J. Brunnée and S. J. Toope, 'Persuasion and Enforcement: Explaining Compliance with International Law' (2002) 13 *Finnish Yearbook of International Law* 1–14.   [7] 993 UNTS 243.

[8] 18 1442 ILM (1979).   [9] 30 ILM 802 (1991).   [10] 38 ILM 517 (1999).

[11] 26 ILM 1550 (1987).

concerning non-compliance procedures. But the Montreal Protocol is well studied and well known.[12] We could furthermore have included the 1997 Kyoto Protocol to the United Nations Framework Convention on Climate Change.[13] But this Protocol only entered into force in 2005 and its substantive commitment period is 2008–12. Parallels will, however, be drawn to both the Montreal Protocol's and the Kyoto Protocol's non-compliance procedures. We could also have included more MEAs on nature conservation, such as the 1979 Convention on the Conservation of Migratory Species of Wild Animals (the Bonn Convention)[14] or the 1992 Convention on Biological Diversity,[15] but, since these agreements are less developed as regards non-compliance mechanisms, they would not add much to our discussion.

5.2 Dispute settlement procedures

Various dispute settlement systems have been established in recent years, for example the International Tribunal for the Law of the Sea (ITLOS) and the WTO Dispute Settlement Understanding (DSU). Regional courts have been created in international human rights, like the European Court of Human Rights and the Inter-American Court of Human Rights. International courts have also established special procedures to resolve international environmental disputes. The International Court of Justice established a seven-member Chamber for Environmental Matters in 1993, and the Permanent Court of Arbitration adopted the Optional Rules for Arbitration of Disputes Relating to the Environment and/or Natural Resources (the 'Environmental Rules') in 2001.

---

[12] See M. Koskenniemi, 'Breach of Treaty or Non-Compliance? Reflections on the Enforcement of the Montreal Protocol' (1992) 3 *Yearbook of International Environmental Law* 123–63; R. E. Benedick, *Ozone Diplomacy: New Directions in Safeguarding the Planet* (Cambridge, MA: Harvard University Press, 1998); D. Victor, 'The Operation and Effectiveness of the Montreal Protocol Implementation Committee', in D. Victor *et al.* (eds.), *The Implementation and Effectiveness of International Environmental Commitments: Theory and Practice* (Cambridge, MA: MIT Press, 1998); and O. Yoshida, 'Soft Enforcement of Treaties: The Montreal Protocol's Noncompliance Procedure and the Functions of Internal International Institutions' (1999) 10(Winter) *Colorado Journal of International Environmental Law* 95.

[13] 37 ILM 22 (1998). See J. Werksman, 'Compliance and the Kyoto Protocol: Building a Backbone into a Flexible Regime' (1998) 9 *Yearbook of International Environmental Law* 48–01; J. Brunnée, 'A Fine Balance: Facilitation and Enforcement in the Design of a Compliance Regime for the Kyoto Protocol' (2000) 13 *Tulane Environmental Law Journal* 223; and J. Brunnée, 'The Kyoto Protocol: Testing Ground for Compliance Theories?' (2003) 63 *Zeitschrift für ausländisches öffentliches Recht und Völkerrecht* 255–81.   [14] 19 ILM 15 (1980).   [15] 31 ILM 818 (1992).

International environmental law was in its earlier days developed by some landmark decisions, such as the *Behring Sea Fur Seals Arbitration* (1898),[16] the *Trail Smelter* case[17] and the *Lake Lanoux* case.[18] While States are currently reluctant to use international courts in environmental disputes, we nevertheless find some environmental cases, for example the *Gabcikovo–Nagymaros Dam* case[19] and the *Southern Bluefin Tuna Arbitration*.[20] It has been claimed that the last decade has shown an increased willingness to use international adjudicatory mechanisms.[21]

The principal advantages of using international courts and tribunals for dispute settlement are that they represent impartial organs with legal expertise, and have a procedure well suited to resolving legal disputes. They also provide binding and final decisions in the form of *res judicata*, and may impose obligations of restitution and payment of reparations for damage suffered. But, as already mentioned, the disadvantage of using these mechanisms in international environmental law is that they represent bilateral approaches to multilateral problems, that they are available only *ex post facto*, and that they are of a confrontational character. It may also be difficult to prove causality between breach of an international obligation and environmental damage, and such damage may be difficult to rectify.

A common feature of multilateral environmental agreements is an obligation to accept negotiations in cases of dispute.[22] Some MEAs also provide for unilateral declarations accepting compulsory jurisdiction under the International Court of Justice or by arbitration, in relation to any other States submitting a similar declaration.[23] An innovative facet of the

[16] 1 Moore's *International Arbitration Awards* 755, reprinted in (1999) 1 *International Environmental Law Reports* 43.

[17] (1939) 33 *American Journal of International Law* 182; and (1941) 35 *American Journal of International Law* 684.   [18] 24 ILR 101 (1957).   [19] ICJ Reports 1997, p. 7.

[20] 39 ILM 1359 (2000).

[21] P. Sands, *Principles of International Environmental Law* (Cambridge: Cambridge University Press, 2nd edn, 2003), p. 227.

[22] See e.g. art. XVIII of the 1973 Convention on International Trade in Endangered Species; and art. 13 of the 1979 Convention on Long-Range Transboundary Air Pollution.

[23] Art. 11 of the Protocol to Abate Acidification, Eutrophication and Ground-Level Ozone under the Convention on Long-Range Transboundary Air Pollution provides an example. Art. 15(2) of the Espoo Convention and art. 16(2) of the Aarhus Convention both establish that arbitration shall be conducted in accordance with an annex to the respective Conventions. But only four States have submitted a declaration accepting compulsory jurisdiction under the Espoo Convention. Art. 11(5) of the Protocol to Abate Acidification, Eutrophication and Ground-Level Ozone also establishes that, if the parties in their declarations on compulsory adjudication have not chosen the same procedure of dispute settlement, one of the parties to the dispute may require compulsory conciliation.

Espoo Convention is its inquiry commissions. If the parties disagree about the extent to which an activity may cause 'significant adverse transboundary impact' – and therefore be covered by the scope of the Convention – one of the parties may call upon an inquiry commission.[24] Such a commission will be composed of experts and, although only being advisory, its opinion may put pressure on the State that plans an activity to respect the commission's recommendations. Inquiry commissions are of particular interest in selecting one possible bone of contention, i.e. the issue of significant transboundary impact, for a compulsory dispute resolution mechanism. But none of the agreements examined goes as far as establishing compulsory binding adjudication. This is similar to other MEAs, where compulsory dispute settlement is rarely found.[25]

Dispute settlement, to the extent available, is also rarely used. As is reported in the case study on the Espoo Convention, Poland has requested negotiations with Germany over the Convention's obligations to take into account comments from the public and the outcome of consultations, in the management of the River Oder. Furthermore, the Convention's inquiry commission procedure has been invoked in one case between Romania and Ukraine on the building of a navigation canal in the Danube. If we also include MEAs outside the scope of the present case studies, Ireland has used the compulsory jurisdiction provided by the 1992 Convention for the Protection of the Marine Environment of the North-East Atlantic (the OSPAR Convention)[26] against the United Kingdom in the so-called MOX case on access to information under article 9 of the Convention.[27]

The Espoo and OSPAR agreements demonstrate that dispute settlement procedures may be invoked in cases under MEAs having bilateral aspects, i.e. activities in one State having concrete effect in a neighbouring State. In such cases, the affected State may want a binding determination that an obligation provided by the relevant Convention has been violated, and possibly to obtain reparation for damages.

Such bilateral aspects may, however, not only transpire between neighbouring States. Several MEAs have bilateral effects in a wider sense, such as

---

[24] Art. 3(7) of and Annex IV to the Espoo Convention.

[25] P. Birnie and A. Boyle, *International Law and the Environment* (Oxford: Oxford University Press, 2nd edn, 2002), p. 226.

[26] Art. 32(1) of the 1992 Convention for the Protection of the Marine Environment of the North-East Atlantic (the OSPAR Convention), 32 ILM 1072 (1993).

[27] The Final Award of 2 July 2003 can be found on the website of the Permanent Court of Arbitration, www.pca-cpa.org.

the trade in endangered species under CITES or the control of the export and import of hazardous substances under the 1989 Basel Convention on the Control of Transboundary Movements of Hazardous Wastes and their Disposal.[28]

States may even have an interest in pursuing a violation having multilateral effects, but where certain States are particularly affected. One example may be the effects of rising sea level on small island States as a result of violation of the Kyoto Protocol on climate change. Another example could be States suffering particularly serious damages as a result of air pollution due to a combination of particular wind conditions and precipitation and a sensitive nature, caused by violations of relevant Protocols under the LRTAP Convention.

Finally, it cannot be excluded that a State may want to act also in cases where it does not have a special interest other than being a party to the relevant MEA. This may occur either to prevent the other party from acting as a 'free-rider' or out of concern for the threat against the environment represented by the violation. The more intrusive commitments and more threatened the environment, the more compelled other States may feel to act. We may see more of such commitments in the future, such as the measures undertaken in the Kyoto Protocol.

It is true that, unlike the non-compliance procedure discussed below, traditional dispute settlement has a confrontational character, and that they apply *ex post facto*. It has also been claimed by the 'managerial school' that the main reason for non-compliance with international commitments is not bad will, but lack of resources and capacity.

There obviously exists a need to prevent violations by providing developing countries with necessary resources, expertise and technology. But there may be examples where both developing and developed States have the capacity to honour their commitments, but are not willing to do so due to domestic political or economic costs. The existence of persistent non-complying States may in itself create confrontations and obstruct a political co-operation. If non-compliance procedures are unable to deal with the situation in an effective way, concerned States may choose to have recourse to dispute settlement procedures. Such procedures may also represent an option if parties disagree on whether a violation has occurred, and a binding settlement therefore is sought. On the other hand, the dispute

---

[28] 28 ILM 657 (1989).

settlement mechanisms in MEAs do not provide for adjudication if a party feels that the treaty bodies, including the Conference of the Parties, have adopted an unlawful decision. The latter aspect may, however, become more important to the extent treaty bodies are allocated power to make binding decisions, possibly including sanctions against the offender.

If a State is prepared to invoke dispute settlement procedures, it must fulfil relevant procedural requirements. The provisions on dispute settlement establish that the parties to the MEAs have a right to make use of such procedures, and no requirements for standing are instituted. Article 42 of the 2001 Draft Articles on Responsibility of States for Internationally Wrongful Acts provides, however, that a State is only 'entitled as an injured State to invoke the responsibility of another State if the obligation breached is owed to . . . (b) A group of States including that State, or the international community as a whole, and the breach of the obligation (i) Specially affects that State; or (ii) Is of such a character as radically to change the position of all the other States to which the obligation is owed with respect to the further performance of the obligation'.[29]

A State will obviously have standing to the extent that a breach of an MEA 'specially affects' that State, such as in cases of transboundary pollution between neighbouring States. It could be more questionable to what extent all parties have a right of standing in cases of violation of regional or global MEAs based on the requirement 'radically to change the position of all the other States to which the obligation is owed with respect to the further performance of the obligation'. Referring to a similar phrase in article 60(2)(c) of the Vienna Convention on the Law of Treaties, the International Law Commission states that this phrase would 'include a disarmament treaty, a nuclear free zone treaty, or any other treaty where each party's performance is effectively conditioned upon and requires the performance of each of the others'. As participation in MEAs is based on other parties' compliance, all parties should be considered 'injured' under the law on State responsibility in cases of non-compliance, and thus have a right to invoke dispute settlement procedures.[30]

It may furthermore be asked whether the claimant must have exhausted local remedies before invoking dispute settlement procedures. Such a

---

[29] Reprinted in J. Crawford, *The International Law Commission's Articles on State Responsibility: Introduction, Text and Commentaries* (Cambridge: Cambridge University Press, 2002). pp. 69–70.　　[30] See also Sands, *Principles of International Environmental Law*, p. 187.

requirement applies in general international law in cases where an injury has been suffered by private subjects, but not if the State as such has suffered damage. There may, however, be 'mixed' cases, where both States and private subjects suffer damage, typically in environmental cases. In mixed cases, the International Law Commission suggests that what is the preponderant interest should be decisive.[31] Although it will ultimately be individuals that suffer from environmental degradation, MEAs are generally construed as inter-State relations and have their principal purpose in protecting State interests. They should therefore generally not require exhaustion of local remedies. This may, however, be different in MEAs having more of a human rights approach, such as the Aarhus Convention on Access to Information, Public Participation in Decision-Making and Access to Justice in Environmental Matters[32] and possibly also the Espoo Convention on Environmental Impact Assessment in a Transboundary Context.

The bilateral character of dispute settlement may, to a certain extent, be mitigated by the possibility of intervention by other States parties to the relevant MEA. In cases before the International Court of Justice, article 63(2) of its Statute establishes a right of intervention, which should be considered open to any State party to the MEA in questions regarding interpretation of the agreement.[33] A possible right of intervention in arbitration depends on the rules of the arbitration procedure. Annex VII on arbitration under the Espoo Convention provides that '[a]ny Party to this Convention having an interest of a legal nature in the subject-matter of the dispute, and which may be affected by a decision in the case, may intervene in the proceedings with the consent of the tribunal'.[34]

NGOs have gained an increasing role in decision-making and compliance control under MEAs. The dispute settlement procedures of the examined MEAs do not explicitly provide for NGO participation. It seems, however, that nothing would prevent a dispute settlement body from allowing such participation, either in the form of their submitting *amicus curiae* briefs or by acting through one or more of the disputing States.[35]

---

[31] Report of the International Law Commission, 56th Session (2004), GAOR, Supp. No. 10 (A/59/10), p. 73.   [32] See Koester, chapter 8 in this volume, pp. 179–218.

[33] Birnie and Boyle, *International Law and the Environment*, p. 221.

[34] The Espoo Convention, Annex VII, para. 15.

[35] See Birnie and Boyle, *International Law and the Environment*, pp. 222–3; and Sands, *Principles of International Environmental Law*, pp. 199–200.

Dispute settlement is usually considered a last resort in cases where one or more parties are unsatisfied with inaction or the result of the specially designed non-compliance procedures. It may be claimed that there is a legal requirement that such procedures should be tested before parties make use of dispute settlement procedures. In this respect, it could be asked to what extent the non-compliance procedures represent a 'self-contained regime' in the sense that this avenue should be exhausted before recourse is had to dispute settlement. There is no basis in the wording of the relevant MEAs or decisions by the Conference of the Parties to this effect, indicating that no such requirement exists.[36] It may, however, be argued that a *de facto* determination of a party's non-compliance is excluded if a case is *sub judice* before an international court.[37]

In cases where a causal link can be established between a private person, company or association suffering damage and the failure of a State to fulfil its obligations under an MEA, use of domestic remedies may be a viable option. This could represent complementary ways to redress, but it is difficult to see such remedies as an effective approach to ensuring compliance with MEAs.[38] Some have also proposed the establishment of a specialized international environmental court, but it is difficult to see how such a court would be more attractive to States than existing courts, and States have shown no inclination to follow up these ideas in practice.[39]

5.3 Compliance control

Non-compliance procedures, including the establishment of a non-compliance or implementation committee, are innovative and significant features of MEAs.[40] The 1987 Montreal Protocol on Substances that Deplete the Ozone Layer was the first MEA to establish what has been known as the non-compliance procedures of environmental agreements.

---

[36] The Espoo Convention provides, however, that, when a matter is being considered by an inquiry commission, it may not be submitted to any other dispute settlement mechanism under the Convention. See Koivurova, chapter 9 in this volume.

[37] Koskenniemi, 'Breach of Treaty or Non-Compliance?' (1992) 3 *Yearbook of International Environmental Law* 157–9.

[38] Birnie and Boyle, *International Law and the Environment*, p. 232.

[39] See Birnie and Boyle, *International Law and the Environment*, pp. 224–6, with further references. See also Sands, *Principles of International Environmental Law*, p. 214; and E. Hey, *Reflections on an International Environmental Court* (The Hague: Kluwer Law International, 2000).

[40] See Birnie and Boyle, *International Law and the Environment*, p. 207; and Sands, *Principles of International Environmental Law*, p. 205.

Article 8 of the Protocol provides that the parties at their first meeting 'shall consider and approve procedures and institutional mechanisms for determining non-compliance with the provisions of this Protocol and for treatment of parties found to be in non-compliance'. An Implementation Committee was established by the Meeting of the Parties on an interim basis in 1990, and made permanent in 1992.

In all the MEAs under examination here, whether they are global, regional or having bilateral aspects, or deal with protection of nature, pollution, access to information and justice, or environmental impact assessments, a need has been felt to develop non-compliance mechanisms. While CITES, the oldest of the four examined MEAs here, does not have a specialized non-compliance committee, questions of non-compliance are dealt with by its Standing Committee. These procedures do not have a basis in CITES itself, but have been developed through secondary rules in the form of decisions by the Conference of the Parties. There are ongoing negotiations on Guidelines on Compliance with the Convention, which are to be completed by 2007.

Non-compliance procedures are increasingly legally formalized by being explicitly based in the respective MEAs, rather than merely in decisions by COPs. Following the establishment of a compliance mechanism in the 1994 Sulphur Protocol, the Executive Body (i.e. the plenary organ) of the LRTAP Convention on Long-Range Transboundary Air Pollution established in 1997 an Implementation Committee for all Protocols to the Convention. Subsequent Protocols provide that compliance review shall take place according to the 1997 decision and any amendments thereto. The Espoo Convention on Environmental Impact Assessment in a Transboundary Context does not contain provisions on compliance control. But the Meeting of the Parties (MoP) established an Implementation Committee in 2001, and an amendment was proposed by an *ad hoc* subsidiary body to the MoP that a formal basis for an implementation body was included in the Convention. Article 15 of the Aarhus Convention on Access to Information, Public Participation in Decision-Making and Access to Justice in Environmental Matters provides that the MoP 'shall establish, on a consensus basis, optional arrangements of a non-confrontational, non-judicial and consultative nature for reviewing compliance with the provisions of this Convention'.

Non-compliance committees are generally composed of representatives of the parties. In this sense, they differ from supervisory bodies of human rights conventions in being political organs rather than expert bodies. The Aarhus Convention provides an exception in the sense that its members are acting in their personal capacity. Furthermore, candidates may be nominated by parties and signatories, as well as by relevant NGOs. Members shall be persons of 'high moral character and recognized competence in the fields to which the Convention relates, including persons having legal expertise'. They shall 'make a solemn declaration in a meeting of the Committee that he or she will perform his or her functions impartially and conscientiously'. The reason for these features of the Aarhus Convention is presumably that its obligations are comparable to those of human rights conventions, by giving individuals access to information, participation in decision-making and access to justice. The requirements of high moral character and qualifications are akin to the 1966 International Covenant on Civil and Political Rights, but the Aarhus Convention goes even further in openness by allowing for nomination by NGOs, while the Covenant reserves this right to States.[41]

The Compliance Committee of the Kyoto Protocol consists also of independent experts, even though it bears no resemblance to human rights conventions. The reason is probably the importance States attach to the determination of non-compliance in cases that may involve heavy economic and political costs. Hence, independence from political control may be considered important both when it comes to protection of obligations towards individuals and in order to secure the interests of States where important economic and political interests are at stake.

Non-compliance committees generally have a limited membership. The CITES Standing Committee has seventeen members, the Implementation Committee of the Montreal Protocol has ten members, the Implementation Committee of the Convention on Long-Range Transboundary Air Pollution has nine members, the Espoo Convention's Implementation Committee will have eight members, and similarly the Aarhus Convention's Compliance Committee has eight members. The Facilitative Branch and the Enforcement Branch of the Kyoto Compliance Committee will each have ten members. This restricted representation may advance the effectiveness of compliance review, and may also add to the independent status of these bodies in relation to COPs.

Non-compliance procedures may be triggered by the non-complying party itself, by other States parties or by the secretariat. While States are

---

[41] Arts. 28 and 29 of the International Covenant on Civil and Political Rights.

reluctant to bring non-compliance cases against other States, it is not unusual that States notify their own implementation problems. The Aarhus Convention is special also in this respect, in providing for a right of individuals and NGOs to trigger cases of non-compliance, presumably an aspect of the Convention's human rights character. The Implementation Committee of the Espoo Convention has, however, decided by majority vote not to consider communications from NGOs. While the role of the secretariat varies between different MEAs, it has been a concern under certain MEAs that an active role of the secretariat may compromise their neutral role in the treaty co-operation. The CITES secretariat has, however, been exceedingly active in securing compliance with treaty commitments.

The principal basis for compliance control in MEAs is reports on implementation of commitments by the States parties. Both the Montreal Protocol and the Convention on Long-Range Transboundary Air Pollution establish that the respective Implementation Committees shall base their recommendations on information forwarded by the Secretariat.[42] We find, however, arrangements for transparency both when it comes to access to information and NGO participation. The Aarhus Convention establishes that its Compliance Committee may consider 'any relevant information submitted to it'.[43] The Espoo Convention is representative in providing that the meetings of the Implementation Committee are open to the public, unless the Committee decides otherwise.[44]

There are also procedural safeguards, such as the requirements of CITES about notice to be given to the non-compliant party and allowing time to respond. The Implementation Committee of the Convention on Long-Range Transboundary Air Pollution shall allow the relevant party to participate in the work of the Committee, but it shall not take part in the preparation and adoption of the Committee's conclusions.[45] The Aarhus Convention also allows such a right of participation, and furthermore provides that the party shall receive the Committee's draft conclusions, and the Committee shall 'take into account' any comments received from the party.[46] The Marrakesh Accords of the Kyoto Protocol set out even more extensive procedural rights for the party, including notifications, access to information, issuing of preliminary findings, allowing comments, and in

---

[42] The Montreal Protocol Non-Compliance Procedure, paras. 7 and 8; and the Convention on Long-Range Transboundary Air Pollution Decision 1997/2, Annex V, para. 6.

[43] Decision I/7, para. 25(c).   [44] Decision III/2, para. 3.

[45] Decision 1997/2, Annex V, para. 8.   [46] Decision I/7, para. 34.

the setting of time limits.[47] The rationale doubtlessly is that the use of 'hard' sanctions in cases of non-compliance requires more of 'due process' assurances.

Non-compliance committees do not have the power to adopt binding decisions, but may recommend measures to be taken by the supreme political organ of the co-operation, i.e. the COP. The Kyoto Protocol is an exception in setting out that the Enforcement Branch of the Compliance Committee takes the final decision, unless overturned by the Meeting of the Parties in its limited role as an appeals body.[48]

More generally, the legal status of a finding by the COP that a State is in non-compliance with one or more of its obligations may be questioned. First, the mandate of the COP is to determine the objective fact of non-compliance with the legal obligations under the MEA.[49] The COP will not, however, express any opinion about the availability of measures allowed under the law of treaties, such as suspension or termination of the MEA, or about the conditions for invoking State responsibility, such as the existence of circumstances precluding responsibility. Furthermore, a finding of non-compliance is not binding in the sense that it itself entails substantive legal consequences for the non-complying State. But it will establish an internal legal obligation of the other MEA organs to recognize the non-compliant status of the relevant State party.[50] It is finally clear that a finding by the COP of non-compliance is different from a *res judicata* decision of an international tribunal.

5.4 Enforcement

The term 'enforcement' may have different connotations, such as measures to ensure respect for legislation at the domestic level,[51] to obtain an international ruling, or taking measures against a State not fulfilling its obligations.[52] In our context, the concept is used to identify measures taken by MEA treaty bodies in order to induce States to comply with their commitments by exerting some kind of pressure on the parties.

---

[47] Decision 24/CP.7, Sections VII, VIII and IX.   [48] Decision 24/CP.7, Section XI.

[49] See Birnie and Boyle, *International Law and the Environment*, p. 207; and Koskenniemi, 'Breach of Treaty or Non-Compliance?' (1992) 3 *Yearbook of International Environmental Law* 128.

[50] See R. R. Churchill and G. Ulfstein, 'Autonomous Institutional Arrangements in Multilateral Environmental Agreements: A Little-Noticed Phenomenon in International Law' (2000) 94 *American Journal of International Law* 623–60, at 634.

[51] UNEP Guidelines, para. 38(d); and Kiev Guidelines, para. 4(c); see note 2 above.

[52] See Sands, *Principles of International Environmental Law*, p. 182.

Material breach of an MEA may give other States parties a right to suspend or terminate the agreement in accordance with article 60 of the Vienna Convention on the Law of Treaties. Termination or suspension of mutual obligations is, however, rather counter-productive when it comes to protection of the environment. While counter-measures under the law of State responsibility may provide effective pressure on a non-complying State, they represent a disadvantage common to measures under treaty law, i.e. that they are in principle unilateral measures, whereas measures adopted by MEA bodies represent concerted approaches to common problems. Furthermore, measures taken under MEAs may have a facilitative rather than a confrontational character. Such measures may thus substitute or supplement measures under general treaty law as a response to a breach of an MEA.

Non-compliance procedures in MEAs emphasize their non-confrontational character. This is reflected in the mandate of the Implementation Committee of the Montreal Protocol, which shall seek an 'amicable solution';[53] the Implementation Committee established under the Convention on Long-Range Transboundary Air Pollution shall address non-compliance with a view to securing a 'constructive solution'; the Aarhus Convention refers to 'non-confrontational, non-judicial and consultative measures';[54] and the deliberations of the Multilateral Consultative Process under the Climate Change Convention shall be conducted in a 'facilitative, co-operative, non-confrontational, transparent and timely manner, and be non-judicial'.[55] Such facilitation may consist in economic and professional assistance, with the contributions from funds, such as the Multilateral Fund under the Montreal Protocol or the Global Environment Facility (GEF).

States may feel that 'shaming' by being named as non-complying is in itself a form of pressure. The Implementation Committee of the Convention on Long-Range Transboundary Air Pollution, with the support of the Executive Body, has, however, brought to bear more extensive, but still gentle, pressure on non-complying States, such as requesting progress reports on the fulfilment of obligations, and urging the head of delegation together with an expert to visit the secretariat to find ways to achieve compliance. These measures are seen as providing an effective incitement to improve compliance, and no State has protested against being the subject of such measures.

---

[53] MoP Decision IV/5, para. 8.   [54] Decision I/7 Review of Compliance, para. 37(g).
[55] Climate Change COP Decision 10/CP.4, Annex, para. 3.

In addition to assistance, the Montreal Protocol provides for the use of cautions and suspension 'in accordance with the applicable rules of international law concerning the suspension of the operation of a treaty, of specific rights and privileges under the Protocol'.[56] We find an almost similar wording in the Aarhus Convention.[57] The non-compliance committee of the Montreal Protocol has issued several cautions that further measures, including suspension of the right to trade in ozone-depleting substances under article 4 of the Protocol, might be considered.[58] So far, however, it has not taken a step further in putting these cautions into operation.

CITES employs what could be termed a 'hard' sanction, i.e. trade measures in listed species against non-complying parties. Other forms of sanctions, such as financial penalties and suspension of rights and privileges have, however, been rejected by the parties. The trade measures seem to be effective in inducing States to take steps to bring about compliance. The Kyoto Protocol also makes use of measures of a penal character if a State violates its emission limits. In these cases, the Enforcement Branch will reduce the party's emission quota for the second commitment period by an amount equal to 1.3 times the excess emissions.[59]

Trade measures under CITES are of a recommendatory character, and accordingly are not binding. Binding measures of this kind would require a formal basis in the agreement itself. Correspondingly, article 18 of the Kyoto Protocol establishes that mechanisms 'entailing binding consequences shall be adopted by means of an amendment to this Protocol'. The parties have, however, deferred this decision in the Marrakesh Accords by stating that 'it is the prerogative of the Conference of the Parties serving as the meeting of the Parties to the Kyoto Protocol to decide on the legal form of the procedures and mechanisms relating to compliance'.[60] Hence, so far, it seems that 'hard' sanctions are only acceptable to the extent that they are non-binding. It should also be recalled that there is a continuing potential that sanctions in the

---

[56] Ozone Secretariat, United Nations Environment Programme, *Handbook for the International Protection of the Ozone Layer* (Nairobi: 6th edn, 2003), Section 2.7, 'Indicative List of Measures that Might Be Taken by a Meeting of the Parties in Respect of Non-Compliance with the Protocol', p. 297.   [57] Decision I/7 Review of Compliance, para. 37.

[58] See e.g. Decision XIII/16.   [59] Decision 24/CP.7, Section XV, para. 5(a).

[60] Decision 24/CP.7, seventh preambular paragraph.

form of trade measures may be struck down as violating WTO commitments.[61]

It may be concluded that 'hard' sanctions are the exceptions rather than the rule. The reluctance towards imposing measures of a more penal character against non-complying States may have diverse causes. First, it may be a matter of protecting State sovereignty from international pressure. Secondly, the motivation may be that facilitative approaches are regarded as more effective, as is advocated by the 'managerial school', especially taking into account the need to preserve a constructive political co-operation. Thirdly, it may be that the sort of environmental problems regulated by MEAs has not required hard sanctions, while environmental challenges requiring more stringent regulations would presuppose the utilization of harder sanctions.

Finally, the use of hard sanctions may be seen in the light of international law as being essentially of a horizontal character. In the context of State responsibility, States have not been willing to accept certain violations of international law as 'international crimes'.[62] While there is in principle nothing to prevent the use of penalties in international law, there are as yet no effective international organs to put into effect enforcement measures. States may also choose to leave an MEA that apply sanctions of a penal character. But, as stronger international institutions are developed, they may be entrusted with more enforcement power. States may also be more reluctant to bear the political and legal costs of leaving such institutions, including the institutional framework of MEAs. In any case, it would seem that MEAs should make use of the full repertoire of measures to combat non-compliance, measures of both a facilitative and an enforcement character.

5.5 Overall evaluation

MEAs do not provide much creativity when it comes to *dispute settlement* procedures. Traditional dispute settlement procedures are only a last resort if the non-compliance procedures fail, and are only exceptionally used in practice. But there are examples of their use, and such procedures may be

---

[61] On trade measures under the Montreal Protocol, see J. Werksman, 'Compliance and Transition: Russia's Non-Compliance Tests the Ozone Regime' (1996) 56 *Zeitschrift für ausländisches öffentliches Recht und Völkerrecht* 750, at 773.

[62] See Crawford, *The International Law Commission's Articles on State Responsibility* (Cambridge: Cambridge University Press, 2002). pp. 16–20.

resorted to if a violation is of particular importance to a State, or concerns a question considered as being of general importance. The inquiry commissions of the Espoo Convention provide an example of the use of non-binding dispute settlement in cases having mainly bilateral aspects.

The non-compliance procedures establish a distinct new feature in international law and embody an aspect of its further *institutionalization* (or constitutionalization) as well as its *formalization* (or legalization).[63] The combined roles of the MEA secretariats, non-compliance committees and the conferences of the parties represent a multilateral rather than a bilateral approach to environmental problems. Although comparisons have been drawn to dispute settlement procedures, such as alternative dispute resolution (ADR) or conciliation, non-compliance procedures of MEAs are in fact very different by releasing the disputing parties from pursuing violations of MEAs on their own, and entrusting it to the MEA institutions.[64]

An essential difference between human rights treaties and MEAs is that, while the former have established expert supervisory organs, the non-compliance procedures of MEAs are basically of a *political* character, with States parties represented on the non-compliance committees and the final decisions taken by COPs. We have, however, seen a development of a more independent role for non-compliance committees by restricting the membership on the committees, and even appointing independent experts, such as in the cases of the Aarhus Convention and the Kyoto Protocol. Under the Kyoto Protocol, the Meeting of the Parties has only a limited role in its function as an appeals body.

The non-compliance procedures of MEAs are generally of a *facilitative* character. Many MEAs have arrangements for assistance to developing countries in fulfilling their commitments. There has, however, been a considerable creativity in designing measures that may be considered non-confrontational but which still put pressure on States to comply. Furthermore, CITES applies trade measures against non-complying States, and the Kyoto Protocol uses sanctions in the form of a penalty reduction of emission quotas. Applying measures of a penal character is rather unique in international law. But such an *enforcement* approach may become more common as MEAs incorporate more stringent restrictions on States' economic activities.

---

[63] See the literature referred to in footnotes 2 and 10 in the Introduction to this book.

[64] See Birnie and Boyle, *International Law and the Environment*, p. 208; and Sands, *Principles of International Environmental Law*, p. 205.

A development towards an *enforcement* approach may bring new challenges to the treaty regime. First, similarly to the development of more effective decision-making in MEAs, the use of binding sanctions may raise questions about their democratic legitimacy.[65] Secondly, such sanctions may provoke claims to include 'due process' guarantees. In this sense, we may experience a convergence between dispute settlement and non-compliance procedures. But MEAs will continue to need facilitative elements under the political control of the Conference of the Parties.

[65] On decision-making and legitimacy, see D. Bodansky, 'The Legitimacy of International Governance: A Coming Challenge for International Environmental Law?' (1999) 93 *American Journal of International Law* 596–625.

6

The Convention on International Trade in Endangered Species of Wild Fauna and Flora (CITES)

ROSALIND REEVE*

6.1 Introduction

The 1973 Convention on International Trade in Endangered Species of Wild Fauna and Flora (CITES) is one of the oldest multilateral environmental agreements (MEAs).[1] A specific tool rather than a global solution, it addresses one of the principal causes of biodiversity loss – the international wildlife trade. Since its inception, CITES has been seen as the flagship wildlife agreement. Most *perceive* it as effective, although there has never been a thorough empirical assessment of the effectiveness of CITES – or of the extent to which it is truly implemented and enforced at national level.

The origin of CITES lies in a 1963 resolution of the General Assembly of the International Union for Conservation of Nature and Natural Resources (IUCN), now the World Conservation Union, calling for 'an international convention on regulation of export, transit and import of rare or threatened wildlife species or their skins and trophies'. Successive draft texts were prepared and circulated by the IUCN Environmental Law Centre in Bonn, then revised in 1969 and 1971 in light of comments received from governments and non-governmental organizations (NGOs). The IUCN initiative coincided with a US prohibition of imports of wildlife 'threatened with worldwide extinction', except for scientific or breeding purposes, under the

---

* Chatham House (the Royal Institute of International Affairs) is an independent body which promotes the rigorous study of international questions and does not express opinions of its own. The opinions expressed in this publication are the responsibility of the author. Chatham House, 10 St James's Square, London SW1Y 4LE (www.chathamhouse.org.uk); charity registration no. 208223.

[1] Convention on International Trade in Endangered Species of Wild Fauna and Flora, Washington DC, 3 March 1973, in force 1 July 1975, 993 UNTS 243 (No. 14537, 1976). The Convention text can be accessed at www.cites.org/eng/disc/text.shtml.

1969 Endangered Species Conservation Act.[2] Complaints of competitive disadvantage from US traders led to efforts by the US Government to seek a binding international convention on endangered species conservation.

These initiatives, reinforced by a recommendation of the 1972 UN Conference on the Human Environment in Stockholm,[3] culminated in the adoption of CITES by twenty-one countries on 3 March 1973. Entering into force after the tenth ratification on 1 July 1975, the Convention subjected imports of species listed in three appendices to mandatory licensing with permits and certificates to be issued by trading countries in accordance with specific criteria. As of 8 November 2005, the number of CITES parties had grown to 169.

The primary objective of CITES, though not explicitly stated in the Convention, is to ensure that international trade in specimens of wild animals and plants does not threaten their survival.[4]

The three CITES Appendices contain over 30,000 species of fauna and flora, over 25,000 of which are plants. Most listed species are on Appendix II and comprise the bulk of CITES trade. Appendix I includes 'all species threatened with extinction which are or may be affected by trade'.[5] In effect, this is a 'black list' of species whose trade for 'primarily commercial purposes' is prohibited. Other trade, largely confined to specimens required for scientific and educational purposes and hunting trophies, is subject to the grant of both an import and an export permit under specific conditions, including a finding that that trade will 'not be detrimental to the survival of that species' – the so-called 'non-detriment' finding.[6] Appendix II includes 'all species which although not necessarily now threatened with extinction may become so unless trade in specimens of such species is subject to strict regulation'.[7] In effect, it is a precautionary or 'grey list' of controlled species for which commercial trade is allowed under certain conditions, including the grant of an export permit subject to a non-detriment finding. Appendix III includes species listed unilaterally by parties as being subject to regulation within their jurisdiction and for which international co-operation is needed to control trade.[8] Permits

---

[2] Public Law No. 91–135, 83 Stat 275, entry into force 3 June 1970; superseded by a comprehensive new Endangered Species Act, 7 USC 136 (1973), after the adoption of CITES in 1973.

[3] Recommendation 99 of the Stockholm Action Plan called for 'a plenipotentiary conference to be convened as soon as possible, under appropriate governmental or intergovernmental auspices, to prepare and adopt a convention on export, import and transit of certain species of wild animals and wild plants'.　[4] www.cites.org/eng/disc/what.shtml.

[5] Art. II(1) of CITES.　[6] *Ibid.*, Art. III.　[7] *Ibid.*, Art. II(2).　[8] *Ibid.*, Art. II(3).

differ depending on whether exports originate in the listing country or in another range State (a State where the species occurs naturally); non-detriment findings are not required.

6.2 Compliance control

6.2.1 Legal basis

CITES differs from other multilateral environmental agreements in that it does not have a specific treaty article mandating the development of procedures to address compliance control. Instead, its compliance system has evolved through secondary rules (Resolutions and Decisions of the Conference of the Parties, or CoP[9]) and practice over nearly three decades on the basis of broad provisions in treaty articles. These broad provisions mandate:

- parties to report annually on CITES trade and biennially on implementation and enforcement measures;[10]
- the Secretariat to review national reports, communicate problems on implementation to parties and make recommendations;[11]
- parties to respond with remedial action and report to the CoP;[12] and
- the CoP to review parties' responses and make recommendations.[13]

This in effect is the foundation and legal basis of the compliance control system. There is no CITES implementation or compliance committee. This role is played by the Standing Committee which was established permanently by resolution in 1979.[14] The system has evolved considerably over the last three decades such that several mechanisms now exist to effect compliance control. These mechanisms, and the role of the Standing Committee, have developed largely through consensus. Although their legal basis has been questioned from time to time, particularly by parties found in non-compliance and faced with the ultimate sanction of a recommended CITES trade suspension, little need was seen to formalize them until recently when

---

[9] Resolutions remain in effect until repealed or amended by a meeting of the CoP, while Decisions remain in effect from one CoP to the next (three years).   [10] Art. VIII of CITES.

[11] *Ibid.*, Arts. XII and XIII.   [12] *Ibid.*, Art. XIII.   [13] *Ibid.*, Art. XI.

[14] CITES Resolution Conf. 2.2, 'Establishment of the Standing Committee of the Conference of the Parties' (1979). CITES Resolutions and other documents may be found on the CITES website, www.cites.org.

negotiations for Guidelines on Compliance with the Convention were initiated following the threat of trade sanctions against a large number of parties (discussed further below). Even so, these Guidelines when adopted will still constitute only another form of secondary rules in addition to Resolutions and Decisions. Formalization through a treaty amendment is considered not only undesirable because of the controversy it would raise, particularly in regard to the use of trade sanctions, but also impractical because of the delay involved. Two-thirds of parties are required to deposit an instrument of acceptance of an amendment to the Convention before it enters into force for those parties that have accepted it; the Gaborone amendment to allow the European Union (EU) to accede to CITES was approved in 1983 but has still not entered into force.

6.2.2 Compliance information

CITES was one of the first MEAs to provide for an information system. The regime relies largely on self-reporting by parties, but also on information provided by other intergovernmental organizations such as Interpol, the World Customs Organization (WCO) and the Lusaka Agreement Task Force (LATF), as well as NGOs.

6.2.2.1 Party reporting

On the basis of records that parties are obliged to keep on importers, exporters and trade in CITES-listed species, parties are required to transmit annual reports to the Secretariat.[15] These reports are to contain information on permits and certificates granted as well as the States with which trade occurred and details of traded specimens listed in the Appendices, including the names of species, types of specimens and their quantities.[16] In addition, parties are required to provide biennial reports containing information on 'legislative, regulatory and administrative measures taken to enforce the provisions of the present Convention'.[17]

Annual reports on trade have two primary purposes:

- to provide the basis for monitoring trade in listed species, including reviews of significant trade in Appendix II species by the Animals and Plants Committees; and

---

[15] Arts. VIII(6) and (7) of CITES.   [16] *Ibid.*, Arts. VIII(6)(b) and (7)(a).
[17] *Ibid.*, Art. VIII(7)(b).

- to provide information on implementation of the Convention, including the detection of illegal trade by highlighting discrepancies between reported imports and exports and assessment of compliance with quotas.

The requirements for annual reporting have been greatly elaborated over the years through a series of resolutions.[18] Guidelines, which are regularly updated, have also been provided since 1982 for their preparation and submission. The deadline for the submission of annual reports is 31 October of the year following that in which the trade took place. The Secretariat, however, may approve a valid request for an extension, provided the party submits a written request containing adequate justification before the 31 October deadline.[19]

The Secretariat's functions include 'studying' parties' reports; requesting any further information it deems necessary to ensure implementation of the Convention; and preparing annual reports on, *inter alia*, implementation.[20] Some of these functions are contracted out. A table of parties that have submitted annual reports was recently published on the CITES website but the reports themselves are not publicly available. Under an annual consultancy contract, data from annual reports are maintained in a computerized database by the United Nations Environment Programme–World Conservation Monitoring Centre (UNEP–WCMC) based in Cambridge, UK. Formerly an NGO, the WCMC now falls under UNEP as part of its environmental monitoring and assessment system. The database, going back to 1975 and to which half a million trade records are added every year, can be accessed through the Internet and allows import and export records to be cross-matched. It also enables export records to be compared with export quotas. Where the records do not match, or parties report possible illegal trade, UNEP–WCMC informs the Secretariat. However, the disadvantage to this system is the considerable delay between the infraction and its detection, as a result of the time taken to record, report and analyze the data. The unreliability of wildlife trade records presents another shortcoming. A recent study comparing CITES data with US Customs data found wide-ranging discrepancies which 'may distort the perceived risk of targeted wildlife exploitation'.[21]

---

[18] All recommendations on annual reporting are consolidated in CITES Resolution Conf. 11.17 (Rev. CoP13) 'National Reports' (2004).   [19] *Ibid.*   [20] Art. XII of CITES.

[21] Discrepancies ranged from a CITES-reported volume 376 per cent greater than that reported by US Customs (live coral exports, 2000) to a Customs-reported volume 5,202 per cent greater than CITES (conch exports, 2000). Arthur Blundell and Michael Mascia, 'Discrepancies in Reported Levels of International Wildlife Trade' (2005) 19 *Conservation Biology* 2020.

Biennial implementation reporting has been virtually moribund. A recent initiative, however, aims to stimulate it. At the 13th meeting of the Conference of the Parties (CoP13), a new format was agreed for the submission of biennial reports – essentially a detailed questionnaire on implementation and enforcement. New provisions on biennial reporting were also incorporated into the Resolution on National Reports[22] (which previously only addressed annual reporting):

- parties are urged to submit biennial reports using the new format and covering the same two-year periods beginning with the period from 1 January 2003 to 31 December 2004;
- the deadline for submission of biennial reports is 31 October following the year for which they are due;
- the Secretariat may approve a valid request for an extension of time to the October deadline; and
- parties are urged to co-ordinate the submission of the two types of reports.

The generalized lack of compliance with the biennial reporting requirement to date means that information on national implementation and enforcement of CITES is patchy. It is hoped that this latest and most concerted initiative to date to stimulate biennial reporting will result in the development of an information base which will assist compliance control, though at the moment there seems to be no provision to make the reports publicly available.

In addition to the legally binding requirement to submit annual and biennial reports, parties may be requested to provide specific information. This is usually in relation to particular species for which additional monitoring is needed but may also be on such issues as mortalities in transport or ranching operations.

6.2.3 Monitoring of compliance

6.2.3.1 Institutional roles

The role of monitoring and reporting on compliance is assigned to the Secretariat. Its mandate comes from article XII of CITES. This article outlines the functions of the Secretariat, which include, in paragraph 2:

> (d) to study the reports of Parties and to request from Parties such further information with respect thereto as it deems necessary to ensure implementation of the present Convention;

---

[22] CITES Resolution Conf. 11.17 (Rev. CoP13).

(e) to invite the attention of the Parties to any matter pertaining to the aims of the present Convention; [and]
(h) to make recommendations for the implementation of the aims and provisions of the present Convention, including the exchange of information of a scientific or technical nature.

The recommendatory function in sub-paragraph (h) has been exercised to the full by the CITES Secretariat which plays an unusually strong role in implementation and compliance control. Almost all cases of non-compliance with CITES have been notified by the Secretariat to the Standing Committee and/or the Conference of the Parties. In other MEAs, there has been a concern that too strong a role for the secretariat in non-compliance issues may compromise its neutrality. This similarly has been a concern of some of the NGOs participating in CITES, particularly in relation to decisions concerning the ivory trade but in compliance control in general the secretariat's role has contributed to the system's strength.

Although parties generally do not bring cases of non-compliance, there was an exception in the case of Bolivia in 1985. A resolution recommending that parties refuse to accept CITES shipments from Bolivia if it did not implement the Convention within ninety days was sponsored by Latin American countries whose wildlife was being depleted by Bolivia's illegal trade.[23]

The Secretariat, which is provided by UNEP, may be 'assisted by suitable intergovernmental or non-governmental international or national agencies and bodies technically qualified in protection, conservation and management of wild fauna and flora' (article XII(1)). Work is often contracted out to NGOs, particularly IUCN, TRAFFIC (Trade Records Analysis of Fauna and Flora in Commerce) and FFI (Fauna and Flora International). TRAFFIC provides information on trade and illegal trade which has in some cases triggered action leading to recommended suspensions of CITES trade.[24] Other NGOs have also provided information, but their relationship with the Secretariat is not as close. On the whole, parties perceive the role of contracted NGOs in a positive light and have not questioned the legitimacy of their work. However, some elephant range States have at times criticized the Elephant Trade Information System (ETIS), a database of elephant product seizures managed by TRAFFIC, and, in the early stages of its development, the system

---

[23] CITES Resolution Conf. 5.2, 'Implementation of the Convention in Bolivia' (1985).
[24] Rosalind Reeve, *Policing International Trade in Endangered Species: The CITES Treaty and Compliance* (London: Earthscan and the Royal Institute of International Affairs, 2002), p. 91.

for Monitoring Illegal Killing of Elephants (MIKE). Generally, though, the work of contracted NGOs is questioned more by other NGOs who believe they wield too much influence in the development of CITES policy.

Recommendations for specific measures to address non-compliance are usually made by the Standing Committee on the basis of a mandate provided by the CoP in Resolutions and Decisions that outline the different compliance mechanisms. Under the mechanisms to address lack of national legislation, failure to submit annual reports and significant trade in Appendix II species (detailed below), the Standing Committee has a mandate specified in several Resolutions to recommend measures, which can include a suspension of trade in CITES-listed species (although in the case of non-reporting only a trade suspension is prescribed). However, the procedure to address cases of generalized non-compliance does not specifically mandate the Standing Committee to recommend measures. Instead, the Committee is mandated to 'find a solution'.[25] This has been interpreted over the years to enable the Standing Committee to make specific recommendations, including trade suspensions. This prominent role by the Standing Committee has evolved over twenty years, prompted in part by a general tendency of the parties not to want to name other parties in the more public CoP meetings and in part by the need to make decisions on measures in between CoP meetings, which have in the past occurred every two-and-a-half years but will now be held only every three years. Occasionally, the CoP has fulfilled a more specific recommendatory role, an example being the case of serious generalized non-compliance by Bolivia in 1985,[26] but the more usual practice is for it to set the framework enabling the Standing Committee to act.

The Standing Committee is an executive committee composed of fourteen regional party representatives, plus Switzerland (as the depositary government), the previous host country of the CoP and the next host country. In effect, it functions as a 'mini-CoP', making decisions regarding implementation, enforcement, finance and administration in between CoP meetings. Compliance is just one issue with which it deals, albeit an important one. Six geographic regions are represented by between one and four members depending on the number of parties in the region. With the revision of the Committee's terms of reference in 2000, Africa, as the region with the most parties, gained a fourth representative. Those attending

---

[25] CITES Resolution Conf. 11.3 (Rev. CoP13), 'Compliance and Enforcement' (2004).
[26] Reeve, *Policing International Trade in Endangered Species*, p. 95.

142 INTERNATIONAL ENVIRONMENTAL LAW

Standing Committee meetings are usually from the parties' Management Authorities. Thus the Committee differs from implementation and compliance committees under other MEAs which have a narrower mandate and in some cases consist of nominated experts.

Regional representatives are elected for a term lasting from the close of the CoP meeting at which they are elected to the close of the second CoP meeting thereafter (five to six years). They are the only voting members, the depositary government voting to break a tie. In practice, however, decision-making is by consensus. Other parties may participate as observers in Standing Committee meetings but they cannot vote. NGOs with expertise in CITES issues may be approved to participate as non-voting observers, though they have only been allowed to participate since 2003. Most issues concerning compliance and enforcement by specific parties used to be considered in closed session, with NGOs making presentations to the Committee beforehand, but in October 2006 the Standing Committee decided to open discussions on these issues to NGO observers for the first time.

No CITES institution is empowered to make binding determinations of non-compliance. Furthermore, obligations to comply cannot be set aside, except where parties take out reservations to listings of species in the Appendices.[27] The treaty provides that, in the case of reservations, parties shall be treated as non-party States with respect to the species concerned. However, parties who enter reservations with respect to Appendix I species are recommended to treat the species as if it were listed in Appendix II, and to report trade accordingly in their annual reports.[28]

6.2.3.2 Compliance mechanisms

Several compliance mechanisms have evolved through secondary rules and practice.

Procedure to address serious generalized non-compliance[29]   The procedure in place since 1989 to deal with countries with major implementation problems (see Figure 6.1) provides for due notice to be given to the non-compliant party, time to respond in cases of an alleged infraction, the provision of advice and technical assistance by the Secretariat, and notification

---

[27] Arts. XV, XVI and XXIII of CITES.
[28] CITES Resolution Conf. 4.25, 'Effects of Reservations' (1983).
[29] CITES Resolution Conf. 11.3 (Rev. CoP13), 'Compliance and Enforcement' (2004); Reeve, *Policing International Trade in Endangered Species*, p. 91.

> Regarding application of Article XIII (from Resolution Conf. 11.3 (Rev. CoP 13))
>
> (a) when, in application of Article XIII, the Secretariat requests information on an alleged infraction, Parties reply within a time-limit of one month or, if this is impossible, acknowledge within the month and indicate a date, even an approximate one, by which they consider it will be possible to provide the information requested;
>
> (b) when, within a one year time-limit, the information requested has not been provided, Parties provide the Secretariat with justification of the reasons for which they have not been able to respond;
>
> (c) if major problems with implementation of the Convention in particular Parties are brought to the attention of the Secretariat, the Secretariat work together with the Party concerned to try to solve the problem and offer advice or technical assistance as required;
>
> (d) if it does not appear a solution can be readily achieved, the Secretariat bring the matter to the attention of the Standing Committee, which may pursue the matter in direct contact with the Party concerned with a view to helping to find a solution; and
>
> (e) the Secretariat keep the Parties informed as fully as possible, through Notifications, of such implementation problems and of actions taken to solve them, and include such problems in its report of alleged infractions.

Figure 6.1 Procedure to address serious generalized non-compliance

to parties and the CoP. It also mandates the Standing Committee to pursue the matter with the party concerned and 'find a solution'. The procedure does not, however, specify the measures to be taken in cases of non-compliance. Instead, these have evolved through practice based on the advice of the Secretariat.

National legislation project[30]   Dating back to 1992, the project's aim is to induce parties to enact CITES implementing legislation. It has evolved

---

[30] CITES Resolution Conf. 8.4 (1992) and Decisions 13.79–13.83 (2004) 'National Laws for Implementation of the Convention'; Reeve, *Policing International Trade in Endangered Species*, p. 134; R. Reeve, 'The CITES Treaty and Compliance: Progress or Jeopardy?', Chatham House Briefing Paper, BP04/01, September 2004, pp. 4–6.

144 INTERNATIONAL ENVIRONMENTAL LAW

through several CoP Decisions, all based on Resolution Conf. 8.4 which directed the Secretariat to identify parties whose legislation did not enable them to implement four basic requirements of the Convention:

1. designation of at least one Management Authority and one Scientific Authority (article IX(1)); or
2. prohibition of trade in specimens in violation of the Convention (article VIII(1)); or
3. penalization of such trade (article VIII(1)(a)); or
4. confiscation of specimens illegally traded or possessed (article VIII(1)(b)).

Under the national legislation project, the Secretariat reviews national legislation and categorizes it according to whether it meets all (category 1), some (category 2) or none (category 3) of the above requirements for CITES implementation. Parties without adequate legislation, i.e. legislation in categories 2 or 3 with only some or none of the requirements for implementation, are required to provide national legislation plans (plans for drafting and enacting legislation) and enact legislation within specified deadlines. The Secretariat provides technical assistance if requested. If parties fail to provide a plan of either drafted or enacted legislation by the stated deadline, the Standing Committee can, on the basis of a Secretariat recommendation, recommend a suspension of trade in all CITES-listed species with the non-compliant party. Such a suspension is used as a penalty. In practice, however, parties have been given extensions of their deadlines and allowed extra time to respond before a suspension is recommended. If they demonstrate legislative progress, for example by providing a legislation plan, the recommended suspension is lifted even though the party may not yet have the necessary implementing legislation in place.

Non-compliance with annual reporting[31]   To address a persistent failure by parties to provide annual reports on their CITES-related trade, in 2000 it was decided by the CoP that parties failing to provide reports for three years in a row would be subject to a recommendation to suspend all trade in all CITES-listed species (the Secretariat identifies the offending parties and the Standing Committee makes the recommendation for a suspension). At

---

[31] CITES Resolution Conf. 11.17 (Rev. CoP13), 'National Reports' (2004); Reeve, *Policing International Trade in Endangered Species*, p. 147; Reeve, 'The CITES Treaty and Compliance', pp. 3–4.

CoP13 in October 2004, it was decided to incorporate this provision, which was originally in the form of two Decisions, into the Resolution on National Reports, giving it greater permanence.

The provision is as follows:

> The Conference of the Parties . . .
>
> INSTRUCTS the Standing Committee to determine, on the basis of reports presented by the Secretariat, which Parties have failed, for three consecutive years and without having provided adequate justification, to provide the annual reports required under Article VIII, paragraph 7(a), of the Convention within the deadline (or any extended deadline) provided in the present Resolution;
>
> RECOMMENDS that Parties not authorize trade in specimens of CITES-listed species with any Party that the Standing Committee has determined has failed, for three consecutive years and without having provided adequate justification, to provide the annual reports required under Article VIII, paragraph 7(a), of the Convention within the deadline (or any extended deadline) provided in the present Resolution . . .

The provision has been applied in many cases (discussed further below). No similar provision exists for failure to provide biennial reports.

Significant trade review[32]   This procedure reviews status and trade in Appendix II-listed species believed to be traded in significant numbers. On the basis of the reviews (which are usually desk-based and contracted out to IUCN, TRAFFIC and occasionally FFI), species are categorized according to the level of concern, and recommendations for action are made by the Animals or Plants Committee as appropriate (both are technical/scientific committees). These recommendations are directed to range States. If range States do not respond within specified time limits (which should normally be no less than ninety days and not more than two years), they may be subject to a recommendation by the Standing Committee to suspend trade in the Appendix II-listed species concerned. Many of these species-specific trade suspensions have been recommended since the Standing Committee was given the mandate to do so in 1992.

In 2001, the first country-based significant trade review was initiated. This involved a review of trade in all Appendix II-listed species found in

---

[32] CITES Resolution Conf. 12.8 (Rev. COP13), 'Review of Significant Trade in Specimens of Appendix II Species' (2002); Reeve, *Policing International Trade in Endangered Species*, p. 159.

Madagascar and the preparation of an action plan based on the results of the review. The case is being seen as a pilot project, the outcome of which will determine whether a country-based approach is repeated.

Urgent action for Appendix I species[33]   Case-specific action may be recommended for species in serious trouble. Rhinos and tigers have been addressed so far through CoP Resolutions and Standing Committee Decisions. The tools used have included technical and political missions to generate recommendations for action and political support; threats of recommended trade suspensions with non-compliant consumer States; and the CITES Tiger Enforcement Task Force, established by a CoP Decision in 2001 to encourage co-operation between tiger range and consumer States on enforcement. This *ad hoc* task force conducted enforcement training for range States but became inactive for lack of funds; it was revived recently following a Decision at CoP13. Great apes have most recently been highlighted for urgent action; a Great Ape Enforcement Task Force is due to meet in October 2006.

Control of internal ivory trade[34]   This is a relatively new initiative. On the basis of an analysis of seizure data by TRAFFIC, ten countries were targeted in 2002 for further investigation by the Secretariat in relation to their internal ivory trade controls. On the basis of desk studies, the Secretariat made recommendations to the Standing Committee, which included restrictions on CITES trade with non-responsive countries, but the Standing Committee postponed a decision. At CoP13 in October 2004, an action plan was agreed. This is designed to clamp down on uncontrolled domestic markets in Africa. The plan includes a provision for non-compliance response – a recommendation that 'parties should not engage in commercial trade in specimens of CITES-listed species with the country in question' if it fails to implement the action plan or if ivory is found to be sold illegally.[35] At Standing Committee meetings in 2005 and 2006, however, NGOs expressed disappointment at the lack of action against non-compliant countries. It will be interesting to see how the plan evolves given that CITES does not have a mandate to control internal trade.

---

[33] Reeve, *Policing International Trade in Endangered Species*, p. 189.
[34] Reeve, 'The CITES Treaty and Compliance', p. 7; CITES Resolution Conf. 10.10 (Rev. CoP12), 'Trade in Elephant Specimens' (2002); CITES Decisions 12.36–12.39 (2002) and 13.26 (2004).
[35] CITES Decisions, Annex 2, 'Action Plan for the Control of Trade in African Elephant Ivory' (2005).

6.2.3.3 Technical assistance and capacity-building

The Secretariat provides technical assistance to parties through the provision of guidelines (e.g. on reporting), checklists (e.g. on making non-detriment findings), model legislation through the national legislation project, and identification manuals of listed species and their parts and derivatives. It also conducts *ad hoc* missions to parties to investigate compliance problems, provide advice and assistance, formulate recommendations and verify compliance. However, these missions are limited due to a lack of funds and personnel.

Capacity-building is conducted largely through regional workshops organized by the Secretariat which are currently addressing scientific issues and national legislation. Enforcement training has been conducted intermittently, most recently through the Tiger Enforcement Task Force. But efforts fall far short of the needs and once again are compromised by lack of funds. A number of independent initiatives by international NGOs are attempting to fill this gap.

6.2.4 Guidelines under negotiation

A recent development in the CITES compliance regime that needs to be watched carefully is the negotiation of Guidelines on Compliance with the Convention, due to be completed by CoP14 in 2007. These originated as a result of the large number of parties found to be affected by Decisions agreed at CoP11 in 2000 recommending trade suspensions for persistent failure to provide annual reports or to enact CITES implementing legislation. A backlash in the Standing Committee resulted in calls for clarification of the existing system, consideration of other measures available to deal with non-compliance (which as yet have not materialized), and eventually a Decision in 2002 (prompted by a Secretariat proposal) to negotiate compliance guidelines. The final draft of the Guidelines is now being prepared by a working group under Standing Committee auspices from which NGOs have been excluded except at the June 2005 meeting of the Standing Committee.

The negotiations have not been smooth. Several concerns were raised at the Standing Committee meeting in March 2004 which delayed the drafting process. These concerns included comments on legal basis, lack of agreement on the nature of the guidelines (should they just provide guidance or should they prescribe detailed procedures), and the need for more encouragement and capacity-building measures rather than sanctions. The meeting gave cause for concern that the guidelines could undermine the existing system.[36] Negotiations by the working group since CoP13, however, have been less contentious. It has been agreed that the function of the guidelines will be to describe or clarify the existing system, and it has largely been accepted that the existing system will provide a baseline, i.e. any provisions that weaken it will not be acceptable. Nevertheless, the process has to be watched carefully to ensure that the gains of the last thirty years are not lost. The negotiations are not straightforward since the guidelines are in effect being grafted onto existing procedures, whereas in other more recent MEAs negotiations started with a blank sheet. To what degree the guidelines will formalize the existing system is unclear. Since they are secondary rules which will be in effect until amended by the CoP their status is equivalent to a Resolution, but in practice they may help to avert complaints by affected parties concerning the legal basis of recommended trade suspensions and the role of the Standing Committee.

6.3 Enforcement

In the context of CITES, enforcement generally relates to national enforcement of implementing legislation, and to co-operative mechanisms at national, regional and international level between different enforcement agencies (which are few and far between). However, in the context of this case study, enforcement is interpreted to mean international enforcement, i.e. methods used to exert pressure on States to comply. Under CITES, such methods include:

- technical and political missions;
- warnings;
- formal cautions;
- legislation plans;
- compliance action plans (or, in the case of non-payment of arrears, 'payment plans'); and
- recommendations to suspend trade in CITES-listed species.

[36] Reeve, 'The CITES Treaty and Compliance', pp. 7–11.

Some of these, notably legislation plans and formal cautions, have been introduced only recently. The use of recommended CITES trade suspensions, on the other hand, dates back to 1985. The Secretariat has suggested other forms of sanctions such as financial penalties and suspension of rights and privileges, but these have not been received positively by some members of the Standing Committee, notably from Latin America, until June 2005 when they were raised again in connection with non-payment of arrears to the CITES Trust Fund (the treaty's financial mechanism) and did not provoke the usual objections. Although such sanctions were not formally agreed, they were raised again in October 2006 and once again did not provoke objections though as before were not formally approved.

Two types of recommended trade suspensions can be characterized: country-specific suspensions of trade in all CITES-listed species and species-specific suspensions of trade in Appendix II-listed species under the significant trade review. Country-specific trade suspensions may be recommended for persistent generalized non-compliance, lack of adequate national legislation and failure to demonstrate legislative progress under the national legislation project, and persistent failure to submit annual trade reports. These are considered voluntary suspensions and not binding. Furthermore, in what is effectively a voluntary import suspension, parties are advised not to accept export permits from countries that fail to notify the Secretariat of their Scientific Authorities since the issuance of permits by a Management Authority without appropriate Scientific Authority findings breaches the Convention.[37] Non-payment of contributions by parties to the CITES Trust Fund has been raised as another possible cause for trade suspensions but the Standing Committee has been reluctant to agree, recommending instead that payment plans be drawn up and pressure exerted through visits by the Secretary-General to missions in Geneva.[38] Progress, however, has been slow with this approach.

Since 1985, trade suspensions have been recommended against eight parties for generalized non-compliance (one on two occasions) as well as three non-parties and one dependent territory whose illegal trade posed a major problem (see Table 6.1). In all but the most recent case, parties responded, at least on paper, and had their sanctions lifted. Also, the

[37] CITES Resolution Conf. 10.3, 'Designation and Role of the Scientific Authorities' (1997).
[38] CITES SC46 Doc. 9.1.3 (Rev. 1), 'Payments of Contributions by Parties', prepared by the Secretariat for SC46 (March 2002): see SC46: Summary Report (March 2002), p. 5.

150   INTERNATIONAL ENVIRONMENTAL LAW

Table 6.1   *Countries and territories subjected to recommended CITES trade suspensions*

Country/territory	Suspension recommended	Suspension lifted
Parties with major implementation/enforcement problems		
Bolivia	1985/6	1987
United Arab Emirates (withdrew from CITES 1988–90)	1985	1990
Thailand	1991	1992
Italy	1992	1993 (temporary) 1995 (permanent)
Greece	1998	1999
Democratic Republic of Congo (DRC)	July 2001	December 2002
United Arab Emirates	November 2001	November 2002
Nigeria	July 2005	Still in force[a]
Non-parties		
Macau	1986	1986
El Salvador (joined 1987)	1986	1987
Equatorial Guinea (joined 1992)	1988	1992
Grenada (joined 1999)	1991	1992[b]
Parties subject to suspensions under national legislation project		
Guyana	September 1999	November 1999
Senegal	October 1999	January 2000
Fiji	January 2002	December 2002 (temporary)
	October 2003	November 2003
Vietnam	January 2002	March 2002
Yemen	January 2002	October 2002
Djibouti	April 2004	Still in force
Equatorial Guinea	April 2004	June 2004
Guinea-Bissau	April 2004	Still in force
Liberia	April 2004	Still in force
Mozambique	April 2004	June 2004
Panama	April 2004	May 2004
Rwanda	April 2004	Still in force
Sierra Leone	April 2004	June 2004
Mauritania	July 2004	Still in force
Somalia	July 2004	Still in force

CONVENTION ON INTERNATIONAL TRADE IN ENDANGERED SPECIES 151

Table 6.1   (*cont.*)

Country/territory	Suspension recommended	Suspension lifted
Gambia	December 2004	August 2005
India	December 2004	March 2005
Parties subject to suspensions for persistent non-reporting		
Afghanistan	December 2002	May 2003
[Bangladesh	December 2002	February 2003]ᶜ
Djibouti	December 2002	June 2003
Dominica	December 2002	March 2003
Liberia	December 2002	February 2005
Rwanda	December 2002	March 2003
Somalia	December 2002	Still in force
Vanuatu	December 2002	March 2003
Mauritania	May 2003	Still in force
Algeria	April 2004	April 2005
Central African Republic	April 2004	June 2004
Guinea-Bissau	April 2004	7 May 2006

Notes:
ᵃ In force at the time of writing (October 2006).
ᵇ It appears that no notification of the lifting of the suspension was sent to the parties.
ᶜ Bangladesh was included by accident.

targeted non-parties have all adhered to CITES.[39] Since 1999, seventeen parties have been subject to recommended trade suspensions under the national legislation project, eleven of which have responded and had sanctions lifted. Meanwhile, since 2002, twelve parties have been subject to a recommended trade suspension for failure to submit annual reports, ten of which have responded (one having been targeted by mistake). Suspensions currently in effect for non-reporting (two parties) apply to all CITES trade, while those under the national legislation project (six parties) apply to commercial trade only. (The use of more severe sanctions for non-reporting than under the national legislation project appears to be because the original Decisions introducing such measures were produced by different drafters.) At the time of writing, twenty-seven parties are subject to a species-specific trade suspension under the significant trade review; the

---

[39] Reeve, *Policing International Trade in Endangered Species*, p. 91.

suspensions affect twenty-six species and three genera (some species are subject to suspensions involving more than one range State).[40]

Technical and political missions were introduced to exert pressure on States involved in illegal trade in rhino horn and tiger parts which has driven these species to the brink of extinction. Conducted in the mid-1990s, the missions appear to have helped curb the rhino horn trade (probably because they were backed by increased security to protect rhinos in range States) but seem to have been less effective against the illegal trade in tiger parts. While most parties responded on paper to the mission's recommendations, in practice the illegal trade in tiger parts continued and is still rampant.[41] Technical missions are also being used to assess compliance by selected parties with CITES recommendations on ivory trade controls. The mission team is selected by the Secretariat, not from a roster of independent experts as is the practice under some other MEAs. The most recent mission agreed by the Standing Committee addressed the illegal trade in orangutans in South East Asia.

A formal caution was introduced in 2003 to exert pressure on fifty-seven parties to enact national implementing legislation.[42] It was an interim measure to stave off recommended trade suspensions since so many parties were affected. All but fourteen parties responded by making some legislative progress or by communicating with the Secretariat.[43] Of the fourteen, nine ended up with a trade suspension being recommended for non-compliance.

A warning was also introduced once in 2000 to alert fifty-three parties that they could be subject to a recommended trade suspension for persistent failure to submit annual reports.[44] Six months later, the number of parties still in non-compliance had declined to twenty.[45]

6.4 Effectiveness of the compliance and enforcement mechanisms

It is difficult to comment on the effectiveness of CITES compliance and enforcement mechanisms since there has been little empirical study or

---

[40] A regularly updated table of parties currently subject to a recommendation to suspend trade has recently been published on the CITES website, www.cites.org.

[41] Reeve, *Policing International Trade in Endangered Species*, p. 189.

[42] CITES SC49 Summary Report (Rev. 1) (April 2003).

[43] CITES SC50 Doc. 29, 'National Legislation Project' (March 2004).

[44] CITES Notification to the Parties No. 2000/057 (September 2000).

[45] CITES SC45 Doc. 13.1, 'Late or Non-Submission of Annual Reports' (June 2001).

on-site verification of compliance except in a few cases of serious generalized non-compliance. Nevertheless, it is possible to conclude that the CITES compliance procedures have had effect, and most parties have moved towards compliance, at least on paper. As noted above, issuing a formal caution and warning drew responses from the majority of affected parties. Most of the countries subject to recommended trade suspensions under the national legislation project or for non-reporting have responded and the suspensions have been lifted, though several still have not actually enacted legislation. All parties targeted with trade suspensions for generalized non-compliance, except for the most recent case of Nigeria, have subsequently come into compliance, though not all were subject to on-site verification.

There has been no survey to determine how many parties actually implement the recommendations to suspend trade. Informal reports indicate that some do but not all. In some of the cases of serious generalized non-compliance, countries complained of the economic costs caused by recommended trade suspensions, particularly Italy and Thailand. Italy, interestingly, now has one of the better enforcement systems among CITES parties – inspired by the CITES sanctions that were recommended in 1992 for its laundering of illegally obtained wildlife into the EU. Even if economic costs and a corresponding response cannot be demonstrated, it is apparent that countries dislike being targeted with recommended trade sanctions and generally appear to respond positively, even if they initially object to the measure. The United Arab Emirates is the only exception – it withdrew from CITES after a trade suspension was recommended, but later rejoined. When it was targeted with trade sanctions a second time, it responded positively. It could be argued that, if trade suspensions were binding, they would be more effective. But such a move would need a treaty amendment and in any case would not be approved by parties for whom trade suspensions remain a sensitive subject, even though their use in CITES has increased markedly since 2000.

Progress on the national legislation project has been slow but sure.[46] As of June 2005, the number of CITES-compliant parties with category 1 legislation stood at fifty-nine compared with twenty-nine in 1997, thirty-seven in 2000, forty-five in 2002 and fifty-one in 2004 (see Table 6.2 and Figure 6.2). The use of trade suspensions has been effective. Of the seventeen parties subject to suspension since 1999, 65 per cent have responded

---

[46] Reeve, 'The CITES Treaty and Compliance', p. 13.

Table 6.2   *Progress in the national legislation project (1992–2005)*[a]

Year	Total no. of parties	Category 1[b]		Category 2[c] and 3[d]		Pending[e]		Under review[f]	
		No. of parties	% total	No. of parties	% total	No. of parties	% total	No. of parties	% total
1992	115	15	13	66	57	34	30	–	–
1997	134	29	22	96	72	9	7	–	–
2000	146	37	25	99	68	–	–	10	7
2002	158	45	29	90	57	10	6	13	8
2004	166	51	31	80	48	10	6	25	15
2005	166[g]	59	36	93[h]	56	10	6	4	2

Notes:
[a] Compiled from the following CITES documents on the national legislation project: Doc. 9.24 (Rev.) Annex 1; Doc. 10.31 (Rev.) Annexes 1 and 2; Doc. 11.21.1 Annex 2; CoP12 Doc. 28 Annex 1; CoP13 Doc. 22 Annex 1; SC53 Doc. 31 Annex. This analysis excludes dependent territories.
[b] Legislation believed generally to meet the requirements for CITES implementation.
[c] Legislation believed generally not to meet all the requirements for CITES implementation (i.e. to meet only some of the requirements).
[d] Legislation believed generally not to meet the requirements for CITES implementation.
[e] Pending submission of legislation.
[f] Includes new parties whose legislation is under review and parties whose category is under review.
[g] Parties numbered 167 but Samoa had joined too recently to be included in the figures.
[h] Of the 93 parties in categories 2 and 3 in June 2005, 53% had submitted draft legislation for comment by the Secretariat and 14% had enacted legislation which was under review.

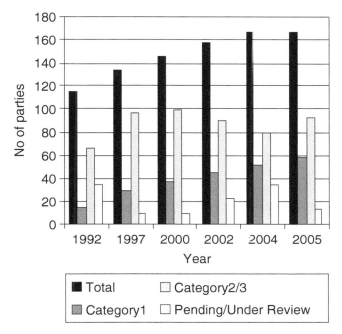

Figure 6.2 Progress in the national legislation project (1992–2005)

and had them lifted (see Table 6.1). Nevertheless, as of August 2005, an unacceptably high number of parties – ninety-three (56 per cent) – still did not have adequate legislation to implement the basic requirements of CITES. However, 14 per cent of the ninety-three had enacted legislation which was under review by the Secretariat and 53 per cent had submitted draft legislation for comment. The number of non-compliant parties is therefore expected to reduce in the near future, though only if pressure is maintained through the threat of sanctions.

Interestingly, CoP13 saw the first backlash against the use of sanctions in the national legislation project. Argentina proposed the deletion of language on using recommended trade suspensions to address non-compliance (language which has been used in CoP Decisions on the national legislation project since 1997). The move was defeated but achieved majority support (a two-thirds majority was needed for it to pass). This move by Argentina reflects the fact that the sanctions-based approach is biting – although suspensions have been recommended against only seventeen parties so far, many more are potentially affected if they fail to demonstrate legislative progress.

The use of sanctions to encourage annual trade reporting has also been effective. At CoP11 in early 2000, a steady decline in the level of trade reporting was noted. In the last four years, however, the threat and use of trade sanctions has notably improved annual reporting. In 1999, prior to the introduction of the new measures, only eighty partial or complete reports had been received, but in 2000 this number rose to 158 and in 2001 it increased again to 179.[47] In its report to CoP13, the Secretariat states that recommended trade suspensions 'have proven useful in obtaining the submission of annual reports'; that they 'complement the ongoing availability of prompt and expert assistance from UNEP–WCMC'; and that 'overall, the level of submission of annual reports is rather high'.[48] It is interesting to note that an improvement in compliance was seen soon after the new measures were approved even though no sanctions were actually recommended until December 2002. Thus the mere threat of sanctions drew a response.

The significant trade review is more difficult to assess. The process is lengthy, so sometimes years can pass before recommendations are made. A 2001 study by the Species Survival Network (SSN) of birds reviewed under the significant trade review programme found quota recommendations exceeded by some parties and some exporting countries excluded from reviews.[49] An evaluation of the significant trade review agreed at CoP13 should shed some light on the effectiveness of the procedure, but results will not be seen for at least four years since the evaluation is not due to start until after CoP14, to be held in 2007. Meanwhile, questions have been raised about the effectiveness of the country-based review since Madagascar failed initially to report adequately on implementation of its action plan, and although the deadline had passed for short-term actions no recommendations for measures were made.

Technical assistance has been effective, particularly in relation to the national legislation project. However, its effectiveness is largely due to the backing provided by the threat of sanctions. Technical assistance alone was not effective in the early days of the national legislation project from 1992 to 1997; parties generally did not seek assistance with preparing implementing legislation until a sanctions-based approach was introduced. In relation to annual reporting, parties were offered technical assistance to

---

[47] CITES CoP12 Doc. 22.1, 'Annual Report' by the Secretariat (November 2002).
[48] CITES CoP13 Doc. 18, 'Regular and Special Reports: Reporting Requirements'.
[49] Ann Michels, 'History of Species Reviewed under Resolution Conf. 8.9 (Rev.): Part I: Aves' (unpublished study, Species Survival Network, 2001).

compile their reports but few took up the offer. A consistent improvement in annual reporting was not seen until a sanctions-based approach was introduced in 2000.

These comments on effectiveness need to be tempered with a recognition that enforcement of CITES at the national level is highly variable and in some countries weak to non-existent. Progress has been made with national implementing legislation, though the situation is far from ideal with a significant number of parties still not possessing adequate legislation. Moreover, parties need only enact legislation complying with four *basic* requirements of the Convention; parties with category 1 legislation may still not comply with all the requirements elaborated in Resolutions and Decisions. Whether CITES legislation is adequately enforced is an entirely different question. In many parties it is not, through lack of political will as much as lack of financial and human resources.

6.5 Dispute resolution

Article XVIII of CITES provides for dispute settlement using the Permanent Court of Arbitration in The Hague. It states:

> 1. Any dispute which may arise between two or more Parties with respect to the interpretation or application of the provisions of the present Convention shall be subject to negotiation between the Parties involved in the dispute.
>
> 2. If the dispute cannot be resolved in accordance with paragraph 1 of this Article, the Parties may, by mutual consent, submit the dispute to arbitration, in particular that of the Permanent Court of Arbitration at The Hague, and the Parties submitting the dispute shall be bound by the arbitral decision.'

These provisions have never been interpreted or expanded on by a CoP Resolution or Decision. The parties involved must consent to the submission of the dispute; thus it is not compulsory. However, parties are bound by the outcome.

The Permanent Court of Arbitration, established by the Hague Conventions of 1899 and 1907,[50] has sponsored the adoption of arbitration rules specifically designed to address needs arising from the arbitration of

---

[50] Philippe Sands and Pierre Klein, *Bowett's Law of International Institutions* (London: Sweet & Maxwell, 2001), p. 348.

disputes relating to the environment and natural resources. These were adopted on 19 June 2001.[51] The Rules provide for the *optional* use of a panel of arbitrators with experience and expertise in environmental or conservation of natural resources law and an indicative list of experts in environmental science. The arbitral panel may be composed of one, three or five persons. The Rules empower the arbitral tribunal to order any interim measures necessary to prevent serious harm to the environment, unless the parties agree otherwise, and provide for arbitration in a shorter period of time than under previous PCA Optional Rules.[52] NGOs play no role in the process and there seems to be no provision for *amicus curiae* briefs.

Article XVIII of CITES has never been invoked. Some CITES parties have voiced objections to recommendations by the Standing Committee for suspensions of trade in CITES-listed species and questioned the legal basis for these, but they have never acted on their objections, other than to respond to the problem of non-compliance in question. Reference to dispute settlement is a last resort in the event a compliance system fails. The multilateral nature of issues dealt with by MEAs renders a bilateral dispute settlement procedure largely irrelevant, particularly where an effective compliance system exists, as is the case with CITES.

6.6 Lessons learned

As one of the earliest MEAs, CITES has developed its compliance control mechanisms largely uninfluenced by other treaty regimes. An exception is the recent attempt to stimulate biennial reporting which was influenced by some of the other MEA regimes where reporting is being redefined as an implementation tool, for example the Ramsar Convention on Wetlands.[53]

The CITES regime does not seem to have had much influence on other treaty regimes with respect to dispute resolution, compliance control or enforcement – for obvious reasons as far as dispute resolution is concerned. With regard to compliance control and enforcement, although CITES does have important lessons to provide, there has been little written about the regime and consequently there is a general lack of awareness. When the

---

[51] The Rules are available at www.pca-cpa.org/EDR/ENRrules.htm.

[52] Philippe Sands, *Principles of International Environmental Law* (Cambridge: Cambridge University Press, 2003), p. 214.

[53] Convention on Wetlands of International Importance Especially as Waterfowl Habitat, Ramsar, 2 February 1971, in force 21 December 1975, 996 UNTS 243 (No. 14583, 1976).

author embarked on an analysis of the CITES compliance and enforcement system in 1998, there was little of consequence in the literature reviewed, apart from one paper by Peter Sand, the first Secretary-General of CITES.[54] Neither was there anything available on the Internet. It was necessary to visit the Secretariat in Geneva to obtain original documentation from CoP and Committee meetings dating back to 1976 and piece together a picture of a regime that had evolved over many years through secondary rules and practice.

However, the CITES experience could be applied to other regimes and should be used as a model more so than currently. Trade sanctions and even the threat of trade sanctions have provoked responses from CITES parties. The national legislation project provides a particularly good example of the effectiveness of technical assistance backed by sanctions; under the threat of trade suspensions parties have been prompted to seek technical assistance. Thus sanctions have indirectly been responsible for capacity-building.

CITES is particularly dependent on a sanctions-based approach because of its lack of resources to support capacity-building. The US$5 million annual budget is shrinking in real terms every year, with cost-cutting measures featuring at every CoP meeting; a shortage of funds is one of the reasons for a reluctance to establish a separate compliance or implementation committee. Other trade-related MEAs, particularly those facing restrictions on funding which limit capacity-building, could benefit most from lessons learned under CITES. The Basel Convention[55] comes to mind, but others include the Biosafety Protocol[56] and the Rotterdam and Stockholm Conventions concerning chemicals.[57] Although concerns have been expressed from time to time (usually by parties faced with trade

---

[54] Peter H. Sand, 'Commodity or Taboo? International Regulation of Trade in Endangered Species', in Helge Ole Bergesen and Georg Parmann (eds.), *Green Globe Yearbook of International Co-operation on Environment and Development 1997* (New York: Oxford University Press, 1997).

[55] Basel Convention on the Control of Transboundary Movements of Hazardous Wastes and their Disposal, Basel, 22 March 1989, in force 5 May 1992, Doc. UNEP/WG.190/4.

[56] Cartagena Protocol on Biosafety to the Convention on Biological Diversity, Montreal, 29 January 2000, in force 11 September 2003, 1760 UNTS 79.

[57] Stockholm Convention on Persistent Organic Pollutants, Stockholm, 22 May 2001, in force 17 May 2004, Depositary notification C.N.531.2001.TREATIES-9€ of 19 June 2001; C.N.1204. 2002.TREATIES-63 of 19 November 2002 (Proposal of corrections to the original text of the Convention (authentic Spanish text)); and C.N.157.2003.TREATIES-6 of 21 February 2003 (Correction of the original text of the Convention (authentic Spanish text)). Rotterdam Convention on the Prior Informed Consent Procedure for Certain Hazardous Chemicals and Pesticides in International Trade, Rotterdam, 10 September 1998, in force 24 February 2004, Doc. UNEP/FAO/PIC/CONF/5.

suspensions) that the use of trade measures under CITES could conflict with obligations under the WTO, none of the affected parties has brought a complaint under the WTO's dispute settlement mechanism. Moreover, an analysis of WTO case law indicates that CITES trade suspensions could be acceptable if they are applied to parties in a non-discriminatory way and if serious good faith efforts have been made to settle the problem by negotiation first.[58]

[58] Reeve, *Policing International Trade in Endangered Species*, p. 311.

7

The Convention on Long-Range Transboundary Air Pollution

TUOMAS KUOKKANEN[*]

7.1 General

In the late 1960s and the 1970s, scientists demonstrated the interrelationship between the long-range transport of air pollutants and the acidification of lakes and forest death in Scandinavia, Central Europe and North America. To describe this phenomenon, the concept of transboundary air pollution was introduced to underscore the fact that air pollutants do not respect national boundaries, and that there was a need for international action.[1]

Intensive diplomatic activities finally led, in 1979, to the conclusion of the Convention on Long-Range Transboundary Air Pollution (the 'LRTAP Convention') under the auspices of the United Nations

---

[*] The views expressed are my own and are not statements of or on behalf of the Implementation Committee. The chapter is based partly on the following articles: Tuomas Kuokkanen, 'Putting Gentle Pressure on Parties: Recent Trends in the Practice of the Implementation Committee under the Convention on Long-Range Transboundary Air Pollution', in Jarna Petman and Jan Klabbers (eds.), *Nordic Cosmopolitanism: Essays in International Law for Martti Koskenniemi* (Leiden and Boston Martinus Nijhoff Publishers, 2003), pp. 315–26; Patrick Széll, Volkert Keizer and Tuomas Kuokkanen, 'Compliance and Consensus', in Johan Sliggers and Willem Kakebeeke (eds.), *Cleaning the Air: 25 Years of the Convention on Long-Range Transboundary Air Pollution* (New York and Geneva: United Nations, 2004), pp. 119–31; and Tuomas Kuokkanen, 'Practice of the Implementation Committee under the Convention on Long-Range Transboundary Air Pollution', in Ulrich Beyerlin, Peter-Tobias Stoll and Rüdiger Wolfrum (eds), *Ensuring Compliance with Multilateral Environmental Agreements: A Dialogue Between Practitioners and Academia* (Leiden: Brill Academic Publishers, 2006), pp. 39–51.

[1] See Lars Björkbom, 'Resolution of Environmental Problems: The Use of Diplomacy', in John Carroll (ed.), *International Environmental Diplomacy: The Management and Resolution of Transfrontier Problems* (Cambridge and New York: Cambridge University Press, 1988), pp. 123–37, at p. 127.

162   INTERNATIONAL ENVIRONMENTAL LAW

Economic Commission for Europe.[2] The Convention was concluded by almost all countries of Western and Eastern Europe and by the United States and Canada. Currently, there are forty-nine parties to the Convention.

The Convention includes general provisions on policies and strategies, research, exchange of information and institutional setting. In order to monitor the deposition and concentration of air pollutants, the Convention integrated the EMEP monitoring programme ('Co-operative Programme for the Monitoring and Evaluation of the Long-Range Transmission of Air Pollutants in Europe') into its framework.[3] Furthermore, the Convention contains provisions that the Executive Secretary of the United Nations Economic Commission for Europe serves as the Secretariat of the Convention.[4]

The Convention does not include specific reduction limits or control measures, but rather provides a framework within which the contracting parties can agree on specific regulations. To this end, the Executive Body[5] was established to serve as the supreme body of the Convention. The Executive Body, composed of the contracting states, is responsible for implementing and developing the Convention and for establishing subsidiary bodies as appropriate. Thus, it functions in a similar way as the conferences or meetings of the parties under other multilateral environmental agreements.

The Convention started to develop dynamically through a close

---

[2] Convention on Long-Range Transboundary Air Pollution, Geneva, 13 November 1979, Doc. E-ECE (XXXIV)-L-18, www.unece.org/env/lrtap/. For background, see e.g. Amy A. Fraenkel, 'The Convention on Long-Range Transboundary Air Pollution: Meeting the Challenge of International Co-operation' (1989) 30 *Harvard International Law Journal* 447–76. The Executive Body of the Convention held a special event on 1 December 2004 to celebrate the 25th anniversary of the Convention. See www.unece.org/env/lrtap/. See also Sliggers and Kakebeeke (eds.), *Cleaning the Air*.

[3] See Toni Schneider and Jürgen Schneider, 'EMEP – Backbone of the Convention', in Sliggers and Kakebeeke (eds.), *Cleaning the Air*, pp. 31–44.

[4] The secretariat has played an important role in the further development of the co-operation under the Convention. See Lars Nordberg, Keith Bull, Radovan Chrast, Oddmund Graham, Andrzej Jagusiewicz, Peter H. Sand, Arne Tollan and Henning Wuester, 'The Role of the Secretariat: Building the Protocol Tree', in Sliggers and Kakebeeke (eds.), *Cleaning the Air*, pp. 97–117.

[5] See art. 10(1) ('The representatives of the Contracting Parties shall, within the framework for the Senior Advisers to ECE Governments on Environmental Problems, constitute the Executive Body of the present Convention and shall meet at least annually in that capacity.').

co-operation between policy-makers and scientists. Instead of amending the Convention itself, the parties decided to establish separate agreements, called protocols, relating to the Convention. So far, the parties have adopted eight specific protocols to further implement the Convention.

As a first step, the parties agreed in 1984 on long-term financing for the EMEP Programme.[6] Thereafter, in 1985, they agreed to reduce sulphur emissions by 30 per cent,[7] and, in 1988, to put a freeze on nitrogen emissions.[8] In 1991, they adopted a protocol on the control of volatile organic compounds (VOCs).[9] In consequence of increased scientific knowledge, a new protocol on further reduction of sulphur emissions was adopted in 1994.[10] Four years later, two more protocols were adopted, one on heavy metals[11] and the other on persistent organic compounds.[12] The most recent protocol, on the abatement of acidification, eutrophication and ground-level ozone, was adopted in 1999.[13]

In 1997, the Executive Body established an Implementation Committee

---

[6] Protocol to the 1979 Convention on Long-Range Transboundary Air Pollution on Long-Term Financing of the Co-operative Programme for Monitoring and Evaluation of the Long-Range Transmission of Air Pollutants in Europe (EMEP), Geneva, 28 September 1984, Doc. EB.AIR-A.C.1–4, Annex, and EB.AIR-CRP.1-Add.4, www.unece.org/env/lrtap/.

[7] Protocol to the 1979 Convention on Long-Range Transboundary Air Pollution on the Reduction of Sulphur Emissions or their Transboundary Fluxes by at Least 30 Per Cent, Helsinki, 8 July 1985, 1480 UNTS 215, www.unece.org/env/lrtap/.

[8] Protocol to the 1979 Convention on Long-Range Transboundary Air Pollution Concerning the Control of Emissions of Nitrogen Oxides or their Transboundary Fluxes, Sofia, 31 October 1988. Depositary notification C.N.252.1988.TREATIES-1 of 6 December 1988, www.unece.org/env/lrtap/.

[9] Protocol to the 1979 Convention on Long-Range Transboundary Air Pollution on the Control of Emissions of Volatile Organic Compounds and their Transboundary Fluxes, Geneva, 18 November 1991, Doc. ECE-EB.AIR-30, www.unece.org/env/lrtap/.

[10] Protocol to the 1979 Convention on Long-Range Transboundary Air Pollution on Further Reduction of Sulphur Emissions, Oslo, 14 June 1994, Doc. EB.AIR-R.84. For discussion, see R. R. Churchill, G. Kütting and L. M. Warren, 'The 1994 UN ECE Sulphur Protocol' (1995) 7 *Journal of Environmental Law* 169–97.

[11] 1998 Protocol to the 1979 Convention on Long-Range Transboundary Air Pollution on Heavy Metals, Aarhus, 24 June 1998, Doc. EB.AIR-1998–1, www.unece.org/env/lrtap/.

[12] 1998 Protocol to the 1979 Convention on Long-Range Transboundary Air Pollution on Persistent Organic Pollutants, Aarhus, 24 June 1998, Doc. EB.AIR-1998–2, www.unece.org/env/lrtap/.

[13] 1998 Protocol to the 1979 Convention on Long-Range Transboundary Air Pollution to Abate Acidification, Eutrophication and Ground-Level Ozone, Gothenburg, 30 November 1999, Doc. EB.AIR-1999–1, www.unece.org/env/lrtap/. The new protocol is based on the multi-pollutant and multi-effect critical load approaches.

to review compliance[14] with all the protocols to the Convention.[15] It developed the Committee's structure and functions in light of experience already gained in operating such a committee under the Montreal Protocol and in furtherance of its own decision on compliance taken three years earlier when adopting the 1994 Sulphur Protocol. The Committee has three main functions: to review compliance by parties with their reporting obligations, to consider any submission or referral and to prepare in-depth reviews of compliance with specified obligations in individual protocols. The non-compliance procedure can be triggered by means of submissions by parties or referrals by the secretariat. A submission may be brought either by one or more parties against another party or by a party with respect to itself. If the secretariat becomes aware of a case of possible non-compliance, it may bring the matter to the attention of the Committee by means of a referral. The mandate of the Committee is contained in the Annex to this chapter.

[14] For discussion on compliance in general, see e.g. Jutta Brunnée and Stephen J. Toope, 'Persuasion and Enforcement: Explaining Compliance with International Law' (2002) 13 *Finnish Yearbook of International Law* 272–95; Abram Chayes and Antonia Handler Chayes, *The New Sovereignty: Compliance with International Regulatory Agreements* (Cambridge, MA: Harvard University Press, 1995); D. G. Victor, K. Raustiala and E. B. Skolnikoff (eds.), *The Implementation and Effectiveness of International Environmental Commitments: Theory and Practice* (Cambridge, MA: MIT Press, 1998); Patrick Széll, 'Introduction to the Discussion on Compliance', in Marko Berglund (ed.), *International Environmental Law-Making and Diplomacy Review 2004* (Joensuu: UNEP and University of Joensuu, 2005), pp. 117–24; Durwood Zaelke, Donald Kaniaru and Eva Kruûíková (eds.), *Making Law Work: Environmental Compliance and Sustainable Development*, vols. 1–2 (London: Cameron May Ltd, 2005); U. Beyerlin, P. T. Stoll and R. Wolfrum (eds.), *Ensuring Compliance with Multilateral Environmental Agreements: A Dialogue Between Practitioners and Academia* (Leiden: Brill Academic Publishers, 2006).

[15] Decision 1997/2 Concerning the Implementation Committee, Its Structure and Functions and Procedures for Review of Compliance. The Executive Body amended the Committee's mandate in 2001 (see Report of the 19th session, ECE/EB.AIR/75, Annex V). Executive Body Decision 1997/2, as amended in 2001, is annexed to this chapter. Article 3(3) of the 1991 VOC Protocol and art. 7 of the 1994 Sulphur Protocol contained a provision on the establishment of a compliance mechanism. However, instead of setting up individual compliance regimes for each protocol, the Executive Body decided to establish one single mechanism to be applied to all protocols. By separate decisions (1997/3 and 1998/3), the parties to the 1991 VOC and the 1994 Sulphur Protocol decided to apply the same mechanism for the purposes of those protocols. In Decision 1998/3, the Executive Body also decided that any amendment to Decision 1997/2 and any other decision of the Executive Body pertaining to the Implementation Committee or its procedures shall be made by consensus between the parties to the Convention. All the subsequent protocols adopted after the establishment of the Implementation Committee contain a provision stating that the compliance review shall be carried out in accordance with the terms of Decision 1997/2 and any amendments thereto. See art. 11 of the 1998 POPs Protocol; art. 8 of the 1998 Heavy Metals Protocol; and art. 9 of the 1999 Gothenburg Protocol.

7.2 Dispute resolution

The LRTAP Convention contains the following dispute settlement clause:

> If a dispute arises between two or more Contracting Parties to the present Convention as to the interpretation or application of the Convention, they shall seek a solution by negotiation or by any other method of dispute settlement acceptable to the parties to the dispute.[16]

A similar dispute settlement clause is included in the 1984 EMEP Protocol,[17] the 1985 Sulphur Protocol,[18] the 1988 Nitrogen Oxides Protocol[19] and the 1991 VOC Protocol.[20] The subsequent protocols contain more specific provisions on dispute settlement.[21] In addition, they provide a compulsory conciliation procedure[22] unless both sides to a dispute have accepted arbitration or submission of the dispute to the International Court of Justice as a compulsory means of dispute settlement.

Despite the fact that the Convention and individual protocols contain dispute settlement clauses, the parties nevertheless recognized a need for a separate compliance mechanism dealing with compliance issues under the protocols. This was due to the fact that it was considered unlikely that a dispute procedure would be applied in relation to non-compliance with the provisions of the individual protocols. The difficulty of establishing environmental impact on one particular party was another reason for having a regime beyond bilateral dispute settlement. Moreover, it was recognized that a compliance mechanism would serve the interests of the parties in general while a dispute settlement procedure appears to be inherently bilateral in nature.[23]

To date, none of the arrangements for dispute settlement has been used under the Convention or under its protocols.

---

[16] See art. 13 of the LRTAP Convention.   [17] See art. 7 of the 1984 EMEP Protocol.

[18] See art. 8 of the 1985 Sulphur Protocol.

[19] See art. 12 of the 1988 Nitrogen Oxides Protocol.   [20] See art. 9 of the VOC Protocol.

[21] See art. 9 of the 1994 Sulphur Protocol; art. 12 of the 1998 POPs Protocol; art. 11 of the 1998 Heavy Metals Protocol; and art. 11 of the 1999 Gothenburg Protocol.

[22] See art. 9(5) of the 1994 Sulphur Protocol; art. 12(5) of the 1998 POPs Protocol; art. 11(5) of the 1998 Heavy Metals Protocol; and art. 11(5) of the Gothenburg Protocol.

[23] See e.g. a background document submitted by the United Kingdom in the Working Group on Environmental Impact Assessment, MP.EIA/WG.1/1997/7 (28 July 1999), para. 4.

166 INTERNATIONAL ENVIRONMENTAL LAW

7.3 Compliance control

7.3.1 Institutional setting

The Implementation Committee, established by the Executive Body in 1997, consists of nine parties to the Convention. Each member of the Committee must, according to the mandate, be a party to at least one protocol. The independence, personal expertise and continuity of participation of the individual members of the Committee are all seen as important for the success of Committee's work, although, formally speaking, the members represent the parties from which they come.

According to its mandate, the Committee may request an evaluation of the quality of data reported by a party by a relevant technical body under the Executive Body and/or by an expert nominated by the Bureau of the Executive Body before it adopts a report or recommendation on a submission or referral concerning the party.[24] So far, this option has not been used.

The Implementation Committee makes recommendations to the Executive Body – the entity to which it is answerable. In accordance with paragraph 9 of its mandate, the Committee is required to report on its activities at least once a year to the Executive Body and to make such recommendations as it considers appropriate.

The Implementation Committee, and subsequently the Executive Body, has in several cases concluded that there has been non-compliance with either reporting or substantive obligations. For instance, the Executive Body has in a number of decisions concluded, on the recommendation of the Implementation Committee, that a party has failed to fulfil its obligation to take effective measures to reduce its annual emissions as required by the VOC Protocol or by the Nitrogen Oxides Protocol (see Table 7.1 below).

7.3.2 Review of compliance by the parties with the reporting obligations

Under its mandate, the Implementation Committee periodically reviews compliance by the parties with the reporting requirements of the protocols. Parties are required to report two types of information: information on strategies and policies that serve as a means of reducing emissions, and information on emissions data.

---

[24] Para. 3(c) of the mandate, note 16 above.

With regard to information on strategies and policies, the Committee reviews both the timeliness and completeness of reporting. While most parties eventually submit complete reports, a number have failed to respect the deadlines. The quality of national reporting has improved markedly over the years, though parties' reporting has, and continues to be, uneven in length, depth and content.

To achieve its goal, the Committee has used various innovative means to put gradually increasing pressure on parties to comply with their reporting obligations relating to emissions data and information on strategies and policies. Such means have ranged from merely noting the non-compliance of a party in its report to advising the Executive Body to urge the head of delegation of the party, together with an expert familiar with the data that should be reported, to visit the secretariat to discuss how and when the material can be presented.

The completeness of emissions data reporting has improved significantly since the Implementation Committee began to review it as a matter of course each year. For example, the level of emissions data reported for the 1985 Sulphur Protocol was 99 per cent in 2003 while it had been 86 per cent in 1998. Similarly, the level reported for the 1988 Nitrogen Oxides Protocol was 99 per cent in 2003 while in 1998 it had been 82 per cent. Parties have clearly made a great effort to fulfil their reporting obligations because of the scrutiny carried out by the Committee and the related decisions of the Executive Body.[25] But, despite such improvements, the situation is not yet entirely satisfactory and the Committee has found it necessary constantly to remind parties of the importance of complying fully with their reporting obligations, in particular with their obligations to report on strategies and policies.

7.3.3 Consideration of submissions by parties and referrals by the secretariat

By the end of 2005, the Implementation Committee had considered a total of ten individual submissions and referrals relating to compliance by individual parties with substantive obligations. Five were self-submissions and five were referrals by the secretariat (see Table 7.1).

---

[25] E.g. Executive Body Decisions 2001/4, 2002/9 and 2003/9.

168 INTERNATIONAL ENVIRONMENTAL LAW

Table 7.1 *Submissions and referrals received by the Implementation Committee*

Party	Protocol	Obligation	Submission/ referral	IC/EB action
Slovenia	1994 Sulphur	Article 2(5)(b), limit value	Self-submission	• EB Decision 2000/1 • EB Decision 2004/5
Norway	1991 VOC	Article 2.2, emission reduction	Self-submission	• EB Decision 2001/1 • Follow-up Decisions 2002/2, 2003/1, 2004/6 and 2005/2
Finland	1991 VOC	Article 2.2, emission reduction	Self-submission	• EB Decision 2001/2 • Follow-up Decision 2002/3 • Closed pursuant to Decision 2003/2 (Finland achieved compliance)
Italy	1991 VOC	Article 2.2, emission reduction	Self-submission	• EB Decision 2001/3 • Follow-up Decisions 2002/4 and 2003/3 • Closed pursuant to Decision 2005/3 (Italy achieved compliance)
Sweden	1991 VOC	Article 2.2, emission reduction	Self-submission	• EB Decision 2002/5 • Closed pursuant to Decision 2003/4 (Sweden in compliance all along)

Table 7.1 (*cont.*)

Party	Protocol	Obligation	Submission/ referral	IC/EB action
Greece	1988 NO_x	Article 2.2, emission reduction	Secretariat referral	• EB Decision 2002/6 • Follow-up Decisions 2003/5, 2004/7 and 2005/4
Ireland	1988 NO_x	Article 2.2, emission reduction	Secretariat referral	• EB Decision 2002/7 • Follow-up Decisions 2003/6 and 2004/8 • Closed pursuant to Decision 2005/5 (Ireland achieved compliance)
Spain	1988 NO_x	Article 2.2, emission reduction	Secretariat referral	• EB Decision 2002/8 • Follow-up Decisions 2003/7, 2004/9 and 2005/6
Luxembourg	1991 VOC	Article 2.2, emission reduction	Secretariat referral	• Closed pursuant to Decision 2004/11 (Luxembourg in compliance all along)
Spain	1991 VOC	Article 2.2, emission reduction	Secretariat referral	• EB Decision 2003/8 • Follow-up Decisions 2004/10 and 2005/7

In eight of the ten cases, the Committee, and subsequently the Executive Body, concluded that there had been non-compliance, namely, the cases of Norway, Finland, Italy, Greece, Ireland, Spain (twice) and Slovenia. The two exceptions were Sweden and Luxembourg. With regard to Sweden's submission, it became apparent in 2003 – as a result of a reappraisal of its VOC emissions data and the method of calculation – that Sweden had in fact been in compliance with the Protocol from the outset. A similar conclusion was reached in the case of Luxembourg in 2004. None of the submissions to date has involved one party commencing the compliance procedure against another party. The parties involved have not questioned the finding of non-compliance but rather have sought to explain the background and the factors that led to their breaches.

Due process requirements are taken into account in the consideration of submissions and referrals. Under the mandate of the Committee, a party in respect of which a submission or referral is made is entitled to participate in the consideration by the Committee of that submission or referral, but may not take part in the preparation and adoption of any report or recommendations.[26] Moreover, the Committee has in the case of all submissions and referrals striven to establish an active and meaningful dialogue with the party concerned.

In most of the ten cases, the parties have identified one or more sectors that have been particularly problematic for them. For instance, the main reason for the failure by Norway to reduce its VOC emissions in accordance with the 1991 VOC Protocol was the technical difficulty of controlling emissions of VOCs in the offshore oil sector (which is responsible for a large share of Norway's emissions) and the consequent delay in developing the necessary technologies to control such emissions. In Ireland, the extraordinary economic growth in the 1990s caused an unexpectedly large increase in its VOC emissions. In addition, so-called 'fuel tourism' between Northern Ireland and the Republic of Ireland increased Ireland's emissions. In Finland, emission reductions in the road transport sector – its largest source of VOC emissions – had fallen below expectations due to the economic recession in the beginning of the 1990s. As a consequence, the renewal of its vehicle fleet was slower than anticipated. The mobile source sector was one of the principal causes of Italy's, Greece's and Spain's difficulties as well. One problem that has been common to many of the referrals and submissions has been the uncertainty and/or inaccuracy of the national data.

The Implementation Committee has first considered the background to the submissions and referrals and then the pertinent provisions of the Protocol in question. It has then determined whether the party concerned has failed to comply with its obligations. Finally, it has produced a

---

[26] Para. 8 of the mandate.

recommendation to the Executive Body. To date, the Executive Body has adopted all the recommendations presented to it by the Committee.

One can identify three main elements in the recommendations of the Committee and the related decisions of the Executive Body in those cases where non-compliance has been established. First, there has been a conclusion of non-compliance. Secondly, the party concerned has been urged to fulfil its obligations as soon as possible. Thirdly, the party has been requested to provide a periodic progress report to the Committee. Depending on the circumstances, the Committee and Executive Body have used different nuances of language in their reports. For instance, their recommendations 'express disappointment', 'note with concern', 'remain concerned', 'urge' or 'strongly urge' in order gradually to increase the pressure on parties in breach.

Regarding the third of these elements, each party found in breach is called on to report by a specified date on the steps it has taken to achieve compliance, to set out a timetable that specifies the year by which it expects to be in compliance, to list the specific measures taken, or scheduled to be taken, to fulfil its emission-reduction obligations under the protocol and to set out the projected effects of each of these measures up to and including the year of compliance. The purpose of such requirements is to place pressure on the parties in question to bring about full compliance as quickly as possible. The Committee has placed a heavy emphasis on the preparation of timetables and on offering practical suggestions to accelerate emission reductions. Each year it has reviewed the steps taken by those parties to which Executive Body decisions have been addressed and, as necessary, made recommendations for follow-up decisions by the Executive Body until the parties concerned have achieved compliance. At that stage, the Executive Body decides that there is no reason for the Implementation Committee to continue to review the particular submission or referral.

To date,[27] of the ten parties in respect of which individual proceedings have been commenced, the Executive Body has decided in three instances to close the proceedings. While Finland, Italy and Ireland achieved compliance,[28] in the cases of Sweden and Luxembourg it was eventually established that they had been in compliance all along.[29] With regard to other pending cases, it is

---

[27] November 2005. [28] Executive Body Decisions 2003/2, 2005/3 and 2005/5.
[29] Executive Body Decisions 2003/4 and 2004/11.

172   INTERNATIONAL ENVIRONMENTAL LAW

envisaged that Slovenia and Norway will achieve compliance quite soon, while the two Spanish cases and the Greek case will continue for several years.[30]

7.3.4 In-depth reviews

In accordance with its mandate and at the request of the Executive Body, the Implementation Committee regularly prepares reports on parties' compliance with the principal obligations in a given protocol. The aim has been to review a different protocol every one or two years.

So far, the Committee has conducted four in-depth reviews: on the 1985 Sulphur Protocol, the 1988 Nitrogen Oxides Protocol, the 1991 VOC Protocol and the 1994 Sulphur Protocol. Typical of the conclusions it has reached was the one in 2001 with regard to the 1991 VOC Protocol where it noted with regret that as many as one-third of the parties to that protocol were not in compliance, and that this was in stark contrast to the 1985 Sulphur Protocol and 1988 Nitrogen Oxides Protocol where compliance had been achieved by almost all parties.

The difference between such in-depth reviews and the Committee's consideration of submissions and referrals is that in-depth reviews are collective in nature and are principally concerned with the overall effectiveness of the protocol under scrutiny, while referrals and submissions are concerned with the performance of individual parties in respect of a particular protocol obligation. This said, in-depth reviews have provided raw material for triggering referrals by the secretariat. The Committee has stated that, even though it may become aware of an instance of non-compliance while carrying out in-depth reviews, due process dictates that the Executive Body should not take specific action with respect to it unless and until the Committee has properly and individually reviewed the matter, including listening to any arguments that the party concerned might wish to make. The Executive Body may, however, take general measures as a consequence of the findings of an in-depth review to promote and improve implementation by the parties to a particular protocol.

7.4 Enforcement

According to paragraph 11 of the mandate of the Implementation Committee, the parties to the protocol concerned, meeting within the

[30] The Eighth Report of the Implementation Committee, EB.AIR/2005/3, 13 September 2005, paras. 15–20 and 24–36.

Executive Body, may, upon consideration of a report and any recommendations of the Committee, decide upon measures of a non-discriminatory nature to bring about full compliance with the protocol in question, including measures to assist a party to enter into compliance. Such decisions must be taken by consensus. The decisions taken by the Executive Body so far have been described above.

In its seventh report, the Implementation Committee discussed possible additional compliance-related measures.[31] Having looked first to the underlying treaties and Decision 1997/2 establishing the compliance review procedure, the Committee noted that the decision was apparently 'drafted with the aim of walking a fine line between the creation of a mechanism that would promote compliance and the avoidance of compliance-related measures that are not authorized by the treaties in question'.[32] The Committee was of the view that additional measures should be applied case by case, taking into account relevant legal, political and practical factors as well as the need to avoid discrimination among parties in similar situations. Furthermore, the Committee considered that measures might involve increasing the publicity, engaging another forum within UNECE and promoting the provision of technical assistance.[33] So far, these kind of additional measures have not been applied.

7.5 Overall evaluation

In light of the above, one may conclude that the operation of the Implementation Committee has brought added value to the management of the Convention. Even though the Committee and Executive Body have only limited powers, they have managed, through the application of innovative means, to put gentle, but persistent, pressure on parties that are in breach. Thereby, it has sent a clear message to all parties about the need to take their obligations seriously.

The completeness and timeliness of emissions data reporting have undoubtedly improved since the Committee started regularly examining parties' compliance with their reporting obligations. The Committee's workload in reviewing individual submissions and referrals has steadily increased and, although it has been difficult at times to get parties in breach

---

[31] The Seventh Report of the Implementation Committee, EB.AIR/2004/6/Add.1, 15 September 2004, paras. 42–56.   [32] *Ibid.*, para. 54.   [33] *Ibid.*, para. 56.

174   INTERNATIONAL ENVIRONMENTAL LAW

to accelerate their schedules for achieving compliance as much as the Committee and the Executive Body would wish, the pressure they have applied has achieved positive results.

So far, no party has challenged the recommendations of the Committee or the way in which it has gone about its work. On the contrary, they have been very supportive of the activities of the Committee and, for the most part, have co-operated fully and constructively with its requests, even when they have been criticized in its recommendations. Most have been ready – indeed keen – to explain the difficulties they have experienced in trying to fulfil their obligations and, in its turn, the Committee has always sought to offer practical suggestions that parties might follow in order to facilitate and accelerate full compliance. True to the spirit and intention of the parties to the Convention when establishing the implementation process in 1997, the Committee has at all times operated on the principle that a co-operative and facilitative approach towards those in breach of their protocol commitments is more likely than a confrontational approach to produce positive results for the Convention and for the environment.

The establishment of the Implementation Committee does not mean that the traditional principles and procedures of international law for breach of treaty would not apply any more in the context of the LRTAP Convention. Rather, the operation of the compliance mechanism complements these traditional means. As to the characteristics of the traditional and new approaches, one may note both similarities and differences. First, the non-compliance procedure has moved beyond a traditional dispute settlement process to a more managerial type of mechanism that serves general interests as opposed to bilateral relations. Secondly, a declaration of non-compliance is comparable to the traditional determination of breach of treaty. However, because the non-compliance procedure is merely quasi-judicial in nature and operates without prejudice to dispute settlement, different terminology has been deliberately used to draw a distinction between it and a judicial determination. Thirdly, one may compare the traditional duty to make reparation which must, as far as possible, restore the *status quo ante*, to the approach by the Implementation Committee and the Executive Body to urge a party concerned to bring about full compliance as soon as possible and to take the measures necessary to that end. Fourthly, by being deliberately non-confrontational in character, the non-compliance process is calculated not to aggravate or alienate parties that are in non-compliance with their treaty commitments but rather to ease or cajole them back into compliance.

Annex: Structure and Functions of the Implementation Committee and Procedures for Review of Compliance

Structure

1. The Committee shall consist of nine Parties to the Convention; each member of the Committee shall be Party to at least one protocol. The Executive Body shall elect Parties for terms of two years. Outgoing Parties may be re-elected for one consecutive term, unless in a given case the Executive Body decides otherwise. The Committee shall elect its own Chairman and Vice-Chairman.

Meetings

2. The Committee shall, unless it decides otherwise, meet twice a year. The secretariat shall arrange for and service its meetings.

Functions of the Committee

3. The Committee shall:

(a) Review periodically compliance by the Parties with the reporting requirements of the protocols;

(b) Consider any submission or referral made in accordance with paragraphs 4 and 5 below with a view to securing a constructive solution;

(c) Where it deems it necessary, be satisfied, before it adopts a report or recommendation on such a submission or referral, that the quality of data reported by a Party has been evaluated by a relevant technical body under the Executive Body and/or, where appropriate, by an expert nominated by the Bureau of the Executive Body; and

(d) Prepare, at the request of the Executive Body, and based on any relevant experience acquired in the performance of its functions under subparagraphs (a), (b) and (c) above, a report on compliance with or implementation of specified obligations in an individual protocol.

Submissions by Parties

4. A submission may be brought before the Committee by:

176   INTERNATIONAL ENVIRONMENTAL LAW

(a) One or more Parties to a protocol that have reservations about another Party's compliance with its obligations under that instrument. Such a submission shall be addressed in writing to the secretariat and supported by corroborating information. The secretariat shall, within two weeks of receiving a submission, send a copy of it to the Party whose compliance is at issue. Any reply and information in support thereof shall be submitted to the secretariat and to the Parties involved within three months or such longer period as the circumstances of a particular case may require. The secretariat shall transmit the submission and the reply, as well as all corroborating and supporting information, to the Committee, which shall consider the matter as soon as practicable; or

(b) A Party that concludes that, despite its best endeavours, it is or will be unable to comply fully with its obligations under a protocol. Such a submission shall be addressed in writing to the secretariat and explain, in particular, the specific circumstances that the Party considers to be the cause of its non-compliance. The secretariat shall transmit the submission to the Committee, which shall consider it as soon as practicable.

Referrals by the secretariat

5. Where the secretariat, in particular upon reviewing the reports submitted in accordance with a protocol's reporting requirements, becomes aware of possible non-compliance by a Party with its obligations, it may request the Party concerned to furnish necessary information about the matter. If there is no response or the matter is not resolved within three months or such longer period as the circumstances of the matter may require, the secretariat shall bring the matter to the attention of the Committee.

Information gathering

6. To assist the performance of its functions under paragraph 3 above, the Committee may:

(a) Request further information on matters under its consideration, through the secretariat;

(b) Undertake, at the invitation of the Party concerned, information gathering in the territory of that Party; and

(c) Consider any information forwarded by the secretariat concerning compliance with the protocols.

7. The Committee shall ensure the confidentiality of any information that has been provided to it in confidence.

Entitlement to participate

8. A Party in respect of which a submission or referral is made shall be entitled to participate in the consideration by the Committee of that submission or referral, but shall not take part in the preparation and adoption of any report or recommendations of the Committee in accordance with paragraph 9 below.

Committee report to the Executive Body

9. The Committee shall report at least once a year on its activities to the Executive Body and make such recommendations as it considers appropriate, taking into account the circumstances of the matter, regarding compliance with the protocols. Each report shall be finalized by the Committee no later than ten weeks in advance of the session of the Executive Body at which it is to be considered.

Competence of Committee members

10. Only those Committee members that are Parties to the protocol in respect of which compliance procedures in accordance with paragraphs 3, 6, 7 and 9 above are being undertaken may participate in those procedures. If as a result of the operation of this paragraph the size of the Committee is reduced to five members or less, the Committee shall forthwith refer the matter in question to the Executive Body.

Consideration by the Executive Body

11. The Parties to the protocol concerned, meeting within the Executive Body, may, upon consideration of a report and any recommendations of the Committee, decide upon measures of a non-discriminatory nature to bring about full compliance with the protocol in question, including measures to assist a Party's compliance. Any such decision shall be taken by consensus.

Relationship to settlement of disputes

12. Application of the present compliance procedures shall be without prejudice to the settlement of disputes provisions of the protocols.

8

The Convention on Access to Information, Public Participation in Decision-Making and Access to Justice in Environmental Matters (Aarhus Convention)

VEIT KOESTER*

8.1 Introduction

The Convention on Access to Information, Public Participation in Decision-Making and Access to Justice in Environmental Matters (the 'Aarhus Convention')[1] was adopted at the Fourth Ministerial 'Environment

---

* Any opinions expressed in this chapter are those of the author in his personal capacity. The author would like to thank Cesare Pitea, PhD candidate in International Law, University of Milan, for his comments and suggestions which provided invaluable help. Any errors or omissions are of course the sole responsibility of the author.

[1] 2161 UNTS 447. The Convention text can be accessed on the Convention's website, www.unece.org/env/pp/. For an analysis of the Aarhus Convention's compliance mechanism, see V. Koester, 'Compliance Review under the Aarhus Convention: A Rather Unique Compliance Mechanism' (2005) 2 *Journal for European Environmental and Planning Law* 31–44; and V. Koester, 'The Compliance Committee of the Aarhus Convention: An Overview of Procedures and Jurisprudence' (2007) 37 *Environmental Policy and Law* (forthcoming). On the Aarhus Convention in general as well as on human rights and the environment, see, *inter alia*, P. Birnie and A. Boyle, *International Law and the Environment* (Oxford: Oxford University Press, 2nd edn, 2002), pp. 262 and 252; P. Sands, *Principles of International Environmental Law* (Cambridge: Cambridge University Press, 2nd edn, 2003), pp. 209 and 294; K. Brady, 'New Convention on Access to Information and Public Participation in Environmental Matters' (1998) 28 *Environmental Policy and Law* 69–75; M. Fitzmaurice, 'Public Participation in the North American Agreement on Environmental Co-operation' (2003) 52 *International and Comparative Law Quarterly* 333–68, at 340; S. Stec and S. Casey-Lefkowitz, *The Aarhus Convention: An Implementation Guide* (New York and Geneva: United Nations, 2000); L. R. Rodriguez-Rivera, 'Is the Human Right to Environment Recognized under International Law? It Depends on the Source' (2001) 12 *Colorado Journal of International Environmental Law and Policy* 1–45; N. J. Robinson, 'Enforcing Environmental Norms: Diplomatic and Judicial Approaches' (2003) 26 *Hastings International and Comparative Law Review* 387–415, at 409; B. E. Hill, S. Wolfson and N. Targ, 'Human Rights and the Environment: A Synopsis and Some Predictions' (2004) 16 *Georgetown International Environmental Law Review* 359–400; and M. Pallemaerts, 'The Aarhus Convention on Access to Information, Participation in Decision-Making and Access to Justice in Environmental Matters: A Model for Engaging the Disenfranchised in Decision-Making Through the

for Europe' Conference in Aarhus, Denmark, on 25 June 1998, and signed by thirty-five countries and the EC. The Russian Federation, as well as Canada and the USA (which are members of the United Nations Economic Commission for Europe (UN/ECE)) are among the non-signatory States that have not ratified or otherwise acceded to the Convention at a later stage. The Aarhus Convention entered into force on 30 October 2001. The first Meeting of the Parties (MoP) was held in Lucca, Italy, in October 2002, and

Institutionalization of Procedural Rights?', in J. Green (ed.), *Engaging the Disenfranchised: Developing Countries and Civil Society in Sustainable Development Governance* (Tokyo and New York: United Nations University Press, 2005), which also traces the origin and history of the Convention. On the Convention and NGOs, see C. Pitea, 'NGOs in Non-Compliance Mechanisms under Environmental Agreements: From Tolerance to Recognition?', in T. Treves, M. Frigessi di Rattalma, A. Tanzi, A. Fodella, C. Pitea and C. Ragni (eds.), *Civil Society, International Tribunals and Compliance Bodies* (The Hague: TMC Asser Press, 2004), pp. 205–24 (which, in note 1, contains references to the recognition of NGOs, in general, as subjects of international law and also, in Part 6 of its Annex, contains an extremely useful list of compliance mechanisms; the list includes very detailed references to all relevant documents and also includes compliance mechanisms under negotiations); J. Wates, 'NGOs and the Aarhus Convention', in T. Treves, M. Frigessi di Rattalma, A. Tanzi, A. Fodella, C. Pitea and C. Ragni (eds.), *Civil Society, International Tribunals and Compliance Bodies* (The Hague: TMC Asser Press, 2004), pp. 167–85; and J. Wates, 'The Aarhus Convention: A Driving Force for Environmental Democracy' (2005) 2 *Journal for European Environmental and Planning Law* 2–11. On the Convention in a human rights perspective, see V. Koester, 'Aarhus-konventionen om "borgerlige rettigheder" paa miljoeomraadet' ('The Aarhus Convention on "Civil Rights" in the Field of Environment') (1999) *Juristen* (Copenhagen) 87–102; M. Pallemaerts, 'Human Rights and Environmental Protection', in M. Déjeant-Pons and M. Pallemaerts (eds.), *Human Rights to the Environment* (Strasbourg: Council of Europe Publishing, 2002), pp. 11–21; and Y. Lador, 'The Challenges of Human Environmental Rights', in *Human Rights and the Environment: Proceedings of a Geneva Environment Roundtable* (Geneva: UNEP for the Geneva Environment Network, 2004), pp. 7–13. On environmental human rights as procedural rights, see A. Boyle, 'The Role of International Human Rights Law in the Protection of the Environment', in A. Boyle and M. Anderson (eds.), *Human Rights Approaches to Environmental Protection* (Oxford: Clarendon, 1997), pp. 43 *et seq.*; J. Ebbesson, 'The Notion of Public Participation in International Environmental Law' (1997) 8 *Yearbook of International Environmental Law* 51; M. Déjeant-Pons, 'Human Rights to Environmental Procedural Rights', in M. Déjeant-Pons and M. Pallemaerts, *Human Rights to the Environment* (Strasbourg: Council of Europe Publishing, 2002), pp. 23–46; A. Kiss, 'Environmental Information and Public Participation in Decision-Making', in A. Kiss, D. Shelton and K. Ishibashi (eds.), *Economic Globalization and Compliance with International Environmental Agreements* (London: Kluwer Law International, 2003), pp. 193–209; M. Pallemaerts, 'Proceduralizing Environmental Rights: The Aarhus Convention on Access to Information, Public Participation in Decision-Making and Access to Justice in Environmental Matter in a Human Rights Context', in *Human Rights and the Environment: Proceedings of a Geneva Environment Roundtable* (Geneva: UNEP for the Geneva Environment Network, 2004), pp. 14–22; and Alfred Rest, 'Access to Justice in International Environmental Law for Individuals and NGOs: Efficacious Enforcement by the Permanent Court of Arbitration' (2004) 1 *Macquarie Journal of International and Comparative Law* 1–28.

the second MoP in Almaty, Kazakhstan, in May 2005.[2] The Convention has (as at October 2006) thirty-nine contracting parties, among them most of the twenty-five EC countries. The majority of the remaining contracting parties are Central and Eastern European countries. The Convention may, in addition to States being members of the ECE, or having consultative status with the ECE, and economic integration organizations, be acceded to by any State that is a member of the UN upon approval by the MoP.[3]

An Extraordinary MoP of the Aarhus Convention, held within the framework of the Fifth Ministerial 'Environment for Europe' Conference (Kiev, May 2003), adopted the Protocol on Pollutant Release and Transfer Registers (the '2003 PRTR Protocol').[4] The Protocol was signed by thirty-six States and the EC. The Protocol, which has (as at October 2006) only been ratified by the EC and Luxembourg, requires sixteen ratifications to enter into force. The second MoP adopted an amendment to the Aarhus Convention.[5]

The present paper examines dispute settlement, enforcement and compliance in the context of the Aarhus Convention. However, enforcement provisions of the Convention are more or less restricted to those dealing with reporting and review of compliance.[6] Compliance procedures of the Convention include compliance with reporting requirements. Hence, there is no basis for making a clear distinction between compliance and enforcement and between non-compliance response measures and enforcement measures. Accordingly, this chapter examines enforcement as part of or in the context of compliance control. Beyond the scope of the analysis is the relationship between the Aarhus Convention regime relating to dispute settlement, enforcement and compliance and the EC regime relating to the similar aspects.[7] Dispute resolution is examined in section 8.3 and compliance in section 8.4 (rules), section 8.5 (bodies), section 8.6 (procedures) and section 8.7 (determination of non-compliance and non-compliance response measures). Section 8.8 summarizes the relationship between dispute resolution and review of compliance and section 8.9 deals with the issue of a self-contained regime. Finally, section 8.10 presents an overall evaluation.

---

[2] Report of the First Meeting of the Parties, Doc. ECE/MP.PP/2002/2; and Report of the Second Meeting of the Parties, Doc. ECE/MP.PP/2005/2.   [3] Arts. 17 and 19(3).

[4] ECE/MP.PP/7 rooted in the Aarhus Convention arts. 5, 9 and 10(2)(i).

[5] Decision II/1 on Genetically Modified Organisms, Doc. ECE/MP.PP/2005/2/Add.2. Annex, substituting art. 6(11) and inserting a new art. 6*bis* and a new Annex I*bis*.

[6] Art. 10(2) on regular reporting and Art. 15 on review of compliance.

[7] J. Jendroska, 'Aarhus Convention and Community Law: The Interplay' (2005) 2 *Journal for European Environmental and Planning Law* 12–21.

182   INTERNATIONAL ENVIRONMENTAL LAW

8.2 Summary contents of the Aarhus Convention and the nature of the Convention

8.2.1 The three pillars of the Convention

Articles 1, 2 and 3 of the Aarhus Convention contain provisions on objective, definitions and general obligations, while articles 4–9 regulate in a detailed manner the three pillars of the Convention: (1) access to environmental information[8] and collection and dissemination of environmental information;[9] (2) public participation in decisions on specific activities,[10] public participation concerning plans, programmes and policies relating to the environment,[11] and public participation during the preparation of executive regulations and/or generally applicable legally binding normative instruments;[12] and (3) access to justice.[13]

8.2.2 Convention organs

Article 10 establishes the Meeting of the Parties (MoP) as the supreme body of the Convention. The Executive Secretary of the Economic Commission for Europe (ECE) carries out the secretariat functions.[14] The Rules of Procedure of the MoP establish a bureau of seven members.[15] The tasks of the Bureau are decided by the MoP. Pursuant to the mandate of the MoP to establish subsidiary bodies, the Working Group of the Parties was established to oversee the implementation of the work programme for the Convention between MoPs.[16] Permanent Convention organs include the Compliance Committee (section 8.5.3 below).

8.2.3 The Convention in a human rights perspective

In a human rights perspective, some provisions in the Preamble and the provision on the objective of the Convention are particularly interesting. These provisions refer directly to rights to 'an environment adequate to . . . health and well-being', but there are other human rights aspects reflected as well (e.g. inter-generational equity and non-discrimination).[17] The most

---

[8] Art. 4.   [9] Art. 5.   [10] Art. 6 and Annex I.   [11] Art. 7.   [12] Art. 8.   [13] Art. 9.
[14] Art. 12.   [15] Decision I/1, Doc. ECE/MP.PP/2002/2/Add.1. Annex, Rules of Procedure, Rule 22.
[16] Rule 23 and Decision I/14, Doc. ECE/MP.PP/2002/2/Add.15.
[17] Preamble, paras. 5, 6 and 7 and arts. 1 and 3(9).

important human rights aspects are, of course, reflected in the procedural environmental rights accorded by the Convention, which constitute its nucleus, although the rights are provided indirectly by the imposition of obligations on States.

8.2.4 The nature of the obligations of the Convention

The Convention is dominated by obligations that are concrete, and relatively clear and concise. With regard to access to environmental information '[e]ach Party shall ensure that . . . public authorities make [environmental] information available to the public . . . as soon as possible and at the latest within one month after the request has been submitted'.[18] Concerning public participation in decisions on specific activities, '[t]he public concerned shall be informed . . . early in an environmental decision-making procedure . . . *inter alia*, of: (a) The proposed activity . . . and [e]ach Party shall require the competent public authorities to give the public concerned access for examination . . . to all information relevant to the decision-making'.[19] In respect of access to justice, '[e]ach Party shall . . . ensure that any person who considers that his or her request for information . . . has been ignored, wrongfully refused . . . inadequately answered, or otherwise not dealt with . . . has access to a review procedure before a court of law, or another independent and impartial body'.[20] These few examples are illustrative of the majority of the substantive provisions of the Convention. At the same time, they also demonstrate that the question of whether parties are in compliance with their obligations, generally speaking, might be easier to determine in relation to the Aarhus Convention than in relation to MEAs containing more general obligations. At the same time, however, to establish the facts, including the precise contents of national legislation, might cause some difficulties.

8.3 Dispute resolution

8.3.1 Nature and scope of the dispute resolution arrangements

The article of the Convention on dispute settlement is rather traditional. It pertains in its first paragraph to negotiation or any other means of dispute

---

[18] Art. 4(1) and (2).   [19] Art. 6(2) and (6).   [20] Art. 9(1).

184 INTERNATIONAL ENVIRONMENTAL LAW

settlement acceptable to the parties in case of a conflict about the interpretation or application of the Convention. Pursuant to the second paragraph of the article, a party may declare that it accepts the compulsory jurisdiction of either the ICJ or an arbitral tribunal established in accordance with the procedure set out in Annex II to the Convention (constituting an integral part of the Convention). The third paragraph states that, if the parties to the dispute have accepted both means of dispute settlement, the ICJ is competent, unless the parties agree otherwise.[21] Due to the provisions on arbitration/judicial settlement, it would be logical to interpret *other means* in the first paragraph to include other (peaceful) measures with a non-legally binding outcome, such as good offices, consultation, mediation and conciliation.[22]

The scope (jurisdiction) of the dispute settlement mechanism (DSM) concerns disputes (1) between two or more parties, (2) about the interpretation or application of the Convention. So, it is obvious that the provision is only applicable for conflicts between parties, and that a decision on whether the defendant was in breach of its treaty obligations is binding only on the parties to the conflict. The DSM does not leave room for conflicts between parties and non-State actors, although this might be considered relevant taking into consideration the special nature of the

---

[21] Art. 16. The DSM of the Convention is also traditional in the sense that 'irrespective of the issue of whether the Convention does or does not afford individual rights, the implementation of . . . obligations under dispute settlement is left to States'. See A. Tanzi and C. Pitea, 'Emerging Trends in the Role of Non-State Actors in International Water Disputes', in International Bureau of the Permanent Court of Arbitration (ed.), *Resolutions of International Water Disputes*, The PCA/Peace Palace Papers, vol. 5 (The Hague: Kluwer Law International, 2003), pp. 259–97, at note 53. Similar dispute settlement mechanisms (DSMs) are included in the Vienna Convention for the Protection of the Ozone Layer, Vienna, 22 March 1985, in force 22 September 1988, 1513 UNTS 293; the Montreal Protocol on Substances that Deplete the Ozone Layer, Montreal, 16 September 1987, in force 1 January 1989, 1522 UNTS 3; the Basel Convention on the Control of Transboundary Movements of Hazardous Wastes and their Disposal, Basel, 22 March 1989, in force 5 May 1992, Doc. UNEP/WG.190/4; the United Nations Framework Convention on Climate Change, New York, 9 May 1992, in force 21 March 1994, 1771 UNTS 107; the Kyoto Protocol to the United Nations Framework Convention on Climate Change, Kyoto, 11 December 1997, in force 16 February 2005, 37 ILM 22 (1998); the Rotterdam Convention on the Prior Informed Consent Procedure for Certain Hazardous Chemicals and Pesticides in International Trade, Rotterdam, 10 September 1998, in force 24 February 2004, 38 ILM 1 (1999); and the Stockholm Convention on Persistent Organic Pollutants, Stockholm, 22 May 2001, in force 17 May 2004, 40 ILM 532 (2001).

[22] World Trade Organization, Doc. WT/CTE/W/191, June 2001, Compliance and Dispute Settlement Provisions in the WTO and in Multilateral Environmental Agreements, Note by the WTO and UNEP Secretariats, para. 21.

Convention.[23] This issue was never raised during the negotiations, the focus in this regard being the compliance mechanism of the Convention. Generally speaking, the relevant article was not the subject of any detailed discussion during the negotiations.[24]

The subject of the DSM is defined as interpretation or application of the Convention. Focusing on the non-fulfilment of commitments, the mandate seems to include what is normally understood by the notion of non-compliance.[25] Furthermore, the language also indicates that it is not necessary to claim violation of individual rights under the Convention, i.e. parties can determine that the tribunal/court 'shall address a certain question of interpretation without having to conclude that the action of one Party infringed the right of another Party'.[26] However, the provision is applicable, not only to conflicts on the meaning of commitments, but also to issues of responsibility for breach of the Convention.[27] In that respect it probably exceeds the notion of non-compliance within the context of compliance mechanisms which does not include a formal breach as a trigger of State responsibility.[28]

8.3.2 Compulsory dispute settlement

The only general compulsory means of dispute resolution is negotiation, in the sense that, if a party requests negotiation on an issue within the scope of the provision, the other party has to abide.[29] Parties may at any time declare that, for a dispute not resolved in accordance with the above provision, they accept either the ICJ or arbitration in accordance with the procedures set out in Annex II, or both means of dispute settlement as compulsory in relation to any other party accepting the same obligation. The ICJ is competent if the concerned parties have accepted both means

---

[23] On the issue of *amicus curiae* submissions, see section 8.3.3 below.

[24] The author participated as head of the Danish delegation in all the meetings of the negotiating body. The statement is based on the author's recollection of the negotiations and not on an examination of the reports of the meetings or other material.

[25] See, in general, Birnie and Boyle, *International Law and the Environment*, p. 207.

[26] A. Bree in co-operation with CIEL, *Harmonization of Dispute Settlement Mechanisms of the Multilateral Environmental Agreements and the World Trade Agreements* (Berlin: Erich Schmidt Verlag Berlin und Unweltsbundesamt, 2003), p. 91.

[27] See, in general, Birnie and Boyle, *International Law and the Environment*, p. 226.

[28] M. Koskenniemi, 'Breach of Treaty or Non-Compliance? Reflections on the Enforcement of the Montreal Protocol' (1992) 3 *Yearbook of International Environmental Law* 123, at 144.

[29] See, in general, Bree, *Harmonization of Dispute Settlement Mechanisms*, p. 91.

186   INTERNATIONAL ENVIRONMENTAL LAW

and do not agree otherwise.[30] This provision is rather typical,[31] although a special annex outlining the procedure in case of arbitration is not a common feature for treaties containing similar provisions.[32]

With the reference in the paragraph on arbitration or judicial settlement to the previous paragraph defining the scope of the dispute settlement, it seems obvious that the scope of arbitration or judicial settlement concerns the interpretation or application of the Convention. This is also reflected in the annex, according to which there is an obligation in the event of a dispute being submitted for arbitration to notify the Secretariat of the subject-matter for arbitration and to indicate, in particular, the articles of the Convention whose 'interpretation or application' is at issue.[33]

According to the annex, the tribunal shall render its decision 'in accordance with international law and the provisions of the Convention', thus leaving it to arbitrators to decide what will constitute the applicable body of international law in this context.[34]

8.3.3 Role of non-State actors

Procedural rules of the annex provide for any party to intervene in the proceedings with the consent of the tribunal, if the party has an interest of a legal nature in the subject-matter of the dispute and may be affected by a decision.[35] There are no provisions on interventions by non-State actors

---

[30] Art. 16(2). Only one party, Norway, has so far made a declaration (to the effect that Norway accepts the ICJ).

[31] See, in general, Bree, *Harmonization of Dispute Settlement Mechanisms*, p. 88.

[32] The DSM of the 2003 PRTR Protocol to the Aarhus Convention is in this regard similar to the Aarhus Convention DSM. Examples of other DSMs supplemented by and annexes containing rules on arbitration are the 1989 Basel Convention, the Convention on Environmental Impact Assessment in a Transboundary Context, Espoo, Finland, 25 February 1991, in force 10 September 1997, Doc. E.ECE.1250 (applicable also to its 2003 Protocol on Strategic Environmental Assessment, ECE/MP.EIA/2003/3), the Convention on Biological Diversity, Rio de Janeiro, 5 June 1992. 31 ILM 818 (1992) (applicable also to the Cartagena Protocol on Biosafety to the Convention on Biological Diversity, 39 ILM 1027 (2000)) and the Convention on the Transboundary Effects of Industrial Accidents, Helsinki, 17 March 1992, in force 19 April 2000, 31 ILM 1330 (1992) (including its protocols). Examples of DSMs without such an annex are the Convention on Long-Range Transboundary Air Pollution, Geneva, 13 November 1979, in force 16 March 1983, Doc. E-ECE (XXXIV)-L-18, the 1985 Vienna Convention (including the 1987 Montreal Protocol), the UNFCCC (including the 1997 Kyoto Protocol) and the 2001 Stockholm POPs Convention.   [33] Convention, Annex II, Arbitration, para. 1.

[34] *Ibid.*, para. 5. The same wording is included in the annexes on arbitration to e.g. the 1989 Basel Convention and the 1991 Espoo Convention; see Stec and Casey-Lefkowitz, *The Aarhus Convention*, p. 168.   [35] Convention, Annex II, Arbitration, para. 15.

(*amicus curiae* briefs) which, taking into consideration the explicit provision on State intervention, could indicate that interventions by non-State actors are excluded. Considering the very purpose of the Convention, this could be regarded as an omission due to the fact that the dispute settlement provisions were never the subject of focused discussions during the negotiations of the Convention.[36] The tribunal, on the other hand, shall draw up its own rules of procedure. Nothing seems to prevent the tribunal from including provisions allowing for *amicus curiae* submissions. Quite to the contrary, the purpose of the Convention provides a legitimate incitement, but probably not an obligation, to do this.[37]

8.3.4 Standing

Non-performance of the obligations of the Convention will rarely affect any particular State party. Most of the obligations are of a non-reciprocal character, because the main aim of the Convention is to impose obligations on States in respect of their own citizens.[38] The dispute settlement provisions do not address the issue of standing. So, the question may be posed whether it is necessary for a party to prove that it is 'injured', i.e. to establish a (sufficient) legal interest to invoke State responsibility for a breach of the obligation in question. The response is probably to the negative. First, the Convention contains provisions on dispute settlement in spite of the fact that it is not likely that violation of obligations under the Convention will result in a party being 'injured'. Secondly, 'as a general matter, where a party to a treaty . . . believes that another party is in violation of its obligations under that treaty . . . it will have the right under the treaty . . . to seek to enforce the obligations of the party alleged to be in violation, even if it has

---

[36] The author participated as head of the Danish delegation in all the meetings of the negotiating body. The statement is based on the author's recollection of the negotiations and not on an examination of the reports of the meetings or other material. On *amicus curiae* submissions in the framework of the procedures of the Compliance Committee, see section 8.7.1 below.

[37] See, generally, Tanzi and Pitea, *Non-State Actors in International Water Disputes*; and Ruth Mackenzie, 'The Amicus Curiae in International Courts: Towards Common Procedural Approaches', in T. Treves, M. Frigessi di Rattalma, A. Tanzi, A. Fodella, C. Pitea and C. Ragni (eds.), *Civil Society, International Courts and Compliance Bodies* (The Hague: TMC Asser Press, 2005), pp. 295–311.

[38] Pallemaerts, *Proceduralizing Environmental Rights*, p. 19, observes that the Convention 'is the first multilateral environmental agreement whose main purpose is to impose on its contracting parties obligations *towards their own citizens*'.

not suffered material damage'.[39] In addition, the mere language of the dispute settlement provisions implies that it is not necessary to claim the violation of rights under the Convention in order to invoke dispute settlement. Without having to rely on the dispute settlement provisions of the Convention, it might be argued that the basic procedural rights of the Convention reflect obligations *erga omnes partes* because they are associated with, or by their very nature resemble, human rights.[40] Therefore, an *actio popularis* concept should be applied, enabling any party to invoke judicial proceedings against any other party without being affected by the alleged violation.[41] This conclusion, based on an interpretation of the provisions of the Convention as well as on principles of international human rights law and on general rules on State responsibility, corresponds to rules emerging as *lege ferenda* in the framework of the International Law Commission.[42]

8.3.5 Use of the DSM?

The DSM has not yet been used, which is not surprising since the Convention entered into force only on 30 October 2001. However, it is likely that the DSM is not going to be used much, or at all, in the future either. The objective of the Convention is not the legal protection of individual States but rather to provide for procedural rights to civil society in order to further the protection of the environment and to ensure sustainable development.[43] The underlying argument is that 'adequate protection of the environment is essential to human wellbeing and the enjoyment of basic human rights, including the right to life itself', and that 'to be able to assert this right citizens must have access to information, be entitled to

[39] Sands, *Principles of International Environmental Law*, p. 185.
[40] See generally Boyle, *Human Rights Law in the Protection of the Environment*; Ebbesson, *Public Participation*; Koester, 'Aarhus-konventionen'; and Déjeant-Pons, 'Human Rights to Environmental Procedural Rights'. Art. 1 of the Convention provides that, '[i]n order to contribute to the protection of the *right of every person* of present and future generations to live in an environment adequate to his or her health and well-being, each Party *shall guarantee the rights* of access to information, public participation in decision-making, and access to justice in environmental matters in accordance with the Convention' (emphasis added). This objective is underscored by the Preamble, para. 7 recognizing that every person has the right to live in an adequate environment.
[41] Sands, *Principles of International Environmental Law*, p. 189; and Birnie and Boyle, *International Law and the Environment*, p. 195.
[42] M. A. Fitzmaurice and C. Redgwell, 'Environmental Non-Compliance Procedures and International Law' (2000) 31 *Netherlands Yearbook of International Law* 35, at 52.
[43] Preamble, para. 5.

participate in decision-making and have access to justice'.[44] Thus, the Convention pursues collective goals, but lacks reciprocity.[45]

While a DSM might be useful to resolve a specific dispute between two or more parties, the nature of the obligations of the Convention implies that it is, generally speaking, difficult or impossible to identify a party being directly affected by a violation of an obligation by another party and to evaluate the nature and extent of the harm caused by the violation.[46] Therefore, traditional repressive measures of dispute settlement (e.g. withdrawal of privileges or invocation of liability) would be inappropriate or ineffective, and would not benefit other parties. Judicial procedures would be likely to lead to a mere assessment of a State's failure to comply.[47] This is also why collective supervision is a more effective and realistic remedy than countermeasures, and why the focus of most MEAs is to avoid disputes, especially by means of the establishment of compliance mechanisms.[48] An even more convincing argument for the allegation that the DSM under the Convention is not likely to be used is the experience so far on the use of such procedures, namely, that a DSM of an MEA, so far, has almost never been invoked.[49]

8.4 Rules of the Convention and MoP decisions on reporting and compliance control

8.4.1 Reporting

The Convention presupposes regular reporting by the parties.[50] The reporting requirement of the Convention is not very precise and therefore

---

[44] *Ibid.*, para. 8.   [45] Bree, *Harmonization of Dispute Settlement Mechanisms*, p. 84.

[46] WTO Doc. WT/CTE/W/191, June 2001, Compliance and Dispute Settlement Provisions in the WTO and in Multilateral Environmental Agreements, p. 2, para. 9.

[47] *Ibid.*, p. 8, para. 18; and Birnie and Boyle, *International Law and the Environment*, p. 196.

[48] An analysis of compliance theory, including the reasons for non-compliance, exceeds the scope of this chapter. See, in general, Birnie and Boyle, *International Law and the Environment*, p. 529; Sands, *Principles of International Environmental Law*, p. 171; R. B. Mitchell, 'Compliance Theory: An Overview', in J. Cameron, J. Werksman and P. Roderick (eds.), *Improving Compliance with International Environmental Law* (London: Earthscan, 1996), p. 3; Markus Ehrmann, 'Procedures of Compliance Control in International Environmental Treaties' (2002) 13 *Colorado Journal of International Environmental Law and Policy* 377–443, at 386, with further references; and, generally, D. Zaelke, D. Kaniaru and E. Kruzíková (eds.), *Making Law Work: Environmental Compliance and Sustainable Development* (London: Cameron May, 2005).

[49] Bree, *Harmonization of Dispute Settlement Mechanisms*, pp. 111 and 400; and Ehrmann, 'Procedures of Compliance Control in International Environmental Treaties', p. 383.

[50] Art. 10(2).

has been supplemented by a decision of the MoP.[51] The decision (Decision I/8) recognizes, *inter alia*, that regular reporting by parties will facilitate the assessment of compliance under the Convention and thereby contribute to the work of the Compliance Committee. In the operative part of the decision, each party is requested:

- to submit to the Secretariat, in advance of the first ordinary MoP a report on the necessary legislative, regulatory or other measures that have been taken to implement the provisions of the Convention, and their practical implication in accordance with the format set out in the annex to the decision;
- in advance of each subsequent meeting to review the report and submit an updated version of it to the Secretariat; and
- to prepare the reports through a transparent and consultative process involving the public, inviting the party at the same time to consider adapting the reports to provide guidance to members of the public on the exercise of their rights and the relevant implementing legislation.[52]

The Secretariat is requested to prepare a report for each meeting of the parties summarizing the progress made and identifying significant trends, challenges and solutions.

Furthermore, international, regional and non-governmental organizations engaged in programmes or activities providing support to parties in the implementation of the Convention are invited to submit reports to the Secretariat on their programmes or activities and lessons learned.[53] According to the compliance arrangements, the Compliance Committee shall also report on its activities to the ordinary meeting of the parties in addition, *inter alia*, to its duty to monitor and assess the implementation and reporting requirements of the parties (see section 8.5.3.2 below). Hence, the reporting system as a whole and its many actors – the parties, the Secretariat, the Compliance Committee and other organizations, especially NGOs, all of them dealing in their specific capacities with issues relating to implementation of the Convention and compliance – is, from a logistical point of view, a rather challenging system. However, a further analysis of this issue exceeds the scope of this chapter.

---

[51] Decision I/8 on Reporting Requirements, Doc. ECE/MP.PP/2002/2/Add.9 (hereinafter, Decision I/8) supplemented by Decision II/10, Doc. ECE/MP.PP/2005/2/Add.14.
[52] Decision I/8, paras. 1–3.   [53] *Ibid.*, paras. 5 and 7.

8.4.2 Compliance control

While the provisions of the Convention on reporting are rather traditional, the article concerning the review of compliance is exceptional in several respects.[54] The article provides for the establishment (1) on a consensus basis of (2) optional arrangements for reviewing compliance with the provisions of the Convention. The arrangements (3) shall allow for appropriate public involvement, and (4) may include the option of considering communications from members of the public on matters related to the Convention.[55]

The scope of the compliance arrangements, however, is rather traditional insofar as it is limited to reviewing 'compliance with the provisions of this Convention'[56] corresponding to provisions in other treaties on the establishment of compliance arrangements.[57] Also, the requirements of the arrangements to be of a 'non-confrontational, non-judicial and consultative nature' are common features of compliance arrangements.

At the first MoP (October 2002), the Meeting adopted a decision on the review of compliance (Decision I/7).[58] The compliance mechanism, based solely on the article on compliance review, establishes a Compliance Committee, constitutes the Committee and MoP as the main bodies for the review of compliance, and sets out in an annex the structure and function of the Committee as well as the procedures for reviewing compliance with the Convention.

---

[54] Art. 15.

[55] No other MEAs seem to contain provisions on compliance mechanisms providing for optional arrangements, public involvement or communications from members of the public, although art. 22 of the 2003 PRTR Protocol, which also requires consensus, charges the MoP to consider, *inter alia*, whether to allow for information to be received from members of the public.

[56] Art. 15. The scope of the compliance mechanism, as decided by the MoP, namely, 'review of *compliance* by the Parties *with* their *obligations under the Convention*' (Decision I/7, para. 1, emphasis added), could be interpreted as offering more flexibility, e.g. as including compliance with decisions of the MoP. However, it is not likely that the different wording is intentional. The Annex to Decision I/7 refers simply to 'compliance with the Convention' (para. 37) corresponding to e.g. art. 18 of the 1997 Kyoto Protocol. There is, in parallel with other treaty provisions on compliance, no definition of compliance/non-compliance, neither in art. 15, nor in Decision I/7.

[57] E.g. art. 17 of the 2001 Stockholm POPs Convention and art. 34 of the Biosafety Protocol.

[58] Decision I/7, Doc. ECE/MP.PP/2002/2 (Add.8) (hereinafter, Decision I/7). The decision as a whole is referred to below as the compliance mechanism. On the negotiation history of Decision I/7, see Koester, 'Compliance Review under the Aarhus Convention: A Rather Unique Compliance Mechanism' (2005) 2 *Journal for European Environmental and Planning Law* 31–44m at 33.

8.5 Bodies responsible for monitoring compliance

8.5.1 The Meeting of the Parties

Ordinary Meetings of the Parties (MoPs) shall be held at least once every two years, unless otherwise decided by the parties.[59] According to the Convention, the MoP 'shall keep under continuous review the implementation of [the] Convention on the basis of regular reporting' and shall, with this purpose in mind, *inter alia* review the policies for and legal and methodological approaches to the three pillars of the Convention, with a view to further improving them. The MoP shall also consider and undertake any additional action that may be required for the achievement of the purposes of the Convention.[60] Decision I/7 entitles the MoP, upon consideration of a report and any recommendations of the Compliance Committee, 'to decide upon appropriate measures to bring about full compliance with the Convention',[61] but the MoP is not under an obligation to consider recommendations of the Compliance Committee.

8.5.2 The Secretariat

The functions of the Secretariat, including tasks assigned to it by the MoP, are carried out by the Executive Secretary of the ECE.[62] Among the functions determined by the MoP are those related to reporting of the parties (section 8.4.1 above) and monitoring compliance. With regard to monitoring compliance, the Secretariat has, in addition to its traditional task of convening and preparing meetings of the Compliance Committee, certain duties to examine non-compliance with obligations under the Convention and bringing the matter to the attention of the Compliance Committee.[63] The Secretariat also has specific tasks with regard to submissions by the parties.[64] The Compliance Committee has addressed various issues relating to the role of the Secretariat in the context of the compliance mechanism and the interplay between the Compliance Committee and the Secretariat. Compliance Committee decisions on working methods and procedures are included in the Modus Operandi of the Compliance Committee (see section 8.6.1 below).

---

[59] Art. 10(1).   [60] Art. 10(2)(a) and (g).   [61] Decision I/7, Annex, para. 37.
[62] Art. 12 and section 8.2.2 above.   [63] Decision I/7, Annex, para. 17.
[64] *Ibid.*, paras. 15 and 16.

8.5.3 The Compliance Committee

8.5.3.1 Election of members

Decision I/7 establishes the Compliance Committee. The Committee consists of eight members elected with due regard, *inter alia*, to the geographical distribution of the membership and to diversity of experience.[65] The members serve in their personal capacity, implying that the Compliance Committee is not composed by States parties. This aspect is further underscored by some features that are probably unique regarding members of compliance committees in general:[66]

- members may be nationals not only of parties but also of signatories (two members of the first Compliance Committee were nationals of States being only signatories when those members were elected);
- members shall explicitly be persons of high moral character (and of recognized competence in the field to which the Convention relates);
- every member shall make a solemn declaration in her or his first meeting of the Compliance Committee that she or he will perform the functions impartially and conscientiously; and
- candidates are nominated by parties, signatories and NGOs entitled to participate as observers in MoPs and promoting environmental protection (two members of the first Compliance Committee were nominated by NGOs).

There are other MEA compliance committees where members serve in their personal or individual capacity, but such prerequisites have not prevented parties of those MEAs from nominating members who were at the same time governmental civil servants. None of the candidates nominated to the first Aarhus Convention Compliance Committee and none of the members who were later elected to replace two resigning members were part of or represented an executive branch of a government of a party or a signatory.[67] This independence is underscored by the availability of funds to meet the costs of the Compliance Committee, especially the travel and accommodation costs of its members.[68] The requirements with regard to

---

[65] *Ibid.*, paras. 1 and 8.   [66] *Ibid.*, paras. 1–11.

[67] See Koester, 'Compliance Review under the Aarhus Convention', p. 34.

[68] E.g. members of the 1989 Basel Convention Compliance Committee and members of the Biosafety Protocol Compliance Committee. On members of Expert Review Teams under the compliance mechanism of the 1997 Kyoto Protocol, who are required to serve in their personal

the members of the Compliance Committee have entailed a number of decisions of the Compliance Committee with a view to ensuring its integrity (e.g. on to what extent members of the Compliance Committee may participate in other meetings under the Convention as representatives of NGOs and on conflicts of interest[69]).

Membership of the Compliance Committee is rotating. However, in order to provide for some degree of continuity, only four members are elected at each ordinary MoP for a full term of office, running from the end of an ordinary MoP until the ordinary MoP following the first MoP thereafter (except at the first MoP where four members were elected only for half a term). Outgoing members may be re-elected for a further full term of office.[70]

It is noteworthy that the Compliance Committee is not a subsidiary body of the MoP, as defined in the Rules of Procedure of the MoP.[71] According to the Rules of Procedure, a subsidiary body means a body established by the MoP in accordance with Rule 23 of the Rules of Procedure which refers to the provision on subsidiary bodies of the Convention, namely, article 10(2)(d), on the authority of the MoP to establish such subsidiary bodies as it deems necessary. However, the operative part of Decision I/7 refers only to article 15 of the Convention and not to article 10(2)(d). Hence, it is quite clear that the Compliance Committee cannot be seen as a subsidiary body in the normal sense of that term, and that the observation of the Compliance Committee to that effect is correct.[72] Accordingly, the MoP is not entitled to instruct or guide the Compliance Committee, unless otherwise provided for in rules governing the compliance mechanism, but, of course, the MoP may, by consensus, amend the rules.

---

capacity, and who shall be neither nationals of nor funded by the party under review, see G. Ulfstein and J. Werksman, 'The Kyoto Compliance System: Towards Hard Enforcement', in O. S. Stokke, J. Hovi and G. Ulfstein (eds.), *Implementing the Climate Regime: International Compliance* (London: Earthscan, 2005), pp. 39–62, at p. 43.

[69] Report on First Meeting, Doc. MP.PP/C.1/2003/2, April 2003, para. 22; and Report on Third Meeting, Doc. MP.PP/C.1/2004/2, March 2004, paras. 37–9. A member of the Compliance Committee having declared a conflict of interest with regard to a concrete case may only participate in meetings dealing with that case in the same manner as an observer and cannot attend deliberations on the preparation of a decision in that case, Report on Fifth Meeting, Doc. MP.PP/C.1/2004/6, October 2004, para. 53.

[70] Decision I/7, Annex, para. 9. Outgoing members were re-elected at the second MoP.

[71] Rules of Procedure (note 15 above), Rule 2(7).

[72] Report on First Meeting (note 69 above), para. 12; and Modus Operandi, section 8.6.1 below.

8.5.3.2 Submissions, referrals and communications

The Compliance Committee shall consider any submission, referral or communication made in accordance with the provisions of the compliance mechanism.[73] The compliance mechanism may be triggered[74] by (1) a party *vis-à-vis* itself or another party,[75] (2) the Secretariat,[76] or (3) a member of the public, which, pursuant to article 2(4) of the Convention, means any natural or legal person and, in accordance with national legislation or practice, their associations, organizations or groups.[77] The last-mentioned legal trigger can only be applied following the expiry of one year from the date of Decision I/7 (23 October 2002) or the entry into force of the Convention for the concerned party, whichever is the later, unless that

---

[73] Decision I/7, Annex, para. 13(a). [74] *Ibid.*, paras. 13(a) and 15–18.

[75] This is not the case for all compliance mechanisms. For example, the compliance mechanism of the 1989 Basel Convention limits the party-to-party trigger to 'affected Parties'. See Akiho Shibata, 'The Basel Compliance Mechanism' (2003) 12 *Review of European Community and International Environmental Law* 183, at 189. Party-to-party submissions are probably, generally speaking, extremely rare. For example, the compliance mechanism under the 1979 LRTAP Convention has not received any party-to-party submission: see P. Szell, V. Keizer, and T. Kuokkanen, 'Compliance and Consensus', in J. Sliggers and W. Kakebeeke (eds.), *Cleaning the Air: 25 Years of the Convention on Long-Range Transboundary Air Pollution* (Geneva: United Nations, 2004), pp. 119–31, at p. 123, Table 8.1. However, in 2004, Romania filed a submission to the Aarhus Convention compliance mechanism alleging non-compliance with the Convention by Ukraine, including non-compliance by Ukraine *vis-à-vis* its own citizens. The Compliance Committee concluded that Ukraine in fact did not comply with some provisions of art. 6 of the Convention, which was subsequently endorsed by the second MoP. See section 8.7.1 below, with notes and further references.

[76] The Secretariat of the 1987 Montreal Protocol is also entitled to trigger its compliance mechanism. See M. M. Goote, 'Non-Compliance Procedures and International Law: The Middle Way between Diplomacy and Law' (1999) 1 *International Law FORUM du droit international* 87. Some compliance committees are entitled to receive information from the secretariat on possible non-compliance without having requested such information, e.g. the 1989 Basel Convention (see Shibata, *The Basel Compliance Mechanism*, pp. 190 *et seq.*), while it is a matter of interpretation whether this is true regarding the Biosafety Protocol, Doc. UNEP/CBD/BD/CoP-MoP/1/15 (February 2004), Decision BS-I/7, Annex, section V, para. 2. However, an entitlement to receive such information from the Secretariat does not necessarily mean that the Secretariat has a right to trigger the compliance mechanism.

[77] The compliance mechanism of the Convention on the Protection of the Alps, Salzburg, 7 November 1991, in force 6 March 1995, 31 ILM 767 (1992), permits the Review Committee to investigate requests also from observers on suspected breaches of contractual obligations. See T. Enderlin, 'Alpine Convention: A Different Compliance Mechanism' (2004) 33 *Environmental Policy and Law* 157. See also V. Koester, 'Pacta Sunt Servanda' (1996) 26 *Environmental Policy and Law* 78–91, on the Case File System of the 1979 Convention on the Conservation of European Wildlife and Natural Habitats, Bern, 19 September 1979, in force 6 January 1981, ETS No. 104.

196 INTERNATIONAL ENVIRONMENTAL LAW

party has notified the depositary by the end of the applicable period that it is unable to accept, for a period of not more than four years, the consideration of such communications. Hence, the optional character of the compliance mechanism as laid down in the Convention is reduced to the possibility of opting-out only with regard to communications from the public and only for a maximum period of four years.[78]

The Committee has further tasks. It shall, *inter alia*, also (1) prepare, at the request of the MoP, a report on compliance with or implementation of the provisions of the Convention; (2) monitor, assess and facilitate the implementation of and compliance with the reporting requirements of the Convention; (3) monitor compliance with the implementation of non-compliance measures;[79] and (4) may also examine compliance issues on its own initiative[80] and make recommendations if appropriate.[81] The Committee shall report to the MoP and make such recommendations as it considers appropriate so that the MoP may decide upon appropriate measures to bring about full compliance with the Convention.[82] In certain circumstances, the Committee may take specific actions on an interim basis, in consultation or in agreement with the party concerned.[83]

The Compliance Committee shall meet at least once a year.[84] However, since its first meeting in March 2003, the Compliance Committee has held nine meetings (2003–5), suggesting that an average of four meetings annually is needed in order for the Compliance Committee to discharge its functions.

---

[78] Decision I/7, Annex, para. 18. For the time being, no State party has opted out. As a consequence of Decision I/7, Annex, para. 18, the Compliance Committee may not consider communications from members of the public during the first year after the entry into force of the Convention for a State party. According to the Modus Operandi of the Compliance Committee (see section 8.6.1 above), the Committee is not precluded from considering communications submitted after the 'grace period' of one year, if the significant events occurred during the first year after the entry into force of the Convention in that State party.

[79] With regard to compliance strategies, Decision I/7, Annex, para. 37(c). See, furthermore, decisions of the second MoP on the compliance of various parties referred to in section 8.7.1 below.

[80] An example of monitoring compliance on the Compliance Committee's own initiative is provided by para. 34 of the Report of the Compliance Committee to the MoP, Doc. ECE/MP.PP/2005/13, March 2005, concerning non-compliance with Decision I/7, Annex, para. 23, on the response from parties concerned when they receive a submission or communication, see section 8.7.1 below.   [81] Decision I/7, Annex, paras. 13(b) and (c) and 14.

[82] *Ibid.*, paras. 35 and 37.   [83] *Ibid.*, para. 36 and section 8.7.1 below.

[84] Decision I/7, Annex, Section II, Meetings.

8.6 Procedures of the Compliance Committee

8.6.1 Modus Operandi of the Committee

Decision I/7 contains some procedural rules. However, these rules have proven to be insufficient to govern the work of the Compliance Committee. The Compliance Committee has therefore made a number of decisions relating to its working methods and procedures. These decisions are compiled as 'Modus Operandi' in a guidance document on the compliance mechanism, elaborated by the Compliance Committee, which is regularly updated and posted on the compliance mechanism website.[85] The guidance document also contains information on the nature of the compliance mechanism including that the compliance procedure is not a redress procedure for a specific violation of the rights of the public under the Convention. Furthermore, guidance to the public on how to draft communications etc. is provided. At the second meeting, the MoP welcomed the way in which the Compliance Committee had been working and the procedures it had developed.[86]

8.6.2 Information gathering and meetings of the Compliance Committee

The Compliance Committee has, speaking in practical terms, by virtue of provisions of the compliance mechanism (Decision I/7), an almost unlimited power to gather and consider relevant information. These provisions have been extensively supplemented by decisions of the Compliance Committee, *inter alia* on information gathering, the role of the Secretariat, and on-the-spot information gathering.[87] Based on some rather meagre provisions of the compliance mechanism dealing with the rights of parties involved in submissions, referrals or communications, or of members of the public having made a communication, to participate in the discussions

---

[85] Guidance Document on the Aarhus Compliance Mechanisms (hereinafter, 'Guidance Document') available at www.unece.org/env/pp/compliance.htm. All other documents relating to the compliance mechanism and referred to below are also posted on this website or on the website of the Convention, www.unece.org/env/pp/.

[86] Decision II/5 on general issues of compliance, Doc. ECE/MP.PP/2005/2/Add.6, para. 5.

[87] Unless specifically mandated by the Compliance Committee to collect information, meetings of the Secretariat or members of the Compliance Committee with concerned parties or communicants do not constitute information gathering for the purpose of Decision I/7, Annex, para. 25: Report on Fifth Meeting, para. 50.

of the Compliance Committee,[88] the Compliance Committee has taken the decision that all meetings should in principle be open to the public as observers, which, of course, implies that meetings are also open to other observers. Those directly involved have the right to participate in the discussions (the right to comment, to be heard and to have comments taken into account). However, the deliberations on the preparation of any decision should generally be closed, the same being the case when rules on confidentiality are applicable.[89]

8.6.3 Rules of procedure for handling submissions and referrals

Rules of procedure for handling submissions and referrals laid down in Decision I/7 are rather few and more or less limited to the interaction between the various actors, i.e. the Secretariat and the Compliance Committee as well as concerned parties. However, it should be stressed that the rules include clear timeframes for informing the parties concerned on party-to-party submissions, on replies from those parties, and on replies from parties asked for information by the Secretariat, when it becomes aware of possible non-compliance. Submissions shall be addressed in writing to the Secretariat and supported by corroborating information.[90] The procedures have been widely supplemented and detailed by the Compliance Committee and included in its Modus Operandi.

8.6.4 Rules of procedure for handling communications from members of the public

The compliance mechanism contains more extensive rules on procedure for handling communications (i.e. complaints) from members of the public (i.e. individuals or NGOs).[91] According to these rules, the Compliance Committee shall consider any communication addressed to it in writing (including in electronic form) and supported by corroborating information, unless it determines that the communication is anonymous, an abuse of the right to make a communication, manifestly unreasonable

---

[88] Decision I/7, Annex, paras. 33 and 30.

[89] Decision I/7, Annex, Section VIII, Confidentiality. On meetings to be closed for members of Compliance Committee due to conflicts of interest, see note 69 above.

[90] Decision I/7, Annex, Section IV, Submission by Parties, and Section V, Referrals by the Secretariat.   [91] Decision I/7, Annex, Section VI, Communications from the Public.

CONVENTION ON ACCESS TO INFORMATION ETC.   199

or incompatible with the provisions of Decision I/7 or with the
Convention.[92] The Compliance Committee should also 'at all relevant
stages take into account any available domestic remedy unless the application of the remedy is unreasonably prolonged or obviously does not
provide an effective and sufficient means of redress'.[93] The Compliance
Committee has interpreted this to mean that, although there is no strict
requirement for exhaustion of domestic remedies, the Committee may
decide not to pursue the substance of a communication if it considers that
the communicant has not sufficiently explored the possibilities for resolving the issue through available national administrative or judicial review
procedures.[94]

The procedural rules invite the communicant to indicate also whether
the matter has been submitted to another means of international investigation or settlement. The language suggests that the Compliance Committee
is not prevented from considering a matter which is the subject of another
international compliance or settlement procedure, thus differing in this
regard from comparable procedures under certain human rights instruments.[95] The communications so far received by the Committee have

---

[92] Some of these features are also included in other compliance mechanisms (e.g. the 1987 Basel
Convention compliance mechanism and the Biosafety Protocol compliance mechanism), but
curiously enough these features relate to party-to-party submissions while in the Aarhus
Convention compliance mechanism they relate only to communications. At its fifth meeting,
the Compliance Committee decided that a communication was inadmissible because it did not
seem to fall within the scope of the Convention. See Report on Fifth Meeting, para. 27. Also, at
the seventh meeting, a communication was found inadmissible: see Report on Seventh Meeting,
Doc. MP.PP/C.1/2005/2, March 2005, para. 15.

[93] Decision I/7, Annex, para. 21. At its fifth meeting, the Compliance Committee decided not to
consider a communication, because it appeared from the communication that the relevant
court decision had simultaneously with the communication been submitted for review by
domestic courts of appeals: see Report on Fifth Meeting, para. 28.

[94] See, Guidance Document (section 8.6.1 above), p. 32; and Report on Third Meeting, paras. 5
and 7.

[95] Optional Protocol to the 1966 International Covenant on Civil and Political Rights, 16
December 1966, in force 23 March 1976, UN Doc. A/6316 (1966), 999 UNTS 302. According to
art. 5(a), it is an admissibility criterion that the same matter is not examined under any other
international procedure. A similar provision, included in the draft compliance mechanism of
the Aarhus Convention was deleted during the negotiations: see Koester, 'Compliance Review
under the Aarhus Convention', p. 34. On the issue of competing disputes, see Bree,
Harmonization of Dispute Settlement Mechanisms, pp. 92 and 109; and Report on Fifth Meeting,
para. 11. See, furthermore, file ACC/5/2004/1, Romania/Ukraine (Report on Seventh Meeting,
Addendum 3), on the decision of the Compliance Committee regarding the relationship
between the compliance mechanism and an inquiry commission under art. 3(7) of and
Appendix IV to the 1991 Espoo Convention.

entailed further decisions by the Compliance Committee on procedures in the initial stages of processing communications, on forwarding communications to the Committee, on communications submitted in other languages than English, on confidentiality, on initial steps required by the Committee and on decisions by e-mail.[96] This is not surprising since the compliance mechanism is the first mechanism in the context of an MEA entitled to consider communication from members of the public, which means that precedents and experience to build on do not exist.

According to Decision I/7, a party concerned shall, not later than five months after a communication is brought to its attention by the Committee, submit to the Committee written explanations or statements clarifying the matter and describing any response it may have made.[97] Under the practice of the Compliance Committee, the communication is forwarded to the party concerned when the Committee has made a preliminary determination on admissibility. The letter to the party concerned may contain specific questions, and the party is also invited to comment on questions to the communicant, if any, raised in the letter to the communicant forwarding the provisional determination on admissibility. At the meeting of the Compliance Committee following the expiry of the timeframe of five months the Committee enters into formal discussion of the file, irrespective of whether the party concerned has replied or not. Normally, both the communicant and the party concerned are invited to the formal discussion in order to present their viewpoints.[98] At the meeting, the Committee makes a final decision on admissibility.[99]

8.6.5 Decision-making of the Compliance Committee

Rules on decision-making of the Compliance Committee, contained in the compliance mechanism, are few. Non-compliance issues will mainly be

---

[96] Report on Fourth Meeting, Doc. MP.PP/C.1/2004/4, July 2004, paras. 22–41; and Modus Operandi (section 8.6.1 above).   [97] Decision I/7, Annex, para. 23.

[98] See, generally, Modus Operandi (section 8.6.1 above), Procedures for Discussing Submissions, Referrals and Communications and Preparing and Adopting Findings, Measures and Recommendations; and Report on Ninth Meeting, Doc. ECE/MP.PP/C.1/2005/6, October 2005, para. 20, on two pending files. Travel costs etc. of the communicant are financed by the budget of the Convention, and so possibly are the participation costs of the party concerned according to the normal rules of the ECE. Interpretation in Russian is provided as necessary.

[99] See, generally, the Modus Operandi, and the reports on meetings of the Compliance Committee.

addressed by the Compliance Committee in its report to the MoP, which shall include such recommendations as the Compliance Committee considers appropriate. According to the provisions of the compliance mechanism, every effort shall be made to adopt the report by consensus, and, where this is not possible, the report shall reflect the views of all the members of the Compliance Committee. However, decision-making also includes taking the measures referred to in section 8.7.4 below. Comments made by the parties concerned and concerned members of the public shall be taken into account before the Compliance Committee finalizes its findings, measures and recommendations. The Compliance Committee has agreed on specific procedures for discussing submissions, referrals and communications and preparing and adopting, measures and recommendations.[100]

The Compliance Committee has decided to apply, as a general rule, the Rules of Procedure of the Meeting of the Parties *mutatis mutandis*. However, the limited membership and the equal number of members (eight) have entailed a rather detailed decision on quorum requirements.[101]

8.6.6 Procedural safeguards

A number of the rules referred to in sections 8.6.2 to 8.6.5 above, including several procedural rules decided by the Compliance Committee itself, may be regarded as procedural safeguards. Information gathering include

---

[100] Decision I/7, Annex, Section X, Committee Reports to the Meetings of the Parties (as well as paras. 34 and 36). Substantive decision-making (the word 'decide' or 'make a decision' is not used in Decision I/7, Annex, in connection with the Compliance Committee, but only in connection with the MoP in para. 37) includes: (1) Findings as to whether or not the party concerned is in compliance. Pursuant to Decision I/7, Annex, para. 34, the Compliance Committee 'shall send a copy of its draft findings, draft measures and any draft recommendations' to the parties concerned and the member of the public who submitted the communication if applicable. Thus, 'findings' must pertain to conclusions with regard to non-compliance referred to below as determinations of non-compliance. The Compliance Committee has decided that such findings are needed in concrete cases found to be admissible and having been formally discussed. (2) Measures which the Compliance Committee is entitled to take under para. 36, which may include recommendations to the party concerned. (3) Recommendations to the MoP, including recommendations to take one or more of the measures listed in para. 37 (the Compliance Committee has agreed that measures listed in Decision I/7, Annex, para. 37, should not be interpreted as requiring a specific sequence in which these measures could be applied or recommended) (Report on Fifth Meeting, paras. 42–8), although severe measures should not be applied before mild measures (see section 8.7.4 below).

[101] Report on First Meeting, para. 12; and Modus Operandi (section 8.6.1 above).

rules reflecting procedural safeguards (section 8.6.2 above). Parties concerned, as well as members of the public having made a communication, have a right to participate in the discussions of the Compliance Committee (sections 8.6.2 and 8.6.4 above). There are timeframes, *inter alia*, for informing parties concerned on party-to-party submissions (two weeks) and on communications (as soon as possible) (sections 8.6.3 and 8.6.4 above). Communications must fulfil certain admissibility criteria, for example they must not be anonymous, or constitute an abuse of the right to make communications or be manifestly unreasonable (section 8.6.4 above). Submissions and communications shall be supported by corroborating information (sections 8.6.2 and 8.6.3 above). Draft findings and recommendations shall be sent to those concerned and any comments made by them shall be taken into account in the finalization of the findings and recommendations (section 8.6.5 above). Procedural safeguards also include rules of the Compliance Committee on conflicts of interest (section 8.3.1 above) and rules of the compliance mechanism on confidentiality.[102]

8.6.7 Involvement of NGOs in the compliance mechanism

It appears from the analysis above that NGOs may be or are involved in the compliance mechanism and monitoring of compliance in various respects.[103] Both NGOs and individuals may be sources of information and expertise, *inter alia* by virtue of their right to attend meetings of the Compliance Committee as observers. They are entitled to submit communications and to participate in formal discussions of the Compliance Committee of their communications. NGOs and individuals may also be involved in national reporting, and NGOs are entitled to submit reports on 'lessons learned'. Finally, NGOs are entitled to nominate candidates to the Compliance Committee. Most of the rights accorded to NGOs and individuals are rather unique.[104]

---

[102] Decision I/7, Annex, paras. 26–31, referring to art. 4(3)(c) and (g). See also Report on Fourth Meeting, para. 31.

[103] NGOs are referred to or defined in the Convention and decisions of the MoP in various ways: see Wates, 'NGOs and the Aarhus Convention'.

[104] Pitea, 'NGOs in Non-Compliance Mechanisms'. As to the role of NGOs *vis-à-vis* the compliance arrangements under the 1979 Bern Convention and the 1991 Alpine Convention, see Enderlin, 'Alpine Convention', p. 157; and Koester, 'Pacta Sunt Servanda', pp. 78–91.

8.7 Determination of non-compliance and decision on non-compliance response measures

8.7.1 The role, power and nature of the Compliance Committee

The Compliance Committee has authority under the Convention to make recommendations to the MoP on all measures outlined in the compliance mechanism (section 8.7.4 below). Leaving this authority aside, the Compliance Committee has a very limited authority, because all measures it may take otherwise are subject to either consultation or agreement with the party concerned. Furthermore, such measures are '[p]ending consideration by the Meeting of the Parties with a view to addressing compliance issues without delay'.[105] So, the final decision concerning non-compliance and the consequences thereof rest with the parties as a whole.[106] This includes even the provision of advice and recommendations to individual parties.[107] Consequently, while the compliance mechanism is extremely innovative and far-reaching in respect of the composition of the Compliance Committee and of its entitlement to receive communications, the power of the Compliance Committee is extremely limited compared to that of some other compliance committees, some of which might be considered rather conservative in other respects.[108] Probably, this should be seen as a compromise indicating a kind of *checks-and-balances approach* and some hesitation *vis-à-vis* the prominent role that NGOs (and other members of the public) play in the framework of the Aarhus Convention compliance mechanism.

Since decisions of the Compliance Committee are not final, the legal status of these decisions, including the Compliance Committee's findings

---

[105] Decision I/7, Annex, Section XI, Consideration by the Compliance Committee.

[106] In conformity with compliance mechanisms of other treaties.

[107] In spite of the fact that the compliance mechanism is not a redress procedure (see section 8.6.1 above), the time between a determination of non-compliance by the Compliance Committee and the final decision of the MoP in this regard can be rather long, since MoPs presently tend to be held only every third year (see Report on Ninth Meeting, para. 15, on the considerations of the Compliance Committee in this respect). So, whether the Compliance Committee can accomplish anything between MoPs depends basically on the authority of the Compliance Committee in combination with considerations of the party found to be non-compliant. Such considerations might include an assessment of the political advantages of not being exposed by a compliance decision by the MoP which might be avoided if the compliance problem has been resolved in the meantime in collaboration with the Compliance Committee.

[108] E.g. the 1987 Basel Convention compliance mechanism and the Biosafety Protocol compliance mechanism.

with regard to compliance or non-compliance (determinations of non-compliance), are irrelevant. Equally, it is quite evident that cases pending before the Compliance Committee are not *sub judice* and determinations of non-compliance are not *res judicata*.[109] In spite of that, it is noteworthy that the Compliance Committee has agreed that, in order to make a recommendation in a concrete case, it has implicitly to make a (provisional) determination of non-compliance[110] (presumably, however, except with regard to self-incriminatory submissions). A *de facto* determination of non-compliance, generally speaking, implicitly involves an examination or interpretation of the provisions of the Convention and, therefore, exceeds a mere examination and establishment of the facts.[111] Therefore, determination of non-compliance is necessarily to some extent based on legal considerations. Hence, to consider the Compliance Committee of the Aarhus Convention (also taking into consideration its composition) as a political body[112] would be a mistake. However, neither is it a judicial body. Rather, it should be seen as an independent and impartial review body of a quasi-judicial nature.

As at November 2005, the Compliance Committee had received fifteen communications from members of the public and one party-to-party

---

[109] Fitzmaurice and Redgwell, 'Environmental Non-Compliance Procedures', p. 48, and Koskenniemi, 'Breach of Treaty or Non-Compliance?', both dealing with the Implementation Committee of the 1987 Montreal Convention. The notion 'determination of non-compliance' is used to denominate that part of a recommendation of the Compliance Committee to the MoP which deals with the findings of the Compliance Committee regarding non-compliance (or the findings of the Compliance Committee regarding non-compliance in the event that the substantive matter is resolved in between MoPs), or to that part of an MoP decision which concerns the same issue. 'Decisions' of the Compliance Committee are divided into: I. Introduction; II. Summary of Facts (including only the main facts considered to be relevant to the question of compliance, as presented to and considered by the Committee); III. Consideration and Evaluation; and IV. Conclusions (containing main findings with regard to non-compliance and recommendations): see Report on Seventh Meeting, Addenda 1–5.

[110] Report on Fifth Meeting, para. 42.

[111] M. Koskenniemi, 'New Institutions and Procedures for Implementation, Control and Reaction', in J. Werksman (ed.), *Greening International Institutions* (London: Earthscan, 1996), pp. 236 *et seq.*, at p. 245; and Koskenniemi, 'Breach of Treaty or Non-Compliance?', p. 159, at note 212. The Compliance Committee has decided that it is not restricted to consideration of the legal and factual arguments presented by the parties concerned and is free to draw conclusions going beyond the scope of those presented by the parties concerned. Equally, it is free to decide not to address all the arguments and assertions presented, but rather to focus upon those that it considers most relevant. See Report on Sixth Meeting, Doc. MC.PP/C.1/2004/8, January 2005, para. 17; and Report of the Compliance Committee to the MoP, Doc. ECE/MP.PP/2005/13, March 2005, para. 13. Annex I of the Report reveals that, in all five cases where the Compliance Committee concluded that there was non-compliance, the Compliance Committee found that certain provisions of the Convention not alleged to be violated had not been complied with.

[112] Fitzmaurice and Redgwell, 'Environmental Non-Compliance Procedures', p. 48.

CONVENTION ON ACCESS TO INFORMATION ETC.   205

submission, closely related to one of the communications in its subject-matter and therefore referred to as one case.[113] Findings and conclusions have been adopted in five cases. In four of them, including the party-to-party submission, the Committee found that the respective parties concerned were not in compliance with the Convention. The findings and conclusions of the Committee in the five cases were subsequently endorsed by the MoP, which also accepted the recommendations of the Committee to the MoP on non-compliance response measures to be applied. Seven cases are under consideration, while three communications have been found inadmissible.[114]

8.7.2 MoP determinations of non-compliance

The MoP has the power to decide upon appropriate measures to bring about full compliance with the Convention, raising the question of the

[113] Datasheets on all files are posted on the website of the compliance mechanism at www.unece.org/env/pp/compliance.htm.

[114] The Compliance Committee, at its Fifth Meeting, made the decision to start 'formal discussion' of six of these cases, including the party-to-party submission: see Report on Fifth Meeting, paras. 11 and 17. The general outline for 'formal discussion' includes comments from observers (*ibid.*, para. 40), thus providing in practice for *amicus curiae* submissions. Formal discussions took place at the Sixth Meeting: Report on Sixth Meeting, paras. 16–27. The Compliance Committee finalized and adopted its findings and conclusions at its Seventh Meeting. See Report on Seventh Meeting, para. 10, together with Addenda 1–7, and Report of the Compliance Committee to the MoP, Doc. ECE/MP.PP/2005/13, March 2005, paras. 19–32 on the following files: Association Green Salvation/Kazakhstan Government, ACCC/C/2004/01 (non-compliance with arts. 3(1), 4(1) and (2) and 9(1)) and ACCC/C/2004/02 (non-compliance with art. 6(1)–(4) and (7)–(8)); Ecopravo-Lviv/Ukraine Government, ACCC/C/2004/03, and Romania Government/Ukraine Government, ACCC/S/2004/01 (non-compliance with arts. 3(1), 4(1) and 6(1)–(8)); Clean Air Action Group/Hungary Government, ACCC/C/ 2004/04 (no violation of the Convention); and Biotica Ecological Society, Moldavia/ Turkmenistan Government, ACCC/C/2004/05 (non-compliance with art. 3(1), (3) and (5)). With regard to the decisions of the second MoP (Almaty, Kazakhstan, May 2005), see Decision II/5a on Compliance by Kazakhstan, Doc. ECE/ MP.PP/2005/2/Add.7; Decision II/5b on Compliance by Ukraine, Doc. ECE/MP.PP/ 2005/2/Add.8; and Decision II/5c on Compliance by Turkmenistan, Doc. ECE/MP.PP/ 2005/2/Add.9. Based on the recommendations of the Committee, the MoP also made a decision on general issues of compliance addressing issues relating *inter alia* to reporting by parties and compliance with procedures laid down in Decision I/7: see Decision II/5, Doc. ECE/MP.PP/2005/2/Add.6. An example of monitoring compliance on the Compliance Committee's own initiative is provided by para. 34 of the Report of the Compliance Committee to the MoP, Doc. ECE/MP.PP/2005/13, March 2005, concerning non-compliance with Decision I/7. All decisions referred to are available on the website of the Convention, www.unece.org/env/pp/, and on the website of the Compliance Committee, www.unece.org/env/pp/compliance.htm. Some further cases were finalized at the eleventh meeting of the Compliance Committee in March 2006: see Report on Eleventh Meeting, section VII.

legal status of such decisions. It seems obvious that a decision on measures to bring about 'full compliance' presupposes a determination to the effect that one or more of the provisions of the Convention are not complied with (unless a party has made a submission with regard to itself).[115] As pointed out (section 8.7.1 above), such a determination has legal implications, because it implies, probably in most cases, an examination of relevant provisions of the Convention and an assessment of how they should be interpreted and applied. Those considerations are closely related to the facts of the concrete case, but they may amount – and have in fact hitherto amounted – to more general conclusions about the interpretation and application of specific provisions of the Convention, although they are not, necessarily, formulated in that fashion.

Although MoP decisions on non-compliance are not legally binding, the authority of general decisions of the MoP on interpretation and, as appropriate, determinations of non-compliance should not be underestimated, particularly if they are adopted by unanimity or on a consensus basis. Determinations of non-compliance are not without any legal effect. Clearly, the MoP is entitled to decide on appropriate measures based on determinations of non-compliance. So, they might be considered as determinations (decisions) being binding on the internal plane.[116] Otherwise, a decision on appropriate measures would seem to lack legitimacy.

The present analysis assumes that decisions on compliance measures as a general matter are based on determinations of non-compliance, and that those determinations, generally speaking, involve legal considerations on the interpretation or application of specific provisions of the Convention. Interpretive decisions deal with matters of substance.

---

[115] '[F]ull compliance' in Decision I/7, Annex, para. 37, probably means compliance with all obligations (of the Convention), assuming that (all) parties are complying with several or most of the obligations.

[116] An analysis of whether it is necessary, in order to reach that conclusion, to apply international institutional law, i.e. to consider the Aarhus Convention regime as autonomous institutional arrangements with implied powers, as suggested by R. R. Churchill and G. Ulfstein, 'Autonomous Institutional Arrangements in Multilateral Environmental Agreements: A Little-Noticed Phenomenon in International Law' (2002) 94 *American Journal of International Law* 623, is beyond the scope of this chapter. According to R. Wolfrum, 'Means of Ensuring Compliance with and Enforcement of International Environmental Law' (1998) 272 *Recueil des Cours* 9–154, at 149, 'a decision under the non-compliance procedure is binding upon the community of States parties'. See also Fitzmaurice and Redgwell, 'Environmental Non-Compliance Procedures', p. 48.

Consequently, decisions on compliance measures cannot be considered as procedural decisions, i.e. their adoption needs consensus or qualified majority.[117]

8.7.3 International law applicable in the context of non-compliance determinations

The mandate of the Compliance Committee – and ultimately the task of the MoP – is to determine 'compliance with the provisions of the . . . Convention'/'compliance by Parties with their obligations under the Convention'.[118] There is probably no doubt that the competent bodies should apply internationally, commonly accepted, interpretative principles when defining the meaning of the obligations in question.[119] It would also seem rather odd if the MoP were to disregard its own interpretative decisions, and rather unlikely that the Compliance Committee would not take into account such decisions even if they have only a recommendatory character. On the other hand, due account has to be paid to the fact that determinations by compliance bodies are not judgments, because the bodies – not least the MoP, which is essentially a political body – are not rendering *judgments*, not even in the event of decisions on sanctions.[120] Therefore, a certain degree of flexibility is probably envisaged. To what extent other rules of international law should be taken into account might be questionable.[121] The Compliance Committee, however, in the context of its findings in one of the cases where findings and conclusions have been adopted, has stated that '[it] does not exclude the possibility when determining issues of non-compliance to take into consideration general rules and principles of international law, including international environmental and human rights law'.[122]

---

[117] The compliance mechanism includes provisions on how the Compliance Committee shall reach decisions (see section 8.6.5 above), but is silent about the decisions of MoPs. Therefore, the normal rules on decision-making of the MoP apply (Rules of Procedure, Rule 35(1) and (2)).

[118] Art. 15 of the Convention, and operative para. 1 of Decision I/7, respectively.

[119] VCLT, Section 3, Interpretation of Treaties.

[120] However, political considerations should ideally be irrelevant when determining compliance or non-compliance, while they may play an important role in the context of decision-making in respect of compliance measures.

[121] See T. Gehring, 'International Environmental Regimes: Dynamic Sectoral Legal Systems' (1990) 1 *Yearbook of International Environmental Law* 35, at 52.

[122] Report on Seventh Meeting, Addendum 4, para. 18, concerning the file ACCC/C/2004/04, Clean Air Action Group/Hungary.

208 INTERNATIONAL ENVIRONMENTAL LAW

Another question is to what extent the mandate of the Compliance Committee and the task of the MoP excludes reviewing compliance with MoP decisions of a non-interpretative character, for example decisions providing guidance on the application of the provisions of the Convention or decisions otherwise supplementing the provisions of the Convention.[123] One of the tasks of the Compliance Committee is to monitor compliance with the reporting requirements (section 8.5.3.2 above). This task was defined and adopted at the same time as Decision I/8 on Reporting Requirements was adopted.[124] Therefore, it seems likely that the mandate of the Compliance Committee also includes monitoring implementation and compliance with Decision I/8. In fact, the Compliance Committee did address some non-compliance issues related to Decision I/8 in its first report to the MoP, and suggested some recommendations which were subsequently, by and large, adopted by the MoP.[125] Other decisions of a similar nature, i.e. decisions on how the Convention should be applied, might be adopted in the future. It remains to be seen to what extent the Compliance Committee and subsequently the MoP are going to consider such decisions in the context of compliance considerations.

8.7.4 Consequences of non-compliance (enforcement)

According to the Convention itself, the compliance mechanism shall be of a non-confrontational, non-judicial and consultative nature.[126] These qualities also govern the compliance mechanism.[127] Measures decided upon by the MoP (and presumably also measures recommended by the Compliance Committee) must also take 'into account the cause, degree and frequency of the non-compliance'.[128]

The compliance mechanism includes a number of measures that do not (necessarily) exclude each other, but the way the measures are enumerated suggests, as a normal procedure, some kind of sequential application of the

---

[123] Birnie and Boyle, *International Law and the Environment*, p. 207 (with references).

[124] Decision I/7, Annex, Section III, para. 13(c).

[125] Report of the Compliance Committee to the MoP, Doc. ECE/MP.PP/2005/13, March 2005, paras. 44–50; and Decision II/5.   [126] Art. 15.

[127] Decision I/7 refers to art. 15, but curiously enough there is no reference at all to the nature of the compliance mechanism in the Annex to Decision I/7. This is, compared to other compliance mechanisms, quite striking but does not, of course, change the character of the Aarhus Convention compliance mechanism.

[128] Decision I/7, Annex, para. 37, Consideration by the Meeting of the Parties.

measures (i.e. providing assistance before using more severe measures). Furthermore, the measure of suspension of special rights might be regarded as a counter-measure under the rules of State responsibility for non-material breach of a treaty, and therefore should be applied proportionately.[129]

Compliance refers to the question of whether States in fact adhere to the provisions of the Convention, which is an assessment to be made on a case-by-case basis. Obviously, the same considerations apply to the appropriate measures to be taken. The Aarhus Convention compliance mechanism lists the measures:[130] (a) providing advice and facilitating assistance; (b) making recommendations; (c) requesting the party to submit a strategy to the Compliance Committee regarding the achievement of compliance and to report on implementation of the strategy; (d) making recommendations to the party concerned on specific measures to address the matter raised in a communication; (e) issuing declarations of non-compliance; (f) issuing cautions; (g) suspending, in accordance with the applicable rules of international law concerning the suspension of the operation of a treaty, the special rights and privileges accorded to the party concerned under the Convention; (h) taking such other non-confrontational, non-judicial and consultative measures as may be appropriate.

The measures of providing advice and facilitating assistance (a), making recommendations (b), and requesting a compliance strategy (c) are also available to the Compliance Committee itself. However, they are only available on a provisional basis, pending a final decision by the MoP, and they are only available under certain circumstances (see section 8.7.1 above).

Some of the measures appear (in various formulations) in compliance mechanisms of other MEAs and may therefore be regarded as rather traditional measures. This particularly concerns measures having a clear recommendatory and/or assistive and facilitative character. Although measure (d) on recommendation on specific measures also has the same character, this measure is peculiar for the Aarhus compliance mechanism, because it is strictly related to communications. However, nothing prevents the MoP from making a recommendation to the party concerned on specific measures to address a matter raised by another party in a party-to-party

---

[129] Fitzmaurice and Redgwell, 'Environmental Non-Compliance Procedures', p. 52 (citing UN Doc. A/CN.4/507/Add.3, p. 2, para. 287). On proportionality between measures and the character of the breach, see *ibid.*, p. 53; and Koskenniemi, 'Breach of Treaty or Non-Compliance?', p. 140.

[130] Decision I/7, Annex, para. 37.

submission. The compliance mechanism has no means of providing financial assistance because the Convention does not contain a financial mechanism.[131] Consequently, the funding of special activities in order to further compliance relies solely on funding by other parties. Declarations of non-compliance and the issuing of cautions are included in the compliance mechanisms of a few other MEAs.

It might be argued that declarations of non-compliance, the issuing of cautions and the suspension of rights are confrontational. However, they should probably be seen as measures taken as a last resort, and therefore the concerned party may be perceived as the confrontational party, not the other parties. This is probably why such measures have to some extent also been included in compliance mechanisms of other MEAs. Furthermore, by virtue of measure (h) of the Aarhus compliance mechanism ('other non-confrontational . . . measures'), these measures are by definition non-confrontational.

Part of a decision to bring about compliance concerns the determination of non-compliance, and part of the decision relates to compliance measures. The decision as such is (probably) binding on the internal level (section 8.7.1 above). As to compliance measures, *eo ipsi*, the question of to what extent they are binding is, however, not relevant with regard to some of the measures because of their very nature (i.e. advice or recommendations). Declarations of non-compliance and the issuing of cautions (measures (e) and (f)) are of a factual character, but both presuppose, logically, a determination of non-compliance (section 8.7.2 above). In particular, measure (e), declaration of non-compliance, is only, legally speaking, more or less an extension of the determination of non-compliance, although it is adding the element of 'shaming'.[132] Leaving aside the catch-all measure (h), the question of the legal nature seems relevant only with regard to measure (c), requesting the party concerned to submit a strategy, and measure (g), suspension of special rights and privileges. Failure to comply with a request to submit a compliance strategy (measure (c)) does not, legally speaking, constitute a wrongful act, because the compliance decision is not legally binding. However, non-compliance with the measure may entail further

---

[131] Art. 10(3) empowers the MoP, as necessary, to consider establishing financial arrangements on a consensus basis.

[132] Issuing a declaration of non-compliance in the framework of the 1997 Kyoto Protocol compliance mechanism should, according to Ulfstein and Werksmann, 'The Kyoto Compliance System', p. 56, 'be considered binding', but 'does not in itself establish new obligations on the party'.

compliance decisions, provided that the party concerned continues to be in violation of the obligations of the Convention. Thus, a further compliance decision could proceed to the application of more severe measures.

8.7.5 Suspension of special rights and privileges

The measure on suspension of special rights and privileges (measure (g)) provides for '[suspension], in accordance with the applicable rules of international law concerning the suspension of the operation of a treaty, the special rights and privileges accorded to the party concerned under the Convention'. The provision has some similarities with the measure provided for in the indicative list of non-compliance response measures under the 1987 Montreal Protocol on '[s]uspension, in accordance with the applicable rules of international law concerning the suspension and operation of a treaty, of specific rights and privileges under the Protocol'.[133] However, there are some noteworthy differences: the provision of the Aarhus compliance mechanism refers to 'special rights and privileges' while the Montreal compliance mechanism refers to rights and privileges that are 'specific'. Furthermore, the Aarhus Convention compliance mechanism relates (only) to rights and privileges 'accorded to the Party concerned'. Taking into consideration that the Montreal Protocol compliance mechanism was the only existing compliance mechanism containing a measure on suspension of rights and privileges at the time when the Aarhus Convention compliance mechanism was adopted, it is not likely that the similarities or the differences are accidental. How, then, should the measure of the Aarhus Convention compliance mechanism be interpreted?

Unlike the Montreal Protocol compliance mechanism suspension measure, it would seem logical to interpret special rights and privileges 'accorded to the Party concerned' as rights and privileges that are not general under the Convention, because they have been accorded specifically to that party. No such rights exist under the Convention as such, but may be accorded pursuant to rules established under the Convention, for example the Rules of Procedure of the Meeting of the Parties. Such rights or privileges could, therefore, include membership of the Bureau (section 8.2.2 above), chairmanship of subsidiary bodies, and host of official meetings

---

[133] On the 1987 Montreal Protocol compliance mechanism, see, *inter alia*, Birnie and Boyle, *International Law and the Environment*, p. 206.

under the Convention (and, possibly, financial assistance to attend meetings, although the funds for such assistance are managed by the Secretariat and not by the parties). Furthermore, obligations under the Convention do not create rights and privileges for parties, but in reality only certain rights and privileges for civil society associated with or resembling human rights. The only rules of the Convention which are of a different nature are article 11 providing for one vote to each party, and article 16(1) on the right to request negotiation in case of a dispute. Only article 11 is relevant in the context discussed, but still it is difficult to consider that right as a special right accorded to the party concerned, because the right follows directly from the Convention itself and other parties have the same right.

The above interpretation raises the question of the *raison d'être* of the reference to applicable international law, which provides a link to article 60 (on termination or suspension of the operation of a treaty as a consequence of its breach) of the Vienna Convention on the Law of Treaties (VCLT). However, with the above interpretation of special rights and privileges, which also excludes from the scope of the measure deprivation of a party's voting rights, article 60 of the VCLT seems rather irrelevant.[134]

There is not much sense in discussing whether a suspension of special rights and privileges is binding *eo ipso*. It is a decision on the internal level, and it is for the MoP to determine the rights and privileges as interpreted above.[135]

8.7.6 Can obligations to comply be set aside by the Compliance Committee or the MoP?

None of the compliance-reviewing bodies has authority to set aside obligations to comply. However, the compliance mechanism as such and its

---

[134] Actually, the character of the obligations share many of the features characterizing 'provisions relating to the protection of the human person contained in treaties of a humanitarian character' to which art. 60 of the VCLT does not apply and therefore does not permit a suspension of the treaty (art. 60(5)). It might be argued that this provision is applicable to the Aarhus Convention, rendering suspension or termination of the Convention irrelevant. Consequently, it might further be argued that the reference to art. 60 of the VCLT in the Convention's compliance mechanism serves exactly this purpose. However, the suggested interpretation of art. 60(5) of the VCLT is probably not sustainable, but the philosophy behind the provision is interesting also in the context of the Aarhus Convention.

[135] Granted by the MoP it seems logical that the suspension of such rights and privileges is within the implied powers of the MoP. For similar considerations, see Ulfstein and Werksman, 'The Kyoto Compliance System', p. 58, on suspension under the 1997 Kyoto Protocol compliance mechanism of eligibility to participate in the mechanisms under art. 17.

underlying philosophy – that non-compliance often is caused not by a lack of will but rather by a lack of capacity or the ability to comply – could imply a power to accept, at least temporarily, non-compliance, i.e. a power to set aside compliance with obligations for a certain period. This is inherent, for example, with regard to the measure requesting 'a strategy, including a time schedule . . . regarding the achievement of compliance'.[136]

8.8 The relationship between settlement of disputes and review of compliance

According to Decision I/7, '[t]he present compliance procedure shall be without prejudice to article 16 of the Convention on the settlement of disputes'.[137] Similar clauses are included in a number of other MEA compliance mechanisms.[138] An in-depth analysis of the relationship between the DSM and the compliance mechanism of the Aarhus Convention exceeds the scope of this chapter but, based on various sources, some provisional conclusions can be offered.[139]

It follows directly from the above clause that a compliance decision taken by the MoP does not prevent recourse to the DSM. Thus, the party concerned can move the matter to a dispute about the interpretation or application of the Convention, if the party disagrees with the decision (i.e. the determination of compliance). Since the final outcome of the DSM is binding only on the parties to the dispute, and the judgment will only determine whether the party concerned was in breach of its obligations, an application of the compliance mechanism after the settlement of a dispute is not excluded. The fact that the compliance mechanism has been invoked, and that the alleged breach is under consideration either by the Compliance Committee or by the MoP, does not exclude invocation of the DSM. This also seems to follow directly from the clause. Whether ongoing procedures under the DSM exclude invocation of the compliance mechanism depends

---

[136] Decision I/7, Annex, para. 37(c).

[137] Decision I/7, Annex, Section XIII, Relationship between Settlement of Disputes and the Compliance Procedure, para. 38.

[138] E.g. the 1979 LRTAP Convention, the 1987 Montreal Protocol, the 1991 Espoo Convention, the 1989 Basel Convention and the Biosafety Protocol.

[139] With regard to the provisional conclusions, see, in particular, Bree, *Harmonization of Dispute Settlement Mechanisms*, p. 138; Fitzmaurice and Redgwell, 'Environmental Non-Compliance Procedures', pp. 43, 49 and 50; Koskenniemi, 'Breach of Treaty or Non-Compliance?', pp. 140 and 150; and Wolfrum, 'Means of Ensuring Compliance', p. 119.

probably on the stage of the proceedings. Negotiations or other non-judicial means of resolving the dispute 'do not pose a legal impediment to simultaneous proceedings within the [compliance mechanism]'.[140] Whether the mere fact that the dispute is *sub judice, eo ipso,* prevents the consideration of the case in the framework of the compliance mechanism is questionable. However, as long as the avenue of an amicable solution is being pursued by the compliance mechanism, such proceedings in spite of the dispute being *sub judice* are probably permissible.

8.9 Do the compliance and the dispute settlement mechanisms constitute a self-contained regime?

When considering the DSM and the compliance mechanism of the Aarhus Convention, the question arises whether the mechanisms constitute a self-contained regime in the sense that they preclude sanctions under general international law, i.e. either suspension under the VCLT (breach of treaty as an instrument) or counter-measures under the rules of State responsibility (breach of treaty as an obligation). This is a matter of interpretation.[141] Only the nature of the Aarhus Convention (semi-human rights and semi-environmental) seems to differ to some extent from other MEAs with compliance and dispute settlement mechanisms. This might be an indication that the question should be answered more or less in the same manner as regards the Aarhus Convention as it would in respect of other MEAs.

The compliance mechanism contains a rather clear reference to article 60 of the VCLT. However, it is difficult to see under what circumstances article 60 could be applied, taking into consideration the nature of the Convention, which has a bearing both on human rights and on the environment.[142] Also, with regard to counter-measures under general rules of State responsibility, the nature of the Aarhus Convention must be kept in mind. Obviously, it is possible to construe examples where, from a

---

[140] Fitzmaurice and Redgwell, 'Environmental Non-Compliance Procedures', p. 49.

[141] Churchill and Ulfstein, 'Autonomous Institutional Arrangements', p. 16; Ehrmann, 'Procedures of Compliance Control in International Environmental Treaties', p. 441; Fitzmaurice and Redgwell, 'Environmental Non-Compliance Procedures', p. 58; and Koskenniemi, 'Breach of Treaty or Non-Compliance?', pp. 135 and 155.

[142] Wolfrum, 'Means of Ensuring Compliance', p. 57, argues that art. 60 'only touches upon the fringes of the legal and political problems on how to react to breach of a legal obligation which is not only relevant in a reciprocal context but serves the community of States as a whole'. See, furthermore, note 134 on the reservation in art. 60(5) of the VCLT.

theoretical point of view, counter-measures in consequence of State responsibility could be considered: if party A deprives nationals of party B of their rights to access to party A's environmental information or does not accord them these rights (thus violating the right to access to environmental information and the principle of non-discrimination as to *inter alia* citizenship),[143] could party B then, as a counter-measure, apply the same measure *vis-à-vis* nationals of party A, provided that this measure was preceded by a demand for compliance? The response is probably to the negative, because the compliance mechanism is established, by virtue of a provision in the Convention, in order to deal with breaches of obligations, implying that the compliance mechanism is considered to be a more suitable means of resolving a breach of obligations than unilateral counter-measures.[144] Furthermore, it is not party B which essentially is injured. It is rather the nationals of party B who are victims, and by using the counter-measure nationals of party A rather than party A itself will be victimized. Accordingly, it is doubtful whether such or similar counter-measures will provide an incentive for party A to comply. However, a firm conclusion to the effect that counter-measures may not be taken in response to non-compliance is not possible. Ultimately, this depends on an interpretation of relevant provisions of the Convention, and on whether the existing system provides for effective remedies. In addition, it is rather difficult to envisage which counter-measures would be adequate and feasible, i.e. effective and not disproportionate.

8.10 Overall evaluation

The article of the Convention on dispute settlement is formulated in accordance with traditional dispute settlement articles of, *inter alia*, other ECE environmental conventions, but how it is going to be interpreted and applied still remains to be seen.

As in other MEAs, compliance control is exercised by a special committee, but the final decision rests with the parties. A number of non-compliance response measures resemble those available in other MEAs, and other features of the Aarhus Convention compliance mechanism may also be found in various treaty regimes. On the other hand, the compliance

---

[143] Arts. 4 and 3(9).
[144] Koskenniemi, 'Breach of Treaty or Non-Compliance?', p. 136; and Wolfrum, 'Means of Ensuring Compliance', p. 93.

216 INTERNATIONAL ENVIRONMENTAL LAW

mechanism of the Aarhus Convention has a number of unique features. To these features belong in particular the features that the Compliance Committee is composed of independent members, and that individuals and NGOs may submit complaints (communications) to the Compliance Committee about the non-compliance of parties with the provisions of the Convention. In spite of the fact that the compliance mechanism of the Aarhus Convention was established quite recently, it has already received a number of communications and in addition one party-to-party submission. The findings and conclusions of the Compliance Committee in the six cases concluded so far (as at November 2005), finding non-compliance in five of them, were endorsed by the second MoP, which also adopted the non-compliance response measures suggested by the Compliance Committee. However, it still has to be seen to what extend the parties concerned actually implement the recommendations. The endorsement of the MoP of the above findings and conclusions also implies agreement with some general conclusions of the Compliance Committee referred to in the above analysis.[145] Due to the special nature of the compliance mechanism of the Aarhus Convention, the Compliance Committee has had to develop working methods and procedural rules supplementing the basic decision, referred to in the above analysis as the Compliance Committee's 'Modus Operandi' which was welcomed by the second MoP.

The Aarhus Convention's compliance mechanism has served as a source of inspiration in discussions so far on the establishment of a compliance mechanism under the Protocol on Water and Health (to the 1992 Convention on the Protection and Use of Transboundary Watercourses and International Lakes)[146] and its provision on the establishment of a compliance mechanism.[147] On the other hand, the influence of the Aarhus Convention's compliance mechanism on the compliance mechanism of the Biosafety Protocol, which is so far (as at November 2005) the only compliance mechanism of an MEA which has been adopted since the Aarhus

---

[145] See, generally, Report of the Compliance Committee to the MoP, Doc. ECE/MP.PP/2005/13, March 2005, *inter alia*, paras. 13, 14, 16 and 39; and section 8.7.3 and notes 95 and 111 above.

[146] Protocol on Water and Health to the 1992 Convention on the Protection and Use of Transboundary Watercourses and International Lakes, London, 17 June 1999, in force 4 August 2005, ECOSOC Doc. MP.WAT/A.C.1/1999/1. On the compliance mechanism of the Protocol, see ECE Docs. MP.WAT/WG.4/2004/2, MP.WAT/A.C.4/2004/6, MP.WAT/WG.4/2004/7, MP.WAT/WG4/2004/8 and MP.WAT/WG.4/2005/3.

[147] The provision, art. 15, contains the same wording as art. 15 of the Aarhus Convention, namely, that the arrangements for reviewing compliance 'shall allow for appropriate public involvement'.

Convention, was rather limited. Some common features, however, may owe their existence to the Aarhus Convention (e.g. members of the Compliance Committee shall serve in their personal capacity, and compliance measures such as declarations of non-compliance[148]).

Some experience from the Aarhus Convention regime exists. Accordingly, it might be appropriate to consider the transfer of some of the traits that are typical for the Aarhus Convention compliance mechanism to other regimes, in particular those related to the role of civil society in this respect.[149] After all, these traits have a close connection with Principle 10 of the Rio Declaration.[150] Such transfer might be possible in relation to future or existing ECE environmental conventions, but is not likely to happen in the near future with regard to MEAs in general.

[148] Decision BS-I/7, Annex, Section VI, para. 2(b) and (c), and Section II, para. 3.

[149] For a detailed analysis of the involvement of NGOs in various compliance mechanisms and a discussion on pros and cons with regard to NGO involvement in compliance mechanisms, see Pitea, 'NGOs in Non-Compliance Mechanisms'. On *de lege ferenda*, see also Sands, *Principles of International Environmental Law*, p. 199; and Birnie and Boyle, *International Law and the Environment*, p. 217.

[150] Rio Declaration on Environment and Development, UN Conference on Environment and Development, Rio de Janeiro, 3–14 June 1992. A/CONF.151/26 (vol. I).

9

The Convention on Environmental Impact Assessment in a Transboundary Context (Espoo Convention)

TIMO KOIVUROVA

The 1991 Convention on Environmental Impact Assessment in a Transboundary Context (the Espoo Convention)[1] was negotiated under the auspices of the United Nations Economic Commission for Europe (ECE) and was signed in Espoo, Finland, in 1991.[2] Following six meetings of the signatories, the Convention entered into force in 1997 and the first Meeting of the Parties (MoP) took place in Oslo in 1998. The Strategic Environmental Assessment (SEA) Protocol to the Convention was adopted in 2003, and has been signed by thirty-six States as well as by the EC.[3]

The institutional development within the Espoo regime has progressed over time. The Meeting of the Parties, representing the voice of States parties, has taken place three times, and has adopted many important decisions pertaining to the institutional structure of the Espoo Convention. The Bureau of the Convention was established as an organ to co-ordinate the work pertaining to the development of the system of the Convention between the Meetings of the Parties. Secretariat tasks are handled by the ECE. The MoP is now assisted by the Working Group on Environmental Impact Assessment (EIA) and the Implementation Committee. The Working Group on EIA assists the MoP in the implementation of the Convention and the management of the work-plan, and the Implementation Committee has the dual

---

[1] The Convention on Environmental Impact Assessment in a Transboundary Context, Espoo, Finland, 25 February 1991, in force 10 September 1997, Doc. E.ECE.1250. The Convention text can be accessed via the website of the Convention at www.unece.org/env/eia/documents/conventiontextenglish.pdf.

[2] For an overview of the negotiations, see R. Connelly, 'The UN Convention on EIA in a Transboundary Context: A Historical Perspective' (1999) 19 *Environmental Impact Assessment Review* 37–46.

[3] Protocol on Strategic Environmental Assessment to the Convention on Environmental Impact Assessment in a Transboundary Context, Kiev, 21 May 2003, Doc. ECE/MP.EIA/2003/2. The Protocol can be accessed via the website of the Convention at www.unece.org/ env/eia/documents/protocolenglish.pdf.

task of developing the reporting system and considering individual cases of non-compliance.

Before taking up the main focus of this chapter – namely, the dispute resolution, compliance control and enforcement procedures of the Espoo regime – it will be useful to examine the substantive rules of the Espoo Convention. The Convention regulates situations where a proposed activity in one contracting State (the origin State) is likely to cause a significant adverse transboundary impact on another State's environment. The Convention tries to manage these situations by requiring the parties to co-operate with each other before the activity is undertaken. In order for this procedure to function effectively, the Convention requires the States parties to establish national EIA procedures as well as licensing procedures, with foreign impacts and foreign actors integrated into both.[4]

The origin State is first required to notify the potentially affected State of the likely significant adverse transboundary impact and to provide basic information regarding the proposed activity. The affected State must next confirm that it wants to participate in the procedure.[5] The origin State is then obligated to study the transboundary impacts together with the affected State and allow the public of that State to participate in the process on the same terms as its own public would be entitled to.[6] After the impact assessment, the affected State has an opportunity to comment on the proposed activity and its likely impacts, through consultations with the origin State. The public of the affected State is entitled to provide its comments on the proposed activity on the same terms as apply to the public of the origin State.[7] The final decision taken on the proposed activity in the origin State must take due account of the comments from the potentially affected State and its public, and must be delivered to the affected State.[8] The States parties are not required to determine whether the impacts studied ultimately materialize, as post-project analysis is optional.[9]

The SEA Protocol requires the contracting States to establish a national SEA procedure – a procedure by which the likely environmental effects of a plan, programme or policy are examined with the help of all relevant parties – rather than on establishing a transboundary procedure between States; only one provision in the Protocol, article 10, addresses the latter procedure. The Protocol requires the contracting States to create an SEA

---

[4] Art. 2(2), (3) and (7) of the Espoo Convention.   [5] *Ibid.*, art. 3(1), (2) and (3).
[6] *Ibid.*; see art. 3(4)–(8) and art. 2(6) on non-discrimination.   [7] *Ibid.*, arts. 4 and 5.
[8] *Ibid.*, art. 6.   [9] *Ibid.*, art. 7 and Appendix V.

procedure that evaluates, with the involvement of the environmental and health authorities and the general public, the likely environmental and health impacts of plans and programmes.[10] Evaluation of the environmental and health impacts of policies and legislation is optional for the parties.[11] In the case of likely significant transboundary environmental and/or health impacts, the origin State must notify the potentially affected State, after which consultations may take place.[12]

The substantive rules of the Espoo Convention and the SEA Protocol set out clear obligations and rights for the States parties. This approach stands in direct contrast to that found in many other international environmental treaties, for example the Convention on Biological Diversity, whose primary rules are so loose and open-ended that their legal status can be questioned.[13] The nature of a treaty's substantive rules has an impact on how the compliance control and enforcement systems are organized in the treaty regime. If the parties and the treaty bodies fail to agree on what is required in a treaty, and perhaps even disagree over whether some of the rules in the convention are binding or not (or are soft rules), it becomes much more difficult to establish a compliance control system, as the object of what is controlled and reviewed is uncertain. In the case of the Espoo Convention, substantial consensus exists on the content and scope of the primary rules, which greatly facilitates the creation of a compliance control system.

9.1 Dispute resolution

9.1.1 The basic dispute resolution mechanism under the Convention

The need to have a separate provision for dispute resolution arose in the first (of six) meetings of the *ad hoc* Working Group that was entrusted by the Senior Advisers of the ECE[14] to draw up an international agreement on the matter.[15] The Espoo Convention thus came to include a provision on

---

[10] Arts. 5–9 of the SEA Protocol.   [11] *Ibid.*, art. 13.   [12] *Ibid.*, art. 10.

[13] The Convention on Biological Diversity, Rio de Janeiro, 5 June 1992, 31 ILM 818 (1992). The Convention can be accessed via the Convention's website at www.biodiv.org/convention/articles.asp.

[14] The body known as the Senior Advisers to the ECE governments was transformed in 1994 to become the Committee on Environmental Protection. For the terms of reference of both bodies, see the ECE website at www.unece.org/env/cep/tor.htm.

[15] Connelly, *EIA in a transboundary perspective*, 1999, p. 40.

dispute settlement which also applies to the SEA Protocol.[16] The provision is set out in article 15:

> 1. If a dispute arises between two or more Parties about the interpretation or application of this Convention, they shall seek a solution by negotiation or by any other method of dispute settlement acceptable to the parties to the dispute.
> 2. When signing, ratifying, accepting, approving or acceding to this Convention, or at any time thereafter, a Party may declare in writing to the Depositary that for a dispute not resolved in accordance with paragraph 1 of this Article, it accepts one or both of the following means of dispute settlement as compulsory in relation to any Party accepting the same obligation:
> > (a) Submission of the dispute to the International Court of Justice;
> > (b) Arbitration in accordance with the procedure set out in Appendix VII.
> 3. If the parties to the dispute have accepted both means of dispute settlement referred to in paragraph 2 of this Article, the dispute may be submitted only to the International Court of Justice, unless the parties agree otherwise.

This article is very much in line with the basic premise of dispute settlement provisions in international environmental treaties: the parties remain fully free to resolve their dispute by any means they deem appropriate, although the article does give them the option of making declarations accepting compulsory third-party settlement.

Article 15 sets out two main channels for resolving disputes between contracting States about the interpretation or application of the Convention. First, if a party has declared in writing to the Depositary that it accepts a compulsory dispute settlement – either the procedure in the International Court of Justice (ICJ) or arbitration as set out in Appendix VII, or both – the disputes it has with other contracting States may be decided by compulsory dispute settlement. However, even when both disputants have made such a declaration, they always have the possibility – if they so agree – to have the dispute decided using political dispute settlement methods ('for a dispute not resolved in accordance with paragraph 1 of this Article …'[17]). The declarations become important in cases where no political solution can be

---

[16] Art. 20 of the SEA Protocol.

[17] Art. 15(2) of the Espoo Convention. In other words, the declarations give the parties the option of submitting the dispute to compulsory dispute settlement; the provision does not force them to do so.

found since, depending on the content of the declarations the parties have given, the potentially affected State may take the origin State to the ICJ or initiate arbitration.[18] To date, Austria, Bulgaria, Liechtenstein and the Netherlands have declared that they accept both means of compulsory dispute settlement identified in article 15(2) of the Convention, meaning that, if a dispute between the parties cannot be handled through the political mechanism, the ICJ will have jurisdiction over it.[19]

There is one pending dispute between the parties to the Espoo Convention. The Polish Minister of the Environment has sent a letter to the German Federal Minister of Environment, Nature Conservation and Nuclear Safety with a request to start negotiations. The dispute relates to the management of the River Oder, and focuses on whether Germany has adequately taken into account the comments from the public and the outcome of the consultation in its final decision, as required by article 6(1) of the Convention. The first meeting between the parties took place in Wroclaw on 12 February 2003.[20]

9.1.2 Special dispute resolution: the inquiry commission procedure

If a dispute centres on whether the origin State is required to initiate a transboundary EIA procedure of the Espoo Convention, then the

---

[18] If both have accepted only arbitration, then it is arbitration according to Appendix VII (similarly, if both have accepted only the ICJ, then the ICJ will be the forum used). If both parties have accepted both means of dispute settlement, then the ICJ will be used provided that the parties do not agree otherwise, in which case Appendix VII arbitration will be applied. However, if one party has accepted only arbitration and the other only the ICJ, the provision leaves open the question whether both parties are bound to have the dispute resolved by compulsory dispute settlement since the provision speaks of the 'same obligation', which can be interpreted as referring to the compulsory dispute settlement in general or a means of compulsory dispute settlement.

[19] For the declarations, see the Espoo Convention website at www.unece.org/env/eia/ convratif.html. If the parties, or one of the parties, have not given such a declaration to the Depositary, then para. 1 applies and the parties are free to resolve their dispute via any method of political dispute settlement they deem necessary. If the dispute cannot be resolved by these mechanisms, art. 15 cannot be resorted to, because the compulsory dispute settlement becomes possible only through the declarations. Where these declarations have not been made, the parties may seek remedies under the regime of the Vienna Convention on the Law of Treaties and/or general international law.

[20] See the Review of Implementation, p. 198, which is available from the Implementation Committee website at www.unece.org/env/eia/implementation.htm. According to the German official in charge, Germany commenced this procedure even before the Convention became binding on it; it thus does not regard the procedure in which the Polish state and its nationals were parties as a regular transboundary EIA procedure or consider art. 15 to be applicable. There is currently a bilateral working group studying the issue (e-mail communication on 28 January 2005).

CONVENTION ON ENVIRONMENTAL IMPACT ASSESSMENT   223

Convention provides a special dispute settlement mechanism known as the inquiry commission procedure.[21] This concept came in quite late in the negotiations leading up to the adoption of the Convention, in the fourth meeting of the *ad hoc* Working Group.[22] The particulars of the inquiry commission procedure were then negotiated in the Working Group's fifth and, especially, sixth and final meeting.[23] This particular method of resolving disputes is actually quite rare in international environmental treaties. The only treaty before the Espoo Convention to have had such a procedure is the 1974 Nordic Environment Protection Convention, but this procedure has never, to the author's knowledge, been invoked.[24]

The basic provision establishing an obligation on the part of the origin State to commence a transboundary EIA procedure is article 3(1), which reads:

> For a proposed activity listed in Appendix I that is likely to cause a significant adverse transboundary impact, the Party of origin shall, for the purposes of ensuring adequate and effective consultations under Article 5, notify any Party which it considers may be an affected Party as early as possible and no later than when informing its own public about that proposed activity.

If the origin State does not notify the potentially affected State concerning a proposed activity listed in Appendix I (list of activities known to be environmentally harmful), and the affected State is of the opinion that the activity is likely to cause a significant adverse transboundary impact, the affected State has a right to request information from the origin State for 'the purposes of holding discussions on whether there is likely to be a significant adverse transboundary impact'.[25] If the concerned States cannot agree in their discussions on whether there is likely to be a significant adverse transboundary impact, or if the origin State refuses to discuss the issue, the affected State 'may submit that question to an inquiry commission in accordance with the provisions of Appendix IV to advise on the likelihood of significant adverse transboundary impact, unless they agree

---

[21] The SEA Protocol does not contain an inquiry commission procedure, even though it does have a provision on a transboundary procedure. See art. 10 of the Protocol.

[22] Connelly, 'The UN Convention on EIA in a Transboundary Context', p. 42.

[23] *Ibid.*, pp. 43–4.

[24] Art. 12 of the Nordic Environment Protection Convention, Stockholm, 19 February 1974, in force 5 October 1976, 13 ILM 352 (1974).   [25] Art. 3(7) of the Espoo Convention.

224 INTERNATIONAL ENVIRONMENTAL LAW

on another method of settling this question'.[26] The affected State can thus initiate an inquiry commission procedure even against the origin State's will.

Although many of the relevant terms are defined in the Convention,[27] determining whether a significant adverse transboundary impact is likely to result from a proposed activity listed in Appendix I is bound to be a difficult and relative task, and for this reason both States may opt to seek advice through an inquiry commission procedure. Then again, if the origin State has persistently rejected any discussion of the applicability of the Espoo Convention to the case, it is unlikely to take part in the inquiry commission procedure either. The Convention contains rules for both situations, i.e. when both States initiate an inquiry commission procedure and when only the affected State does so. In both instances, the procedure starts by the parties (or party) notifying the Secretariat of the Convention of their (its) intention to commence it. This notification must also state the subject-matter of the inquiry. The Secretariat then notifies all parties to the Convention of this submission, a measure which broadens the awareness of the dispute to the whole treaty community.

If both parties seek advice through an inquiry commission procedure, each proceeds, in accordance with paragraph 2 of Appendix IV, to appoint a scientific or technical expert as its representative to the commission. The two experts then appoint by common agreement a third expert, who serves as president of the commission and whose impartiality must be ensured.[28] After adopting its own rules of procedure, the inquiry commission may take all appropriate measures to carry out its functions, a task in which it clearly needs assistance from the concerned States.[29] Paragraph 7 of Appendix IV requires the parties to an inquiry commission procedure to facilitate the work of the commission using all means at their disposal.[30] The decision by the inquiry commission as to whether the proposed activity listed in Appendix I is likely to cause a significant adverse transboundary impact is only advisory in nature but, where negative for the origin State,

---

[26] *Ibid.*   [27] *Ibid.*, art. 1.

[28] *Ibid.*, Appendix IV, para. 2, which states that he or she 'shall not be a national of one of the Parties nor have his or her usual place of residence in the territory of one of these parties, nor be employed by any of them, nor have dealt with the matter in any other capacity'. Para. 3 then provides: 'If the president of the inquiry commission has not been designated within two months of the appointment of the second expert, the Executive Secretary of the Economic Commission for Europe shall, at the request of either party, designate the president within a further two-month period.'

[29] *Ibid.*, Appendix IV, para. 6.   [30] *Ibid.*, Appendix IV, para. 7.

certainly puts pressure on that State to initiate the transboundary EIA procedure.[31]

There are special rules for cases where the affected State invokes the inquiry commission procedure against the origin State without the participation of the latter. The procedure commences as described above, with the affected State making a submission to the Secretariat, which then informs the other parties to the Convention. After the affected State has appointed its expert to the commission, if the origin State does not appoint its expert within one month of its being notified by the Secretariat, the affected State may inform the Executive Secretary of the ECE accordingly.[32] The Executive Secretary is empowered by paragraph 4 of Appendix IV to designate the president of the inquiry commission, who will then require the origin State to appoint its expert. If the origin State remains passive and fails to appoint its expert within one month of the president's request, the president must inform the Executive Secretary of the ECE, who then has to make the appointment within the next two months. The affected State can thus invoke the inquiry commission procedure even without any participation by the origin State. According to paragraph 9 of Appendix IV, if the origin State does not appear before the commission or fails to present its case, the affected State may request that the commission continue the proceedings and complete its work, which it must do since 'absence of a party or failure of a party to present its case shall not constitute a bar to the continuation and completion of the work of the inquiry commission'.[33] It should be borne in mind that, if the origin State does not participate at all in the inquiry commission procedure, it becomes very hard for the commission to do its work, given that the origin State has most of the relevant information about the proposed activity.

The inquiry commission procedure has been invoked in one recent case. On 19 August 2004, the Secretariat of the Espoo Convention notified all the parties to the Convention, as required by paragraph 1 of Appendix IV, that Romania had made a submission requesting the establishment of an inquiry commission to advise on the likelihood of a significant adverse transboundary impact arising from the Ukrainian project 'Danube–Black Sea Deep Water Navigation Canal in the Ukrainian Sector of the Danubian Delta'. The concerned States, Romania and Ukraine, were not able to agree

---

[31] *Ibid.*, Appendix IV, paras. 12–14.   [32] *Ibid.*, Appendix IV, para. 3.
[33] *Ibid.*, Appendix IV, para. 9.

whether a significant adverse transboundary impact from the project would be likely, and both nominated their experts to the commission. However, the two experts were not able to agree on a third expert – the president of the commission – within two months of the appointment of the second expert, whereupon, on 17 December 2004, Romania asked the Executive Secretary of the ECE to make the appointment of the president pursuant to paragraph 3 of Appendix IV. The Executive Secretary did so, and the first meeting of the inquiry commission was held on 26 January 2005 in Geneva. Further meetings are scheduled for 24 February and 13 May, with site visits from 10 to 16 April 2005.[34] In principle, according to paragraph 13 of Appendix IV, the inquiry commission is to present its final opinion within two months of the date on which it was established, which did not take place in this case. However, paragraph 13 also provides that the inquiry commission can extend the time limit for an additional two months, a timeframe that may prove to be challenging in this case, given that parties have already scheduled a meeting for 13 May 2005.

The Espoo Convention provides three mechanisms by which parties can resolve their disputes: the Implementation Committee, to be discussed below, the inquiry commission procedure, and the general dispute settlement procedures. This range of alternatives seems like a sound approach in principle, since it enables parties to avoid resorting to third-party dispute settlement, which is a measure to be used only when all others have been exhausted. Thus far, four parties have filed a declaration to have their disputes with other parties decided through compulsory third-party dispute settlement. With the Convention having been in force for seven years, there are two disputes pending between States parties: one is being dealt with in an inquiry commission procedure, the other through general dispute settlement, as discussed above.

9.2 Compliance control

Compliance control is the mechanism whereby the treaty community monitors and reviews whether the States parties have observed their

---

[34] The information about inquiry procedures can be accessed through the Espoo Convention website at www.unece.org/env/eia/inquiry.htm. See also the responses by States parties as to whether they have made use of the inquiry procedure, presented in the full Review of Implementation (Advance Copy, 30 August 2004), p. 197, which can also be accessed through the Espoo Convention's website at www.unece.org/env/eia/implementation.htm.

obligations as set out in the Convention. The principal need here is for an institutional structure by which such compliance can be monitored in general. There is also a need to establish basic rules and procedures by which compliance information flows to the treaty bodies from the States parties, procedures as to how the treaty bodies may ensure that this subjective information corresponds to the reality (the reporting procedure) and procedures by which potential cases of non-compliance are examined by the treaty bodies (the non-compliance procedure).

The Espoo Convention did not originally provide much in the area of compliance control. It did establish the basis for institutional development in article 11 by creating the Meeting of the Parties and defining its terms of reference; otherwise, all legal changes to the Convention are to be made through formal amendments, as set out in article 14. Curiously, article 11 does not explicitly mandate that the MoP create any sub-organs, frequently so relevant in the management of international environmental treaties.[35]

9.2.1 The system for reviewing treaty compliance

In contrast to its SEA Protocol,[36] the Espoo Convention does not impose any reporting obligation on the parties. Unlike some international environmental treaties, the Convention did not require the parties to provide an initial submission of information, nor does it require them to submit regular reports. The farthest the Convention has gone in this respect is article 11(2) setting out the terms of reference of the MoP, essentially requiring the parties to continuously review implementation of the Convention in numerous ways.

The second MoP, held in Sofia in 2001, decided to develop a reporting system 'on how the obligations of the Convention have been complied with, both at the general level and by particular Parties'.[37] A task force[38] was established at the Sofia meeting to handle the review procedure until the system proper under the Implementation Committee became operational. The ensuing review was published at the third MoP, in Croatia in 2004, and

[35] Art. 11(2) of the Espoo Convention.
[36] Art. 14(7) of the Protocol stipulates as follows: 'Each Party shall, at intervals to be determined by the Meeting of the Parties to the Convention serving as the Meeting of the Parties to this Protocol, report to the Meeting of the Parties to the Convention serving as the Meeting of the Parties to the Protocol on measures that it has taken to implement the Protocol.'
[37] Decision II/11, Adoption of the Work-plan (ECE/MP.EIA/4, 7 August 2001).
[38] The delegation of the United Kingdom led the task force, assisted by the Secretariat.

228   INTERNATIONAL ENVIRONMENTAL LAW

it focused on how the parties had applied the obligations of the Convention with regard to the transboundary EIA procedure.[39] In keeping with the mandate of the task force, the review did not analyze whether the parties had complied with their obligations; it only examined the experiences of the parties with a view to improving the regime, basically summarizing what the parties had experienced in implementing and applying the Convention. This task clearly differed from the regular analysis of State reports with a view to detecting non-compliance.

The first review of implementation was carried out by the task force, not the Implementation Committee. The decision establishing the Implementation Committee in the 2001 Sofia MoP gave the Committee the responsibility of developing a reporting procedure, and it is expected to prepare a revised and simplified questionnaire and draft a review of implementation for the fourth MoP.[40] The third MoP adopted an amendment formalizing the regular reporting requirement for the parties, which when it enters into force will provide a formal basis for the reporting of compliance information to the Implementation Committee and the MoP. The amendment inserted a new article, article 14*bis*, into the Convention. Article 14*bis* provides as follows:

1. The Parties shall review compliance with the provisions of this Convention on the basis of the compliance procedure, as a non-adversarial and assistance-oriented procedure adopted by the Meeting of the Parties. The review shall be based on, but not limited to, regular reporting by the Parties. The Meeting of Parties shall decide on the frequency of regular reporting required by the Parties and the information to be included in those regular reports.
2. The compliance procedure shall be available for application to any protocol adopted under this Convention.[41]

The role of the Implementation Committee in examining State reports is still taking shape and it seems that its role in the near future will be largely to do what the task force did, namely, to conduct an evaluation of State behaviour in terms of the future development of the regime rather than to carry out a review focused on detecting non-compliance. The reason for this is that there will be no legal obligation to report until the second amendment

---

[39] Full Review of Implementation (Advance Copy, 30 August 2004).
[40] Decision III/9 of the third MoP (ECE/MP.EIA/6, 13 September 2004).
[41] *Ibid.*, Decision III/7, Second Amendment to the Espoo Convention, para. f.

to the Convention enters into force. Yet, if and when the formal amendment quoted above enters into force, the Implementation Committee will be empowered to develop a regular system of State reporting.

9.2.2 The non-compliance mechanism: the Implementation Committee

The Espoo Convention has no provisions on non-compliance, but the work-plan for the years 1998 to 2000, formulated in 1998 at the first MoP in Oslo, included work on non-compliance guidelines.[42] The delegation of the United Kingdom, which was assigned to lead a task force in this area, produced a background paper entitled 'Compliance with Multilateral Environmental Agreements', in which it outlined the existing non-compliance mechanisms and identified certain trends in these mechanisms for the Working Group on EIA to consider.[43] Decision II/4 by the MoP – setting out the structure and functions of the Implementation Committee – drew heavily from the Implementation Committee which supervised the Convention on Long-Range Transboundary Air Pollution and its protocols, which had been established by that Convention's Executive Body in its Decision 1997/2.[44]

The third MoP, held in Croatia in 2004, changed the structure and functions of the Implementation Committee, but only very slightly. The principal change, seen throughout Decision III/2, is its emphasis on openness and transparency, a development much influenced by the other ECE convention, the Aarhus Convention. The third MoP introduced another change, prompted by the adoption of the SEA Protocol in May 2003 and the concomitant need to determine whether the Implementation Committee is empowered to supervise observance of the Protocol. In its Decision III/2, the MoP 'encourag[ed] the application of the procedure for the review of compliance to the Protocol on Strategic Environmental Assessment and to any future protocols to the Convention, in accordance with their relevant provisions'.[45] Furthermore, as noted above, the MoP adopted an amendment which, when it enters into force, will make it clear that the Implementation Committee procedure also applies to supervision of the

---

[42] Decision I/6, chapter 5 (ECE/MP.EIA/2, 10 November 1998).
[43] MP.EIA/WG.1/1999/7, 28 July 1999.
[44] The first draft, MP.EIA/WG.1/2000/9, 27 March 2000. The Executive Body Decision 1997/2, ECE/EB.AIR/53.
[45] Decision III/2, Review of Compliance, para. 4, ECE/MP.EIA/6, 13 September 2004.

SEA Protocol. What is more, the SEA Protocol itself contains an explicit provision on the applicability of the Implementation Committee procedure to the Protocol.[46] A possible challenge for the Implementation Committee in this respect is how it can adjust its work to include not only inter-State situations and disputes, as set out in the Espoo Convention, but also situations regulated by the SEA Protocol, which focuses primarily on requiring the contracting States to create and implement national SEA procedures.

Where non-compliance is suspected, the contracting States may notify the Secretariat of the Convention with corroborating information.[47] The Secretariat will then inform the State alleged to be in non-compliance and allow it to supply information of its own. Thereafter, the Secretariat will transmit these bodies of information to the Implementation Committee.[48] It is also possible that the origin State will notify the Secretariat that it is unable to comply with the obligations of the Convention, either after the notification by the affected State or on its own initiative. In such cases, the State is obligated to inform the Secretariat of its reasons for non-compliance, and this information is delivered to the Implementation Committee.[49] The Committee may also commence the procedure on its own initiative with the party that has failed to comply with its obligations.[50]

The Implementation Committee has two options in proceeding with a case of suspected non-compliance: it may request further information on the case through the Secretariat or it may even gather information in the territory of the concerned States, but only at its invitation.[51] The Committee must ensure the confidentiality of the information delivered to it.[52] The concerned States and the public are entitled to participate in the proceedings if the Committee does not decide otherwise, but not in the preparation and adoption of any report or recommendations of the Committee.[53] The Implementation Committee Procedure is without prejudice to the general dispute settlement clause, meaning that, even when a procedure is pending, the parties can try to resolve the dispute on their own.[54] When a matter is being considered under the inquiry commission procedure, however, it may not be submitted to any other dispute settlement mechanism under the Convention.[55]

---

[46] Art. 14(6) of the SEA Protocol.
[47] Decision III/2, Annex II, Review of Compliance, Appendix, para. 5(a), ECE/MP.EIA/6, 13 September 2004.   [48] *Ibid.*   [49] *Ibid.*, para. 5(b).   [50] *Ibid.*, para. 6.   [51] *Ibid.*, para. 7.
[52] *Ibid.*, para. 8.   [53] *Ibid.*, paras. 9 and 10.   [54] *Ibid.*, para. 14.   [55] *Ibid.*, para. 15.

As noted above, the Convention did not originally contain any provisions on non-compliance. In the third MoP, in Croatia in 2004, the parties adopted the above-quoted second amendment to the Convention, which, if and when it enters into force, will formalize the status of the Implementation Committee.

To date, while the Implementation Committee has not been called upon to resolve any disputes, it has received a communication from an NGO. This presented a difficult problem for the Committee since, in contrast to the Compliance Committee of the Aarhus Convention, it may not receive direct submissions from other than States parties. The Committee discussed this challenge extensively in its third meeting, outlining various alternatives for the role of the public.[56] In the fourth meeting, the President of the Committee drew the Committee's attention to a letter from an NGO addressed both to the Committee and to the Secretariat; the Secretariat had forwarded the letter to the Committee on 26 August 2003. The Committee did not address the fundamental question of how to deal with such communications but only agreed that the information that had been provided thus far was insufficient for the case to be considered.[57]

However, in the fifth meeting of the Committee, the case came back to the Committee. The Secretariat had received a copy of a letter sent by the same NGO to a party regarding a potential non-compliance issue and then made this letter available to the Committee.[58] It is worth noting here that the rules of the Committee permit it to initiate the procedure when it becomes aware of possible non-compliance. The Committee's conclusion in this respect is worth quoting:

> The Committee agreed that it should acknowledge the latest communication and that its response should reflect the views of all its members. The majority agreed not to consider the information, because considering unsolicited information from NGOs and the public relating to specific cases of non-compliance was not within the Committee's existing mandate. A minority disagreed, interpreting the present mandate (Decision II/4, app., para. 5) to mean that there

[56] Paras. 5–15 of the minutes of the third meeting of the Implementation Committee, MP.EIA/WG.1/2003/8, 10 July 2003.
[57] Para. 10 of the minutes of the fourth meeting of the Implementation Committee, MP.EIA/WG.1/2004/3, 17 December 2003.
[58] Para. 5 of the minutes of the fifth meeting of the Implementation Committee, MP.EIA/WG.1/2004/4, 8 April 2004.

were no restrictions on how the Committee became aware of a case of possible non-compliance, preferring to examine the information further.[59]

In the present author's view, it seems hard to defend the position of the majority except in terms of political realism. The Committee certainly had become aware of a case of possible non-compliance that was not a direct submission from an NGO but a copy of a letter by an NGO that a State party had sent to the Secretariat, which it had then forwarded to the Committee. If the case had been a direct submission from an NGO, there would have been better grounds for refusing to examine it. This decision by the Implementation Committee will most likely serve as a precedent: it is hard to see how after this decision the non-compliance mechanism could be triggered by parties other than the States parties. The Espoo Convention's non-compliance review cannot be started even by the Secretariat, as it is only the Committee that can 'open' a case and contact the State party alleged to be in non-compliance. In the case of, for example, the Convention on Long-Range Transboundary Air Pollution non-compliance mechanism, the Secretariat of that Convention can initiate a procedure with the State alleged to be in non-compliance on the basis of information provided by, for instance, an environmental NGO.[60]

As noted above, the Implementation Committee has neither received any submissions from States parties nor 'become aware' of any non-compliance by a party. With no formal submission from the States parties, a case has to be opened by the Implementation Committee itself, a course of action it has been reluctant to take. The Committee's conclusions quoted above clearly indicate that it will not easily start the non-compliance procedure without formal submissions from States parties, a policy also seen in the MoP's increased emphasis on requiring parties to make self-submissions.[61] When the reporting system becomes obligatory, the Committee will have a good basis for starting a non-compliance procedure on the basis of the information obtained from the State reports.

[59] *Ibid.*, para. 7.
[60] Statement of the secretary to the Executive Body of the LRTAP Convention in the third meeting of the Compliance Committee of the Aarhus Convention, para. 7 of the minutes of the third meeting (MP.PP/C.1/2004/2, 2 March 2004).
[61] See para. 1 of Decision III/2, ECE/MP.EIA/6, 13 September 2004.

9.2.3 Enforcement

According to the rules that govern the work of the Implementation Committee, the Committee cannot take decisions of its own, a mandate differing, for example, from that of the Compliance Committee of the Aarhus Convention.[62] The Implementation Committee can only draft a recommendation on a compliance case to the MoP, which makes the final decision.[63] If consensus cannot be reached in the MoP, the recommendation by the Implementation Committee will be accepted if a three-quarters majority of the parties present and voting favours it.[64] The party suspected of non-compliance cannot block the decision, since consensus is not required. Yet, not even such a decision is binding on the non-compliant State, since it is a decision of the MoP, which, arguably, is non-binding, although arguments to the contrary have been put forth in the legal literature.[65]

Decision III/2, Review of Compliance, of the MoP does not specify the measures that can be taken in the case of non-compliance. It is only stipulated that the MoP may decide 'upon appropriate general measures to bring about compliance with the Convention and measures to assist an individual party's compliance'.[66] This would seem to refer to two basic approaches, enforcement and management. The former entails implementation of negative measures against the party in non-compliance and the latter assistance for parties in complying with the obligations of the Convention. However, it is still very unclear what form these measures might take, as the

---

[62] Para. XI of the Annex to Decision I/7 of the first MoP, ECE/MP.PP/2/Add.8. The Compliance Committee is empowered by its founding document to provide advice and facilitate assistance to individual parties concerning their implementation situation pending consideration by the meeting of the parties. The Committee may also make recommendations and request an implementation strategy pending the decision by the meeting of the parties but only when an agreement has been reached with the non-compliant state.

[63] Para. 13 of the Appendix to Decision III/2 of the MoP, ECE/MP.EIA/6, 13 September 2004.

[64] *Ibid.*

[65] It is of course possible that decisions by the MoP can be seen as 'any subsequent agreement between the parties regarding the interpretation of the treaty or the application of its provisions', as stated in Art. 31(3)(a) of the Vienna Convention on the Law of Treaties. Or, as has been suggested by Churchill and Ulfstein, the regime of the Espoo Convention may qualify as an Autonomous Institutional Arrangement (AIA), an entity comparable to an intergovernmental organization, with the concomitant possibility that the decisions of its plenary organ are binding on the States parties. See Robin R. Churchill and Geir Ulfstein, 'Autonomous Institutional Arrangements in Multilateral Environmental Agreements: A Little-Noticed Phenomenon in International Law' (2000) 94 *American Journal of International Law* 623–59.

[66] Para. 13 of the Appendix to the Decision III/2 of the MoP, ECE/MP.EIA/6, 13 September 2004.

234 INTERNATIONAL ENVIRONMENTAL LAW

Implementation Committee has not had to decide any actual cases of non-compliance nor has it addressed the issue in its meetings. Given the recent amendment to the Convention providing that the 'Parties shall review compliance with the provisions of this Convention on the basis of the compliance procedure, as a non-adversarial and assistance-oriented procedure',[67] it seems likely that the procedure is very much tilted towards using a managerial rather than an enforcement approach.

One problem that the Implementation Committee has been well aware of since its third meeting is that, with MoPs taking place only every three years, a considerable amount of time may elapse before the MoP can take a decision on an issue decided by the Committee and a response to non-compliance made.[68] The trend in this issue might very well be that the Implementation Committee will follow the lead of the Aarhus Compliance Committee and become empowered to take certain decisions by itself, with more severe consequences for the parties being decided by the MoP.[69]

It is hard to evaluate the direction which the collective decisions to counter non-compliance might take, as no case has proceeded that far. To date, the Implementation Committee, which must draw up the particulars of reactions to non-compliance since it recommends them to the MoP, has not started elaborating guidelines as to the kinds of measures the MoP could take if the Committee should discover a case of non-compliance. While this is no doubt due in part to the fact that the Committee has not dealt with any cases, such guidelines are precisely the kinds of measures that should be elaborated before any case even comes before the Implementation Committee and the MoP.

9.2.4 Evaluation

A number of general trends can be identified with respect to reporting, non-compliance mechanisms and enforcement rules and procedures in the

---

[67] Decision III/7, Second Amendment to the Espoo Convention in the third MoP, para. f, ECE/MP.EIA/6, 13 September 2004.

[68] Para. 21 of the minutes of the third meeting of the Implementation Committee, MP.EIA/WG.1/2003/8, 10 July 2003. The same issue was taken up in the fourth (para. 13 of the minutes of the fourth meeting of the Implementation Committee, MP.EIA/WG.1/2004/3, 17 December 2003) and fifth meetings of the Implementation Committee (para. 15 of the minutes of the fifth meeting of the Implementation Committee, MP.EIA/WG.1/2004/4, 8 April 2004).

[69] See Parts XI and XII of the founding document of the Compliance Committee of the Aarhus Convention, Annex, 'Structure and Functions of the Compliance Committee and Procedures for the Review of Compliance', Decision I/7, Review of Compliance, ECE/MP.PP/2/Add.8.

Espoo regime. First, the Convention itself provides no guidance in these matters; the MoPs have developed the compliance system as it presently stands. Secondly, in the third MoP, the second amendment to the Convention was adopted which, if and when it enters into force, will provide a formal basis for a compliance system. Finally, the SEA Protocol has seemingly learned the lesson lost on its parent Convention and provided for a compliance system in its article 14.

Yet, there will be many questions to be answered in the near future where development of a compliance system is concerned. The second amendment to the Espoo Convention, which formalizes the compliance system, was adopted on 4 June 2004 and has not yet[70] been ratified by any State. Even when the amendment enters into force someday – as will happen in all likelihood – it will probably apply to only some parties, making it hard to operate a collective compliance system on an equal basis. Another interesting question is whether the SEA Protocol will formalize the status of the Implementation Committee, for it contains an explicit provision to this effect; then again, the Protocol has yet to be ratified by States. Many questions thus remain to be resolved by not only the entry into force of the relevant instruments but also the number of States that ultimately ratify those instruments.

9.3 Overall evaluation

International environmental treaties – the Espoo Convention among these – exhibit a clear trend towards having similar provisions for dispute resolution: they keep dispute settlement in the hands of the States parties but provide the parties with the possibility of making a declaration that they will have their disputes resolved by a third-party procedure.[71] Significantly, the general dispute settlement clause of the Espoo Convention seems to have established a 'precedent' for other ECE environmental protection conventions. In contrast to the first environmental protection convention of the ECE, the 1979 Convention on Long-Range

---

[70] November 2005.

[71] See, for instance, the Vienna Convention for the Protection of the Ozone Layer, Vienna, 22 March 1985, in force 22 September 1988, UNEP Doc. IG.53/5 (art. 11), the 1992 Convention on Biological Diversity (art. 27), the 1992 United Nations Framework Convention on Climate Change, New York, 9 May 1992, in force 21 March 1994, UN Doc. A/A.C.237/18 (Part II) (Add.1). (art. 14).

Transboundary Air Pollution, article 13 of which only provided the parties with a possibility to settle their disputes through political means,[72] the Espoo Convention's dispute settlement provision allows parties to declare in writing that they accept compulsory third-party settlement as binding. This 'precedent' was embraced in the protocols to the Convention on Long-Range Transboundary Air Pollution, as the protocols adopted from 1994 onwards all contain the option of making a declaration. It was also followed by both of the ECE conventions adopted in Helsinki in 1992, i.e. the Convention on the Transboundary Effects of Industrial Accidents[73] and the Convention on the Protection and Use of Transboundary Watercourses and International Lakes,[74] and the 1998 Aarhus Convention in its article 16.

The inquiry commission procedure was quite unique when it was adopted as a special dispute settlement procedure in the Espoo Convention, there being only one other treaty in the field of international environmental law that contained such a procedure previously.[75] The only other international negotiation process apart from the Espoo Convention that tried to create a transboundary EIA procedure – the outcome of which was the draft Transboundary Environmental Impact Assessment Agreement negotiated under the auspices of the North American Commission for Environmental Co-operation (NACEC) – did not contain an inquiry commission procedure but only a general dispute settlement clause.[76]

---

[72] Art. 13 of the Convention on Long-Range Transboundary Air Pollution, Geneva, 13 November 1979, Doc. E-ECE (XXXIV)-L-18: 'If a dispute arises between two or more Contracting Parties to the present Convention as to the interpretation or application of the Convention, they shall seek a solution by negotiation or by any other method of dispute settlement acceptable to the parties to the dispute.'

[73] Art. 21 of the Convention on the Transboundary Effects of Industrial Accidents, Helsinki, 17 March 1992, in force 19 April 2000, 31 ILM 1330 (1992). The Convention can be accessed via its website at www.unece.org/env/teia/text.htm. See also the Convention's Protocol on Civil Liability and Compensation for Damage Caused by the Transboundary Effects of Industrial Accidents on Transboundary Waters, Kiev, Ukraine, 21 May 2003. The Protocol has not yet entered into force (art. 26).

[74] Art. 22 of the Convention on the Protection and Use of Transboundary Watercourses and International Lakes, Helsinki, 17 March 1992, in force 6 October 1996, Doc. ENVWA-R.53 and Add.1. The Convention can be accessed via the Convention's website at www.unece.org/env/water/text/text.htm. See also the Convention's Protocol on Water and Health, London, 17 June 1999, in force 4 August 2005, ECOSOC Doc. MP.WAT/A.C.1/1999/1, 24 March 1999 (art. 20).

[75] The 1974 Nordic Environment Protection Convention, Stockholm, 19 February 1974, in force 5 October 1976, 13 ILM 352 (1974). The Protocol provides for a commission procedure in its art. 12.

[76] See Timo Koivurova, *Environmental Impact Assessment in the Arctic: A Study of International Legal Norms* (Aldershot: Ashgate Publishing, 2002), pp. 293–5.

The inquiry commission procedure has inspired the use of similar procedures, within the UN and the ECE in particular, in situations where it must be decided whether a proposed major development activity is likely to cause a significant adverse transboundary impact. The 1992 Convention on the Transboundary Effects of Industrial Accidents followed the lead of the Espoo Convention and contains an inquiry commission procedure in its article 4(2) and Annex II that is almost identical to that found in the Espoo Convention. Two International Law Commission (ILC)-sponsored projects – the draft preventative rules produced by the ILC project on International Liability[77] and the 1997 Convention on the Non-Navigational Uses of International Watercourses[78] – both contain fact-finding commissions that are clearly modelled after the inquiry commission in the Espoo Convention.

Another distinct and quite recent trend in the drafting and managing of international environmental treaties has been the creation of compliance control systems that have separate bodies for examining suspected cases of non-compliance and allow the plenary organ the option of taking collective enforcement measures. It is quite interesting that a collective compliance system was also developed in the regime of the Espoo Convention, given that the situations it regulates are far more bilateral in nature than those in the regulative field of other international environmental treaties, which seek to protect a common concern of the treaty community. With this background, the treaty community is more likely to be able to exert greater influence in situations that are often seen as disputes between two parties only. Through the compliance system, the treaty community can prod the

[77] In 2001, at its fifty-third session, the International Law Commission recommended to the UN General Assembly an elaboration of an international convention on the basis of the Draft Articles on Prevention of Transboundary Harm from Transboundary Activities that it had approved. The Draft Articles were clearly inspired by the Espoo Convention: they provide for a fact-finding commission as a method of settling disputes in art. 19, one very much modelled after the inquiry commission procedure. See art. 19 of the Draft Articles on Prevention of Transboundary Harm from Hazardous Activities, Report of the International Law Commission on the Work of Its 53rd Session, A/56/10 (Supp.), pp. 370–436. The Draft Articles are available from the ILC website at www.un.org/law/ilc/texts/prevention/preventionfra.htm. Since the General Assembly decided to include liability in the project again, it is not very likely that negotiations will be taking place in the project in the near future. See paras. 165–74 of the Report of the ILC (56th Session) in 2004, A/59/10 (Supp.), 16 September 2004. The report is available from the ILC website at www.un.org/law/ilc/reports/2004/2004report.htm.

[78] The Convention on the Law of Non-Navigation Uses of International Watercourses, New York, 21 May 1997, not yet in force, Doc. A/51/869. This Convention contains not only an identical fact-finding commission but also a general dispute settlement provision: see art. 33.

States parties to improve their capability in organizing a transboundary EIA procedure, to participate in it as an affected State, and to educate their civil societies to take part in it. This role of the compliance system will become more apparent when the SEA Protocol enters into force.

The Implementation Committee of the Espoo Convention is most clearly based on the non-compliance mechanisms of the two ECE conventions, the Convention on Long-Range Transboundary Air Pollution and the Aarhus Convention. At first, it was extensively based on the Convention on Long-Range Transboundary Air Pollution Implementation Committee model, which itself drew heavily on the first non-compliance mechanism developed under the Montreal Protocol.[79] The work of the Compliance Committee of the Aarhus Convention has become increasingly influential, especially as regards the openness and transparency of the Implementation Committee procedure. All in all, however, it is the Convention on Long-Range Transboundary Air Pollution model that has figured most prominently in the present structure and function of the Implementation Committee of the Espoo Convention.

The institutional environmental protection work within the ECE – ministerial-level meetings in the Environment for Europe process, work among senior officials in the Committee on Environmental Protection, and the environment secretariat of the ECE – has a clear bearing on the capacity of each ECE environmental protection convention and provides a firm platform for incorporating a collective dimension even in treaties that deal primarily with bilateral issues between States.[80] The ECE in general has been very active in advocating non-compliance mechanisms, and it is no wonder that the five treaties have drawn inspiration from each other and prompted the Committee on Environmental Protection to draw up

---

[79] See Annexes IV and V to the fourth meeting of the parties to the Montreal Protocol establishing the Implementation Committee and its terms of reference, UNEP/OzL.Pro.4/15, p. 52. The document is available from the ozone regime website at www.unep.org/ozone/Meeting_Documents/mop/index.asp. For an analysis, see Tuomas Kuokkanen, 'Putting Gentle Pressure on Parties: Recent Trends in the Practice of the Implementation Committee under the Convention on Long-Range Transboundary Air Pollution', in Jarna Petman and Jan Klabbers (eds.), *Nordic Cosmopolitanism: Essays in International Law for Martti Koskenniemi* (Leiden and Boston: Martinus Nijhoff Publishers, 2003), pp. 315–26, at p. 320.

[80] The ECE environmental protection is organized very efficiently: it has an international organization of its own, the environment department in the ECE; senior-level officials of the ECE Member States provide policy direction via the Committee on Environmental Policy; and higher-level guidance is provided by the Environment for Europe process, which convenes the environment ministers in the ECE region.

guidelines on how to make sound non-compliance mechanisms. These guidelines were recently adopted as the Kiev Guidelines in the last ministerial meeting in the Environment for Europe process.[81] Seen from the ECE perspective, a collective dimension is always present in the transboundary EIA procedures, which otherwise are often handled privately, as it were, by States parties. It is this collective dimension, upheld by the Espoo Convention being connected to the general environmental protection structure of the ECE, which provides an important underpinning for its dispute settlement and compliance control system.

On this basis, it seems fairly clear that the experiences gained in applying the regime of the Espoo Convention cannot easily be transferred to the regulation of similar situations in other parts of the world, which often lack a comparably strong institutional backing. Within the ECE, the various international environmental treaties regularly draw inspiration from each other, and the Espoo regime has also inspired developments in other ECE regimes.[82] Yet, as was argued above, it is also possible to use particular elements of the Espoo regime outside of the ECE context, as has been done in the work of the International Law Commission in two instances.

---

[81] The Kiev Guidelines, ECE/CEP/107, 20 March 2003. The Guidelines are available from the Espoo Convention website at www.unece.org/env/eia/implementation.htm.

[82] The Implementation Committee of the Espoo Convention has been used as a model at least in designing a compliance mechanism for the Protocol on Water and Health to the ECE Convention on the Protection and Use of Transboundary Watercourses and International Lakes. See the second draft prepared by the Legal Bureau, MP.WAT/A.C.4/2004/8, 23 July 2004.

PART III

International arms control

10

Dispute resolution, compliance control and enforcement of international arms control law

THILO MARAUHN

10.1 Introduction

Arms control and disarmament can best be understood as processes, both in substance and over time.[1] The initiation of such processes necessitates a favourable political climate among participating States, facilitating communication among them and allowing the preparation of (treaty) negotiations. In order to successfully conduct such negotiations, it is important to define precisely their substance, i.e. the problem to be solved and the objective to be achieved.[2] Traditionally, States have been concerned primarily with the prevention of armed conflict, the establishment of international security and the limitation of damage in case of conflict. Increasingly, however, economic considerations – i.e. restricting armaments expenditure – and confidence-building have become important, enhancing co-operation among States.[3] In light of the complexity of arms control negotiations, States often first agree upon their general set-up, issuing political declarations of intent.[4] Such political agreements indicate the perception of States 'that their individual national security is better

---

[1] Eric P. J. Myjer, 'Supervisory Mechanisms and Dispute Settlement', in Julie Dahlitz (ed.), *Avoidance and Settlement of Arms Control Disputes* (New York: Genf, 1994), pp. 149–69, at p. 149. See also George W. Rathjens, Abram Chayes and Jack P. Ruina, *Nuclear Arms Control Agreements: Process and Impact* (Washington, DC: Carnegie Endowment for International Peace, 1974).

[2] See Michael Bothe, 'Rechtsfragen der Rüstungskontrolle im Vertragsvölkerrecht der Gegenwart' (1990) 30 *Berichte der Deutschen Gesellschaft für Völkerrecht* 31–79, at 41 *et seq.*

[3] Quite a number of multilateral agreements include provisions on economic and technological co-operation: see, among others, the Convention on the Prohibition of the Development, Production, Stockpiling and Use of Chemical Weapons and on their Destruction (CWC), Paris, 13 January 1993, UN Doc. A/RES/47/39, art. XI.

[4] On the concept of soft law, see William Michael Reisman, 'The Concept and Functions of Soft Law in International Politics', in Emmanuel G. Bello (ed.), *Essays in Honor of Judge Taslim Olawale Elias* (Dordrecht: Martinus Nijhoff, 1992), pp. 135–44: see also Bothe, 'Rechtsfragen der Rüstungskontrolle', pp. 69–70.

243

served if the arms competition between them is managed under agreed covenants'.[5] Since the mid-1980s, such processes have eventually led to the conclusion of multilateral arms control agreements, illustrating a 'clearly discernible trend towards greater legalism in arms control'.[6]

While the general public often perceives the conclusion of such arms control agreements as the final outcome of the political process, it may be argued that the entry into force of any arms control and disarmament treaty must be considered to be the beginning rather than the end of the matter. As was already argued in the late 1980s, 'the end of the negotiations is, in fact, only the beginning of the arms control process. The test of arms control's success is whether the parties to an agreement abide by its terms over time, and whether each side recognizes and credits the other side's compliance.'[7] It is the successful implementation of such arms control agreements as well as their ability to solve the security problem at issue which can be considered the litmus test of their effectiveness.

Looking back into history, the implementation of arms control agreements is still a fairly new issue on the agenda, in particular when taking the Hague Conference of 1899 with its focus on dispute settlement as the starting point of modern arms control law. The then prevailing philosophy considered agreement on procedures of dispute settlement and on the reduction of armed forces as improvements in security, without recognizing the importance of implementation, enforcement and related verification of compliance.[8] Arms control agreements were perceived as the culmination of a development from dispute settlement to dispute prevention.

In the immediate aftermath of the Second World War, arms control was not a primary concern – apart from pertinent obligations in peace treaties.[9]

---

[5] Gloria Duffy, *Compliance and the Future of Arms Control: Report of a Project Sponsored by the Center for International Security and Arms Control* (Cambridge, MA: Stanford University and Global Outlook, 1988), p. 1.

[6] Dahlitz, 'Introduction', in Dahlitz (ed.), *Avoidance and Settlement of Arms Control Disputes*, pp. 1–6, at p. 2. But see the critical remarks on the US position of the 1950s and 1960s in Rathjens, Chayes and Ruina, *Nuclear Arms Control Agreements*, p. 56: 'All this reflected, almost to the point of caricature, the well-known American propensity for legalism and judicialism.'

[7] Duffy, *Compliance and the Future of Arms Control*, p. 1.

[8] Cf. Wolfgang Graf Vitzthum, 'Rechtsfragen der Rüstungskontrolle im Vertragsvölkerrecht der Gegenwart' (1990) 30 *Berichte der Deutschen Gesellschaft für Völkerrecht* 95–137, at 104.

[9] On peace treaties after the First World War, see Stefan Oeter, 'Inspection in International Law: Monitoring Compliance and the Problem of Implementation in International Law' (1997) 28 *Netherlands Yearbook of International Law* 101–69, at 110 *et seq.*

This, however, changed in the 1960s when the objective of general and complete disarmament was disbanded in light of its limited practical relevance and its primary use as a propaganda tool during the Cold War of the 1950s.[10] It was the successful completion of negotiations on a number of limited arms control issues in the late 1960s and during the 1970s[11] which eventually made possible the important bilateral and multilateral arms control agreements since the mid-1980s.[12] It is the confidence-building potential of such agreements which may improve inter-State (and thus common) security, which in itself will leave more room for rules-based discourse and the judicial settlement of disputes. However, since this approach will only be successful if armaments are indeed reduced, numerous institutional and procedural elements have been introduced into pertinent agreements since the mid-1980s. Thus, it was not the conclusion of an ever larger number of agreements which can be considered the decisive advancement of arms control at the end of the twentieth century, but the innovative element of verification as part of co-operative compliance control,[13] including challenge inspections at short notice.

It may be argued that these developments in international arms control law contributed to the further development of related mechanisms in other fields of public international law, including international environmental law – although a number of those developments occurred in parallel.[14] The

[10] Bothe, 'Rechtsfragen der Rüstungskontrolle', p. 38.
[11] Cf. the Treaty on the Non-Proliferation of Nuclear Weapons, London, Moscow and Washington, 1 July 1968, 729 UNTS 161; and the Convention on the Prohibition of the Development, Production, and Stockpiling of Bacteriological (Biological) and Toxin Weapons and on their Destruction, London, Moscow and Washington, 10 April 1972, 1015 UNTS 163.
[12] At the bilateral level, the START agreements deserve closer attention, in particular the Treaty between the United States of America and the Union of Soviet Socialist Republics on the Reduction and Limitation of Strategic Offensive Arms, Moscow, 31 July 1991, 729 UNTS 161 (START I). Following the demise of the USSR, the so-called Lisbon Protocol (START I Treaty – Protocol to the Treaty between the United States of America and the Union of Soviet Socialist Republics on the Reduction and Limitation of Strategic Offensive Arms, Lisbon, 23 May 1992) was agreed. Noteworthy at the multilateral level are the Conventional Armed Forces in Europe Treaty (CFE Treaty), Paris, 19 November 1990, 30 ILM 1 (1991) and the CWC. Further reference should be made to the Comprehensive Nuclear Test Ban Treaty, New York, 10 September 1996, 35 ILM 1439 (1996), and to the Convention on the Prohibition of the Use, Stockpiling, Production and Transfer of Anti-Personnel Mines and on their Destruction, Oslo, 18 September 1997, 36 ILM 1507 (1997).   [13] Graf Vitzthum, 'Rechtsfragen der Rüstungskontrolle', p. 104.
[14] Cf. for parallels in international environmental law, Ulrich Beyerlin and Thilo Marauhn, *Law-Making and Law-Enforcement in International Environmental Law after the Rio Conference 1992* (Berlin: Erich Schmidt Verlag, 1997), pp. 73 *et seq.*

findings of implementation and compliance research[15] led commentators and negotiators to move away from termination clauses and sanctions as the primary means to enforce arms control agreements and over to co-operative approaches. In parallel, increasingly, positive incentives were included in arms control agreements. New techniques of governance, complementing and replacing sanctions, were developed in order to increase the effectiveness of arms control agreements. They seek to avoid the 'all or nothing' approach and rather aim at achieving a 'reasonable level of compliance'.[16] It is noteworthy that these developments can build upon an academic debate during the inter-war period which, unfortunately, never reached the political and legal reality of arms control agreements. This debate on the implementation of international obligations contrasted diplomatic and institutional means of enforcement or control.[17]

Before addressing the techniques to make arms control treaties work, this chapter will, in light of recent developments, first address the so-called 'crisis of arms control (law)'. It will demonstrate that, a political environment full of scepticism towards arms control notwithstanding, there are chances to consolidate the achievements that were made in arms control law in the 1980s and the 1990s. Subsequently, it will identify positive and negative incentives to comply with arms control agreements, before entering a conceptual discussion of instruments of dispute resolution, enforcement and compliance control in arms control agreements. The final section will identify a few perspectives on arms control law in general and effective implementation of pertinent agreements in particular.

[15] Cf. Oran R. Young, *Compliance and Public Authority: A Theory with International Applications* (Baltimore: Johns Hopkins University Press, 1979); and Abram Chayes and Antonia Handler Chayes, *The New Sovereignty: Compliance with International Regulatory Agreements* (Cambridge, MA: Harvard University Press, 1995).

[16] With regard to international environmental law, this has been phrased by Antonia Handler Chayes, Abram Chayes and Ronald B. Mitchell, 'Active Compliance Management in Environmental Treaties', in Winfried Lang (ed.), *Sustainable Development and International Law* (London: Graham & Trotman, 1995), pp. 75–89, at p. 80: 'We believe that there are acceptable levels of compliance – not an invariant standard, but one that changes over time with the capacities of the parties and the urgency of the problem'.

[17] See Lang, 'Verhinderung von Erfüllungsdefiziten im Völkerrecht – Beispiele aus Abrüstung und Umweltschutz', in Johannes Hengstschläger *et al.* (eds.), *Für Staat und Recht Festschrift für Herbert Schambeck* (Berlin: Duncker & Humblot, 1994), pp. 817–35, at pp. 817 *et seq.*

10.2 Consolidation rather than crisis?

When considering that, for several years, hardly any multilateral arms control agreement has been successfully negotiated and signed, nor even entered into force, a commentator may easily perceive a standstill, if not a major crisis, in arms control. The plausibility of such a perception depends on whether or not there is a true need for arms control in order to improve international security. Only in a case of divergence between political necessity and normative standstill is the process of arms control at risk. It will be shown that there are indeed several issues on the arms control agenda which deserve to be addressed.

First, in the context of conventional armaments, the problem of small arms is of urgency.[18] After the UN General Assembly in 1995[19] had taken up the issue on the basis of the work of two expert groups,[20] a programme of action was agreed upon in 2001.[21] It aims at an improvement of municipal laws and improved enforcement, including trans-border co-operation. While early on no juridification was envisaged, States seem to have realized by now that – in light of the large number of non-State actors in the field – legislation could be helpful in curbing the proliferation of small arms.

A second issue in conventional arms control which has been tackled is explosive remnants of war. Within the framework of the 1980 UN Convention on Conventional Weapons[22] and on the basis of a mandate, adopted at the second Review Conference in 2001,[23] negotiations have been successfully completed. This is probably due to the fact that explosive remnants of war are equally a matter of arms control and of

---

[18] It would go beyond the scope of this chapter to consider more closely the UN weapons registry; but see the 1999 Inter-American Convention on Transparency in Conventional Weapons, www.oas.org/juridico/english/treaties/a-64.htm.

[19] UN Doc. A/RES/50/70B.   [20] UN Doc. A/52/298 (1997) and UN Doc. A/54/258 (1999).

[21] Programme of Action to Prevent, Combat and Eradicate the Illicit Trade in Small Arms and Light Weapons in All Its Aspects (UN Doc. A/CONF.192/15). For a comprehensive debate, see E. Dahinden, J. Dahlitz and N. Fischer (eds.), *Small Arms and Light Weapons: Legal Aspects of National and International Regulations* (New York: UN, 2002).

[22] On the 1980 Convention, see R. J. Mathews, 'The 1980 Convention on Certain Conventional Weapons – A Useful Framework Despite Earlier Disappointments' (2001) 83 *Revue internationale de la Croix-Rouge* 844, at 991.

[23] UN Doc. CCW/CONF.II/2, pp. 35–6. For a public international law analysis, see D. Kaye and S. A. Solomon, 'The Second Review Conference of the 1980 Convention on Certain Conventional Weapons' (2002) 96 *American Journal of International Law* 922 *et seq.*

248 INTERNATIONAL ARMS CONTROL

humanitarian law. The adoption of the Protocol[24] followed a decision of December 2002 to elaborate a legally binding instrument.[25] Negotiations addressed all important issues ranging from definitions across responsibility for removal, information exchange, as well as assistance and cooperation. The limited mandate contributed to the successful completion of negotiations.

Beyond conventional armaments, the Chemical Weapons Convention (CWC) is currently undergoing a process of consolidation which will only be complete when existing stocks of chemical weapons have been destroyed.[26] In contrast, there is agreement that the institutional deficiency of the Biological and Toxin Weapons Convention (BTWC), namely, its weak verification provisions, must be remedied. However, after the failure of the negotiations to develop a verification protocol, prospects for major improvements appear to be dim. In the meantime, States parties have sought to improve national implementation of the provisions of the Convention.[27] Such a low-level approach may also contribute to consolidation, while avoiding the pitfalls of high-profile negotiations in a more than sensitive environment.

There is an intensive need for action in nuclear arms control. Sometimes it seems that the unlimited and unconditional extension of the Non-Proliferation Treaty (NPT)[28] in 1995 has kept commentators from focusing on the deficiencies. While there can be no doubt that the non-proliferation regime must be enhanced and that its implementation must be improved,[29] there are more pressing problems outside the NPT. For example, there are still no proper rules for the disposal of plutonium. While there is a fairly modest bilateral agreement between the governments of the United States

---

[24] Protocol V on Explosive Remnants of War was adopted on 28 November 2003; see UN Doc. DC/2900 (Press Release) and UN Doc. CCW/MSP/2003/2 (text of the Protocol).

[25] See www.vbs-ddps.ch/Internet/groupgst/de/home/peace/rustungskontrolle/inhumane/internationale.html.

[26] See W. Krutzsch and R. Trapp, *A Commentary on the Chemical Weapons Convention* (Dordrecht: Nijhoff, 1994), pp. 344 *et seq.* On extensions granted to the United States and Russia, see OPCW Doc. C-8/DEC.15 and C-8/DEC.13 (as of 24 October 2003).

[27] Cf. the paper submitted by the German delegation in August 2003, BWC/MSP.2003/MX/WP.35, entitled 'Coherent National Implementation as a Means to Improve the Effectiveness of the BTWC', www.opbw.org/new_process/bwc_msp.2003_mx_wp35.pdf.

[28] Treaty on the Non-Proliferation of Nuclear Weapons, London, Moscow and Washington, 12 June 1968, 729 UNTS 161.

[29] In particular, within the IAEA, but including the UN Security Council. For a critical review of the 1995 conference, see D. Howlett, H. Leigh-Phippard and J. Simpson, 'The 1995 NPT Extension Conference: Can the Treaty Survive the Outcome?' (1996) *VERTIC Yearbook* 13 *et seq.*

and of Russia,[30] the complex problems at the interface of environmental protection and international security have remained largely unresolved. Similarly, there is a need for a fissile material cut-off treaty.[31] The aim is to limit the number of nuclear weapons by cutting off the supply of new fissile material for nuclear explosive devices. In 1993, the UN General Assembly unanimously accepted Resolution 48/75L, calling for the negotiation of a non-discriminatory, multilateral and internationally and effectively verifiable treaty. The 1995 Geneva Conference on Disarmament adopted a negotiation mandate (limited to a ban on the future production of fissile material for nuclear weapons purposes, and excluding available stockpiles).[32] After this, the Conference on Disarmament in August 1998 decided to appoint an *ad hoc* committee with a mandate to negotiate.[33] However, this committee has so far been without success, due to the inability to agree on the reappointment of an *ad hoc* committee in later sessions. Nuclear disarmament is not only a political matter, but an obligation imposed upon – in particular – nuclear-weapon States under article VI of the NPT.[34]

One of the major challenges of today is the development of meaningful non-proliferation regimes. Most of the existing regimes are based on legally non-binding arrangements.[35] Even though most of these arrangements enjoy a remarkable degree of effectiveness, they give rise to many questions, including their certainty and reliability as well as their legitimacy. This is particularly so in relations between industrialized and

---

[30] For the text of the agreement, see www.nti.org/db/nisprofs/russia/fulltext/plutdisp/ pudispft. pdf.

[31] See T. Rauf, 'Fissile Material Treaty: Negotiating Approaches' (1999) *Disarmament Forum*, No. 2, 17 *et seq.*; and M. Sultan, 'The Problems and Prospects of Carving a Verification Mechanism for a Fissile Material Treaty' (2001) 21 *Strategic Studies* 114 *et seq.*   [32] See CD/1364, para. 27.

[33] UN Doc. CD/1547.

[34] ICJ Reports 1996, p. 226 (para. 99). On the advisory opinion, see T. Marauhn and K. Oellers-Frahm, 'Atomwaffen, Völkerrecht und die internationale Gerichtsbarkeit: Anmerkungen zur Spruchpraxis internationaler Organe hinsichtlich der völkerrechtlichen Zulässigkeit von Atomtests, der Drohung mit oder des Einsatzes von Atomwaffen' (1997) 24 EuGRZ 221 *et seq.*

[35] Note the 1996 Wassenaar Arrangement (www.wassenaar.org); see also 'The Wassenaar Arrangement at a Glance', Arms Control Association Fact Sheet, January 2003, www. armscontrol.org/factsheets/wassenaar.asp. See also the 1987 Missile Technology Control Regime, www.mtcr.info/; cf. 'The Missile Technology Control Regime (MTCR) at a Glance', Arms Control Association Fact Sheet, September 2003, www.armscontrol.org/factsheets/mtcr. asp.With regard to weapons of mass destruction, the Australia Group must be referred to (www.australiagroup.net). For a comprehensive discussion of export control regimes, cf. C. Ahlström, *The Status of Multilateral Export Control Regimes: An Examination of Legal and Non-Legal Agreements in International Co-operation* (Uppsala: Iustus, 1999).

developing countries. The latter – in light of the absence of an effective regime for the transfer of technology and know-how for peaceful purposes – often consider export controls rather as instruments of protectionism than as instruments of international security.[36] Integrating export control regimes into multilateral arms control treaties – as in the case of the Chemical Weapons Convention[37] – could compensate for deficiencies in legitimacy, but has so far not been successful either.

In light of these developments and the need for a continuation of effective arms control, it may be argued that, while the process has slowed down, it is actually going through a period of consolidation rather than crisis. Such consolidation is necessary in order to develop arms control strategies which pay tribute to a continuously changing international environment. It would go too far to address the numerous issues related to non-State actors here, but such developments have an impact on traditional inter-State arms control agreements. Also, considerations of cost-efficiency must be borne in mind if multilateral arms control is to continue as one of the building blocks of international security in the future. What must be raised in this context, and what must be debated much more vividly than in the past, is the optimization of governance in the arms control field. This chapter can only give some hints in this direction, first, by identifying some of the negative and positive incentives to comply with arms control agreements, and, secondly, by discussing the existing strategies of enforcement, dispute resolution and compliance control. An issue that should be taken up elsewhere is the adaptation of multilateral arms control to the growing plurality of actors and its questionable cost-efficiency.

10.3 Negative and positive incentives to comply with arms control agreements

Compliance with, and implementation of, arms control agreements largely depends on the incentives States parties perceive with regard to such agreements. Those incentives may be part of, or originate outside, the

---

[36] See A. Latham and B. Bow, 'Multilateral Export Control Regimes: Bridging the North–South Divide' (1998) 53 *International Journal* 465.

[37] Cf. Marauhn, 'National Regulations on Export Controls and the Chemical Weapons Convention', in M. Bothe, N. Ronzitti and A. Rosas (eds.), *The New Chemical Weapons Convention – Implementation and Prospects* (The Hague and Boston: Kluwer Law International, 1998), pp. 487–531, at pp. 487 *et seq.*

agreement. Including incentives in arms control agreements is a matter which should be part of the negotiating process. Those built-in incentives will have to take into account external incentives.

10.3.1 The traditional predominance of negative incentives and sanctions

Until recently, public international law was concerned primarily with negative incentives, such as sanctions.[38] They have been and still are part of arms control agreements. Mostly, such negative incentives are unilateral or non-institutional in character and repressive rather than preventative. State responsibility has never played a prominent role in arms control law. However, enforcement strategies that have been inserted into arms control agreements cover a broad range from retorsion across suspension, withdrawal and termination to collective sanctions adopted on the basis of Chapter VII of the UN Charter.

As will be demonstrated, dispute settlement clauses, sometimes even of an institutional character, have been part of bilateral and a few multilateral arms control agreements. They provide positive incentives, but have never played a major role in the context of implementation and compliance. Further, positive incentives have often been underestimated in arms control law. However, there are some examples which will be taken up here in order to enrich the compliance debate in this regard.

10.3.2 Some thoughts on positive incentives

Discussing positive incentives in the context of implementation and compliance must go beyond the benefits inherent in the conclusion of arms control agreements as such, which States typically perceive as a tool to improve their (national) security. Without such abstract benefits for national security, entry into arms control agreements would be difficult to explain, even beyond a purely utilitarian perspective. Some arms control agreements include further incentives for States to become a party to the agreement such as clauses on economic and technological co-operation.[39]

---

[38] On counter-measures, see generally O. Y. Elagab, *The Legality of Non-Forcible Counter-Measures in International Law* (Oxford: Clarendon Press, 1988).

[39] See Marauhn, 'National Regulations on Export Controls and the Chemical Weapons Convention', in Bothe, Ronzitti and Rosas (eds.), *The New Chemical Weapons Convention*, pp. 487–531, at p. 495; Thilo Marauhn, *Der deutsche Chemiewaffen-Verzicht – Rechtsentwicklungen seit 1945* (Berlin: Springer Verlag, 1994), pp. 342 *et seq.*, in particular p. 343.

In contrast, positive incentives to further compliance with arms control agreements – after having become a party – must convince States that the benefits of abiding by such obligations outweigh the costs thereof.[40]

Security assurances, as reflected in articles VI and VII of the Non-Proliferation Treaty (NPT), can be considered to be such positive incentives.[41] While these clauses also provide an incentive to join the NPT, they deserve closer scrutiny in the context of implementation and compliance. Negative security assurances are guarantees by the five NPT nuclear-weapon States not to use or threaten to use nuclear weapons against States that have formally renounced them; in contrast, positive security assurances are an undertaking to provide assistance, in accordance with the UN Charter, to a State victim of an act of nuclear-weapons aggression or the object of a threat of such aggression.[42] The NPT itself explicitly includes only the possibility of negative security assurances. Positive assurances, however, were declared by nuclear-weapon States before the UN Security Council which confirmed them. In 1996, the International Court of Justice reaffirmed – in its Advisory Opinion on the *Legality of the Threat or Use of Nuclear Weapons* – the obligation included in article VI of the NPT.[43] While there have been some truly substantive steps towards nuclear disarmament by nuclear-weapon States, including the Comprehensive Test Ban Treaty (CTBT),[44] there are too many activities countering the implementation of article VI. The ambivalence inherent in the behaviour of nuclear-weapon States is continuously undermining the credibility of their attitude towards the NPT. The recent agreement between India and the United States on co-operation in the field of nuclear energy[45] must be contrasted with the attitude of the international community towards Iran. While Iran's behaviour

---

[40] Marauhn, 'Routine Verification under the Chemical Weapons Convention', in Bothe, Ronzitti and Rosas (eds.), *The New Chemical Weapons Convention*, pp. 219–47, at p. 219.

[41] Art. VI reads: 'Each of the Parties to the Treaty undertakes to pursue negotiations in good faith on effective measures relating to cessation of the nuclear arms race at an early date and to nuclear disarmament, and on a treaty on general and complete disarmament under strict and effective international control.' Art. VII stipulates: 'Nothing in this Treaty affects the right of any group of States to conclude regional treaties in order to assure the total absence of nuclear weapons in their respective territories.'

[42] UN SC Res. 255 (1968). See also UN SC Res. 984 (1995) (in the period before the 1995 Review Conference). See also para. 8 of the second decision of the Review Conference, UN Doc. NPT/CONF.1995/L.5.   [43] ICJ Reports 1996, p. 226.

[44] Comprehensive Nuclear Test Ban Treaty, New York, 10 September 1996, 35 ILM 1439 (1996).

[45] On the 2006 US–India Civilian Nuclear Co-operation Agreement, see the Opening Remarks Before the Senate Foreign Relations Committee by Secretary of State Condoleezza Rice of 5 April 2006, www.state.gov/secretary/rm/2006/64136.htm.

has indeed been harshly criticized by the IAEA,[46] it is difficult to argue that there is no ambivalence in the related politics of the US administration. Also, in light of the period of time that has elapsed since the entry into force of the NPT, and in light of the major changes since 1989/1990, progress towards implementation of article VI of the NPT must be considered to be insufficient.[47]

Article VII of the NPT only entails the right to establish nuclear-weapon-free zones (NWFZs). It does not define the obligations of nuclear-weapon States *vis-à-vis* those NWFZs. It was only as a consequence of the establishment of NWFZs, and in protocols attached to NWFZ treaties, that nuclear-weapon States undertook pertinent obligations. Thus, article 1 of Additional Protocol I attached to the Treaty of Tlatelolco[48] stipulates that nuclear-weapon States undertake to apply the statute of denuclearization 'in territories for which, *de jure* or *de facto*, they are internationally responsible and which lie within the limits of the geographical zone established in that Treaty'. Article 1 of Additional Protocol II even goes beyond this obligation in stating that the 'statute of denuclearization . . . shall be fully respected by the Parties to this Protocol in all its express aims and provisions'. Finally, article 3 of Additional Protocol II prohibits nuclear-weapon States 'to use or threaten to use nuclear weapons against the Contracting Parties' of the Treaty of Tlatelolco. In light of this prohibition, nuclear-weapon States have declared that they would reconsider their obligations, should one of the parties to the Treaty commit an act of aggression and enjoy the support of a nuclear-weapon State.[49]

A second category of positive incentives are clauses of mutual assistance. Such clauses are included in the Biological and Toxin Weapons Convention (BTWC) and in the Chemical Weapons Convention (CWC). According to article VII of the BTWC, each State party is under an obligation 'to provide or support assistance, in accordance with the United Nations Charter, to any Party to the Convention which so requests, if the Security Council decides that such Party has been exposed to danger as a result of violation of the Convention'. While this clause is fairly restrictive, and not necessarily suited

---

[46] See Resolution of the IAEA Board of Governors on the Implementation of the NPT Safeguards Agreement in the Islamic Republic of Iran of 4 February 2006, IAEA Doc. GOV/2006/14.

[47] Cf. John Simpson, 'The Nuclear Non-Proliferation Regime After the NPT Review and Extension Conference' (1996) *SIPRI Yearbook* 561–609.

[48] Treaty for the Prohibition of Nuclear Weapons in Latin America, Mexico, 14 February 1967, 634 UNTS 326.   [49] See the UK declaration upon ratification of Protocols I and II.

254 INTERNATIONAL ARMS CONTROL

for practical application since it requires a decision of the UN Security Council, article X of the CWC provides a much more realistic incentive. This article is intended to ensure that States parties not having chemical weapons at their disposal can rely on the international community's support. Being entitled to receive protective equipment shall prevent a decrease in security. Protective equipment is a sufficient guarantee not to suffer damage from chemical weapons.[50] The only problem is that the assistance under article X of the CWC is in principle voluntary. However, article X(7) provides for the possibility of a binding commitment by States to provide certain measures of assistance.[51] Thus, States parties, in particular industrialized States parties, can contribute to the universality[52] of the CWC as well as to its effectiveness.

Finally, co-operative implementation can be considered to be a positive incentive. Such co-operative implementation is foreseen, among others, by the CWC. Article IV(12) of the CWC provides that each State party 'undertakes to co-operate with other States Parties that request information or assistance on a bilateral basis or through the Technical Secretariat regarding methods and technologies for the safe and efficient destruction of chemical weapons'. Also, according to article IV(11), the State party which is under an obligation to destroy chemical weapons attributed to another State 'may request the Organization and other States Parties to provide assistance in the destruction of these chemical weapons'.[53] Both provisions can be considered to specify, in a particular context, the more general obligation to co-operate as laid down in article VII(2) of the CWC.[54] Apart from these obligations to co-operate, the CWC also provides for the possibility to modify intermediate destruction deadlines or to extend deadlines for the completion of destruction. Such modifications and extensions are only permissible in the case of exceptional circumstances.[55] As paragraph 26 of the Annex on Verification stipulates, '[a]ny extension shall be the minimum necessary, but in no case shall the deadline for a State party to complete its

---

[50] On protective equipment, see Matthew Meselson and Julian Perry Robinson, 'Antichemical Protection and the CWC', *Chemical Weapons Convention Bulletin*, No. 13, September 1991, p. 18.

[51] See also Krutzsch and Trapp, *A Commentary on the Chemical Weapons Convention*, p. 205.

[52] Cf. Joachim Badelt, *Chemische Kriegführung – Chemische Abrüstung: Die Bundesrepublik Deutschland und das Pariser Chemiewaffen-Übereinkommen* (Berlin: Arno Spitz, 1994), p. 243.

[53] I.e. the Organisation for the Prohibition of Chemical Weapons established pursuant to art. VIII of the CWC.

[54] Krutzsch and Trapp, *A Commentary on the Chemical Weapons Convention*, pp. 73–5 and 117–18.

[55] Part IV(A), paras 20–3 and 24–8 of the Annex on Verification; Badelt, *Chemische Kriegführung*, pp. 122–3; and Krutzsch and Trapp, *A Commentary on the Chemical Weapons Convention*, p. 347.

destruction of all chemical weapons be extended beyond 15 years after the entry into force of this Convention'. Apart from obligations to co-operate as an integral part of arms control agreements, international co-operation has meanwhile led to separate bilateral agreements on arms control assistance.[56] Those agreements are not formally integrated into pertinent arms control regimes, but they refer to multilateral treaties and thus supplement them.

A final category of positive incentives is the very existence of co-operative compliance control and its institutionalized supervision of States parties. This is, however, discussed separately.[57]

10.4 Dispute settlement in arms control agreements

While, in principle, dispute settlement clauses are a common feature of arms control agreements, they play only a limited role in recent multilateral arms control treaties, which focus on compliance control rather than dispute settlement. This necessitates a closer look at the relationship between those two types of procedures. However, it may be useful first to address the issue of dispute settlement as part of earlier arms control agreements. In this regard, it is noteworthy that some of the early agreements, in particular bilateral arms control agreements, do not include specific dispute settlement clauses along the lines of article 33 of the UN Charter. As is well established, the application of such clauses necessitates a dispute, i.e. a 'disagreement on a point of law or fact, a conflict of legal views or interests between two persons'.[58] Normally, such a dispute will only arise with regard to potential violations of treaty obligations. This means that pertinent dispute settlement clauses are primarily repressive tools of implementation. In order to evaluate such clauses, it seems helpful to distinguish between bilateral and multilateral agreements.

Thus, the ABM Treaty[59] does not include a specific dispute settlement clause. However, article XIII of the Treaty provides for the establishment

---

[56] See Marauhn, 'Bilaterale Abkommen über Abrüstungshilfe' (1993) 35 *Neue Zeitschrift für Wehrrecht* 221–9.   [57] See section 10.5 below.

[58] *Mavrommatis Palestine Concessions Case* (*Greece* v. *UK*) (Jurisdiction), PCIJ Reports, Series A No. 2 (1924), pp. 11–12. This was further refined by the ICJ see *South West Africa Cases* (Preliminary Objections), ICJ Reports 1962, p. 319, at p. 328. See generally Gilles Cottereau, 'A Comparative View of Arms Control Disputes', in Dahlitz (ed.), *Avoidance and Settlement of Arms Control Disputes*, pp. 103–21, at p. 103.

[59] Treaty between the United States of America and the Union of Soviet Socialist Republics on the Limitation of Anti-Ballistic Missile Systems, Moscow, 26 May 1972, 944 UNTS 13.

of a Standing Consultative Commission, which is – among others – the framework for parties to 'consider questions concerning compliance with the obligations assumed and related situations which may be considered ambiguous'.[60] A similar approach was adopted by article XIII of the Intermediate Range Nuclear Forces (INF) Treaty[61] establishing a Special Verification Commission. The parties agreed to make use of the Commission in order to 'resolve questions relating to compliance with the obligations assumed'. Indeed, a number of disputes were settled within the framework of the Commission, including the issue of SS-23 missile systems in the German Democratic Republic, Czechoslovakia and Bulgaria.[62] It may also be argued that the Special Verification Commission contributed to the further development of the INF Treaty's verification system. Similar to the other two agreements mentioned here, the START 1 Treaty of 1991 does not include a dispute settlement clause but establishes the institutional framework for dispute settlement.[63]

It is noteworthy that bilateral arms control treaties largely rely on consultations and negotiations as the primary means of dispute settlement. This is often done by establishing an institutional framework, rather than on the basis of explicit dispute settlement clauses providing for particular means of dispute settlement. Such institutional arrangements can be considered an important tool for treaty implementation, since they maintain the political balance within the treaty system and, to this end, even handle substantive obligations in a flexible manner.

A different example of a dispute settlement arrangement within a multilateral arms control agreement is article 25 of the Treaty of Tlatelolco. This provision reads as follows: 'Unless the Parties concerned agree on another mode of peaceful settlement, any question or dispute concerning the interpretation or application of this Treaty which is not settled shall be referred to the International Court of Justice with the prior consent of the Parties to the controversy.' Such a clause is unusual, since it does not specify any particular means or forum of dispute settlement except

---

[60] On related practice, see Göran Lysén, *The International Regulation of Armaments: The Law of Disarmament* (Uppsala: Förlag, 1990), pp. 212 *et seq.*

[61] Treaty between the United States of America and the Union of Soviet Socialist Republics on the Elimination of Their Intermediate-Range and Shorter-Range Missiles, Washington, 8 December 1987, 27 ILM 183 (1988).

[62] Cottereau, 'A Comparative View of Arms Control Disputes', in Dahlitz (ed.), *Avoidance and Settlement of Arms Control Disputes*, p. 111.   [63] Art. XV.

reference to the International Court of Justice, which is available to the parties anyway.[64]

Even recent multilateral arms control agreements, while primarily focusing on compliance control mechanisms, have – perhaps as a matter of routine – included dispute settlement clauses. This necessitates a discussion of the relationship between compliance control and dispute settlement, in particular since it is hard to qualify pertinent compliance control regimes as 'self-contained regimes'.[65] Hardly any of the agreements provide an explicit answer as to the relationship between (traditional) dispute settlement clauses and (more recent) mechanisms of compliance control, including verification and inspection. Rather, they simply exist in parallel, as can be seen, for example, in article VI(6) of the CTBT, dealing with the settlement of disputes arising under that Treaty. The article explicitly states that it is 'without prejudice to Articles IV and V', which are those articles of the CTBT covering verification and measures to redress a situation, including sanctions. Among the few agreements that seem to be more specific are the NWFZ Treaties of Bangkok and Pelindaba.[66] They explicitly distinguish among disputes arising out of the application of the Treaty (article 12 of the Treaty of Pelindaba; article 10 of the Treaty of Bangkok) and those concerning the interpretation of the Treaty (article 15 of the Treaty of Pelindaba; article 21 of the Treaty of Bangkok). In the first case, supervisory mechanisms such as compliance control, verification and inspection apply. The latter refers States parties to traditional mechanisms of dispute settlement.

10.5 Compliance control in arms control agreements: verification and inspections

As has already been indicated above, modern arms control agreements, in particular multilateral arms control treaties, rely primarily upon mechanisms of compliance control, typically including verification and inspection.

---

[64] See also Cottereau, 'A Comparative View of Arms Control Disputes', in Dahlitz (ed.), *Avoidance and Settlement of Arms Control Disputes*, p. 112, arguing that the reference to the ICJ 'simply reminds States of its existence'.

[65] See Bruno Simma, 'Self-Contained Regimes' (1985) 16 *Netherlands Yearbook of International Law* 111–36.

[66] On those treaties, see David Fischer, 'The Pelindaba Treaty: Africa Joins the Nuclear-Free World' (1995/6) 25 *Arms Control Today*, No. 10, pp. 9–14; and Sandra Szurek, 'De Rarotonga à Bangkok et Pelindaba: note sur les traités constitutifs de nouvelles zones exemptes d'armes nucléaires' (1996) 42 *Annuaire français de droit international* 164–86.

258   INTERNATIONAL ARMS CONTROL

Also, as a rule, these procedures, finally, lead up to measures to redress a situation, including enforcement. These will be addressed separately.[67]

As far as verification and inspection are concerned, transparency has been identified as an essential means to reduce distrust and to build confidence.[68] Transparency in arms control agreements has a dual function: it establishes trust among parties and it can pressurize parties into compliance. In particular, transparency can avoid misperceptions as to treaty compliance (or at least clarify them) and it can help a party acting *bona fide* to demonstrate its compliance. Due to the risk of discovery, transparency may, on the other hand, deter potential violators. Thus, transparency – in arms control – is a pre-condition for improved treaty implementation and compliance, enabling parties to better co-ordinate their activities.

Transparency cannot rely exclusively on the exchange of information but necessitates fact-finding in a broader sense. Fact-finding is nothing totally new in public international law, as a reference to article 33 of the UN Charter demonstrates.[69] However, procedures of fact-finding have been refined over recent years. This takes into account that disagreement about facts entails an enormous potential for conflict, and that acceptable procedures of fact-finding can be part of a more comprehensive strategy towards conflict management. In the following, this chapter will provide an overview on different mechanisms of fact-finding in arms control law. Typically, arms-control-related fact-finding is termed 'verification'.[70]

10.5.1 National verification (national technical means of verification)

National technical means of verification (NTMs) are among the oldest, though debated, means of fact-finding in arms control law. They are unilateral in nature and rely on such means as satellites, radar, wiretapping, etc. Provisions in arms control agreements dealing with NTMs thereby implicitly recognize their admissibility in the context of the treaty and thus their (partial) legality.[71] Sometimes, as in the case of the ABM Treaty, there

---

[67] See section 10.6 below.

[68] See Chayes and Chayes, *Compliance with International Regulatory Agreements*, pp. 135 *et seq.*

[69] See Karl Josef Partsch, 'Fact-Finding and Inquiry', in Rudolf Bernhardt (eds.), *Encyclopedia of Public International Law* (Amsterdam: North-Holland, 1995), vol. II, pp. 343–5.

[70] On the different concepts of verification, cf. Lang, 'Compliance with Disarmament Obligations' (1995) 55 *Zeitschrift für ausländisches öffentliches Recht und Völkerrecht* 69–88, at 79 *et seq.*

[71] On the permissibility of remote sensing, cf. Jörg H. Wallner, *Konventionelle Rüstungskontrolle und Fernerkundung in Europa* (Baden-Baden: Nomos, 1995), pp. 191 *et seq.*

is an additional reference to compatibility with the rules and principles of public international law, intended to protect territorial integrity. Thus, article XII(1) of the ABM Treaty states: 'For the purpose of providing assurance or compliance with the provisions of this Treaty, each Party shall use national technical means of verification at its disposal in a manner consistent with generally recognized principles of international law.' Article XII(2) makes it clear that the 'inspected party' is under an obligation to accept such fact-finding: 'Each Party undertakes not to interfere with the national technical means of verification of the other Party operating in accordance with paragraph 1 of this Article.' Finally, article XII(3) even requires parties 'not to use deliberate concealment measures which impede verification by national technical means of compliance with the provisions of this Treaty'. Provisions similar to those of the ABM Treaty have been included in article II(1) and (2) of the 1974 Threshold Test Ban Treaty[72] and in article IV(1) and (2) of the 1976 Peaceful Nuclear Explosions Treaty.[73] Much more detailed provisions dealing with NTMs are included in article XII of the INF Treaty, article XV of the CFE Agreement,[74] article IX of the 1991 START Treaty and article IV(5) and (6) of the CTBT. Finally, the 1992 Open Skies Treaty,[75] which entered into force on 1 January 2002, has established a regime of unarmed aerial observation flights over the entire territory of its participants, enhancing mutual understanding and confidence by giving all participants, regardless of size, a direct role in gathering information about military forces and activities of concern to them.[76] Such aerial surveillance complements monitoring by satellites (remote sensing), which is not available to all parties. While the Treaty is directed at information about military forces and related activities, it is, nevertheless, possible that the Treaty's potential will also have an impact on arms control verification.[77]

---

[72] Treaty between the United States of America and the Union of Soviet Socialist Republics on the Limitation of Underground Nuclear Weapon Tests, Moscow, 3 July 1974, 13 ILM 906 (1974).

[73] Treaty between the United States of America and the Union of Soviet Socialist Republics on Underground Nuclear Explosions for Peaceful Purposes, Washington and Moscow, 28 May 1976, 15 ILM 891 (1976).

[74] Conventional Armed Forces in Europe Treaty (CFE Treaty), Paris, 19 November 1990, 30 ILM 1 (1991).

[75] Treaty on Open Skies, Helsinki, 24 March 1992, www.osce.org/documents/doclib/1992/03/13764_en.pdf.

[76] See generally J. Wallner, 'Das Open-Skies-Regime' (1995) *OSZE-Jahrbuch* 321–30.

[77] On conventional arms control, see J. Wallner, 'Die Implementierung konventioneller Rüstungskontrollvereinbarungen' (1996) *OSZE-Jahrbuch* 253–65.

10.5.2 Notification and reporting in arms control

Obligations of notification[78] and reporting systems[79] form the basis of institutionalized mechanisms of fact-finding in arms control. At a preliminary stage, treaties may simply refer to the exchange of information, such as article 9(2) of the NWFZ Treaty of Rarotonga:[80] 'The Parties shall endeavour to keep each other informed on matters arising under or in relation to this Treaty. They may exchange information by communicating it to the Director, who shall circulate it to all Parties.' Such exchange of information has to be distinguished from a formalized reporting system, which differs as far as the degree of detail is concerned.

Thus, article VII(5) of the Antarctic Treaty[81] includes the obligation of States parties to inform the other parties of 'any military personnel or equipment intended to be introduced by it into Antarctica subject to the conditions prescribed in paragraph 2 of Article I of the present Treaty'. According to article 14 of the NWFZ Treaty of Tlatelolco, States parties have to submit reports explaining 'that no activity prohibited under this Treaty has occurred in their respective territories'. Article 15 of the same Treaty provides that 'the Secretary-General may request any of the Contracting Parties to provide the Agency with complementary or supplementary information regarding any extraordinary event or circumstance which affects the compliance with this Treaty'.[82] Similarly, article 9(1) of the NWFZ Treaty of Rarotonga requires States parties to 'report to the Director of the South Pacific Bureau for Economic Co-operation . . . as soon as possible after any significant event within its jurisdiction affecting the implementation of this Treaty'. An interesting provision is included in article XIII of the INF Treaty. Paragraph 2 thereof establishes a system for the continuous exchange of information: 'The Parties shall use the Nuclear Risk Reduction Centers, which provide for continuous

---

[78] For some detail, cf. Chayes and Chayes, *Compliance with International Regulatory Agreements*, pp. 154 *et seq.*, especially p. 162.

[79] On the power of review conferences to contribute to fact-finding, see Knut Ipsen, 'Explicit Methods of Arms Control Treaty Evolution', in J. Dahlitz and D. Dicke (eds.), *The International Law of Arms Control and Disarmament* (New York: United Nations, 1991), pp. 75–93, at pp. 81 *et seq.*

[80] South Pacific Nuclear Free Zone Treaty, Rarotonga, 6 August 1985, 1445 UNTS 177.

[81] Antarctic Treaty, Washington, 1 December 1959, 402 UNTS 71.

[82] The 'Agency' referred to is the Agency for the Prohibition of Nuclear Weapons in Latin America and the Caribbean, established under art. 7 of the Treaty.

communication between the Parties, to: (a) exchange data and provide notifications . . .'[83]

While these obligations can still be considered to be very general in nature, more modern arms control agreements establish detailed notification requirements and reporting obligations. Among the most detailed obligations are those included in the Chemical Weapons Convention (CWC).[84] A principal distinction included in the CWC is between obligations with respect to the destruction of chemical weapons and related production facilities (article III of the CWC and Part IV of the Verification Annex), and obligations related to the obligation not to produce or otherwise acquire chemical weapons (article VI of the CWC and Part VI of the Verification Annex). In light of those detailed obligations, there was no need to grant the Technical Secretariat of the Organisation for the Prohibition of Chemical Weapons extensive powers to request additional information. Uniformity and comparability of reports is basically ensured already on the basis of the provisions of the Treaty. Nevertheless, the Technical Secretariat in practice must precisely define some of the notification and reporting obligations. This is done, in light of the topic's complexity, on the basis of a handbook.

While reporting obligations are an important element of fact-finding, and thus an important element of verification (and compliance control), States parties face increasing difficulties in meeting the multitude of reporting obligations. Not only do they often have to acquire the necessary data from non-State actors, including undertakings, which means that they have to establish a national system of information gathering. Even more burdensome are the costs involved in data acquisition and data processing. This issue can be addressed properly only if there is a more selective approach to the question of whether all States have to provide all different types of information, or whether criteria should be developed to identify (and select) States as well as the type of information required from them more specifically. This is ultimately a matter of cost-efficiency.

---

[83] See art. XIII of the CFE Treaty and the corresponding Protocol on Notification and Information Exchange.

[84] For a conceptual background, see Julian Perry Robinson, 'The Verification System for the Chemical Weapons Convention', in Daniel Bardonnet (ed.), *The Convention on the Prohibition and Elimination of Chemical Weapons: A Breakthrough in Multilateral Disarmament* (Dordrecht: Martinus Nijhoff, 1995), pp. 489–507, at pp. 494 *et seq.*

10.5.3 Verification

With the development of institutionalized procedures for compliance control and verification, a new qualitative dimension of implementation and enforcement has been achieved in arms control. Most procedures build upon the structure of and experiences gained within the safeguard measures of the IAEA in the context of the NPT. A similar approach was adopted as part of the CWC, whereas the CFE Treaty has a much weaker institutional structure. A comprehensive institutional setting has also been developed for the CTBT, and its institutional backbone, the CTBO.[85] As was already indicated above, such a procedure is missing for the BTWC, although attempts were made to introduce such a mechanism.[86] In order to conceptualize these approaches, this chapter focuses on four characteristic features: the degree of institutionalization; on-site inspections; routine procedures; and challenge inspections.

10.5.3.1 Institutionalization

There are a number of advantages of institutionalized[87] verification (or compliance control) procedures. They do not require any preceding claim of treaty violation, nor any dispute between parties. Institutionalized procedures tend to be more 'objective', sticking to the facts, impartial, and pushing back national political considerations. Also, institutionalized supervision tends to avoid stigmatization and can be performed as a matter of routine. In effect, it supports the preventative and confidence-building nature of multilateral arms control, with built-in mechanisms to prevent the occurrence of a situation that endangers peace and international security. Less pursuant of unilateral or bilateral interests, institutionalized verification entails the typical features of multilateralism. The structure can be described as two-sided, but asymmetric: States do not have to inform each other, but they inform the pertinent treaty body, and this particular organ views and filters information according to the object and purpose of the treaty.

---

[85] See Huw Llewellyn, 'The Nuclear Test Ban Treaty – Keywords: Disarmament, On-Site Inspection, Verification' (1997) 10 *Leiden Journal of International Law* 269–80.

[86] See Oliver Thränert, 'Strengthening the Biological Weapons Convention: An Urgent Task' (1996) 17 *Contemporary Security Policy* 347–64; and Annabelle Duncan and Robert J. Mathews, 'Development of a Verification Protocol for the Biological and Toxin Weapons Convention' (1996) *VERTIC Yearbook* 151–70.

[87] The importance of institutionalization is underlined by Stefan Oeter, 'Inspection in International Law' (1997) 28 *Netherlands Yearbook of International Law* 101–69, at 102 *et seq*.

It goes without saying that it is of major importance how these organs are established and what their powers are. In arms control, States opted for a specialized international bureaucracy.[88] These administrative units, as they may be called, normally are (technical) secretariats, with a workforce of independent civil servants.[89] They enjoy a similar status as independent experts, having been appointed *ad personam*.

10.5.3.2 On-site inspections

On-site inspections is the one mechanism that pierces the veil of sovereignty in the strongest manner. Their main feature is that staff of the treaty's secretariat, or (only in some cases) representatives of other States parties, enter the territory of the inspected party in order to verify whether that party has adopted particular measures in compliance with its treaty obligations. They are interventionist in the sense that the inspectors may look for issues which the inspected party seeks to conceal.[90] It is exactly this feature which makes on-site inspections such a sensitive matter – and which explains why it took so long before States were prepared to agree on this type of procedural element.[91]

Including on-site inspections in arms control verification arrangements is not the end of the matter. Rather, it is now important to limit the powers of inspection in the interests of the inspected party.[92] What must be addressed in particular is confidential information – whether for business purposes or in the interest of national security. This protection of confidential information is supported by a number of procedural safeguards, which have reached such a degree of refinement that it is possible to consider this as international procedural law.[93] Typically, pertinent procedural rules include two elements: procedural steps and procedural principles. As far as procedural steps are concerned, arms control treaties include rules on the initiation of the procedure, the sequencing of procedural steps, the

---

[88] Under the CWC, this is in the hands of the Technical Secretariat; cf. art. VIII(37), second sentence.

[89] Cf. Joachim Badelt, 'Das Pariser Chemiewaffen-Übereinkommen: Probleme der nationalen und internationalen Umsetzung' (1994) 69 *Die Friedens-Warte* 7–37, at 25 *et seq.*

[90] Oeter, 'Inspection in International Law', p. 107.

[91] On the CWC negotiations, see Thomas Bernauer, 'Globales Chemiewaffen-Verbot: Regime-Bildung mit Hindernissen' (1996) 71 *Die Friedens-Warte* 9–26, at 16–17 and 23–4.

[92] From a conceptual background, managed access and the perimeter procedure were relevant.

[93] Cf. considerations by Torsten Lohmann, *Die rechtliche Struktur der Sicherungsmaßnahmen der Internationalen Atomenergie-Organization* (Berlin: Duncker & Humblot, 1993), pp. 90 *et seq.*

duration of the procedure and its outcome. Much more innovative – at least in the 1990s – were procedural principles – less the effectiveness and rationality of the procedure as such, but rather principles protecting the rights of the inspected party (and perhaps even the non-State actors concerned). They include the principle of co-operative implementation, the right to be heard, the principle of equal treatment, the principle of proportionality, and the protection of confidential information.[94]

It is these elements which allow the procedure of verification and on-site inspections in arms control to be characterized as quasi-judicial. This refers neither to the question of whether or not a party has met its treaty obligations, nor to the adoption of measures to redress a situation. It refers, instead, to the legal nature of the structural elements inserted into verification in arms control. Only such procedural rules provide verification in general, and on-site inspections in particular, with the indispensable legitimacy they need in order to encroach upon a State's sovereignty. This is even more necessary should the rights of individuals be concerned, such as in the inspection of industrial facilities.

10.5.3.3 Initiation of the procedure as a matter of routine

Prima facie, the initiation of routine procedures does not entail particular legal problems. Such procedures are performed irrespective of any doubts about treaty compliance, thus avoiding controversies, but contributing to transparency and confidence-building. Whereas challenge inspections (which will be addressed below) primarily provide negative incentives, routine verification procedures must be considered as positive incentives. They do not serve the establishment of a breach of treaty but of treaty compliance. The only sensitive issues in routine procedures are their timing and their intensity.

As they often serve to cross-check notifications and reports submitted by parties, most of the existing arms control agreements provide for a certain period of time within which routine verification should take place. The degree of precision varies among the different agreements. Should specific disarmament matters be included in the treaty, then time limits have to be linked to pertinent deadlines (e.g. for destruction). If verification is more concerned with non-production and non-acquisition, then mostly regular

---

[94] For a similar approach in international environmental law, cf. Marauhn, 'Towards a Procedural Law of Compliance Control in International Environmental Relations' (1996) 56 *Zeitschrift für ausländisches öffentliches Recht und Völkerrecht* 696–731, at 722 *et seq.*

intervals are laid down in the treaty. If no specific timeframe is fixed, then criteria for the determination of the proper point in time are included in the treaty. Thus, Part VI, paragraph 30, of the CWC's Verification Annex determines with respect to facilities dealing with particular listed substances: 'The number, intensity, duration, timing and mode of inspections for a particular facility shall be based on the risk to the object and purpose of this Convention posed by the quantities of chemicals produced, the characteristics of the facility and the nature of the activities carried out there.' This provision illustrates, once again, the problem of cost-efficiency, which necessitates that the risk of treaty violation is taken into account when determining the frequency of verification measures.[95] It is no surprise that the CWC even includes criteria for the determination of such risk. Such determination is relevant not only with regard to the frequency of verification measures, but also in respect of the objects to be inspected or the measures to be verified.

10.5.3.4 Close to enforcement: *ad hoc* or challenge inspections

While challenge inspections[96] are not necessarily linked to institutionalized verification procedures, they are, nevertheless, a common feature thereof. However, they were introduced even earlier. Thus, article XI(3)–(5) of the INF Treaty as well as Part VIII of the CFE Treaty's Inspection Protocol include challenge inspections, although both treaties have a much weaker institutional structure than the CWC or the NPT.[97] The decisive difference between routine and challenge procedures within institutionalized settings is that the initiation of the procedure is not exclusively in the hands of an international body or a treaty organ. Rather, it necessitates some input from one of the parties: a challenge directed at another party. Thus, article IX(8) of the CWC states: 'Each State Party has the right to request an onsite challenge inspection of any facility or location in the territory or in any other place under the jurisdiction or control of any other State Party for the sole purpose of clarifying and resolving any questions concerning possible non-compliance with the provisions of this Convention, and to have this inspection conducted anywhere without delay by an inspection

---

[95] Krutzsch and Trapp, *A Commentary on the Chemical Weapons Convention*, p. 425.
[96] For the CWC context, see Julian Perry Robinson, 'The Verification System', in Bardonnet (ed.), *The Convention on the Prohibition and Elimination of Chemical Weapons*, pp. 498 *et seq.*
[97] But see paras. 73 and 77 of the model safeguards agreement, INFCIRC/153, and the comments by Oeter, 'Inspection in International Law', pp. 117–18.

team designated by the Director-General and in accordance with the Verification Annex.' In order to avoid undermining of the characteristics of the routine procedure, a number of criteria must be met before a challenge inspection actually takes place.

First, corroborating information must go with the request for an *ad hoc* or challenge inspection in order to avoid abuse of the procedure. Secondly, one of the treaty bodies is entitled to assess the conclusiveness of the request. Finally, by way of example, article IX(17) of the CWC stipulates that the 'Executive Council may, not later than 12 hours after having received the inspection request, decide by a three-quarter majority of all its members against carrying out the challenge inspection, if it considers the inspection request to be frivolous, abusive or clearly beyond the scope of this Convention as described in paragraph 8. Neither the requesting nor the inspected State Party shall participate in such a decision. If the Executive Council decides against the challenge inspection, preparations shall be stopped, no further action on the inspection request shall be taken, and the States Parties concerned shall be informed accordingly.'

It is important to realise that challenge and *ad hoc* inspections include an element of enforcement. They do not primarily aim at verifying compliance, but they are motivated by a situation which has given rise to concern that there is already a treaty violation. Even the threat of a challenge inspection may bring States back into compliance. It is against this background that a few remarks on enforcement within arms control agreements will now follow.

10.6 Enforcement

Before addressing the details of traditional and modern enforcement strategies in arms control agreement, it is important to point out that, by their very nature, arms control agreements are preventative. They seek to prevent situations of, or coming close to, international armed conflict. To this end, their normal range of operation must be prior to enforcement – and even at a lower level than UN Security Council action under Chapter VII of the UN Charter. Once a situation has escalated and the preconditions of Chapter VII are met, the essence of multilateral arms control has already been surpassed. Nevertheless, it is important to take into account that Chapter VII can also be used in the context of arms control – since non-implementation or even violation of multilateral arms control agreements will easily come close to a situation where international peace and security is at risk. Thus, the threat of UN Security Council action should always act as a negative incentive for States to abide by their obligations under an arms control agreement. Unfortunately, however, this has not always worked, as in particular nuclear arms control and the attitudes of Iraq, North Korea and Iran have generally or recently shown.

The specifics of modern arms control agreements should never detract from the existence of traditional means of enforcement, which have played a major role in the history of arms control and which can always be brought back onto the agenda, unless an arms control regime would under exceptional circumstances qualify as a 'self-contained regime'.

10.6.1 Counter-measures

Counter-measures are one of the traditional techniques of enforcement in relations between States. They are intended to end or remedy a violation of a rule of public international law. To this end, they must be in conformity with article 2(4) of the UN Charter, they must be proportionate and they can only be directed against the wrongful State. Usually, they are limited to the non-performance of obligations and aimed towards a resumption of performance. Reprisals do not seem to fit the object and purpose of arms control agreements. They necessitate a degree of obstructive behaviour within an arms control regime which could best be met by withdrawing from the regime as such. Keeping recalcitrant parties in a regime by means of counter-measures might endanger the stability of the regime as such and undermine its credibility. However, the case of North Korea demonstrates that there are two sides of a coin, always.[98]

Retorsions, in contrast, seem to be too soft to consider them as tools of enforcement. They are unfriendly but lawful acts of a State, undertaken in response to an unfriendly but normally lawful act of another State. Only if they are a reaction to a treaty violation by the other State do they come into the spectrum of enforcement techniques. In light of the growing degree of juridification in international relations, however, there is little room left for retorsions. Even economic and financial relations are today often governed by international law. Although a retorsion may serve a

---

[98] See Masahiko Asada, 'Arms Control Law in Crisis? A Study of the North Korean Nuclear Issue' (2004) 9 *Journal of Conflict and Security Law* 331–55.

preventative purpose, it is doubtful whether it does this in the context of arms control politics.[99] Retorsion rather may breed mistrust, thus being counter-productive to the primary purpose of arms control: the building of confidence between States.

10.6.2 Withdrawal and termination of arms control agreements

Most of the early arms control agreements include clauses on suspension, withdrawal and termination. They are, however, very general in their wording and usually not specifically addressed to cases of a breach of the treaty. Thus, article IV of the Limited Test Ban Treaty of 1963[100] stipulates that each party 'in exercising its national sovereignty [shall] have the right to withdraw from the Treaty if it decides that *extraordinary events*, related to the subject matter of this Treaty, have jeopardized the *supreme interests* of its country'.[101] Similar provisions are included in article VII of the NPT, article VIII of the 1971 Seabed Treaty,[102] article XIII of the BTWC and article XV(2) of the ABM Treaty and the corresponding interim agreement (article VIII(3)). A slightly different wording is included in article 31(1) of the NWFZ Treaty of Tlatelolco: 'any Party may denounce it by notifying the Secretary-General of the Agency if, in the opinion of the denouncing State, there have arisen or may arise circumstances connected with the content of this Treaty or of the annexed Additional Protocols I and II which affect its supreme interests or the peace and security of one or more Contracting Parties.' By contrast, article 13 of the NWFZ Treaty of Rarotonga explicitly refers to a violation of the Treaty: 'in the event of a violation by any Party of a provision of this Treaty essential to the achievement of the objectives of the Treaty or of the spirit of the Treaty, every other Party shall have the right to withdraw from the Treaty.'

It is noteworthy that clauses referring to 'supreme interests' or 'extraordinary events' were introduced into such agreements in light of the position that had originally been promoted by the USSR, namely, that a State party's right of withdrawal was inherent in State sovereignty. The clauses

---

[99] Cf. Lysén, *The International Regulation of Armaments*, pp. 198 *et seq.*

[100] Treaty Banning Nuclear Weapon Tests in the Atmosphere, in Outer Space and Under Water, Moscow, 5 August 1963, 480 UNTS 43.   [101] Emphasis added.

[102] Treaty on the Prohibition of the Emplacement of Nuclear Weapons and Other Weapons of Mass Destruction on the Sea-Bed and the Ocean Floor and in the Subsoil Thereof, London, Moscow and Washington, 11 February 1971, 955 UNTS 115.

therefore were intended to limit governmental discretion towards withdrawal and termination.[103] In general, however, all these clauses can be considered to include measures in response to treaty violations.[104] Difficulties may arise only with respect to other parties to a multilateral agreement. In such a case, however, article 60(2)(c) of the Vienna Convention on the Law of Treaties would allow at least a suspension by the party that perceives itself to be endangered.[105]

10.6.3 Sanctions adopted by the UN Security Council

Matters of international peace and security always bring the United Nations to the fore. It is noteworthy that a number of arms control agreements explicitly provide for a reference to, or an intervention by, the UN Security Council in cases where treaty compliance is at risk. Thus, article VI of the BTWC stipulates: 'Any State Party to this convention which finds that any other State Party is acting in breach of obligations deriving from the provisions of the Convention may lodge a complaint with the Security Council of the United Nations.' The Security Council can then carry out an investigation and will inform the parties about its findings. Much more relevant at present is article XII, part C, of the IAEA Statute, which is applicable also to all IAEA safeguards. Under this provision, the IAEA Board of Governors 'shall report the non-compliance to all members and to the Security Council and General Assembly of the United Nations'.[106] The recent case of Iran illustrates that this provision is still very much alive. Even modern arms control agreements provide for a reference to the Security Council. Thus, article XII(4) of the CWC empowers the Conference of the Parties 'in cases of particular gravity, [to] bring the issue, including relevant information and conclusions, to the attention of the United Nations General Assembly and the United Nations Security Council'. Finally, article V(4) of the CTBT includes a similar provision.

The type of measures adopted by the UN Security Council depends on the Charter itself. If the Council makes a determination according to article 39 of the Charter, then non-military and military sanctions are an option

---

[103] See Egon Schwelb, 'The Nuclear Test Ban Treaty and International Law' (1964) 58 *American Journal of International Law* 642–70, at 661.

[104] See Lysén, *The International Regulation of Armaments*, p. 176.

[105] Schwelb, 'The Nuclear Test Ban Treaty and International Law', pp. 662–3.

[106] Cf. Lohmann, *Die rechtliche Struktur der Sicherungsmaßnahmen der Internationalen Atomenergie-Organization*, pp. 243–4.

270   INTERNATIONAL ARMS CONTROL

according to articles 41 and 42. However, there is no Security Council practice with regard to multilateral regimes so far, and the Iran case may become a precedent to this end. The measures against Iraq were not adopted on the basis of safeguards,[107] although the Security Council confirmed the assessment of the IAEA Board of Governors.[108] Thus the sanctions were not triggered by the Board of Governors but by 'reports in the hands of Member States'.[109] As the case of Iraq illustrates, the UN Security Council can react to violations of arms control agreements irrespective of the provisions of the agreement concerned, as long as it makes a determination under article 39 of the UN Charter.

10.6.4 Treaty provisions on measures to redress a situation

Coming back to other mechanisms provided for in multilateral arms control agreements in response to the outcome of verification and inspection procedures, one of the essential questions relates to the powers of treaty bodies. Normally, one would expect that the facts will be assessed and evaluated in light of the obligations undertaken by Member States. However, as a rule, the procedure ends with factual evaluation only,[110] providing the basis for a political decision to be taken by the Conference of the Parties or a similar organ. Thus, there is a clear separation of powers between the Technical Secretariat of the CWC – which cannot go beyond factual evaluation – and the Conference of the Parties which is entitled to take a broad variety of measures on the basis of article XII of the Convention.[111] These measures, however, are not limited to traditional enforcement. They can include assistance in order to support the State party in its efforts to comply.

Basically, multilateral treaties thus rely on a more or less consensual solution rather than on an authoritative decision of one of the treaty organs. It is noteworthy that the terms 'legality' or 'illegality' are hardly ever used. Such terms are too close to the concept of State responsibility. This, indeed, is what most multilateral agreements seek to avoid. The complex

---

[107] See *ibid.*, pp. 251–2.   [108] UN SC Res. 707 (1991), para. 2.
[109] UN SC Res. 687 (1991), preamble.
[110] Cf. Marauhn, 'Routine Verification under the Chemical Weapons Convention', in Bothe, Ronzitti and Rosas (eds.), *The New Chemical Weapons Convention*, pp. 241–2.
[111] Cf. A. Rosas, 'Reactions to Non-Compliance with the Chemical Weapons Convention', in Bothe, Ronzitti and Rosas (eds.), *The New Chemical Weapons Convention*, pp. 415–61.

title of article XII[112] of the CWC is illustrative in this regard. Sanctions – and thus enforcement – are not excluded, but they are not the focal point of article XII. This can best be taken from article XII(1) of the CWC, stipulating that the Conference of the Parties may adopt measures 'to ensure compliance with this Convention and to redress and remedy any situation which contravenes the provisions of this Convention'.

It is noteworthy, therefore, that multilateral arms control agreements rely on co-operative means to achieve compliance rather than on unilateral or multilateral enforcement.

10.7 Perspectives

As this overview has sought to illustrate, States have developed a number of strategies to make arms control agreements work. Most of these strategies, however, were developed in the 1980s and the 1990s when arms control politics culminated in the conclusion of a number of highly sophisticated multilateral arms control agreements. While in light of this climax some commentators fear that we are experiencing a period of arms control in crisis today, this chapter has argued that there is a period of, and a need for, consolidation of those techniques. One particular aspect of such consolidation is the need to consider more seriously whether or not compliance control strategies are cost-efficient. This is all the more important if the process of multilateral arms control is to continue.

A second aspect deserves attention in this context. Multilateral arms control as it has developed in the second half of the twentieth century focuses on inter-State relations. This focus – claims to the contrary notwithstanding – remains an important part of national and international security. States are still among the most important actors in international security. However, the situation has changed, in the sense that States are no longer the only actors in the field. There is a certain proliferation of actors, in particular as far as the private sector is concerned. Terrorists today pose a different type of security risk, without, however, totally replacing other security risks. Also, private security firms are a factor which has in the past not been taken into account. But all these new developments do not justify totally turning away from multilateral arms control and rather relying on military power or other unilateral methods. As the non-proliferation

---

[112] 'Measures to Redress a Situation and to Ensure Compliance, Including Sanctions.'

initiative illustrates, the proliferation of weapons of mass destruction (and other types of military equipment) is a major problem today. This can be better addressed by a meaningful international agreement than by isolated – even though sometimes co-ordinated – national politics.

Turning to the main concern of this chapter and this volume, arms control agreements have been made effective primarily on the basis of mechanisms of compliance control, which are typically termed differently in the arms control sector. Traditional dispute settlement is not excluded in the arms control field, but it is only of supplementary value. While early arms control agreements had no other means at hand than dispute settlement, this is different for modern multilateral agreements. Here, notification, reporting, verification and inspection are much more important. The only question that necessitates closer attention in future agreements than in the past is whether or not compliance control mechanisms and dispute settlement should co-exist in parallel, or whether there should be a sequencing of both. In light of some of the reports, this chapter suggests that sequencing might be both more effective and more cost-efficient.[113]

One of the more traditional enforcement options in arms control has been and remains the Security Council. However, this is only a means of last resort – and such last resort often is ample evidence of a failure of the co-operative mechanisms with regard to one particular State party. There are indeed serious cases to be considered for UN Security Council enforcement, but this should not detract from the fact that the very rationale of arms control agreements is to develop mechanisms avoiding the need to resort to the Security Council.

Finally, turning to the procedures developed within arms control agreements in order to make those treaties work, it must be stressed that, in light of arms control practice and politics, two elements are of utmost importance: the establishment of transparency between States parties, and the building of confidence among them. It is only on this basis that arms control can be meaningful and successful. At the same time, there is a need for creativity to optimize governance in the field of arms control, to avoid unnecessary costs and to improve the effectiveness of agreements.

---

[113] See Nancy W. Gallagher, 'The Politics of Verification: Why "How Much?" is Not Enough', in Nancy W. Gallagher, *Arms Control: New Approaches to Theory and Policy* (London: Johns Hopkins University Press, 1999).

11

The Convention on the Prohibition of the Development, Production, Stockpiling and Use of Chemical Weapons and on their Destruction (Chemical Weapons Convention)

LISA TABASSI*

11.1 Introduction

The 1993 Chemical Weapons Convention (CWC)[1] is a true disarmament instrument: in adhering to the treaty all States parties have undertaken to eliminate this category of weapon by destroying all of their existing stockpiles and related production facilities and by taking positive measures to prevent any new proliferation. The Convention has achieved nearly universal adherence, with 179 States parties as of 1 October 2006 and an additional seven signatory States.[2] The CWC contains the most intrusive verification regime established so far. Initially lauded as the model for future arms control and disarmament agreements, after nine years of implementation it remains an important anomaly in the current international political climate.

Expanding upon the one-page 1925 Geneva Protocol, which had effectively banned only the first-use of chemical weapons,[3] the CWC comprises more

---

* The views expressed are the author's own and do not necessarily reflect those of the OPCW Secretariat. The author would like to express her appreciation to Ruth Möhlenkamp, Ralf Trapp and Gordon Vachon for their insight and comments on verification practice under the Convention and, as ever, Walter Krutzsch for his inspiration and critical thought.

[1] Convention on the Prohibition of the Development, Production, Stockpiling and Use of Chemical Weapons and on their Destruction, Paris, 13 January 1993, entered into force 29 April 1997, UN Doc. A/RES/47/39.

[2] Only eight States have stayed totally outside the regime: Angola, Barbados, North Korea, Egypt, Iraq, Lebanon, Somalia and Syria.

[3] Protocol for the Prohibition of the Use in War of Asphyxiating, Poisonous or Other Gases, and of Bacteriological Methods of Warfare, Geneva, 17 June 1925, 94 LNTS (1929) No. 2138. As of 1 October 2006, it has 133 States parties. Thirty-five of them had reduced their obligations to a ban on first use by reservations. Those reservations became void for States parties to the CWC when the CWC entered into force for them.

than 200 pages prescribing that States parties shall *never, under any circumstances*: (a) develop, produce, otherwise acquire, stockpile, retain or use chemical weapons, or transfer them directly or indirectly to anyone; (b) engage in any military preparations to use them; or (c) assist, encourage or induce, in any way, anyone to engage in any activity prohibited to a CWC State party. States parties are under the obligation to destroy all chemical weapons they own, possess, have under their control or have abandoned elsewhere, as well as the production facilities related to them. To close a near loophole, the CWC defines riot control agents and bans their use as a method of warfare. To prevent the proliferation of chemical weapons, States parties are additionally under the obligation to declare certain activities, subject certain chemical production facilities to international inspection, and restrict transfers of certain dual-use chemicals to States not party.

To ensure CWC implementation, including verification of compliance as well as consultation and co-operation among States parties, the CWC established an intergovernmental treaty-implementing body, the Organisation for the Prohibition of Chemical Weapons (OPCW) in The Hague. It comprises three organs – plenary (the Conference of the States Parties), executive (the Executive Council) and secretariat (the Technical Secretariat) – and one subsidiary organ – the Commission for the Settlement of Disputes Related to Confidentiality. Each State party is required to designate or establish a 'National Authority' and these have proven to be essential for effective national implementation and for demonstrating compliance since it is largely through their efforts that implementing legislation is drafted and submitted to the parliamentary process and the Convention's provisions are made known to the relevant community nationally. The respective mandates of all these are discussed further below in the context of dispute resolution, compliance, and enforcement.

11.2 Dispute resolution

In considering dispute resolution under the CWC, it should first be noted that the emphasis in the Convention is on swift and co-operative dispute resolution, with the aim of preserving legitimate interests and achieving the object and purpose of the Convention. The OPCW was established as 'the forum for consultation and co-operation among States Parties'[4] with: a

---

[4] Art. VIII(1).

Secretariat which is engaged full time in verifying compliance and providing implementation support; the Council which meets regularly and on very short notice to address any issue arising under the CWC (including doubts about compliance); and the Conference which meets annually and in special sessions when needed. Those formal activities are supplemented by a continuous cycle of informal consultations in the OPCW as well as bilateral consultations between States parties, which in most cases are not brought to the attention of the organization or other States parties. It is to be expected that so many levels of continuous dialogue lessen the likelihood that an issue could escalate into a full-scale 'dispute' with all the political implications a 'dispute' could entail.

Having said that, the Convention provides for several options and means of dispute resolution, some overlapping, depending upon the nature of the dispute, who the parties are, and the preferences of the parties.

11.2.1 Disputes over the application or interpretation of the Convention

Article XIV ('Settlement of Disputes') regulates the settlement of disputes concerning the application or interpretation of the Convention occurring between two or more States parties or between one or more States parties and the OPCW. It envisages that the disputing parties shall consult together to expeditiously settle the dispute by negotiation or other peaceful means of their choice, including recourse to the OPCW organs or, by mutual consent, to the International Court of Justice (ICJ) in accordance with its Statute. Under the ICJ Statute, if the States concerned have consented to the ICJ's jurisdiction, the court would be competent to resolve a dispute over interpretation of the CWC; the existence of any fact which, if established, would constitute a breach of the CWC; and the nature or extent of reparations for a breach. In such cases, the Court's judgment would be binding.[5]

For its part, under article XIV of the CWC, the Council plays the central role, in that it is empowered to contribute to the settlement of a dispute by whatever means it chooses, including offering its good offices, calling upon disputing States parties to start the settlement process of their choice or recommending a time limit for any agreed procedure.

In contrast, under article XIV, the Conference is limited to considering questions related to disputes raised by States parties or brought to its

---

[5] Art. 36 of the ICJ Statute.

276 INTERNATIONAL ARMS CONTROL

attention by the Council. The Conference is also empowered to establish subsidiary organs or to entrust organs with tasks related to the settlement of those disputes.

The provisions of article XIV are also explicitly applicable to all disputes arising under 'facility agreements' concluded between the OPCW and an inspected State party.[6] The CWC requires that these agreements be concluded, based on models, to specify the detailed arrangements governing OPCW on-site inspections, and they incorporate reference to article XIV. Negotiation and conclusion of these agreements reduces the likelihood that disputes will arise in an eventual inspection since so many details are agreed upon in advance between the OPCW and the State party, with the participation of the facility owner or operator.

There are many potential sources for disagreement between an OPCW inspection team and the inspected State party. In the event the differences cannot be resolved, the inspection team has no enforcement authority – its only recourse will be to report the situation to the Director-General and include it in its final report which, if unresolved, will be brought to the Council's attention, and may also be referred to the Conference if the Council so decides. In practice, no significant problems have occurred – or were made known. Less than five instances have ever been brought to the Council's attention, and those occurred in the early years.

11.2.2 Additional recourse to the International Court of Justice for advisory opinions

The Conference and the Council are also separately empowered, subject to authorization by the United Nations General Assembly, to request the ICJ to give an advisory opinion on any legal question[7] arising within the scope of the activities of the OPCW. As provided for by the Convention, the UN and the OPCW have concluded a relationship agreement[8] for, *inter alia*, this purpose. However, unlike the Relationship Agreement between the UN and the International Atomic Energy Agency (IAEA),[9] the UN General Assembly has not subsequently granted blanket approval to the OPCW to

---

[6] Part III, para. 3, of the Verification Annex.
[7] 'Legal question' could include a determination of compliance or non-compliance.
[8] Art. VII of the Relationship Agreement between the United Nations and the OPCW (OPCW Conference Decision C-VI/DEC.5 (2001)) and UN GA Res. 55/283, dated 7 September 2001, both available at www.opcw.org/legal/.   [9] UN GA Res. 1146 (XII), dated 14 November 1957.

seek such advisory opinions. Thus this dispute settlement option is weakened by the fact that General Assembly approval must first be sought (a time-consuming step) and the advisory opinion eventually rendered by the ICJ, although authoritative, will not be binding.

11.2.3 Disputes over a State party's compliance

Article IX ('Consultations, Co-operation and Fact-Finding') is another basis for dispute settlement since it constitutes the primary mechanism for preventing or resolving disputes among States parties regarding compliance, either through consultation and clarification procedures or by challenge inspection (short notice, no right of refusal). Article IX is discussed further below, in relation to its role in determining or resolving questions of compliance.

Article XII ('Measures to Redress a Situation and to Ensure Compliance, Including Sanctions') could additionally serve as the basis for dispute resolution, in so far as the Conference is required, in cases of particular gravity, to bring the issue to the UN General Assembly and Security Council. Article XII is discussed further below, in relation to its role in enforcement of the Convention.

11.2.4 Disputes over confidentiality

The CWC's intrusive verification regime could coincide with matters of national security, military activities, or confidential business information from the chemicals industry. For that reason, the drafters of the Convention provided for circumstances in which a State party can avoid having its confidential information collected by the OPCW.[10] The Annex on Confidentiality sets forth stringent requirements concerning the protection of any confidential information gathered by the OPCW, shared with States parties or transmitted between them directly. For breaches of confidentiality involving a State party and the OPCW, the CWC established a Commission for the Settlement of Disputes Related to Confidentiality (the 'Confidentiality Commission') as a subsidiary organ of the Conference.[11] Under the Rules Governing the Confidentiality Commission,[12] the Commission membership

---

[10] See W. Krutzsch and R. Trapp, *Verification Practice under the Chemical Weapons Convention* (The Hague: Kluwer Law International, 1999), pp. 163–4.

[11] Annex on Confidentiality, para. 23. [12] Conference Decision C-I/DEC.13 (1997), Part IX.

is composed of twenty persons, appointed in their personal capacity for two-year terms by the Conference from a list of nominees put forward by States parties and drawn from relevant fields of expertise. The Commission and its members individually are required to act without interference or direction from the Secretariat or other OPCW organs, but must follow the mandate of the Conference. No disputes have arisen.

11.2.5 Recourse to arbitration

While not explicitly referring to arbitration, article XIV provides that disputes can be settled 'by other peaceful means of the parties' choice', which would include arbitration.

11.2.6 The Administrative Tribunal of the International Labour Organization: safeguarding the independence of the OPCW Technical Secretariat

In the eight years since entry into force of the CWC, no formal disputes have been submitted under any of the mechanisms described above – either there have been no disputes, or no State party has been willing to come forward publicly with its dispute. Oddly enough, the body to which disputes have been submitted is the Administrative Tribunal of the International Labour Organization (the 'Tribunal'). Recourse to the Tribunal is a right established by the OPCW Staff Regulations; however, three of the cases adjudicated by it were not strictly staff administrative matters. Those three cases concerned the proper functioning of the OPCW and could have constituted disputes between the OPCW and the States parties concerned, if either had been willing to institute proceedings under the Convention. Absent the political willingness to do so, the disputes were ultimately decided by the Tribunal as administrative disputes. The first two cases concerned respect for the tax-free status of the emoluments of staff members, in respect of which the Tribunal instructed the OPCW on its 'duty to protect the staff member against the claims of the authorities of a Member State ... Exemption from national taxes is an essential condition of employment in the international civil service and is an important guarantee of independence and objectivity.'[13] The third case arose out of a disagreement between a State party and

---

[13] Para. 17 of International Labour Organization Administrative Tribunal (ILOAT) Judgment 2032 (2001) and para. 13 of Judgment 2256 (2003), available at www.ilo.org/dyn/triblex/.

the Director-General over his 'actions and overall management of the Secretariat',[14] which eventually resulted in the termination of his appointment by decision of the Conference.[15] In that case, the Tribunal ultimately decided that the Conference decision contravened the general principles of the law of the international civil service:

> the independence of international civil servants is an essential guarantee, not only for the civil servants themselves, but also for the proper functioning of international organisations. In the case of heads of organisations, that independence is protected, *inter alia*, by the fact that they are appointed for a limited term of office. To concede that the authority in which the power of appointment is vested – in this case the Conference of the States Parties of the Organisation – may terminate that appointment in its unfettered discretion, would constitute an unacceptable violation of the principles on which international organisations' activities are founded ... by rendering officials vulnerable to pressures and to political change.[16]

11.3 Compliance control

The CWC provides the most extensive verification regime for ensuring compliance in force today, comprising: (a) State party declarations of chemical weapons, related facilities and production of the toxic chemicals/precursors subject to verification measures; (b) routine on-site inspections to verify those declarations and the destruction of chemical weapons; (c) the option for States parties to request a challenge inspection if they have evidence of non-compliance; and (d) investigations of alleged use of chemical weapons. All of these are to be carried out by, or in conjunction with, the standing organization, the OPCW.

11.3.1 Demonstrating compliance with the CWC

Demonstrating compliance is a fundamental co-operative principle of the verification regime, not a burden of proof, and is in each aspect balanced in some way by the protection for legitimate interests.

---

[14] US Department of State Fact Sheet dated 1 April 2002, available at www.state.gov/t/ac/rls/fs/9120.htm.   [15] Conference Decision C-SS-1/DEC.1 (2002).

[16] ILOAT Judgments 2232 (2003), 2327 (2004) and 2328 (2004), available at www.ilo.org/dyn/triblex/.

The reporting obligations to the OPCW by each State party are the following: initial declarations regarding its chemical weapons (including old or abandoned ones), their present or former production facilities and certain other related information; riot control agents held; and Schedule 1[17] facilities, relevant data on Schedules 2[18] and 3[19] plant sites, as well as other chemical facilities producing unscheduled discrete organic chemicals. These are supplemented by annual updates, including data on scheduled chemicals imported or exported. The Convention establishes the level of detail that is to be included in the required reporting, and, in practice, States parties and the organs of the OPCW have been working diligently to fine-tune and reach consensus on the formats and details of reporting in the declarations. Especially in respect of import/export data, the number of discrepancies has been significant and has not always been clarified to the satisfaction of those concerned.

The second aspect of demonstrating compliance is the State party's obligation to provide access for routine inspections to verify the information contained in its declarations, continuous monitoring of its chemical weapons destruction activities, and access for challenge inspections or alleged use investigations.

The third aspect of demonstrating compliance is the State party's cooperation and willingness to engage in consultations with the Secretariat or other States parties to clarify any doubts or ambiguities about its compliance and to participate in any eventual sessions of the Council or Conference in this regard. Demonstrating compliance is termed as an obligation[20] as well as a right: each State party has the right to request the Council to clarify any situation which has been considered ambiguous or has given rise to a concern about its possible non-compliance with the CWC.[21]

11.3.2 Monitoring compliance with the CWC

The arrangements for monitoring compliance are the inspections or investigations carried out and evaluated by the OPCW. A summary of the mandates and composition of the players in this process is as follows:

---

[17] Schedule 1 chemicals have historically been developed, produced, stockpiled or used as chemical weapons and have little or no use for purposes not prohibited under the CWC.

[18] Schedule 2 'dual-use' chemicals pose significant risk to the object and purpose of the Convention and have few commercial uses.

[19] Schedule 3 'dual-use' chemicals have historically been developed for chemical weapons purposes, pose a risk to the object and purpose of the CWC, and are produced in large commercial quantities for purposes not prohibited under the Convention.   [20] Art. IX(4)(b).   [21] Art. IX(5).

- The OPCW is required to achieve the object and purpose of the CWC, to ensure the implementation of its provisions, including those for international verification of compliance with it, and (as discussed above) to provide a forum for consultation and co-operation among States parties.
- The Conference, as the principal organ, considers any questions, matters or issues within the scope of the CWC and acts to promote its object and purpose. It reviews compliance with the CWC and oversees the activities of the Council and Secretariat and provides guidelines to them. Although its rules of procedure foresee voting, the Conference is required to make an effort to achieve consensus,[22] and in practice all decisions have been adopted by consensus except one (termination of the appointment of the Director-General). The emphasis on consensus is understandable since it ensures the viability of a security instrument and the universal participation of its members.
- The Council is the executive organ that promotes implementation and compliance with the CWC. The Council's forty-one members are drawn from the five regional groups set by the CWC. All members are equal – there is no veto power or permanent seats, although the seats reserved for 'the States Parties with the most significant national chemical industry' in each region mean that some members hold a seat on a quasi-permanent basis. The Council supervises the Secretariat, co-operates with National Authorities, and considers any issue affecting the CWC and its implementation, including concerns regarding compliance and cases of non-compliance, and, as appropriate, brings them to the attention of States parties, the Conference and, in cases of urgency, the UN General Assembly and Security Council. Again, although its rules of procedure foresee voting, in practice all decisions have been adopted by consensus except two (the terms of appointment of the Director-General in 1998 and the removal of the Director-General in 2002). Unlike the Conference, the rules of procedure do not require the Council to make any effort to achieve consensus; thus one could conclude that the Council is expected to vote upon its decisions. The practice of, almost exclusively, taking decisions by consensus in effect means that the veto power exists in reality. This could be an obstacle in the exercise of the Council's dispute resolution function.

---

[22] Rule 69 of the Rules of Procedure of the Conference.

- The Secretariat assists the Conference and Council and carries out the verification measures as a fact-finder. It is required to inform the Council of any problem arising in the discharge of its functions, including doubts, ambiguities or uncertainties about compliance with the CWC that have come to its notice in the performance of its verification activities, and that it has been unable to resolve or clarify through its consultations with the State party concerned. To ensure the impartiality and independence of OPCW verification and the protection of the information obtained thereby, article VIII provides that the Director-General, the inspectors and the other members of the staff shall not seek or receive instructions from any government or from any other source external to the OPCW and each State party is required to respect that independence and not seek to influence them in the discharge of their responsibilities.
- The Director-General is the head and chief administrative officer of the Secretariat. S/he appoints and supervises the inspectorate and the other staff. He or she also appoints and is responsible for the functioning of the Scientific Advisory Board, a Convention-mandated body that renders specialized advice relevant to the CWC to keep the organs abreast of scientific and technological advances which may affect the operation of the Convention. The Director-General establishes the rules for the conduct of inspections and issues the mandate for each inspection, which the team is bound to observe. He or she receives the final inspection reports and, if they contain uncertainties, he or she must approach the State party for clarification. If the uncertainties cannot be removed, or if the facts suggest that CWC obligations have not been met, he or she must inform the Council without delay. During a challenge inspection or alleged use investigation, the Director-General is the primary facilitator of the process. Finally, the Director-General has primary responsibility for ensuring the protection of confidential information.
- States parties are under the obligation to provide access to OPCW inspection teams to verify routinely the accuracy of their declarations as well as short-notice access to any place in their territory or under their jurisdiction or control, for challenge inspection. States parties are each required to designate or establish a National Authority to liaise with the OPCW and other States parties. In practice, an increasing number of National Authorities have been formally established by legislation empowering them to request persons to provide the information needed

for declarations. This is being done to ensure accurate national declarations to the OPCW, co-operation with the OPCW inspection process and effective national implementation of the CWC. The procedures for verification are set forth in the CWC, which establishes the general rules of verification (including pre-inspection activities, conduct of inspections, debriefing and preparation of reports) as well as the periodicity, duration and intensity of inspections depending upon the type of inspection, and the principles for, and order of, destruction of chemical weapons. These have been supplemented by Conference decisions which interpret the relevant CWC provisions, record understandings, or constitute guidelines.[23] The Secretariat has prepared standard operating procedures for most aspects of the verification process.[24] Destruction of chemical weapons and chemical weapons production facilities is carried out, at the cost of the State party concerned, under combined plans for destruction and verification, agreed with the State party, and under continuous monitoring by an OPCW inspection team.

11.3.3 Monitoring compliance: evaluation of declarations and inspections

Under the Annex on Confidentiality, data required by States parties for the purpose of ensuring continued compliance with the CWC by other States parties shall be routinely provided to them. This includes the initial and annual declarations and reports provided by States parties and 'general reports on the results and effectiveness of verification measures'.[25] For the evaluation of compliance, the main document is the Verification Implementation Report, a classified document distributed annually to the Council. That report contains summary information as well as relevant country-specific information submitted to, or gathered by, the Secretariat. In addition to the Verification Implementation Report, informal consultations are held between the Secretariat and Council members immediately prior to each Council session. In those consultations, the Secretariat provides a briefing on such issues, and delegations equally have the opportunity to raise points of their own.

---

[23] See further Part One of L. Tabassi (ed.), *OPCW: The Legal Texts* (The Hague: TMC Asser Press, 1999), pp. 119–255.

[24] Inspection Manual, OPCW Doc. QDOC/INS/IM/01 (1 January 2001).

[25] Annex on Confidentiality, para. 2(b).

11.3.4 Determination of compliance/non-compliance

The Council is the first line for assessing compliance with the CWC. 'In its consideration of doubts or concerns regarding compliance and cases of non-compliance ... the Council shall consult with the States parties involved and, as appropriate, request the State party to take measures to redress the situation within a specified time.'[26] If it considers further action necessary, the Council can inform all States parties, bring the matter to the Conference, and/or recommend to the Conference measures to redress the situation. The Conference is the organ with the mandate to review compliance and act upon its review.

It must be stressed that the Secretariat's mandate is to serve as the independent and impartial fact-finder. The Convention specifies that the Final Inspection Report shall only contain facts relevant to compliance, as provided for under the inspection mandate issued by the Director-General. The Final Inspection Report is a factual account of the inspection team's activities, their findings, and the manner in which the inspected State party co-operated with the inspection team. Any differing observations by the inspectors can be annexed to the Final Inspection Report, together with any comments by the inspected State party. If the report contains uncertainties, or co-operation between the National Authority and the inspectors was substandard, the Director-General is required to approach the inspected State party for clarification. If the uncertainties cannot be removed, or the facts suggest that 'obligations under [the] Convention have not been met',[27] the Director-General is required to inform the Council without delay. Thus, although the Secretariat solely has a fact-finding role, the discretionary authority of the Director-General to determine whether or not the facts require Council attention involves an assessment of whether the facts reflect uncertainty preventing him or her from concluding that no act of non-compliance has occurred. From this description, it is also clear that the negotiation and communication skills of the Secretariat can also impact the extent to which uncertainties can be clarified expeditiously and prevent disputes from arising. Most issues arising during an inspection require interpretation of the Convention, a technical understanding of the site processes, and negotiation (i.e. what needs to be seen to verify non-diversion).

---

[26] Art. VIII(36).   [27] Part II, para. 65, of the Verification Annex.

Any State party in doubt about another State party's compliance has a range of options available to it under article IX ('Consultations, Co-operation and Fact-Finding') of the Convention. Article IX establishes the principle in the broadest possible terms:

> States Parties shall consult and co-operate, directly among themselves, or through the Organization or other appropriate international procedures, including procedures within the framework of the United Nations and in accordance with its Charter, on any matter which may be raised relating to the object and purpose, or the implementation of the provisions, of this Convention ... Without prejudice to the right of any State Party to request a challenge inspection, States Parties should, whenever possible, first make every effort to clarify and resolve, through exchange of information and consultations among themselves, any matter which may cause doubt about compliance with this Convention, or which gives rise to concerns about a related matter which may be considered ambiguous ...[28]

The State party concerned must respond, with sufficient information to answer the doubt or concern, within ten days. (In practice, this mechanism has been used most frequently.) The States parties concerned can also arrange for a bilateral inspection to satisfy the request. The doubting State party can also request assistance from the Council, including any appropriate information the Council has in its possession. If still unsatisfied, the requesting State party can request a special session of the Council to consider the matter and recommend measures to resolve it. If still unsatisfied and if it believes its doubts warrant urgent consideration, the requesting State party can request a special session of the Conference to consider the matter and recommend measures to resolve it.

Whether or not a doubting State party has pursued the above-mentioned options, it can always request a 'challenge inspection'. Article IX establishes the fundamental right of each State party to request an on-site challenge inspection of any facility or location in the territory or in any other place under the jurisdiction or control of any other State party for the sole purpose of clarifying and resolving any questions concerning possible non-compliance and to have this inspection conducted anywhere without delay by an inspection team designated by the Director-General

---

[28] Art. IX(1) and (2).

and in accordance with the Verification Annex.[29] Subject to the inspected State party's agreement, the requesting State party can send an observer on the challenge inspection. The Director-General must give at least twelve hours' notice to the inspected State party and, unless the Council stops the challenge inspection within twelve hours of receiving the request, the inspected State party must provide access to the location. The inspected State party can negotiate 'managed access' to the location, i.e. it has the right, *inter alia*, to shroud certain sensitive items and remove papers unrelated to chemical weapons as well as take measures to protect national security. At the same time, it also has the obligation to make reasonable efforts to demonstrate to the inspection team that the protected areas are not related to the possible non-compliance concerns.[30] The Council reviews the Final Inspection Report to address any concerns as to whether non-compliance has occurred, whether the request fell within the scope of the Convention, and whether the right to request a challenge inspection was abused (in which case, the requesting State party might be held responsible to bear the financial implications). If the Council concludes that further action is necessary, 'it shall take the appropriate measures to redress the situation and to ensure compliance, including recommendations to the Conference'.[31] Investigations of alleged use of chemical weapons, or of alleged use of riot control agents as a method of warfare, can also be initiated under article IX.[32]

In practice, no requests for challenge inspection or alleged use investigation have occurred and may never do so if their mystique as politically charged and even somewhat hostile acts is not overcome. In 2003, the First Review Conference confirmed the viability of both mechanisms, and the OPCW has periodically tested them through mock exercises to develop its procedures and capacity to implement them. One dramatic incident did occur during the First Review Conference when the United States alleged that two States parties, Iran and Sudan,[33] were actively pursuing chemical weapons programmes. Iran exercised a right of reply, denying this

---

[29] Art. IX(8). [30] Part X, paras. 41 and 46–52, of the Verification Annex.
[31] Art. IX(22) and (23). [32] Part XI, para. 1, of the Verification Annex.
[33] The US allegation sharply contrasts with its earlier allegation in 1998 against Sudan. At that time, Sudan was not party to the CWC and the United States bombed a pharmaceutical plant in Khartoum, alleging that it was a chemical weapons production facility. See CNN, 'Sudan Wants UN to Probe US Bombing of Drug Factory', available at www.cnn.com/WORLD/africa/9908/18/sudan/ (18 August 1999).

allegation.[34] No further action has occurred, although obviously the right to request a challenge inspection remains a prerogative.

11.3.5 Standing to initiate an allegation of non-compliance

As is clear from the above, only States or the OPCW organs can initiate action that could result in a recommendation on non-compliance from the Council to the Conference for action, or the matter being brought to the attention of the UN General Assembly and Security Council by the OPCW. Individuals have no standing before the organization, and there is no private right of action created by the Convention.[35] The United Nations and other international organizations and NGOs have only limited possibilities for participation as observers in sessions of the Conference or, by invitation of the Council, in its sessions.[36] The Council also has the power to invite individuals to attend when its agenda so requires. In practice, only three instances have occurred which may be of interest in this regard. In 2002, during the Seventh Session of the Conference, an NGO held a workshop on 'Non-Lethal Chemical Weapons and the CWC' in which it presented its research and allegation that the United States military was developing 'non-lethal' chemicals and long-range mortar projectiles for their delivery, raising 'non-compliance concerns' under the CWC.[37] Media attention increased in late 2002 as a result of the use of a gas by Russian security forces to quell a hostage situation in a Moscow theatre[38] and in

---

[34] D. de Luce and O. Burkeman, 'US Accuses Iran of Stockpiling Chemical Arms', *Guardian*, 16 May 2003; and www.opcw.org/cwcrevcon/doc/NAT/UnitedStates_s.pdf. A recent submission to the United States Congress indicated that 'a 2001 Department of State report assesses that China, Iran, Russia and Sudan have not fully declared the extent of their chemical weapons programs'. See United States General Accounting Office Report to the Chairman, Committee on Armed Services, House of Representatives, 'Nonproliferation: Delays in Implementing the Chemical Weapons Convention Raise Concerns About Proliferation', Report No. GAO-04–361 (March 2004), p. 2.

[35] Civil society has only limited insight into the workings of the OPCW. Only some official documents are publicly available: some Conference documents following the conclusion of the session and some Secretariat documents, but no Council documents. At present, only the Harvard Sussex Program on CBW Armament and Arms Limitation routinely reports publicly on the Council's activities (www.sussex.ac.uk/spru/hsp/).

[36] Respectively, Rules 31–33 of the Rules of Procedure of the Conference, and Rule 50 of the Rules of Procedure of the Council.

[37] The Sunshine Project, 9 October 2002; leaflets on file with the author and available at www.sunshine-project.org.

[38] J. Miller and W. Broad, 'US Suspects Opiate in Gas in Russia Raid', *New York Times*, 29 October 2002; J. Whalen, 'US Envoy Criticizes Russian Secrecy on Gas', *Wall Street Journal Europe*, 30 October 2002.

2003 when the US Defense Secretary was seeking to include the use of non-lethal agents in the rules of engagement for US troops in Iraq.[39] As a result, the International Committee of the Red Cross (ICRC) held an informal briefing for OPCW delegations on 'Implications of the use of chemical incapacitants for law enforcement purposes'.[40] During the OPCW's First Review Conference, the ICRC submitted a request to address the session (denied under the rules of procedure)[41] and was permitted to distribute its 'Appeal on Biotechnology, Weapons and Humanity' during the session.[42] Finally, during the First Review Conference session, the OPCW Technical Secretariat facilitated the organization of an 'Open Forum' to which members of the public were invited to speak on issues related to the CWC. Some of the speakers raised their concerns about the risk 'non-lethal' weapons pose to the object and purpose of the CWC.[43] This issue has continued to be raised by NGOs.[44]

11.3.6 Compliance, pragmatism and treaty evolution

One challenge for treaty negotiators, framing a regime intended to regulate the behaviour of States over the long term, is that incentives or disincentives which were relevant politically or technically at that point in time may be surpassed by events. One such example could be the deadlines set by the CWC which, for late joiners, have already passed. The deadlines are relevant only to a chemical weapons possessor State and they were included in the CWC as disincentives for States which could have been contemplating retaining their stockpiles for whatever reason and joining the CWC later on. The purpose of such provisions was to maximize the universality of the

---

[39] P. Hess, 'New Rules for Non-Lethal Combat', *Urban Operations Journal (UPI)*, 5 February 2003; A. Hay, 'Out of the Straitjacket', *Guardian*, 12 March 2003.

[40] ICRC briefing on 28 March 2003; leaflet on file with the author.

[41] D. Ruppe, 'Red Cross Says It Was Muzzled over Stand on Incapacitating Weapons', *Global Security Newswire*, 30 April 2003.

[42] Distributed 1–9 May 2003; available at www.opcw.org.

[43] 'Open Forum' papers available at www.opcw.org.

[44] Among others, the ICRC, the Harvard Sussex Program on CBW Armament and Arms Limitation, the Pugwash Study Group on the Implementation of the Chemical and Biological Weapons Conventions, and the Working Group on Chemical and Biological Weapons Control of the Federation of American Scientists. Most recently, during the Tenth Session of the OPCW Conference of the States parties in November 2005 in The Hague, the Center for Arms Control and Non-Proliferation, Washington, DC, organized a panel discussion on 'Incapacitating Chemical Weapons: Debating the Pros and Cons'.

CWC from the outset. Now, however, they no longer serve as incentives for universality since a late joiner would have lost the opportunity to adjust certain fundamental destruction obligations and this may be deemed punitive enough to discourage the State from joining at all. Since the organs have no power to set aside obligations, they may find themselves faced with the need to consider amending the Convention. Indeed, the OPCW has amended the Convention through the 'change' process under article XV(5) in order to approve the request by Libya to convert two former chemical weapons production facilities to pharmaceutical factories for purposes not prohibited.[45] Another, earlier example was the amendment to the provision requiring States parties to notify the OPCW thirty days in advance of any transfer of Schedule 1 chemicals. One such chemical is saxitoxin which coastal States may need on short notice to test for the presence of paralytic shellfish poisoning in shellfish intended for human consumption. In view of the public health dimension of timely access to saxitoxin, States parties pursued the change process to amend the Convention and allow small amounts of saxitoxin being transferred for medical/diagnostic purposes to be notified by the time of transfer.[46]

Some of the Convention's deadlines have proven complex to meet in practice, for reasons unanticipated by the negotiators of the treaty. The most critical of these has been the intermediate deadlines for the destruction of chemical weapons which have not been met for various reasons by some of the six possessor States.[47] This has been recognized within and

---

[45] Conference Decision C-9/DEC.9 (2004) and United Nations Depositary Notification C.N.610.2005.TREATIES-4, issued on 29 July 2005.

[46] Executive Council Decisions EC-MII/DEC.1 (1999) and EC-XV/DEC.5 (1999); and UN Depositary Notifications C.N.1112.1999.TREATIES-8, dated 10 December 1999 and C.N.157.2000.TREATIES-1, dated 13 March 2000.

[47] Citing plant safety issues, environmental requirements and funding shortfalls, the US General Accounting Office indicated that the US will be unable to complete the destruction of its chemical weapons stockpile even by the final extended deadline of 2012: United States General Accounting Office Report to the Chairman, Committee on Armed Services, House of Representatives, 'Nonproliferation: Delays in Implementing the Chemical Weapons Convention Raise Concerns About Proliferation', Report No. GAO-04–361 (March 2004), p. 11. The extremely high costs of destruction continue to plague the Russian Federation's ability to destroy its stockpile on time, despite increasingly significant voluntary contributions from other States. See, for example, SIPRI, *SIPRI Yearbook 2004: Armaments, Disarmament and International Security* (Oxford: Oxford University Press, 2004), p. 673; and the US General Accounting Office Report, pp. 3 and 7–10; and the extensions approved by the OPCW Conference of the States Parties, C-8/DEC.13 (2003). Faced with the technical complexities of destroying chemical weapons, both Albania and Libya have sought and received extensions on their intermediate deadlines for destruction: see, respectively, Decisions C-9/DEC 8 and 7 (2004).

outside the OPCW as a matter of concern. Pending destruction, chemical weapons stockpiles need to be adequately secured so that they are not vulnerable to theft or diversion.[48] In 2004, the United Nations Secretary-General's High-Level Panel on Threats, Challenges and Change characterized the delays in the destruction of chemical weapons stockpiles by CWC States parties as one of the current threats to international peace and security.[49] The CWC sets a strict maximum deadline of 2012 to complete the destruction of all declared chemical weapons: for States adhering to the treaty in the first decade, there is no possibility to extend destruction activities beyond that date.[50] A recent US Government report has indicated that, based on the current schedule, the US will not meet that deadline and estimated that the Russian Federation will not complete destruction of its stockpile until 2027.[51] If so, this situation will need to be addressed by States parties and the policy-making organs in due course, while at the same time preserving the object and purpose of the Convention. Other implementation difficulties are being addressed pragmatically and co-operatively, as is discussed in the following section.

11.4 Enforcement

In considering enforcement, the starting point is to bear in mind that all States parties joined the treaty voluntarily and generally exhibit a marked willingness to comply with their obligations under it. At the same time, only six States parties have declared possession of chemical weapons, and only twelve have declared former chemical weapons production facilities. The remainder of the other 167 States became parties out of their interest in participating with the international community in banning chemical weapons and preventing their proliferation and/or to avoid being locked out of the market for Schedules 1 and 2 chemicals and/or a desire to develop their own peaceful uses of chemistry in co-operation with other States parties. For many of these others, especially those with little or no chemical industry declarable under the Convention, scarce resources are

---

[48] Para. 7.42 of the Report of the First Review Conference (RC-1/5 (2003)); and the US General Accounting Office Report (note 47 above), p. 3.

[49] Report of the High-Level Panel on Threats, Challenges and Change, 'A More Secure World: Our Shared Responsibility', UN Doc. A/59/565 (2004), p. 40, para. 114.

[50] CWC art. IV(6); and Part IV(A), para. 26, of the Verification Annex.

[51] US General Accounting Office Report (note 47 above), pp. 10–11.

being allocated to other matters of greater national priority than the CWC. It is difficult to argue against this when a technically non-compliant State party is experiencing famine, environmental disaster or political unrest or is faced with other grave circumstances. Rather than adopting a confrontational approach to this problem, true to the spirit of the OPCW being a forum for consultation and co-operation, a large number of States parties have increasingly joined the Secretariat in its implementation support programme to assist such States, and over time a partnership has formed between the Secretariat and States parties which is unique among international organizations. Just as dialogue is preventing adversarial disputes from developing, 'soft' enforcement through assistance programmes has established itself as the prevailing mode of operation, rather than coercive measures, although the Conference has made it clear that stronger measures are not ruled out.[52]

11.4.1 National law and national enforcement mechanisms

Article VII(1) of the CWC requires States parties to adopt national measures to implement the Convention, including enacting penal legislation, and to *not permit* in any place under its control any activity prohibited to a State party under the CWC, which implies positive enforcement action. Article VII(2) requires States parties to co-operate with each other and afford the appropriate form of legal assistance to one another to facilitate the implementation of those commitments. Article VI(2) requires that each State party adopt the 'necessary measures' to ensure that toxic chemicals and their precursors are only developed, produced, otherwise acquired, retained, transferred or used within its territory or in any other place under its jurisdiction or control for purposes not proscribed under the CWC,[53] again implying positive enforcement action. Finally, to secure universality and prevent proliferation of chemical weapons, the Verification Annex to the CWC requires States parties to ban transfers of

---

[52] Final paragraph of Conference Decision C-8/DEC.16 (2003) and para. 14 of C-10/DEC.10 (2005) on Follow-up to the Plan of Action Regarding the Implementation of Article VII Obligations: 'decide on any appropriate *measures* to be taken, if necessary, in order to ensure fulfilment by States parties of their Article VII obligations' (emphasis added).

[53] The concept established by the CWC definition of chemical weapons – that all toxic chemicals and their precursors are chemical weapons except where intended for purposes not prohibited under the Convention as long as the types and quantities are consistent with such purposes – is referred to by some commentators as the 'general purpose criterion'.

Schedules 1 and 2 chemicals to or from States not party and to adopt restrictions on transfers of Schedule 3 chemicals to States not party. To meet those obligations, States parties, regardless of their legal system, need to adopt and enforce effective import/export controls.

In such a system of horizontal enforcement, the question as to what extent the CWC is enforceable in the jurisdictions of States parties becomes particularly important. Even without specific implementing legislation, all States parties would probably be able to charge persons *using* chemical weapons with the ordinary crime of murder. It is the related offences of development, production, stockpiling and transferring directly or indirectly chemical weapons that might go uninvestigated and/or unpunished if comprehensive penal legislation has not been enacted. In addition, absent specific penal legislation, it may not be possible to bring charges against co-conspirators who assisted.

Offences are currently being reported much more frequently in the press. It is unclear whether this is because transgressions are on the rise, specific implementing legislation has been enacted criminalizing a wider range of chemical weapons offences, enforcement authorities have become more vigilant due to heightened fears of terrorism, or because the subject is receiving greater media attention. In 2003, there were several media reports of chemical weapons offences being committed. The United Kingdom was reported to have charged suspects under its Terrorism Act 2000 and Chemical Weapons Act 1996 in respect of ricin-related crimes. In the United States, it was reported that a man had been sentenced to fourteen years in prison for producing ricin, that another had been sentenced to thirteen years in prison for violating the federal chemical weapons statute (possession of sodium cyanide and potassium cyanide), and that a third had been arrested under the same statute and had later been found to have had sodium cyanide and nitric acid at his residence. There were even more reports in 2004 concerning alleged chemical weapons offences. For instance, six people were detained in Lyon, France, in connection with an earlier arrest related to plans to produce ricin and botulinum toxin, several individuals were apprehended in connection with a plot in Jordan to use a chemical bomb and deadly gases, eight British nationals were arrested in the United Kingdom in connection with a conspiracy to explode a bomb containing osmium tetroxide, a series of primitive bombs containing chlorine were thrown by youths into a bar and residences in New Jersey, and information obtained off a computer seized by authorities in Pakistan led to arrests in the United Kingdom and disruption of planned chemical weapons attacks there and in the United States.[54]

Heightened fears of terrorist activity have made the issue of whether persons violating the norms of the CWC anywhere in the world might be detected, apprehended, prosecuted and punished ever more urgent. The Council has identified the full implementation of the legislative measures required by article VII as one of the main contributions that the OPCW can make to anti-terrorist efforts,[55] a focus reaffirmed by the First Review Conference.[56]

11.4.2 Assistance to non-compliant States parties ('soft' enforcement by the OPCW)

As of 1 October 2006, 63 per cent of States parties had met their article VII(5) obligation to inform the OPCW of legislative or administrative measures they have introduced to implement the Convention. However, according to self-assessment undertaken by States parties in a legislation questionnaire on penal measures, only 39 per cent have legislation in force that covers all areas key to the enforcement of the CWC. Furthermore, a significant number of the National Authorities have been only nominally established – a designated contact person in the ministry of foreign affairs, for example, rather than a functioning governmental body – and require assistance and/or training in order to effectively implement the Convention. As could be expected, resources (both funding and personnel) pose a challenge.

The Conference and Council adopted a series of decisions encouraging States parties to comply with their implementation obligations, urging them to assist each other with that task, assigning a more proactive role to the Secretariat and providing increased funding for this area of work. Foremost among these was the 2003 'Plan of Action Regarding the Implementation of Article VII Obligations' which gave a deadline of November 2005 for States to institute national implementation measures.[57] At its conclusion, the Action Plan was assessed to be a success since it created an unprecedented

---

[54] See further L. Tabassi and R. Silvers, 'Enforcing the CWC: Actual Investigations and Prosecutions of Offenders' (2004) 2 *Chemical Disarmament*, No. 4, pp. 18–25; S. Tendler *et al.*, 'Eight Britons Charged in Dirty Bomb Plot', *Ottawa Citizen*, 18 August 2004, p. A1; N. Lathem, 'Chemical "Plotters" Charged: Citigroup Center Link', *New York Post*, 18 August 2004, p. 10.

[55] Para. 2(b) of OPCW Executive Council Decision EC-XXVII/DEC.5 (2001).

[56] Report of the First Review Conference (RC-1/5 (2003)), para. 7 10.

[57] Conference Decision C-8/DEC.16 (2003).

294   INTERNATIONAL ARMS CONTROL

momentum among States parties to implement the Convention effectively. While the number of States with comprehensive legislation did not increase significantly by the deadline, 152 drafts had been submitted by 92 States parties to the Secretariat for review and comment and 25 per cent of States parties had bills pending in the parliamentary process.[58] The process under the Action Plan led to greater dialogue, organizational change, more intensive reporting and other concrete outcomes. Several earlier implementation support efforts (programmes to assist States parties with identifying declarable chemical industry, drafting implementing legislation and conducting outreach and training of National Authority personnel) were folded into the Action Plan rubric. Significant voluntary contributions were made by a number of States parties and the European Union to augment those implementation support activities and create new initiatives. As the deadline approached, consultations on the results and possible follow-up became intense as disagreement among States parties over the usage of the terms 'non-compliance' and 'measures' became apparent, as will be discussed further below. The decision[59] on follow-up to the Action Plan ultimately adopted by the Conference aimed at sustaining the momentum created for national implementation. The implementation support efforts will continue, and the Conference will conduct a new review of article VII implementation in December 2006. The challenge facing States parties in meeting the objectives set by the Conference will be to attract the political willingness of their parliaments to give priority to adopting the necessary legislation.[60] Practice has shown that a robust National Authority is key to ensuring that comprehensive legislation is drafted, shepherded through the parliamentary process, and enforced. Establishment of such National Authorities was one of the aims of the Action Plan and continues to be the first objective under the follow-up action.

11.4.3 Measures to redress non-compliance ('hard' enforcement by the OPCW)

Other Convention provisions not yet invoked are article VIII(36) (stipulating Council action to request a State party to redress a situation of

---

[58] Report by the Director-General on the Plan of Action Regarding the Implementation of Article VII Obligations, OPCW Doc. C-10/DG.4/Rev.1, Add.1 and Corr.1 (2005).

[59] Conference Decision C-10/DEC.10 (2005).

[60] See further R. Münch, S. Oñate, R. Trapp and L. Tabassi, 'Follow-up to the Action Plan on Article VII: What Is at Stake in 2006?', (2006) 4 *Chemical Disarmament Quarterly* 13.

non-compliance) and article XII ('Measures to Redress a Situation and to Ensure Compliance, Including Sanctions').

Under article VIII(36), in considering doubts or concerns regarding compliance and non-compliance, the Council is required to consult with the States parties involved and, as appropriate, to request the State party to take measures to redress the situation within a specified time. If the Council considers further action to be necessary, it can, *inter alia*: (a) inform all States parties of the issue or matter; (b) bring the matter to the Conference; (c) make recommendations to the Conference regarding measures; and (d) in cases of particular gravity and urgency, bring the matter to the UN General Assembly and Security Council.

Under article XII, the Conference is required to take the necessary measures to redress and remedy any situation which contravenes the CWC, taking into account all information and recommendations on the issues submitted by the Council. Article XII sets forth the measures as the following:

- in cases where a State party has been requested by the Council to take measures to redress a situation and it has not done so within the deadline, the Conference may, *inter alia*, restrict or suspend the State party's rights and privileges under the Convention until the State undertakes the necessary action to conform with its CWC obligations;
- in cases where serious damage to the object and purpose of the CWC may result from activities prohibited by the CWC, in particular the general obligations under article I (development, production, stockpiling, use, etc.), the Conference may *recommend* collective measures to States parties in conformity with international law;
- in cases of particular gravity, the Conference is required to bring the issue, including relevant information and conclusions, to the attention of the UN General Assembly and Security Council.

It will be noted that these measures are drafted leaving the maximum flexibility for the Conference to determine which measure would be most appropriate and effective for the situation at issue. What is clear from the words 'in conformity with international law', and as is already evident from the preamble to the CWC, and goes without saying in any event, is that only recourse to peaceful measures is permissible. This, however, would not rule out the UN Security Council authorizing Chapter VII action if the situation referred by the OPCW were considered to be a threat to international peace and security.

As noted above in the section on soft enforcement, both article VIII(36) and article XII were the subject of intense debate at the conclusion of the Action Plan since there was no consensus on what 'measures' could be taken and when they would be appropriate, especially any recourse to the UN. During consultations over a period of weeks prior to and during the Conference session, it became apparent that States parties are not in agreement on the usage of the terms 'compliance', 'cases of non-compliance', 'violation' and 'breach' and in what situations articles VIII(36) or XII could be appropriately invoked to take action in respect of 'non-compliance'. The most pointed disagreement centred on whether those provisions could be invoked in respect of obligations other than the most fundamental chemical-weapons-related ones in article I. In the negotiated text eventually adopted by consensus by the Conference,[61] preambular paragraph 6 refers to 'compliance by all States Parties with article VII', and no explicit reference is made to either article VIII(36) or article XII, although operative paragraphs 12 and 14 of the decision mirror words expressed in those provisions. The adopted decision continues soft enforcement through implementation support by the Secretariat and States parties for a further year, reserving the option to consider 'measures' again in December 2006 at the Eleventh Session if some States parties have not completely fulfilled their obligations in respect of national implementation of the CWC under article VII.

11.4.4 Enforcement outside the CWC regime

A new global security environment has emerged in the wake of 11 September 2001 which has led to a number of initiatives designed to prevent or eliminate the proliferation of weapons of mass destruction. Since measures under the current arms control or disarmament treaties, including the CWC, are aimed at preventing the transfer or development of militarily significant quantities of weapons of mass destruction, the new initiatives are designed also to address prevention of the transfer of even the small quantities that could be of interest to, and serve the purposes of, non-State actors. As a consequence, the focus in non-proliferation efforts has enlarged.

The UN adopted two resolutions in 2004 which arguably legitimize some of the earlier unilateral or plurilateral initiatives which had been

---

[61] C-10/DEC.16 (2005).

criticized.[62] The General Assembly adopted a resolution on measures to prevent terrorists from acquiring weapons of mass destruction, urging Member States to take and strengthen national measures in this regard and report them to the UN Secretary-General. On its part, the Security Council adopted a new resolution in 2004 which goes even further than all its previous ones on counter-terrorism.[63] UN Security Council Resolution 1540 (2004) requires a number of measures which were heretofore only CWC treaty obligations, including adopting penal legislation criminalizing the proliferation of chemical weapons by non-State actors and improving export controls and enforcement at the borders. Since the resolution was adopted under Chapter VII and thus binds all UN members, these measures are now extended to States not party to the CWC as well, thus reinforcing the argument that much of the CWC is now universally binding.[64] In respect of the CWC, its States parties and the OPCW, the Security Council explicitly decided that none of the obligations set forth in the resolution shall be interpreted so as to conflict with or alter the rights and obligations of States parties to the CWC or alter the responsibilities of the OPCW.

In the discussions in the OPCW on the follow-up to the Action Plan, some States parties viewed Resolution 1540 as further reinforcement of the Action Plan and wanted specific reference to it in the Conference decision. This was rejected by other States parties which resisted any attempt to explicitly link the actions taken by the two separate organizations.

---

[62] See further S. Oñate Laborde and L. Tabassi, 'Enforcement of the CWC Transfers Regime Against Non-State Actors in the New Global Security Environment: Current Multilateral, Regional, Plurilateral and Unilateral Initiatives', conference paper presented at the Technical Meeting of National Authorities on Practical Aspects of the Transfers Regime in Connection with the Current Implementation of the Chemical Weapons Convention: Customs, in Buenos Aires, Argentina, 6–8 September 2004, available at www.opcw.org.

[63] The resolution was initially announced by US President Bush in a speech to the UN General Assembly in 2003. After seven months of negotiations, the resolution (co-sponsored by France, the Philippines, Romania, the Russian Federation, Spain, the UK and the US) was adopted. One-quarter of the entire UN membership appeared before the Security Council to speak to the proposed resolution. Pakistan expressed several concerns, questioning the right of the Security Council to assume the role of prescribing legislative action by Member States, especially when the CWC, BWC and NPT already prescribe those obligations See S. D. Murphy, 'Security Council Resolution on Nonproliferation of WMD' (2004) 98 *American Journal of International Law* 607.

[64] See L. Tabassi, 'Impact of the CWC: Progressive Development of Customary International Law and Evolution of the Customary Norm against Chemical Weapons', *The CBW Conventions Bulletin*, March 2004, pp. 1–7; and L. Tabassi, 'A Note on UN Security Council Resolution 1540 (2004)', *The CBW Conventions Bulletin*, June 2004, pp. 12–13.

298 INTERNATIONAL ARMS CONTROL

In parallel, the Statute of the International Criminal Court (the 'Rome Statute') entered into force in 2002. The object and purpose of the ICC is to ensure that 'the most serious crimes of concern to the international community as a whole' will be investigated and, if possible, prosecuted and punished. The Rome Statute recognizes that it is the duty of each State to exercise its criminal jurisdiction over those responsible for international crimes. If the State concerned does not and the facts meet certain criteria, the ICC was established to do so as a complement to national criminal jurisdictions. Under its Statute, the ICC has jurisdiction over war crimes, including use of asphyxiating gases – echoing the ban as originally expressed in the 1925 Geneva Protocol. Under that narrow definition, the ICC only has jurisdiction over cases involving the *use* of chemical weapons in *international armed conflict* when a State that has jurisdiction over the case is unwilling or genuinely unable to carry out the investigation or prosecution. Cases involving the use of chemical weapons would not be prosecuted by the ICC if the act occurred in internal armed conflict or was a terrorist act, unless the act was on such a scale that it can be deemed to fall within the scope of the crime of genocide or crimes against humanity as defined by the Rome Statute.[65] Other acts prohibited by the CWC (developing etc. chemical weapons) fall outside the court's jurisdiction. However, the use of riot control agents as a method of warfare in international armed conflict arguably would fall within the scope of ICC jurisdiction as a war crime.[66]

11.5 Overall evaluation

11.5.1 Inspiration from other treaty regimes

The drafters of the CWC built upon lessons learned from the model of verification of the Treaty on the Non-Proliferation of Nuclear Weapons (NPT)

[65] In the case against Frans van Anraat in the Netherlands, in December 2005, the accused was found guilty of complicity in war crimes committed by Iraq. Van Anraat, a Dutch businessman, supplied chemicals to Iraq that were eventually used by Saddam Hussein in the chemical attacks on Kurdish villages in Iraq in 1988 and in the Iraq–Iran war of 1984–8. Although the court considered that the attacks on the Kurdish villages did constitute genocide, and that van Anraat knew that the chemicals he was supplying could be and were used to produce chemical weapons, the charges of complicity in genocide failed, since the prosecution was unable to prove that van Anraat knew of the genocidal intent of the former Iraqi regime. Judgment LJN: AU8685, Rechtbank 's-Gravenhage, 09/751003–04 (available at www.trial-ch.org).

[66] See further L. Tabassi, 'The OPCW and the ICC: Where Do They Meet?' (2007) *CBW Conventions Bulletin* (forthcoming).

by the IAEA. There are significant differences: the NPT is not a disarmament instrument; the IAEA carries out verification for a number of nuclear treaties, not just the NPT; OPCW inspections cover a wider range of activities and are more intrusive than those of the IAEA, and the CWC covers potentially thousands of chemicals while the IAEA verifies specifically identified nuclear materials.[67] In a synergistic effect, the drafting of the CWC inspired the IAEA to add short-notice inspections to its safeguards agreements.[68]

11.5.2 Inspiration for other treaty regimes

In broad terms, the OPCW structure and mandate were the model followed for the Comprehensive Test Ban Treaty Organization (CTBTO), although verification by the OPCW under the CWC is quite distinct from that which will be performed by the CTBTO under the Comprehensive Test Ban Treaty (CTBT), if it ever enters into force. The CTBT provides for a verification regime, including on-site inspections and an International Monitoring System, the data of which are reported to an 'International Data Centre' and made available to all States parties. All States parties will be under the obligation to accept verification. The confidentiality of information obtained during verification activities is to be protected. The Secretariat will carry out on-site inspections (which each State party will have the right to request to be carried out on the other State parties), will operate the International Data Centre and will be responsible for supervising and co-ordinating the International Monitoring System (321 stations located around the globe to register sound and energy vibrations underground, in the sea and in the air, and to detect radionuclides released into the atmosphere). The CTBTO Conference and Council will have limited enforcement powers similar to those of the OPCW. Each State party will designate or set up a National Authority.

Lastly, the treaty regime of the OPCW could potentially have provided excellent inspiration for what was intended to be an additional protocol to

---

[67] See further A. Walter Dorn and A. Rolya, 'The Organisation for the Prohibition of Chemical Weapons and the IAEA: A Comparative Overview' (1993) 3 *IAEA Bulletin* 44–7; and T. Lohmann, 'The Law of IAEA Safeguards: A Framework for the Legal Issues of Chemical Weapons Verification?', in M. Bothe, N. Ronzitti and A. Rosas (eds.), *The New Chemical Weapons Convention – Implementation and Prospects* (The Hague and Boston: Kluwer Law International, 1998), pp. 79–118.

[68] See further Laura Rockwood, chapter 12 below.

strengthen the 1972 Biological Weapons Convention. The 'Organization for the Prohibition of Biological Weapons' was hoped to be the newest addition to the group of international organizations headquartered in The Hague. In contrast to the CWC, the Biological Weapons Convention did not provide for the establishment of a verification mechanism and a corresponding treaty-implementing body. Multilateral efforts to conclude a protocol creating such a body to strengthen the Biological Weapons Convention were frustrated in 2001 and remain at an impasse.[69]

11.6 Conclusion

In conclusion, the experience of the OPCW has shown that the organs of the organization, working jointly and in parallel, have been able to significantly improve the universality of the treaty and qualitatively improve implementation. The treaty cannot prevent a determined State or non-State actor from acquiring the banned weapon but the treaty will act as a deterrent in most other cases.

Over the nine years the treaty has been in force, the organization's dedicated attention, regular participation in the organs by States parties, and political pressure by States and the UN and regional organizations, are leading most States parties to engage in the processes of enacting legislation criminalizing violations of the Convention, establishing the administrative mechanisms needed to implement the Convention's provisions, sensitizing its public to the Convention's requirements, and monitoring implementation more vigilantly. These activities contribute to global public order and threat reduction. As recent efforts by the UN Security Council have shown, a concerted effort is needed to prevent weapons of mass destruction from falling into the hands of non-State actors, engaging the treaty-implementing bodies, the United Nations, States and, one could conspicuously add, NGOs and civil society at large. The OPCW is actively enrolled in that effort, making this treaty work.

---

[69] See further L. Tabassi and S. Spence, 'Arms Control II: The Case of the OPBW', in P. Krieken and D. MacKay (eds.), *The Hague: Legal Capital of the World* (The Hague: TMC Asser Press, 2005).

12

The Treaty on the Non-Proliferation of Nuclear Weapons (NPT) and IAEA Safeguards Agreements

LAURA ROCKWOOD

The International Atomic Energy Agency (the 'IAEA' or 'Agency') is an independent intergovernmental organization with a current membership of 139 States. It was created by the Statute of the IAEA, which was approved on 23 October 1956 by the Conference on the Statute of the IAEA, held at the headquarters of the United Nations, and entered into force on 29 July 1957.[1]

The IAEA is headed by the Director General, and is composed of six Departments headed by Deputy Directors General[2] and a Secretariat staff of some 2,300 individuals. The policy making organs of the IAEA are its Board of Governors and General Conference. The Board consists of thirty-five members, ten of whom are designated as the most advanced in the technology of atomic energy within geographically specified country groups. The others are elected to membership by the General Conference. The Board of Governors is authorized to carry out the functions of the Agency in accordance with the Statute, subject to its responsibilities to the General Conference. The General Conference of the IAEA consists of representatives of all Member States, and is convened annually, usually in September.

Although the IAEA is considered to be part of the United Nations common system, and, as a consequence, implements, and participates in the development of, administrative rules and practices for United Nations organizations, it is, formally speaking, not a body of the United Nations nor is it a specialized organization thereof. The Director General does not report to the Secretary-General or to any of the UN organizations. The IAEA does, however, have an agreement with the United Nations which

---

[1] 276 UNTS 3 (No. 3988).

[2] The Departments of the IAEA are: Department of Safeguards, Department of Technical Cooperation, Department of Nuclear Energy, Department of Nuclear Safety and Security, Department of Nuclear Sciences and Applications, and Department of Management.

301

provides for a unique relationship between the IAEA and the Security Council: the IAEA is authorized to submit reports directly to the Security Council, not through the Economic and Social Council, the General Assembly or any other body of the United Nations.

Pursuant to Article III.B.4 of the Agency's Statute, the IAEA reports on its activities annually to the General Assembly of the United Nations and, when appropriate, to the Security Council. If in connection with the activities of the Agency there should arise questions that are within the competence of the Security Council, the Statute provides that the Agency is to notify the Security Council, as the organ bearing the main responsibility for the maintenance of international peace and security.[3]

In terms of substantive authority, the IAEA is also not only a 'nuclear watchdog' – it is responsible for the promotion of the safe and peaceful uses of nuclear energy, and its contribution to peace, health and prosperity. The Agency is constructed on the basis of three pillars: safety and security; science and technology; and safeguards and verification. It engages in activities as diverse as: helping developing countries in the detection and treatment of cancer; developing and implementing nuclear techniques for the eradication of pests such as the tse-tse fly; and helping States in the safe and secure construction and operation of nuclear research and power reactors through the establishment of codes of practice, safety standards and other international instruments, and the provision of advisory services.

The focus of this article is, however, on the third of these pillars, safeguards and verification, and includes a review of disputes resolution, compliance and enforcement issues in connection with the IAEA's verification activities.

12.1 The IAEA's safeguards system

Pursuant to the Statute of the IAEA, the Agency is authorized to establish and administer safeguards: (1) in connection with nuclear material, facilities and services made available by the Agency (generally in connection with Agency projects); (2) at the request of the parties to any bilateral or multilateral arrangement; or (3) at the request of a State, to any of that State's nuclear activities.[4]

---

[3] Art. 24 of the Charter of the United Nations confers on the Security Council 'primary responsibility for the maintenance of international peace and security'.

[4] IAEA Statute, Art. III.A.5.

The Statute sets out the rights and responsibilities of the Agency that may be included, to the extent relevant, in the Agency project or other arrangement as a consequence of which the Agency is requested to apply safeguards (Article XII.A). These include, *inter alia*:

- the right to examine the design of nuclear facilities;
- the right to require States to maintain and produce operating records and to report to the Agency; and
- the right to send into the territory of the State concerned inspectors designated by the Agency, who shall have access at all times to all places and data and to any person who by reason of his occupation deals with items required to be safeguarded, as necessary to account for nuclear material and to determine whether there is compliance with any other conditions in the agreement with the State concerned.

The drafters of the Statute also included a provision of specific relevance to the subject at hand, Article XII.C, which describes the actions the Agency is authorized to take in the event of non-compliance with the conditions of such projects or arrangements. These actions include the reporting of non-compliance by the Director General to the Board of Governors, and the reporting of non-compliance by the Board to all Member States of the Agency, and to the Security Council and General Assembly of the United Nations. In the event of failure of the State to take fully corrective action within a reasonable time, the Statute provides that the Board may direct the curtailment or suspension of assistance and/or call for the return of materials and equipment made available to that State. A Member State found to have persistently violated the provisions of any agreement entered into by it pursuant to the Statute may also be suspended from the exercise of the privileges and rights of Agency membership by the General Conference, acting by a two-thirds majority and voting upon recommendation by the Board of Governors.

The statutory authority of the IAEA to apply safeguards, however, is not self-executing. Membership in the IAEA in itself does not require a State to accept safeguards. In fact, the Agency can only insist on the acceptance of safeguards in connection with assistance provided by it to a State, such as where the IAEA assists a State in the acquisition of nuclear material or a nuclear facility from a supplier State. Even in such cases, safeguards can only be applied by the Agency to the extent the State concerned has undertaken to accept safeguards.

304 INTERNATIONAL ARMS CONTROL

The acceptance of safeguards by a State can be manifested in one of three ways:

- the conclusion of a Safeguards Agreement with the IAEA;
- the voluntary acceptance of Agency verification (e.g. granting the Agency access to information and/or locations in addition to that required by a Safeguards Agreement concluded with that State, such as was done by South Africa in permitting verification by the Agency of the dismantling of its nuclear weapons); and/or
- the acceptance of verification as a consequence of a decision taken by the Security Council pursuant to Chapter VII of the Charter of the United Nations (such as was done by Iraq as required pursuant to Resolution 687 (1991)).[5]

In the early days of the IAEA, the Agency's verification system was focused on the safeguarding of items specified in the individual Safeguards Agreements (such as nuclear material, facilities or equipment), largely in response to requests by recipient States and/or supplier States as a precondition for the supply of such items.[6] The Agency's safeguards system underwent a dramatic transformation in 1970, however, with the entry into force of the Treaty on the Non-Proliferation of Nuclear Weapons.

12.2 The Treaty on the Non-Proliferation of Nuclear Weapons

The text of the Treaty on the Non-Proliferation of Nuclear Weapons (NPT), largely negotiated in the forum of the Eight Nation Disarmament Committee in Geneva, was commended by the General Assembly in June 1968[7] and opened for signature on 1 July 1968 to all States. It entered into force on 5 March 1970, with the Soviet Union, the United Kingdom and the United States identified as the Depositary Governments of the Treaty. It currently has 189 parties.[8]

---

[5] Under Chapter VII of the United Nations Charter, the Security Council is authorized to 'determine the existence of any threat to the peace, breach of the peace, or act of aggression and shall make recommendations, or decide what measures shall be taken . . . to maintain or restore international peace and security' (Art. 39). Chapter VII further requires that all Member States of the United Nations, directly and through their action in the appropriate international agencies of which they are members, to carry out the decisions of the Security Council for the maintenance of international peace and security (Art. 48).

[6] The IAEA continues to implement such item-specific Safeguards Agreements in India, Israel and Pakistan.   [7] A/RES/2373, UN Doc. A/7016/Add.1, p. 5, 10 June 1968.

[8] This number includes the Democratic People's Republic of Korea.

The Treaty was the result of delicately balanced negotiations, involving exchanges of commitments between the nuclear-weapon States[9] and the non-nuclear-weapon States. For their part, the nuclear-weapon States committed not to transfer nuclear weapons or other nuclear explosive devices, or control over them, to any recipient, and not to assist any non-nuclear-weapon State in the manufacture, acquisition or control of such weapons or devices,[10] and to pursue negotiations relating to cessation of the nuclear arms race and to nuclear disarmament, and on a treaty on general and complete disarmament under strict and effective international control.[11]

The non-nuclear-weapon States, for their part, undertook not to receive the transfer from any transferor whatever of nuclear weapons or other nuclear explosive devices or of control over such weapons or explosive devices directly or indirectly; not to manufacture or otherwise acquire nuclear weapons or other nuclear explosive devices; and not to seek or receive any assistance in the manufacture of nuclear weapons or other nuclear explosive devices.[12]

The non-nuclear-weapon States also undertook to accept safeguards, as set forth in an agreement to be negotiated and concluded with the IAEA (within 180 days of becoming party to the NPT) in accordance with the Statute of the IAEA and the Agency's safeguards system, for the exclusive purpose of verification of the fulfilment of its obligations assumed under the NPT with a view to preventing diversion of nuclear energy from peaceful uses to nuclear weapons or other nuclear explosive devices (Article III(1) of the NPT). The fundamental assumption of the drafters of the Treaty was that, without nuclear material, a State could not produce a nuclear weapon, and, if all nuclear material in that State were controlled, then the State could not divert that material for use in proscribed purposes. Thus, the NPT required that the agreements to be concluded with the IAEA apply to all source and special fissionable material in all peaceful nuclear activities within the State's territory, under its jurisdiction, or carried out under its control anywhere.

Article III.2 of the NPT requires all States parties not to provide source or special fissionable material, or equipment or material especially designed or prepared for the processing, use or production of special

---

[9] Which, for the purposes of the NPT, are defined as those States which had manufactured and exploded a nuclear weapon or other nuclear explosive device prior to 1 January 1967, Art.IV.3.

[10] NPT, Art. I.   [11] NPT, Art. VI.   [12] NPT, Art. II.

306 INTERNATIONAL ARMS CONTROL

fissionable material,[13] to any non-nuclear-weapon State for peaceful purposes unless the source or special fissionable material is subject to the safeguards required by Article III.

An integral part of this balance of obligations was the acknowledgment of the inalienable right of parties to the Treaty to develop research, production and use of nuclear energy for peaceful purposes in conformity with Articles I and II of the Treaty, and the undertaking by all parties to facilitate, and have the right to participate in, the fullest possible exchange of equipment, materials and scientific and technological information for the peaceful uses of nuclear energy.[14]

The NPT contains a number of provisions which, although more of a procedural nature, have taken on substantive aspects over the Treaty's thirty-five year history. Among those provisions is Article X, which required that, twenty-five years after the Treaty's entry into force, a conference be convened to decide whether the Treaty should continue in force indefinitely or be extended for an additional fixed period or periods. In 1995, the States parties of the NPT agreed to the indefinite extension of the Treaty.

The NPT has no standing secretariat but convenes, with the support of the United Nations, a conference for review of the operation of the Treaty every five years. And, while the IAEA is requested to apply its safeguards system in States parties to the Treaty, the IAEA is neither a depositary for, nor a party to, the NPT.

12.3 Comprehensive NPT Safeguards Agreements

Having been requested by the parties to the NPT to apply safeguards to all of the nuclear activities of non-nuclear-weapon States – that is, full scope, or comprehensive, safeguards as opposed to item-specific safeguards – the IAEA, in 1970, established an open-ended committee of the Board of Governors to negotiate a standardized text for such agreements. The resulting document, 'The Structure and Content of Agreements between the Agency and States Required in Connection with the Treaty on the Non-Proliferation of Nuclear Weapons', was approved by the Board of Governors in 1971, and is reproduced in INFCIRC/153 (Corr.).

The agreements concluded by the IAEA with the non-nuclear-weapon States of the NPT are all based on INFCIRC/153, and are highly standardized,

---

[13] Often referred to as 'EDP' or Single-Use Items.   [14] NPT, Art. IV.2.

and remain in force for so long as the State concerned is a party to the NPT. These agreements are commonly referred to as Comprehensive Safeguards Agreements, to distinguish them from the item-specific Safeguards Agreements (referred to above), and from the Voluntary Offer Agreements (VOAs) concluded with the five nuclear-weapon States party to the NPT – so called because the NPT does not require nuclear-weapon States to conclude Safeguards Agreements with the Agency. While the VOAs are based in some respects on INFCIRC/153, they are less standardized, not comprehensive in scope, and permit the State to withdraw nuclear material and/or facilities from safeguards at the State's discretion.

Safeguards Agreements, regardless of the type, are international treaties, and are concluded by the IAEA with a State or States (and in some circumstances with non-States parties[15]), following approval by the Board of Governors. A Safeguards Agreement may enter into force, at the discretion of the State or States concerned, either upon signature by the parties, or upon receipt by the IAEA of written notification from the other party or parties that their respective statutory and constitutional requirements for entry into force have been met. Upon entry into force, these agreements are published by the IAEA and are available to the public.

Following the discovery by the Agency in 1991 of Iraq's clandestine nuclear weapons programme, the IAEA Member States decided to strengthen the safeguards system of the Agency. In 1995, the Board approved a number of measures that could already be taken within existing legal authority under Comprehensive Safeguards Agreements (such as environmental sampling; access to undeclared locations; and the receipt, evaluation and use of information from all sources). It also agreed that additional measures, beyond those possible within the legal confines of a Comprehensive Safeguards Agreement, were necessary, and tasked another open-ended working group of the Board of Governors with the negotiation of a model protocol which would contain measures designed to provide the IAEA with more and better tools with which to carry out its responsibilities under Comprehensive Safeguards Agreements.

The text negotiated by that Committee, the 'Model Protocol Additional to the Agreement(s) between State(s) and the IAEA', was approved by the Board of Governors in May 1997, and is reproduced in IAEA document

---

[15] Such as EURATOM, the safeguards inspectorate of the European Community, or the Brazilian–Argentine Agency for Accounting and Control of Nuclear Materials (ABACC).

INFCIRC/540 (Corr.). In approving the text, the Board requested the Director General to use this Model Protocol as the standard for Additional Protocols concluded with States parties to Comprehensive Safeguards Agreements. Thus, Additional Protocols concluded with non-nuclear-weapon States parties to the NPT are, as are the Comprehensive Safeguards Agreements with those States, highly standardized.[16]

Additional Protocols are not stand-alone documents. They are, by definition, additional to a Safeguards Agreement. The relationship between the Safeguards Agreement and the Additional Protocol is described in Article 1 of the Model Additional Protocol, which states that the provisions of the Safeguards Agreement shall apply to the Protocol to the extent that they are relevant to and compatible with the provisions of the Protocol. It provides further that, in case of conflict between the provisions of the Safeguards Agreement and those of the Protocol, the provisions of the Protocol shall apply.

It is worth noting that, although the NPT requires a non-nuclear-weapon State to conclude a Safeguards Agreement 'in accordance with the Statute of the IAEA and the Agency's safeguards system', neither the States parties to the NPT, nor the Member States of the IAEA, have agreed that the conclusion of an Additional Protocol by such States is obligatory.

12.4 Verification

The basic undertaking of a non-nuclear-weapon State under Article III.A of the NPT is reiterated in paragraph 1 of INFCIRC/153,[17] specifically, that the State undertakes to accept safeguards, in accordance with the terms of the Safeguards Agreement, on all source or special fissionable material in all peaceful nuclear activities within its territory, under its jurisdiction or carried out under its control anywhere, for the exclusive

---

[16] The Board also requested the Director General to negotiate Additional Protocols or other legally binding agreements with nuclear-weapon States incorporating those measures provided for in the Model Protocol that each nuclear-weapon State has identified as capable of contributing to the non-proliferation and efficiency aims of the Protocol, when implemented with regard to that State, and as consistent with the State's obligations under Art. I of the NPT. All five of the NPT nuclear-weapon States have signed such protocols; as at the time of writing, only three had entered into force. The Board further requested the Director General to negotiate Additional Protocols with other States that are prepared to accept measures provided for in the Model Protocol in pursuance of safeguards effectiveness and efficiency objectives.

[17] The references to provisions in INFCIRC/153 (Corr.) are to paragraphs, whereas the corresponding provisions in the individual Comprehensive Safeguards Agreements are to articles.

purpose of verifying that such material is not diverted to nuclear weapons or other nuclear explosive devices. Pursuant to paragraph 2 of INFCIRC/153, the IAEA has a corresponding right and obligation to ensure that safeguards will be applied to *all* such material.[18]

The Agency verifies compliance by a State with the basic undertaking through the implementation of the safeguards provided for in the State's Safeguards Agreement. This is achieved through the evaluation of all information available to the Agency, including that resulting from activities undertaken by it in connection with on-site access, with a view to verifying the correctness and completeness of States' declarations concerning nuclear material, facilities and activities.

12.4.1 Information

Upon entry into force of a Comprehensive Safeguards Agreement, a State is required to provide the Agency with an initial report of its inventory of nuclear material, and a list and description of all existing nuclear facilities in the State. The State is required thereafter to maintain operating records with respect to all activities involving nuclear material and to report on a regular basis to the Agency on any changes in that inventory (e.g. imports, exports, production). The State is also required to provide information on the operation and modification of existing nuclear facilities, and to inform the Agency in the event of a decision to construct a new nuclear facility.

To ensure that States are able effectively to track all nuclear material in the State and to carry out its reporting and record-keeping obligations, these Agreements require the State to establish a system for the accounting for and control of nuclear material (referred to as 'SSACs').

The State is also obliged to conclude with the IAEA Subsidiary Arrangements, which are to specify in detail, to the extent necessary to permit the Agency to fulfil its responsibilities under the Agreement in an effective and efficient manner, how the procedures laid down in the agreement are to be applied. These Subsidiary Arrangements, which consist of a General Part and facility-specific documents referred to as Facility Attachments, are concluded at the operational level (normally at the level of the Deputy Director General for the IAEA's Department of Safeguards

---

[18] The NPT Safeguards Agreements do not provide for verification by the IAEA of compliance with the Art. III.2 requirement for controls on the export of equipment or material especially designed or prepared for the processing, use or production of special fissionable material.

and by the head of the relevant body responsible for safeguards implementation in the State), and, unlike the Safeguards Agreements, are not approved by the Board of Governors.

If a State has also concluded an Additional Protocol, it undertakes to provide the IAEA with declarations supplementing those provided for under the Safeguards Agreement. These declarations are to include not only information concerning nuclear material not subject to inspection under the Agreement (such as material exempted from safeguards), but information on the State's nuclear fuel cycle infrastructure, including nuclear fuel cycle-related research and development activities that do not involve nuclear material.

The State's records and reports are treated by the Agency as confidential. In accordance with paragraph 5 of INFCIRC/153, the IAEA is required to take every precaution to protect commercial and industrial secrets and other confidential information coming to its knowledge in the implementation of the Safeguards Agreement. It is prohibited from publishing or communicating to any State, organization or person any information obtained by it in connection with the implementation of the Agreement, except that specific information relating to such implementation in the State may be given to the Board and to such IAEA staff members as require such knowledge by reason of their official duties in connection with safeguards, but only to the extent necessary for the Agency to fulfil its responsibilities in implementing the Agreement. Summarized information on nuclear material being safeguarded by the Agency may, however, be published upon decision of the Board if the States directly concerned agree. Thus, the reports submitted by the States are not normally made available to the public (except to the extent necessary when matters require the Director General to report to the Board of Governors).

12.4.2 On-site access

On-site access is carried out under the Safeguards Agreement in the form of facility design information verification, and through inspections (*ad hoc*, routine and special). Design information verification is used to ensure that a facility is constructed and operating consistently with the design information provided by the State, with a view to ensuring that all possible diversion routes are subject to Agency control. The Agency carries out *ad hoc* inspections predominantly in the course of verifying the State's initial declarations to the Agency. Once Subsidiary Arrangements are brought into force, the Agency carries out routine inspections. These inspections are carried out at nuclear facilities, as well as at other locations where nuclear material is customarily used. The frequency of routine inspections, and the locations at which they may be carried out, are limited by the provisions of the Safeguards Agreement. Special inspections are available to the Agency if it considers that information available by the State is not adequate for the Agency to fulfil its responsibilities under the Agreement, and may involve access to information or locations in addition to the access permitted for *ad hoc* and routine inspections.

Under Additional Protocols, the IAEA has yet another form of on-site access, referred to as complementary access. As the name was intended to convey, such access was designed to complement the access provided for under the Safeguards Agreement, not to modify the terms and conditions relevant to design information verification or inspections. Complementary access is much broader in scope, and ensures Agency access anywhere on the site of a nuclear facility, and at any location where the State declares nuclear material to be located (even if exempted from safeguards or otherwise not subject to inspection under the Agreement), to ensure the absence of undeclared nuclear material and activities. It also provides for Agency access, for the purpose of resolving questions or inconsistencies, to any other location declared by the State. In the case of a question or inconsistency, complementary access may also be carried out by the IAEA at any other location in the State for the purposes of conducting environmental sampling.

During its on-site access, the IAEA may carry out a variety of activities, including: the sampling of nuclear material; environmental sampling (e.g. swipe sampling); installing and checking surveillance cameras, including remote monitoring equipment; and applying containment measures, such as tamper indicating seals, to provide assurances that, in the Agency's absence, the equipment or material placed under seal is not moved or operated. The Agency also reviews the operating records of the facilities for internal consistency, and compares them with the reports submitted by the States.

12.4.3 State-based evaluations

Perhaps the most significant development in the implementation of IAEA safeguards since 1991 has been the shift from a quantitative facility-based approach to a more qualitative analysis of the State's nuclear activities as a

312 INTERNATIONAL ARMS CONTROL

whole. This process involves the preparation of State Evaluation Reports, containing a compilation and assessment of all of the information available to the Agency concerning each State which has a Safeguards Agreement with the Agency, as well as an analysis of that State's nuclear activities, including supporting infrastructure.

The information used in these evaluations is derived from a variety of sources, including not only State declarations and reports, facility operating records, and commercially available satellite imagery and the results of on-site access, but sources external to the State. Outside sources can include open-source data, such as journals and newspapers, as well as intelligence information. Should information be made available to the Agency which it concludes is credible and actionable, whatever its source, the Agency may consider this information in its assessment of the correctness and completeness of the State's declarations concerning its nuclear activities.

12.5 Dispute resolution

The standardized text of Comprehensive Safeguards Agreements contains three articles related to the interpretation and application of such agreements and the settlement of disputes. In reverse order, they provide for arbitration, consultations with the Board of Governors and consultations among the parties to the relevant Agreement. Neither individuals nor non-governmental organizations have legal standing to invoke these provisions or to participate in the resolution of disputes.

Paragraph 22 of INFCIRC/153 provides that any dispute arising out of the interpretation or application of the Agreement which is not settled by negotiation or another procedure agreed to by the parties should, on the request of either party, be submitted to an arbitral tribunal. Disputes concerning any finding by the Board pursuant to paragraph 19 (that is, a finding that the Agency is unable to verify the non-diversion of nuclear material: see the discussion below) on action by the Board pursuant to such a finding are expressly excluded from arbitration.

The arbitral tribunal is to be composed of one arbitrator designated by each party, and the two arbitrators so designated are to elect a third, who would be the chairman. If, within thirty days of the request for arbitration, either party has not designated an arbitrator, either party to the dispute may request the President of the International Court of Justice to appoint an arbitrator. The same procedure is to apply if, within thirty days of the designation or appointment of the second arbitrator, the third arbitrator has not been elected. A majority of the members of the arbitral tribunal would constitute a quorum, and all decisions would require the concurrence of two arbitrators. The arbitral procedure would be fixed by the tribunal and its decisions would be binding on both parties.

However, arbitration in connection with the implementation of safeguards has never been invoked either by the Agency or by a State. Indeed, it is difficult to imagine a situation in which a State, or the IAEA for that matter, would seek arbitration as a means for adjudicating an issue associated with the implementation of a Safeguards Agreement, given the sensitivities of the issues likely to be involved. Arbitration may be more suitable for the resolution of disputes which are of a nature more akin to those arising in commercial settings, rather than political contexts.

Paragraph 20 of INFCIRC/153 provides that the parties to the Safeguards Agreement shall, at the request of either, consult about any question arising out of the interpretation or application thereof; there is no exclusion from this provision. Paragraph 21 provides that the State shall have the right to request that any question arising out of the interpretation or application of the Agreement shall be considered by the Board of Governors of the IAEA; and that the State shall be invited by the Board to participate in the discussion of any such question by the Board.

The Secretariat frequently consults with States on the implementation of safeguards, either at its own initiative or at the request of the State or States concerned. The use of such consultations is, in fact, the most common and most successful, although often time-consuming, means of resolving State-specific questions that arise out of the interpretation or application of Safeguards Agreements. The Secretariat has also consulted with the Board of Governors on State-specific matters related to the implementation of NPT safeguards agreements (for example, in connection with the conclusion of Subsidiary Arrangements under the Agreement with the European non-nuclear-weapon States and EURATOM, the European safeguards inspectorate). However, it has never been necessary to formally invoke paragraphs 20 or 21; consultations are simply a regular aspect of safeguards implementation.

From time to time, the Secretariat has also sought the views, recommendations and/or decisions of the Board of Governors on issues of general concern related to the implementation of safeguards. These have included matters such as the interpretation of specific provisions of INFCIRC/153 (e.g. the early provision of facility design information by a State) and financial responsibility for the costs of certain verification activities. The Board was also actively involved, between 1991 and 1997, in the efforts to strengthen the IAEA's safeguards system which resulted in the Board's approval of the Model Additional Protocol.

The discussion of such issues in the Board is frequently preceded by informal consultations between the Secretariat and the Board members, either individually or collectively. Such matters are then generally debated at the regional level (e.g. within the European Community) or interest group level (e.g. the G-77 or the Non-Aligned Movement) in the margins of the Board meetings, and a decision is taken thereafter by the Board as a whole following a formal discussion on the record. While these debates and the related consultations can sometimes result in protracted informal negotiations, this form of engagement eventually produces a decision. The decisions themselves, reflected in resolutions of the Board or in summary statements by the Chairman of the Board, may be taken either by consensus, by a 'decision taken without a vote' (which conveys the concept of a decision taken, but without the same degree of accord as a consensus decision), or, as a last resort, by a vote. Although the Rules of Procedure of the Board of Governors provide for the taking of decisions by a vote, the practice of the IAEA is rather to take decisions, to the extent possible, by consensus.

12.6 Compliance

The technical objective of IAEA safeguards under Comprehensive Safeguards Agreements is the timely detection of diversion (i.e. through the misuse of declared nuclear material or the failure to declare nuclear material) of significant quantities of nuclear material from peaceful nuclear activities to the manufacture of nuclear weapon or of other nuclear explosive devices or for purposes unknown, and the deterrence of such diversion by the risk of early detection.[19]

Should the Agency be unable to carry out the activities necessary for it to draw the required conclusions about the absence of diversion of nuclear material, the Director General may seek from the Board of Governors a determination, pursuant to paragraph 18 of INFCIRC/153, that certain actions are 'essential and urgent' for the Agency to fulfil its responsibilities

---

[19] INFCIRC/153, para. 28.

under the Agreement. In the event that the Board makes such a determination, the State becomes obliged to take the requested action.

Such a situation arose in the early 1990s in connection with the IAEA's efforts to verify the correctness and completeness of the initial declarations of the Democratic People's Republic of Korea (DPRK) concerning nuclear material and facilities in the DPRK. In that instance, the IAEA had, in the course of its verification activities, detected an anomaly that suggested that the State was concealing nuclear material and activities required to have been declared to the Agency. Following a series of intensive consultations between the Secretariat and the DPRK, an impasse was reached, and no further progress was possible without resort to a more formal resolution of the problem. Accordingly, the IAEA formally requested access to carry out special inspections at certain locations identified by the Agency, which the DPRK declined to provide. Following a report by the Director General, and the Board's consideration of this matter in a closed session, the Board of Governors determined, in accordance with Article 18 of the DPRK's Safeguards Agreement, that the granting of Agency access to those locations was 'essential and urgent'. Notwithstanding, the DPRK refused to provide the Agency with the requested access.

The next step involved reporting by the Director General to the Board of Governors that the IAEA was unable to verify that there had been no diversion of nuclear material required to be safeguarded under the DPRK's Safeguards Agreement, as foreseen in paragraph 19 of INFCIRC/153.

Paragraph 19 provides that, if the Board upon examination of relevant information reported to it by the Director General finds that the IAEA is unable to verify that there has been no diversion of nuclear material required to be safeguarded under a Comprehensive Safeguards Agreements, it may make the reports provided for in Article XII.C of the Statute (to the members of the IAEA, to the Security Council and to the General Assembly), and may also take, where applicable, the other measures provided for in that article. Paragraph 19 further requires that the Board take account of the degree of assurance provided by the safeguards measures that have been applied and shall afford the State every reasonable opportunity to furnish the Board with any necessary reassurance. Implicit in this provision is the concept that a State, given the opportunity to take corrective action, could resolve the issue and thereby enable the Agency to verify that there has been no diversion to nuclear weapons or other nuclear explosive devices, and thereby obviate the need for the Board of Governors to report the situation to the Security Council.

In the case of the DPRK, the Board found that, as a result of the DPRK's denial of access, which it considered to be in non-compliance with the DPRK's obligations under its Safeguards Agreement, the Agency was unable to verify that there had been no diversion, and decided to report the non-compliance to the Security Council.[20]

Pursuant to the Statute of the Agency, and the relevant Safeguards Agreements, the Board of Governors is the policy-making organ of the IAEA with the primary responsibility for drawing conclusions concerning non-compliance with IAEA Safeguards Agreements. While there is nothing to prohibit a Member State of the Agency from raising an issue of compliance in the Board of Governors, there is no standing for such a State to compel the conduct of an inspection in another State (so-called 'challenge inspections'). However, neither individuals nor NGOs have standing in either regard.

There is no mechanism for setting aside a State's obligation to comply with a Safeguards Agreement. However, a distinction has been drawn by the Board of Governors in terms of the appropriate response to non-compliance of a less significant nature (e.g. delays or minor oversights in reporting), as distinguished from non-compliance of a nature fundamental to the treaty obligation (e.g. diversion of nuclear material to a proscribed use) or where there is intentional non-compliance and/or a pattern of concealment, as indicated below.

The Board of Governors has made formal findings of non-compliance with respect to five countries: Iraq, Romania, the DPRK, Libya and Iran. In the cases of Iraq and the DPRK, the findings were prompted by actions taken by the State, discovered by the IAEA, to conceal nuclear activities, and the non-compliance of those States was reported to the Security Council. Iraq's non-compliance was detected by the IAEA in the course of inspections carried out by the Agency pursuant to Security Council Resolution 687 (1991), the cease-fire resolution adopted by the Council under Chapter VII at the end of the first Gulf War, and was reported to the Security Council in July and September of 1991. The Board decided to report to the Security Council non-compliance on the part of the DPRK in response to the DPRK's denial of access in 1993, and twice again in 1994, for furthering its non-compliance. In the second 1994 resolution of the Board on the

---

[20] It is important to point out that a determination under para. 18 is not a prerequisite for the carrying out by the Agency of special inspections, or for the Board to make a finding of non-compliance.

DPRK's non-compliance, the Board also decided, 'in conformity with article XII.C of the Statute, to suspend non-medical assistance to the DPRK'.[21] The Board of Governors reported to the Security Council again in January 2003 following the DPRK's announcement of its withdrawal from the NPT, its dismantling of the Agency's containment and surveillance equipment and its expulsion of IAEA inspectors at the end of 2002.

In the case of Romania and Libya, the findings of non-compliance were prompted by admissions volunteered by the States themselves of undeclared nuclear activities. In both of these instances, the Board of Governors requested that its findings of non-compliance be reported to the Security Council for information purposes only.

Recently, the Director General informed the Board of Governors of failures by the Republic of Korea (ROK) and Egypt to report to the IAEA nuclear material and activities required to be declared under their respective Safeguards Agreements. In both instances, the Board, through the mechanism of the chairperson's summary, expressed the view that the failure of each State to report in accordance with its Safeguards Agreement was of concern, but decided not to report the matter to the Security Council. In doing so in connection with the ROK's failures, the Board noted that the quantities of nuclear material involved had not been significant and that, to date, there had been no indication that the undeclared experiments had continued. With regard to Egypt, the Board expressed the view that, bearing in mind the nature of the activities, the fact that some of them had been the subject of open domain publications and therefore not clandestine, the fact that some of them had taken place fifteen to forty years previously, and the small amount of nuclear material involved, the issue was not a matter of proliferation concern.

Since early 2003, the Board of Governors has had under consideration Iran's nuclear programme and Iran's failures to fulfil its obligations under its Safeguards Agreement to report nuclear material, facilities and activities to the IAEA. The Director General has reported regularly to the Board, in oral and in written reports, on Iran's efforts, over a period of some twenty years, to conceal the scope and nature of its nuclear programme, in particular its previously undeclared enrichment programme, and on the Agency's efforts to verify that there are no further undeclared nuclear material, facilities and activities in Iran.

---

[21] In response to that resolution, the DPRK withdrew from membership in the IAEA.

In a number of resolutions, the Board of Governors has emphasized the importance of the fulfilment by Iran of its commitments under its Safeguards Agreement. It has also encouraged Iran to ratify the Additional Protocol that Iran has signed and to implement it on a voluntary basis pending its entry into force. The Board has also called on Iran to cease all enrichment-related and reprocessing activities pending resolution of the verification issues as a voluntary, non-legally binding, confidence-building measure.

In parallel with the activities of the IAEA, the Governments of the United Kingdom, France and Germany (the so-called E3), and the European Union (EU), concluded an agreement with Iran in November 2004 which provided for the expansion and sustaining by Iran of its voluntary suspension of all enrichment-related and reprocessing activities (including the conversion of uranium to produce feed material for its enrichment facilities) while negotiations on a long-term agreement are underway. The E3/EU and Iran agreed to begin negotiations with a view to reaching a mutually acceptable agreement on long-term arrangements to provide objective guarantees that Iran's nuclear programme is exclusively for peaceful purposes, and equally to provide firm guarantees on nuclear, technological and economic co-operation and firm commitments on security issues. At the request of the E3/EU and Iran, the Agency monitored all elements of Iran's voluntary suspension of those activities.

Following Iran's resumption of uranium conversion activities in August 2005, the Board of Governors adopted a resolution in September 2005 in which it found that Iran's many failures and breaches of its obligations to comply with its NPT Safeguards Agreement constituted non-compliance in the context of Article XII.C of the Agency's Statute. It also found that the history of concealment of Iran's nuclear activities, the nature of the activities, the issues brought to light in the course of the Agency's verification of Iran's declarations and the resulting absence of confidence that Iran's nuclear programme is exclusively for peaceful purposes have given rise to questions that are within the competence of the Security Council, as the organ bearing the main responsibility for the maintenance of international peace and security. However, the Board did not decide to report the matter to the Security Council at that time, but rather to address the timing and content of the report required under Article XII.C and the notification required under Article III.B.4 at its next meeting.

As 2005 was drawing to a close, while a great deal of progress had been made, the IAEA was still not in a position to draw conclusions regarding the completeness of Iran's declarations, and its verification activities in Iran were continuing. The discussions between the E3/EU and Iran, which were suspended following Iran's actions in August 2005, were expected to resume before the end of the year. In light of these discussions, and the fact that the Agency was still making some progress on the verification issues, the Board had not, as of December 2005, decided to report the matter to the Security Council.

12.7 Enforcement

While it is for the States party to the NPT to determine whether there is compliance with the NPT itself, the IAEA is recognized as the sole body responsible for verifying, in accordance with its Statute and its safeguards system, compliance with the Safeguards Agreements concluded by States parties undertaken in fulfilment of their obligations under Article III.1 of the NPT. The quinquennial Conferences of the NPT parties have also expressed the conviction that nothing should be done to undermine the authority in this regard, and that States parties to the NPT that have concerns regarding non-compliance with the Agreements should direct such concerns, together with supporting evidence and information, to the IAEA so that it may consider, investigate, draw conclusions and decide on necessary actions in accordance with its mandate.

However, while the IAEA is responsible for verifying a State's compliance with its nuclear non-proliferation undertakings, the Agency's safeguards system is not intended as an enforcement mechanism, but rather is more in the nature of an 'early warning system', hence the reference to the Agency as 'the nuclear watchdog'.

In fact, apart from the withdrawal of Agency assistance (such as acting as a broker for nuclear supplies, providing safety or security support, and/or the provision of humanitarian assistance), and the suspension of the rights and privileges of Agency membership, the IAEA has little in the way of enforcing its decisions. And, while such actions may have a greater impact on some countries, only in the case of the DPRK did the Board decide to withdraw Agency assistance, which clearly had little impact on the country in terms of enforcing compliance with its non-proliferation obligations. And the threat of suspension of the rights and privileges of Agency

320 INTERNATIONAL ARMS CONTROL

membership was rendered useless by the withdrawal of the DPRK from Agency membership.

The real mechanism for enforcement in connection with safeguards is the Security Council, to which the IAEA has direct access. As noted above, that access can be achieved through notification to the Council, in accordance with Article III.B.4 of the Agency's Statute, should questions arise that are within the competence of the Security Council, or, in accordance with paragraph 19 of INFCIRC/153, reporting to the Security Council on the IAEA's inability to verify the non-diversion of nuclear material.

On 31 January 1992, at the conclusion of a meeting of the Security Council held at the level of Heads of State and Government, in connection with an item entitled 'The responsibility of the Security Council in the maintenance of international peace and security', the President of the Security Council made a statement on behalf of the members of the Security Council, in which he said, *inter alia*:

> The proliferation of all weapons of mass destruction constitutes a threat to international peace and security. The members of the Council commit themselves to working to prevent the spread of technology related to the research for or production of such weapons and to take appropriate action to that end.
>
> On nuclear proliferation, they note the importance of the decision of many countries to adhere to the Non-Proliferation Treaty and emphasize the integral role in the implementation of that Treaty of fully effective IAEA safeguards, as well as the importance of effective export controls. The members of the Council will take appropriate measures in the case of any violations notified to them by the IAEA.

The Security Council's response to IAEA reports of non-compliance has varied, depending on the circumstances, ranging from diplomatic engagement to the imposition of financial and trade sanctions.

Following the IAEA's report to the Security Council in 1991 of Iraq's non-compliance, the Security Council adopted a resolution[22] under Chapter VII of the Charter in which it condemned the non-compliance, and demanded, *inter alia*, that Iraq halt all nuclear activities of any kind, except for the use of isotopes for medical, agricultural or industrial purposes until the Security Council determines that Iraq is in full compliance with that resolution and the relevant provisions of the ceasefire resolution,

---

[22] S/RES/707 (1991), para. 3(vi).

and the IAEA determines that Iraq is in full compliance with its Safeguards Agreement with the Agency.[23] The Security Council also prohibited the export to and import by Iraq of nuclear-related items.

In the case of the DPRK, in 1993 the Security Council called on the DPRK to reconsider its announced intention to withdraw from the NPT, and to honour its non-proliferation obligations under the Treaty and comply with its Safeguards Agreement. It also requested the Director General of the IAEA to continue to consult with the DPRK with a view to resolving the issues reported by the Agency, and urged all Member States to encourage the DPRK to respond positively to the resolution and to facilitate a solution.[24] In response to the IAEA's reports of expanded non-compliance in 1994, the President of the Security Council issued another statement on behalf of the Council, in which he expressed the Council's grave concern, urged the DPRK to take certain actions to permit IAEA verification, called for immediate consultations between the IAEA and the DPRK, and requested the IAEA to maintain inspector presence in the DPRK to monitor activities at one of the reactors.[25]

This was followed by bilateral negotiations between the United States and the DPRK of an Agreed Framework, signed in Geneva on 21 October 1994, calling for the IAEA to monitor a 'freeze' on certain nuclear activities of the DPRK.[26] In considering the Agreed Framework, the Security Council, in a Presidential statement of 4 November 1994, requested the IAEA to take all steps it may deem necessary to verify full DPRK compliance with its Safeguards Agreement, and to take all steps it deemed necessary as a consequence of the Agreed Framework to monitor the freeze. The IAEA was permitted to carry out limited safeguards activities in the DPRK until December 2002, when, as indicated above, it was expelled from the DPRK. The matter since became the subject of the 'Six Party Talks' between the DPRK, the ROK, China, Japan, Russia and the United States.

12.8 Overall evaluation

As one of the foremost treaty regimes that provide for international verification, the IAEA's safeguards system has served as an example for other

---

[23] As of 20 December 2005, the Security Council has not yet taken a decision revoking this prohibition.

[24] Note by the President of the Security Council, S/25562, 8 April 1993; S/RES/825 (1993).

[25] S/PRST/1994/13, 31 March 1994. [26] IAEA Doc. INFCIRC/457.

treaty-based verification systems. The IAEA was frequently consulted in the development of the Chemical Weapons Convention and the Comprehensive Nuclear Test Ban Treaty. The Agency has also been engaged in the development of a regime for the verification of nuclear material released by nuclear-weapon States from their respective defence programmes. The Agency's experience is of equal relevance to the future consideration of arms control and non-proliferation inspection regimes, in particular in the development of a treaty on the cut-off of the production of fissile material for weapons purposes.

The development of IAEA safeguards has, likewise, benefited from the prevailing appreciation of security concerns as reflected in other verification regimes. It is reasonable to conclude that the stronger and more effective any individual regime for international verification is, the more support there will be for strong and effective verification in the context of other regimes.

The Agency's ability to detect non-compliance by a State with its obligations under Safeguards Agreements has improved dramatically since the early 1990s. In the case of Iraq, the effectiveness of the Agency's broad Security Council-mandated inspection authority was clearly demonstrated. Using the verification tools developed by the Agency in Iraq, and in its verification of South Africa's dismantled nuclear-weapons programme, the Agency was able to detect the possible diversion of nuclear material in the DPRK, and to detect previously undeclared nuclear activities in Iran and, on a smaller scale, the Republic of Korea and Egypt. The IAEA is using innovative tools and measures in its efforts to obtain a complete picture of Iran's nuclear activities.

However much the verification techniques have developed, however, the available enforcement mechanisms have not changed. They are: discussion, dialogue and diplomacy.

On 10 October 2005, the Norwegian Nobel Committee awarded the Nobel Peace Prize for 2005 to the 'IAEA and its Director General, Mohamed ElBaradei, for their efforts to prevent nuclear energy from being used for military purposes and to ensure that nuclear energy for peaceful purposes is used in the safest possible way'. In its press release, the Committee provided some insight into its decision:

> At a time when the threat of nuclear arms is again increasing, the Norwegian Nobel Committee wishes to underline that this threat must

be met through the broadest possible international co-operation. This principle finds its clearest expression today in the work of the IAEA and its Director General. In the nuclear non-proliferation regime, it is the IAEA which controls that nuclear energy is not misused for military purposes, and the Director General has stood out as an unafraid advocate of new measures to strengthen that regime. At a time when disarmament efforts appear deadlocked, when there is a danger that nuclear arms will spread both to States and to terrorist groups, and when nuclear power again appears to be playing an increasingly significant role, IAEA's work is of incalculable importance.

In his Nobel Lecture given in Oslo on the occasion of the award ceremony, Mr ElBaradei had these words to say about the IAEA and its role in international peace and security:

> [A]rmed with the strength of our convictions, we will continue to speak truth to power. And we will continue to carry out our mandate with independence and objectivity. The Nobel Peace Prize is a powerful message for us – to endure in our efforts to work for security and development. A durable peace is not a single achievement, but an environment, a process and a commitment.

13

The Convention on the Prohibition of the Use, Stockpiling, Production and Transfer of Anti-Personnel Mines and on their Destruction (Ottawa Convention)

KATHLEEN LAWAND[*]

Since the Convention on the Prohibition of Anti-Personnel Mines (also known as the Ottawa Convention)[1] entered into force in 1999, its implementation has been characterized by a high degree of co-operation and transparency rarely seen in multilateral treaty regimes, at least in the disarmament and humanitarian fields in which the Convention is rooted. The treaty's success so far is a reflection of the success of its formal and informal mechanisms to oversee and support compliance, in particular of those created by States parties after the treaty's entry into force, and of the monitoring, advocacy and support provided by non-governmental and other organizations. These mechanisms have been driven by the political will of States parties, notably those States that were key players in the negotiation of the treaty, and by the active involvement of non-State actors, in particular the International Campaign to Ban Landmines (ICBL) and the International Committee of the Red Cross (ICRC), as well as UN agencies engaged in 'mine action'.[2]

The 'compliance culture' of the Ottawa Convention, including the significant role of non-State actors in monitoring and supporting implementation,

---

[*] The author thanks Dr Walter Krutzsch and the editors for comments and suggestions on earlier drafts. The article reflects the views of the author alone and not necessarily those of the ICRC.
[1] The Convention on the Prohibition of the Use, Stockpiling, Production and Transfer of Anti-Personnel Mines and on their Destruction, Ottawa, 3 December 1997, in force 1 March 1999, 36 ILM 1507 (1997). The Convention is alternately referred to in publications as the 'Anti-Personnel Mine Ban Convention', the 'Mine Ban Treaty' or the 'Ottawa Convention'. This paper will use the latter term as shorthand. As of 1 April 2006, 150 States were party to the Convention and an additional four States had signed but not yet ratified the treaty.
[2] The International Mine Action Standards (IMAS) define 'mine action' as 'activities which aim to reduce the social, economic and environmental impact of mines and UXO [unexploded ordnance]'. Among the group of activities which comprise mine action, the IMAS include 'advocacy against the use of anti-personnel mines'. See IMAS 04.10, 2nd edn, 1 January 2003, available at www.mineactionstandards.org/imas.htm.

can best be understood by reference to the unique negotiation process that led to its adoption. This paper will therefore begin with a brief presentation of the Convention's negotiating history, followed by an overview of its key obligations, achievements and challenges. It will then describe the compliance control mechanisms, both those provided by the Convention itself and those created by the States parties after it entered into force. This will be followed by a description of the as yet unused dispute resolution and enforcement mechanisms available to States parties. The snapshot of the regime will end with an overview of the compliance monitoring initiatives of non-governmental organizations (NGOs) and compliance support by other organizations. The paper will conclude with an assessment of the regime's effectiveness and of whether its experiences can be transferred to other treaty regimes.

13.1 Negotiating history of the Ottawa Convention[3]

The Ottawa Convention is part of the international response to the humanitarian crisis caused by the worldwide proliferation and use of anti-personnel mines. The calls for a total ban on anti-personnel mines made in 1993 by the ICBL[4] and in 1994 by the ICRC and the growing public abhorrence with the devastating effects of anti-personnel mines on civilians led like-minded governments to begin negotiating the treaty in October 1996. The manner in which these negotiations began and were conducted set the tone that still permeates the work of the Convention today.

Under increasing pressure to effectively deal with the scourge of anti-personnel mines, States first attempted to address the problem in the context of the 1980 Convention on Certain Conventional Weapons

---

[3] For a more detailed history of the negotiation process, see S. Maslen, *Commentaries on Arms Control Treaties*, vol. I, *The Convention on the Prohibition of the Use, Stockpiling, Production, and Transfer of Anti-Personnel Mines and on Their Destruction* (Oxford: Oxford University Press, 2004) (hereinafter, *Commentary*), pp. 21–48; and S. Maslen and P. Herby, 'An International Ban on Anti-Personnel Mines: History and Negotiation of the Ottawa Treaty' (1998) 325 *International Review of the Red Cross* 693–713. For a history and analysis of the international efforts to ban anti-personnel mines, see M. A. Cameron *et al.*, *To Walk Without Fear – The Global Movement to Ban Landmines* (Oxford: Oxford University Press, 1998); and D. Hubert, *The Landmine Ban: A Case Study in Humanitarian Advocacy* (Providence: Thomas J. Watson Institute for International Studies, 2000).

[4] The ICBL and its then co-ordinator, Ms Jody Williams, were co-awarded the Nobel Peace Prize in 1997. Today, the ICBL is a network of 'more than 1,400 groups in over 90 countries'. See www.icbl.org.

(CCW).[5] This seemed logical at the time. Protocol II to the CCW was the only multilateral treaty imposing some restrictions on the use of landmines for humanitarian reasons. At the conclusion of the CCW Review Conference in May 1996, the States parties adopted Amended Protocol II, which included stronger restrictions on the use of anti-personnel mines, but fell far short of the complete ban on these weapons sought by many governments, the ICRC, the ICBL and several UN agencies.[6] Its provisions were considered overly complex and difficult to apply.[7]

Disappointment with the inability of the CCW to deliver an effective remedy to the 'epidemic' of death and injury caused by anti-personnel mines[8] led Canada to host a strategy meeting of some fifty pro-ban States, NGOs and international organizations in October 1996. At the close of this meeting, the Canadian Foreign Minister stunned government delegations by calling for negotiations to begin on a treaty to comprehensively ban anti-personnel mines. This launched the so-called 'Ottawa process', a negotiation process involving like-minded States which would take place outside of the traditional fora for multilateral disarmament negotiations, notably of the United Nations and the Conference on Disarmament, and therefore outside of the rigid confines of consensus-based diplomacy. This process was unique in that it was conducted in a spirit of equal partnership between governments, NGOs and international organizations, with the ICRC and the ICBL particularly active participants.

In September 1997, less than one year after the Ottawa process was launched, a diplomatic conference hosted by Norway adopted the Convention on the Prohibition of the Use, Stockpiling, Production and Transfer of Anti-Personnel Mines and on their Destruction. It was opened for signature on 3 December 1997 in Ottawa and entered into force barely fifteen months later on 1 March 1999, after receiving the requisite forty ratifications.

---

[5] Convention on Prohibitions or Restrictions of the Use of Certain Conventional Weapons which may be deemed to be Excessively Injurious or to have Indiscriminate Effects (CCW), Geneva, 10 October 1980, in force 2 December 1983, 1342 UNTS 137. The CCW is a framework treaty complemented by five protocols containing prohibitions and restrictions applying to specific weapons.

[6] Calls for a ban on anti-personnel mines had been made in the mid-1990s by the Secretary-General of the UN, the UN High Commissioner for Refugees and UNICEF, following those of the ICBL and the ICRC.   [7] Maslen, *Commentary*, pp. 21–3, §§ 0.40–0.42.

[8] In the early 1990s, the ICRC's medical staff qualified as an 'epidemic' in medical terms the level of death and injury caused by anti-personnel mines. See *The Worldwide Epidemic of Landmine Injuries: The ICRC's Health-Oriented Approach* (Geneva: ICRC, 1995).

It is the strategic partnership between pro-ban States, the ICBL, the ICRC and UN agencies that achieved the Ottawa Convention.[9] This 'dynamic interaction' continues today between States parties and these non-State actors in the context of the Convention's formal and informal compliance control mechanisms. It is a key factor explaining the impressive strides made by States parties so far in implementing the Convention.

13.2 Key obligations, achievements and challenges

The Ottawa Convention provides a comprehensive prohibition of anti-personnel mines. Each State party to the treaty undertakes never under any circumstances to use, develop, produce, otherwise acquire, stockpile, retain or transfer anti-personnel mines, and to destroy all anti-personnel mines it owns or possesses, or that are within its jurisdiction or control.[10] Each may exceptionally retain or transfer anti-personnel mines for the development of and training in mine detection, mine clearance and mine destruction techniques, but the number of mines so retained 'shall not exceed the minimum absolutely necessary' for these purposes.[11]

The adoption of the Ottawa Convention marked the first time that States agreed to ban completely a weapon that was already in widespread use. They did so on the basis of international humanitarian law, in particular the principle that the right of the parties to an armed conflict to choose methods or means of warfare is not unlimited, the rule prohibiting the use of weapons of a nature to cause superfluous injury or unnecessary suffering, and the rule requiring that a distinction be made between civilians and combatants.[12]

In addition to imposing disarmament obligations, the Ottawa Convention requires States to remedy the human cost of anti-personnel mines by committing them to clear mines that are already in the ground,[13] to take

---

[9] For an excellent analysis of the interplay between States and non-State actors in achieving the Ottawa Convention, see Hubert, *The Landmines Ban*, Chapter 2, 'The Path to the Landmines Treaty'. See also M. Dolan and C. Hunt, 'Negotiating in the Ottawa Process: The New Multilateralism', in Cameron *et al.*, *To Walk Without Fear*, pp. 392–423.

[10] See arts. 1, 4 and 5.   [11] Art. 3(1).

[12] See the last paragraph of the Preamble to the Ottawa Convention.

[13] Art. 5(1) reads: 'Each State Party undertakes to destroy or ensure the destruction of all anti-personnel mines in mined areas under its jurisdiction or control, as soon as possible but not later than ten years after the entry into force of this Convention for that State Party.' Paragraphs (3) to (6) provide a procedure by which a State party may request an extension of its mine clearance deadline. Such request must contain a detailed explanation of the reasons for the proposed extension and be submitted to a Meeting of the States Parties or a Review Conference for approval.

measures to reduce the risk that civilians will enter mined areas (including through 'mine awareness' programmes),[14] and to provide assistance for the care, rehabilitation and socio-economic reintegration of mine victims.[15] In the latter respect, the Ottawa Convention is the first treaty banning a weapon to require that assistance be provided to the weapon's victims.

Article 6 of the Convention represents the formal basis of the Convention's compliance culture. It requires States parties to assist each other in implementing their mine clearance, stockpile destruction, awareness, and victim assistance obligations, and in exchanging relevant technology. This obligation is formulated as a 'right' of each State party 'to seek and receive assistance' and an obligation of 'each State Party in a position to do so' to provide assistance, either directly to the concerned State or through *inter alia* the UN system, regional organizations, the ICRC or NGOs.[16] Financial, material and technical assistance provided under article 6 constitutes an important incentive for States parties to comply with the Convention and has helped to resolve implementation difficulties. In financial terms, between 1998 and 2004, an estimated US$1.2 billion was generated by States parties for mine action, bilaterally or through international agencies or NGOs.

At the First Review Conference of the Ottawa Convention,[17] States parties took stock of achievements in the implementation of the Convention since it entered into force. Among these is the fact that three-quarters of States are party to the treaty,[18] including most severely mine-affected countries. Worldwide production and use of anti-personnel mines have decreased significantly, including by States not party, and international trade in these weapons has effectively ceased.[19] The compliance rate with the Convention's anti-personnel mine stockpile destruction deadlines is almost 100 per cent, with all States parties whose deadlines have passed reporting completion of

---

[14] Risk reduction measures are required by arts. 5(2) and 6(3).   [15] See art. 6(3).

[16] See in particular art. 6(1), (3) and (4).

[17] The First Review Conference, also called the 'Nairobi Summit on a Mine-Free World', took place from 29 November to 3 December 2004. The Review Conference adopted a Final Report, UN Doc. APLC/CONF/2004/5, 9 February 2005 (available at www.reviewconference.org), which includes a number of substantive policy documents: Part II contains the 'Review of the Operation and Status of the Convention on the Prohibition of the Use, Stockpiling, Production and Transfer of Antipersonnel Mines and on their Destruction: 1999–2004'; Part III contains a five-year action plan, entitled 'Ending the Suffering Caused by Anti-Personnel Mines: Nairobi Action Plan 2005–2009' (the 'Nairobi Action Plan'); and Part IV contains the 'Programme of Meetings to Facilitate Implementation 2005–2009'.

[18] As of 1 April 2006, there were 150 States parties to the Convention.

[19] See 'Review of the Operation and Status of the Convention', p. 12, paras. 6–8.

their destruction programmes.[20] Moreover, the ICRC has found that, in States parties where the Convention's norms are being fully implemented, the annual number of new mine victims has fallen significantly, in some cases by two-thirds or more.[21] And, as shown below, compliance with the annual reporting requirement of article 7, which is one of the Convention's principal compliance control mechanisms, has been exemplary.

While noting these impressive achievements, among others, the Review Conference concluded that much more still needs to be done to meet the humanitarian and disarmament objectives of the Convention. Key challenges include successfully meeting mine clearance deadlines, which will begin to fall as of 2009, improving assistance for mine victims and achieving universal adherence to the Convention.[22] The latter is essential if the Convention's goal of a world free of anti-personnel mines is to be reached, especially in view of the fact that a number of States not party hold vast stockpiles of anti-personnel mines.[23] In order to face these and other challenges, the States parties adopted a key policy document – the Nairobi Action Plan 2005–2009 – in which they have committed to taking seventy specific 'actions' over the next five years. The Nairobi Action Plan is now serving as the framework for efforts to universalize and implement the Convention and as a benchmark for monitoring compliance.

13.3 Compliance control, dispute resolution and enforcement mechanisms managed by the States parties

13.3.1 Compliance control mechanisms provided by the Convention or established by decisions of the States parties

The term 'compliance control' is used in this chapter to mean mechanisms, both formal and informal, to oversee and support the implementation of

---

[20] Art. 4 of the Ottawa Convention requires each State party to destroy all stockpiled anti-personnel mines it owns or possesses, or that are under its jurisdiction or control, 'as soon as possible but not later than four years after the entry into force' of the Convention for the State party. As of December 2004, States parties had together destroyed a total of over 37.2 million anti-personnel mines. See 'Review of the Operation and Status of the Convention', p. 16, para. 23.

[21] See *Caring for Landmine Victims* (Geneva: ICRC, June 2005); and *Ending the Landmine Era – Victim Assistance* (ICRC Factsheet, August 2004), p. 2.

[22] See Final Report of the Review Conference, p. 8, paras. 25(3), (4) and (1).

[23] The ICBL's *Landmine Monitor Report 2005* (Human Rights Watch, October 2005), p. 14, estimates that China, Russia, the United States, Pakistan, India and South Korea, among others, together hold some 160 million stockpiled anti-personnel mines.

330   INTERNATIONAL ARMS CONTROL

the Convention's obligations and to monitor compliance with its prohibitions. Three types of formal compliance control mechanisms are provided by the Ottawa Convention: annual meetings of the States parties, annual reporting by each State party, and a procedure for facilitating and clarifying compliance. The first two are the Convention's 'routine' compliance control mechanisms. Both are supported by complementary mechanisms set up by formal and informal decisions of the States parties after the entry into force of the treaty. In many respects, these complementary mechanisms have had a greater impact on compliance control up to now than the mechanisms formally envisaged by the Convention.

Taken together, the formal and complementary compliance monitoring mechanisms can be divided into three categories: (1) bodies set up to monitor or to facilitate compliance with the Convention's obligations; (2) annual reporting by each State party and mechanisms to facilitate such reporting; and (3) a special multi-step procedure for 'clarifying compliance', including on-site verification.

13.3.1.1 Bodies set up by the Convention or by decision of the States parties to monitor or facilitate compliance

Annual meetings of the States parties under article 11   The Meeting of the States Parties, the decision-making authority set up under article 11 of the Ottawa Convention, plays an important role in compliance control. It is empowered 'to consider any matter with regard to the application or implementation' of the Convention, including, but not limited to, the operation and status of the Convention, matters arising from the annual reports submitted under article 7,[24] submissions of States parties pursuant to the compliance procedure under article 8,[25] and decisions relating to requests by individual States for the extension of their mine clearance deadlines under article 5.[26] The Meeting of the States Parties' broad powers include considering and taking decisions on any matter relating to compliance and enforcement.

Meetings of the States Parties have been convened each year since the Convention's entry into force in 1999, with the exception of 2004 when the First Review Conference took place.[27]

---

[24] Discussed in section 13.3.1.2 below.   [25] Discussed in section 13.3.1.3 below.

[26] Art. 11(1) and art. 5.

[27] Pursuant to art. 11, the Meeting of the States Parties meets once a year until the convening of the Convention's First Review Conference. In 2004, the latter decided to continue holding Meetings of the States Parties on an annual basis. See 'Programme of Meetings', p. 108, para. 2(a).

The Meetings of the States Parties are intended 'as a mechanism to track implementation and compliance and to provide an opportunity for mine-affected States to present their respective situations. [They] have become a major decision-making event, turning the [Ottawa Convention] and its implementation mechanisms into a more dynamic process.'[28] The Meetings of the States Parties have made significant decisions in relation to compliance control. Notable among these is the decision to establish an Intersessional Work Programme and an Implementation Support Unit and the decision to adopt a standard format for annual article 7 reports, discussed below.

Non-state actors such as the ICRC, the ICBL and UN agencies, as well as many other international and regional organizations and NGOs, participate in the Meetings of the States Parties as observers and intervene in the exchanges of views.

The Standing Committees and the Intersessional Work Programme
Two months after the Convention entered into force, the First Meeting of the States Parties established the Standing Committees, to meet in between the annual Meetings of the States Parties in what is known as the Intersessional Work Programme. [29] The latter's purpose is to ensure 'the systematic, effective implementation of the Convention through a more regularized programme of work by establishing informal, open-ended intersessional working groups which could engage a broad international community for the purpose of advancing the achievement of the humanitarian objectives of the Convention'.[30] In so doing, States parties intended to replicate the same informal, co-operative, transparent and inclusive framework that was the hallmark of the negotiations leading to the adoption of the Convention in 1997, based on a strategic partnership between governments and non-State actors with the aim of facilitating the implementation of the Convention.[31]

There are currently four Standing Committees, dealing respectively with (1) stockpile destruction, (2) mine clearance, mine risk education and mine action technologies, (3) victim assistance and socio-economic reintegration,

---

[28] Maslen, *Commentary*, p. 260, § 11.1.
[29] See First Meeting of the States Parties to the Convention on the Prohibition of the Use, Stockpiling, Production and Transfer of Anti-Personnel Mines and on their Destruction, Final Report, UN Doc. APLC/MSP.1/1999/1, para. 25 and Annex IV.
[30] *Ibid.*, Annex IV, p. 26 (emphasis added). [31] See section 13.1 above.

and (4) the general status and operation of the Convention.[32] Every year, for each of the Standing Committees, the Meeting of the States Parties appoints two co-chairs and two co-rapporteurs. In practice, each pair is usually composed of one mine-affected or stockpile-holding State party and one 'donor' State party.[33] This ensures that the Convention's main stakeholders are directly involved in managing the Intersessional Work Programme.

The Standing Committees report to the Meeting of the States Parties, which sets the dates of the Committees' meetings for the following year. In the period 1999–2004, the Standing Committees met twice a year, in between the annual Meetings of the States Parties. At the end of 2004, the Convention's First Review Conference decided to reduce the frequency of Standing Committee meetings to once a year.[34] It is too early to tell what effect this will have on the Convention's compliance rate, which has been impressive so far.[35] The meetings are held in Geneva with the support of the Implementation Support Unit, discussed below.

The work of the Standing Committees is overseen by a Co-ordinating Committee, established in 2000 by the Second Meeting of the States Parties.[36] It is made up of the co-chairs and co-rapporteurs of the Standing Committees and presided by the President of the previous Meeting of the States Parties.[37] The ICRC and the ICBL attend the Co-ordinating Committee Meetings as observers.

Attendance at the Standing Committee meetings has increased incrementally since 2000. Representatives of more than ninety States parties,

---

[32] The First Meeting of the States Parties in 1999 originally set up five 'Standing Committees of Experts': Final Report, p. 6, para. 25. The Second Meeting of the States Parties in 2000 reduced these to four, merging 'mine action technologies' and 'mine clearance', and dropping the word 'experts' from the name of the Standing Committees: Final Report, UN Doc. APLC/MSP.2/2000/1, p. 8, para. 28. The Third Meeting of the States Parties in 2001 shifted the responsibility for mine awareness from the Standing Committee on Victim Assistance to the Standing Committee on Mine Clearance: Final Report, UN Doc. APLC/MSP.3/2001/1, p. 6, para. 28.

[33] In 2005, co-chairs and co-rapporteurs were as follows: for the Standing Committee on General Status and Operation of the Convention, South Africa and New Zealand (co-chairs) and Guatemala and Belgium (co-rapporteurs); for the Standing Committee on Stockpile Destruction, Bangladesh and Canada (co-chairs) and Tanzania and Japan (co-rapporteurs); for the Standing Committee on Mine Clearance, Algeria and Sweden (co-chairs) and Jordan and Slovenia (co-rapporteurs); for the Standing Committee on Victim Assistance, Nicaragua and Norway (co-chairs) and Afghanistan and Switzerland (co-rapporteurs).

[34] See Programme of Meetings, p. 109, para. 2(b).   [35] Discussed in section 13.2 above.

[36] Second Meeting of the States Parties, Final Report, para. 29.

[37] In 2005, the Co-ordinating Committee was presided by the President of the First Review Conference, H. E. Ambassador Wolfgang Petritsch of Austria.

thirty States not parties, the United Nations, the ICBL, the ICRC and numerous other international and non-governmental organizations participated in the 2003 meetings, a total of well over 400 delegates.[38] Consistent with the open negotiation process that led to the adoption of the Ottawa Convention in 1997, international organizations, the ICRC and NGO representatives – including mine victims themselves – actively participate in the Standing Committee meetings and intervene as of right in the discussions.

Though the Intersessional Work Programme is an informal process not envisaged by the treaty and though the Standing Committees are not vested with any binding decision-making authority, it is fair to say that this is where the real compliance control work of the Ottawa Convention is being done. The Standing Committees' meetings have evolved to become 'clearing houses' for detailed information on all aspects of the implementation of the Convention, focusing on mine clearance, victim assistance, stockpile destruction and universalization, considered the Convention's four 'core humanitarian objectives'. This is the result of the significant preparatory work done by the Standing Committee co-chairs, with the crucial support of the Implementation Support Unit (see next section). In practice, co-chairs write to States parties well in advance of the Standing Committee meetings, asking them to prepare and present interventions on the basis of detailed questionnaires regarding implementation of specific obligations.[39] These questionnaires are based on the so-called '4-P' approach, whereby States are asked to present information on their 'problems, plans, progress and priorities for assistance' in mine clearance, stockpile destruction and victim assistance. Likewise, 'States Parties in a position to do so' are asked to share information on the support they can provide to States parties in need of assistance to fulfil their Convention obligations.[40] In this, the Standing Committee meetings aim at facilitating the implementation of the Convention's requirements for international assistance and co-operation under article 6.[41]

Thus, the Intersessional Work Programme complements 'the official and legally required exchange of information' conducted through annual

---

[38] See Fifth Meeting of the States Parties, Final Report, Annex VI, p. 52, para. 2.

[39] For example, regarding documents used to prepare the Standing Committee Meetings of 13–17 June 2005, see www.gichd.ch/mbc/iwp/SC_june05/documents.htm.

[40] See Review of the Operation and Status of the Convention, p. 39 para. 114.

[41] Art. 6 is discussed under section 13.2 above.

334   INTERNATIONAL ARMS CONTROL

reporting pursuant to article 7 and discussed below.[42] Most records of the Standing Committee meetings are posted on the website of the Geneva International Centre for Humanitarian Demining (GICHD), as are those of the Meetings of the States Parties.[43]

Implementation-related information is also provided by international organizations and the ICBL, with the latter often providing comments on compliance by particular States parties. In this connection, the ICBL has played a critical role in the Standing Committee meetings by regularly exposing compliance concerns.[44] In addition, the ICRC regularly raises general issues of concern regarding the Convention's implementation, without singling out specific countries.

The Implementation Support Unit   The Ottawa Convention does not provide for a secretariat. During the negotiations of the treaty, 'it was argued that resources should be devoted to mine clearance and victim assistance rather than set up new structures'.[45] Conference services for the Meetings of the States Parties are rendered by the UN Secretariat.

In order to ensure effective administrative support to States parties in the implementation of the Convention and the conduct of the Intersessional Work Programme, in 2001 the Third Meeting of the States Parties mandated the GICHD, a non-governmental institution, to establish an Implementation Support Unit (ISU). Its duties include providing secretarial assistance and advice to the Standing Committees and the Co-ordinating Committee, and supporting 'liaison/interaction with States Parties, the ICBL, ICRC, the UN, and other international organizations and agencies'.[46]

The ISU is funded by States on a voluntary basis. It is composed of a small but dedicated staff. With an annual budget of some US$500,000, its running costs are low by the standards of the secretariats of other multilateral treaties, partly because its infrastructure and basic support services are covered by the GICHD.

The ISU has played a crucial role in collecting, managing and making available to States parties compliance-related information, thereby facilitating compliance monitoring. It has been instrumental in assisting States

---

[42] Review of the Operation and Status of the Convention, p. 39, para. 114.
[43] See www.gichd.ch.
[44] The role of NGOs and civil society in compliance control is addressed below in section 13.4.
[45] Maslen, *Commentary*, pp. 262–3, § 11.8.
[46] Third Meeting of the States Parties, Final Report, Annex II, p. 17. See also *ibid.*, para. 33.

CONVENTION ON ANTI-PERSONNEL MINES 335

parties to develop the Intersessional Work Programme into the key compliance monitoring mechanism that it has become today.

The Sponsorship programme   Several 'donor' States parties have set up a sponsorship programme to ensure the participation of developing States parties, in particular mine-affected States, in the Meetings of the States Parties and the Intersessional Work Programme. The sponsorship programme is funded by voluntary contributions of States parties and is administered by the GICHD and the ISU. [47] The participation of fifty-four States at the June 2004 Standing Committee meetings was supported in this fashion, as was the attendance of some ninety delegates at the First Review Conference in December 2004. This has ensured widespread representation at meetings of States parties, thereby facilitating effective exchanges of information on the implementation of the Convention and on issues of compliance.

13.3.1.2 Annual reporting obligation under article 7 and measures to facilitate reporting

Article 7, entitled 'Transparency Measures', requires each State party to provide initial and annual reports to the UN Secretary-General. As the title suggests, the annual reports are meant to provide a window on whether the State party has obligations to fulfil under the Convention and, if so, on the status of the implementation of its obligations. The reports must contain the compliance-related information listed in article 7(1), such as the location of all mined areas under its jurisdiction or control, the type and quantity of stockpiled anti-personnel mines, the status of stockpile destruction and mine clearance programmes, the types and quantities of anti-personnel mines destroyed, the measures taken to provide warnings to mine-affected populations, and so on. As is the case in all multilateral reporting regimes, the quality of the reports varies, but on the whole they provide relevant and detailed information.

Article 7 obliges the Secretary-General to transmit all such reports to all States parties. This is done in practice by the United Nations Department for Disarmament Affairs (UNDDA), which posts the reports on its website.[48] As such, the reports are accessible to the public.

---

[47] See Review of the Operation and Status of the Convention, at p. 44, para. 133.
[48] See http://www.unog.ch (Disarmament > APLC > Article 7 Reports).

At the First Review Conference in December 2004, each of the 143 States parties which was required to submit an initial report under article 7 had done so, with the exception of four States parties. This represents a compliance rate of 97 per cent with the initial reporting requirement. Each State party which was required to provide an annual update of their report in 2004 had done so except for twenty-four States parties, representing a compliance rate of 81.7 per cent.[49]

In 1999, the First Meeting of the States Parties made an important decision to facilitate the implementation of article 7 by recommending standard reporting formats, which are now used by the vast majority of States parties, and by agreeing on guidelines for 'the technical ways and means to circulate reports'.[50]

The Second Meeting of the States Parties followed up on this by adopting an additional *voluntary* reporting form – known as Form J – 'in order to provide States Parties with the opportunity to report voluntarily on matters pertaining to compliance and implementation not covered by the formal reporting requirements contained in article 7'.[51] The meeting recommended that this form be used to report in particular on the implementation of the Convention's requirements to provide assistance for the care and rehabilitation, and socio-economic reintegration, of mine victims. Over sixty States parties have made use of Form J since its adoption.[52]

At the Third Meeting of the States Parties, Belgium tabled a comprehensive 'Guide to Reporting under Article 7 of the Ottawa Convention', prepared by an NGO, the Verification Research, Training and Information Centre (VERTIC).[53]

In addition, an informal Contact Group on article 7 chaired by Belgium gathers interested States parties, as well as the ICBL, the ICRC, the United Nations Mine Action Service (UNMAS) and other observers, approximately twice a year on the margins of meetings of States parties to exchange information and strategies aimed at encouraging compliance with article 7. Assisted by the ISU, the Contact Group has been instrumental in ensuring the high rates of compliance with article 7.

---

[49] See Review of the Operation and Status of the Convention, p. 38, paras. 105–6.
[50] See First Meeting of the States Parties, Final Report, p. 6, paras. 23–4, and Annexes II and III.
[51] Second Meeting of the States Parties, Final Report, para. 27 and Annex III.
[52] Review of the Operation and Status of the Convention, p. 39, para. 112.
[53] APLC/MSP.3/2001/INF/1, 20 August 2001.

The accuracy of the information set out in article 7 reports can be verified *in situ* through the as yet unused procedure under article 8, described in the next section. In practice, article 7 reports may be clarified, corrected and/or supplemented in the presentations made by States parties to the Standing Committees, discussed above. Their reliability is also tested against the information provided in the annual *Landmine Monitor Report*, a country-by-country analysis of compliance with and implementation of the Ottawa Convention entirely compiled and prepared by the ICBL, discussed in section 13.4 below.

13.3.1.3 Special procedure for dealing with compliance issues (article 8)

Entitled 'Facilitation and Clarification of Compliance', article 8 is the longest provision of the Ottawa Convention, consisting of twenty paragraphs. The first paragraph states the general rule that 'States Parties agree to consult and co-operate with each other regarding the implementation of [the] Convention, and to work together in a spirit of co-operation to facilitate compliance by States Parties with their obligations under [the] Convention'. The remaining paragraphs set up a formal procedure available to States parties if they are unable to resolve compliance issues through 'consultation and co-operation'.

The article 8 compliance procedure can be triggered by one or more States parties, and is carried out through the UN Secretary-General.[54] It begins with a 'Request for Clarification' to the concerned State, which has twenty-eight days to respond.[55] If the requesting States parties are dissatisfied with the requested State's clarification, they may refer the matter to the next Meeting of the States Parties[56] or to a Special Meeting of the States Parties,[57] which may decide to send a fact-finding mission to the requested State.[58] The fact-finding mission consists of experts nominated by the UN Secretary-General in consultation with the requested State party.[59] In-country, it must be given the opportunity to speak with all relevant persons and must be granted access to all relevant areas and installations, subject *inter alia* to the protection of any constitutional obligations.[60]

---

[54] For a more detailed discussion of the art. 8 procedure, see T. Hajnoczi *et al.*, 'The Ban Treaty', in Cameron *et al.*, *To Walk Without Fear*, pp. 292–313; and Maslen, *Commentary*, pp. 223–4, §§ 8.19–8.24.   [55] Art. 8(2).   [56] Art. 8(3).   [57] Art. 8(5).   [58] Art. 8(8).

[59] *Ibid.* and art. 8(9)–(10). So far, eleven States parties have provided names of qualified experts to the Secretary-General for this purpose: see Review of the Operation and Status of the Convention, p. 41, para. 126.   [60] Art. 8(13)–(14).

338   INTERNATIONAL ARMS CONTROL

Once it has the fact-finding mission's report, the Meeting of the States Parties 'may request the requested State Party to take measures to address the compliance issue within a specified period of time'.[61] The Meeting may further 'suggest to the States Parties concerned ways and means to further clarify or resolve the matter under consideration, including the initiation of appropriate procedures in conformity with international law'.[62] In extreme cases, this could include referring the matter to the UN Security Council or adopting other enforcement measures provided by the UN Charter.[63]

Maslen notes that article 8 'was one of the hardest provisions to agree on as the negotiating position of certain States on the twin issues of verification and compliance were often far apart . . . The outcome represents a compromise between the intrusive verification measures typical of disarmament treaties and the relatively light model traditionally favoured by international humanitarian law.'[64]

Article 8 remains untested, as there has as yet been no issue of compliance that could not be resolved through the informal or 'soft' compliance control means described earlier. At the Convention's First Review Conference, States parties noted that '[t]his fact, combined with the overall exceptional level of compliance with the Convention, underscores the States Parties' commitment to the aims of the Convention and is a testament to their agreement . . . "to work together in a spirit of co-operation to facilitate compliance by States Parties with their obligations under this Convention" '.[65]

But calls have been made by the ICBL and some States parties to put into place structures and means to ensure that article 8 can be quickly 'operationalized' when required. The ICBL has also called on States parties to make systematic use of the article 8 procedure in response to compliance concerns, rather than keeping it as an exceptional eventuality.[66] States have resisted this due to their traditional aversion to openly confronting issues of compliance, as opposed to their preferred 'quiet diplomacy'. However, it is only a matter of time before States parties will have to seriously consider

---

[61] Art. 8(18).   [62] Art. 8(19).

[63] International Committee of the Red Cross, *Banning Anti-Personnel Mines – The Ottawa Treaty Explained* (Geneva: ICRC, 1998), p. 9.

[64] Maslen, *Commentary*, p. 214, § 8.1 (footnotes omitted).

[65] Review of the Operation and Status of the Convention, p. 42, para. 125.

[66] See Maslen, *Commentary*, pp. 224–7. At the request of some States parties, in 2002 the NGO VERTIC prepared a *Guide to Fact-Finding Missions under the Ottawa Convention* to assist States parties in planning and preparing for receiving a fact-finding mission under art. 8.

making use of the article 8 procedure, notably in view of the potentially serious compliance issues that may arise in relation to the Convention's looming mine-clearance deadlines, which will begin to fall in 2009.

At the First Review Conference, States parties made clear that they see the compliance control procedure of article 8 as a mechanism of last resort in case of the failure of national enforcement measures under article 9 of the Convention, including penal sanctions for acts prohibited by the treaty, discussed in section 13.3.3 below.[67]

13.3.2 Dispute resolution

As is the case for most other multilateral treaties, the Ottawa Convention does not set up a formal judicial dispute settlement procedure, but this option is of course available to the disputing States if they agree, either of their own initiative or if called upon by the Meeting of the States Parties.

Article 10, entitled 'Settlement of Disputes', does not refer to any one specific dispute settlement mechanism, but imposes a general obligation on States parties to 'consult and co-operate with each other to settle any dispute that may arise with regard to the application or interpretation' of the Convention.

Article 10 goes on to allow any State party to 'bring any such dispute before the Meeting of the States Parties', which 'may contribute to the settlement of the dispute by whatever means it deems appropriate, including offering its good offices, calling upon the States Parties to a dispute to start the settlement procedure of their choice and recommending a time-limit for any agreed procedure'. The Convention does not give the Meeting of the States Parties the authority to impose a settlement on the parties.

Article 10 concludes by specifying that it is 'without prejudice to the provisions of this Convention on facilitation and clarification of compliance'. This refers to the procedure on clarification of compliance set out in article 8 and described above. Pursuant to article 8(4), pending the convening of a Meeting of the States Parties to deal with a Request for Clarification, any of the concerned States parties 'may request the Secretary-General of the United Nations to exercise his or her good offices to facilitate the clarification request'.

---

[67] See Nairobi Action Plan, Action #63.

States parties to the Ottawa Convention have not yet made use of any formal dispute resolution procedures under article 10.

13.3.3 Enforcement

The Ottawa Convention does not provide for any specific means of enforcement of obligations. In the event of non-compliance by a State party amounting to a serious breach of the Convention, the States parties are left with the usual means of collective enforcement under international law, such as those under the UN Charter. In the context of the 'facilitation and clarification of compliance' procedure of article 8, the Meeting of the States Parties 'may suggest to the States Parties concerned ways and means to further clarify or resolve the matter under consideration, including the initiation of appropriate procedures in conformity with international law' (article 8(19)). This could conceivably include more robust enforcement measures ranging from the suspension of the State party's voting rights under the Convention, which in the case of a serious breach may do little to redress the situation, to referring the matter to the UN Security Council.

With respect to bilateral enforcement, it is difficult to identify what kind of counter-measures – in the sense of non-belligerent reprisals permissible under international law and consistent with the humanitarian objectives of the Ottawa Convention – may be used. The most probable bilateral enforcement measure would be the imposition of some form of economic sanctions on the concerned State, for example through the suspension or withdrawal of assistance for mine clearance or stockpile destruction, but it is not clear how this would be effective in redressing the situation.

Although international enforcement mechanisms are not specified in the Ottawa Convention, *national* enforcement is an important requirement of the treaty. Article 9, entitled 'National Implementation Measures', obliges each State party to 'take all appropriate legal, administrative and other measures, including the imposition of penal sanctions, to prevent and suppress any activity prohibited to a State Party under [the] Convention undertaken by persons or on territory under its jurisdiction or control'. During the negotiation of the treaty, an early draft of article 9 was entitled 'Compliance with the Convention', and included a paragraph requiring States parties 'to consult each other and to co-operate with each other' to resolve any implementation problems.[68] This paragraph was later moved to a draft article entitled 'Verification of Compliance', now article 8. The fact that both the obligation to consult and co-operate and the obligation to prevent and suppress prohibited activities were grouped in the same draft article underscores the complementary nature of national enforcement and international compliance control.

13.4 The involvement of non-State actors in compliance control[69]

As previously mentioned, NGOs and international organizations and institutions have played a key role in monitoring and supporting the implementation of the Ottawa Convention. They are actively involved in the Meetings of the States Parties and in the Intersessional Work Programme, and are present on the ground where the Convention's obligations are to be implemented.

In addition to the ICBL and the ICRC, whose role in bringing about a ban on anti-personnel mines is expressly recognized in the Convention's preamble,[70] interested non-State actors include the GICHD, UNMAS and other UN agencies engaged in mine action in the field (in particular, the UNDP and UNICEF), the programmes of other intergovernmental organizations such as the EU and the OAS, non-governmental mine clearance operators such as the Mines Advisory Group and Norwegian People's Aid, and issue-specific NGOs such as the Landmine Survivors Network, which focuses on the Convention's mine victim assistance obligations, and Geneva Call, which aims at getting armed non-State actors to respect the Convention's norms. The active involvement of all of these actors, interacting with States parties on implementation matters both inside and outside of formal meetings of the States parties, creates the dynamic and potent mix that characterizes the compliance culture of the Ottawa Convention.

---

[68] See Maslen, *Commentary*, p. 244, § 9.3.

[69] The term 'non-State actor' is used here in the broadest sense to refer to all actors other than States, and therefore it also includes programmes and agencies of intergovernmental organizations such as the UN and the OAS.

[70] The eighth preambular paragraph to the Ottawa Convention reads: 'Stressing the role of public conscience in furthering the principles of humanity as evidenced in the call for a total ban on anti-personnel mines and recognizing the efforts to that end undertaken by the International Red Cross and Red Crescent Movement, the International Campaign to Ban Landmines and numerous other non-governmental organizations around the world.'

342 INTERNATIONAL ARMS CONTROL

The important role of non-State actors in compliance control was expressly acknowledged in the Nairobi Action Plan, which in the context of 'transparency and exchange of information' commits all States parties to continuing 'to encourage the invaluable contribution to the work of the Convention by the ICBL, the ICRC, the United Nations, the GICHD, and regional and other organizations'.[71]

The ICBL in particular has been very effective in publicly calling attention to implementation and compliance issues, both in the Intersessional Work Programme and in the Meetings of the States Parties where it presents its analysis of the status of implementation in key areas including stockpile destruction, mine clearance and victim assistance, and calls on States parties to take measures to redress compliance issues.

In this connection, arguably the most significant NGO contributions to compliance control of the Ottawa Convention is the ICBL's annual publication, *Landmine Monitor Report*.[72] Containing some 1,000 pages, it provides a comprehensive review and a critical but constructive analysis of the country-by-country status of mine action (including in States not party to the Convention), and of implementation of and compliance with the Convention by States parties. In addition to the information submitted by States parties in their annual article 7 reports and in the Standing Committee meetings, the *Landmine Monitor Report* relies on data provided by hundreds of in-country researchers worldwide. It is a thorough and influential publication, referred to frequently by States parties themselves, and its findings generally have a significant impact on the behaviour of States, which are usually quick to attempt to respond to any issue of compliance that may be raised there. At the First Review Conference, States parties acknowledged the significance of the *Landmine Monitor Report* in the following terms:

> Non-governmental organizations have played an important role in the exchange of information related to the implementation of the Convention. In particular, the ICBL's *Landmine Monitor* initiative has provided States Parties and others with a detailed independent information source on the actions of all States regarding the pursuit of the Convention's aims.[73]

The first edition of the *Landmine Monitor Report* was published in 1999 and was released at the First Meeting of the States Parties to the Ottawa

---

[71] Nairobi Action Plan, Action #56.   [72] See www.icbl.org/lm/.
[73] Review of the Operation and Status of the Convention, p. 40, para. 116.

Convention in May of that year. From 1999 through to 2004, it was edited by Human Rights Watch, a founding member of the ICBL, and as of 2005 it is edited by Mines Action Canada. It is funded mainly by governments party to the Ottawa Convention and by independent institutions.

In addition to the ICBL, other non-State actors play a significant role in monitoring and facilitating compliance. For its part, the ICRC raises issues of interpretation and implementation of the Convention in meetings of the States parties although it refrains from naming specific States, consistent with its long-standing policy not to comment publicly on whether or not a State is respecting international humanitarian law. Instead, it engages the individual States concerned in a confidential bilateral dialogue. It also provides advice and technical assistance to States parties in the implementation of their Convention obligations relating to mine risk reduction and education, victim assistance and national implementing legislation.[74]

UN agencies, including UNMAS, have also been active in promoting implementation of the Convention. In addition, the UNDP and UNICEF, as well as agencies of other intergovernmental organizations such as the EC and the OAS, have played a critical role in supporting national mine action efforts.

13.5 Conclusions: assessing the strengths and weaknesses of the Ottawa Convention's compliance control regime

As described above, the Ottawa Convention's compliance control mechanisms are of three types: (1) those provided by the treaty itself, consisting of annual reporting by each State party, oversight by the annual Meetings of the States Parties, and a special procedure to resolve difficult compliance issues with the possibility of on-site verification; (2) those established by decisions of the Meeting of the States Parties, including the Standing Committees and the Implementation Support Unit; and (3) those established by non-State actors, including the annual *Landmine Monitor Report* published by the ICBL. The combination of these mechanisms, formal and informal, State and non-State, makes up the Convention's compliance control regime.

---

[74] The role of the ICRC in assisting States parties in implementing these Convention obligations is recognized in the Nairobi Action Plan, Action points #8, 22, 56 and 60 and Part IV on victim assistance.

344 INTERNATIONAL ARMS CONTROL

The key ingredients that made the success of the treaty's negotiation in 1996–7 have been identified as: (a) 'favourable negotiating conditions' including a strong chairperson and NGO access; (b) 'effective coalition building' among NGOs, governments and international agencies; and (c) 'clear campaign messaging (advocating stringent provisions within an explicitly humanitarian discourse)'.[75] These ingredients have persisted *mutatis mutandis* in the Ottawa Convention's implementation phase, and have been crucial to fostering the Convention's 'culture of compliance' characterized by a high degree of trust, transparency and ownership relative to other multilateral treaties. With the support of the Implementation Support Unit, the leadership of the Meeting of the States Parties and the Standing Committees on the whole has remained strong. This is backed up by the continued political and financial support of key stakeholders in the Convention, notably those States parties that were instrumental in negotiating the treaty. The strategic partnerships forged between NGOs, international organizations and governments during the campaigns to ban anti-personnel mines have lived on. Non-state actors have full access to formal and informal meetings of the States parties, where they express themselves freely on matters of compliance. The goals of the Convention are relatively simple and straightforward: States parties focus on the 'core humanitarian objectives' of the Convention that are clearing all mined areas, destroying all stockpiled mines, assisting mine victims and working towards universal adherence to the Convention.

Whether this formula can be applied to other treaty regimes may depend on a number of factors, including the sensitivity of the treaty's subject-matter and the complexity of its objectives. In any case, it ultimately (and tritely) depends on the political will of the States party to the treaty to allow a high level of transparency, inclusiveness and co-operation to enter the treaty's compliance control regime. This will of course be made more difficult where the treaty has been negotiated and is being implemented in a climate of suspicion, hostility or coercion. A significant fact in this regard is that the Ottawa Convention States parties do not include several major military powers, notably three permanent members of the UN Security Council and several other notorious rivals.[76] The non-participation of these States, which stockpile large quantities of anti-personnel mines, poses a serious challenge to the Convention's goal of the global elimination

---

[75] Hubert, *The Landmine Ban*, p. 57.   [76] See footnote 23 above and the accompanying text.

of these weapons and may threaten the treaty's credibility in the long run. But, paradoxically, their absence may account for the Convention's open and co-operative compliance culture, inclusive of non-State actors, that has made it a model for multilateral treaty regimes.

It is perhaps not surprising that the Convention's special compliance control procedure and its dispute resolution and enforcement mechanisms have never been used.[77] Like other treaty regimes, most of the Convention's compliance issues have stemmed not from 'wilful disobedience but the lack of capability or clarity or priority',[78] or understanding of the Convention's requirements. There is a general propensity of States to comply with their treaty obligations, not out of fear of sanction or enforcement, but because of their need to be accepted as members in good standing of the treaty regimes of which they are members and more broadly of the international community.[79]

When faced with more serious compliance concerns, States party to the Ottawa Convention have rarely raised them openly in meetings of the States parties, but have preferred instead to use 'quiet diplomacy', i.e. persuasion through bilateral dialogue and démarches. This reflects the general aversion of States to use 'hard' mechanisms to control and enforce treaty compliance except in extreme cases. For its part, the ICRC pursues bilateral dialogue to encourage individual States to respect and implement their Convention obligations. These discreet approaches are complemented by the more public 'straight-talking' advocacy of the ICBL. It is the synergy of these different but complementary approaches that has driven progress in the implementation of the Convention and in resolving issues of compliance.

In one notable case, the announcement by one State party in 2003 that it intended to retain over 69,000 anti-personnel mines for training in detection, clearance and destruction techniques pursuant to article 3,[80] well in excess of the 'hundreds, thousands but not tens of thousands' generally understood as the legitimate threshold for mines so retained, sparked strong criticism by the ICBL, which saw this as a potential violation of articles 1 and 3 of the Convention.[81] This was followed by intense parallel pressure on the concerned State by a number of States parties, bilaterally and

---

[77] Described respectively in sections 13.3.1.3, 13.3.2 and 13.3.3 above.

[78] A. Chayes and A. H. Chayes, *The New Sovereignty: Compliance with International Regulatory Agreements* (Cambridge, MA: Harvard University Press, 1995), Chapter 1, 'A Theory of Compliance', p. 22.   [79] See *ibid.*, p. 27.   [80] See above, text referring to note 11.

[81] See *Landmine Monitor Report 2004*, p. 829.

through regional organizations. One year later, the State party in question reversed its position, declaring it would proceed with the destruction of all of its stockpiled anti-personnel mines, which it has now completed. It invited the ICBL and others to observe parts of the destruction. This is a good example of complementary efforts of State and non-State actors to ensure compliance with the Convention.

The Ottawa Convention's compliance control regime will face a number of important challenges in the near future. The most significant of these will be the test to its ability to effectively facilitate implementation and deal with clear compliance problems in relation to the Convention's first mine clearance deadlines, which will begin to fall in 2009. In this context, States parties may have to give serious consideration to applying 'harder' forms of compliance control, notably the article 8 procedure, including on-site inspections. The credibility of the Convention's compliance control regime will depend on whether States parties are capable of applying the Convention's formal compliance control procedures in cases of serious issues of compliance, when they are most needed.

In this connection, another significant challenge is how well the regime will manage divergences of interpretation and practice among States parties in the application of certain key provisions of the Convention. These divergences include the practice of some States parties to retain so-called 'anti-vehicle' mines designed with sensitive fuses making them function as anti-personnel mines within the meaning of article 2 of the Convention. They also include the wide discrepancies in numbers of mines retained for permitted purposes under article 3, although attempts are being made to address this issue through enhanced information exchange and reporting.[82] In the long run, the regime's credibility will be put to the test if these issues remain unresolved.

For now, the 'new multilateralism' of the mid- and late-1990s heralded by the 'Ottawa process' has survived in the implementation of the Ottawa Convention in the form of a successful culture of compliance based on co-operation between governments and non-State actors. Some other treaty regimes have attempted to replicate this approach, with mixed results.[83] What is certain is that the world of 2006 is far different from that of the

---

[82] See in particular Nairobi Action Plan, p. 103, Action #54.
[83] See Hubert, *The Landmine Ban*, Chapter 4, which discusses the campaigns for the International Criminal Court, to end the use of child soldiers, and to restrict the availability of small arms and light weapons.

mid-1990s, when 'the post-Cold-War environment [was] highly conducive to effective humanitarian advocacy'.[84] It would undoubtedly be more difficult today to transfer the experiences of the Ottawa Convention to other treaty regimes, but it is by no means impossible. It depends only on the courage and will of governments, international organizations and NGOs, and especially of the individuals behind them, to make it happen.

[84] *Ibid.*, p. 71.

General comments

14

Dispute resolution

ANDREAS L. PAULUS

14.1 Dispute settlement in a fragmented legal order

In the twenty-first century, we are witnessing an astonishing revival of judicial instruments in international law: from the increasing use of the International Court of Justice by States to the establishment of the International Criminal Court, of the Dispute Settlement Body of the World Trade Organization and also of the International Tribunal for the Law of the Sea. Even the services of the Permanent Court of Arbitration established in 1907 are increasingly used.[1] On the other hand, when browsing through the relevant political science literature, one hardly finds an explanation for this development. International adjudication is supposed to be slow, cumbersome, expensive and, ultimately, ineffective. Recently, American scholars have attempted to undermine the last prerogative of international courts and tribunals, namely, the presumption of impartiality, neutrality and fairness.[2] Submission to international adjudication would thus appear to be exceptional and risky. And yet, States are using judicial bodies with increasing frequency, in particular in issue areas such

---

[1] For an overview of current dispute settlement mechanisms, see J. Collier and V. Lowe, *The Settlement of Disputes in International Law* (Oxford: Oxford University Press, 1999), pp. 19–44; P. Sands, R. Mackenzie and Y. Shany (eds.), *Manual on International Courts and Tribunals* (London: Butterworths, 1999); Project on International Courts and Tribunals, 'Synoptic Chart', available at www.pict-pcti.org/publications/synoptic_chart.html (visited 21 June 2005).

[2] See E. Posner and J. Yoo, 'A Theory of International Adjudication', University of Chicago Law and Economics, Olin Working Paper No. 206 (February 2004), available at http://papers.ssrn.com/sol3/papers.cfm?abstract_id=507003 (visited 21 June 2005); and E. Posner, 'The Decline of the International Court of Justice', University of Chicago Law and Economics, Olin Working Paper No. 233, available at http://papers.ssrn.com/sol3/papers.cfm? abstract_id=629341 (visited 21 June 2005). But see J. Goldstein *et al.*, 'Legalization and World Politics' (2000) 54 *International Organization* 3; R. O. Keohane, A. Moravcsik and A.-M. Slaughter, 'Legalized Dispute Resolution: Interstate and Transnational' (2000) 54 *International Organization* 457; A.-M. Slaughter, 'A Global Community of Courts' (2003) 44 *Harvard International Law Journal* 191 *et seq.*, at p. 194.

352 GENERAL COMMENTS

as world trade or international criminal law. In addition, recent studies indicate that the compliance with international judicial pronouncements is in general positive.[3]

The example of international criminal law demonstrates that the development of dispute settlement is far from uniform. International criminal courts and tribunals deal with the violation of international legal rules by individuals, whether acting on behalf of States or not. Recent developments thus point to a certain 'fragmentation' of dispute settlement in different areas of international law.[4] The current book draws the conclusion from this development by specifically analyzing different issue areas instead of jumping to general conclusions. The role that judicial adjudication plays is very different from issue area to issue area – from a large role in European human rights litigation to a virtually non-existent one in disarmament.

Classical international dispute settlement consists in the resolution of a dispute between two or more parties by a third party applying international law, ideally a court or an arbitral tribunal. According to the *Mavrommatis* formula of the Permanent Court of International Justice and used by its successor, the International Court of Justice, a 'dispute is a disagreement on a point of law or fact, a conflict of legal views or of interests between two persons'.[5] Speaking of 'a specific disagreement relating to a question of rights or interests in which the parties proceed by way of claims, counter-claims,

---

[3] C. Schulte, *Compliance with Decisions of the International Court of Justice* (Oxford: Oxford University Press, 2004); C. Paulson, 'Compliance with Final Judgments of the International Court of Justice Since 1987' (2004) 98 *American Journal of International Law* 434.

[4] See generally J. Charney, 'Is International Law Threatened by Multiple International Tribunals?' (1998) 271 *Recueil des Cours* 101; 'Symposium Issue: The Proliferation of International Courts: Piecing Together the Puzzle' (1999) 31 *New York University Journal of International Law and Politics* 679; P. S. Rao, 'Multiple International Judicial Forums: A Reflection of the Growing Strength of International Law or Its Fragmentation?' (2004) 25 *Michigan Journal of International Law* 929; and Y. Shany, *The Competing Jurisdictions of International Courts and Tribunals* (Oxford: Oxford University Press, 2003).

[5] *Mavrommatis Palestine Concessions*, 1924, PCIJ, Series A No. 2, p. 11. For the ICJ, see *East Timor* (*Portugal* v. *Australia*), Judgment, ICJ Reports 1995, p. 99, para. 22; *Land and Maritime Boundary between Cameroon and Nigeria* (*Cameroon* v. *Nigeria*), Preliminary Objections, Judgment, ICJ Reports 1998, p. 314, para. 87; *Questions of Interpretation and Application of the 1971 Montreal Convention arising from the Aerial Incident at Lockerbie* (*Libyan Arab Jamahiriya* v. *United States of America*), Preliminary Objections, Judgment, ICJ Reports 1998, p. 122, para. 21; *Questions of Interpretation and Application of the 1971 Montreal Convention arising from the Aerial Incident at Lockerbie* (*Libyan Arab Jamahiriya* v. *United Kingdom*), Preliminary Objections, Judgment, ICJ Reports 1998, p. 17, para. 22; *Certain Property* (*Liechtenstein* v. *Germany*), Preliminary Objections, 10 February 2005, para. 24, available at www.icj-cij.org (visited 13 June 2005).

denials and so on',[6] Collier and Lowe use a narrower definition which better captures the process of dispute settlement. As opposed to mere supervision, the procedure is adversarial[7] and takes place before a more or less neutral third party. Our main focus here is on dispute settlement before an international judicial or quasi-judicial body.[8]

In most of the areas under discussion in the present volume, there is little dispute settlement of this 'classical' kind. They concern 'community interests' that transcend those of individual States.[9] Disputes in the areas of human rights involve, at least on one side, the interests of individuals against States, usually against the State of their nationality. The protection of the environment concerns not only, or even primarily, States, but all human beings or the international community as a whole. In a world in which weapons of mass destruction are proliferating, arms control goes to the heart of State self-preservation, but also to the survival of humanity at large. The legal resolution, or at least clarification, of such disputes is seldom possible in the classical adversarial setting. One judicial mechanism used for this purpose is the advisory proceeding before the ICJ, which has played an important role in arms control and environmental questions, but also regarding humanitarian law.[10] Advisory proceedings take place in a quasi-judicial form before an independent third party, but they do not result in a solution of a concrete dispute, but in an opinion of an advisory character.

In classical dispute settlement, the 'persons', or rather parties,[11] are States. In human rights issues, however, at least one party to the dispute is an individual.[12] There are two possibilities to cure this 'defect'. In the more

---

[6] Collier and Lowe, *Settlement of Disputes*, p. 1; cf. C. Tomuschat, in B. Simma (ed.), *Charter of the United Nations* (Oxford: Oxford University Press, 2nd edn, 2002), art. 2(3), marginal note 17, fn. 25 (criticizing the Charter definition as being too broad).

[7] See Marauhn, chapter 10 in this volume, pp. 255–7.

[8] For a list of other means, see art. 33 of the UN Charter as well as Tomuschat, in Simma, *Charter*, art. 33, marginal notes 26–34.

[9] See B. Simma, 'From Bilateralism to Community Interest in International Law' (1994) 250 *Recueil des Cours* 221.

[10] See the most important advisory opinions in the last decade, *Legality of the Threat or Use of Nuclear Weapons*, Advisory Opinion, ICJ Reports 1996, p. 226; and *Legal Consequences of the Construction of a Wall in the Occupied Palestinian Territory*, Advisory Opinion, 9 July 2004, 43 ILM 1009 (2004), available at www.icj-cij.org (visited 13 June 2005).

[11] The ICJ is now using 'parties' rather than 'persons': see *Certain Property* (*Liechtenstein* v. *Germany*), Preliminary Objections, 10 February 2005, available at www.icj-cij.org (visited 13 June 2005).

[12] Tomuschat, in Simma, *Charter*, art. 2(3), marginal note 24, excludes these disputes from those covered by art. 2(3) of the UN Charter, but, when we look at contemporary dispute settlement, they play an indispensable role.

354 GENERAL COMMENTS

traditional case of diplomatic protection, States take up the claim of their nationals.[13] In some treaty regimes, in particular in the human rights field, States may complain about violations of human rights by other States parties regardless of the nationality of the victims.[14] The question of whether, in the case of so-called obligations *erga omnes*, States may bring infringements of the rights of non-nationals to international courts is hotly debated, but not yet resolved.[15] One further alternative to the extension of standing may consist in allowing the UN Secretary-General to request advisory opinions.[16] Finally, the third party need not be of a judicial kind *stricto sensu*. Human rights treaty bodies are composed of independent individuals, or even State representatives, and issue non-binding opinions. In disarmament cases, recourse to the Security Council, a political body, may substitute for the involvement of judicial or quasi-judicial bodies.[17]

To accommodate for these cases, the term 'dispute settlement' should be interpreted broadly as to include judicial proceedings between individuals and States, advisory procedures on questions of law involving international

---

[13] For two recent examples before the ICJ, see *LaGrand* (*Germany* v. *US*), ICJ Reports 2001, p. 466; and *Avena and other Mexican Nationals* (*Mexico* v. *US*), Judgment of 31 March 2004, 43 ILM 581 (2004), available at www.icj-cij.org (visited 13 June 2005).

[14] For the non-use of the State complaint mechanism of the ICCPR, see Scheinin, chapter 2 in this volume, pp. 20–1.

[15] See, famously *Barcelona Traction, Light and Power Company Ltd* (*Belgium* v. *Spain*), ICJ Reports 1970, p. 3, paras. 33–4; but see also *ibid.*, para. 91 (requiring a concrete treaty mechanism). See also *East Timor* (*Portugal* v. *Australia*), ICJ Reports 1995, p. 90 (requiring States nevertheless to fulfil the requirement of consent to the Court's jurisdiction); *Legal Consequences of the Construction of a Wall in the Occupied Palestinian Territory*, Advisory Opinion, 9 July 2004, 43 ILM 1009 (2004) (available at www.icj-cij.org (visited 13 June 2005)), paras. 154–60 (drawing consequences of the violation of such obligations beyond the question of standing). The WTO Dispute Settlement Body has accepted some claims of parties to the GATT without a more than theoretical interest in the trade of the goods in question: see *Report of the Appellate Body on the European Communities Regime for the Importation, Sale, and Distribution of Bananas*, AB-1997–3, 9 September 1997, Doc. WT/DS27/AB/R, para. 136, available at www.wto.org (visited 20 June 2005), short version in 37 ILM 243 (1998), at 245. For further discussion of this topic, see A. Paulus, *Die internationale Gemeinschaft im Völkerrecht* (Munich: Beck, 2001), pp. 363–86; C. Tams, *Enforcing Obligations Erga Omnes* (Cambridge: Cambridge University Press, 2005); and C. Günther, *Die Klagebefugnis der Staaten in internationalen Streitbeilegungsverfahren* (Cologne: Heymann, 1998).

[16] See H. Mosler and K. Oellers-Frahm, in Simma, *Charter*, art. 96, marginal note 15, with further references.

[17] Treaty for the Non-Proliferation of Nuclear Weapons, New York, 12 July 1968, in force 5 March 1970, 729 UNTS 161. On the general problem, see R. Higgins, 'The Place of International Law in the Settlement of Disputes by the Security Council' (1970) 64 *American Journal of International Law* 1; and V. Gowlland-Debbas, 'Security Council Enforcement Action and Issues of State Responsibility' (1994) 43 *International and Comparative Law Quarterly* 55.

organizations and not especially interested States, and non-judicial third parties, such as mediators, or political organs, such as the UN Security Council. But I would suggest excluding common interpretations by the States parties[18] because they avoid a dispute rather than solving an existing one.[19]

A further development relevant for us is the emergence of specialized sectors, or 'issue areas',[20] with a great number of different dispute settlement mechanisms. It may well be that there are not many traits that dispute settlement procedures in the areas under discussion in this book have in common. Rather, we may find a panoply of different regimes and divergent trends on the continuum between formality and informality, inter-State and individual–state, judicial and non-judicial proceedings. The proliferation of international legal mechanisms has led to concerns regarding the fragmentation of international dispute settlement.[21]

As lawyers, we tend to emphasize formal legal regimes in a court-like setting. However, courts and tribunals are mostly involved only after the fact. More innovative means centre on prevention rather than repression. Violations of human rights, international environmental regulation or disarmament obligations will often be difficult to assess. Thus, recent trends emphasize non-judicial means rather than formal adjudication.

In each issue area discussed here – human rights, environment, disarmament – we will first look to the character of the dispute settlement mechanisms provided for in the respective instruments. Secondly, the subjects of dispute settlement will be discussed – both regarding the participants in the respective dispute settlement mechanism and the interests served. We will see that States are neither the exclusive actors in modern forms of dispute settlement, nor are they the only beneficiaries. Finally, we will look at the 'dynamics' of dispute settlement in the respective area.

There is an assumption behind this symposium that formal inter-State dispute settlement is superseded by non-judicial means of treaty implementation that are more prospective rather than reactive. If there is a space for dispute settlement, it regards, as in the area of human rights, the relationship

---

[18] See Kicker, chapter 4 in this volume, pp. 101–2.

[19] For a case where the ICJ saw the threshold clearly passed, see *Certain Property* (*Liechtenstein* v. *Germany*), Preliminary Objections, 10 February 2005, para. 25, available at www.icj-cij.org (visited 13 June 2005).

[20] For an explanation of the term, see D. W. Leebron, 'Linkages' (2002) 96 *American Journal of International Law* 5 *et seq.*, at 6–10.

[21] For recent literature, see note 4 above and the accompanying text.

356   GENERAL COMMENTS

between individuals and the State rather than international relations as such. In the conclusion, we will nevertheless point out the lasting relevance of both traditional inter-State and more novel means of judicial dispute settlement.

14.2 International human rights

Human rights constitute the main field demonstrating the trend to the 'individualization' of international law. Traditional inter-State procedures are not hospitable to human rights issues. States are reluctant at best to bring cases in the public interest before a judicial forum. They usually limit themselves to advancing claims in their own or their citizens' interests. As an example, one may take the almost complete non-use of the State complaint mechanisms of both the International Covenant on Civil and Political Rights and the European Convention on Human Rights.[22] If States deal with human rights violations by their brethren, human rights are politicized instead of legalized. The fate of the UN Human Rights Commission is the best example. Its substitution by a permanent Human Rights Council, whose members are chosen by the UN General Assembly with stronger regard to their human rights record, is unlikely to remedy for the reluctance of States towards exposing their equal sovereigns. Regional mechanisms such as the European Convention on Human Rights have also shown that inter-State complaint procedures will remain the exception, and are used almost exclusively to advance the State's individual interest.[23]

The reason for this reluctance can be explained by their lack of a direct interest in the implementation of human rights obligations by another State, as long as the human rights violations do not have transboundary effects such as refugees. The global condemnation of human rights

---

[22] For the non-use of the State complaint mechanism of the ICCPR, see Scheinin, chapter 2 in this volume, pp. 20–1.

[23] On the reform proposals for the formation of a permanent Human Rights Council as a substitute for the Commission, see K. Annan, 'In Larger Freedom: Towards Development, Security and Human Rights for All', Report of the Secretary-General, 21 March 2005, UN Doc. A/59/2005, paras. 181–3. But see the more modest approach of the 2005 World Summit Outcome, UN GA Res. 60/1, UN Doc. A/RES/60/1 (2005), 24 October 2005, paras. 157–60, adopted on 16 September 2005 by the Summit of Heads of State and Government, UN Doc. A/60/PV.8 (2005), that leaves most details open to further negotiations. The Options Paper on Human Rights Council, of 3 November 2005, available at www.reformtheun.org/index.php?module=uploads&func=download&fileId=1157/ (visited 21 November 2005), still a 'non-paper', does not provide for new quasi-judicial mechanisms.

violations, and the increasing realization of the collective interest in the observation of international human rights law, has, however, resulted in more serious efforts to struggle against the most egregious breaches of human rights law. Calls for collective military intervention in cases of massive human rights abuses, the so-called 'responsibility to protect',[24] have centred on the obligations rather than the rights of States. The recent discussion on UN reform appears to indicate that States are increasingly willing to accept this responsibility.[25] But the 2005 summit of heads of State and government failed to strengthen the judicial aspect of the pacific settlement of disputes.[26] While States remain reluctant to submit situations in other States to independent judicial review, they will not necessarily hesitate to go before an international court or tribunal to secure individual rights of their own citizens, in particular when other States have walked down that route in similar cases.[27]

While clauses providing for ICJ jurisdiction in human rights treaties are largely a failure, individual complaint mechanisms are thriving. Thus, article 29 of the Convention on the Elimination of All Forms of Discrimination Against Women (CEDAW)[28] establishes a competence of the ICJ which is invoked extremely rarely, but an optional protocol with an individual complaint mechanism has garnered more than eighty States parties in five years.[29] Recent attempts to argue that human rights are better

[24] 'The Responsibility to Protect', Report of the International Commission on Intervention and State Sovereignty (ICRC, 2001), available at http://web.idrc.ca/en/ev-9436-201-1-DO_TOPIC.html (visited 20 June 2005). The report has been taken up by the Report of the High-Level Panel on Threats, Challenges and Change, A More Secure World: Our Shared Responsibility, UN Doc. A/59/565, 2 December 2004, paras. 199–203, and endorsed by UN Secretary-General Annan, note 23 above, para. 135.

[25] See World Summit Outcome document, note 23 above, para. 139: '[W]e are prepared to take collective action . . . should peaceful means be inadequate and national authorities are manifestly failing to protect their populations from genocide, war crimes, ethnic cleansing and crimes against humanity.'

[26] See World Summit Outcome document, note 23 above, para. 73, which mentions recourse to the International Court of Justice as an option only for the peaceful settlement of disputes.

[27] The most relevant example of the use of diplomatic protection to secure the rights of nationals, if not necessarily human rights, are the *LaGrand* and *Avena* cases (see note 13 above) dealing with the individual right to consular information under art. 36 of the Vienna Convention on Consular Relations, 24 April 1963, 596 UNTS 291.

[28] Convention on the Elimination of All Forms of Discrimination Against Women, New York, 18 December 1979, in force 3 September 1981, 1245 UNTS 13.

[29] Optional Protocol to the Convention on the Elimination of All Forms of Discrimination Against Women, New York, 6 October 1999, in force 22 December 2000, A/RES/54/4. For the status, see Multilateral Treaties Deposited with the Secretary-General, available at http://untreaty.un.org.

preserved in States not subject to an individual complaint mechanism[30] completely disregard the deepening of domestic human rights regimes such mechanisms are bringing about. For States not subject to these institutions, violations can only be determined when of a sufficiently egregious nature. Many violations of human rights will thus remain undiscovered. For human rights protections to be effective, special mechanisms are thus required.

Recent years have seen a remarkable widening and deepening of a truly judicial approach to the implementation of human rights in special regimes – from the expansion of the membership of the European Convention on Human Rights to the establishment of an African Court and Commission on Human Rights and the establishment of the International Criminal Court.[31] This is a trend towards judicial forms of settlement with compulsory jurisdiction and a strict application of legal standards rather than loose supervisory systems. Even the latter, such as the individual complaint mechanism of the International Covenant on Civil and Political Rights, are 'judicializing' and tend to pronounce quasi-judgments rather than loose advisory opinions. This does not imply, however, that their 'views' are regularly followed by States. Rather, their effectiveness largely depends on State willingness to implement them, in other words, on their political clout.[32]

As to the subjects of human rights litigation, whereas inter-State complaints have remained the exception, the prosecution of individuals for the most egregious abuses against human rights and humanitarian law has made remarkable progress in recent years. Forty-seven years after the Nuremberg precedent, the Security Council established, in the cases of the Former Yugoslavia and Rwanda, international criminal tribunals for the prosecution of individuals responsible for mass-scale atrocities.[33] Beyond the UN framework, States have ratified, in record time, the 1998 Rome Statute of the International Criminal Court (ICC) to prosecute genocide, crimes against humanity and war crimes on the basis of territori-

---

[30] See O. A. Hathaway, 'Do Human Rights Treaties Make a Difference?' (2002) 111 *Yale Law Journal* 1935. Against her, see R. Goodman and D. Jinks, 'Measuring the Effects of Human Rights Treaties' (2002) 13 *European Journal of International Law* 171. See also her response, Hathaway, 'Testing Conventional Wisdom' (2003) 14 *European Journal of International Law* 185.

[31] See Rome Statute of the International Criminal Court, 17 July 1998, 2187 UNTS 3.

[32] See Scheinin, chapter 2 in this volume, pp. 64–6.

[33] SC Res. 827, 25 May 1993; SC Res. 955, 8 November 1994.

ality and nationality of the (now 100) States parties.[34] Remarkably, the prosecution of offenders does not necessarily require a State or UN Security Council referral, but can be initiated by an independent prosecutor, under the control of a trial chamber.[35] In spite of the vigorous opposition of the United States to the very idea of an international criminal court, the UN Security Council referred the situation in Sudan regarding the Darfur region to the ICC.[36] The ICC's dealing with no less than four situations in the very first year of its operation referred to it by States or the UN Security Council[37] demonstrates the willingness of States to use the mechanism of the Court for bringing individuals to justice.

The trend in human rights thus clearly goes beyond classical inter-State dispute settlement into the direction of individual complaint mechanisms and the criminal prosecution of individual perpetrators. Classical international law litigation is increasingly sidelined, or, indeed, puts itself into the margins by leaving human rights to others, as the example of the International Court of Justice demonstrates.[38] By distinguishing between individual rights in multilateral conventions and human rights in general, the ICJ implied that it was not its main function to deal with human rights issues, while also proving that it is willing to deal with individual rights in 'classical' inter-State treaties such as the Vienna Convention on Consular Relations. The Court is even more inclined to

---

[34] Rome Statute of the International Criminal Court, 17 July 1998, 2187 UNTS 3, art. 12.

[35] *Ibid.*, art. 13.   [36] SC Res. 1593, 31 March 2005.

[37] In the cases of the Central African Republic, Uganda and Congo, these States have actually referred situations on their territory to the ICC. In the Ugandan case, the Court has issued its first five arrest warrants: see www.icc-cpi.int/cases.html (visited 21 November 2005). In a fifth situation, the government of the non-Member State of Côte d'Ivoire, accepted the Court's jurisdiction *ad hoc* under art. 12(3) of the Rome Statute: see 'Registrar Confirms that the Republic of Côte d'Ivoire Has Accepted the Jurisdiction of the Court', Press Release, 15 February 2005, available at www.icc-cpi.int/press/pressreleases/93.html (visited 21 November 2005).

[38] *Avena and Other Mexican Nationals (Mexico* v. *United States)*, available at www.icj-cij.org (visited 20 June 2005), 43 ILM 581, para. 124: 'Whether or not the Vienna Convention rights are human rights is not a matter that this Court need decide. The Court would, however, observe that neither the text nor the object and purpose of the Convention, nor any indication in the *travaux préparatoires*, support the conclusion that Mexico draws from its contention in that regard.' But see Inter-American Court of Human Rights, Advisory Opinion OC-16/99, 1 October 1999, 'The Right to Information on Consular Assistance in the Framework of the Guarantees of the Due Process of Law', as well as the UN Declaration on the Human Rights of Individuals Who Are Not Nationals of the Country in which They Live, UN GA Res. 40/144, 13 December 1985, General Assembly, Official Records, Supp. No. 53, Resolutions and Decisions, UN Doc. A/40/53, p. 253.

360 GENERAL COMMENTS

apply international humanitarian law, in particular in its advisory opinions in the *Legality of the Threat or Use of Nuclear Weapons*[39] and the *Wall in the Occupied Territories*[40] cases. However, the latter opinion may also signal a change by emphasizing the continual applicability of human rights instruments in times of armed conflict.[41] State responsibility and diplomatic protection are centred on State interests and are rarely used to resolve human rights disputes between States and individuals. Nevertheless, as Andreas Zimmermann has pointed out,[42] general mechanisms remain useful for the protection of aliens, for instance regarding consular rights. Thus, traditional dispute settlement procedures and human rights instruments can exist side-by-side.

Dealing with more or less precise individual rights, the human rights field seems an unlikely candidate for an exclusively managerial approach[43] that would substitute individual protection by inter-State diplomacy. However, pioneered by the European Convention Against Torture,[44] more and more treaty instruments are developing mechanisms for the pro-active and preventive protection of human rights.[45] Truth commissions are increasingly complementing the establishment of international or 'hybrid' (mixed domestic–international) criminal tribunals.[46] Thus, human rights are becoming an example for the combination rather than the exclusion of judicial and non-judicial fora of treaty implementation. Nevertheless, in order to receive redress for a human rights violation, individuals are still in need of a judicial or quasi-judicial pronouncement in their favour. Informal mechanisms may often not help against States that violate human rights obligations. However, human rights violations are not limited to States. Terrorist non-State groups can also violate the most basic rights of the human person. Both on the side of the victim and on the side of the perpetrator, the concept of human rights thus requires a transformation of traditional international law models.

---

[39] *Legality of the Threat or Use of Nuclear Weapons*, Advisory Opinion, ICJ Reports 1996, p. 226.
[40] *Legal Consequences of the Construction of a Wall in the Occupied Palestinian Territory*, Advisory Opinion, 9 July 2004, 43 ILM 1009 (2004), also at www.icj-cij.org (visited 20 June 2005).
[41] See *ibid.*, paras. 102–13.   [42] See chapter 1 in this volume, pp. 38–9.
[43] See Brunnée, chapter 15 in this volume, pp. 373–90.
[44] See Kicker, chapter 4 in this volume, pp. 91–6.
[45] Cf. Scheinin, chapter 2 in this volume, pp. 57–60.
[46] See e.g. the example of Sierra Leone, Agreement between the United Nations and the Government of Sierra Leone on the Establishment of a Special Court for Sierra Leone, in UN Doc. S/2002/246, 8 March 2002, Appendix II.

Human rights also confirm a trend towards regionalization. Global systems are based on informal supervisory mechanisms and subject to opt-ins or opt-outs. Participation in compulsory dispute settlement at a global scale remains relatively low. But with the exception of parts of Asia and Cuba, most States are now also subject to at least some regional scrutiny. In addition, the co-operation between international and domestic courts and tribunals becomes increasingly dense. As most disputes are individual–state, most mechanisms require the exhaustion of local remedies. Local courts are increasingly dealing with human rights cases and are referring to these instruments. Complementing the role of courts, NGOs play an increasingly active role. However, States and international tribunals remain reluctant to accord NGOs a role within judicial proceedings, although some tribunals accept so-called *amicus curiae* briefs of NGOs when added to government submissions.[47] With the involvement of that many actors, the human rights field becomes increasingly complex. Indeed, since the 1980s, warnings of too much proliferation abound.[48]

The trend towards individualization is probably unstoppable. Security considerations in the age of terrorism may slow down the general dynamics, but, *pace* Michael Ignatieff,[49] the era of human rights is not over. Dispute settlement in this regard requires special legal mechanisms tailored to the relationship between individual claimant and State. Preventive mechanisms such as at the Council of Europe Convention Against Torture[50] may contribute to this task, but cannot substitute for the binding determination of individual claims for redress.

---

[47] For the rather timid practice of the ICJ, see the newly adopted Practice Directive XII, available at www.icj-cij.org/icjwww/ibasicdocuments/ibasictext/ibasic_practice_directions_20040730_I-XII.htm (visited 21 November 2005). On the debate in the WTO, see *United States – Importation of Certain Shrimp and Shrimp Products*, Report of the Appellate Body, WT/DS58/AB/R, 12 October 1998, paras. 101–8; *US – Imposition of Countervailing Duties on Certain Hot-Rolled Lead and Bismuth Carbon Steel Products Originating in the United Kingdom*, WT/DS/138/AB/R, Report of the Appellate Body, 10 May 2000; and *European Communities – Measures Affecting Asbestos-Containing Products*, Report of the Appellate Body, WT/DS135/AB/R, 12 March 2001, paras. 50–7. For a more detailed critique see, G. C. Umbricht, 'An "Amicus Curiae Brief" on Amicus Curiae Briefs at the WTO' (2001) 4 *Journal of International Economic Law* 773–94; A. Paulus, in A. Zimmermann, C. Tomuschat and K. Oellers-Frahm (eds.), *Statute of the International Court of Justice* (Oxford: Oxford University Press, 2006), pp. 1427–43, at pp. 1439–43, art. 66, marginal notes 23–30.

[48] See P. Alston, 'Conjuring Up New Human Rights: A Proposal for Quality Control' (1998) 78 *American Journal of International Law* 607.

[49] M. Ignatieff, 'Is the Human Rights Era Ending?', *New York Times*, 5 February 2002, p. 29.

[50] On which, see Kicker, chapter 4 in this volume.

14.3 Environment

Compared to the human rights field, the implementation of environmental accords appears almost as the opposite: it is informal rather than formal, dominated by negotiation rather than adjudication; often applies informal standards rather than precise rules, and is facilitative rather than confrontational. However, even if judicial dispute settlement, such as the *Gabcikovo*[51] or *Trail Smelter*[52] cases, constitutes the exception rather than the rule and uses general rather than specific environmental treaty mechanisms, it has the non-negligible effect of clarifying the rules and developing the law. Nevertheless, even such litigation usually does not lead to definitive results. As the judgment of the ICJ in the *Gabcikovo* litigation exemplifies, with its insistence on negotiation rather than a clear and unequivocal pronouncement, environmental situations are often too complex and technical to be adjudicated in a classical manner. Negotiation between the parties cannot be substituted by judicial *fiat*.

As the analysis contained in this volume shows, in most contemporary environmental treaties, compulsory dispute settlement is more or less absent. Where newer treaty instruments contain traditional dispute settlement clauses, as it were,[53] they are not used by States. The main instrument for both

---

[51] *Gabcikovo–Nagymaros Project (Hungary v. Slovakia)*, ICJ Reports 1997, p. 7.

[52] *Trail Smelter (US v. Canada)*, 3 UNRIAA 1905 (1941). The arbitration related to compensation for damage in the United States allegedly caused by fumes emanating from a smelter operating in Canada.

[53] See the 'optional clause' contained in art. 14 of the Framework Convention on Climate Change, New York, 9 May 1992, in force 21 March 1994, 1771 UNTS 107 (English version at *ibid.*, p. 165). Of the no less than 189 States parties, only the Solomon Islands has made the declaration under art. 14(2) that provides for binding dispute settlement by arbitration. Similarly, of the twenty-three States parties to the Aarhus Protocol to the 1979 Convention on Long-Range Transboundary Air Pollution on Persistent Organic Pollutants, Aarhus, 24 June 1998, in force 23 October 2003, UNTS No. 21623, only Liechtenstein and Norway have accepted the jurisdiction of the ICJ according to art. 12(2). The other parties are limited to negotiation and conciliation, involving, however, notification to the Executive Body and, eventually, a Conciliation Commission (art. 12(1), (5) and (6)). See Kuokkanen, chapter 7 in this volume, p. 165: 'To date, none of the arrangements for dispute settlement have been used under the [LRTAP] Convention or under its protocols.' The UNECE Convention on Access to Information, Public Participation in Decision-Making and Access to Justice in Environmental Matters, Aarhus, 25 June 1998, in force 30 October 2001, 2161 UNTS 447, contains an elaborate procedure for inter-State dispute resolution, but is unlikely to be used: see Koester, chapter 8 in this volume, pp. 188–9. Similarly, of the forty parties to the Espoo Convention on Environmental Impact Assessment in a Transboundary Context, Espoo, 25 February 1991, in force 10 September 1997, 1989 UNTS 309, only four have used the possibility provided by art. 15 to recognize binding dispute settlement: on the details, see Koivurova, chapter 9 in this volume, pp. 220–2, in particular regarding the

negotiation of treaties and the supervision of their implementation is the Conference of the Parties (CoP), in which traditional 'dispute settlement' is difficult or impossible to separate from the further development of the relevant treaty document. Nevertheless, in exceptional cases, general dispute settlement bodies will deal with environmental issues. This happened in the most prominent environmental law case before the International Court of Justice, on the *Gabcikovo–Nagymaros Project*. In 1977, at a time when environmental concerns did not play the role they do today, Hungary and Czechoslovakia had concluded a treaty on the construction and operation of a system of locks in the Danube to produce hydroelectricity. Having turned a democracy in the late 1980s, Hungary wished to abandon the project, partly for environmental reasons.[54] However, the Court asked the parties to continue the search for a negotiated settlement. Thus, litigation failed to provide a solution to the dispute in question. In addition, advisory opinions of the ICJ deal with environmental law and armed conflict, but in very general terms.[55] Environmental litigation before generalized international judicial bodies remains the exception rather than the rule.

Environmental treaty making and monitoring are dominated by States. Increasingly, however, non-governmental organizations such as Greenpeace contribute to the drafting and implementation of environmental treaties. A positive example for their involvement is the Aarhus Convention, whose article 10(5) allows for NGO participation in the meeting of States parties. Some participation of NGOs in international dispute settlement may also prove helpful. It will only be admitted, however, if and to the extent NGOs do not claim representative status, but limit themselves to the provision of information and expertise.[56] The informality of the developing law does not render formal dispute settlement redundant, as the *Gabcikovo* case has shown. But judicial pronouncements serve rather to elucidate important principles than to achieve a concrete and detailed settlement by themselves. Negotiation by the parties remains indispensable.

---

inquiry commission procedure which is being used in one case only. The one pending dispute is not resolved in the framework of the Convention, but by direct negotiation: *ibid*. Neither has the arbitration provision contained in the CITES Convention been used so far: see Convention on International Trade in Endangered Species of Wild Fauna and Flora, Washington DC, 3 March 1973, in force 1 July 1975, 993 UNTS 243; and Reeve, chapter 6 in this volume, pp. 157–8.

[54] *Gabcikovo–Nagymaros Project (Hungary v. Slovakia)*, para. 140.
[55] *Legality of the Threat or Use of Nuclear Weapons*, ICJ Reports 1996, p. 226, paras. 27–33.
[56] See note 15 above and the accompanying text.

364 GENERAL COMMENTS

Dispute settlement in environmental matters thus constitutes not a moment, but a dynamic, a movement of negotiations and decisions which engender further negotiations and decisions. However, the one treaty with the most elaborate dispute settlement mechanism, the Montreal Protocol on Substances that Deplete the Ozone Layer,[57] seems to be the one that works most effectively. Even if this is hardly due to the dispute settlement provision – which has been accepted only by the European Communities and four of its Member States, and apparently never been used[58] – strong dispute settlement procedures at least indicate the seriousness of States in their treaty undertakings. The importance of the non-compliance procedures rather than dispute settlement is striking.

The interests protected by environmental mechanisms are mostly community interests – such as the interest not to be harmed by global warming – but they may translate into very concrete State interests. In the case of the Kyoto Protocol, one may mention the danger for certain island States of being completely submerged and destroyed in the case of a further rise in the level of the sea. In addition, in most cases, States will incur a mere *risk* of damage by a transboundary hazardous activity, not an actual damage. Thus, traditional dispute settlement will often miss a concrete claimant. The concept of so-called obligations *erga omnes*,[59] or, in a treaty setting, obligations *erga omnes partes*,[60] which would allow each and every State to demand implementation of the respective agreement and to sue other States to that end without evidence of concrete injury to themselves, has so far not been applied to environmental issues, although the International Law Commission, in its Commentaries on its Draft Articles on State Responsibility, has included

[57] Montreal Protocol on Substances that Deplete the Ozone Layer, Montreal, 16 September 1987, in force 1 January 1989, 1522 UNTS 3, 26 ILM 1550 (1987).

[58] Vienna Convention for the Protection of the Ozone Layer, Vienna, 22 March 1985, in force 22 September 1988, 1513 UNTS 293, art. 11. Only the European Communities have accepted compulsory dispute settlement by way of arbitration however, and only Finland, the Netherlands, Norway and Sweden also recognize the competence of the International Court of Justice.

[59] *Barcelona Traction, Light and Power Company Ltd* (*Belgium* v. *Spain*), ICJ Reports 1970, p. 3, paras. 33–4; but see also *ibid.*, para. 91 (requiring a concrete treaty mechanism). See also *East Timor* (*Portugal* v. *Australia*), ICJ Reports 1995, p. 90 (requiring States nevertheless to fulfil the requirement of consent to the Court's jurisdiction).

[60] For the difference, see arts. 42(11) and 48(7), in J. Crawford (ed.), *The International Law Commission's Articles on State Responsibility* (Cambridge: Cambridge University Press, 2002), pp. 259 and 277.

the protection of the environment in the list of obligations eligible for its application.[61]

For all the impact of dispute settlement on environmental questions, however, the dynamics is clearly in favour of informal mechanisms instead of judicial dispute settlement. The way States dealt with the ozone layer problem provides a perfect example. There was no real 'dispute' between States on whether one of them had violated the Protocol. Rather, problems of implementation were considered a collective issue requiring technical support, not penalties or damages.[62] One can call such an implementing mechanism non-confrontational and non-judicial, flexible, co-operative. For sure, there is peer review and considerable pressure for enforcement, but there is no authoritative third party who would 'settle' the dispute. Even more formal procedures such as in the ozone layer treaty aim at fostering compliance, not sanctioning deviant behaviour.

There are many reasons for the absence of judicial dispute settlement in environmental treaties. States are unwilling to bring charges against others when they do not directly benefit from the pronouncement and may open themselves up to counter-criticism. After all, no State can claim a clean slate on environmental issues. The facts and the issues are often complex and technical and cannot be decided by lawyers. Allocation of responsibility for harm to specific actors is difficult, if not impossible. Finally, international adjudication cannot provide States with the funds and the expertise needed to comply with environmental obligations. Problem-solving thus requires a less confrontational, more co-operative approach.

14.4 Arms control

Arms control is probably the most political of the three issues discussed in this volume. In the particular instruments under discussion here, the implementation is left to the political organs rather than to judicial dispute settlement. The 1972 Biological Weapons Convention,[63] for example, contains, in its article VI, a State complaint mechanism, but the complaints are

---

[61] Art. 48(7), in Crawford, *ibid.*, p. 277. For its potential relevance in environmental matters, see Koester, chapter 8 in this volume, pp. 187–8.

[62] See the contributions to this volume cited in note 53.

[63] Convention on the Prohibition of the Development, Production and Stockpiling of Bacteriological (Biological) and Toxin Weapons and on their Destruction, 10 April 1972, in force 26 March 1975, 1015 UNTS 163.

addressed to the UN Security Council, not to a judicial body. The 1968 Treaty on the Non-Proliferation of Nuclear Weapons (NPT) provides for the co-operation of non-nuclear-weapon States with the International Atomic Energy Agency which may refer issues of non-compliance to the UN Security Council.[64] It is oriented towards fact-finding and on-site inspection rather than to adjudication of inter-State claims,[65] aiming at future compliance rather than the righting of past wrongs. Multilateral enforcement is based on political rather than legal criteria. The most appropriate body for these issues is the political organ mandated by the UN Charter with the maintenance of international peace and security, namely, the UN Security Council.

However, this necessarily raises the question of the limits of Security Council activity. For the present commentator, both quasi-legislative and quasi-adjudicative roles of the Security Council require close scrutiny, because the Security Council is a political organ acting according to political, not legal, criteria.[66] The role of international adjudication proper is largely limited to advisory opinions requested by the relevant treaty body with the assent of the UN General Assembly, as explicitly provided for by article 14 of the Chemical Weapons Convention.[67] Nevertheless, in the *Legality of the Threat or Use of Nuclear Weapons* case, the International

[64] For action of the Security Council, see e.g. the case of North Korea, SC Res. 825 (1993), 11 May 1993, which seems to imply that the Council may prohibit withdrawal from the NPT regime against the wording of the treaty.

[65] See e.g. arts. 8 and 10 of the Convention on the Prohibition of the Use, Stockpiling, Production and Transfer of Anti-Personnel Mines and on their Destruction (Landmines Convention), Oslo, 18 September 1997, in force 1 March 1999, 2056UNTS 211, on which see Lawand, chapter 13 in this volume, pp. 337–40; and the NPT and IAEA regime of inspections and reporting to political bodies, on which see Rockwood, chapter 12 in this volume, pp. 301–23. See also art. 11 of the Geneva Protocol on Explosive Remnants of War to the Convention on Prohibitions or Restrictions on the Use of Certain Conventional Weapons which may be deemed to be Excessively Injurious or to have Indiscriminate Effects (Protocol V), 28 November 2003 (not yet in force), UN Doc. CCW/MSP/2003/2 (2003), providing for bilateral consultation and co-operation, but also for the involvement of the UN Secretary-General as a channel of co-operation.

[66] For similar criticism, see Simma, *From Bilateralism to Community Interest*, paras. 39–42 (considering judicial review of the Council); see also the recent discussion on the purported quasi-legislative functions of the Security Council, S. Talmon, 'The Security Council as World Legislature' (2005) 99 *American Journal of International Law* 175; J. A. Frowein and N. Krisch, in Simma, *Charter*, Introduction to chapter VII, marginal note 33; and A. Zimmermann and B. Elberling, 'Grenzen der Legislativbefugnisse des Sicherheitsrats' (2004) 52 *Vereinte Nationen* 71; all with further references.

[67] Convention on the Prohibition of the Development, Production, Stockpiling and Use of Chemical Weapons and on their Destruction, Geneva, 3 September 1992, in force 29 April 1997, 1974 UNTS 47.

Court of Justice had the occasion to pronounce an advisory opinion on disarmament issues on a request by the UN General Assembly.[68] But this case was not a result of a treaty mechanism.

Dealing with the core State task of international security, arms control law is almost exclusively inter-State law. Nevertheless, non-governmental organizations such as the International Association of Lawyers against Nuclear Arms have played an important role in organizing and supporting States willing to submit the nuclear weapons issue to the ICJ. Thus, States seem less to rely on judicial means to control the spread of weapons of mass destruction than non-governmental organizations. However, the lack of support by the most important States reduces the impact of such litigation. Mindful of the problematic character of its task, the ICJ was reluctant to denounce the politics of deterrence. In the end, both sides claimed to have won.[69] As a result, however, this inconclusive opinion was deprived of any real effect. No nuclear-weapon State felt compelled to change, or even to newly justify, its policies. The 'obligation to pursue in good faith and bring to a conclusion negotiations leading to nuclear disarmament in all its aspects under strict and effective international control' enunciated by the Court has not yet led to discernible results. For example, although complied with in practice, the Comprehensive Nuclear Test Ban Treaty[70] did not enter into force in spite of 135 ratifications or accessions, because China, the United States and other nuclear-weapon States are unwilling to ratify it.

Nevertheless, the lack of judicial dispute settlement is not identical with a lack of compliance. In particular, since the terrorist attacks on the United States on 11 September 2001, political pressure to prevent the proliferation of weapons of mass destruction has considerably increased. Where such strong pressure is absent, as is arguably the case with the Conventional Weapons Convention,[71] effectiveness rather depends on the vigilance of NGOs and, in particular, the ICRC, than on the availability of

---

[68] *Legality of the Threat or Use of Nuclear Weapons*, Advisory Opinion, ICJ Reports 1996, p. 226. The General Assembly may request such opinions, according to art. 96 of the Charter, 'on any legal question'.

[69] See J. B. Rhinelander *et al.*, 'Testing the Effectiveness of the International Court of Justice in the Nuclear Weapons Case' (1997) 91 *ASIL Proceedings* 1.

[70] UN Doc. A/50/1027, 10 September 1996; for the status of ratification, see Multilateral Treaties Deposited with the Secretary-General, chapter XXVI, No. 4, http://untreaty.un.org (visited 9 June 2005).

[71] Convention on Prohibitions or Restrictions on the Use of Certain Conventional Weapons which may be deemed to be Excessively Injurious or to have Indiscriminate Effect, Geneva, 10 October 1980, in force 2 December 1983, 1342 UNTS 137.

dispute settlement. States will rarely get involved except when their own interests are at stake. But there are positive examples, such as the Landmines Convention, where individual and State interests intersect, and NGOs and governments co-operate for a common goal. Collective interests will thus be served by conferences, informal mechanisms and, in particular, the involvement of humanitarian organizations, in particular the ICRC.

Since 11 September 2001, the political dynamics of the field are getting stronger, surpassing the long and arduous legal mechanisms of dispute settlement. Some are advocating a differentiation of obligations between 'rogue States' – those in danger of proliferating weapons of mass destruction – and liberal States controlled by democratic processes of a more peaceful nature.[72] However, such differentiated responsibility – which is not alien to arms control with regard to the non-proliferation regime for nuclear weapons – sidelines the legal regimes and fails to provide for the necessary incentives to join. Here lies the strength of a formalized legal regime as opposed to the arbitrariness of 'coalitions of the willing'. In the arms control regime, politics will remain more important than judicial dispute settlement. But the advisory opinion on the *Legality of the Threat or Use of Nuclear Weapons* has demonstrated the latter's relevance for enlisting a broader public to the protection of global interests.

14.5 Conclusion

The three regimes under discussion here have very different dispute settlement procedures, and they seem hardly to present a completely coherent picture. Whereas the environmental and arms control regimes may signal a trend away from traditional dispute settlement, the human rights field is characterized by an increasing formalization of the regional regimes. In other areas, from the law of the sea to diplomatic immunity, more traditional mechanisms of dispute settlement are more frequently used. Regional arrangements may also play a significant role. The general impression may be one of fragmentation – indeed, fragmentation appears

---

[72] See L. Feinstein and A.-M. Slaughter, 'A Duty to Protect', *Foreign Affairs*, January/February 2004, pp. 136 *et seq.*, at pp. 144–5. But see G. Evans, 'Uneasy Bedfellows: The Responsibility to Protect' and Feinstein and Slaughter's 'Duty to Prevent', available at www.crisisgroup.org/home/index.cfm?id=2560&l=1 (last visited 20 June 2005).

at the forefront of the attention of international lawyers today.[73] However, there are trends in more than one direction.

Two other areas of international law which are increasingly gaining importance, namely, international criminal law and international trade law, have created new dispute settlement mechanisms of a judicial or quasi-judicial character. They exemplify the need for special regimes – not necessary self-contained regimes[74] – for dealing with issues going beyond inter-State relations. The WTO dispute settlement system and international criminal bodies, from the Security Council-mandated tribunals via 'hybrid' tribunals to the International Criminal Court, have been particularly impressive in this regard.[75] In addition, much of international law is adjudicated by domestic courts – in particular those rules of international law that are of a self-executing character within the internal legal order. In addition, regional courts such as the European Court of Justice also play an increasing role.

However, mechanisms of general international law continue to enjoy a residual function. We always look at special regimes and tend to forget that many States are either not a member of an adjudicatory mechanism or even of no special treaty at all. Here, the United Nations provides a fall-back position to address disputes in diplomatic ways or, in extreme cases, by the sanctioning mechanisms of the Security Council, which plays an important role not only in the implementation of arms control treaties. The reaction to violations of international law cannot be limited to courts, domestic or international. In many cases, it may also comprise non-formal instances such as non-governmental organizations or the public opinion in general that may exert pressure on governments to comply with international legal rules and standards.

---

[73] See ILC, *Fragmentation of International Law: Difficulties Arising from the Diversification and Expansion of International Law*, Report of the International Law Commission on its 56th Session, GAOR, 59th Sess., Supp. No. 10 (A/59/10 (2004)), pp. 281–304, paras. 296–358; M. Koskenniemi and P. Leino, 'Fragmentation of International Law? Postmodern Anxieties' (2002) 15 *Leiden Journal of International Law* 553; see also the contributions to the 'Symposium on Diversity or Cacophony? New Sources of Norms in International Law' (2004) 25 *Michigan Journal of International Law* 845–1375. For an argument for unity rather than fragmentation, see P.-M. Dupuy, 'L'unité de l'ordre juridique international: Cours général de droit international public (2000)' (2002) 297 *Recueil des Cours* 207–489.

[74] On self-contained regimes, see the ground-breaking article by B. Simma, 'Self-Contained Regimes' (1985) 16 *Netherlands Yearbook of International Law* 111.

[75] For a general overview of the criminal tribunals, see A. Paulus, in Simma, *Charter*, art. 29, marginal notes 61–86; for a critical overview of WTO dispute settlement, see P. C. Mavroidis, 'Remedies in the WTO Legal System: Between a Rock and a Hard Place' (2000) 11 *European Journal of International Law* 763.

Nevertheless, the international legal regime is still lacking a true advocate of the general interest. As to obligations *erga omnes* as a means of bringing cases of a general character before international adjudicatory bodies, the theoretical input has not been matched by real practical relevance. No court or tribunal has yet admitted a complaint by a 'non-injured' State (or rather a State injured only in its general interest to uphold the law) based on the *erga omnes* nature of the claim. Two reasons exist for this reluctance. First, States rarely, if ever, lodge such a complaint. The extension of standing thus shares the fate of the inter-State complaint in human rights treaties.[76] Global vigilantism would also have its pitfalls. Secondly, tribunals are reluctant to assume jurisdiction when this may endanger their 'customer base', so to speak, by encouraging new reservations to the submission of States to compulsory jurisdiction. Some potential may lie in the greater use of (quasi-)judicial bodies for advisory rulings of a non-binding nature. The general character of such opinions may help to define the obligations stemming from general provisions of treaties, without necessarily dubbing one State the 'evildoer'.

Considerable potential lies in a greater input of non-governmental organizations. Their influence on contemporary multilateral treaty-making can hardly be overstated, and the same is probably true for compliance in all areas under discussion here. However, their participation in dispute settlement is minuscule. It is not so much the self-appointed representation of public interests, but rather NGO expertise which qualifies them for some sort of participation in questions of dispute settlement, in particular by the provision of information which may serve as a check on the evidence provided by States. Understandably, however, the will of States to permit such involvement is modest, the *Asbestos* case in WTO dispute settlement[77] constituting only the most prominent example. On the other hand, small States may depend on support from NGOs to be able to participate in dispute settlement mechanisms. An emphasis on information rather than formal participation may provide an avenue for both States and international dispute settlement bodies to overcome considerations of sovereignty and legitimacy.[78]

---

[76] See Scheinin, chapter 2 in this volume.

[77] See, in particular, *European Communities – Measures Affecting Asbestos-Containing Products*, Report of the Appellate Body, WT/DS135/AB/R, 12 March 2001, paras. 50–7.

[78] For an argument for a larger role of NGOs in advisory proceedings, see A. Paulus, in Zimmermann, Tomuschat and Oellers-Frahm, *Statute of the International Court of Justice*, art. 29, marginal note 30.

In addition, one should not disregard rarely used clauses authorizing the International Court of Justice or another dispute settlement mechanism to adjudicate the interpretation and application of a treaty. Dispute settlement provisions are often dormant for quite some time before they are used. As an example, to the surprise of many, Paraguay, and then Germany and Mexico, used the optional protocol to the Vienna Convention on Consular Relations to bring the violation of the right to consular information by the United States before the ICJ.[79]

Thus, the examples chosen here should not lead us to overestimate informality. Nevertheless, we should also ask why, at least in some issue areas, judicial dispute settlement is unpopular with States. Third party dispute settlement may be regarded as too confrontational, emphasizing the discord of States rather than their willingness to compromise. Dispute settlement goes much more deeply against sovereignty than the acceptance of obligations without compliance control. The very public nature of international dispute settlement may also contribute to deter States from submitting to it. Finally, States sometimes know quite well that their behaviour is unlawful, and try to elude judicial condemnation by limiting their exposure to international courts and tribunals as far as possible.[80]

But there also exist considerable advantages to formal dispute settlement. Dispute settlement may actually resolve a dispute according to legal, not political, criteria. Traditional dispute settlement results in binding pronouncements that may lead to damages. Binding dispute settlement will contribute to convincing domestic courts to implement international obligations. Many of those advantages may turn into disadvantages, however, preventing risk-averse States from engaging in legal relationships altogether. Soft implementation may help by providing low-key solutions instead of open political confrontation.

The respective tasks of (quasi-)judicial and of political organs for dispute settlement and the relationship of judicial and political forms, as well as their respective legal and political limits, needs further research. It seems not to be sufficient to simply exclude 'political' means from the

---

[79] See *Vienna Convention on Consular Relations* (*Paraguay* v. *US*), Order on Provisional Measures, ICJ Reports 1998, p. 248; and the cases cited in note 13 above.

[80] See e.g. the case of *Spain* v. *Canada* and the limitation of the Canadian submission, ICJ Reports 1998, p. 432; or the recent limitation of the Australian submission, see Multilateral Treaties Deposited with the Secretary-General, chapter I, No. 4, available at http://untreaty.un.org (visited 20 June 2005). In both cases, however, a settlement has finally been reached that more or less protects the legitimate interest of the other side.

purview of legal analysis. And it may ultimately hurt our main purpose, namely, the better implementation of legal obligations. As pointed out by Professors Delbrück and Zimmermann,[81] the central task consists in keeping the political process within the law and making extra-treaty dispute settlement activity useful for and not disruptive of treaty implementation.

The role of the Security Council in this process seems to be both legal and political. I would be hesitant to regard the Security Council itself as a dispute settlement body in the full legal sense, but I also believe that a clear separation of the conventions as 'legal' and the Security Council as 'political' is impossible – and indeed would let the Security Council entirely off the hook regarding respect for existing international law.[82] The Security Council may indeed contribute to a legal assessment of State compliance with international obligations. Both North Korea and Iraq come to mind.[83] However, the Security Council itself should become subject to a judicial or quasi-judicial assessment. The *Lockerbie* case strongly suggests that existing legal mechanisms are not sufficient to allow targeted States – and even less so individuals and business – to defend themselves against accusations of wrongdoing emanating from the Security Council (and some of its members).[84]

For the time being, in the environmental field, but also in arms control, co-operative approaches will dominate over traditional judicial dispute settlement. They should not be regarded as illegitimate competitors, but rather as necessary complements to international adjudication. On the other hand, the trend to informality should not blind us to the advantages of formal judicial dispute settlement and adjudication of international rights and duties, both State and individual.

---

[81] In the discussion at the symposium resulting in this volume.

[82] For a thorough and critical discussion, see e.g. Frowein and Krisch, in Simma, *Charter*, Introduction to chapter VII, marginal notes 25–31.

[83] See note 64 above (North Korea 1993), and SC Res. 687, 3 April 1991 (Iraq, 1991 *et seq.*).

[84] See *Questions of Interpretation and Application of the 1971 Montreal Convention arising from the Aerial Incident at Lockerbie* (*Libya* v. *UK*; *Libya* v. *US*), Provisional Measures, 14 April 1992, ICJ Reports 1992, pp. 3, 114, where the ICJ failed to rule on the legality *vel non* of the respective Security Council resolutions on the matter. I do not mean to say that the Council was at fault here. The point is that there was no third party legal mechanism in place that would protect affected parties. For a comprehensive presentation of the problematic, see E. de Wet and A. Nollkaemper (eds.), *Review of the Security Council by Member States* (Antwerp: Intersentia, 2003).

15

Compliance control

JUTTA BRUNNÉE

In their highly influential 1995 book on *The New Sovereignty*, Abram Chayes and Antonia Handler Chayes argue for a 'co-operative, problem-solving approach' to compliance with international regulatory agreements.[1] Drawing upon examples from the areas of human rights, environmental protection and arms control, Chayes and Chayes assert that States generally enter into commitments with an intention to comply and that non-compliance more often results from norm ambiguities or capacity limitations than from deliberate disregard.[2] Therefore, apart from the fact that 'sanctioning authority is rarely granted by treaty, rarely used when granted', sanctions are 'likely to be ineffective when used'.[3] Compliance strategies should focus instead on the actual causes of non-compliance and 'manage' these through positive means, consisting in a blend of transparency (regarding both the regime's requirements and procedures and the parties' performance), dispute settlement and capacity-building.[4] The main engine of this 'managerial' approach is continuous processes of argument and persuasion, 'justificatory discourse' that ultimately 'jawbones' States into compliance.[5]

As it turns out, the active treaty management that Chayes and Chayes advocate has indeed established itself as central to compliance strategies in the three areas. While there is considerable variation in the precise configuration of compliance control approaches, strong managerial elements can be found in the practice of virtually all the treaties examined in this book. Focusing upon reporting requirements, monitoring and assessment of compliance, the role of compliance bodies, and the range of outcomes of compliance procedures, this essay will sketch out the contours of treaty management in the three areas. It will highlight the key features of the

---

[1] Abram Chayes and Antonia Handler Chayes, *The New Sovereignty: Compliance with International Regulatory Agreements* (Cambridge, MA: Harvard University Press, 1995), p. 3.
[2] *Ibid.*, pp. 10–15.   [3] *Ibid.*, pp. 32–3.   [4] *Ibid.*, pp. 22–5.   [5] *Ibid.*, pp. 25–6.

374   GENERAL COMMENTS

compliance control strategies employed in the regimes under review,[6] and identify the main commonalities and differences among these strategies.

15.1 Reporting

In all three areas, compliance control is anchored in extensive reporting requirements. These can pertain to implementation measures, such as legislative or administrative steps, or to indicators of performance towards a specified outcome, such as emissions or weapons data. The latter type of reporting requirements would appear to be more common in the environmental and arms control areas.[7]

Reporting plays at least two important roles in the context of compliance control. First, the reported information enhances transparency and trust as to parties' performance, an effect that is reinforced by the publication of the reports among parties, or their release to the general public. However, in many treaties today, reporting serves a second crucial function, providing the foundation for compliance assessment processes within the regime.[8]

For both functions it is essential that parties' reports be complete, reliable and comparable.[9] The significance of rigorous reporting in all three areas is illustrated by the progressive standardization and refinement of reporting requirements under most regimes reviewed in this volume. Under some of the treaties, decisions of the plenary body flesh out the basic requirements enshrined in the treaty itself.[10] In other cases, the treaty body

---

[6] Where relevant, reference will also be made to treaty regimes other than those covered in this book.

[7] For example, under the Convention on Long-Range Transboundary Air Pollution (LRTAP Convention), parties report both on strategies and policies to reduce emissions and on emissions data. See Kuokkanen, chapter 7 in this volume, section 7.3.2. Under the Convention on International Trade in Endangered Species (CITES), parties submit annual reports on trade and biennial reports on legislative or administrative implementing measures. See Reeve, chapter 6 in this volume, section 6.2.2.1. Under the Chemical Weapons Convention (CWC), parties must report both on weapons stocks, production facilities and destruction measures, and on the adoption of implementing legislation. See Tabassi, chapter 11 in this volume, section 11.3.1.

[8] For a detailed review in the environmental context, see Kal Raustiala, *Reporting and Review Institutions in 10 Multilateral Environmental Agreements* (Nairobi: UNEP, 2001), p. 11 (available at www.unep.org/GEO/techreports.htm).

[9] Note the very differently structured reporting system under the European Convention on the Prevention of Torture (CPT). Rather than by States parties, reports are prepared by a treaty committee on the basis of country visits. These reports then serve as the basis for 'constructive dialogue' with the party concerned. See Kicker, chapter 4 in this volume, section 4.1.1.1.

[10] In the environmental area, see e.g. Decision 1/8 on Reporting Requirements (2002) under the Aarhus Convention. See Koester, chapter 8 in this volume, section 8.4.1; Resolution Conf.11.17

entrusted with the review of parties' reports elaborates on existing requirements through its operating procedures or through its communications with the party concerned.[11] In all three areas, the relevant requirements thus tend to be developed as a matter of evolving practice under a regime. The process is consensual and typically operates without recourse to formal treaty amendments.

In view of the fact that treaty regimes in all three areas have experienced, and continue to experience, shortfalls in parties' reporting practice,[12] one might ask how compliance with reporting requirements themselves is promoted. A degree of pressure results from the publication not just of reported information as such, but also of information on the extent to which parties meet reporting requirements. This transparency exposes parties to peer pressure and, to the extent that parties place a premium on being seen as trustworthy, it may in itself induce compliance. However, given the foundational importance of reporting for all efforts at compliance control, most regimes today provide for additional steps to ensure that comprehensive and reliable information is provided by parties. Reference was already made to the progressive refinement of reporting requirements. Further, under many treaties, parties with capacity problems receive assistance designed to enable them to meet reporting requirements.[13] In

---

(rev. CoP13) on 'National Reports' (2004) under CITES; and Reeve, chapter 6 in this volume, section 6.2.2.1. In the arms control area, see e.g. the standard formats and reporting guidelines adopted at the first meeting of the parties to the Landmines Treaty. See Lawand, chapter 13 in this volume, section 13.3.1.2.

[11] In the human rights area, see e.g. ICCPR, Consolidated Guidelines for State Reports under the International Covenant on Civil and Political Rights, CCPR/C/66/GUI/Rev.2 (26 February 2001); CEDAW, 'Compilation of Guidelines on the Form and Content of Reports to Be Submitted by States Parties to the International Human Rights Treaties', UN Doc. HRI/GEN/2/Rev.1/Add.2 (5 May 2003). In the arms control area, see e.g. the standard operating procedures for verification processes developed by the Secretariat under the CWC, in Tabassi, chapter 11 in this volume, section 11.3.2.

[12] In the human rights area, see e.g. ICCPR, 'Overview of the Working Methods of the Human Rights Committee', para. V (available at www.ohchr.org/english/bodies/hrc/workingmethods.htm); CEDAW, 'Overview of the Current Working Methods of the Committee on the Elimination of Discrimination Against Women', para. 27 (available at www.un.org/womenwatch/daw/cedaw/wk-methods/Overview-English.pdf). On reporting problems under multilateral environmental agreements, see Raustiala, *Reporting and Review Institutions*, pp. 10 and 63. In the arms control area, see e.g. Tabassi, chapter 11 in this volume, section 11.4.2, noting that, as of October 2005, only 60 per cent of parties to the CWC had met reporting requirements regarding legislative and administrative implementing measures.

[13] See e.g. CEDAW, 'Overview of the Current Working Methods', where 'United Nations and other entities are encouraged to provide technical assistance to States parties' with significant reporting problems.

376 GENERAL COMMENTS

addition, in cases of persistent non-compliance, various practices have evolved to exert pressure on parties,[14] or even for parties to lose access to certain treaty-based benefits or privileges.[15]

15.2 Monitoring and assessment of compliance

15.2.1 Reporting

At least in the environmental field, reporting (and subsequent publication) of performance-related information by parties was the primary tool for compliance monitoring in many earlier treaties.[16] Only in the early 1990s, with the creation of a compliance regime under the Montreal Protocol on Substances that Deplete the Ozone Layer, was there a significant shift in the practice of multilateral environmental agreements (MEAs) towards more active compliance assessment.[17]

15.2.2 Implementation review

Under some treaties, the reported information is utilized for reviews of overall implementation patterns. Such surveys are prepared, for example, under the Montreal Protocol or the Convention on Long-Range Transboundary Air Pollution (LRTAP Convention), where they can assist in determining the overall success of the regime.[18] In both the

---

[14] Under the LRTAP Convention, the Implementation Committee applies gradual pressure on States that fail to report. See Kuokkanen, chapter 7 in this volume, section 7.3.2. Under CITES, parties that persistently fail to submit annual reports receive warnings and may be subject to recommendations for trade suspensions. See Reeve, chapter 6 in this volume, section 6.3. Under the ICCPR, the Human Rights Committee may decide to schedule a session during which the implementation performance of a party is examined, notwithstanding its failure to submit a report. See ICCPR, 'Working Methods of the Human Rights Committee'.

[15] For example, under the Montreal Protocol, developing country parties or parties with economies in transition may not be eligible for grace periods in implementation requirements or for financial assistance unless they meet specified reporting requirements. See Raustiala, *Reporting and Review Institutions*, pp. 34 and 37. Similarly, under the Kyoto Protocol, parties' eligibility for participation in international emissions trading will be contingent upon compliance with emissions monitoring and reporting requirements. See Jutta Brunnée, 'The Kyoto Protocol: Testing Ground for Compliance Theories' (2003) 63 *Zeitschrift für ausländisches öffentliches Recht und Völkerrecht* 255 and 271.

[16] A notable exception is the extensive compliance control practice that developed early on under the 1973 CITES.   [17] See Brunnée, 'The Kyoto Protocol', p. 262.

[18] On the Montreal Protocol, see Raustiala, *Reporting and Review Institutions*, pp. 25 and 34. On the LRTAP Convention, see Kuokkanen, chapter 7 in this volume, section 7.3.4, commenting on in-depth reviews.

environmental and the arms control fields, performance assessment tends to focus on implementing measures as well as compliance with substantive commitments.[19]

In the human rights field, where compliance with treaty commitments and implementation through various governmental measures are closely connected, implementation review is a central compliance control technique. For example, under the International Covenant on Civil and Political Rights (ICCPR) or the Convention on the Elimination of All Forms of Discrimination Against Women (CEDAW), parties must report on legislative, judicial and administrative measures adopted to implement the convention. The respective treaty bodies, the Human Rights Committee for the ICCPR and the Committee for the Elimination of Discrimination Against Women for CEDAW, will then engage individual parties in 'constructive dialogue' regarding their performance.[20] While these processes serve similar functions as compliance assessments, and proceed in comparable fashion, they do not make explicit determinations regarding a party's compliance with treaty commitments. For example, under the ICCPR, the dialogue with a party about its report leads to 'concluding observations', in which the Human Rights Committee highlights positive aspects of the party's implementation efforts, flags subjects of concerns, and offers recommendations for improved performance.[21]

15.2.3 Compliance assessment and control

In the environmental and arms control areas, performance reviews appear to be more explicitly cast as compliance assessment. Careful analysis of party reports is usually the first step in this process. Frequently, efforts are made to de-politicize these initial analyses by stressing their technical focus and placing them in the hands of neutral or expert bodies. However, in many cases, they do provide the basis for compliance assessment by a designated treaty body or the treaty's plenary body. For example, the Kyoto Protocol to the Climate Change Convention provides for expert review teams to scrutinize parties' reports and to raise 'questions of implementation', which can

---

[19] See note 7 above.

[20] See ICCPR, 'Working Methods of the Human Rights Committee'. And see CEDAW, 'Overview of the Current Working Methods'.

[21] See ICCPR, 'Working Methods of the Human Rights Committee'. A similar process takes place under CEDAW.

then trigger a compliance assessment by the treaty's compliance commit-tee.[22] The compliance procedure, in turn, specifically provides that the tasks of this committee will include 'determining whether a Party . . . is not in compliance' with emission reduction and related inventory and reporting commitments.[23] Under the Convention on International Trade in Endangered Species (CITES), the treaty Secretariat reviews the reports submitted by parties, identifies implementation problems and makes recom-mendations to a Standing Committee of the treaty's plenary body. This com-mittee then makes suitable determinations and recommendations.[24] Under the Chemical Weapons Convention (CWC), the Secretariat acts as an impar-tial fact-finder and identifies potential compliance problems. But it is the treaty's Executive Council that ultimately considers 'doubts or concerns regarding compliance and cases of non-compliance'.[25]

15.2.4 Inspections

A final tool for compliance monitoring and assessment consists in various types of inspections undertaken in the territories of individual parties. Such in-country inspections are the exception in the environmental field.[26] Environmental agreements tend to be preoccupied with the transboundary implications of a State's performance, leaving the details of how to meet commitments to the discretion of the party. In addition, to the extent that the sources of emissions or other types of pollution are highly diffuse, inspections would be difficult if not impossible.[27]

By contrast, human rights treaties are concerned precisely with the specifics of domestic performance and compliance that may be difficult to

---

[22] See art. 7 of the Kyoto Protocol. And see Brunnée, 'The Kyoto Protocol', p. 272.

[23] UNFCCC, Procedures and Mechanisms on Compliance under the Kyoto Protocol, FCCC/KP/CMP/2005/8/Add.3, Decision 27/CMP.1, para. V.4.

[24] See Reeve, chapter 6 in this volume, section 6.2.3.1.

[25] See art. VIII(36) of the CWC; and Tabassi, chapter 11 in this volume, section 11.3.4.

[26] Of the environmental agreements reviewed in this volume, only CITES appears to have an actual inspection practice. The CITES Secretariat undertakes at least a limited number of *ad hoc* country visits to investigate compliance problems: see Reeve, chapter 6 in this volume, section 6.2.3.3. The compliance mechanism of the LRTAP Convention contemplates country visits, but only at the invitation of the party concerned. See UN Doc. ECE/EB/AIR/79, Annex V(6)(c). A similar arrangement exists under the Espoo Convention: see Koivurova, chapter 9 in this volume, section 9.2.2.

[27] But note that there are exceptions. For example, the 'in-depth reviews' of national implementa-tion of the UNFCCC involves country visits by expert review teams. See Raustiala, *Reporting and Review Institutions*, pp. 43–4.

verify without country visits. Nonetheless, due to the sensitivity of direct scrutiny of a country's actions, inspection systems remain rare in the human rights field as well. Under the Convention Against Torture and Other Cruel, Inhuman or Degrading Treatment or Punishment (the 'Convention Against Torture'), an Optional Protocol that would permit in-country inspections of places of detention was adopted in 2002, but has not entered into force.[28] The European Convention for the Prevention of Torture, however, does have an active system of country visits.[29] The Convention attempts to strike a balance between the sensitivity of inspections and their importance as a compliance tool by casting the goals of the 'visits' as preventative. Thus, country visits are not intended to inquire into a State's compliance or non-compliance, but aim to create an opening for the development of recommendations and an ongoing dialogue towards progressive improvement of conditions in the country.[30]

It is in the arms control area that inspection systems are most common. The old adage of 'trust but verify' encapsulates the importance of inspection regimes to the mutual reassurance that is crucial to the strategic considerations underlying arms control agreements. Accordingly, all of the arms control treaties surveyed in this volume provide for inspections, although there appear to be significant differences in the degree to which inspections are actually carried out.[31] The most extensive inspection practice would seem to have evolved under the Conventional Forces in Europe (CFE) treaty, which may be all the more remarkable in view of the fact that the inspections in one State party are actually carried out by another. According to one expert, around 200 intrusive and largely unhampered on-site inspections are undertaken by the parties every year, providing accurate and reliable information on the performance of parties under the treaty.[32]

---

[28] To date, the protocol has received only eight of the twenty ratifications required for its entry into force. See www.ohchr.org/english/countries/ratification/9_b.htm.

[29] As of May 2005, the Convention has seen 193 country visits, including 123 periodic visits and 70 *ad hoc* visits. See www.cpt.coe.int/en/about.htm.

[30] See Kicker, chapter 4 in this volume, sections 4.1.1.1 and 4.1.1.4.

[31] Inspections are carried out under the Non-Proliferation Treaty (NPT): see Rockwood, chapter 12 in this volume, sections 12.2 and 12.4.2. Under the CWC, the Secretariat carries out routine inspections: see Tabassi, chapter 11 in this volume, section 11.3.2. To date, no party has initiated a 'challenge inspection': see *ibid.*, section 11.3.4. Under the Landmines Treaty, the compliance procedure, which would entail fact-finding missions, remains untested: see Lawand, chapter 13 in this volume, section 13.3.1.3.

[32] Presentation by Wolfgang Richter, Senior Military Adviser, German Mission to the Organization of Security and Co-operation in Europe, Kiel, 22 January 2005 (notes on file with the author).

15.3 Compliance bodies

15.3.1 Mandate

In very general terms, it can be said that the various types of compliance bodies operating within human rights, environmental and arms control agreements are mandated to establish facts, facilitate compliance, and assess performance. However, within this spectrum of tasks, a considerable variety of approaches can be found.

In the context of fact-finding, the mandates of MEA compliance bodies are noteworthy in that they explicitly encompass identification and consideration of the causes of compliance problems.[33] Similarly, while technical or other assistance appears to be provided to parties with compliance problems in all three areas,[34] the mandates of MEA compliance bodies tend to specifically include assistance functions. Indeed, MEA-based compliance bodies are in the business of 'co-operative problem-solving' as much as in the business of compliance control, and MEA compliance procedures are usually cast as facilitative exercises.[35] Of course, whether specifically mandated or not, facilitative rather than adversarial approaches are also common in the practice under human rights and arms control treaties.[36]

When it comes to the tasks of assessing parties' performance, compliance bodies must typically tread lightly. As previously noted, in the human

---

[33] See e.g. UNEP, Report of the Tenth Meeting of the Parties to the Montreal Protocol on Substances that Deplete the Ozone Layer, Annex II: Non-Compliance Procedure, UNEP Doc. OzL.Pro.10/9, 3 December 1998, para. 7(d).

[34] For example, the Landmines Treaty envisages that parties in a position to do so provide assistance to non-complying parties: see Lawand, chapter 13 in this volume, section 13.2.

[35] See Jutta Brunnée, 'Enforcement Mechanisms in International Law and International Environmental Law', in Ulrich Beyerlin, Peter-Tobias Stoll and Rüdiger Wolfrum (eds), *Ensuring Compliance with Multilateral Environmental Agreements: A Dialogue Between Practitioners and Academia* (Leiden: Brill Academic Publishers, 2006), p. 18. To date, the compliance procedure under the Kyoto Protocol is the exception in that its mandate is to 'facilitate, promote and *enforce* compliance' (emphasis added); see UNFCCC, Procedures and Mechanisms on Compliance, para. I.

[36] See for example ICCPR, 'Working Methods of the Human Rights Committee' and CEDAW, 'Overview of the Current Working Methods' on the 'constructive dialogue' to promote implementation of the ICCPR and CEDAW. In some cases, financial assistance appears to be provided to CPT parties: see Kicker, chapter 4 in this volume, section 4.5. See also note 34 above on the Landmines Treaty. Under the CWC, parties are encouraged to assist each other in implementing their commitments, and an Action Plan was adopted in this context: see Tabassi, chapter 11 in this volume, section 11.4.2. Under the CFE Treaty, technical and financial assistance seems to be provided only rarely: see Presentation by Wolfgang Richter (note 32 above).

rights field, the conclusions drawn by the treaty committees do not explicitly focus on compliance with treaty commitments but on the implementation efforts of parties. In the environmental field, while the relevant treaty bodies do focus on compliance, they normally do not make final determinations. As in the arms control field, while their conclusions may amount *de facto* to findings of non-compliance, MEA compliance body mandates are usually limited to recommendations to the treaty's plenary body.[37] The blending of pragmatic, political and quasi-judicial features that is typical for the mandates of MEA compliance bodies is nicely captured in the Montreal Protocol compliance procedure, which is aimed at 'securing an amicable solution . . . on the basis of respect for the provisions of the Protocol'.[38]

15.3.2 Composition

In keeping with the different tasks undertaken by compliance bodies, and the different combinations of such tasks, the bodies entrusted with compliance-related mandates also display some variation. Indeed, a variety of treaty institutions may discharge compliance-control-related tasks, including both bodies with general tasks and bodies specifically established as compliance bodies.

As to treaty bodies with general tasks, in most regimes, treaty secretariats are in one way or another involved in compliance matters. In human rights regimes, the role of the secretariat is usually limited to neutral, technical tasks (e.g. receipt and forwarding of party reports; convening and assisting of meetings).[39] The same is true for certain MEA secretariats,[40] while others

---

[37] In the arms control area, see e.g. the CWC, where compliance assessments are left to the Council (see Tabassi, chapter 11 in this volume, section 11.3.3), or the NPT, where conclusions concerning non-compliance are drawn by the Board (see Rockwood, chapter 12 in this volume, section 12.6). In the environmental field, see e.g. the LRTAP Convention, where the Implementation Committee submits recommendations to the Executive Body (see Kuokkanen, chapter 7 in this volume, section 7.3.1), or the Aarhus Convention, where the Compliance Committee makes recommendations to the Conference of the Parties (see Koester, chapter 8 in this volume, section 8.6.5). An exceptional case is the Compliance Committee to be established under the Kyoto Protocol's compliance procedure: its enforcement branch will both make determinations of compliance and apply relevant consequences. See UNFCCC, Procedures and Mechanisms on Compliance, paras. V.4–V.6.

[38] UNEP, Montreal Protocol Non-Compliance Procedure, para. 8.

[39] See e.g. ICCPR, 'Working Methods of the Human Rights Committee', para. V.

[40] See e.g. Koivurova, chapter 9 in this volume, section 9.2.2.

382 GENERAL COMMENTS

may refer cases involving individual parties for compliance assessment.[41] The particularly active role of the CITES Secretariat in the review of national reports and identification of implementation problems is unusual in the environmental field.[42] An active role is also played by the Secretariat under the CWC, including even in-country inspections.[43]

In the environmental and arms control areas,[44] the plenary bodies of treaties too usually discharge some compliance-related functions. Indeed, these political bodies normally retain ultimate control over compliance matters. Upon the recommendation of the relevant treaty body, the COP or other plenary body reviews compliance assessments, makes determinations of non-compliance and adopts decisions on suitable responses.[45]

For present purposes, the creation of specific compliance control bodies may be the most significant institutional distinction between MEAs and treaties in the other two areas. To be sure, human rights treaties too can be said to have designated compliance bodies. However, as noted earlier, the work of these treaty committees tends to be cast as implementation review rather than as explicit compliance control.[46] Of course, whether a treaty body engages in constructive dialogue about implementation issues or engages in co-operative solving of compliance problems may at times be a fine distinction to draw. In any case, most MEAs now contemplate a designated compliance body operating alongside other treaty bodies.[47] This fact may account in part for the relatively more limited, technical role that MEA secretariats play in compliance control matters. It may also account for the sensitive nature of questions relating to the composition of MEA compliance bodies. Unlike the human rights treaty committees,[48] they tend to be composed of party delegates (usually representing a mix of geographical

[41] See notes 59–62 below and the accompanying text.
[42] Even more unusual is the fact that the CITES Secretariat contracts some of the assessment work out to NGOs: see Reeve, chapter 6 in this volume, section 6.2.2.1.
[43] See note 31 above.
[44] Human rights treaties, such as the ICCPR, the Convention Against Torture or CEDAW, do not have plenary bodies that would be comparable to those of MEAs or of the arms control agreements reviewed in this volume. [45] See note 37 above.
[46] See ICCPR, 'Working Methods of the Human Rights Committee'. And see CEDAW, 'Overview of the Current Working Methods'. See also the text accompanying notes 20–1 above.
[47] Brunnée, 'Enforcement Mechanisms in International Law'.
[48] The ICCPR's Human Rights Committee is a representative example, being composed of '18 independent experts who are persons of high moral character and recognized competence in the field of human rights'. See www.ohchr.org/english/bodies/hrc/members.htm.

backgrounds, and of legal, technical and diplomatic expertise) rather than independent experts.[49] Given the blend of political and legal considerations that characterizes compliance assessment, MEA parties appear to be more comfortable with peer review processes than reviews by expert bodies, notwithstanding the fact that final decision-making is generally left to the treaty's plenary body.[50]

If the creation of specific compliance bodies is the rule rather than the exception in MEAs today, it should be noted that this fact represents a remarkable shift over a relatively short period of time. The non-compliance procedure of the Montreal Protocol, adopted in 1992, is generally seen as marking the turning point in MEA design in this respect.[51] The relatively recent vintage of the MEA compliance body phenomenon may explain in part why the compliance machinery of CITES does not fit the emerging MEA pattern. Under CITES, compliance-related tasks are shared between treaty bodies with general mandates – the Secretariat and a Standing Committee of the COP.[52]

15.3.3 Triggers: standing to raise compliance issues

15.3.3.1 States parties

MEAs usually allow parties both to raise concerns about the compliance of other parties and to bring themselves before the compliance body when they are experiencing compliance problems.[53] The latter possibility must be understood against the backdrop of the collective action problems that MEAs typically address. As a result, the primary objective of compliance regimes is not to lay the blame for violations of treaty commitments but to achieve the greatest possible degree of compliance by the largest possible number of treaty parties. The self-triggering option is in line with the pragmatic emphasis of MEA compliance regimes on facilitation and collective problem-solving, especially when it comes to parties that experience

---

[49] The compliance body under the Aarhus Convention is the exception, as its members serve in a personal capacity. Perhaps even more unusual is the fact that expert members can be drawn from States that have only signed and not ratified the Convention: see Koester, chapter 8 in this volume, section 8.5.3.1.   [50] See note 37 above.

[51] Brunnée, 'The Kyoto Protocol', pp. 262–5.

[52] See Reeve, chapter 6 in this volume, section 6.2.3.1.

[53] See e.g. UNEP, Montreal Protocol Non-Compliance Procedure, paras. 1 and 4. And see the compliance mechanisms of the LRTAP Convention (Kuokkanen, chapter 7 in this volume, section 7.3.1) and the Aarhus Convention (Koester, chapter 8 in this volume, section 8.5.3.2).

384 GENERAL COMMENTS

capacity limitations. Indeed, in the practice of MEA compliance procedures to date, procedures have been initiated by States parties primarily
with respect to their own performance.[54] The dearth of complaints about
other parties' performance, in turn, is in keeping with the general desire to
conduct compliance proceedings in a co-operative rather than adversarial
manner. The pattern is hardly surprising, given that the formal party-to-
party dispute settlement processes provided for in most MEAs have also
remained unused.[55]

In the human rights and arms control areas, there does not appear to be
any comparable practice of parties triggering compliance proceedings
regarding their own performance. Arguably, this fact is rooted in the nature
and sensitivity of the commitments in each of these areas. One might also
expect that there would be no instances of States initiating compliance
control processes with respect to other parties. This expectation appears to
be borne out in the human rights field, where available inter-State complaint options remain unutilized, for example, under the ICCPR, CEDAW
or the Convention Against Torture.[56] Under the European Convention on
Human Rights, there have been some inter-State complaints, but they have
remained rare. While party complaints also seem to be relatively rare in the
arms control field,[57] there is one striking exception. Under the CFE treaty,

[54] See e.g. Raustiala, *Reporting and Review Institutions*, p. 36, on the practice under the Montreal
Protocol.

[55] There appear to be only three exceptions, one relating to compliance assessment, the others to
dispute settlement. First, in 1985, several Latin American countries raised the issue of Bolivia's
non-compliance with CITES obligations. See Reeve, chapter 6 in this volume, section 6.2.3.1.
Secondly, Ireland triggered the OSPAR Convention's dispute settlement procedure in the
context of its differences with the United Kingdom in relation to British nuclear installations on
the Irish Sea coast. See *Dispute Concerning Access to Information under Article 9 of the OSPAR
Convention (Ireland v. United Kingdom of Britain and Northern Ireland)*, Permanent Court of
Arbitration, 2 July 2003 (available at www.pca-cpa.org). Thirdly, Poland relied on the Espoo
Convention's dispute settlement procedure to request that Germany begin negotiations regarding management of the River Oder. However, Germany does not appear to consider the negotiations to be a matter of dispute settlement under the Espoo Convention. See Koivurova, chapter
9 in this volume, section 9.1.1.

[56] See Office of the United Nations High Commissioner for Human Rights (OHCHR), 'Human
Rights Bodies – Complaints Procedures' (available at www.ohchr.org/english/bodies/peti-
tions/index.htm). Under the European Convention on Human Rights, there have been some
inter-State complaints, but they have remained rare. There have been twelve such complaints
since the Convention's adoption in 1950: see Villiger, chapter 3 in this volume, section 3.2.4.
However, as this complaints process is a form of judicial dispute settlement, it is not further
reviewed in the present discussion.

[57] The CWC permits parties to raise concerns about other parties' performance and to seek short-
notice 'challenge inspections' of other parties' facilities. No challenge inspection has been

parties regularly request and even conduct inspections of other parties' operations.[58]

15.3.3.2 Treaty secretariats

Within MEAs, given the reluctance of States to complain about other parties' performance, treaty secretariats might be expected to play a significant role. Indeed, many MEA compliance procedures do provide for a secretariat trigger.[59] However, MEA secretariats exercise these triggering options to varying degrees. As previously noted, under some agreements, parties appear to prefer a neutral, largely technical role for the treaty secretariat.[60] By contrast, in the practice of the two longest-standing MEA compliance procedures, those under the Montreal Protocol and the LRTAP Convention, the secretariat trigger appears to have become well established.[61] The CITES secretariat is an atypical case in this context, given that it plays a central compliance control role, leaving only final determinations and recommendations regarding measures to address non-compliance to a Standing Committee of the COP.[62]

Although they may not be explicitly cast as 'triggers', some treaty secretariats in the arms control area seem to play roughly comparable roles in initiating individual compliance reviews. For example, the CWC secretariat plays a significant fact-finding and verification role and, in the process, brings potential compliance problems to the attention of the CWC

---

requested to date: see Tabassi, chapter 11 in this volume, section 11.3.4. Under the Landmines Treaty, the formal compliance procedure can be triggered only by request of States parties. The procedure remains untested: see Lawand, chapter 13 in this volume, section 13.3.1.3.

[58] Presentation by Wolfgang Richter (note 32 above).

[59] See e.g. UNEP, Montreal Protocol Non-Compliance Procedure, para. 3. And see the compliance mechanisms of the LRTAP Convention (Kuokkanen, chapter 7 in this volume, section 7.3.1) and of the Aarhus Convention (Koester, chapter 8 in this volume, section 8.5.3.2).

[60] For example, under the Espoo Convention, a stronger role for the Secretariat was contemplated, but ultimately rejected by the parties. Under the Espoo Convention, compliance proceedings can be triggered only by submissions from States parties (Koivurova, chapter 9 in this volume, section 9.2.2).

[61] Under the Montreal Protocol, the secretariat analyzes the national reports submitted by parties, prepares a synthesis report for the MoP, and refers questions regarding the performance of individual parties to the treaty's compliance body, the Implementation Committee. See Raustiala, *Reporting and Review Institutions*, pp. 34 and 37. Similarly, under the LRTAP Convention, the secretariat has triggered compliance reviews on a number of occasions, bringing the performance of individual parties before the treaty's Implementation Committee. See Kuokkanen, chapter 7 in this volume, section 7.3.3, Table 7.1.

[62] See Reeve, chapter 6 in this volume, section 6.2.3.1.

Council.[63] However, not all arms control treaties envisage a secretariat role in the triggering of compliance procedures,[64] or even have a secretariat that could undertake that function.[65] Finally, in the human rights area, secretariats play no role in initiating reviews of party performance.

15.3.3.3 Individuals or non-governmental organizations

Individuals or non-governmental organizations (NGOs) cannot initiate compliance reviews in the so quintessentially sovereign domain of arms control.[66] The Landmines Treaty, which was initiated and shaped to a significant degree through NGO involvement, is an atypical case in this context. Under the treaty, non-State actors cannot trigger compliance proceedings. But NGOs nonetheless make important informal contributions to compliance control. Most notably, the International Campaign to Ban Landmines releases an influential annual country-by-country review of implementation of and compliance with the Landmines Treaty.[67]

It may be more surprising that, by and large, environmental agreements too take a restrictive approach to non-State actor involvement in compliance matters. It is worth bearing in mind, however, that the procedures that have been emerging under MEAs, their facilitative language notwithstanding, do scrutinize the performance of States in relation to their binding treaty commitments. So, just as that scrutiny has been acceptable only when undertaken by peers and with appropriate regard for the need to blend political and legal considerations, States have sought to keep the triggering functions in State, or at least intergovernmental, hands. Therefore, although – or precisely because – individuals or NGOs could be expected to bring a much wider range of compliance problems to the attention of treaty bodies than is uncovered and addressed through existing reporting and monitoring channels,[68] the role

---

[63] See art. VIII(36) of the CWC; and Tabassi, chapter 11 in this volume, section 11.3.4.

[64] Under the Landmines Treaty, the formal compliance procedure can be triggered only by a request of States parties. The procedure remains untested. See Lawand, chapter 13 in this volume, section 13.3.1.3.

[65] Under the CFE Treaty, compliance control remains in the hands of individual parties, albeit co-ordinated within the forum of the Joint Consultative Group: see the presentation by Wolfgang Richter (note 32 above).

[66] See e.g. the practice under the CWC (Tabassi, chapter 11 in this volume, section 11.3.4) and under the NPT (Rockwood, chapter 12 in this volume, section 12.6).

[67] See Lawand, chapter 13 in this volume, sections 13.3.1.2 and 13.3.1.4.

[68] This is borne out, for example, through the experience of the citizen complaints process under the North American Agreement for Environmental Co-operation. See Kal Raustiala, 'Police

of non-State actors in MEA compliance procedures remains relatively limited. It may involve the option to submit 'factual and technical information' relevant to the compliance review,[69] access to meetings of the compliance bodies unless parties object,[70] and access to the findings of the compliance body.[71] Only under the Aarhus Convention may individuals or NGOs actually make submissions to the compliance body.[72] Of course, given its concern with access to environmental information and decision-making by individuals, the Aarhus Convention arguably has more in common with human rights agreements than with the typical MEA.

And, indeed, it is under the various human rights treaties that the triggering of proceedings by individuals is most common. However, it is not the case that individuals or NGOs could trigger the previously discussed implementation reviews, such as those under the ICCPR, CEDAW or the Convention Against Torture.[73] Rather, through optional protocols or other devices through which parties can opt in, these and other human rights treaties allow the treaty committees to consider complaints or communications from individuals.[74] But, in view of the fact that these proceedings deal with individual cases and lead to determinations regarding the violation of

Patrols and Fire Alarms in the NAAEC' (2004) 26 *Loyola of Los Angeles International and Comparative Law Review* 389.

[69] UNFCCC, Procedures and Mechanisms on Compliance, para. VIII.4. Under CITES, NGOs provide information on trade and illegal trade in endangered species. On some occasions, such information has led to compliance control measures. See Reeve, chapter 6 in this volume, section 6.2.3.1. CITES is unusual in that, as a matter of established practice, the Secretariat contracts out the analysis of implementation data to two NGOs, the World Conservation Union and TRAFFIC. See Raustiala, *Reporting and Review Institutions*, p. 26

[70] See UNFCCC, Procedures and Mechanisms on Compliance, para. IX.2; and Koivurova, chapter 9 in this volume, section 9.2.2. Under CITES, NGOs now appear to be permitted to observe compliance discussions: see Reeve, chapter 6 in this volume, section 6.2.3.1.

[71] See e.g. UNFCCC, Procedures and Mechanisms on Compliance, para. VIII.7.

[72] Such a non-State actor communication must be 'in accordance with national legislation', and parties may opt out of this triggering mechanism for up to four years. See Koester, chapter 8 in this volume, section 8.5.3.2. Under the Espoo Convention, the compliance body received a communication from an NGO, but decided that its mandate did not permit it to do so. See Koivurova, chapter 9 in this volume, section 9.2.2.

[73] Presumably, however, it could be through individuals or NGOs that the Committees under the Convention Against Torture and under CEDAW receive the 'reliable information containing well-founded indications of serious or systematic violations of the conventions in a State party' that enables them to initiate inquiries. The applicability of the inquiry procedure to individual States is contingent upon their opt-in in the case of the Convention Against Torture, and their ratification of the optional protocol in the case of CEDAW. See OHCHR, 'Human Rights Bodies' (note 56 above).   [74] See *ibid*.

388 GENERAL COMMENTS

human rights by a State party in that case, they are more appropriately seen as dispute settlement than as compliance control.[75]

15.4 Outcomes

For the purposes of this book, questions of dispute settlement, compliance control and enforcement were divided into distinct analytical categories. In practice, of course, these categories blend into one another. In particular, the topics of compliance control and enforcement overlap to a considerable extent. The possible outcomes of compliance control processes encompass a wide spectrum, ranging from measures designed to prevent non-compliance, to determinations of non-compliance, to measures to address causes of non-compliance, to more enforcement-oriented measures designed to respond to cases of non-compliance.[76] In the analytical framework of this book, all of these measures are grouped under the rubric of 'enforcement', and so are not treated in any detail in this essay.

However, for the sake of a reasonably complete account of compliance control processes, at least brief reference must be made to the range of possible outcomes. It would be misleading to leave the reader with the impression that compliance control processes lead merely to more or less explicit determinations of non-compliance, possibly coupled with recommendations for improvement of a party's performance. Of course, as the preceding discussion suggested, even such determinations and recommendations are sensitive matters in the three areas under review, and their significance should not be underestimated.[77]

However, findings of non-compliance and recommendations for improved performance alone are unlikely to bring a party into compliance where capacity limitations are at the root of its failure. Various forms of advice and assistance are therefore among the possible outcomes of

---

[75] See also Kicker, chapter 4 in this volume, section 4.2 at note 43 (citing Steiner and Crawford). Of course, such procedures nonetheless serve compliance control functions. See Kicker, *ibid.* See also Raustiala, 'Police Patrols and Fire Alarms', p. 59, highlighting the 'fire alarm' function that individual complaints can serve in compliance control strategies.

[76] For a detailed discussion of 'enforcement' and 'compliance' mechanisms, see Brunnée, 'Enforcement Mechanisms in International Law'.

[77] See e.g. Kicker, chapter 4 in this volume, section 4.4, on the positive impact of the 'ongoing dialogue' with treaty parties regarding their implementation of committee recommendations under the CPT; and Kuokkanen, chapter 7 in this volume, section 7.5, on the 'gentle, but persistent, pressure' that the LRTAP Convention Implementation Committee has been able to exert on parties through its findings of non-compliance and recommendations.

compliance processes in all three areas.[78] Similarly, facilitative approaches alone may not suffice to induce compliance where strong countervailing interests are at play. Environmental agreements, for example, can engage significant financial and competitiveness considerations. In such cases, enforcement-oriented outcomes may be required, both to induce a party's compliance and to assure other parties of a level playing field. Accordingly, notwithstanding their emphasis on facilitation and co-operation, most MEA compliance regimes do have enforcement-oriented features, at least in the wider sense of creation of costs or removal of benefits.[79] Compliance regimes usually allow for the publication of parties' compliance records, or the issuance of 'cautions' to non-complying parties. Some compliance regimes also envisage the suspension of certain 'privileges' under the MEA (such as access to funds) when a party fails to meet its commitments. Finally, while rare, under some MEAs non-compliance may result in trade restrictions, such as under CITES,[80] or in other hard-edged consequences.[81]

One more point is worth making: arguably, none of the outcomes of the compliance control processes reviewed in this volume, be they findings of compliance bodies, recommendations for improvement, or even decisions on trade restrictions, are legally binding. Compliance control, it seems, operates on the basis of two contradictory but also mutually reinforcing phenomena. On the one hand, it would seem that the non-legally binding nature of the compliance control enterprise is what makes it acceptable to treaty parties. One can surmise that few, if any, of the compliance processes reviewed in this volume would operate if their outcomes were legally binding. Yet, on the other hand, it also appears that their non-binding nature does not make them any less effective than binding measures might be. Trade measures under CITES seem to operate quite well, notwithstanding the fact that they are based on non-binding recommendations. And the findings of non-compliance under the various compliance procedures appear to derive their force from the ongoing interactions in which they are anchored, not from legal status. The studies in this volume suggest that it is these interactions – continuous cycles of deliberation, justification and

---

[78] See notes 34 and 36 above, and the accompanying text.
[79] See Brunnée, 'Enforcement Mechanisms in International Law', p. 19.
[80] See Reeve, chapter 6 in this volume, section 6.3.
[81] Under the Kyoto Protocol, if a party fails to meet its emissions target, its excess emissions will be deducted (at a penalty rate of 1.3) from future emission allowances. See UNFCCC, Procedures and Mechanisms on Compliance, para. XV.5(a).

judgment – that power compliance control, and develop and legitimate the specific contours of a regime's responses to non-compliance, be they facilitative or enforcement-oriented.

15.5 Conclusion

This book offers in-depth accounts of the compliance control strategies that have evolved within treaties in the human rights, environmental and arms control areas. What they reveal is that, in all three areas, compliance control builds on what Chayes and Chayes referred to as active treaty management. Of course, many questions lurk beneath the surface of this conclusion. It does not provide an answer to the big theoretical questions about why States comply with international law (or not). Nor does it illuminate exactly why the managerial approach works, or under what circumstances it may work more or less well.[82] Answering these questions would require engagement with the rich theoretical literature on compliance.[83] It would also require the formulation and empirical testing of hypotheses and specific research questions.[84] Indeed, some of managerialism's critics have suggested that its central weakness is precisely that it provides policy advice without sufficient attention to the conditions under which it is likely to succeed, and without sufficient evidence.[85] The studies of treaty practice assembled in this volume might help fill this gap. They show that managerial approaches operate in a wide variety of settings, and can be configured in a variety of ways to suit the needs of the regime in which they operate. To be sure, what the case studies offer is 'raw material' for further empirical and theoretical investigation, not 'evidence'. But one is tempted to surmise that the engine that ultimately makes treaties work is just that – the hard work of collective deliberation, justification, persuasion and judgment.

---

[82] See e.g. Kyle Danish, 'Management v. Enforcement: The New Debate on Promoting Treaty Compliance' (1997) 37 *Virginia Journal of International Law* 809; and Anastasia A. Angelova, 'Compelling Compliance with International Regimes: China and the Missile Technology Control Regime' (1999) 38 *Colorado Journal of Transnational Law* 445–9.

[83] For an overview and references to key sources, see Kal Raustiala and Anne-Marie Slaughter, 'International Law, International Relations and Compliance', in Walter Carlsnaes *et al.* (eds.), *Handbook of International Relations* (Thousand Oaks, CA: Sage Publications, 2002), p. 541. See also Jutta Brunnée and Stephen J. Toope, 'Persuasion and Enforcement: Explaining Compliance with International Law' (2002) 13 *Finnish Yearbook of International Law* 273.

[84] See e.g. Steven R. Ratner *et al.*, 'Empirical Work in Human Rights', in American Society of International Law, *Proceedings of the Annual Meeting, Washington: 2004*, p. 197.

[85] See George Downs *et al.*, 'Is the Good News about Compliance Good News about Co-operation?' (1996) 50 *International Organization* 397.

16

Enforcement

CHRISTIAN J. TAMS[*]

The different contributions assembled in this volume clearly bring out the complexity and sophistication of treaty regimes aimed at securing the observance of rules of international law in the fields of human rights law, international environmental law and arms control law. It is not possible, in the space of this short comment, to assess the different contributions in any detail. However, some general perspectives on the role of enforcement within the process of securing compliance with international law may be offered. More specifically, three points will be covered. First, the contributions prompt a number of remarks about issues of terminology and about the basic features of the concept of 'enforcement'. Secondly, and most importantly, on the basis of the distinctions thus introduced, this comment will briefly review the different enforcement strategies pursued in the fields of human rights law, international environmental law and arms control law. And, lastly, it may be fruitful to reflect about the specific features of the three fields of law from the perspective of the general law of State responsibility, as elaborated by the UN International Law Commission in its Articles on State Responsibility, adopted after second reading in August 2001.[1]

16.1 Terminology and basic distinctions

It seems necessary to begin by seeking to define what is meant by 'enforcement'. To begin with a literal interpretation, a prominent online dictionary defines 'enforcement' as the process of 'ensuring observance of' the laws,[2] and most writers and practitioners would agree with that understanding. However, this is a rather broad, generic, way of using the term 'enforcement',

---

[*] Comment presented at the Workshop 'Making Treaties Work', held at Kiel University, 21–22 January 2005. The format of the oral presentation has largely been retained.
[1] Annex to GA Res. 56/83. In 2004, the General Assembly once more commended the ILC's text: see GA Res. 59/35.   [2] Cf. www.thefreedictionary.com/law%20enforcement.

391

392 GENERAL COMMENTS

which does not allow us to distinguish enforcement from other forms of ensuring the observance of rules, such as managerial approaches, often labelled 'compliance control' (an issue dealt with in the contribution by Jutta Brunnée),[3] or the implementation of international rules at the national level. It therefore seems required to define more clearly what is meant by 'enforcement'. In this respect, the above-given generic definition needs to be complemented in two ways. First, in contrast to the use within a number of treaty bodies, 'enforcement' here is meant to denote measures of ensuring the observance of rules *on the international plane*. It only covers conduct between States, or between a treaty body and a State, but is not meant to encompass the national 'enforcement' (or rather 'implementation') of international legal rules, within the domestic legal order of treaty members. Admittedly, a number of treaties in the field of international environmental law or arms control law use 'enforcement' when describing action to be taken at the national level.[4] However, because of the very different legal regime applicable, it seems crucial to retain a distinction between the domestic and the international. Secondly, and more importantly, within the spectrum of responses available at the international plane, enforcement shall be understood to describe attempts to ensure the observance of rules *prompted by a previous case of non-observance*. Measures of enforcement therefore are reactive, in that they respond to a case of non-observance.[5] Thus used, 'enforcement' is still a very broad concept, comprising both soft and hard forms of enforcement – an issue to be addressed below.[6] But it is considerably narrower than the generic definition quoted above, since it excludes from the

---

[3] See Brunnée, chapter 15 in this volume, pp. 373–90.

[4] See e.g. the use of terminology in the Chemical Weapons Convention (see Tabassi, chapter 11 in this volume, pp. 290–8), the Convention on International Trade in Endangered Species (see Reeve, chapter 6 in this volume, pp. 148–52) and in the 'Kiev Guidelines' of the Economic Commission for Europe (see Koivurova, chapter 9 in this volume, pp. 233–4, note 3).

[5] For similar definitions, see Georg Dahm, Jost Delbrück and Rüdiger Wolfrum, *Völkerrecht* (Berlin: Gruyter, 2nd edn, 1989), vol. I/1, pp. 90–1; O. Schachter, *International Law in Theory and Practice* (Dordrecht: Martinus Nijhoff Publishers 1991), p. 227.

[6] Others have adopted a narrower approach than the one pursued here, e.g. by restricting enforcement to measures requiring justification: see Morrison, 'The Role of Regional Organizations in the Enforcement of International Law', in J. Delbrück (ed.), *Allocation of Law Enforcement Authority in the International System: Proceedings of an International Symposium of the Kiel Institute of International Law, March 23–25, 1994* (Berlin: Duncker & Humblot, 1995), pp. 39 and 43. Art. 53 of the UN Charter, addressing the role of regional arrangements in the enforcement of UN sanctions, is equally based on a narrower (treaty-specific) understanding: see G. Ress and J. Bröhmer, in B. Simma (ed.), *Charter of the United Nations* (Oxford: Oxford University Press, 2nd edn, 2002), art. 53, marginal notes 3–7.

scope of the concept all attempts to promote norm adherence that exist independently of non-compliance. These notably include preventative measures, which are future-oriented and, by definition, aim at preventing the occurrence of a breach.[7] Also, enforcement, as defined here, does not cover measures by which States or treaty bodies seek to assess *whether* there has been non-compliance, notably fact-finding, verifications or inspections.[8] In addition, in order to qualify as an enforcement measure, the conduct in question has to aim at bringing the target State back into compliance, which introduces a subjective element. This notably helps to distinguish between, on the one hand, enforcement measures, and, on the other, decisions, by a State, to suspend the performance of an obligation in response to a previous non-performance by another State, such as responses justified under article 60 of the Vienna Convention on the Law of Treaties (sometimes referred to as 'reciprocal measures').[9]

On the basis of these qualifications, it seems possible to clarify the scope of 'enforcement', and of related concepts. Notably, given their 'reactive' character as responses against breaches, enforcement measures can be distinguished from managerial approaches of ensuring the observance of international rules, which operate independently of breaches, and which in this volume are addressed under the rubric of 'compliance control'.[10] On

---

[7] On prevention within environmental agreements, see Chayes, Chayes and Mitchell, 'Active Compliance Management in Environmental Treaties', in W. Lang (ed.), *Sustainable Development and International Law* (London and Boston: Graham & Trotman/Martinus Nijhoff Publishers, 1995), pp. 75 and 83–7; for trends towards a 'preventative approach' in international human rights law, see M. Nowak, *Introduction to the International Human Rights Regime* (Leiden and Boston: Martinus Nijhoff Publishers, 2003), pp. 277 *et seq.*

[8] For details on the concepts of 'inspection', 'monitoring' and 'verification', see in particular S. Oeter, 'Inspection in International Law – Monitoring Compliance and the Problem of Implementation in International Law' (1997) 28 *Netherlands Yearbook of International Law* 101–69 (with many further references).

[9] See e.g. J. Crawford and S. Olleson, 'The Exception of Non-Performance: Links between the Law of Treaties and the Law of State Responsibility' (2001) 21 *Australian Yearbook of International Law* 55–74. For further details on the distinction between art. 60 of the VCLT and measures of enforcement, see B. Simma, 'Reflections on Article 60 of the Vienna Convention on the Law of Treaties and Its Background in General International Law' (1970) 20 *Österreichische Zeitschrift für Öffentliches Recht* 5–83; B. Simma and C. Tams, 'Commentaire de l'article 60 de la Convention de Vienne sur le droit des traités', in O. Corten and F. Klein (eds.), *La Convention de Vienne sur le Droit des Traités* (forthcoming, 2006), paras. 3–5. For a broader concept of 'enforcement', covering measures under art. 60 of the VCLT, contrast, however, Ulfstein, chapter 5 in this volume, pp. 128–31.

[10] As Jutta Brunnée notes, the distinction may be less evident in practice: see Brunnée, chapter 15 in this volume, pp. 388–90.

the other hand, it deserves to be mentioned that the notion of 'enforcement' as defined here comprises means of dispute settlement, whether judicial or quasi-judicial, as these, almost by definition, presuppose a prior breach of the law. While the two issues are addressed separately in the framework of the present debate,[11] it is worth underlining that judicial or quasi-judicial dispute settlement is indeed a primary form of law enforcement. In fact, Sir Robert Jennings once put matters very clearly when he described court orders and judgments as 'the acid test of enforcement'.[12]

On the basis of these remarks, it must be assessed what forms of enforcement exist in international law, and in the three branches relevant to the present debate (i.e. human rights law, international environmental law and arms control law) in particular. The short answer is that enforcement can take a variety of forms. On the basis of the above description – and without assessing their legality – any of the following forms of conduct would qualify as an enforcement measure:

- a critical remark at a meeting of treaty parties (MoP);
- the exercise of political pressure outside the treaty framework (e.g. the public condemnation of the other State's failure to comply);
- the severance of diplomatic relations;
- an offer to assist a non-complying State to meet the standard it had previously failed to comply with;
- a trade sanction to force a non-complying State to comply with its obligations;
- the suspension of membership in a treaty, or the expulsion of a non-complying State from an international regime;
- the suspension of other treaties, such as development aid treaties, or air services agreements; and
- a military attack.

In terms of their gravity or effects, these different means of redressing breaches may have very little in common. But all of them would qualify as enforcement measures as all of them constitute responses against breaches of the law, which a State or other actor takes in order to bring the target State back into compliance. The concept of 'enforcement' therefore needs to be further refined. When trying to do this, a number of contributors

---

[11] For comment on dispute settlement, cf. Paulus, chapter 14 in this volume, pp. 351–72.
[12] Robert Jennings, 'The Judicial Enforcement of International Law' (1987) 47 *Zeitschrift für ausländisches öffentliches Recht und Völkerrecht* 3, p. 3.

have relied on the distinction between 'soft' and 'hard' enforcement.[13] When looking into the literature,[14] we find a great number of similar terms, which, by and large, evoke the same dichotomy:

- confrontational v. non-confrontational means of enforcement;
- command/control v. incentives;
- sticks v. carrots.

Admittedly, the dichotomy may be somewhat simplistic – who, for example, could say whether a decision not to pursue the negotiation of a development aid agreement would be enforcement of the 'hard' kind (because it was a means of exercising pressure) or 'soft' kind (because it represented a perfectly legitimate course of conduct). Yet, at least for practical purposes, it is unproblematic and, for descriptive purposes, may be helpful.

There is, however, a second basic distinction which has not been referred to frequently in the different contributions. Quite naturally, these have largely focused on the means of enforcement recognized in the different treaty regimes.[15] Since they are part and parcel of the respective treaty systems, these means of enforcement may be called 'systemic' enforcement. However, not all forms of enforcement mentioned above are expressly recognized in treaties. In order to ensure the observance of the law, States at times also resort to forms of enforcement that are not expressly referred to in the respective treaty (and therefore are not 'systemic'), but which may be recognized outside the treaty, notably under general international law. There is, in short, a second distinction between 'systemic' (or 'conventional') and 'non-systemic' (or 'extra-conventional') forms of enforcement. To give but one example, not deriving from the areas of law relevant here, many bilateral treaties concerning friendship, commerce and navigation ('FCN treaties') provide for recourse to the International Court of Justice as a means of enforcement. While the breach, by one of the parties,

---

[13] Cf. e.g. Tabassi, chapter 11 in this volume, pp. 293–6; Scheinin, chapter 2 in this volume, pp. 64–6.

[14] See *inter alia* Michael Bothe, 'International Obligations: Means to Secure Performance', in Rudolf Bernhardt (ed.), *Encyclopedia of Public International Law*, vol. II (Amsterdam and Oxford: North-Holland, 1995), p. 1278; Michael Bothe, 'The Evaluation of Enforcement Mechanisms in International Environmental Law: An Overview', in Rüdiger Wolfrum (ed.), *Enforcing Environmental Standards: Economic Mechanisms as Viable Means?* (Berlin and New York: Springer, 1996), p. 13.

[15] Contrast, however, Tabassi, chapter 11 in this volume, section 11.4.4, discussing 'Enforcement outside the CWC regime'.

of its obligations under the treaty might prompt the other party to refer a dispute to the ICJ (which would be a form of systemic enforcement), that other State might also consider responding by cutting development aid, i.e. respond in a way hardly ever expressly regulated in the FCN treaty. These latter forms of response would be 'non-systemic'.

It is submitted that the distinction between systemic and non-systemic forms of enforcement deserves more attention than has been given to it so far. It may therefore serve as a starting point for a comparative assessment of the different areas of law relevant in the present context.

16.2 Enforcement in the different treaty systems

In fact, when analyzing human rights law, international environmental law and arms control law from the perspective of 'systemic' versus 'non-systemic' enforcement, a number of differences emerge. This is particularly striking because, on the face of it, the three fields of law have a lot in common. They all protect general interests of the international community – an issue to be addressed below.[16] They are all heavily regulated, subject to different (often overlapping) sets of norms – to the point where a particular human right such as the right to be free from torture (to give but one example, specifically addressed by Renate Kicker in her contribution) is protected by general international law, by universal and regional general human rights agreements,[17] but also forms the subject of specific treaty regimes of universal and regional application, namely, the United Nations Convention Against Torture and the European Convention for the Prevention of Torture.[18] Furthermore, the regimes established to secure compliance with the international regimes of human rights, environmental law or arms control law are highly complex and diverse, typically involving treaty bodies, States parties and sometimes also individuals or NGOs. And, finally, compared to other areas of international law (such as the law of the sea or international humanitarian law) human rights law, international environmental law and arms control law are heavily institutionalized, often leaving international lawyers specializing in other areas wondering how the different committees, commissions, Meetings of the Parties, Conferences

---

[16] See below, section 3, for brief comment.

[17] See e.g. art. 7 of the International Covenant on Civil and Political Rights, or art. 3 of the European Convention on Human Rights.

[18] For comment on the respective regimes, see Kicker, chapter 4 in this volume, pp. 91–113.

of the Parties, and judicial and quasi-judicial bodies involved could ever be told apart.

However, notwithstanding these commonalities, important differences remain, as the following summary assessments suggests.

16.2.1 International environmental law

First, what are the enforcement strategies pursued in international environmental law? In their presentations, a number of contributors as well as most participants in the discussion – echoing a dominant trend in the literature – have dealt with enforcement rather briefly, focusing instead on compliance control, or managerial approaches to securing the observance of rules of international environmental law. For example, in Tuomas Kuokkanen's paper assessing the practice of the Implementation Committee under the Convention on Long-Range Transboundary Air Pollution, the detailed analysis of compliance control is followed by a mere two paragraphs addressing enforcement.[19] It is not intended to suggest that this approach is incorrect. Clearly, one of the most important lessons to learn from treaty-making in the field of international environmental law concerns the important role that managerial approaches may play in the process of inducing norm-compliance.[20] Still, there is a risk of focusing too much on the new, and of neglecting (or taking for granted) the traditional. On that premise, it may be worth underlining that many multilateral environmental agreements (MEAs) have a lot to say about enforcement as well.

Although the point is not always made (maybe because of the terminological uncertainties noted at the outset[21]), this is hardly disputed insofar as 'soft enforcement' is concerned. And, indeed, the different contributions clarify that most MEAs incorporate very specific strategies of soft enforcement, including, at times, mechanisms for the monitoring of bringing States back into compliance. For example, Veit Koester[22] notes that, pursuant to Decision I/7 on Review of Compliance,[23] the Compliance Committee established under the Aarhus Convention can *inter alia* agree to 'provid[e] advice and facilitate assistance', or request a non-complying treaty party 'to submit a strategy to the Compliance Committee regarding the achievement of

---

[19] Cf. Kuokkanen, chapter 7 in this volume, pp. 172–3.
[20] See e.g. Bothe, 'The Evaluation of Enforcement Mechanisms'; and Ulrich Beyerlin, *Umweltvölkerrecht* (Munich: C. H. Beck, 2000), pp. 231–40.   [21] See section 16.1 above.
[22] Koester, chapter 8 in this volume, pp. 179–210.   [23] Doc. ECE/MP.PP2/Add.8.

compliance and to report [presumably to the Compliance Committee] on implementation of the strategy'.[24] Similarly, Rosalind Reeve's paper highlights the role of the Secretariat established under the Convention on International Trade in Endangered Species of Wild Fauna and Flora (CITES) in providing technical assistance and capacity-building.[25]

But enforcement under MEAs should not be reduced to soft enforcement. At least some of the relevant agreements also expressly recognize forms of enforcement that would come within the scope of 'hard' or 'confrontational' enforcement. The possibility of curbing membership rights (a measure whose confrontational character is brought out well by Wolfgang Friedmann's description as 'the sanction of non-participation'[26]) is one example. The Aarhus Convention provides a case in point. As Veit Koester shows, it envisages the suspension of special rights and privileges accorded to treaty members as a regular measure in case of non-compliance,[27] thereby following the direction of an earlier provision adopted under the Montreal Protocol.[28] However, it is worth noting that a number of agreements – such as CITES or the Montreal Protocol – despite their general focus on non-confrontational forms of enforcement, clearly go beyond the suspension of membership rights. In the case of CITES, a considerable number of States showing a pattern of generalized non-compliance have been targeted by trade sanctions suspending trade in endangered species.[29] Furthermore, Geir Ulfstein notes that '[t]he non-compliance committee of the Montreal Protocol has issued several cautions that further measures, including suspension of the right to trade in ozone-depleting substances under article 4 of the Protocol, might be considered'[30] in order to bring recalcitrant States back into compliance.

[24] See Koester, chapter 8 in this volume, p. 209; and cf. Decision I/7, Doc. ECE/MP.PP2/Add.8, Annex, para. 37.

[25] Reeve, chapter 6 in this volume, p. 147. For further details, cf. Ulfstein, chapter 5 in this volume, pp. 128–31.

[26] Friedmann, *The Changing Structure of International Law* (London: Stevens & Sons, 1964), p. 88.

[27] Cf. e.g. Koester, chapter 8 in this volume, pp. 208–11.

[28] Cf. Ozone Secretariat, United Nations Environment Programme, *Handbook for the International Protection of the Ozone Layer* (Nairobi: 6th edn, 2003), Section 2.7, 'Indicative List of Measures that Might Be Taken by a Meeting of the Parties in Respect of Non-Compliance with the Protocol', p. 297.

[29] Cf. Reeve, chapter 6 in this volume, pp. 152–7, for details. The fact that these sanctions are recommendatory in nature, and therefore strictly speaking not binding, does not affect their status as 'hard enforcement'. Insofar as CITES only encourages, rather than mandates, sanctions, it is in line with general international rules on enforcement, which almost inevitably are permissive.

[30] Ulfstein, chapter 5 in this volume, p. 130 (referring to Decision XIII/16).

Lastly, while not covered in any of the in-depth studies assembled in the present volume, the Kyoto Protocol may be briefly referred to. As is widely recognized,[31] this agreement is characterized by an increased reliance on forms of 'hard enforcement'. Notably, the Kyoto Protocol Enforcement Branch can penalize States violating their emission limits by reducing their emission quotas, and by suspending their right to make emission transfers under article 17 of the Protocol. In a recent article, Gerhard Loibl has described this in the following terms: 'The enforcement branch of the Kyoto Protocol has added a new dimension to compliance procedures [in the environmental field]. It includes many elements that have only been known from judicial procedures before, such as [the possibility of] sanctions.'[32]

These examples do not affect the general assessment that international agreements in the field of international environmental law primarily seek to secure compliance through non-confrontational means, such as managerial approaches and/or soft enforcement. However, they show that there is more to MEAs than compliance control or soft enforcement. Contrary to the firmly held views of many writers, many of the more recent agreements rely on hard enforcement as well, and seem to do so increasingly.

16.2.2 Human rights law

The picture thus sketched may be contrasted to enforcement in the human rights field. A quick look at the text of the respective agreements (i.e. at systemic measures) reveals that their main enforcement strategy is dispute settlement – which is assessed elsewhere.[33] Of course, the development of dispute settlement in the human rights field is one of the most striking features of modern international law; besides, it is one of the major successes of the human rights movement, and of the move towards a more mature system of international law more generally. Precisely because of this success, other forms of enforcing human rights, however, have not received the same degree of attention. When looking at the text of the relevant agreements, one finds comparatively little about enforcement outside the field of dispute settlement. Furthermore, measures of enforcement that are

---

[31] For a clear analysis, cf. Gerhard Loibl, 'Environmental Law and Non-Compliance Procedures: Issues of State Responsibility', in Fitzmaurice and Sarooshi (eds.), *Issues of State Responsibility Before International Judicial Institutions* (Oxford: Hart, 2004), pp. 201–17.

[32] See *ibid.*, p. 217.   [33] Cf. Paulus, chapter 14 in this volume, pp. 351–72.

400   GENERAL COMMENTS

provided often come into play once dispute settlement has been exhausted, or, more precisely, in order to secure that the result of the dispute settlement process is complied with. Article 46(2) of the European Convention on Human Rights provides a well-known example.[34] However, this provision does not confer upon the Committee of Ministers any specific powers to secure the judgment's implementation.[35] Perhaps more importantly, it is a form of enforcement 'after the fact' (or, rather, 'after the judgment'), in that it is only available after an independent court has established non-compliance. While this does not render article 46(2) meaningless, it shows that, under the ECHR system, court proceedings are the primary means of enforcement, whereas non-judicial enforcement through the Committee of Ministers plays an ancillary role. And the same can be said of enforcement under the European Convention on the Prevention of Torture, as Renate Kicker's paper shows.[36]

This of course does not mean that human rights are not enforced through non-judicial procedures. In fact, States use a great variety of strategies to redress human rights breaches, some of which are 'soft' (or facilitative), others 'hard' (or coercive). However, these manifold processes of enforcing human rights law often take place outside the treaty regimes in question. In line with the terminology suggested above, it may be said that, in order to enforce international human rights (outside the field of dispute settlement), States and other actors often rely on non-systemic means of enforcement. In this respect, three different approaches may be distinguished:

1. For a start, very often, other, global, mechanisms are used as fora for human rights enforcement, notably the UN:[37] often, a UN condemnation, or a sanction mandated by the UN Security Council,[38] may be the substitute for action under the specific treaties. By way of example, suffice it to refer to the regular condemnations of human rights abuses by the United Nations Security Council, which on several occasions has deplored human rights violations[39] or, with respect to Côte

---

[34] Cf. Villiger, chapter 3 in this volume, pp. 83–5, for comment.   [35] *Ibid.*, pp. 83–5.

[36] Kicker, chapter 4 in this volume, pp. 107–109.

[37] See Riedel, in Simma, *Charter*, art. 68, marginal notes 61–93, for an overview of available mechanisms.

[38] For a brief analysis of Security Council sanctions adopted in response to human rights violations, cf. J. A. Frowein and N. Krisch, in Simma, *Charter*, art. 39, marginal notes 19–21.

[39] Cf. G. Nolte, 'Practice of the UN Security Council with Respect to Humanitarian Law', in K. Dicke *et al.* (eds.), *Weltinnenrecht: Liber Amicorum Jost Delbrück* (Berlin: Duncker & Humblot, 2005), pp. 487–501.

ENFORCEMENT

d'Ivoire, has 'emphasize[d] again the need to bring to justice those responsible for the serious violations of human rights'.[40] In terms of the specific treaties whose breaches are at stake, this form of responding to breaches of human rights treaties would be a non-systemic form of enforcement, as it is not mandated by the specific human rights treaty regime concerned.

2. More important, perhaps, are assertions of a right to employ hard enforcement strategies unilaterally. A particularly clear example is the coercive human rights enforcement through counter-measures or the use of force. Unsurprisingly, no human rights treaty provides for a right to use force in order to secure the observance of human rights norms. However, at least in the case of persistent and egregious breaches of human rights, a right to use force in defence of humanitarian purposes seems to be (increasingly) claimed.[41] When leaving aside cases of forcible intervention (which, contrary to Reisman's assertion, can hardly be considered 'a primary means cf enforcing . . . human rights'[42]), a similar point can be made with respect to non-forcible counter-measures. None of the human rights treaties discussed in the present symposium provides for a right to take counter-measures in response to treaty breaches. Still, this is what States rather frequently do. Of course, it is highly controversial whether there exists, under present-day international law, a right to adopt unilateral counter-measures in response to serious human rights breaches, or at least breaches of those fundamental human rights which qualify as obligations *erga omnes*.[43] However, even sceptics would have difficulties denying that, in a considerable number of instances, States have claimed such a right, and have acted accordingly. By way of example, suffice it to mention the suspension of bilateral aviation agreements, by European countries, in response to the mounting Kosovo crisis (1998),[44] of trade

---

[40] SC Res. 1479 of 13 May 2003; and earlier SC Res. 1464 of 4 February 2003.

[41] This is not the place to engage in a discussion, however brief, of the legality or legitimacy of these claims. For a critical assessment, cf. Christine D. Gray, *International Law and the Use of Force by States* (Oxford and New York: Oxford University Press, 2nd edn, 2004), pp. 31 *et seq.*

[42] Cf. W. M. Reisman, 'Comment', in Delbrück (ed.), *The Future of International Law Enforcement: New Scenarios – New Law?* (Berlin: Duncker & Humblot, 1993), pp. 168 and 171.

[43] For a detailed analysis, see Christian J. Tams, *Enforcing Obligations Erga Omnes under International Law* (Cambridge: Cambridge University Press, 2005), pp. 198 *et seq.*

[44] See Common Position 98/326/CFSP, OJ 1998, L143/1; and Common Position 98/426/CFSP, OJ 1998, L190/3. For the implementation, see Regulation (EC) No. 1091/98, OJ 1998, L248/1.

402 GENERAL COMMENTS

agreements concluded with Argentina during the Falklands war (1982),[45] or the more recent sanctions adopted, by a number of States, against the Zimbabwean government.[46] Quite clearly, this form of human rights enforcement (however one judges its legality or effectiveness) is non-systemic in that it takes place outside the treaty framework.

3. Lastly, there is the interesting tendency to 'humanize' treaties not primarily concerned with human rights. For example, many development aid treaties today incorporate human rights conditionality – the Lomé and Cotonou agreements between European and ACP States are particularly prominent examples.[47] Again, there is much discussion about the scope of the respective conditionality clauses.[48] However, in terms of the present debate, it is beyond doubt that, in order better to ensure the observance of human rights standards, States have felt the need to include enforcement mechanisms in treaties *outside* the human rights field. This means that mechanisms established under, for example, development assistance treaties are used to enforce human rights agreements, and make up for the lack of effective systemic human rights enforcement.

It is submitted that it is this last feature which brings out the difference between human rights law on the one hand and international environmental law on the other with particular clarity. Both human rights law and

---

[45] See Regulation (EEC) No. 877/82, OJ 1982, L102/1; and Regulation (EEC) No. 1176/82, OJ 1982, L136/1; and the parallel measures adopted by the European Coal and Steel Community, Decision 82/221/ECSC, OJ 1982, L102/3; and Decision 82/320/ECSC, OJ 1982, L136/2.

[46] See e.g. Common Position 2002/145/CFSP, OJ 2002, L50/1 (arts. 3 and 4); for the implementation, see Regulation (EC) No. 310/2002, OJ 2002, L50/4, for sanctions adopted by EU Member States; and, for the United States' response, Executive Order of 7 March 2003 ('Blocking Property of Persons Undermining Democratic Processes or Institutions in Zimbabwe'), available at www.ustreas.gov/offices/eotffc/ofac/sanctions/t11zimb.pdf.

[47] Cf. OJ 2000, L317/3 for the text of the Cotonou Agreement; and arts. 9 and 96(2) for references to human rights as an essential condition of the EC–ACP co-operation. On the evolution of human rights clauses in the external relations of the European Community, see B. Brandtner and A. Rosas, 'Human Rights and the External Relations of the European Community: An Analysis of Doctrine and Practice' (1998) 9 *European Journal of International Law* 468 *et seq.*

[48] See notably Brandtner and Rosas, 'Human Rights and the External Relations of the European Community'; as well as Frank Hoffmeister, *Menschenrechts- und Demokratieklauseln in den vertraglichen Außenbeziehungen der Europäischen Gemeinschaft* (Berlin and New York: Springer, 1998); E. Riedel and M. Will, 'Human Rights Clauses in External Agreements of the EC', in Philip Alston and Joseph Weiler (eds.), *An 'Ever Closer Union' in Need of a Human Rights Policy: The European Union and Human Rights* (Cambridge, MA: Harvard Law School, 1999), p. 723.

international environmental law, for some cases, seem to envisage economic sanctions as a potentially effective form of 'hard enforcement'.[49] In the latter field, these enforcement measures are systemic – as has been noted, they are provided for in MEAs such as CITES or the Kyoto Protocol.[50] With respect to human rights agreements, trade sanctions operate as a non-systemic enforcement measures – they exist under, for example, the Cotonou and Lomé agreements, or are claimed under general international law.

In short, with the huge exception of dispute settlement, human rights provide for a less developed system of systemic enforcement. Not surprisingly, the demand for non-systemic enforcement is considerable.

16.2.3 Arms control law

Finally, it is necessary to consider the enforcement of arms control law. As is made clear in the papers by Laura Rockwood and Lisa Tabassi, at least the Chemical Weapons Convention (CWC) and the Non-Proliferation Treaty (NPT) contain a number of provisions allowing for enforcement in the sense in which that term is used here. For example, under article XII(C) of the NPT, the IAEA may suspend any non-complying member from the exercise of the privileges and rights of IAEA membership, and can also curtail or suspend assistance being provided by the Agency or by a Member State.[51] For example, article XII of the CWC confers upon the Conference of the Parties the right to respond to breaches by 'restrict[ing] or suspend[ing] the State Party's rights and privileges under the Convention', or by 'recommend[ing] collective measures to States Parties in conformity with international law'.[52] Notwithstanding this normative assessment, most commentators argue that arms control treaties generally rely on non-confrontational means of enforcement.[53] One reason for this approach may

---

[49] For details, see the many contributions in Rüdiger Wolfrum (ed.), *Enforcing Environmental Standards: Economic Mechanisms as Viable Means?* (Berlin and New York: Springer, 1996).

[50] See section 16.2.1 above.

[51] For further details, see Rockwood, chapter 12 in this volume, pp. 303–19.

[52] Tabassi, chapter 11 in this volume, p. 295.

[53] See e.g. Tabassi, chapter 11 in this volume, pp. 290–8; and Marauhn, chapter 10 in this volume, pp. 266–71. This is particularly evident from the fact that arms control treaties hardly ever provide for enforcement in the form of institutionalized dispute settlement. For a detailed analysis of this aspect (which is outside the scope of the present comment), see S. Seidel, *Aufsichts- und Streitbeilegungsverfahren im Recht der Abrüstung und Rüstngskontrolle* (Frankfurt am Main: Peter Lang, 2005), especially pp. 297 *et seq.*

404 GENERAL COMMENTS

be particular to the field of arms control law, and thus deserves particular emphasis. More than in other areas of law, the different agreements seek to establish an atmosphere of mutual trust. In her paper focusing on the Chemical Weapons Convention, Lisa Tabassi explains the rationale underlying this approach in very clear terms:

> [The OPCW's] formal activities are supplemented by a continuous cycle of informal consultations in the OPCW as well as bilateral consultations between States parties, which in most cases are not brought to the attention of the organization or other States parties. It is to be expected that so many levels of continuous dialogue lessen the likelihood that an issue could escalate into a full-scale 'dispute' with all the political implications a 'dispute' could entail.[54]

It is not difficult to understand why mutual trust and confidence (which of course are relevant to other areas of international law as well) should play such a crucial role in arms control law. Especially in the different agreements regulating the use of weapons of mass destruction, any single breach potentially undermines the system as a whole.[55] As a consequence, the focus of many arms control treaties is on verification, fact-finding and inspection rather than on means of responding to breaches.[56] These specific features also affect the enforcement provisions adopted under the relevant agreements. Two features are of particular relevance here.

The first point to make concerns withdrawal clauses. As Thilo Marauhn's paper clarifies,[57] many arms control treaties contain such clauses, allowing States to withdraw from the regime in cases which include qualified breaches by another treaty member.[58] This recognition of a relatively liberal

---

[54] Tabassi, chapter 11 in this volume, p. 275.

[55] As will be shown below in the section on State responsibility, it is precisely this factor that informs the general rules governing standing to respond against breaches: cf. section 16.3 below.

[56] For a more detailed assessment, see Marauhn, 'Die Durchsetzung von Rüstungskontroll- und Abrüstungsvereinbarungen' (1999) 74 Friedens-Warte 159, at 174–84; Lang, 'Compliance with Disarmament Obligations' (1995) 55 Zeitschrift für ausländisches öffentliches Recht und Völkerrecht 69 et seq.

[57] Marauhn, chapter 10 in this volume, pp. 268–9; and further Marauhn, 'Rüstungskontroll- und Abrüstungsvereinbarungen', pp. 164–6.

[58] See e.g. art. XVI(2) of the Chemical Weapons Convention (CWC), which provides: 'Each State Party shall, in exercising its national sovereignty, have the right to withdraw from this Convention if it decides that extraordinary events, related to the subject-matter of this Convention, have jeopardized the supreme interests of its country. It shall give notice of such withdrawal 90 days in advance to all other States Parties, the Executive Council, the Depositary and the United Nations Security Council. Such notice shall include a statement of the extraordinary events it regards as

right to withdraw from a treaty would seem to be a consequence of the specific features of arms control law just referred to; it follows from, and operationalizes, the importance of mutual trust. However, in light of the previous comments,[59] it is doubtful whether withdrawal clauses can really be qualified as means of enforcement. The better view seems to be that they aim at re-establishing the contractual balance between the States parties (albeit at a lower level of normative regulation), but do not seek to bring the non-complying State back into compliance.

The second specific feature of arms control treaties is the degree to which they rely on institutions established by other treaties in order to enforce treaty obligations. A great number of the treaties in question envisage a role for UN organs, in particular the Security Council.[60] If the Security Council (e.g. following an information by the Conference of the Parties to the CWC under article XII(4) of the CWC[61]) adopts measures to redress breaches, it exercises an enforcement function with respect to arms control law. What is peculiar about the treaties in question is that they expressly anticipate this forms of enforcement through the Security Council.[62] When taking action with respect to the CWC or the NPT, the Council therefore can act as an enforcement agent with respect to arms control law. When seeking to assess this function in light of the terminology adopted here, one might speak of a 'quasi-systemic' role – 'systemic' in that measures by the Security Council are anticipated in the respective treaties, but different from the previous instances of systemic enforcement because the enforcement organ in question (i.e. the Security Council) has not been set up by the treaty.

It should be added that the specific provisions providing for a referral by treaty bodies are not the only way in which the Security Council can get

---

having jeopardized its supreme interests.' It is important to note that States parties retain a considerable margin of appreciation in deciding whether 'extraordinary events' jeopardize their 'supreme interests'. For similar provisions in the treaties addressed in this volume, see art. 20(2) of the Convention on the Prohibition of Anti-Personnel Mines (Ottawa Convention) and art. X(1) of the Non-Proliferation Treaty.   [59] See section 16.1 above.

[60] See e.g. art. XII of the Statute of the IAEA; art. XII(4) of the CWC. With respect to the Ottawa Convention, Lawand, chapter 13 in this volume, p. 338, notes that measures taken under art. 8 could '[i]n extreme cases, this could include referring the matter to the UN Security Council or adopting other enforcement measures provided by the UN Charter'. However, unlike in the case of the CWC or the NPT, this is not expressly stated in the treaty.

[61] Art. XII(4) of the CWC provides: 'The Conference shall, in cases of particular gravity, bring the issue, including relevant information and conclusions, to the attention of the United Nations General Assembly and the United Nations Security Council.'

[62] See Marauhn, 'Rüstungskontroll- und Abrüstungsvereinbarungen', pp. 166–7.

406 GENERAL COMMENTS

involved in the enforcement of arms control law.[63] Provisions such as article XII(4) of the CWC or article XII of the Statute of the IAEA provide for *additional* forms of involving the Security Council. As commentators rightly note,[64] they cannot be interpreted to mean that the Security Council could only address issues of arms control law at the instigation of the relevant treaty bodies. Just as in other fields of international law, it can always make use of its general competence to react if it considers that a particular situation qualifies as a breach of or threat to international peace and security in the sense of article 39 of the UN Charter, or even amounts to an aggression. For present purposes, it is important to note that this form of enforcement of arms control law would have to be qualified as non-systemic. Insofar as the Security Council responds to breaches of arms control agreements on its own initiative (i.e. in the absence of treaty body referral) it performs its regular role as the international community's primary guardian of international peace and security. As is well known, more recently it has begun to make use of this power in a rather spectacular (and problematic) way, namely, by laying down, in a binding Security Council resolution, general obligations for States in the field of non-proliferation of weapons of mass destruction.[65] This is not the place to assess the legality of the Security Council's new role as a 'legislator' in the field of arms control law. However, the recent developments in the field bring out the Security Council's dual role with particular clarity, and highlight a specific feature of the enforcement system of arms control law. Because of the sensitivity of the issues, breaches of arms control law are particularly apt to amount to breaches of or threats to international peace and security, and thus trigger non-systemic enforcement measures, decided upon by the Security Council upon its own initiative. However, fully aware of this proximity, a number of treaties provide for additional ways of referring situations to the Security Council.

---

[63] Cf. Tabassi, chapter 11 in this volume, p. 295, noting that the specific means of redress set out in art. XII of the CWC 'would not rule out the UN Security Council authorizing Chapter VII action if the situation referred by the OPCW were considered to be a threat to international peace and security'.

[64] See especially Tabassi, chapter 11 in this volume, pp. 294–6 *et seq.*; and Rockwood, chapter 12 in this volume, pp. 314–19.

[65] See in particular SC Res. 1540 of 28 April 2004. For comment on the conceptual problems raised by the Security Council's role as a 'legislator', see A. Zimmermann and B. Elberling, 'Grenzen der Legislativbefugnisse des Sicherheitsrates' (2004) 52 *Vereinte Nationen* 71; R. Wolfrum, 'Der Kampf gegen eine Verbreitung von Massenvernichtungswaffen: Eine neue Rolle für den Sicherheitsrat', in K. Dicke *et al.* (eds.), *Weltinnenrecht: Liber Amicorum Jost Delbrück* (Berlin: Duncker & Humblot, 2005), p. 865.

As has been shown, it is this latter feature, allowing for a quasi-systemic enforcement, that is peculiar to arms control law and has no equivalent in the fields of human rights or international environmental law.

16.3 The role of State responsibility

One final point deserves to be mentioned. It concerns the role of State responsibility in the process of securing observance with the rules of the respective systems. In this respect, the relative absence of references, in the different contributions, to the work of the International Law Commission (ILC) on the law of State responsibility[66] is striking. This may be due to the fact that the ILC has sought to elaborate *general* rules of State responsibility, including *general* (i.e. non-systemic) forms of enforcement,[67] while most of the contributions to the present volume have focused on treaty regimes and systemic forms of enforcement. Still, a look at the ILC's work may be helpful, if only because it clarifies one of the important specificities of treaties in the field of human rights law, international environmental law and arms control law. This specific feature is the general standing of all States parties to a treaty to raise issues of non-compliance. This issue has largely been taken for granted in the different contributions, since it is usually expressly recognized in the relevant treaties.[68] However, it is much more controversial in the absence of express provisions.[69] At least traditionally, standing to raise

---

[66] Literature on the topic is enormous. Cf. notably James Crawford, *The International Law Commission's Articles on State Responsibility* (Cambridge: Cambridge University Press, 2002); James Crawford, 'The ILC's Articles on State Responsibility of States for Internationally Wrongful Acts: A Retrospect' (2002) 96 *American Journal of International Law* 874; C. J. Tams, 'All's Well That Ends Well? Comments on the ILC's Articles on State Responsibility' (2002) 62 *Zeitschrift für ausländisches öffentliches Recht und Völkerrecht* 759; and the many contributions to the symposia organized by the American and European Journals of International Law: (2002) 96 *American Journal of International Law* 773 *et seq.*; (2002) 13 *European Journal of International Law* 1053 *et seq.*

[67] See para. 1 of the Introductory Commentary to the ILC's work, reproduced in Crawford, *State Responsibility*. Similarly, art. 55 of the ILC's text provides: 'These articles do not apply where and to the extent that the conditions for the existence of an internationally wrongful act or the content or implementation of the international responsibility of a State are governed by special rules of international law.'

[68] See e.g. art. 33 of the ECHR, referred to by Villiger, chapter 3 in this volume, p. 33; art. 41 of the ICCPR, referred to by Scheinin, chapter 2 in this volume, pp. 53–7; as well as Koester, chapter 8 in this volume, pp. 183–9; and Kuokkanen, chapter 7 in this volume, p. 165. For more detailed assessments of the underlying issue of standing, cf. Ulfstein, chapter 5 in this volume, pp. 118–24; and Koester, chapter 8 in this volume, pp. 179–218.

[69] For detailed considerations on the following aspect, see notably K. Sachariew, *Die Rechtsstellung betroVener Staaten bei Verletzungen multilateraler Verträge* thesis manuscript, Institut für

violations of international law – at least by means of coercion, i.e. in the case of 'hard enforcement' – has been said to be the prerogative of States individually injured by a wrongful act, or of States suffering some form of measurable damage.[70] Quite clearly, these traditional approaches are difficult to apply to legal obligations States are supposed to observe, at least primarily, *vis-à-vis* their own nationals (as in the case of human rights law) or within their own sphere of jurisdiction (as with respect to most obligations of international environmental or arms control law). To give but two examples, the breach, by State A, of its obligation not to torture its own citizens simply does not injure any other State in its individual capacity; and the same holds true for State B's failure to provide for procedures for environmental impact assessment in its national laws.[71]

It is therefore worth noting that, in its work on State responsibility, the ILC has moved beyond the traditional paradigm, and has justified this progressive approach at least partly with reference to treaties in the three areas of law relevant to the present debate. Hence article 48(1) of its Articles on State Responsibility[72] accepts that, even in the absence of a specific regulation, all States (irrespective of individual injury) are entitled to redress breaches of collective obligations protecting general community interests.[73] As the explanatory commentary suggests, obligations in the fields of human rights law and international environmental law are counted among the most

---

Theorie des Staates und des Rechts, East Berlin, 1986); C. J. Tams, *Enforcing Obligations*; J. Crawford, 'The Standing of States: A Critique of Article 40 of the ILC's Draft Articles on State Responsibility', in M. Andenas and D. Fairgrieve (eds.), *Liber Amicorum in Honour of Lord Slynn of Hadley* (The Hague and Boston: Kluwer Law International, 2000), vol. II, p. 23.

[70] Hence, Riphagen ('Third Report on State Responsibility', *ILC Yearbook 1982*, vol. II, Part One (1982), p. 38) described traditional international law as 'bilateral-minded', while Alfred Verdross (*Völkerrecht* (in collaboration with Stephan Verosta and Karl Zemanek, Vienna: Springer, 5th edn, 1964), p. 126) spoke in more guarded terms of the 'essentially relative character of international obligations'.

[71] Cf. Koester, chapter 8 in this volume, p. 187, who observes that: 'Non-performance of the obligations of the [Aarhus] Convention will rarely affect any particular State party. Most of the obligations are of a non-reciprocal character, because the main aim of the Convention is to impose obligations on States in respect of their own citizens.'

[72] Reproduced in Crawford, *State Responsibility*.

[73] '*Any State* . . . is entitled to invoke the responsibility of another State . . . if: (a) the obligation breached is owed to a group of States including that State, and is established for the protection of a collective interest of the group; or (b) the obligation breached is owed to the international community as a whole' (emphasis added). It must be admitted though that the ILC adopted a more cautious approach with respect to counter-measures: cf. art. 54 of its text; and further Tams, *Enforcing Obligations*, pp. 198 *et seq.*

prominent examples of such community interest obligations.[74] It would seem to follow that, even in the absence of an express provision and even though they are not injured, States are entitled to redress human rights breaches or breaches of obligations in the field of international environmental law, simply because these obligations safeguard general interests.

As far as arms control law is concerned, the situation again is different. Following the ILC's approach, which in turn is modelled on article 60(2)(c) of the 1969 Vienna Convention on the Law of Treaties, obligations under disarmament or arms control treaties are 'interdependent'. Put differently, the performance, by one party, of obligations arising under these treaties is 'effectively conditioned upon and requires the performance of each of the others'.[75] This means that the breach, by one State, of its obligations under an arms control or disarmament agreement, 'is of such a character as radically to change the position of all the other States to which the obligation is owed with respect to the further performance of the obligation'.[76] As a consequence, all States parties would be considered injured States in the sense of article 42 of the ILC's text.[77]

In short, with respect to human rights law, arms control and international environmental law, the ILC's text moves beyond the traditional, bilateral approach, and recognizes a right of all States bound by the obligation to respond to breaches. Of course, the Commission's progressive view, in its generality, is still controversial. However, it is clearly defensible, and, given the importance of the Articles on State Responsibility, it is likely to influence the development of the law. Last but not least, it is important to underline that the move from a traditional, restrictive, regime of standing towards the broader approach now embodied in article 42(b)(ii) and article 48 has been largely influenced by examples of human rights conventions, arms control agreements and MEAs. Developments in the law of State responsibility thus illustrate the importance of human rights, environmental law and arms control law in the evolution of general international law.

---

[74] See the ILC's commentary to art. 48(7), which expressly refers to obligations protecting the environment or human rights.   [75] See the ILC's commentary to art. 42(13).

[76] Cf. art. 42(b)(ii) of the ILC's text.

[77] The point is made with particular clarity in para. 13 of the ILC's commentary to art. 42, where the Commission clarifies that art. 42(b)(ii) would *inter alia* cover 'a disarmament treaty, [or] a nuclear free zone treaty'.

INDEX

Aarhus Convention
  Compliance Committee, 182
    composition, 126, 193–4
    decision making, 200–1
    experts, 132
    influence, 238
    information gathering, 197–8
    meetings, 196, 198
    powers, 203–5
    procedural guidance, 197
    procedures, 197–202
    reports, 190
    submissions to, 195–6, 198–200
  compliance control, 125, 198–215
    and dispute settlement, 213–15
    individuals' complaints, 127
    institutions, 192–6, 383
    international law principles,
      207–8, 214
    Meetings of Parties, 192, 205–7
    NGO participation, 127, 190, 193,
      194, 198–200, 202, 387
    non-compliance measures, 203–13
    procedures, 197–202
    public participation, 198–200
    record, 204–5, 216
    reporting obligations, 189–91
    safeguards, 201–2
    sanctions, 208–12
    Secretariat, 192
    setting obligations aside, 212–13
    suspension of privileges, 209, 210,
      211–12
  contents, 182–3
  contracting parties, 180–1
  dispute settlement, 183–9
    amici curiae, 187

and compliance review, 213–15
    extent of use, 188–9
    ICJ jurisdiction, 184–6
    non-state actors, 186–7
    standing, 187–8
  enforcement, 129, 130, 181, 208–12,
    397–8
  evaluation, 215–17
  generally, 179–217
  human rights approach, 123, 182–3
  influence, 216–17, 229, 238
  institutions, 182
  origins, 179–80
  PRTR Protocol, 181
  Secretariat, 182, 192
ABM Treaty
  dispute resolution, 255–6
  enforcement, 268
  verification, 258–9
acidification, 163
Afghanistan, 99, 151
African Charter on Human and
    Peoples' Rights
  Court and Commission, 358
  monitoring, 34–5, 37
  reporting obligations, 28
African Union, 35, 46
air pollution. *See* LRTAP Convention
airports, 104
Albania, and CWC, 289
Algeria, and CITES, 151
Alpine Convention, compliance
    control, 195, 202
American Convention on Human
    Rights (ACHR)
  reporting obligations, 28
  standing, NGOs, 20

411

INDEX

amici curiae
Aarhus Convention, 187
environmental treaties, 123
human rights treaties, 21, 361
ICCPR, 56
Permanent Court of Arbitration, 158
Amnesty International, 109
Angola, and CWC, 273
Antarctica, 260
anti-vehicle mines, 346
apes, 146
arbitration
Aarhus Convention, 184, 185, 186
CWC, 278
environmental disputes, 123
Espoo Convention, 221
NPT, 312–13
Argentina, 155, 402
Argentine–Brazilian Agency for
Accounting and Control, 307
arms control
See also specific treaties
consolidation, 250
cooperation, 243, 254–5, 264, 372
crisis, 246, 247–50
dispute settlement, 255–7
commentary, 365–8
NGO role, 367
enforcement, 266–71
comparisons, 403–7
counter-measures, 267–8
reprisals, 267
termination of agreements, 268–9,
404–5
treaty measures, 270–1
UN role, 266, 269–70, 272, 369,
372, 405–6
and environmental treaties, 245–6
focus on, 6–7
history, 244–6
mutual assistance, 253–4
non-state actors, 271
nuclear-weapon-free zones, 253, 260
treaty processes, 243–4
verification
aerial surveillance, 259
challenge inspections, 264, 265–6,
285–7, 316

confidential information, 263, 264
generally, 257–66
incentives to comply, 246, 250–5
institutional mandates, 381
institutions, 262–3, 382
national verification, 258–9
notifications and reporting, 260–1
on-site inspections, 263–4, 379
principles, 259, 264
quasi-judicial procedure, 264
routine procedures, 264–5, 280
transparency, 258
triggers, 385–6
weapons of mass destruction, 297,
366, 367–8
Association for the Prevention of
Torture, 104, 111
Austria, 18, 222
aviation agreements, 401
Azerbaijan, and UN CAT, 98

Bangkok Treaty, 257
Bangladesh, and CITES, 151
Barbados, and CWC, 273
Basel Convention
compliance mechanism, 195, 199, 203
dispute settlement, 213
Belgium, and Ottawa Convention, 336
Bern Convention, compliance control,
202
Biodiversity Convention, 118, 186, 220,
235
Biological and Toxin Weapons
Convention (BTWC)
deficiencies, 248, 262, 300
enforcement, 268, 269, 365–6
mutual assistance, 253
Biosafety Protocol, 159, 186, 191, 199,
203, 213
Bolivia, and CITES, 150
Bulgaria, 222, 256
Burundi, and UN CAT, 98
Bush, George W., 297

Canada, 180, 326
capacity building
CITES, 147, 159
compliance mechanism, 373

INDEX

Casale, Silvia, 111
CCW Convention
  2003 Protocol, 248
  effectiveness, 367
  and landmines, 326
  success, 247–8
CEDAW
  Committee case load, 21
  enforcement, 47
  ICJ jurisdiction, 357
  monitoring, 29
  Optional Protocol, 68
  reporting obligations, 377
  standing, 20
  state complaints, 384
CEE countries, 24, 80
Central African Republic, 151, 359
CERD, 21, 26, 68
CFE Treaty, 259, 379, 384–5
Chayes, Abram and Antonia, 373, 390
Chechnya, 95, 107
chemical weapons
  definition, 291
  ICC jurisdiction, 298
  non-state actors, 297
Chemical Weapons Convention (CWC)
  Conference, 281
  consolidation, 248
  contents, 274
  contracting parties, 273
  Council, 281
  definition of chemical weapons,
    291
  Director-General, 282
  dispute settlement, 274–9
    arbitration, 278
    compliance disputes, 277
    confidentiality disputes, 277–8
    ICJ jurisdiction, 275
    ICJ opinions, 276–7
    ILO Administrative Tribunal,
      278–9
    interpretation disputes, 275–6
  enforcement, 403–4
    assistance, 291, 293–4
    decision making, 270
    domestic measures, 291–3
    export control, 250

    generally, 290–8
    hard enforcement, 294–6
    media reports, 292–3
    outwith CWC regime, 296–8
    provisions, 271
    UN sanctions, 269, 295–6
  evaluation, 298–300
  generally, 273–300
  model, 273, 299–300, 322
  mutual assistance, 253–4
  national authorities, 274
  NGO participation, 287–8
  OPCW
    establishment, 274
    independence safeguards, 278–9
    mandate, 274–5, 281
    Secretariat, 281, 282, 284
  verification, 261
    challenge inspections, 285–7
    compliance pragmatism, 288–90
    cooperation, 280, 285
    demonstrating compliance,
      279–80
    determination of non-
      compliance, 284–7
    evaluation of declarations, 283
    inspections, 265, 266, 280–3
    institutions, 281–3, 382, 385–6
    monitoring, 280–3
    regime, 273, 279–90
    reporting obligations, 280
    routine procedures, 280
    standing, 287–8
    state parties, 282–3
    treaty evolution, 288–90
    Verification Implementation
      Report, 283
children's rights, ICCPR, 49
China, 99, 321, 329, 367
CITES
  Appendices, 135
  budget, 159
  compliance control
    capacity building, 147, 159
    effectiveness, 152–7
    generally, 136–48
    Guidelines, 125, 136–7, 147–8
    legal framework, 136–7

414 INDEX

CITES (*cont.*)
  compliance control (*cont.*)
    mechanisms, 142–6, 378
    monitoring, 139–42
    national legislation project, 143–4,
      153–5, 159
    procedures, 125, 127
    reporting obligations, 136, 137–9
    Secretariat, 127, 381, 385
    technical assistance, 144, 147, 152,
      156–7, 398
  dispute settlement, 157–8
  enforcement, 148–57
    cautions, 152
    effectiveness, 152–7
    methods, 148
    missions, 152
    trade sanctions, 130, 132, 136,
      149–52, 153–6, 159–60, 389, 398
    warnings, 152
  generally, 134–60
  Great Ape Enforcement Task Force,
    146
  ivory trade, 146
  lessons learned, 158–60
  listed species, 135
    urgent action, 146
  model, 134, 158, 383
  monitoring, 139–42
  NGO participation, 140–1, 142, 145,
    158
  objective, 135
  origins, 134
  reporting obligations, 137–9
    database, 138
    guidelines, 138
    implementation and enforcement,
      138–9, 144–5
    rules, 136
    sanctions, 156
  reservations, 142
  Secretariat, functions, 139–40, 144
  significant trade reviews, 145–6, 156
  Standing Committee, 125
    composition, 126, 141
    decision-making, 142
    establishment, 136
    mandate, 141

  Tiger Enforcement Task Force, 146
  transparency, 159
civil service, international civil service,
  278–9
Climate Change Convention, 129, 377
Cold War, 245
Collier, J., 353
Colombia, and ICCPR, 64
comparative approaches, 7
compliance control
  advantages, 9–10
  arms control
    CWC, 279–90
    generally, 257–66
    NPT, 308–12, 314–19
    Ottawa Convention, 329–39
    START I Treaty, 259
  assessment of compliance, 376–9
  cooperation, 373
  discussion, 373–90
  effectiveness, 388–90
  environmental treaties, 116–17,
    124–8, 132
    Aarhus Convention, 125, 189–215
    Alpine Convention, 195, 202
    Basel Convention, 195, 203
    Bern Convention, 202
    Biosafety Protocol, 203
    CITES, 136–48
    Espoo Convention, 213, 226–35,
      237–9
    LRTAP Convention, 166–72, 195,
      213
    Montreal Protocol, 124–5, 127,
      195, 211, 385
  human rights treaties
    ECHR, 47, 87
    ECPT, 101–2, 104–6
    generally, 22–37
    ICCPR, 57–64
    UN CAT, 101–2
  inspections, 378–9
  institutions, 10
    commentary, 380–8
    composition, 381–3
    mandates, 380–1
    secretariats, 383–4
  issues, 10–11

managerial approach, 373, 390
meaning, 6, 9
monitoring. *See* monitoring
reporting obligations. *See* reporting
  obligations
screening, 22–5
technical assistance. *See* technical
  assistance
triggers, 383–8
  individuals, 386–8
  NGOs, 386–8
  secretariats, 385–6
  state parties, 383–5
compliance mechanisms
  case studies, 12
  comparative approach, 7
  dispute settlement. *See* dispute
    settlement
  enforcement. *See* enforcement
  importance, 4–5
  international law remedies, 5–6
  non-compliance procedures. *See*
    compliance control
  state responsibility. *See* state
    responsibility
  treaty mechanisms, 6–7
Comprehensive Test Ban Treaty
  (CTBT)
  confidentiality, 299
  CTBO, 262
  dispute settlement, 257
  enforcement, 269, 299
  monitoring, 299
  NPT model, 322
  ratifications, 367
  substantive step, 252
  verification, 259, 299
confidentiality
  arms control inspections, 263, 264
  CTBT, 299
  CWC, 277–8
Congo (DRC), 150, 359
Convention Against Torture. *See* UN
  Convention Against Torture
  (UN CAT)
Convention on the Rights of the Child
  (CRC), 20
conventional weapons

CCW. *See* CCW Convention
CFE Treaty, 259, 379, 384–5
explosive remnants, 247–8
landmines. *See* Ottawa Convention
small arms, 247
cooperation
  arms control, 243, 254–5, 264, 372
  compliance control, 373
  CWC, 280, 285
  ECPT, 94
  environmental treaties, 129
  Ottawa Convention, 337, 340–1
Costa Rica, and UN CAT Protocol, 110
Côte d'Ivoire, 359, 400–1
Cotonou Agreement, 402
Council of Europe
  country visits, 87
  and European Union, 90
  execution of ECtHR judgments, 71,
    73, 83–5
  expulsion of members, 85, 109
  monitoring systems, 30–1
  origins, 90
  recommendations and declarations,
    73
  screening states, 22–4
courts. *See* international tribunals
Cuba, 361
Cyprus, and ECPT, 92, 93
Czechoslovakia, and INF Treaty, 256

damages, ECHR, 81–3
death penalty, and ICCPR, 49, 67–8
Delbrück, Jost, 372
detention, 49, 107
developing countries
  arms control, 250
  common but differentiated
    responsibilities, 115
  and environmental treaties, 121
  Montreal Protocol, 376
diplomatic protection, 38–9
dispute settlement
  advantages, 8, 371
  amici curiae. See amici curiae
  arms control treaties, 255–7
    ABM Treaty, 255–6
    commentary, 365–8

INDEX

dispute settlement (*cont.*)
  arms control treaties (*cont.*)
    CTBT, 257
    CWC, 274–9
    NPT, 312–14, 366
    Ottawa Convention, 339–40
    START 1 Treaty, 256
    Tlatelolco Treaty, 256–7
  bilateral character, 10
  consent, 8
  courts and tribunals. *See*
    international tribunals
  definition of dispute, 352–3
  environmental treaties, 118–24, 131–2
    Aarhus Convention, 183–9
    Basel Convention, 213
    Biosafety Protocol, 213
    CITES, 157–8
    commentary, 362–5
    Espoo Convention, 120, 213,
      220–6, 235–7
    LRTAP Convention, 165, 235–6
    Montreal Protocol, 213, 364
    Nordic Environment Convention,
      223
  erga omnes. See erga omnes
    obligations
  extent of use
    Aarhus Convention, 188–9
    human rights, 21–2
    ICCPR, 56
  fragmented legal order, 351–6
  human rights treaties, 16–22, 353–4
    commentary, 356–61
    compulsory procedures, 16–17
    ECHR, 17–18, 73–89
    ECPT, 103–4
    extent of use, 21–2
    general courts and tribunals,
      17–18
    ICCPR, 53–6
    mandates, 18
    procedures, 19
  issues, 8–9
  meaning, 6, 7
  NGO role, 370
  standing. *See* standing
  WTO, 8, 351, 369

Djibouti, and CITES, 150, 151
domestic courts
  environmental disputes, 124
  reopening proceedings, ECHR, 85–6
domestic remedies, exhaustion, 77,
  122–3
Dominica, and CITES, 151
Dugard, John, 38

ECE
  Espoo Convention, 218
  Kiev Guidelines, 229, 392
  non-compliance methods, 238–9
Egypt, 273, 317, 322
El Baradei, Mohamed, 322–3
El Salvador, and CITES, 150
Elephant Trade Information System
  (ETIS), 140
endangered species. *See* CITES
enforcement
  arms control
    ABM Treaty, 268
    BTWC, 268, 269, 365–6
    comparisons, 403–7
    CTBT, 269, 299
    CWC, 290–8, 403–4
    generally, 266–71
    Limited Test Ban Treaty, 268
    NPT, 268, 319–21, 403
    Ottawa Convention, 340–1
    Rarotonga Treaty, 268
    Tlatelolco Treaty, 268
  by other states
    meetings of contracting parties,
      40–1
    state responsibility norms, 5–6,
      41–3, 407–9
  commentary, 396–407
  environmental treaties, 116–17,
    128–31, 133
    Aarhus Convention, 129, 130, 181,
      208–12, 397–8
    assistance, 129
    CITES, 148–57, 159–60, 389, 398
    comparisons, 397–9
    Espoo Convention, 233–4
    Kyoto Protocol, 130, 132, 212,
      399

INDEX

LRTAP Convention, 129, 172–3, 397
Montreal Protocol, 129, 130
shaming, 129
hard enforcement v. soft law, 395–6
human rights treaties
  binding determinations of non-compliance, 44–5
  by other states, 39–44
  CEDAW, 47
  comparisons, 399–403
  diplomatic v. treaty procedures, 38–9
  ECHR, 400
  ECPT, 107–9, 400
  generally, 38–45
  ICCPR, 64–6
  issues, 38–40
  non-treaty measures, 43–4
  sanctions, 46
  setting obligations aside, 45
  state responsibility norms, 41–3
issues, 11–12, 38–40
meaning, 6, 391–6
measures, 394
state responsibility. *See* state responsibility
termination of agreements, 5, 268–9, 404–5
environmental impact assessments. *See* Espoo Convention
environmental treaties
  See also specific treaties
  and arms control, 245–6
  case law, 119
  compliance control, 116–17, 124–8, 132
    complaint procedures, 126–8
    compliance committees, 125–6
    NGO participation, 127, 386
    political character, 132
    recommendations, 128
    transparency, 127
  conferences, 115
  and developing countries, 115, 121
  dispute settlement, 118–24, 131–2
    amici curiae, 123
    arbitration, 123

commentary, 362–5
erga omnes obligations, 364–5
exhaustion of domestic remedies, 122–3
international tribunals, 118
NGO participation, 123, 363
standing, 122
enforcement, 128–31, 133
  comparisons, 397–9
  v. managerial approach, 116–17
evaluation, 131–3
focus on, 6–7
generally, 115–33
implementation issues, 116
institutions, 115–16, 382
sustainable development approach, 115
UNEP guidelines, 116
equality and non-discrimination
  arms control, 264
  ECHR, 70–1
  ICCPR, 50
Equatorial Guinea, 99, 150
erga omnes obligations
  Aarhus Convention, 188
  enforcement by other states, 42–3
  environmental obligations, 364–5
  human rights treaties, 20
  practical effect, 370
  standing, 354, 370
Espoo Convention
  arbitration, 123
  compliance control, 213, 226–35
    evaluation, 234–5, 237–9
    inter-state negotiations, 120
    NGO participation, 231–2
    notification of non-compliance, 230
    reporting obligations, 227–9
  contents, 219
  dispute settlement, 120, 213, 220–6
    arbitration, 221
    evaluation, 235–7
    ICJ jurisdiction, 221–2
    inquiry commissions, 120, 222–6, 236–7
  enforcement, 233–4
  evaluation, 235–9

418   INDEX

Espoo Convention (*cont.*)
  generally, 218–39
  human rights approach, 123
  Implementation Committee, 125
    composition, 126
    evaluation, 238
    mandate, 228
    model, 239
    public meetings, 127
    record, 231–2
  institutions, 218
  NGO participation, 127, 231–2
  origins, 218
  SEA Protocol, 219–20, 229–30, 235,
    238
EURATOM, 307, 313
European Commission on Human
    Rights, 70
European Convention on Human Rights
  See also Council of Europe
  compliance control, 47, 87
  dispute settlement, 73–89
    compulsory settlement, 17
    damages, 81–3
    general international courts,
      17–18, 76
    individual applications, 71
    judgments, 33–4, 40, 71, 72, 80–7
    mandates, 18
    restitutio in integrum, 82–3
    subsidiarity principle, 80–1
    See also European Court of
      Human Rights
  enforcement, 47, 400
  and European Union, 90
  generally, 70–90
  monitoring, 33–4
  proportionality principle, 77
  Protocols, 70
  ratifications, 24, 358
  reporting obligations, 26–7
  subsidiarity principle, 73
  substantive rights, 70–1
European Convention on Torture
    (ECPT)
  Committee (CPT)
    annual reports, 96
    composition, 92

    cooperation, 94
    expert assistance, 92
    functions, 92–4
    inspections, 105, 379
    pilot project, 108
    public statements, 107
    recommendations, 108
    Rules of Procedure, 95–6
  compliance control, 101–2, 104–6
    country reports, 92–3, 95, 101,
      105, 110–11, 379
    public statements, 94–5
  dispute settlement, 103–4
  enforcement, 107–9, 400
  evaluation, 109–11
  Explanatory Report, 95
  mandate, 101–2
  origins, 91
  preventive role, 360, 361
  reporting obligations, 27–8
  UN CAT compared, 101–2
European Court of Human Rights
  admissibility of cases, 75, 76–7
    disadvantage, 77
    NGOs, 76, 79
    time limits, 77
    victims, 76, 79–80
  amici curiae, 21
  case load, 21, 79, 80
  Committees, 75–6
  composition, 74–5
  creation, 70
  exclusive jurisdiction, 41
  function, 70
  Grand Chamber, 72, 75, 87
  individual applications, 71, 78–9
  influence, 89–90
  judgments, 80–7
    binding nature, 80–1
    compliance, 71, 85
    costs, 82
    damages, 81–3
    execution, 40, 71, 73, 83–5, 86–7
    monitoring compliance, 33–4
    precedents, 72
    reopening domestic proceedings,
      85–6
    subsidiarity principle, 80–1

jurisdiction, 76–7
Practice Directions, 72
procedures
  individual applications, 78–9
  inter-state applications, 79
  languages, 78
  legal aid, 79
  NGO participation, 80
  principles, 78–9
  transparency, 78
Rules of Court, 71–2, 78
settlements, 78
state use, 22, 356, 384
success, 21, 47, 87–8
European Human Rights
    Commissioner, 87
European Minorities Convention,
    27
European Minority Languages Charter,
    reporting obligations, 27
European Social Charter
  monitoring, 31, 34
  reporting obligations, 27
  standing, NGOs, 21
European Union
  Cotonou Agreement, 402
  and ECHR, 90
  and Iran, 318–19
  Lomé Agreement, 402
  and Montreal Protocol, 364
exhaustion of domestic remedies, 77,
    122–3

fair trial, 49, 83
Falklands war, 402
Fauna and Flora International (FFI),
    140, 145
Fiji, and CITES, 150
Finland, 64, 168, 169, 170, 171,
    364
fissile material, 249
France, 292, 297, 318
Franck, Thomas M., 5
freedom of association, 48
freedom of movement, 49
freedom of thought, conscience and
    religion, 49
Friedmann, Wolfgang, 3

Gambia, 58, 151
Gautier, Jean-Jacques, 109–10
Geneva Call, 341
Geneva Conventions, 18, 40
Geneva Disarmament Conference
    1995, 249
Geneva International Centre for
    Humanitarian Demining
    (GICHD), 334, 335, 342
Genocide Convention, ICJ jurisdiction,
    17, 41
Germany, 95, 120, 222, 256, 318, 384
Global Environment Facility, 129
Greece, 102, 109, 150, 169, 170, 172
Greenpeace, 363
Grenada, and CITES, 150
Guatemala, and UN CAT, 98
Guinea-Bissau, and CITES, 150
Guyana, and CITES, 150

Hague Conference 1899, 244
heavy metals, 163
Henkin, Louis, 4–5
human rights treaties
  See also specific treaties
  assessment, 47
  compliance control
    country visits, 378–9
    generally, 22–37
    institutional mandates, 381
    monitoring systems, 29–37
    reporting obligations, 25–9
    screening, 22–5
    standing, 37
    triggers, 384
  courts, composition, 19
  derogations, 45
  dispute settlement, 353–4, 356–61
    amici curiae, 21, 361
    compulsory procedures, 16–17
    extent of use, 21–2
    general international courts,
      17–18
    generally, 16–22
    ICJ jurisdiction, 17–18, 357, 359
    individualisation, 359–61
    mandates, 18
    procedures, 19

420 INDEX

human rights treaties (*cont.*)
  dispute settlement (*cont.*)
    standing, 20–1
    state responsibility, 360
  effect, 15
  enforcement
    by other states, 39–44
    comparisons, 399–403
    diplomatic v. treaty procedures, 38–9
    generally, 38–45
    issues, 38–40
    meetings of contracting parties, 40–1
    non-treaty measures, 43–4
    setting obligations aside, 45
    soft enforcement, 45, 46
    state responsibility norms, 41–3
  focus on, 6–7
  instruments, 15
  international institutions, 381
  NGO participation, 361
  overlapping procedures, 16
  regionalisation, 360–1
  victims, 20–1
Human Rights Watch, 343
humane treatment, 48–9
humanitarian interventions, 357, 401
Hungary, and Aarhus Convention, 205, 207

IAEA
  annual reports, 302
  Comprehensive Safeguards Agreements, 306–8
    Protocols, 307–8, 310, 311
  El Baradei, Mohamed, 322–3
  establishment, 301
  evaluation, 321–3
  and Iran, 253
  mandate, 302
  model, 262
  non-compliance reports, 269, 303
  NPT verification, 308–12, 319
  nuclear watchdog, 302, 319
  Safeguards Agreements, 304, 305
  safeguards system, 302–4

status, 301–2
structure, 301
ICCPR
  compliance control, 50, 57–64
    individual complaints, 52, 60–4
    reporting procedures, 57–60, 377
    state complaints, 384
  contracting parties, 50
  and death penalty, 49, 67–8
  dispute settlement, 53–6
    alternative procedures, 18, 54
    amici curiae, 56
    Conciliation Commissions, 54, 55
    extent of use, 56
    individuals, 52, 60–4, 358
    inter-state complaints, 51–2, 56, 356
    procedure, 54–6
  enforcement, 64–6
  evaluation, 66–9
  generally, 48–69
  interim protection measures, 61, 63
  meetings of state parties, 52
  NGO participation, 59, 60
  reporting
    delay, 25, 59, 66
    effectiveness, 59–60
    implementation, 66
    model, 68
    NGO participation, 59, 60
    obligations, 50–1, 52
    procedures, 57–60
  right to remedy, 52
  Rules of Procedure, 53
  substantive rights, 48–50
  UNHCR General Comments, 53
  UNHCR Guidelines, 53
ICESCR, 26, 47
Ignatieff, Michael, 361
India, 252, 304, 329
individuals
  Aarhus Convention, 127, 198–200, 202
  compliance control, 386–8
  CWC, 287
  ECHR complaints, 71, 78–9, 79–80
  Espoo Convention, 231–2

human rights field, 20, 359–61
ICCPR complaints, 52, 60–4, 358
standing, 8–9, 20
UN CAT complaints, 98–9
institutions. *See* international
institutions
Inter-American Commission on
Human Rights, 21, 35–6
Inter-American Court of Human
Rights, 21, 35–7, 36
Intermediate Range Nuclear Forces
Treaty (INF)
exchange of information, 260–1
verification, 256, 259, 265
International Association of Lawyers
against Nuclear Arms, 367
International Atomic Energy Agency.
See IAEA
International Campaign to Ban
Landmines (ICBL), 324, 325,
326, 327, 332, 336, 338, 341,
342, 343, 345, 346, 386
international civil service, 278–9
international constitutionalism, 3
International Convention on Civil and
Political Rights. *See* ICCPR
International Court of Justice
Aarhus Convention, 184
advisory proceedings, 353
alternative jurisdictions, 41
CEDAW jurisdiction, 357
CWC jurisdiction, 275, 276–7
environmental issues, 118
Espoo Convention, 221–2
Genocide Convention, 17, 41
and human rights treaties, 17–18,
357, 359
and ICCPR, 54
increased use, 351
jurisdiction, 8
Tlatelolco Treaty, 256–7
international courts. *See* international
tribunals
International Criminal Court, 298, 351,
358–9
international criminal law, 369
International Criminal Tribunal for
Rwanda, 358

International Criminal Tribunal for the
Former Yugoslavia (ICTY), 93,
358
international humanitarian law, 327
international institutions
Aarhus Convention, 182, 192–6, 383
BTWC, 262
CITES, 125, 126, 139–40, 144
compliance control, 10, 380–8
composition, 381–3
environmental treaties, 115–16, 382
Espoo Convention, 218
LRTAP Convention, 162, 166
mandates, 380–1
Ottawa Convention, 330–1
secretariats, 385–6
International Labour Organization
Administrative Tribunal, and CWC,
278–9
reporting obligations, 25, 68
International Law Commission
diplomatic protection, 38–9
exhaustion of domestic remedies,
123
state responsibility. *See* state
responsibility
international tribunals
advantages, 8
and American scholarship, 351
compliance with, 352
criminal courts, 352, 358–9
environmental treaties, 118–19
human rights treaties, 19
International Union for Conservation
of Nature and Natural
Resources (IUCN), 134, 140,
145
Iran
arms control, 267, 269, 270
and CWC, 286–7
and NPT, 317–19, 322
nuclear weapons, 253
Iraq
arms control, 267, 270, 372
chemical weapons, 273, 288, 298
and NPT, 316, 320–1, 322
nuclear weapons programme, 307
Ireland, 120, 169, 170, 171, 384

422 INDEX

Israel, 40, 99, 304
Italy, 18, 150, 153, 168, 169, 170, 171
ITLOS, 8, 118
ivory trade, 146

Japan, 98, 321
Jennings, Robert, 394
Jordan, chemical weapons, use, 292
judgments
    ECtHR, 33–4, 40, 71, 72, 80–7
    human rights disputes, 19–20
    Inter-American Court, 35–7
    international tribunals, compliance,
        352
jus cogens, 42

Kazakhstan, and Aarhus Convention,
    205
Kiev Guidelines, 229, 392
Kosovo, 41, 65, 92–3, 401
Kuwait, and UN CAT, 99
Kyoto Protocol
    Compliance Committee, 126
    decision-making powers, 128
    declarations of non-compliance, 210
    enforcement, 130, 132, 212, 399
    experts, 132, 377
    recent treaty, 118
    transparency, 127–8
    violations, multilateral effects, 121

Landmine Monitor Report, 337, 342–3
Landmine Survivors Network, 341
landmines. *See* Ottawa Convention
Latvia, and ECPT, 95
League of Nations, 88
Lebanon, and CWC, 273
legal costs, ECHR applications, 79, 82
legality principle, ICCPR, 49
Liberia, and CITES, 150, 151
liberty and security, 49
Libya, 289, 316, 317
Liechtenstein, 222, 362
Limited Test Ban Treaty, 268
Loibl, Gerhard, 399
Lomé Convention, 402
Lowe, V., 353
LRTAP Convention

acidification, 163
compliance control, 166–72, 195,
    213
    in-depth reviews, 172, 376
    institutions, 166
    model, 229, 238
    monitoring, 162
    NGO participation, 232
    record, 167–72
    reporting obligations, 166–7
    Secretariat referrals, 176, 385
contents, 162
dispute settlement, 165, 213, 235–6
effect of violations, 121
EMEP Programme, 162, 163
enforcement, 129, 172–3, 397
evaluation, 173–5
Executive Body, 162
generally, 161–78
heavy metals, 163
Implementation Committee, 125
    compliance control, 166
    composition, 126, 175
    establishment, 163–4
    information gathering, 176–7
    mandate, 129, 164, 175
    meetings, 175
    procedures, 175–8
    recommendations, 127
    submissions to, 127, 175–6
influence, 229, 238
nitrogen oxide, 163
origins, 161–2
persistent organic pollutants (POPs),
    163
protocols, 163
Secretariat, 162, 176, 385
sulphur emissions, 163
volatile organic compounds (VOCs),
    163
Luxembourg, 108, 169, 170, 171

Macau, and CITES, 150
Madagascar, and CITES, 156
Malta, 24
managerial approach, 116–17, 373, 390
Maslen, S., 338
Mauritania, and CITES, 150, 151

media, and chemical weapons, 292–3
Mexico, and UN CAT, 98
Migrant Workers Convention, 38
mine actions, 324
Mines Action Canada, 343
Mines Advisory Group, 341
minority rights, 48, 49–50, 88
Moldova, 27, 108, 205
monitoring
  arms control, 259
    CTBT, 299
    CWC, 280–3
    Ottawa Convention, 330
  commentary, 376–9
  environmental treaties
    CITES, 139–42
    LRTAP Convention, 162
  human rights treaties, 29–37
    Africa, 34–5, 37
    Americas, 35–7
    case-specific, 31–7
    Council of Europe, 30–1
    Europe, 33–4
    general compliance, 29–31
    torture, 111
    UN CAT, 98–9
  ICTY, 93
Montreal Protocol
  compliance control, 124–5, 127, 195, 211, 385
  dispute settlement, 213, 364
  enforcement, 129, 130
  Implementation Committee, 125, 126, 129, 164
  model treaty, 117–18, 376, 383
  Multilateral Fund, 129
Morocco, and UN CAT, 99
Mozambique, and CITES, 150
mutual assistance, arms control, 253–4

Netherlands, 222, 298, 364
NGOs
  and arms control, 367
  compliance control, 386–8
  dispute resolution, 370
  and environmental treaties, 123, 127, 363, 386

Aarhus Convention, 127, 190, 193, 194, 198–200, 202, 387
  amici curiae, 123
  CITES, 140–1, 142, 145, 158
  CWC, 287–8
  Espoo Convention, 127, 231–2
  LRTAP Convention, 232
and human rights treaties, 361
  amici curiae, 21
  ECHR, 76, 79, 80
  ICCPR, 59, 60
  standing, 20–1
  UN CAT, 102
Ottawa Convention. *See* Ottawa Convention
Nigeria, and CITES, 150
nitrogen oxide, 163
Non-Proliferation Treaty (NPT)
  See also IAEA
  commitments, 305–6
  Comprehensive Safeguards Agreements, 306–8
    Protocols, 307–8, 310, 311
  deficiencies, 248
  dispute resolution, 312–14, 366
  enforcement, 319–21
    rights and privileges, 209, 210, 211–12, 403
    termination of agreement, 268
  evaluation, 321–3
  generally, 301–23
  model, 298–9, 321–2
  nuclear-weapon-free zones, 253
  origins, 304
  progress, 253
  sanctions, 252
  verification, 308–12, 314–19
    challenge inspections, 316
    information, 309–10
    site inspections, 310–11
    state evaluations, 311–12
  Voluntary Safeguards Agreements, 307
non-state actors
  Aarhus Convention, 186–7
  compliance control, 386–8
  individuals. *See* individuals
  NGOs. *See* NGOs

424 INDEX

non-state actors (*cont.*)
  Ottawa Convention, 324, 331, 332,
    333, 336, 341–3, 386
  weapons of mass destruction, 297,
    300
Nordic Environment Convention,
  223
North Korea, arms control, 267, 273,
  304, 315, 316–17, 321, 322, 366,
  372
Norway, 168, 169, 170, 172, 362, 364
Norwegian People's Aid, 341
NPT. *See* Non-Proliferation Treaty
  (NPT)
Nuclear Test Ban Treaty, 4
nuclear-weapon-free zones, 253, 260
nuclear weapons. *See* Non-
  Proliferation Treaty (NPT)
Nuremberg trials, 358

Open Skies Treaty, 259
Organization of American States, 46
OSPAR Convention, 120, 384
Ottawa Convention
  anti-vehicle mines, 346
  challenges, 329
  commitments, 327–9
  compliance control, 329–39
    institutions, 330–1
    Meetings of the Parties, 330–1
    non-compliance procedures,
      337–9
    non-state actors, 331, 332, 333,
      334, 341–3
    reporting obligations, 335–7
    Sponsorship Programme, 335
    Standing Committees, 331–4
  compliance culture, 324–5
  cooperation, 337, 340–1
  dispute settlement, 339–40
  enforcement, 340–1
  evaluation, 343–7
  generally, 324–47
  implementation, 324
  Implementation Support Unit,
    334–5
  Nairobi Action Plan, 329, 342
  negotiating history, 325–7

NGO participation, 324, 328, 332,
  334, 341–3, 368, 386
success, 324, 328–9, 368
technical assistance, 328, 343
Ottawa Process, 326, 346

Pakistan, 292–3, 297, 304, 329
Panama, and CITES, 150
Pelindaba Treaty, 257
Permanent Court of Arbitration
  and CITES, 157–8
  environmental issues, 118
  increased use, 351
Peru, human rights, 44
Philippines, 297
plutonium, 248–9
Poland, 120, 222, 384
Portugal, new democracy, 23
private and family life, 49
property rights, ECHR, 83
proportionality principle, 77, 264

Ramsar Convention, 158
Rarotonga Treaty, 260, 268
Red Cross, 110
  and CWC, 288
  landmines campaign, 324, 325, 326,
    327
  and Ottawa Convention, 329, 332,
    334, 336, 341, 343, 345
Reisman, W. M., 401
reporting obligations
  arms control, 260–1
    CWC, 280
    Ottawa Convention, 335–7
  commentary, 374–6
  environmental treaties
    Aarhus Convention, 189–91
    CITES, 136, 137–9, 144–5
    Espoo Convention, 227–9
    LRTAP Convention, 166–7
  human rights treaties
    Africa, 28
    Americas, 28
    arrears, 25
    CEDAW, 377
    Europe, 26–8
    generally, 25–9

ICCPR, 50–1, 57–60, 377
UN CAT, 98, 100
universal level, 25–6
violations, 26
ILO conventions, 25, 68
meaning, 10
res judicata, 10, 86, 119
rhinos, 146
ricin plot, 292
right to life, 49
Romania, 120, 195, 199, 205, 225–6,
297, 316, 317
Russia
and Aarhus Convention, 180
Council of Europe membership, 24
counter-terrorism, 297
and CWC, 287, 289, 290
and ECPT, 95, 107, 109
landmines, 329
and North Korea, 321
Rwanda, and CITES, 150, 151

Sand, Peter, 159
Saudi Arabia, and UN CAT, 99
saxitoxin, 289
screening, 22–5
Seabed Treaty, 268
self-contained regimes, 7
self-determination, 48, 49
Senegal, and CITES, 150
September 11 events, 296, 367, 368
Serbia-Montenegro, 24–5, 41, 65,
92–3
Seychelles, and UN CAT, 98
Sierra Leone, 150, 360
Simma, Bruno, 3–4
slavery and forced labour, 49
Slovenia, 168, 172
soft law
assistance. *See* technical assistance
compliance control, 389
ECPT, 107–9
v. hard enforcement, 395–6
human right treaties, 45, 46
ICCPR, 64–6
Somalia, 150, 151, 273
South Korea, 317, 321, 322, 329
Spain, 23, 169, 170, 172, 297

standing
Aarhus Convention, 187–8
CWC non-compliance allegations,
287–8
dispute settlement procedures, 8–9
environmental treaties, 122
erga omnes obligations, 354, 370
human rights treaties, 20–1, 37
START I Treaty, 245, 256, 259
state parties
CWC compliance, 282–3
ECHR
applications, 79
compliance with judgments, 72–3
extent of use, 22, 356, 384
human rights complaints, 384
ICCPR complaints, 51–2, 356
responsibility to protect, 357
standing, 20, 37
triggering compliance control, 383–5
UN CAT complaints, 98, 384
state practice, international law, 44
state responsibility
alternative procedures, 39
enforcement by norms of, 5–6
Aarhus Convention, 187–8
commentary, 407–9
environmental treaties, 122
human rights, 41–3, 360
environmental protection, 364–5
fact-finding commissions, 237
ILC Articles, 407–9
state succession, Yugoslavia, 41
Stockholm Conference 1972, 135
subsidiarity principle, ECHR, 73, 80–1
Sudan, 286, 359
sulphur emissions, 163
Suriname, 58
sustainable development, 115
Sweden, 168, 169, 171, 364
Switzerland, and CITES, 141
Syria, and CWC, 273

taxation, international civil service, 278
technical assistance
Aarhus Convention, 209, 397–8
arms control, 253–4
BTWC, 253

426 INDEX

technical assistance (*cont.*)
 CITES, 144, 147, 152, 156–7, 398
 compliance function, 388–9
 CWC, 291, 293–4
 ECPT Committee, 92
 environmental treaties, 129
 human rights, 46
 institutional mandates, 380
 Ottawa Convention, 328, 343
termination of treaties, 5, 268–9, 404–5
terrorism
 and arms control, 271
 chemical weapons, 293
 and torture, 107–8
 and United Nations, 296–8
 weapons of mass destruction, 297, 300
Thailand, and CITES, 150, 153
tigers, 146
Tlatelolco Treaty, 253, 256–7, 260, 268
torture
 Association for the Prevention of Torture, 104, 111
 Convention Against Torture. *See* UN Convention Against Torture (UN CAT)
 definition, 97
 ECPT. *See* European Convention on Torture (ECPT)
 Gautier project, 109–10
 international instruments, 109, 396
 practice, 109
 prevention, 110–11
trade agreements, suspension, 401–2
trade sanctions, CITES, 130, 132, 136, 149–52, 153–6, 159–60, 389
TRAFFIC, 140, 145, 146
tribunals. *See* international tribunals
truth commissions, 360
Turkey, and ECPT, 95, 107
Turkmenistan, 205

Uganda, 98, 359
Ukraine, 120, 195, 199, 205, 225–6
UN Committee Against Torture (UN CAT)
 case load, 21
 composition, 97

follow-up procedures, 100–1
 mandate, 97–8
 missions, 43–4
 Rules of Procedure, 100
 Sub-Committee, 99–100, 111
UN Convention Against Torture (UN CAT)
 compliance control, 98, 101–2
 ECPT compared, 101–2
 generally, 96–101
 individual complaints, 98–9
 inquiries, 99, 102
 inspections, 99, 379
 mandate, 101–2
 monitoring, 29, 98
 NGO participation, 102
 objectives, 96–7
 origins, 96
 reporting obligations, 98
  guidelines, 100
 state complaints, 98, 384
 state declarations, 98, 99
 UN Committee Against Torture (UN CAT), 21, 97–101, 111
UN High Commissioner for Human Rights, 61, 66, 111
UN Human Rights Commission, 30, 43–4, 356
UN Human Rights Committee, and ICCPR
 case load, 21
 compliance control guidance, 37
 composition, 126
 country visits, 45
 disputes, 55–6
 General Comments, 53
 Guidelines, 53
 ICCPR Rules of Procedure, 53
 implied powers, 69
 individual complaints, 61–4
 individual complaints to, 52
 inter-state complaints to, 51–2
 methodology, 377
 model, 68
 powers, 52–3
 report requests, 26
 reports, 25–6, 51, 57–60, 66, 67, 68
 torture remit, 97

UN Human Rights Council, 30
UNDP, 341
UNEP, 116, 140
UNEP–WCMC, 138
UNICEF, 341
United Arab Emirates, and CITES, 150,
153
United Kingdom, 98, 107, 120, 229,
292, 297, 318
United Nations
  arms control
    CWC, 277, 295–6
    fissile material, 249
    NPT, 320–1
    sanctions, 269–70, 272
    Security Council role, 366–7, 369,
    372, 405–6
    terrorism, 296–8
    weapons registry, 247
  Chapter VII
    and IAEA, 304
    interventions, 266, 295–6, 297
    Iraq intervention, 316
  Department for Disarmament
    Affairs (UNDDA), 335
  human rights role, 25, 400–1
  Mine Action Service (UNMAS), 336,
    341, 343
  reform, 357
United States
  Aarhus Convention, 180
  chemical weapons, 287–8, 292–3
  counter-terrorism, 297
  CTBT, 367

CWC, 286, 287, 289, 290
endangered species, trade, 134
and ICC, 359
India, nuclear cooperation, 252
Iran nuclear weapons, 253
landmines, 329
North Korean policy, 321
Sudan bombing, 286
Sunshine Project, 287
UN CAT, 98
UNMAS, 336, 341, 343

Vanuatu, and CITES, 151
VERTIC, 336, 338
victims, human rights treaties, 20–1
Vietnam, and CITES, 150
volatile organic compounds (VOCs),
  163

Wassenaar Arrangement, 249
weapons of mass destruction, 297, 366,
  367–8
Williams, Jody, 325
women. See CEDAW
World Bank, 68
World Conservation Union, 134
WTO, 8, 160, 351, 369

Yemen, and CITES, 150
Yugoslavia, 23, 24, 41, 46, 65, 93,
  358

Zimbabwe, 402
Zimmermann, Andreas, 372